D1565644

LATIN AMERICA'S
DEMOCRATIC CRUSADE

LATIN AMERICA'S DEMOCRATIC CRUSADE

The Transnational Struggle against Dictatorship,

1920s–1960s

ALLEN WELLS

Yale

UNIVERSITY PRESS

New Haven and London

Published with assistance from the foundation established
in memory of Henry Weldon Barnes of the Class of 1882,
Yale College.

Yale University Press books may be purchased in quantity for
educational, business, or promotional use. For information, please
e-mail sales.press@yale.edu (U.S. office) or sales@yaleup.co.uk
(U.K. office).

Set in Janson type by IDS Infotech Ltd.
Printed in the United States of America.

Library of Congress Control Number: 2022944419
ISBN 978-0-300-26440-1 (hardcover : alk. paper)

A catalogue record for this book is available from the British Library.

This paper meets the requirements of ANSI/NISO Z39.48-1992
(Permanence of Paper).

10 9 8 7 6 5 4 3 2 1

For David, Emily, and Anna

Soldiers with pen or sword, for the liberty of humankind
. . . against the dictatorships of America.

—ALBERTO BAYO, 1950

Contents

Abbreviations

AAA	Acción Armada Auténtica (Cuba)
ABC	Clandestine Cuban organization opposed to Machado's dictatorship
AD	Acción Democrática (Venezuela)
AID	Agency for International Development
AIE	Ala Iqzuierda Estudiantil (Cuba)
ANERC	Asociación Nuevos Emigrados Cubanos
APRA	Alianza Popular Revolucionaria Americana (Peru)
AGELA	La Asociación General de Estudiantes Latinoamericanos (Paris)
ARDE	Alianza Revolucionaria Democrática (Nicaragua)
ARDI	Agrupación Revolucionaria de Izquierda (Venezuela)
ATLAS	Agrupación de Trabajadores Latinoamericanos Sindicalizados
CC	Comité Coordinador de las Actividades de AD en el Exterior (Venezuela)
CCRLA	Committee on Cultural Relations with Latin America
CEN	Comité Ejecutivo Nacional (AD, Venezuela)
CI	Communist International
CIT	Confederación Interamericana de Trabajadores
COPEI	Comité de Organización Electoral Independiente (Venezuela)
CROM	Confederación Regional Obrera Mexicana
CTAL	Confederación de Trabajadores de América Latina
DEU	Directorio Estudiantil Universitario (Cuba)
DRE	Directorio Revolucionario Estudiantil (Cuba)
ECLA	United Nations Economic Commission for Latin America and the Caribbean (Spanish acronym CEPAL)
EDSNN	Ejército Defensor de la Soberanía Nacional de Nicaragua
ERP	Ejército Revolucionario del Pueblo (Argentina)
FEU	Federación Estudiantil Universitaria (Cuba)
FEV	Federación Estudiantil Venezolano

FOR	Fellowship of Reconciliation
FSLN	Frente Sandinista de Liberación Nacional
GOU	Grupo Obra de Unificación (Argentina)
IADF	Inter-American Association of Democracy and Freedom
IAPC	Inter-American Peace Committee
ISI	import substitution industrialization
JP	Junta Patriótica (Venezuela)
LADLA	Liga Antiimperialista de las Américas
MAFUENIC	Comité Manos Fuera de Nicaragua
MIR	Movimiento Izquierdista Revolucionario (Venezuela, Peru, Chile)
MNR	Movimiento Nacional Revolucionaria (Bolivia)
MSR	Movimiento Socialista Revolucionario (Cuba)
NCFPW	National Council for the Prevention of War
NSC	National Security Council
OAS	Organization of American States
ORIT	Organización Regional Interamericana de Trabajadores
ORVE	Movimiento de Organización Venezolano
PCC	Partido Comunista Cubano
PCCR	Partido Comunista de Costa Rica
PCM	Partido Comunista Mexicano
PCV	Partido Comunista Venezolano
PDN	Partido Democrático Nacional (Venezuela)
PGT	Partido Guatemalteco del Trabajo
PLN	Partido Liberación Nacional (Costa Rica)
PRC-A	Partido Revolucionario Cubano or Partido Auténtico (Cuba)
PRD	Partido Revolucionario Dominicano
PRI	Partido Revolucionario Institucional (Mexico)
PRV	Partido Revolucionario Venezolano
PVP	Partido Vanguardia Popular (Costa Rica)
PSP	Partido Socialista Popular (Cuban Communist Party)
SIM	Servicio de Inteligencia Militar (Dominican State Security)
SN	Seguridad Nacional (Venezuelan State Security)
UFCO	United Fruit Company
UIR	Unión Insurrecional Revolucionario (Cuba)
ULA	Unión Latinoamericana
UPGP	Universidad Popular González Prada (Peru)
UPJM	Universidad Popular José Martí (Cuba)
URD	Unión Revolucionario Democrática (Venezuela)

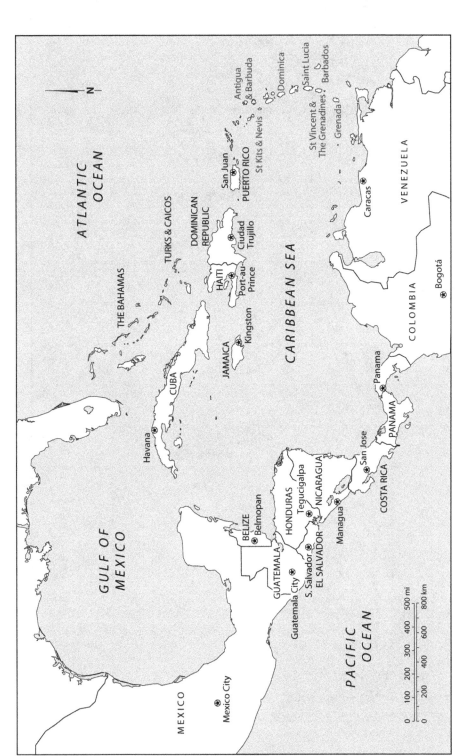

Caribbean Basin

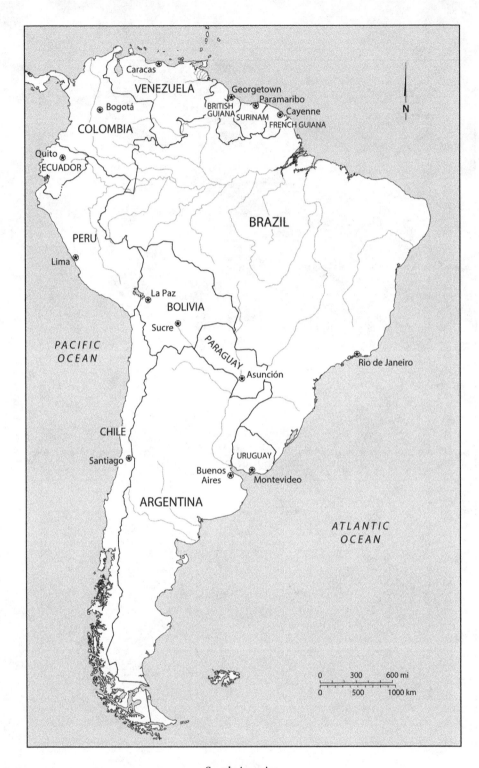

Caracas

VENEZUELA

Bogotá

COLOMBIA

Georgetown
Paramaribo
BRITISH
GUIANA SURINAM Cayenne
FRENCH GUIANA

Quito
ECUADOR

BRAZIL

PERU

Lima

La Paz

BOLIVIA

Sucre

PACIFIC
OCEAN

PARAGUAY

Asunción

Rio de Janeiro

CHILE

Santiago

URUGUAY

Buenos
Aires Montevideo

ARGENTINA

ATLANTIC
OCEAN

N

0   300   600 mi
0   500   1000 km

South America

Introduction

IN JULY 1958, TWO months after Vice President Richard Nixon was taunted and pelted with rocks and trash and his limousine smashed by baseball bats in Caracas, Venezuela, during an ill-fated "goodwill" tour through South America, a thirty-seven-year-old, first-term member of Congress from Oregon drew an enthusiastic crowd of twenty thousand, who cheered his every word at a political rally at the Nuevo Circo bullring in the Venezuelan capital. This reception was hardly unique. Representative Charles Porter had just drawn effusive crowds in Puerto Rico, Costa Rica, Panama, and Colombia. How did a political neophyte who barely spoke a word of Spanish become an overnight sensation, earning the moniker Latin America's Representative in the U.S. Congress? What resonated so well was Porter's championing of democracy and his searing criticism of Washington's coddling of brutal, corrupt dictators, such as Fulgencio Batista, Anastasio Somoza, and Rafael Trujillo.

Nixon, who chalked up his hostile reception to communist agitators, scarcely left the U.S. embassy for the duration of his visit, cancelling much of his itinerary and cutting short his stay. The vice president needed a "superabundant military escort" just to leave the country. So concerned was President Dwight Eisenhower about the safety of the vice

Note: During the five decades of this study, the Dominican Republic's capital changed names on two occasions: from Santo Domingo to Ciudad Trujillo in 1936, before reverting back to Santo Domingo in 1961. Brazil's capital was moved from Rio de Janeiro to Brasília in 1964, and British Guiana received its independence in 1966, when it changed its name to Guyana.

president, his wife, Pat, and the rest of their entourage that he rattled sabers by dispatching one thousand Marines and paratroopers from North Carolina to Guantánamo and Ramey Air Force Base in Aguadilla, Puerto Rico, and ordered the Navy to send six destroyers, a missile cruiser, and an aircraft carrier to the area.[1]

By comparison, Rep. Porter's visit was a love-in. His jam-packed schedule featured wide-ranging interviews with the press and a local television station and meetings with leaders of the major political parties, the president of the provisional junta, labor organizers, and the Venezuelan Chamber of Commerce. In addition, he participated in a three-hour roundtable at the Central University, a notorious leftist hotbed, where anti-American feelings ran high and two campus dormitories bore the nicknames Stalingrad I and II. No matter; the opinionated Oregonian gave as good as he got. And while Nixon's meetings were held at the embassy for security reasons, Porter, according to one local newspaper account, sampled *comida criolla* (native cuisine) and met with Venezuelans in their own element, "where he was received as if he were at home."[2]

The congressman's message could not have been more dissimilar from Nixon's Cassandra-like warnings about the communist threat. At the *plaza de toros*, for instance, Porter commended those in attendance for their participation in the popular upheaval that had ousted General Marcos Pérez Jiménez from power seven months earlier. He framed the restoration of democratic rule in Venezuela as part and parcel of an unmistakable hemispheric trend. "Pérez Jiménez is overthrown. Trujillo is teetering. Batista's days are numbered, [Paraguayan dictator Alfredo] Stroessner and Somoza know they must soon answer to their people for their sins."[3] He also had strong words for Venezuela's military, lecturing them to "defend their country, not to try to govern it." In appreciation of his message, the packed house at the bullring waved white handkerchiefs, an honor usually reserved for gallant bullfighters. Porter was deeply moved by the tribute. The reception he received in Caracas and elsewhere during his visits to other Latin American capitals indicates that on the eve of the Cuban Revolution, a transnational battle against the region's dictatorships was foremost in the minds of many.

Latin Americans' very different responses to an inveterate Cold Warrior like Nixon and a liberal critic raise intriguing questions about why scholars persist in framing the Cold War as a Manichaean battle between left and right, one in which the Global South is cast as either a witting or an unwitting proxy. What if that era were told from the perspective of the many who preferred reform instead of revolution? Just as Latin America became a flashpoint of the Cold War as a result of the Cuban Revolution, reformers, unhappy with what they viewed as Washington's and Moscow's simplistic "us versus them" mindset, forged a different path, rejecting right-wing militarism *and* leftist totalitarianism.

Politicians like José "Pepe" Figueres (Costa Rica), Rómulo Betancourt (Venezuela), Alberto Lleras Camargo (Colombia), Víctor Paz Estenssoro (Bolivia), Juan Bosch (Dominican Republic), Ramón Villeda Morales (Honduras), and Eduardo Frei (Chile) came to power in the 1950s and 1960s articulating policies that would have resonated with New Dealers: electoral democracy, a safety net for the poor, the curbing of exploitative monopolies, and a modest agrarian reform. They may have opposed the policies of a particular administration in Washington, but they never once questioned the inevitability of North American hegemony in the hemisphere. Reformers built formidable political machines, enlisting the support of tens of thousands of professionals, teachers, students, small business owners, union rank and file, and peasants.

How does the periodization of the Cold War as a discrete era hinder our understanding of the region's political evolution during the twentieth century? *Latin America's Democratic Crusade* boldly contends that the Cold War came late to Latin America. Until the Cuban Revolution, the battle was not between capitalism and communism for many Latin Americans— that was Washington's abiding preoccupation—but democracy versus dictatorship. Beginning in the 1920s, the fight against authoritarianism was contested on multiple fronts—political, ideological, and cultural—taking on the dimensions of a crusade. Grafted onto this extended conflict was a belated Cold War with all its convulsions. Indeed, the political aftershocks of the struggle between reformers and dictators are still felt today, long after the Cold War ended.

Broad multiclass parties, such as Venezuela's Acción Democrática (AD), the Peruvian Alianza Popular Revolucionaria Americana (APRA), Colombia's Liberal Party, Costa Rica's Partido Liberación Nacional (PLN), Chile's Christian Democrats, and Argentina's Radical Party, enjoyed widespread support, in contrast to the region's weak, fractious, leftist parties, which were badly tarnished by opportunistic alliances with dictators. One might presume that leftists were the chief preoccupation of autocrats, but social democrats and their followers troubled them far more.

Reformers earned the respect of their political base because for decades they had fought courageously against tyranny. As student activists in

the 1920s and 1930s, they battled the region's many caudillos and the repressive militaries and reactionary oligarchies that propped them up. Experiencing partial victories, bitter defeats, repression, and exile, members
of this historical generation were marked in ways that would not become
fully apparent until they were much older. Some owed an intellectual debt
to the Mexican Revolution, while others dabbled with communism before
cutting ties with what they concluded was an imported, rigid ideology ill-
suited to local realities. Student militants also forged ties with like-minded
peers throughout the hemisphere and cultivated the support of progressives in Europe and the United States. When they became the political establishment of the 1950s and 1960s, they replicated this strategy, reaching
out to liberal politicians, such as Porter, as well as to the leaders of the
U.S. labor movement, academics, and journalists.

Just as reformers built cosmopolitan alliances, so too did dictators, a
phenomenon that Venezuela's Betancourt aptly called *La Internacional de la
Espada* (The International of the Sword). That informal pact enabled dictators to extend their reach far beyond the confines of national borders. A tyrant like Trujillo could act with impunity, eliminating dissidents and political
rivals abroad. He hounded dissidents relentlessly in the diaspora and purposefully destabilized democratic governments that were in league with his
political enemies. Strategies that the Dominican dictator honed on the island
to guarantee his political survival were exported with deadly effect. He even
went as far as to hire *pistoleros* (gunmen) to assassinate the elected heads of
state of Haiti, Cuba, Venezuela, Costa Rica, and Guatemala. Moreover, Trujillo and his peers in La Internacional knew just how to curry favor in Washington, tarring and feathering their opponents with a "red" brush. They, too,
built transnational networks, expending what for their poor countries were
vast sums to lobby anticommunist politicians on the Hill.

Convinced that La Internacional represented an existential threat to
their cause, reformers declared that no civilian government was safe until
the cancer of dictatorship was excised entirely from the hemisphere.
Where they were sorely mistaken was in their unshakable belief that
democratic rule was inevitable, that their authoritarian enemies were on
the verge of extinction, and that the future was theirs.

Bedeviling their efforts was the *eminence grise* of La Internacional,
the Argentine general Juan Perón, whose diplomats and labor attachés
were, in the words of Betancourt, "conspiring, whispering, and encouraging" fellow strongmen to defend their interests against the region's democracies.[4] Also lending inspiration to La Internacional was the Spanish

dictator Francisco Franco, who hosted sumptuous state visits for his Latin American brethren. Especially problematic for democrats was Washington's cozying up to the region's dictatorships. Indeed, successive Democratic and Republican administrations were not only loath to criticize authoritarian regimes, but by providing military and economic assistance they made it easier for their armies to repress the internal opposition and to subvert neighboring democracies.

To be sure, reformers paid a high price for their principles. Some were murdered, and many were tortured, imprisoned, or spent years in exile. Often they found common cause with ideologically diverse exiles who populated the capitals of the Caribbean, as well as Mexico City, Miami, New York, and Paris. An understated feature of the war against dictatorships was the willing and able participation of battle-tested Spanish Civil War veterans. Hardened by the fight against fascism in Europe, exiled Spanish Republicans brought both convictions and military expertise to the circum-Caribbean theater. Even a confirmed Marxist like Alberto Bayo appreciated the importance of the democratic crusade against La Internacional, personally risking life and limb to oust Somoza. Years before he instructed the likes of Fidel Castro and Che Guevara on the finer points of guerrilla warfare, the author of this book's epigraph dedicated his 1950 memoir *Tempestad en el Caribe* to those intrepid "soldiers with pen or sword" fighting "against the dictatorships of America." Among those Bayo singled out for special commendation were Betancourt, Figueres, Bosch, and the Guatemalan president Juan José Arévalo (1944–1950).[5]

Indeed, multiple political agendas were in play—official and informal, legal and unlawful—with a host of political actors seeking to shape and influence the course of reform and U.S.–Latin American relations. The collective efforts of democrats and their allies did not go unrewarded. Between 1952 and 1961, ten dictators either stepped down voluntarily or were driven from power.

Cold Warriors like Nixon and Secretary of State John Foster Dulles viewed this democratic wave with trepidation, convinced that strongmen were more likely to thwart communist infiltration than democrats. In fact, U.S. foreign policy goals remained remarkably consistent and bipartisan for much of the century. Washington sought to preserve its sphere of influence in Latin America, contain international communism, protect and defend the investments of its nationals and corporations, promote regional stability, and ensure support for its policies. As Assistant Secretary of State for Inter-American Affairs Henry Holland put it matter-of-factly in 1955, "the objective of United States inter-American policy is to persuade the Latin American Governments and peoples to adhere to our political and economic policies."[6]

It should come as little surprise that a young Fidel Castro received material assistance from reformers while he was in the Sierra Maestra mountains. Betancourt and Figueres were persuaded that the young Cuban's fight was theirs—that is, until Castro embraced communism. Fidel's early calls for continental unity against authoritarianism and his attempts to oust Trujillo, Somoza, and Haiti's François Duvalier in the spring and summer of 1959 appeared to validate moderates' support for the young *comandante*. Watchful waiting, however, soon gave way to disillusionment, especially after Cuba's bear hug of the Soviet Union. The revolution's sudden radicalization, its provision of assistance to budding leftist insurgencies across the region, and Washington's determination to prevent another Cuba from happening elsewhere placed reformers in an untenable position, necessitating the taking of sides.

The bitter half-century fight left its mark on reformers. It is no small irony that when they finally achieved political success, these democrats governed with a heavy hand. Now ensnared in the Cold War's web, they turned on a new generation of politicized students who were enamored of Castro's Revolution. For their part, student activists ridiculed their political elders, calling them "bourgeois lapdogs of imperialism" while scheming to depose them. After 1960, moderates had the ear of the Kennedy administration, which implemented both altruistic (for example, Alliance for Progress, Peace Corps) and counterinsurgent strategies. As guerrilla insurgency escalated, reformers fought a rearguard action against the right and the left that circumscribed their options, undermining their legitimacy at home and abroad.

A new generation of military commanders quickly concluded that civilian politicians were too weak to defeat leftist subversion, so they restored authoritarian rule in eight countries between 1962 and 1964. Coupled with the unanticipated emergence of the United States and Cuba as parties to the region's longstanding border wars, the few remaining democracies were forced to tack to the right, moderate their agendas, and align their foreign policies with Washington's. Just as a democratic wave gained momentum, Havana, Washington, and Moscow indelibly altered the hemisphere's political calculus.

Most of the new democracies thus became casualties of a belated Cold War. (Porter, too, paid a price for his candor: his principled stance unleashed a concerted campaign by his political opponents, and a once-promising career was derailed at the polls in 1960.) By the end of the 1960s, repressive military regimes, noticeably more ideological than their predecessors, dominated the political landscape, as hundreds of thousands perished on the hemisphere's killing fields.

I became acquainted with this democratic crusade while researching an international history of Central European refugees who fled one racist dictator (Hitler) and were then welcomed by another. The refugees and their donors rallied to Trujillo's defense after he was widely criticized for having his henchmen abduct a prominent dissident off the streets of New York in 1956. When the despot tried to cover his tracks by silencing those linked to the disappearance, he inadvertently turned Representative Porter into the darling of reformers.[7]

Until recently, students of U.S.–Latin American relations during the Cold War era, relying heavily on U.S. diplomatic records, have adhered uncritically to an East-West binary, obscuring as much as it reveals about the multifaceted nature of inter-American relations during this turbulent period. To give but one example, an otherwise splendid synthesis correlates the region's history during those decades with the accepted North American periodization of the conflict. "The Latin American Cold War began not in 1959, with the triumph of the Cuban Revolution, nor in 1954, with the United States' first intervention (Guatemala), but in the years following World War II."[8] Several innovative anthologies, which counter the traditional overreliance on English-language materials by tapping sources in Latin American archives to illuminate the Cold War's impact at the grassroots, remain wedded to that binary.[9] Not surprisingly, state terror, guerrilla insurgencies, dirty wars, mass graves, and the plight of the *desaparecidos* monopolize the literature, and much of that is filtered through the prism of U.S.–Latin American relations.[10] Too often, historical accounts of what preceded 1959 become an exercise in teleology, markers set down anticipating the Cuban Revolution's arrival. Meanwhile, moderates are scarcely mentioned. Why has much of the scholarship relegated reformism to an ephemeral role?[11]

My research underscores that hemispheric relations were not just reflected in an East-West mirror; they also were refracted through the lenses of Latin American liberalism and nationalism. Until now, the literature has largely glossed over reformers and their accomplishments, or alternatively, has written them off as *vendepatrias* (sellouts) or ineffectual, careerist politicians who stymied meaningful reform. That scholarship privileges the national context, neglects the movement's transnational character, and accentuates the period when reformers came of political age during the Cold War. Furthermore, studies of these politicians, whether in Spanish or English, are often uncritical or unabashedly partisan.[12] Absent is a fine-grained examination of why these movements resonated so deeply for many Latin Americans across the twentieth century. In keeping with the latest scholarship in international history, I illustrate how both internal and external forces affected the prospects for democratic rule in nations where reformers enjoyed sustained success (most notably, but not exclusively, in Venezuela, Costa Rica, and Colombia) and where they petered out or failed (for example, Cuba, Peru, the Dominican Republic). While much of the attention here is devoted to the countries of the Caribbean littoral, where the struggle for democratic rule was joined between the 1920s and the 1960s, similar battles were ongoing to a greater or lesser degree in the Southern Cone and the Andean region as well.[13]

Latin American democrats' decades-long fight to overcome authoritarian rule has much to teach us at a time when our own political institutions appear increasingly fragile, when there have been once-unthinkable calls in some quarters for our armed forces to crush domestic discontent, where at home and abroad a flagrant disregard for the rule of law by populist strongmen has been increasingly normalized, and when terms like *coup, insurrection, disinformation,* and *the big lie* are no longer considered artifacts of a distant time and place. Comparisons across political cultures and eras are always fraught, but Latin America's reformers, who had firsthand experience with all of these disturbing trends, learned at their peril that democracy could not be taken for granted and had to be defended at any cost.

What's in a Label?

The politicians at the heart of this study initially referred to themselves as democratic leftists, a descriptor they may have aspired to during their formative years, but over time, as circumstances dictated their pivot away from a progressive agenda, became a political albatross. They did not help their cause by making repeated promises to bring about a "revolution" in their respective societies. Also complicating matters was that early on, some reformers proudly declared that they were democratic socialists. By the late 1940s, however, anything that hinted at socialism became a distinct liability, and not just with policymakers in Washington.

Dictators and their conservative allies were quick to pounce on reformers' earlier admissions to paint them as fellow travelers or communists. Leftists, of course, never missed the chance to highlight the disparity between what their rivals promised and how modest their accomplishments really were.

Reformers did enjoy several advantages over their leftist competitors. While they were not averse to invoking Marxist precepts, especially when they denounced foreign investors, they were not constrained by ideological orthodoxy and enjoyed much greater latitude when it came to how and when they rallied their supporters. In contrast, the region's Communist parties had to wait for the right objective conditions before mobilizing their supporters, and even then, not before seeking the approval of a notoriously cautious Comintern. In addition, reformers' emphasis on bread-and-butter trade union demands often gave them a leg up in the fight to win over organized labor. They also had the luxury of casting themselves as homegrown, a feature that parties reputed to be joined at the hip to Moscow could not gainsay. On the other hand, since moderates posed a far more formidable threat to the political establishment, they were much more likely to experience repression.[14]

Some political theorists classify reformers as populists or protopopulists. Unfortunately, such terms have been applied to so many different historical actors—militarists, civilian politicians, progressives, reactionaries—that the terminology has almost lost its meaning. The more successful populists, such as Perón and Brazil's Getúlio Vargas, were charismatic leaders who built lasting political movements. Decrying "politics as usual," they denounced real and imagined members of the political establishment while invoking a black-and-white struggle between "the people" and their adversaries (for example, oligarchs, foreign companies, Washington, unwanted immigrants). Enemies of the state were labeled traitors or instruments of foreign powers.[15]

Although they were elected to office, once in power, populist politicians evinced scant respect for democratic norms or the rule of law. Under their watch, legislatures and judiciaries became rubber stamps to an omnipotent executive branch. Although dissent was tolerated in the breach, political opponents and the fourth estate were intimidated and repeatedly branded as enemies of the people. Attacks on critics by armed thugs or paramilitaries loyal to populist leaders were tolerated or encouraged.

Even though they challenged and undermined the legitimacy of the political system, populists stopped short of destroying it. Instead, they used and abused democratic institutions to weaken the opposition and consolidate their authority. The result was an authoritarian version of democracy that upended society but rarely survived the leader's political decline or death. In fact, populist movements nosedived in Peru, Chile, and Colombia immediately after their leaders were chased out of office, defeated at the polls, or assassinated. The glaring exception was the resilient Peronists, who, against all odds, managed to overcome not only their leader's death in 1974 but the disastrous term in office of Perón's successor in the Casa Rosada, his second wife, Isabel Martínez de Perón. Even the savage Dirty War (1976–82), which expressly targeted movement organizers, failed to throttle Peronism.

Like reformers. populists constructed broad coalitions that cut across class lines, but they gave pride of place to those from below. They sought to dignify and elevate the standing of the popular classes, who, they insisted, were not just demeaned, but were defrauded of their rights as citizens by a rigged political game. Although populist parties were fundamentally personalistic vehicles, the relationship between the leader and the masses was reciprocal. Supporters made demands and expected their *jefe* to deliver on his promises. And while it is true that a populist's party apparatus mobilized workers and enforced discipline, that relationship was never, as their adversaries insisted, a simple case of the leadership's manipulation of the masses.[16]

All populists promised redistributive measures to redress social and economic disparities and were critical of laissez-faire liberal policies. Instead, they emphasized economic sovereignty and self-sufficiency. Even as populists reserved their harshest slings and arrows for wealthy capitalists—especially foreign investors—in practice, they rarely challenged the sanctity of private property.[17]

Populists and reformers overlapped in their policy prescriptions, their methods of political persuasion, and their reliance on multiclass coalitions. Both preached the gospel of economic nationalism and believed that the state should play an outsized role in promoting development. While populists deserve credit for policies that improved the quality of life for the urban working classes, they were not alone in bringing about meaningful change to their constituents. The agrarian reform of the Movimiento Nacional Revolucionario (MNR), for example, arguably was more successful in transforming the Bolivian countryside than the policies of the Mexican president Lázaro Cárdenas, while Frei's Revolution in Liberty did more to alter land tenure in Chile than did his Marxist successor, Salvador Allende. Figueres's nationalization of the banks, expansion of the social safety net, and astute renegotiation of labor contracts with the United Fruit Company (UFCO) testify to his commitment to improving the lives of everyday Costa Ricans.

Methods of political organizing were comparable. Both populists and reformers utilized patronage, mass gatherings, and propaganda to reinforce links between the leadership and their rank-in-file. As we shall see, AD and APRA assembled powerful political machines in Venezuela and Peru that were comparable to the Peronist party apparatus and were the envy of their domestic competitors.

But there were clear-cut differences as well. Reformers were strongly committed to the liberal democratic project, voicing opposition to dictatorships of any kind and insisting that the military should distance itself from the political arena and remain in the barracks. Unlike their populist rivals, they accepted the need for checks and balances and, for the most part, permitted freedom of expression and association. Virtually every reformist president accepted defeat at the polls and endeavored to ensure an orderly transition of power. Democrats detested *continuismo*, the common practice of succeeding oneself in office. The one exception was the Bolivian president Paz Estenssoro, who tried to override the constitutional mandate against succeeding himself in power in 1964. He was summarily ousted, in large part because disenchanted members of his own party abandoned him and supported a coup d'état. With these political traits in mind, a progressive like Cárdenas, who is often pegged as a populist, fits far more comfortably in the reformist camp.

On the other hand, moderates were not averse to decreeing martial law and clamping down on domestic protest when threats arose that endangered the survival of democratic rule. And when they perceived that the electoral playing field was so tilted that they did not stand a chance, opportunistic politicians enlisted the support of disgruntled members of the military in order to establish (or reestablish) democratic rule.

Rather than stake their political fortunes on the direct, unmediated bond between a personalistic politician and the masses, reformist movements used the vehicle of the political party to secure victory at the polls. Given the heterogenous nature of these broad-based parties, it was not surprising that intraparty debates turned downright contentious. In some cases, rump factions emerged, rupturing party unity, and at other times, splinter groups broke away to form their own parties. AD, for instance, faced an existential crisis during the early 1960s when two factions waged a fierce campaign contesting the party's political direction. So acrimonious were the disputes that the party's leader, President Betancourt, threatened to resign on two occasions if dissidents within his own party made their objections to his policies public. In sum, although populists and reformers shared several attributes, the differences were stark enough that contemporaries had little trouble differentiating between the two.

There were moderate politicians, though, such as Peru's Víctor Raúl Haya de la Torre and Colombia's Jorge Eliécer Gaitán, whose cultish appeal and authoritarian propensities blurred the line between the two prototypes. The reformist movement that most closely resembled populism was Peru's APRA, which propagated a cult of personality around its charismatic leader. Often a groomsman, never a groom, Haya never governed Peru during his lifetime, making comparisons with other populist rulers speculative. Given his magnetic hold over his followers and APRA's use of heavy-handed tactics, however, it is certainly understandable why Aprismo has elicited such comparisons. Assessments of what kind of ruler Gaitán would have been are even more problematic, since the charismatic politician was cut down by an assassin's bullet just as he was making his mark in Colombian politics.[18]

Like civilian politicians, dictators were products of distinctive political cultures, and as a result, their methods of governing and their conduct of foreign affairs varied widely. A Somoza or a Trujillo had a military background, but their regimes could not have been more different from Colonel Perón's or Peru's military dictator Manuel Odría. At first glance, Trujillo's thirty-one-year reign (1930–1961) and the Somoza family dynasty (1936–1979) appear to be throwbacks to an earlier age of strongman rule. Yet both experimented and evolved over the course of their tenure, even incorporating populist rhetoric and strategies to mobilize their supporters and buy off the opposition.[19]

One might assume, given their martial background, that the Somozas and Trujillo would view their militaries as pillars of their regimes. In fact, high commands were perceived as potential threats. To assure their political survival, they instead relied on family members, cronies, and a pervasive security apparatus. Personalistic dictators, however, were not the only ones to govern in this manner. Pérez Jiménez, the epitome of the professionally trained modern officer, ruled in a similar fashion, with soldiers relegated to the barracks. Considering Venezuela's chronic history of *golpes* (coups), it was incumbent on his surveillance state to keep especially close tabs on the leadership of the armed forces. Given how marginalized the high command became during the Pérez Jiménez era, it was not surprising when disgruntled officers joined the popular insurrection that toppled the dictator in 1958. Other despots, such as Batista and Colombian general Gustavo Rojas Pinilla, co-opted key officers by incorporating them into the upper echelons of their administrations.

All dictators harassed dissidents at home and employed their diplomatic corps to monitor the movements of troublesome exiles in the diaspora. Their secret police watched the comings and goings of the opposition and shared that intelligence with their colleagues in La Internacional. But a stubborn few refused to cooperate with fellow autocrats and bristled when they felt that another dictator's diplomats acted too intrusively in domestic matters.

What strongmen had in common was the belief that civilian politicians were incompetent, corrupt, or self-serving. Some deemed their countries not yet ready for democratic rule, concluding that their tutelage was essential to prepare the nation for a democratic transition in the future; others contended that importing an alien political system like liberal republicanism to their countries made for a poor fit, considering the region's colonial heritage, and the long, dispiriting history of failed experiments with civilian governance since independence. This rarely deterred autocrats from paying lip service to constitutional formalities in order to legitimize their claims to power.

Mobilizing against Dictatorship

Part I of this book tracks a university reform movement that spread like wildfire throughout the hemisphere during the 1920s. What began in June 1918 as a spirited call by students in Córdoba, Argentina to bring about modest reforms to their university soon mushroomed into a full-throated critique of the ills besetting Latin American societies. Peru's student leader Haya de la Torre spearheaded a transnational movement to depose autocrats, employing the vehicle of the popular university to forge ties between workers and students.

Subsequent chapters scrutinize student movements in Venezuela and Cuba, where entrenched autocrats barred the doors to democratic reform. In the former, two student leaders, who followed markedly different political trajectories—Betancourt and the communist Gustavo Machado—are examined to illustrate how some youthful activists experimented with leftist ideology before rejecting it, while others embraced it wholeheartedly. For Betancourt, leftist radicalization represented a temporary interlude, a period he would spend the rest of his life explaining away as a moment of youthful indiscretion. Like many former believers, his antipathy for his former colleagues turned increasingly visceral. The dogmatic Machado, on the other hand, remained a loyal and faithful servant of the party, no matter the inconsistencies and ideological twists and turns in position dictated by Moscow. He had no tolerance for the likes of Betancourt and Haya, whom he dismissed as bourgeois pseudorevolutionaries.

Nowhere was student protest more successful than in Cuba, where the island's proximity to the Colossus of the North fueled nationalistic fervor and calls for the ouster of the ruthless dictator Gerardo Machado. What was distinctive about the Cuban student movement was its determination to thoroughly transform the island's neocolonial relationship with the United States. To students at the University of Havana, the North American intervention in 1898, successive military occupations, the Platt Amendment, and the ceding of Guantánamo to the U.S. military represented a betrayal of the principles for which heroic *mambises* (guerrilla fighters) had fought and died during the wars of independence (1868–1898).

Later chapters assess how the Mexican Revolution and U.S. foreign policy in the region simultaneously motivated and inflamed student militancy. When youthful refugees were forced to flee their homelands, Mexico's capital was their destination of choice. Seeking to counter Washington's influence in the isthmus, President Plutarco Calles's support for liberal parties in Central America during the mid-1920s buoyed militants across the region. A diplomatic showdown between Washington and Mexico City, however, made it apparent that the United States, even when confronted with widespread criticism of its policies at home and abroad, would not brook interference in its backyard. By the end of the 1920s, a chastened Calles, facing daunting domestic constraints and a concerted U.S. diplomatic and economic offensive, settled his differences with the Coolidge administration and tacked sharply to the right. Once considered the darling of Latin American progressives, Mexico's revolutionary regime now cracked down on homegrown leftists and political exiles to whom it had granted sanctuary.

Meanwhile, extended U.S. military interventions in the Dominican Republic, Haiti, and Nicaragua and boots on the ground for shorter stints in Cuba, Panama, Puerto Rico, Honduras, and Mexico during the first decades of the century galvanized opposition at home and abroad. By the late 1920s, so-called peace progressives in the U.S. Congress and their allies in the media, the labor movement, academia, and women's organizations, emboldened by growing global opposition to the lingering Nicaraguan and Haitian interventions, raised their collective voices in protest. Although their disapproval was always more about the means than the ends, the peace progressives' campaign dovetailed with growing domestic weariness and skepticism about the moral and material costs of intervention.

Part I concludes with an analysis of the surprisingly influential role Cuban student activists played in Ramón Grau San Martín's one-hundred-day provisional government (1933–34). The transcendent figure of this period was Antonio "Tony" Guiteras, a former pharmaceutical student, who, at the age of twenty-seven, held down three posts in Grau's cabinet. His saga was emblematic of an idealistic, if ultimately tragic, strain of Cuban student radicalism. In just over three months, Guiteras pushed through landmark legislation, which had as its objective a fundamental redesign of the island's land and labor relations. His call for an autonomous, egalitarian revolution, free from external influence, whether from Washington or Moscow, won him the admiration of many of his peers. But Guiteras's principled stance and a dogged unwillingness to compromise unnerved and threatened elements across the political spectrum. He was assassinated by a strongman (Batista) and became a martyr for the cause of *Cuba libre*. Not surprisingly, Guiteras would be an inspiration to Fidel Castro and his followers.

Democratic Effervescence and Authoritarian Retrenchment

Part II delineates the transnational struggle against dictatorships between the 1940s and the 1970s. If the 1920s and 1930s were a time of thwarted ambition for social democrats, over the course of the next three decades, civilian rule alternated in power with dictatorship. A democratic wave emerged in the years immediately after World War II, as despots were booted from power in nine countries. Former student activists who had spent years in exile returned home to contribute to the new democracies. Reformist political parties, such as Venezuela's AD, Cuba's Auténticos, and Costa Rica's PLN, began the task of implementing much-needed reforms to their respective societies. Despite the postwar trend toward civilian rule, military high commands, either directly or indirectly, continued to play an intrusive role in the political arena in all

but four countries in the hemisphere. Moderates were soon disabused of
the idea that representative government was here to stay. By the end of
the 1940s, a resurgence of authoritarianism had crushed the democratic
offensive.

Ensuing chapters examine the decades-long fight to overturn Trujillo's dictatorship and consider in some detail the 1950s, a turbulent period when reformers, many of them in exile, pooled their limited
resources to make common cause with the region's remaining democracies. To elude Trujillista aggression, stateless Dominican refugees were
continually on the move, forced to seek out one safe haven after another.
The exiles' best-laid plans to oust the tyrant often foundered in the
maelstrom of regional politics. The entire Caribbean littoral was awash
in political intrigues, rivalries, and undeclared border wars during the
entire half-century, and policymakers in Washington were often stymied
in their efforts to get reformers and dictators to stand down. The Dominican case, then, is emblematic of the enduring transnational struggle
to overcome dictatorial rule, while it illustrates the great lengths tyrants
went to remain in power.

Reformers also banded together to overthrow Pérez Jiménez. By
early 1954, AD's efforts to remove him had reached an inflection point.
The underground's leadership had been decimated, and the lines of communication between it and AD-in-exile were frayed. At a desperate moment, Betancourt and Figueres announced a boycott of the upcoming
Inter-American Conference, scheduled to be held in Caracas in March of
that year. The boycott campaign shined a spotlight on the regime's atrocious human rights violations and sought to publicly embarrass Pérez Jiménez. The Caracas Conference is cast in the historical literature as a
crucible of the Cold War. I push back on that U.S.-centric assessment.
Dulles may have used the meetings to ram through an anticommunist
resolution that cleared the way for the CIA's successful overthrow of Jacobo Árbenz's democratically elected government in Guatemala, but
what was apparent from the acrimonious debate in Caracas was that only
the United States actually believed that international communism represented a threat to the region's security.

The 1954 intervention posed a challenge for reformers, who supported Árbenz's removal from power but were uncomfortable with U.S.
intervention. From their perspective, his ouster was not a harbinger of
the Cold War but another in a series of regional conflicts pitting dictatorships against democracies. Proof of that, they were quick to point out,

were Somoza's, Trujillo's, and Pérez Jiménez's behind-the-scenes involvement in the Guatemalan *golpe*. Moderates quickly recognized that the CIA's Operation PBSUCCESS was a no-win proposition. If they spoke out publicly against Árbenz, they would be assailed by those who were staunchly opposed to North American interference. If they condemned the Eisenhower administration, they feared it would only strengthen Washington's support for their mortal enemies. Their silence was deafening, costing them dearly in the court of public opinion, especially with a new generation of student militants.

Between 1952 and 1961, ten dictators either stepped down voluntarily or were driven from power. I scrutinize why liberals like Porter, Wayne Morse, J. William Fulbright, and Hubert Humphrey raised their voices in favor of reformers at this opportune moment. Just as in the 1920s, North American progressives signaled their displeasure with their government's Latin American policy. To be sure, this new generation of liberal politicians never once questioned the Cold War binary. As a result, they remained vulnerable to attacks from both the right and the left. But with dictators falling by the wayside, progressives on both sides of the border had reason to believe that democracy was finally on the march.

The democratic surge at the end of the 1950s dovetailed with Nixon's and Porter's visits to the region in 1958. I examine those trips in some detail to tease out the implications for reformers as they sought to navigate a moment that was at once promising and perilous. Columnist Walter Lippmann fittingly referred to the vice president's goodwill mission as a "diplomatic Pearl Harbor," as voices that had been silenced by years of repression now seized the opportunity afforded by democratic openings to express their dissatisfaction with Washington's policies. Latin Americans were savvy enough to realize that North American politicians were not all cut from the same cloth, however. In fact, "Charley" Porter's triumphal reception in Caracas, coming as it did so soon after the Nixon debacle, proved to be a balm for the many who aspired to a democratic future. The jarringly dissimilar responses to the two visits prompted a long-overdue reckoning in U.S. policy.

Fresh on the heels of those visits, Fidel Castro was given a hero's welcome in Caracas in late January 1959. Just two weeks after forcing Batista to flee the island, his message of transnational unity in the fight against La Internacional resonated with Venezuelans who had just overthrown their own despot. Believing that Castro's agenda was similar to their own and recognizing how popular he was with their constituents, reformers initially backed the young *comandante*. That honeymoon was short-lived. A backlash against the revolution's leftward drift polarized the region and a renewed war without borders, in which the Kennedy and Johnson administrations and Cuba were now active participants, contributed to the restoration of authoritarian rule in eight countries between 1962 and 1964. By the end of the decade, reformist governments had, with few exceptions, run aground on the shoals of revolution and reaction. Based on recent history, democrats had every reason to believe that the political pendulum would swing back and soon return them to power. But the protracted wars between guerrilla insurgencies and anti-communist military regimes meant that reformers would be sidelined for years to come.

This story begins with an unusual partnership during the late 1920s between the Nicaraguan rebel Augusto Sandino and an obscure Honduran poet and bookdealer, Froylán Turcios. The goals they articulated—opposition to dictatorship, anti-imperialism, the internationalization of the Panama Canal, Central American unification, economic nationalism, and a panhemispheric, Indo-Hispanic unity—reflected an ambitious cross-fertilization of ideas shared by two generations of public intellectuals and activists. Idealistic students from around the Caribbean rim enlisted in Sandino's "crazy little army," as the Chilean poet Gabriela Mistral affectionately dubbed the rebel's ragtag band of guerrilla fighters. To volunteer in Sandino's Latin American Legion they first traveled to Turcios's bookshop in Tegucigalpa, Honduras to meet with the poet, where he personally vetted prospective recruits before sending them on to the rebels' remote, mountainous redoubt in neighboring Nicaragua.

PART I

Mobilizing against Dictatorship

CHAPTER ONE

The Poet and the Rebel

I resolved to lend my services to Nicaragua because one was fighting there . . . not just for the Nicaraguan people but also for Venezuela and for the entire continent.

—CARLOS APONTE

Turcios then was the only door by which those of us coming from away could enter the fields of liberty in Nicaragua . . . his decision was final, and those whom he closed his doors to also were banned from the rebel camp.

—GREGORIO GILBERT

IN THE SUMMER OF 1928, a fifty-three-year-old poet, journalist, and book-dealer who hailed from the capital of Honduras, Tegucigalpa, was something of an international celebrity. Froylán Turcios's three-year-old, bimonthly literary and political review, *Ariel*—its title a homage to José Enrique Rodó's critique of North American materialism—reputedly enjoyed a circulation of somewhere between twenty-five thousand and fifty thousand copies an issue. One number, Turcios claimed, reached a remarkable one hundred thousand readers. Ever the self-promoter, the poet crowed that his audience extended from Alaska to Argentina, from Russia to Portugal, and from North Africa to Asia and Oceania.[1]

The figures are even more astonishing if we consider just how isolated Tegucigalpa was in the 1920s. Located in Honduras's central highlands, "this very simple, remote and rather lonely little mountain capital," as a North American travel writer described it in 1928, lacked railway service, and the road from it to the nation's principal port on the Atlantic coast had yet to be completed.[2]

What explains such a broad readership? Certainly not the hodgepodge of poems, short stories, and essays *Ariel* contained in each issue, even if Latin America's most renowned writers were occasional contributors.[3] Perhaps of greater interest was the reprinting of selected editorials and syndicated columns from newspapers all over Latin America, Europe, and the United States, carefully selected by the editor to echo his and his audience's progressive biases. To be sure, constraints on book publishing contributed to *Ariel*'s popularity; during the 1920s, literary and topical magazines were the principal vehicles of intellectual conversation throughout Latin America.

No doubt what really piqued the interest of many was the correspondence he included, coming from an even more remote backwater than Tegucigalpa, the rugged, mountainous Segovias of northern Nicaragua, just across Honduras's southern border. Turcios's journal was the principal purveyor of Augusto Sandino's letters and manifestos; the general, whose small army was conducting a guerrilla insurgency against the U.S. Marines, had chosen *Ariel* as his mouthpiece and Turcios as his spokesperson.[4] In a letter to the poet confirming their collaboration in September 1927, the rebel expressly authorized Turcios "to make it known to Central America, to the community of intellectuals, to the workers and artisans, and to the Indo-Hispanic race, that I will be intransigent and that I will not abandon my position until I have thrown the invaders and traitors from my country and from power those who have for so many years have trafficked with the nation's honor." Several months later he detailed the Honduran's responsibilities. As the rebel's exclusive representative "in the whole Hispanic continent," Turcios should, as he saw fit, "accept and deliver statements to the world press, to corporations, and to private persons."[5] Soon, sympathetic newspapers and magazines around the globe helped popularize *Ariel* by reprinting correspondence between the two that had been first published in the magazine.[6]

Turcios not only acted as Sandino's press service, he was a tireless propagandist for the cause. To counter Washington's cynical tarring of the rebel as a bloodthirsty bandit who preyed on U.S. soldiers and companies, he, by his own account, wrote four thousand letters on Sandino's behalf to prominent individuals and organizations in Europe, the United States, and Latin America, painting the Segovian as a noble patriot, fully justified in his heroic struggle to defend his homeland against imperialist aggressors. For his part, Sandino sent the poet detailed, sometimes overly embellished accounts of his army's encounters with the Marines, which, in turn, became fodder for Turcios's pressroom.[7] The Honduran then relayed the rebel's communiqués from the front to another propagandist, Nicaraguan physician Pedro Zepeda, then residing in Mexico City, who, in turn, forwarded the accounts to the wire services.[8] Referring to Turcios's efforts, Sandino later acknowledged, "We learned the tremendous value of publicity in terms of world opinion." In fact, the general was certain that thanks to the poet's labors he was much better known abroad than he was in his homeland.[9]

Encomiums of Turcios's political spadework were everywhere in the Latin American press. Typical was Haya de la Torre, who was so taken with him that he made the poet an honorary member of APRA. Writing in a sister publication, Haya praised Turcios for his determination and his principles. "*Ariel* represents the most brilliant press campaign against North American imperialism and is inspired by the highest ideals of Latin American unity." Nicaragua's poet laureate, Rubén Darío, was less effusive, however, drolly declaring Turcios a "typical representative of our zone. He writes books, publishes journals, and makes revolutions."[10]

From Paris, in a series of columns syndicated throughout Latin America, Mistral tweaked armchair critics who only paid lip service to the rebellion and praised Turcios for fixing the gaze of the Hispanic world on Sandino. The rebel's *Ejército Defensor de la Soberanía Nacional de Nicaragua* (EDSNN, or Army for the Defense of Nicaragua's National Sovereignty) became a pan-Latin symbol for a David versus Goliath struggle against the forces of reaction.[11] Sandino, she rhapsodized, "honors us with his struggle," and she had nothing but admiration for idealistic Latin American youth who were willing to leave their homes, universities, and countries to enlist in his army: they contributed "young blood and a reckless loyalty that only youth can offer."[12] In another column, "The Hunt for Sandino," she observed that Sandino's guerrilla army had united the region in a manner not seen since the Independence era, comparing the Nicaraguan to heroes like José Artigas, José Paéz, and José María Morelos. Washington should be wary, she prophesied, lest the pursuit of the rebel end in the freedom fighter's martyrdom.[13]

Newspapers across the region, such as the Buenos Aires daily *La Crítica*, with a print run of three hundred thousand, issued a call to arms, imploring readers to form a brigade to enlist in such a noble undertaking.[14] This helps to explain why some made the pilgrimage to Turcios's bookshop and the Segovias. Indeed, the Nicaraguan rebel cobbled together a Latin American Legion of sorts. Largely composed of volunteers from the greater Caribbean and Central America, their influence on the rebel was significantly greater than their numbers. More than a few would take up positions of leadership in his army, including the Dominican Gregorio Gilbert; Venezuelan communists Carlos Aponte and Gustavo Machado; the Salvadoran communist Farabundo Martí; Hondurans Porfirio Sánchez and José de la Rosa Tejada; the Guatemalan Manuel María Girón Ruano; a Colombian student, Rubén Ardila Gómez; the Peruvian Esteban Pavletich; and the Mexicans Manuel Chávarri and José de Paredes.[15] The reasons foreigners gave for joining Sandino's army differed, but more than a few expressed dissatisfaction and frustration with their own nation's inability or unwillingness to stand up to the United States. For instance, Ardila Gómez said he joined because he was humiliated by his nation's loss of Panama.[16] The general was heartened by the steady influx of Latin Americans into his army, calling it "eloquent proof of the immense value of the ties of blood, language and race that unite the Latin American peoples."[17]

The varied ideas and perspectives the volunteers carried with them to the Segovias and the unusual collaboration between the poet and the rebel help us to understand the rebellion's ambitious agenda and its continental reach. Although driving out the Marines was always nonnegotiable for Sandino—after all, U.S. military forces had occupied his homeland, with one six-month exception, since 1912—the rebel's objectives transcended Nicaraguan nationalism. As this chapter argues, virtually all of Sandino's lofty objectives—an end to strongman rule, the internationalization of the Panama Canal, the unification of the isthmus, anti-imperialism, economic nationalism, and a panhemispheric, Indo-Hispanic unity—resonated with the aspirations of two generations of Latin American *pensadores* (intellectuals) and activists.

The breadth, if not the depth, of the response to the uprising was staggering. Sandino's manifestos were read aloud and endorsed at

General Sandino and members of the Latin American Legion. Left to right, Rubén Ardila Gómez, José de Paredes, Sandino, Farabundo Martí, and Gregorio Gilbert, c. 1928. Photographic Prints Used in Marine Corps Exhibits, ca. 1913–1937; Record Group 127; Photograph No. 127-EX-1(6); National Archives at College Park, MD.

anti-imperialist congresses in Brussels and Frankfurt, and solidarity committees sprang up all over Latin America and in New York, Chicago, and Detroit. A broad swath of the international press and a considerable number of mainstream U.S. newspapers condemned the intervention; youthful nationalist Jawaharlal Nehru and Madame Sun Yat-Sen sent messages of support to the rebel; and improbably, Chiang Kai-Shek's nationalist army not only named a battalion after Sandino, but his image graced the Kuomintang army's banners as it marched into (then) Peking to celebrate its victory over the Japanese in 1928.[18]

In addition to his promotional work, during an eighteen-month period from July 1927 to January 1929 Turcios acted as both resident quartermaster and gatekeeper for the EDSNN, procuring arms and supplies and forwarding donations that had been raised abroad. A steady stream of men, arms, medicine, clothes, and information flowed from Honduras to the Segovias—"all we needed," according to one of Sandino's soldiers.[19] Stationed in Tegucigalpa, U.S. military attaché Fred Cruse sent detailed reports to the War Department about the comings and goings of messengers between Turcios's home and the Segovias. Owing to the absence of telegraph lines, the poor condition of roads, and the densely forested, mountainous terrain, he estimated, correspondence carried by go-betweens took a minimum of seven days from the Nicaraguan border town of Jalapa to the Honduran capital.[20]

Those who felt moved by Sandino's cause to join the rebellion had first to travel to Turcios's bookstore to meet with the poet, who vetted prospective recruits. If he thought they could be of value, he arranged for a guide to escort them two hundred miles overland to Sandino's camp in El Chipotón. A typesetter by trade who had fought against the North American occupation of his homeland, Gilbert recalled in his memoirs that he arrived in Tegucigalpa carrying two letters of introduction, one for the poet and the other for the general. Gilbert recalled that Turcios took his responsibilities seriously: "His decision was final, and those he closed his doors to also were banned from the rebel camp." He added that the Honduran was so strongly committed "that it would have been difficult, if not impossible, to determine who felt the most for it, Sandino the guerrilla or Turcios the poet."[21] Echoing Gilbert's testimonial was Sandino's personal secretary, Farabundo Martí, who urged a colleague back home in San Salvador to encourage others to join the fight. "There are many in El Salvador who want to join the ranks of the liberators ... they must obtain a passport ... travel to Tegucigalpa, and try to obtain an audience with Froylán Turcios. ... Don Froylán will tell them the way to our camps."[22]

Further evidence of the trust Sandino placed in the poet occurred when a North American peace delegation, led by a pacifist Episcopal minister, John Nevin Sayre, and composed of members of the Fellowship of Reconciliation (FOR) and the American Friends Service Committee, traveled to Nicaragua on a fact-finding mission in December 1927. Sayre's intent, not shared with the other members of the delegation, was to meet with the rebel in the Segovias and with U.S. officials in the hopes of brokering an end to hostilities and the withdrawal of the Marines. The FOR-Quaker Mission of Peace and Good Will in Central America made the mistake, however, of first traveling to Managua, the Nicaraguan capital, instead of Tegucigalpa. As the best analysis of the mission noted, if only Sayre had "told the others of his plan to meet Sandino ... it might have been possible to make contact with Sandino from Honduras where the rebel leader may have felt considerably less threatened and less suspicious of their intentions." Instead, in Managua, the U.S. legation dissuaded the delegation from visiting the rebel, and even though Sayre secured audiences with both Sandino's father and his wife in order to ask for their assistance in arranging a meeting with the general, a skittish Sandino, then under attack from the Marines, refused to meet with the delegation.[23] Considering how savvy Turcios was about promoting the cause and how opposed the Mission of Peace was to U.S. intervention, there seems little doubt about how the Honduran would have reconciled the costs and benefits of such an encounter.

Honduran authorities and erstwhile recruits were not the only ones to show up at Turcios's doorstep, although not all came away impressed. A German journalist passing through Tegucigalpa pegged the poet as a misguided, star-struck romantic: "Only by hearsay and from letters does he know his hero [Sandino], and . . . he will not allow himself to be robbed of his happy illusion. . . . Buried under a mass of manuscripts, newspapers and books, he has created the protagonist of a drama which is imaginary but which the world has taken seriously."[24] The Venezuelan Machado also was not an admirer. He stayed long enough in Tegucigalpa before joining Sandino's army to cast a disapproving eye, dismissing Turcios as "one of those ivory tower, literary old-timers that live in abstract clouds of thought. . . . All that *Ariel* publishes is drum-beating and flattery."[25]

Others were far more complimentary. Carleton Beals, an intrepid North American writer then living in Mexico City, had persuaded his editor at *The Nation* in New York that he could obtain an exclusive interview with the general at his base camp. With the assistance of Sandino sympathizers in Mexico City and San Salvador in late January 1928, Beals was shepherded to Turcios's bookstore. Cognizant of the potential propaganda value of an empathetic treatment in English, Turcios quickly arranged for a guide to take Beals to Sandino's camp.[26]

All told, Beals filed six stories for *The Nation*, which collectively humanized the man Washington had denounced as a bandit and helped to alter public opinion in the United States. He also thought highly of Sandino's liaison, describing the poet as "a truly noble and free soul" who was under "constant police surveillance and is probably protected from arrest only by his international prominence as a man of letters."[27] Characterizing Turcios as "a middle-aged man of charming simplicity," with "just a hint of [the] politician along with the poet," Beals provided his readers with an intimate account of the Honduran in his element: "His office proved a combination bookstore, editorial headquarters, and parlor. He appeared clad in a sweater and cap. . . . He brought out some new books on Latin America." The journalist then let the bookdealer explain what works captured his fancy. "You see, I am a very foolish bookseller. I only keep books which I think worthwhile—in every literature. And I try to make my magazine *Ariel* not only a Sandino organ, but a guide to the best new books."[28]

Intentionally or not, Beals neglected to mention that the bookshop also served as a partial repository for the archive of Sandino's army. The rebel considered the documents "a moral treasure of great historical value," which he was keen to preserve for posterity.[29]

After meeting with Turcios in his bookshop and interviewing Sandino in the Segovias, Beals became an advocate. Speaking in April 1928 to a packed house at a fundraiser for the rebel at the Virginia Fábregas auditorium in Mexico City, he received an especially warm welcome. Beals was taken aback by the reception, joking, "frankly, this ovation scares me more than the [U.S.] airplanes" that routinely conducted bombing raids in the Segovias. In addition to Beals's recounting of his trip, a brief telegram from Turcios was read aloud, saluting the "noble Mexican people," and two hundred fifty pesos were raised for Sandino's army.[30]

Then, suddenly, only eighteen months after their fruitful collaboration began, the Honduran and the Nicaraguan went their separate ways. Six months after the breakup an increasingly isolated Sandino would feel compelled to leave his lair in the mountains and travel to Mexico in hope of obtaining assistance from its government. From his exile in Mérida, Yucatán, far removed from the fight, he discussed his reasons for temporarily abandoning the struggle and reflected on the value of his collaboration with Turcios in a newspaper interview. "What we lacked was not weapons or money or bullets, but moral support, the sympathy that we have always had from all the countries of America. We were overwhelmed by the silence, by the isolation, the desperation of being ignored. We missed the world knowing that we were still in the fight; it is for this reason that I left Nicaragua. Froylán Turcios's resignation brought this isolation. We have agents, but, unfortunately, many of them have been selfish; others, frankly, traitors; others, merely inactive. When Turcios was our representative in Honduras, we were in contact with the world. . . . But Turcios was gone and we were left isolated."[31]

We will address the reasons for and the implications of this awkward political divorce later, but what makes Turcios such a fascinating figure is not his ephemeral alliance with Sandino; it is that he and his bookstore in remote Tegucigalpa became an intellectual and political crossroads for the greater Caribbean. Activists and intellectuals of every conceivable ideological stripe paid a visit on their way to the Segovias, submitted their work for publication, or corresponded with him. Although Turcios's political work and mentorship of Sandino have received the most scholarly attention, the friendship between the Honduran and the Nicaraguan, as we shall see, was emblematic of a deeper-rooted synergy between members of two distinctive generations during the turbulent 1920s.

Porous Borders

The U.S. chargé d'affaires Dana Munro, who met with the Sayre delegation in Managua, was certainly cognizant of the difficulties that a porous border and a propagandist like Turcios posed for North American interests. He cabled Secretary of State Frank Kellogg: "Sandino . . . is unquestionably receiving arms and supplies from Honduran sources. . . . It would be most helpful if the Honduran government could be induced to exercise a more effective vigilance on the frontier and to remove officials who are in sympathy with the bandits."[32]

Although unclear, Munro's reference to "officials" suggests that Turcios may not have acted alone. Five days later, the secretary relayed Munro's message to the U.S. minister in Tegucigalpa, George Summerlin, with explicit instructions: "Department expects you to impress upon [Honduran] President [Miguel] Paz [Barahona] necessity" of preventing "the rebels from receiving material assistance from Honduras."[33] A follow-up telegram on January 4, 1928, from Kellogg to Summerlin drove home the point: "Should the Government of Honduras be unable to undertake this, it would be very helpful if you could have the Government of Honduras request the Government of the United States to prevent the bandits from entering Honduras, using the territory of Honduras as a base of operations if necessary."[34]

Policymakers in Washington were not the only ones aware of the problem. UFCO, which had significant investments in Honduras, wrote the State Department in July 1928 about Turcios's and Sandino's alleged ties to the Mexican Communist Party (*Partido Comunista Mexicano*, PCM) and fretted that "Turcios might support a rebellion [in Honduras]."[35] Summerlin seems to have taken the company's allegations at face value. Although the name of the "agent" was redacted out of a letter the minister sent to Kellogg, it is clear that he was referring to Turcios: "There is no doubt that [. . .] who is Sandino's openly avowed agent in Tegucigalpa, is sending money in considerable amounts to Sandino, although it would be difficult to prove in a court of law. . . . There appears to be little doubt, although there is no tangible proof, that [. . .] is in touch with, if he is not actually an agent of, the All-America Anti-Imperialist League in the United States. . . . In view of widespread native sympathy for Sandino, and the weakness of Dr. Paz's Government, it is not within reason to expect him to take such action unless an appropriate demand is made upon him."[36]

El pulpo (the octopus), the pejorative term for the banana company in the isthmus, was certainly correct that communist front organizations in New York and Mexico City, such as the Anti-Imperialist League of the Americas (*Liga Antiimperialista de las Américas* or LADLA) were funneling funds for Sandino's rebellion via Turcios, but the inference that the poet might be a fellow traveler was a red herring.[37]

Not until the middle of 1928 did Summerlin's entreaties produce results. Brigadier General Frank McCoy, the commander of U.S. forces in Nicaragua, persuaded Paz Barahona to permit his troops to cross the Honduran border in pursuit of Sandino's troops. As a result, sixteen hundred rebels surrendered that summer alone.[38] Then, citing Central American treaty obligations requiring authorities to contain revolutionists from fomenting unrest in neighboring countries, Summerlin persuaded the Honduran president to clamp down on Turcios's activities and to shut down *Ariel*.[39]

Undeterred, the poet began smuggling issues of his magazine out of the country and had the content published by sympathetic venues in Guatemala, El Salvador, Costa Rica, and Mexico.[40] He also unleashed a screed in *El Cronista*, a Tegucigalpan newspaper, accusing the president of suborning Honduran sovereignty: "Our politicians, who grovel at the feet of the arrogant *yanquis*, are securing the chains of the most vile servitude . . . they are drowning our autonomy in an abyss of abjection and infamy."[41]

Yet sealing the frontier remained a challenging proposition. As late as May 1929, the U.S. minister in Managua, Charles Eberhardt, advised Kellogg's successor, Henry Stimson, that despite "repeated representations," Nicaraguan president José Moncada was "greatly perturbed" by the Honduran government's failure to curtail the flow of "arms and other material" to the rebels.[42] Infuriated by Marine bombing of their villages, Honduran peasants living on or near the frontier defied their government's orders and continued to offer shelter to fleeing rebels.[43] One incident in particular drove home the point that Turcios's propagandizing had an impact at home as well as abroad. In March 1929, two conscripts from the Nicaraguan National Guard deserted and crossed the border into Honduras. When they reached the capital, the Nicaraguan government filed a request for their extradition, and the Honduran Supreme Court complied. But protests in the capital were so great that the prisoners "escaped." And when the new Honduran president, Vicente Mejía Colindres, declared martial law along the frontier two months later, it caused such an uproar that the Congress undercut the president's authority by enacting legislation to reduce the size of the army. After a trip through the region in 1930, the journalist Raymond Buell noted that Hondurans continued to regard Sandino "as a great Central American patriot" and that efforts to curb the flow of weapons and goods had been largely unsuccessful.[44]

Bosom Buddies

The son of a well-to-do rancher who exported cattle to Cuba and Puerto Rico, Turcios was born in 1874 in the small district seat of Juticalpa in Olancho Department, some 250 kilometers from the Honduran capital. As a young man, he threw himself into journalism, writing for and then editing a number of magazines. His early contributions were largely literary, but in 1910, writing under a pseudonym, he penned his first anti-imperialist tract, criticizing North American intervention.

He became increasingly strident in his opposition to the United States when the U.S. Marines occupied his country in 1924. The poet swung into action, forming a patriotic committee, publishing a newspaper aptly named the *Boletín de la Defensa Nacional*, and distributing issues of the paper gratis.[45] In one issue, he implored his countrymen to unify and defy foreign intervention: "We are the only ones who must find solutions to our problems. . . . This is a moment when silence would be a crime."[46]

Ariel's inaugural issue appeared on March 15, 1925. In it, Turcios outlined his aspirations for the magazine. In addition to disseminating cultural production, he hoped the journal would elicit a greater sense of "public-spiritedness" (*civismo*) among his countrymen. As historian Volker Wünderich notes, inherent in this concept was a steadfast opposition to militarism and caudillo rule and a renewed commitment to liberal democratic norms.[47]

Well before he enlisted in Sandino's cause, Turcios garnered attention beyond the isthmus. The young Cuban communist Julio Antonio Mella, who had been driven into exile by the dictator Machado, was an early admirer. Writing from Mexico City in July 1926, the rabble-rouser congratulated the poet for "the beautiful chaos of your crusades . . . for Honduras's right to be free."[48]

It is quite possible that Sandino first learned of Turcios when Sandino worked for the Cuyamel Fruit Company in La Ceiba, Honduras during the early 1920s.[49] He alluded to this in a letter to Turcios in September 1927 when he first asked the poet if he would act as his personal secretary outside of Nicaragua. "What a coincidence! Before you even knew about my attitude and ideas, I felt a kinship and affection for you, since I was enthusiastic about all that you had written."[50]

Public intellectuals like Turcios moved effortlessly from one genre to the other. As the literary critic Ángel Rama has noted more generally about writers during this period, "poetry and journalism were intermixed in their daily work, going unceasingly from one to the other, in the same day, over the same writing desk."[51] Turcios's bookshelves reflected his erudition and eclectic interests. Classics by Maxim Gorky, Marcel Proust, and H. G. Wells were interspersed with works by the Argentine political theorist José Ingenieros, the Spanish dramatist Ramón del Valle-Inclán, and the Cuban poet and revolutionary José Martí.

A highly regarded North American journalist and travel writer, Arthur Ruhl, befriended Turcios during his stay in the capital, where he had a "pleasant chat" on a number of topics, including Walt Whitman's poetry, "which Señor Turcios greatly admired." The Honduran shared some of his publications with his guest, including his unpublished novel, *Annabel Lee*. Delighted to meet a kindred spirit during his travels, Ruhl quoted liberally from the novel's foreword, penned by fellow Honduran poet Juan Ramón Molina. As early as 1906, Molina had praised Turcios's decision to forsake loftier intellectual circles, to bloom where he was planted, as it were, in his *patria*. "The poet is of medium stature, somber without being dark, like the Moors of Teneriffe [*sic*]," Ruhl wrote. "Perhaps his life might have been happier in a more aromatic world, but in default of that he has set about to make a world of his own, building little by little on the azure plateau, a palace of faith, love and dreams."[52]

The well-read Honduran had a special interest in theosophy—Rudolf Steiner was a particular favorite. Spiritism and spiritualism were subjects of keen interest to the autodidact Sandino as well. A mélange of eastern spiritual concepts, ranging from universal brotherhood, a tolerance of all faiths, a commitment to personal ethical behavior, communing with the dead, and reincarnation, animated liberal *pensadores* in the

1920s. Visits by the prominent spiritualist Jiddu Krishnamurti, his lieu-tenant Curuppumullage Jinarajadasa, and Annie Besant drew enthusiastic audiences across the isthmus.[53] Sandino's biographer contends that this "interest in Eastern learning, and above all, theosophy, marked a genera-tion of Central American poets and intellectuals."[54] It also helped forge cultural and political ties between *pensadores* and the popular classes. As historian Catherine LeGrand points out, these ideas did not just inhabit urban centers. They permeated provincial regions, such as Colombia's banana zone on its Caribbean coast.[55]

The poet and the rebel's fascination with alternative spiritual tradi-tions was not unusual. Liberals and progressives were disheartened with the Catholic Church's steadfast backing of oligarchs and dictators. The pair was especially taken with the nonsectarian teachings of the Bengali polymath Rabindranath Tagore, a fierce critic of British colonial rule, who had made a triumphal tour of the Southern Cone in the fall of 1924.[56] Tagore's call for a synthesis of the knowledge and teachings of all the great religions resonated with *pensadores*. Sandino's own eclectic spir-ituality would become apparent during his stay in Mexico, when he joined the Argentine-based Magnetic Spiritual School of the Universal Commune.[57] His melding of such distinctive spiritual traditions with the armed struggle baffled supporters and opponents alike.

Just how often Sandino and Turcios actually met is unclear. One ac-count claimed that Sandino stayed with Turcios early on when he came down with malaria and needed treatment from the Honduran's doctor, and there is evidence in the form of a photograph that Turcios made at least one trip to the Segovias during the eighteen-month period they worked most closely together. A group portrait of Sandino, Turcios, and four members of the Latin American Legion appears in a short bio-graphical sketch of Farabundo Martí. Turcios is dressed for the occasion, fitted out in a sport jacket and bowtie.[58]

Sandino and Turcios knew enough about each other that the general sent condolences to the poet on the passing of his sister and then thanked Turcios for sending birthday wishes. We do know they corre-sponded faithfully at least twice a month because the poet published much of that correspondence in *Ariel*. Their letters make clear that for a time Sandino regarded Turcios as both mentor and muse. Typical of this high regard was a letter in which Sandino invoked the honorific *maestro* (teacher) in referring to Turcios and praised the poet's efforts on behalf of the rebellion: "your pen has stirred the heart of my valiant army, as it has mine ... there's no one better than yourself to serve as the faithful representative of our sacred right to defend our national sovereignty."[59] Returning the compliment, Turcios praised Sandino for having "stirred a powerful movement of universal awareness abroad ... which will force imperialism to retreat from your country."[60]

Moreover, both were dyed-in-the-wool Liberals. Party identification was deeply ingrained throughout the isthmus, allegiances were passed down from one generation to the next, and partisan loyalties often transcended national borders. Harold Dodds, a North American professor and electoral consultant working in Nicaragua at the behest of Warren Harding's administration, remarked that Conservative and Liberal "Party leaders and their followers display a bitterness towards their opponents which makes ordinary social and business intercourse between members of opposite parties almost impossible." It would not have surprised Dodds to learn that the Honduran and the Nicaraguan were political confederates. "A man is a Liberal or a Conservative before he is a Nicaraguan," he related, "and the bond between a Liberal of Nicaragua and another of Honduras or Guatemala is closer than that between Liberal and Conservative Nicaraguans."[61] The result, according to Buell, was "a curious combination of internal revolution and international war," with Liberals and Conservatives in one country not infrequently providing arms and funds to like-minded colleagues in another.[62]

From the outset, Sandino made clear that his fight meant more than driving the Marines from his homeland. In May 1927, the general had refused to lay down his arms and accept a power-sharing agreement between Liberals and Conservatives, a pact brokered by Washington. Among the concessions agreed to was that U.S. officials would supervise upcoming national elections. To demilitarize the countryside before the vote, partisans on both sides of the conflict were offered amnesty and encouraged to turn in their weapons for cash. More than two thousand combatants accepted the amnesty.[63]

In one of his first manifestos, Sandino explained why he summarily rejected the Tipitapa Pact—named for the locale outside Managua where the talks were held. He drew a bright line between "puritanical and honorable" Liberals like himself and those "chicken" Liberals who sold out to the *yanqui* "machos." True Liberals, he insisted, "will never permit the division of their party in the next elections, because this would mean allowing the triumph of the Conservatives." His army would never "surrender our weapons as long as the government is Conservative," but would, however, hand over "our weapons only to a (true) Liberal government, even if we should not be followers of that government."[64] If observers were needed to ensure clean, verifiable elections, he wrote Turcios, let it be Latin Americans, not North Americans, "because they do not constitute a threat to our sovereignty and they are bound to us by ties of race, religion, and language."[65]

The Liberal Moncada would win the 1928 presidential election, but Sandino's forces refused to relinquish their arms, since the rebel viewed the elections as a farce and an imposition, certain that the "turncoat and traitor" Moncada had been promised the presidency during the negotiations with *los yanquis* in return for his capitulation at Tipitapa. In a letter to one of his chief lieutenants in November 1927, Sandino condemned Moncada for not acting "with the duty that a soldier's honor requires of him. . . . That man made use of Liberal blood to attain sinecures and public jobs." He vowed to continue the fight until the Marines left Nicaragua.[66]

The poet and the rebel were of like mind about the illegitimacy of the Tipitapa agreement and U.S. intervention in the isthmus. Turcios, in particular, was livid about recent North American meddling in his country, which, he contended, violated his nation's sovereignty and kept corrupt, self-serving despots in power.

Turcios and Sandino also shared a fervent desire for Central American reunification. Soon after independence, the five Central American countries of Costa Rica, Nicaragua, Honduras, El Salvador, and Guatemala established a federation that lasted for fifteen years until it was dissolved in 1838. Ever since that time, periodic efforts had been made to revive the union, most recently in 1921 on the centenary of Central American independence. Both Sandino and Turcios were convinced that the State Department was opposed to the idea and that it was conspiring with isthmian governments to derail any attempt to bring about reunification. Here they echoed the suspicions of Ingenieros, who contended that Washington's opposition was rooted in a deliberate divide-and-conquer strategy that turned small countries against each other, thereby facilitating North American hegemony in the region. As he wryly remarked, "all prey is easy to devour if divided into small mouthfuls."[67] In fact, Washington was not alone in its misgivings about unification; ample opposition to the unionist cause existed throughout the isthmus.

Turcios was undeterred. He had been a rabid supporter of union since his youth, and his first magazine, *Revista Hispano América*, which began publication in 1922, made the cause its *raison d'être.*[68] He praised Sandino for embodying his hopes and aspirations for Central American unity. "All of my hard work for the complete sovereignty of our five republics finds in you today a potent, luminous and resonant affirmation." The poet believed Sandino to be the figurative reincarnation of the first president of the federation, Honduran patriot Francisco Morazán, who was executed when he unsuccessfully tried to revive the idea of unification in 1842. Turcios proved alarmingly prophetic in one letter when he wrote, "Morazán died for the Union; you will die for liberty."[69] Not surprisingly, a Honduran contingent of fighters who joined Sandino's Army of National Sovereignty bore the name *Caballería Morzánica* (Morazán's Cavalry).[70]

Turcios's and Sandino's views about solidarity, moreover, clearly transcended the isthmus. Petty nationalisms, they agreed, had played into the hands of local elites and foreign investors. In a speech delivered on the floor of the Honduran Congress, Turcios decried the "regionalist intolerance" that national politicians had falsely propagated ever since independence. "Until those regionalist barriers ... disappear from our political geography, every attempt made in favor of a Grand Continental Nation—the dream of the American Quixote—is a wasted effort." The answer, he added, was a successful Ibero-American Union.[71]

Despite their mutual admiration and shared enthusiasms, however, the poet and the rebel were unlikely partners, since they came from such different backgrounds and their responsibilities were so dissimilar. Whereas Sandino was focused on the day-to-day realities of keeping his peasant army together, Turcios's daily life was far more sedentary, taken up with his journal, books, and propagandizing.[72]

Unlike the poet, the rebel had been exposed to anarcho-syndicalism and Marxism while he lived and worked among oil workers in Mexico during the early 1920s. Of far greater import ultimately was an unanticipated divergence in their political thinking and goals, which would, much to Sandino's lasting regret, bring an abrupt end to their collaboration in January 1929. It would be Turcios who initiated the breakup, chalking it up to "two brothers who cannot understand each other."[73]

The crux of the disagreement stemmed from Sandino's surprising decision in late 1928 to form a coalition with two minor political parties to challenge the Liberal and Conservative Parties. Sandino wrote Turcios that his intention was to establish a junta composed of representatives from his army, the two parties, and a Mexico City–based solidarity organization, *Comité Manos Fuera de Nicaragua* (Hands Off Nicaragua Committee or MAFUENIC), a Communist International (CI) offshoot that raised funds and political awareness for his cause. Should this gambit succeed, he would then ask Zepeda to head up the junta. Sandino closed the letter by informing Turcios of his decision to offer the Nicaraguan physician the position that the Honduran presently held as his army's authorized representative abroad.[74]

Stung by the news, Turcios tried unsuccessfully to get Sandino to forgo this new partnership. He believed that such a coalition would weaken the Nicaraguan Liberal Party, undermine kindred parties in neighboring countries, and paint the general as just another opportunistic caudillo. What had attracted international support to their cause was his fight against the occupation, not meddling in domestic politics, the poet contended. When Sandino did not budge, Turcios was devastated. "I have become entirely convinced that calamity looms over our cause, and that with the new ideology that you present to me, you are taking rapid steps toward your certain failure." As much as he remained committed to ousting the Marines, he could not support Sandino's efforts to "change an internal political regime, using civil war to attain this end." He closed his letter with a bitter lament: "Your teacher, as you call me, no longer has any influence over your soul."[75]

Sandino may not have reconciled with Nicaragua's Liberal Party establishment, but it was he who pursued the fight until the Marines left the country in 1934, while the poet abandoned the cause, closing down his beloved *Ariel* and taking a post as a commercial representative of the Honduran government in Paris. Embittered, Turcios never forgave the general. In his memoirs, he fumed, "I cannot forget his ingratitude."[76]

From the middle of 1927 to early 1929, however, Sandino and Turcios forged a successful partnership. Their plentiful correspondence during that span attests to a broader dialogue occurring during the 1920s between members of two generations—youthful militants, like Sandino and his lieutenants, and their intellectual fathers. Like fathers and sons, the two generations did not always see eye to eye, especially when it came to methods and tactics, but there is little doubt that the young activists benefited greatly from the public intellectuals who first put words to their grievances about the perils of dictatorship and imperialism after the Spanish-Cuban-American War.

Generational Conversations

Turcios's decision to name his journal after the Uruguayan Rodó's *Ariel* (1900), an allegory of Shakespeare's *The Tempest*, speaks to the Honduran's identification with the turn-of-the-century aesthetic and elitist modernist movement that Rodó's essay spawned. *Ariel* warned Spanish Americans that they should be leery of being swept up in North American materiality, lest their own spiritual identity be lost. By stressing the value of a shared heritage and culture, Rodó sought to correct Latin Americans' perception of their own inferiority. Although he never rejected North American values outright, some of his less nuanced followers, Turcios included, certainly interpreted *Ariel* that way. The Honduran saw Sandino as the fulfillment of Rodó's literary prophecy, the idealistic Indo-Hispanic Ariel battling the materialistic, Caucasian Caliban of the Colossus of the North.[77]

Only by accentuating commonalities, Rodó believed, could Latin America best counter North American cultural hegemony. "I have always believed that in our America it was not possible to talk about many *patrias*, but only one great *patria* ... the American *patria* transcends the national *patria*."[78] His affirmation of a shared cultural and spiritual tradition struck a responsive chord, as *Ariel* became a touchstone for an entire generation of *pensadores*.[79]

Cultural nationalists did more than fix their critique on dichotomous values. They were concerned by the Colossus's repeated interventions in the Caribbean Basin. Rodó would later admit that the impetus for *Ariel* was the Spanish-Cuban-American War.[80] He and his cohort witnessed subsequent U.S. military occupations of Mexico (1913–14), the Dominican Republic (1916–24), Haiti (1915–34), and Nicaragua (1912–33), and Washington's unwelcome forging of protectorates in Cuba, Puerto Rico, and the Philippines. They interpreted such interpositions as arrogant displays of empire building.

These intellectuals were just as incensed by the United States' carving up of Panama, its tight-fisted control of the canal, and the subsequent Bryan-Chamorro Treaty (1916) with Nicaragua, which precluded the possibility that European or Asian competitors would build a second canal in the isthmus. The treaty was widely regarded with suspicion, because in the opinion of its critics, it sowed discord among Central American governments, undermined reunification aspirations, and contributed to the demise of the Central American Court of Justice, a regional tribunal created in 1907 to arbitrate disputes.

To policymakers in Washington, however, the canal's security was paramount. The entire circum-Caribbean theater was now a strategic zone. To protect the region and deter European rivals, the United States not only established a military base in the Canal Zone but added naval bases in Key West, Guantánamo (Cuba), Samaná Bay (Dominican Republic), Mole St. Nicholas (Puerto Rico), the Virgin Islands, and the Corn Islands and Fonseca Bay (Nicaragua). In addition to a robust military presence, Washington determined that it would not, to the best of its capabilities, tolerate political disorder in the region. As Lippmann observed, "from this point it was but a short step to the theory that the United States must insure itself in the Caribbean region against supposedly unfriendly governments." This explains why the internationalization of the Panama Canal became such an article of faith for Turcios, Haya, Sandino, and their peers.[81]

As intellectual historian Nicola Miller notes, "in the wake of *Ariel*, to be an intellectual was to be an anti-imperialist, and to be an anti-imperialist was to be anti-American." To be clear, what Miller refers to as anti-American is a rejection of North American cultural values and Washington's interference. By the 1920s, "anti-yanquísmo" was something that liberals, conservatives, and leftists could all agree upon.[82] After *Ariel's* publication, a succession of hard-hitting polemics on the subject appeared in print, including the Colombian José María Vargas Vila's *Ante los bárbaros* and Venezuelan Rufino Blanco-Fombona's "La americanización del mundo," which caricatured and mocked U.S. society, juxtaposing Latin America's Hispano-Catholic heritage with an overtly materialistic Protestant individualism.[83] Typical was Vargas Vila's diatribe against North American expansionism: "American filibusterism makes for brutality. Proofs of this are seen in the Filipinos, hunted like wild beasts; in the disappearing Hawaiians, in the despoiled natives of Panamá and in the Puerto Ricans, compelled by oppression to emigrate . . . wherever the Yankee goes, a race dies."[84]

Turcios never missed a chance to denigrate the North American Mammon. After a visit to New York City he confided, in prose typical of the genre: "I did not like New York. . . . Its stupendous material magnificence is admirable, but only in a physical sense. . . . My spirit remains untouched, if not indifferent, before the monstrous elevation of a race for whom material force, audacity and gold constitute the highest human ideals."[85]

Sandino echoed those sentiments in a letter he penned to President Herbert Hoover in 1929. Blaming his country's plight on Wall Street bankers, who "knelt down before their strong boxes full of metal, their hands and eyes lifted toward heaven, giving thanks to the god *Gold*" (emphasis in original). The rebel then explicitly invoked Arielismo by paraphrasing Darío's poem "Ode to Roosevelt": "I am not unaware of the material resources that your nation has at its disposal. In fact, you have everything, but 'what you lack is God.' "[86]

More thoughtful critics, however, drew a distinction between a critique of capitalism and Washington's propensity for interventionism, and North America's rich cultural heritage. In 1925, the Peruvian Marxist José Carlos Mariátegui penned a column, "Iberoamericanismo y Panamericanismo," in which he asked: "Is it the United States' fault that Ibero-Americans know more about Theodore Roosevelt's ideas than those of Henry Thoreau? The United States is certainly the homeland of Pierpont Morgan and Henry Ford; but it is also the country of Ralph Waldo Emerson, of William James, and of Walt Whitman. The nation that has produced the greatest captains of industry, has also produced the brightest teachers of continental idealism."[87]

Anti-Americanism in Latin America was more than a critique of U.S. foreign policy. It developed from dissatisfaction closer to home. According to historian Max Friedman, critics rarely considered U.S. hegemony in the region in isolation. Opposition to the United States "was an effect, not a cause of their beliefs, which were diverse and evolving (and debatable), but stemmed from an intense commitment to engagement with the problems of their own societies."[88]

To be sure, not all of Rodó's contemporaries penned invectives. José Martí, who spent much of his adult life in exile in the United States, had a far more nuanced appreciation for North American society because his journalistic vocation required it. His thoughtful "insider" columns, syndicated throughout Latin America, suggest political divisions in Washington that begged to be exploited by Latin Americans. He thought it essential to cultivate alliances with like-minded North American progressives who could work from within to alter U.S. policy and cautioned Latin Americans not to overstate North American shortcomings "out of a desire to deny it all virtue." Cultural historian Christopher Abel believes that even though Martí's time spent in exile in the United States left him wary of its economic and financial might, he expressed "neither an uncritical adulation nor total condemnation" of North America.[89]

Martí did share the Uruguayan's conviction that the only way for Latin Americans to defend themselves against foreign aggression was by allying with each other. A violation of one country's sovereignty should be considered an attack on the rest of the region. He also warned of the slippery slope of indebtedness. North American loans came at the cost of sovereignty. But unity for Martí began at home; Cubans needed first to forge a broad-based, multiclass movement against their common enemies. When Martí became a martyr for the cause of independence in 1895 and his island and Puerto Rico exchanged Spanish colonial rule for the unsatisfactory status of a U.S. protectorate after 1898, his admonitions about the need for solidarity took on a decidedly more prophetic character.[90]

Another public intellectual, the Argentine democratic socialist Manuel Ugarte, also had a nuanced understanding of the U.S.-Latin American relationship. He enjoyed an especially devoted following, since his columns were featured prominently in the liberal press and because he was a roving advocate for his causes, presenting lectures and meeting with students and professors across the region during an extended tour between 1911 and 1913. In all, Ugarte visited twenty countries throughout the hemisphere and spent considerable time on the Continent, forging networks with European intellectuals, such as Henri Barbusse, Maxim Gorky, Miguel de Unamuno, and Albert Einstein. One memorable gathering, held at the Maison de Savantes on Rue Danton in Paris on June 29, 1925, is suggestive of the Latin American intelligentsia's transnational character and its camaraderie with like-minded Europeans. The meeting, which featured lectures by Ingenieros and Haya, brought together the Spaniards Unamuno and José Ortega y Gasset, Miguel Ángel Asturias (Guatemala), and Carlos Quijano (Uruguay), among others.[91]

Like Turcios, Ugarte's talents extended to political organizing. He repeatedly issued calls for pan-Latin American student unity, and his 1927 "Manifesto a la juventud latinoamericana" backed Sandino and criticized U.S. aggression in Mexico and Central America.[92] The Argentine also established contacts with four expatriate Latin American student organizations, La Federación Universitaria Hispanoamericana and La Federación Universitaria Escolar in Madrid, La Asociación General de Estudiantes Latinoamericanos (AGELA) in Paris, and La Asociación General de Estudiantes Latinoamericanos of Berlin, which all signed on to his call for support of the Sandino insurgency.[93]

His early writings, such as "El peligro yanqui" (1901), written in the aftermath of the Spanish-Cuban-American War, were polemical, but his classic work, *El porvenir de América Latina* (1911), was equal parts travelogue, thoughtful analysis, and screed against U.S. hegemony. Like Martí, he opined that Latin Americans had much to learn and profit from North America and that they would do well to take a lesson from the Meiji regime in Japan, which, in the nineteenth century, adapted what it felt useful from the West without relinquishing its cultural identity. Latin

America, Ugarte contended, should take advantage of U.S. economic and technological assistance, and he chided those *Arielistas* who felt themselves spiritually superior to North Americans. Latin American states had only themselves to blame for their plight because they repeatedly caved to U.S. aggression. "If the U.S. has not shown us more respect, it has perhaps been because of the obsequiousness with which we have always bowed down before them [and] also because of the selfishness with which we have postponed the advantages of union in favor of the short-term interests of one man, one oligarchy or one particular region."[94]

But he also did not refrain from denouncing the more devious aspects of U.S. support for dictators in Latin America. Calling the U.S. a New Rome, he fulminated that Washington benefited from "the clash of factions" and that it worked surreptitiously by "taking advantage of the instability of governments in these unruly and impressionable democracies. . . . Here it foments tyrannies, there it supports attempts at revolutions, always constituting itself the conciliator or the arbiter."[95] "Tyrants, oligarchs, legal presidents," Ugarte explained to the *New York Times* in 1927, were at the heart of the problem.[96]

The only solution for Ugarte was hemispheric solidarity. In *El porvenir de América Latina,* he emphasized cultural commonalities: "except for subtle differences, the social environment, customs, inclinations and tastes are identical. From a racial perspective, the Hispanic republics couldn't be more similar." *The Times* of London, in its review of the book, paid the author what he would have perceived as a sterling compliment when it concluded, "The author speaks as a citizen of South America and defends the unity of these nations with such eloquence that we do not know which republic he is from."[97]

Nicknamed the Champion of the Latin American Cause, Ugarte held the Mexican Revolution in high regard and promoted its ideals at every opportunity. The revolution was, in his words, "the model of an American democracy ruled by cultural forces rather than by privilege and convenience."[98] His views on the pernicious impact of North American intervention and Washington's support for dictatorships found an especially receptive audience in Mexico.

Like Ugarte, Mexican secretary of education José Vasconcelos traveled extensively throughout the region. Dispatched by his government to spread the gospel of its revolution, his speaking tours were part diplomatic mission, part cultural exchange. A case in point was his address "Letter to Colombian Youth" at a student congress in Bogotá in May

1923. In it he challenged his youthful audiences to bring about meaningful reforms at home and to identify with peers throughout the hemisphere who faced similar challenges.[99]

Vasconcelos rarely missed an opportunity to criticize authoritarianism. Two dictators had been ousted in 1920, Mexico's Venustiano Carranza and Manuel Estrada Cabrera in Guatemala, and for Vasconcelos, that was a trend that deserved emulation. He pronounced Venezuela's dictator Juan Vicente Gómez (1908–1935) the worst of the lot—"a human swine that dishonors our race"—and encouraged Mexican students to show solidarity with their peers in Venezuela. Students took him at his word and responded with a concerted campaign, composing broadsides, holding a massive demonstration through the streets of the Mexican capital, and sending a letter to Harding demanding that his administration sever diplomatic ties with Venezuela.[100] Then he penned a blistering salvo that reproached patriots in Venezuela and throughout the hemisphere for venting their spleen against the United States when the enemy was much closer to home: "It is the fashion nowadays in our part of America to protest loudly against the imperialism of the Yankees. Let us not forget however that in remaining under the heel of our local dictators we are admirably serving the schemes of our Northern neighbors. . . . It is useless to talk about dangers from abroad which we cannot ward off while at the same time we consent to, or at least accept, all those misdeeds at home which we could and should seek to prevent or punish. It is natural that on such a soil should spring up those 'Gomezes,' which today dishonor several countries of Spanish America."[101]

The Mexican intellectual went on to warn that "all America is likely to become 'Gomezised' unless we can stamp out the coals of iniquity in Venezuela." Vasconcelos did more than write, however. He welcomed (and in some cases found employment in his ministry for) Venezuelan refugees, prevailed on Mexican president Álvaro Obregón to provide arms and funds to the exiles, and persuaded the former revolutionary general to sever relations with the Gómez regime.[102] He also praised Peruvian students in their fight to unseat the dictator Augusto Leguía and made sure that Mexico's doors remained open to political exiles who had experienced repression at the hands of regional caudillos.[103]

Vasconcelos was just as critical of the outsized role that militaries played in the political life of Latin American countries as he was of tyrants. In Santiago, Chile, he inveighed against "an unwitting force, that doesn't know its destination or who is leading it. Mexico's disgrace,

Chile's disgrace, Latin America's disgrace is that we have been governed by the sword and not by intelligence."[104]

Intellectual travelers like Martí, Vasconcelos, and Ugarte, whether they were driven into exile, in demand on the lecture circuit, or just the nomadic type, experienced a kind of cultural displacement, according to literary critic Beatriz Colombi. This helps explain why they made a point of emphasizing Hispanoamericanism or Latin Americanism in their writings. Ugarte, who spent much of his life away from his native Argentina, believed that travel had its own rewards: "We traveled to find ourselves and to find a hemispheric identity." The appearance of such a charismatic public intellectual in foreign capitals was a cause for celebration. The most important ritual of the visits, the *conferencia*, or public lecture, invariably elicited a rousing response from the audience.[105]

Pensadores sought out and found allies in the United States as well. They were particularly taken with the philosophical writings of Waldo Frank, with whom Ugarte and others had come into contact in Paris during the early 1920s. Frank embraced the idea of inter-American solidarity and, unlike the Arielistas, extended it to include the entire Western Hemisphere, arguing that the North had much to learn from the South. Appalled at how Protestantism and capitalism distorted and corrupted North American society, he viewed Latin America's cultural and spiritual character as a necessary antidote to a North American corporate "propensity to approach the earth only in the spirit of possession." Frank's ideas were music to the ears of Latin American intellectuals who sought to counter deeply ingrained European and North American stereotypes of Latin American inferiority.[106]

In "What is Hispano-America?" Frank commended the region's public intellectuals and artists who evoked a revolutionary spirit, unlike his peers in the United States, whom he dismissed as "Platonic" and "powerless." North American intellectuals had lost contact with the spiritual and had embraced "the superstitious dogmatisms of science ... and servilely submitted to a rationale (called Pragmatism) of enslavement to the external order of industrial expansion, whose superficial comforts drug us and unman us." In contrast, Frank did not conceal his admiration for Mexican muralists like Diego Rivera and José Clemente Orozco, whose art and political activism illustrated how "the holiness of man must be expressed through the harmonious interplay of individual, social, aesthetic, and political forms."[107]

Revolution was not something to be feared as a destabilizing force but welcomed as a sign of maturity, Frank averred, since it had the potential of removing backward-looking dictators from power. What was troublesome were the ties between foreign investors and "tyrants whose source of power is the product not of the people at all but of American finance." He added: "Such tyrants stifle the process of natural selection; such tyrants ... introduce an alien element into the delicate biology of national formation. And when that alien element is backed by the force of a country vastly greater than the victims, it is an element that dominates, that destroys, and that the people themselves are powerless to cope with."[108]

At some point in the not-too-distant future, Frank, recasting a cabalist myth, believed, a new America would be created from a masculine, if spiritually starved, North America, so captivated by the rational, the empirical, and the mechanistic, and the "instinctive, introspective and vitalistic world views" of a feminized Hispano-America. The integration of the two "half-worlds' " into an androgynous "mystical organic whole" would combine the best virtues of both the North and the South.[109]

Like Ugarte, Frank undertook an extensive lecture tour through nine countries in Latin America in 1929–30. Speaking in Spanish, he was compared to Thoreau, Emerson, and Whitman and "evoked an almost frenzied response from Latin American intellectuals."[110] In his memoirs, Frank immodestly recalled a lecture he gave in an auditorium at Mexico's National University that included an overflow crowd of one thousand students who "heard me by loudspeaker in the yard." The next day his lecture was accorded space on the front pages of Mexico City's dailies. Coverage continued in this vein all over South America, where newspapers published daily summaries of his invited lectures.[111]

Ugarte, Frank, and their colleagues had nothing but contempt for regional elites who worked hand-in-glove with North American capitalists and Washington. They contended that the ruling classes selectively adopted Western theories of modernity like positivism and social Darwinism solely to legitimate their undemocratic rule. It is perhaps understandable why the cultural nationalist critique of dictatorships and imperialism resonated so well with contemporaries. Many came to view imperialism as a symptom, not a cause, of a more pervasive and insidious evil. Wall Street, North American companies conducting business in Latin America, and the State Department, they contended, were complicit with local oligarchies, the church, and militaries, which collectively made certain that self-serving dictators or elites remained in power in their homelands indefinitely. Even conservative Peruvian diplomat and historian Francisco García Calderón did not mince words: "If the U.S. in its efforts to avoid anarchy tolerates the reelection of presidents in countries which have no political liberty, they are enthroning dictatorship—that is a kind of government out of which cannot emerge normal life, the untrammeled function of institutions and the development of a critical spirit."[112]

Leftist student activists, who might have disagreed with many of the diplomat's modest prescriptions for reform, nevertheless saw eye to eye with him when it came to decrying U.S. support for dictators in "the backyard." For García Calderón, a disciple of Rodó, Latin Americans were their own worst enemy because they permitted strongman rule to eclipse the democratic impulse. The dictator sowed divisions among political parties, García Calderón contended; "without ideals or unity of action the parties are transformed into greedy cliques."[113]

Two Argentine socialists, Ingenieros and Alfredo Palacios, became indispensable mentors for the younger generation of student activists. In 1925 they founded the Unión Latinoamericana (ULA), in part to repudiate the Pan American Union, an elitist organization based in Washington, which had been established in 1890 to promote U.S.-Latin American trade and cultural exchanges. Ingenieros rightfully viewed that organization as an ineffectual creature of U.S. foreign policy.[114] In contrast, the ULA's journal *Renovación* urged students to assume leadership roles in society, to repudiate colonial legacies and the "ignorance" of the masses, and to fashion an "aristocracy of merit."[115] The ULA's charter did not just attack North American imperialism, however. It explicitly railed against caudillos, the Catholic Church, bloated bureaucracies, and the political class's penchant for taking on ruinous debts from abroad. It vowed to contest dictatorships and to work for social justice.[116]

Sandino's rebellion encapsulated many of the Unión's causes. The Monroe Doctrine's original intent as a defensive statement of principles against European intervention, Ingenieros claimed, was distorted grossly by the U.S. spate of occupations, so much so that the doctrine's motto, "America for Americans," was really just a euphemism for "America for North Americans." In 1922 Ingenerios delivered an impassioned speech at an event honoring Vasconcelos's visit to Buenos Aires in which he denounced North America's pervasive influence: "The danger does not begin with annexation, as in Puerto Rico, nor with intervention, as in Cuba, nor in wardship, as in Nicaragua, nor in territorial secession, as with Colombia, nor in armed occupation, as in Haiti, nor in purchase, as in the Guyanas. The danger, in its first phase, begins with the progressive mortgaging of national independence through loans ... that diminish the sovereignty of those who agree to them. ... We know that over the last years North American infiltration is felt with growing intensity in all the political, economic and social machinery of South America. Do we continue to ingenuously believe that imperialist ambitions will cease with Panama?"[117]

Invoking the Bolivarian ideal of hemispheric unity, Ingenieros called for the creation of a "collective conscience" to put a brake on North American expansionism.[118] His prolific writings became required reading for a generation of students. The prominent Aprista Manuel Seoane later remarked after witnessing Ingenieros give a speech that he was the "true gospel of anti-imperialism ... he represents the essential thoughts of Latin America's new generations."[119]

For all their rhetorical outrage, with the notable exception of Martí, the preferred weapon of these elders remained the pen, not the sword. As a result, both contemporaries and scholars have often pigeonholed them as political dilettantes who had little apparent impact. The future Nobel Prize winner Asturias, then living in Paris, issued a withering critique of these armchair thinkers: some, he complained, only sought notoriety, others were little more than "future parasites" intent on securing government sinecures, while still others, although well-meaning, were blind to the political realities. As far as Asturias was concerned, the incessant talk, meetings, broadsides, letter writing, and telegrams were a waste of time and energy without action to accompany it.[120]

Despite such misgivings among critics, there is little doubt that the corpus of these *pensadores'* writings and their outsized role as public intellectuals helped educate and fire the imagination of a younger generation of students, professionals, and activists who took to the streets during the 1920s. Perhaps it is not surprising that when Haya first visited Uruguay in 1922, he paid his respects at Rodó's crypt in Montevideo.[121]

Students sought to democratize the region, most notably in Cuba, Chile, Venezuela, and Peru, where authoritarian rule was most entrenched. Their political mobilization informed their perspective of Sandino's rebellion. His was not just a principled fight against North American intervention but an illustration of a more significant battle much closer to home. Students, faculty, and progressive elements of the middle and working classes came to the collective realization that dictatorships and oligarchical rule had to be eliminated, root and branch.

Some youthful critics readily acknowledged their debt to their elders. Cuban columnist Eugenio d'Ors, in the Havana journal *Social,* called intellectuals, such as Vasconcelos, Ugarte, and Palacios and their Cuban colleague Enrique José Varona, "apostles and propagandists for the ideals that Sandino is fighting for today in Nicaragua." In his column, "Only Sandino Represents Our America," d'Ors zeroed in on "two great inter-related evils" that fed off each other: dictatorships and imperialism. "in return for selling the country and its riches to North Americans, the ruler stays in power indefinitely. . . . Sandino is our hero; he aims to defeat this alliance."[122] Sandino never missed an opportunity to make a similar point, praising, for instance, the Haitian rebel leader Joseph Jolibois Fils, who was in the midst of a struggle against corrupt strongmen who were col-laborating with the U.S. occupation of that island.[123]

When tyrants did not lord over small nations like Sandino's Nicara-gua and Turcios's Honduras during the 1920s, small, elitist political par-ties monopolized power and collaborated with U.S. corporate interests. Ousting the Marines from the isthmus and dismantling oligarchic politi-cal parties, which held sham elections to legitimate their rule and crush dissent, was viewed increasingly as a principled act of pan-Latin Ameri-can solidarity.

Typical was the call to action by Dominican intellectual Américo Lugo, an outspoken opponent of U.S. intervention in his homeland. Lugo urged his countrymen to leave the island and join Sandino's army. In the Dominican journal *Patria*, he wrote a column titled "Sandino," in which he extolled the rebel army's exemplary struggle. "Nicaragua is the heart, soul, mind, and strength of Hispanic America." Reminding his readership of a Dominican general who had left his homeland to play such an instrumental role in Cuba's struggle for independence against Spanish colonialism, he asked, "where is the new Máximo Gómez who will assist Sandino in his liberating enterprise?" For Lugo, the U.S. was the "caudillo of caudillos," and the North American public's perception of Latin Americans was, at its core, "implacably racist." He was openly contemptuous of local *vendepatrias*, who handed over their nations lock, stock, and barrel to the *yanquis*.[124]

A Call to Arms

Indeed, Sandino's cause resonated powerfully for Lugo and his peers. As the German leftist Alfons Goldschmidt noted after he traveled through-out Latin America in 1929: "In Europe, they have no idea of the enor-mous importance Sandino has for liberation movements in Latin

America. Around this figure revolve the hopes and aspirations for liberty of the peasants of the continent. The children of Central America pretend at playing Sandino. Sandino now has been converted into a type of continental hero."[125]

Goldschmidt was not entirely accurate; Sandino's clarion call did, in fact, reach the Old World. During the interwar period, Paris was a hotbed of anticolonial and anti-imperialist activity. In one notable show of strength, APRA's Parisian cell, acting in concert with AGELA, organized a boisterous protest against the former dictator of Nicaragua, Emiliano Chamorro. When Chamorro's train arrived at the Paris station, he was booed by hundreds of Mexican, Cuban, Argentine, Uruguayan, Peruvian, and Venezuelan students.[126]

Latin American students in Paris also voiced their displeasure with other regional dictators. In early 1928 AGELA, which boasted two hundred fifty members, met at the Salles des Sociétés Savantes to show solidarity for three hundred fellow students in Venezuela who had been imprisoned that spring by the dictator Gómez. Later that year, the Association of New Cuban Revolutionary Emigrants (*Asociación Nueva de Emigrantes Revolucionarios Cubanos*, ANERC) organized a demonstration against Machado. At another high-profile meeting in January 1927, Vasconcelos, Haya, and Asturias, among others, spoke out against North American meddling in Mexico.[127]

In Paris, Latin American students also found common cause with anticolonial refugees from Asia and Africa. All manner of clubs, advocacy groups, and mutual aid societies gave students the sense that they were part of a global generational movement committed to fighting imperialism. As the historian Michael Goebel, in his study of the interwar period, relates: "The ideal of regional solidarity became a lived reality . . . encounters between Latin Americans of different nationalities fostered a sense of a shared regional identity, which in turn formed a crucial bedrock of anti-imperialism."[128]

A case in point was the political awakening of a Colombian law student then studying in Paris, who, after listening to Vasconcelos deliver an eloquent lecture on the symbolic import of Sandino's struggle for the liberation of Latin America, decided to forgo his studies and enlist in the rebel's army. He was not disappointed when he reached Sandino's headquarters: "Do you know," he reflected, "I have a true veneration for him [Sandino]. He is the only man that I would give my life for . . . and the same is true for everyone else [in this army]."[129]

The solidarity of the international progressive community for Sandino's rebellion would prove short-lived, but for an extraordinary moment from the middle of 1927 until early 1929, the rebel's cause became its own. And Sandino did nothing to discourage the mystique that was emerging about him on both sides of the Atlantic. His political thinking, inflected with messianic overtones and mysterious-sounding spiritual bromides, was so amorphous that to many contemporaries it appeared bewildering at best.[130] Its essence, however, reflected a judicious melding of the critiques and political aspirations of two generations.

Borrowing a page from APRA's platform, Sandino seconded Haya's call for solidarity in his first manifesto, "Nicaraguans, Central Americans and the Indo-Hispanic Race." A product of *mestizaje* himself, Sandino, however, was at best diffident about Indigenous communities in his own country, and his writings more generally about Indians reflected a paternalistic, civilizing mission common to the *indigenista* movement at the time. Championed by ideologues of the Mexican Revolution, *mestizaje* offered, in Sandino's mind, the best possible hope of unifying very disparate, heterogeneous elements.[131]

Like Haya, Sandino also was upset with U.S. control of the Panama Canal and the Bryan-Chamorro Treaty. (Sandino's strident opposition to the latter was inculcated at an early age; his father, Gregorio, had been jailed for his outspoken opposition to the treaty.)[132] Sandino was troubled by the fact that the U.S. alone had funded the construction of the canal. At least half of the capital, he insisted, should have come from Latin American sources.[133] Thrilled by the rebel's articulation of his principles, Haya moved heaven and earth to visit Sandino in the Segovias in 1928, but Honduran and Nicaraguan authorities would not permit it.[134]

Why had the internationalization of the canal become a *sine qua non* for critics of U.S. foreign policy? Successive Democratic and Republican administrations in the 1910s and 1920s had made it clear to Central American governments that the U.S. geopolitical stake in protecting the canal required a North American sphere of influence that extended far beyond Panama's borders. In that sense, the Bryan-Chamorro Treaty was emblematic of a broader North American policy designed to keep European and Asian governments and their financiers and concessionaries out of the isthmus. To economic nationalists like Haya and Sandino, Washington's proscription of such investment in the isthmus left the door open to North American companies, such as *el pulpo*, while making a mockery of Central American governments' claims of sovereignty.[135]

In fact, Sandino wrote the Argentine president Hipólito Yrigoyen asking him to host a regional conference of Latin American governments in Buenos Aires to discuss the Aprista call for the internationalization of the canal. When Yrigoyen's reply was not forthcoming, the Nicaraguan extended the invitation to attend the conference to other Latin American presidents. Such solidarity was critical, he insisted, because North American occupations had, for all intents and purposes, politically and culturally isolated those countries from their neighbors.[136]

Echoing Haya, Sandino claimed that the handiwork of imperialism was in plain sight when it stoked nationalism and exploited minor boundary disputes in the isthmus. Taking advantage of permeable frontiers and weak states, caudillos, elite political parties, and exiles, sometimes egged on by North American proconsuls and U.S. companies, were persistently destabilizing regional politics. In fact, elitist political parties were more apt to ally with like-minded counterparts in neighboring countries, if it suited their political agenda, than to reach accommodation with the opposition at home. What Central America needed, Sandino contended, was reconciliation, not fratricidal conflict.

If political differences sundered the relationship between the poet and the rebel, a boundary dispute may have been the final straw. An acrimonious quarrel between Guatemala and Honduras was triggered by a land concession that the Guatemalan government awarded the United Fruit Company near the border between the two countries. Upset with what it viewed as an incursion into its territory, United's chief rival, the Cuyamel Fruit Company, pressured the Honduran government to protest the concession. More so than elsewhere in the isthmus, competition among the banana companies often seeped into the fabric of Honduran regional and national politics during the 1920s. Members of the political class were often hired by the companies as either employees or consultants.[137] Undue influence of the fruit companies was perhaps unavoidable, since 25 percent of government revenues came from taxes assessed to them.[138]

Turcios's Liberal Party was beholden to Cuyamel, while *el pulpo* favored (and provided funds for) what would ultimately become the National Party. (In fact, it was United Fruit's largesse that helped make it possible for the caudillo Tiburcio Carías Andino to dominate national politics during the 1930s and 1940s).[139] Complicating matters, the Liberal Party was itself badly divided. Turcios was a leader of its more progressive, anti-imperialist wing, which decried the influence of the banana companies and sought to emulate the nationalist path taken by Mexico after its revolution. This explains why the poet, in the May 1, 1928, issue of *Ariel*, was critical of the Guatemalan government's concession to *el pulpo*.[140]

For their part, Sandino and Haya both decried the boundary dispute as fabricated and symptomatic of how U.S. companies, acting in concert with the State Department, manipulated corrupt and weak isthmian governments to suit their interests.[141] A month later, the rebel weighed in on the matter, lecturing his propagandist in a letter on the need to promote unity, not division in the isthmus: "you have an obligation to make the people of Central America understand that there should be no frontiers between us and that concern for the fate of each and every Latin American people is our common duty."[142]

Like many progressives, Haya and Sandino also were strong proponents of Emiliano Zapata's agrarian ideals. In his "Open Letter to America's Governments," Sandino praised Mexico for its inspirational revolution, its resistance to U.S. intervention when Woodrow Wilson sent in marines to occupy Veracruz in 1913, and its vocal championing of hemispheric solidarity. In 1930 Sandino told a Mexican journalist, "our struggle in Nicaragua . . . is nothing more than the daughter of the Mexican Revolution."[143]

Echoing the *Arielistas*, Sandino called for a plan to fulfill Bolívar's dream and urged Latin American states to forge a united front against the U.S. and corrupt dictators like Machado and Gómez, who had profited from kickbacks and concessions from U.S. companies.[144] He rejected the Monroe Doctrine out of hand, calling instead for a confederation of twenty-one Latin American countries with its own Supreme Court to resolve disputes and a pan-Latin army to be made up of three hundred fifty soldiers from each nation.[145] Even as Turcios and Sandino were on the verge of breaking up their collaboration, the former reminded the latter that he had devoted his "best energies to making the general shine forth as the new Bolívar under the American sky." And Sandino embraced this comparison. In an interview in June 1928, he explained his ideological transformation: "My country, for which I struggle, has Spanish America for its frontiers. At the beginning of my campaign I thought only of Nicaragua. Afterward my ambition grew. I thought of the Central American Republic whose coat of arms has been sketched by one of my comrades. Tell Hispano-America that as long as Sandino breathes, the independence of Central America will have a defender. I shall never betray my cause. That is why I am the son of Bolívar."[146]

Although historians understandably have focused on Sandino's seven-year struggle against the Marines, there is ample evidence in the general's correspondence with the poet and in his manifestos of his bitter frustration with reactionary forces in Nicaragua, which, in his mind, squelched efforts to bring about an authentic democracy. What made Turcios and Sandino such kindred spirits is that for a time they shared—with like-minded activists scattered all over Latin America—the common goal of dismantling dictatorial regimes.[147]

The poet, however, lost his appetite for the cause. During the last years of his life he became disenchanted with politics. He spent those years in exile in San José, Costa Rica, where, fittingly, he opened a bookshop. When Honduran exiles tried to coax the former firebrand to join their struggle to overthrow Carías, he spurned them, refusing to criticize the despot, perhaps because the caudillo had granted him a lifetime pension "for literary services" to the nation.[148]

Three additional factors encouraged cross-generational conversations: a university reform movement that began in Córdoba, Argentina in 1918 and then spread across the region; the Mexican and Russian Revolutions' liberating agendas; and Haya's militancy. Each of these identified viable solutions to the problems of authoritarian rule, foreign economic and political penetration, and social injustice.

CHAPTER TWO
The Obligation to Think

[The university reform movement] aspired to forge a new moral conscience, to subvert the ominous political, economic and social reality of our peoples and to unify, under its banners, Hispanic American youth; hence, its struggle against dictatorships, its anti-imperialist flavor, its linkages with the workers, its solidarity with oppressed peoples, its appeal to social justice, and its insistence on a true democracy.

—RAÚL ROA GARCÍA

PARTICIPATION IN THE UNIVERSITY reform movement marked Latin American students as members of a distinctive generation. As the young Cuban student Roa García noted, the course set and the causes fought for in the 1920s and 1930s—opposition to strongman rule, economic nationalism, solidarity between students and workers, social justice, and democratic governance—shaped the political trajectories and agendas of militant student leaders when they entered politics during the 1950s and 1960s. The Peruvian Haya de la Torre, Venezuelans Rómulo Betancourt and Gustavo Machado, and Cubans, such as Roa, Eddie Chibás, and Aureliano Sánchez Arango, may have had their political and philosophical disagreements, but their participation in the university reform movement instilled a lifelong commitment to bringing about meaningful change in their respective countries.

One of Argentina's most conservative institutions of higher learning, La Universidad de San Carlos de Córdoba (founded in 1663) was an unlikely site to initiate such sweeping changes. Like many of its peer institutions, the university underwent institutional changes after independence, evolving from a colonial scholastic model of education to a more secular curriculum. Patterned on the Napoleonic model of higher education, nineteenth-century Latin American universities increasingly took on a utilitarian function; their *raison d'être* became the education of future generations of professionals and civil servants culled from the ranks of the elite. Even so, Argentine socialist Juan Justo found the University of Córdoba's religious iconography so austere that a walk through its principal buildings felt like stepping back in time to the Middle Ages. He was stunned that the library lacked books by Darwin, Huxley, Marx, or Engels.[1]

Student demands initially were modest, focusing on modernizing the tradition-bound, religious vestiges of the provincial university's course offerings and ousting officious faculty who, in the words of one student manifesto, perceived their position as "a species of divine right."[2] However, change did not come without a fight. Administrators dug in and refused to accede to student demands. One of the leaders of the university reform movement recalled: "The masters of the Latin American universities exercised a truly implacable dictatorship. For them, the 'old' was symbolic of wisdom, and they denied all attention to every suggestion of the students, whatever it was."[3]

In the face of such intransigence, students went on strike in June 1918, demanding more say in their education, university autonomy, free tuition, and a shared role in governance (*co-gobierno*). This last goal was of critical importance to the strike committee; student representatives should, they argued, have a voice in removing incompetent instructors. The advancement of professors, the strike committee argued in its manifesto, should be based on merit, not patronage, and the curricula should be more relevant: "The universities have been, until now, the secular refuge of the mediocre, a sinecure of the ignorant and worse still, the place in which every form of tyranny could be preached and practiced. The university is thus the exact image of a decadent society, a senile man who will neither retire or die."[4]

Co-gobierno went hand in hand with university autonomy. According to the strike committee secretary, Julio González, students insisted that the university govern itself as if it were a republic, not a dictatorship, wherein its key constituents—students as well as permanent and adjunct faculty—all had a voice. If Argentina's government was constituted as a republic, then so too should students have representation in their universities. Once staff, faculty, and students exercised shared governance, government oversight of the university would no longer be necessary.[5]

In addition, the strike committee insisted that the working classes, long denied access to higher education, be afforded that opportunity and that it was incumbent on the state to provide financial assistance to make that possible. Palacios, then a professor in the School of Medicine at the University of Buenos Aires, told the daily *La Razón* that what was occurring in Córdoba was nothing short of "a war to the death between the spirit of progress and tradition."[6]

Córdoba's students also staged public rallies and demonstrations, and reached out to labor unions, peers at comparable institutions of higher education, and local and national politicians. Fifteen thousand turned out in support of the students in Córdoba in late August 1918, and sympathy strikes took place at the Universities of Buenos Aires, La Plata, Tucumán, and the Litoral (Santa Fe). Soon student leadership at other institutions made similar demands.[7] Several labor unions joined the strike, and moderate political parties even adopted the students' cause as their own. After eight months of agitation and negotiations, a reform-minded President Yrigoyen signed an executive decree incorporating the strike committee's demands into the University of Córdoba's system of governance.[8]

The decree had far-reaching implications. No longer would the university's role in society be simply to train civil servants to fill the bureaucracy. As Rama notes, "Now the university was to operate in a wider field of endeavors, participating in the processes of national integration. Amid a reigning climate of agnosticism, the academy took on many of the functions that had pertained to the established church."[9]

Students throughout Argentina did not just dwell on the university itself, but were reacting to a host of external stimuli. Disturbed by the barbarism and devastation of World War I, students questioned whether Europe deserved its status as a beacon of civilization. The virtues of liberalism and democracy increasingly were called into question. Students were particularly taken by the Prussian philosopher Oswald Spengler's *Decline of the West* (1918), which contended that Europe was far from a pinnacle of progress and, like earlier civilizations, was destined to decline.[10] A leader of the reform movement and later its chief historian,

Gabriel del Mazo, recalled that "the intellectual leadership of Europe was broken and there arose for the youth the vital need to save our people from the fate of the European people." For a nation like Argentina, with such close ethnic, cultural, and economic ties to the Continent, such questioning cut to the heart of its national identity. Indeed, conditions specific to each country influenced the degree and nature of politicization of its student reform movement. As Haya noted, the Argentine iteration was a product of a constellation of forces—immigration, demographic increase, reform-minded governments of the 1910s and 1920s—factors quite distinct from what transpired in his native Peru.[11]

But one factor that the movement had in common throughout the hemisphere was the greater socioeconomic diversity of the student body. For the first time, significant numbers of students from the middle class were attending university. Reflecting the concerns of their class, they were, for the most part, prodemocracy, anticlerical, anticolonial, and anti-imperialist.[12] Given the pervasive poverty, unemployment, and underemployment throughout the region, the skewed distribution of wealth, and economic dislocations, progressive *and* reactionary students increasingly viewed capitalism as the problem.[13] Casting about for alternative models, two recent revolutions in particular—the Mexican and the Russian—afforded the students intriguing templates. Authorities, who had been initially sympathetic to student demands, grew increasingly concerned with the student-worker alliance. Union activities were repressed and the student movement was disparaged.[14]

From the movement's inception, activists sought out allies among their peers at home and abroad. The Córdoban strike committee issued a plea to students at universities throughout the hemisphere to join them in their struggle. Evidence of how quickly the movement spread was a 1920 pact signed by the Argentine, Peruvian, and Venezuelan student federations obliging their organizations to advocate for university reform, promote intellectual exchanges, and address social problems in their respective countries.[15]

A year later, Vasconcelos convened an International Student Congress in Mexico City. The idea for the conference came from one of the leaders of the Argentine movement, the University of La Plata student Héctor Ripa Alberdi. Twenty-three nations sent student representatives, which affirmed many of the Córdoban students' goals. Proof of a shared sense of purpose was the approval of planks about the *desiderata* of free tuition, *co-gobierno*, university autonomy, extension classes for workers and peasants, and a commitment to confront dictatorship, militarism, and imperialism throughout the hemisphere.[16] In the same year, the presidents of the student federations of Argentina (Del Mazo), Peru (Haya de la Torre), and Chile (Alfredo Demaría) signed agreements pledging that their organizations would actively promote "americanismo."[17]

There were a number of prominent Argentine *pensadores*, some of them professors themselves, whose insights and commitment to social justice energized the student body.[18] Del Mazo recalled that Ugarte was held in especially high regard; they were taken with his advocacy of pan-Latin solidarity and grateful for his unflinching support. In fact, students had invited him to address the inaugural meeting of the Argentine Student Federation in April 1918. Socialists Justo, Ingenieros, and Palacios provided additional inspiration and encouragement. Their party's newspaper, *La Vanguardia*, applauded student strikers at a time when mainstream newspapers were critical of the students' methods.[19]

Ingenieros's *El hombre mediocre*, which emphasized the importance of the pursuit of high-minded ideals, resonated particularly well, selling an extraordinary twenty thousand copies in a span of four months. The Argentine zeroed in on the malaise that many students felt about the ills of contemporary society. "When a generation feels fed up with deception, duplicity, servility, it has to seek in the geniuses of its race, the symbols of thought and action which will stimulate it to new efforts."[20] In 1915, he delivered a provocative lecture in Washington titled "The University of the Future," which later became a student blueprint for reform. He argued that higher education should be less professionally oriented and instead must become a site of social action; if students and faculty were not actively engaged in the "emancipation of humanity," they bore responsibility for the mistreatment of the working class.[21]

Agitate, Think, and Act

Nowhere did the university reform movement resonate more forcefully than in Lima. Unlike their peers in Argentina, Peruvian student militants during the early 1920s mobilized against a dictator who used both carrot and stick to first appease and then repress the movement.

As at Córdoba, the initial impetus for change in Peru was reform of the university. One of the student leaders, Luis Alberto Sánchez, fumed that "professors were there by divine right. ... Sons usually inherited faculty professorships from their fathers. ... No one questioned their privileges."²² Students at the nation's most prestigious university, the Universidad de San Marcos, demanded the removal of eighteen professors, the elimination of certain religion courses, academic freedom for professors, and a greater role for students in university governance. After a four-month strike, the students received support from an unlikely quarter: President Leguía embraced their concerns, firing twenty-four professors, granting academic freedom, providing fellowships for needy students, and permitting student participation in university governance.²³

The Argentine mentors Palacios and Ugarte visited and spoke at San Marcos and at other venues in Lima in 1919, praising the achievements of the Córdoban reform. According to Haya, Ugarte's lectures, with his admonitions about the consequences of complicity between Washington and Latin American governments and the *desideratum* of pan-Latin American unity, earned him the "ardent affection of the students." Haya's lieutenant Seoane had a similar reaction to Palacios's speech at the university. "Palacios's fierce words ignited the spark in [19]19. San Marcos was shaken to its core."²⁴

The young Haya also drew intellectual inspiration from the teachings of the aging anarchist Manuel González Prada, who had been critical of the Catholic Church, the landed elite, strongman rule, and the military's meddling in politics. González Prada counseled his charges that the relationship between workers and teachers must be synergistic; the ideas of intellectuals may be presented to the workers, but it is the working class that appropriates their perspectives and implements them.²⁵ Many of these views would be incorporated into Haya's writings.

Haya's baptism by fire occurred in 1919 when he persuaded the Peruvian University Student Federation to take to the streets of Lima in support of a strike called by urban workers, who were fighting for an eight-hour workday and a 25 percent wage increase. Thirty thousand workers and students flooded the streets of the capital. What was unusual about this strike was the degree of collaboration between workers and students. Unions had always advocated for themselves. But this time the union leadership decided to elect Haya and other student leaders to negotiate on their behalf, perhaps in hope that the regime would respond less harshly if middle-class students were involved.²⁶

Haya served on the student commission that negotiated with authorities. The workers did not get the salary increase, but the eight-hour workday was approved. That partial victory spawned greater trust and collaboration between anarcho-syndicalist union leaders and student militants. To show their gratitude, textile workers named Haya honorary president of their new Federation of Textile Workers.[27]

Two years later, representatives from San Marcos and three provincial universities held the First Congress of Peruvian Students in Cuzco. Haya overcame conservative student opposition to win support for a program of evening extension courses for workers.[28] The Universidad Popular González Prada (UPGP), named in honor of his mentor, began modestly enough on January 22, 1921, with a lecture series, and was later expanded to include student-taught evening classes in hygiene, anatomy, arithmetic, grammar, and geography. Courses ranged from "The Life of Rachmaninoff" to "The Obligation to Think." Instruction in Indigenous culture and history and the Quechua language was later added to the curriculum. Occasional cultural events featuring traditional dances and instrumentation were not infrequently brought to a close with a teacher calling for the vindication of "the rights of Peru's long-oppressed Indians."[29] Some classes were held at 3 a.m. so that waiters and other restaurant personnel could attend after their work shifts had concluded. Sanitation drives in working-class communities were organized, lectures about sex education—unheard of at that time—were offered, and the consumption of alcohol was discouraged.[30]

The UPGP's credos were consistent with anarcho-syndicalist values. The curricular emphasis on moral purity, for instance, of living a "clean life" free of temptations, followed from anarchist precepts.[31] Its motto, "one for all and all for one," also reflected an anarchist emphasis on solidarity. The slogan "8–8–8" signified that eight hours of each working day should be dedicated to work, study, and rest. A colorful maxim, "Ignorance is the godmother of tyranny and the pimp of exploitation," encouraged workers to educate themselves. Still another saying, "The popular university has no other dogma than social justice," reflected its dedication to improving the deplorable living conditions of Peru's urban and rural poor.[32] In retrospect, this commitment to social justice among student-teachers is not surprising. They had steeped themselves in the writings of advocates for social reform. As one instructor recalled, "all UPGP professors had the same cultural formation as Haya: the books of Tolstoy, Kropotkin, Hugo, Barbusse, Zola, Ingenieros, and González Prada."[33]

Although the Popular University presented itself as apolitical, that often depended on the particular instructor and the subject matter. A few, like Mariátegui, who gave seventeen lectures at the UPGP, felt that the Popular University's purpose was to raise the consciousness of the working class: "The UPs [popular universities] are not institutions of ag-nostic and apolitical university outreach. They are not night schools for workers. They are schools of revolutionary culture. Schools of class con-sciousness. The reason they exist is not only to foster the simple primi-tive adoption of bourgeois culture: they exist to develop and create a proletarian culture."[34]

Popular University adult education centers met from 9 to 11 p.m., three times a week in Lima and twice a week in Vitarte, a small textile-manufacturing center east of the capital. Later, additional campuses opened in urban centers all over the country.[35] Since the schools offered no formal degrees and charged no tuition, the UPGP subsisted on contributions in kind from idealistic students and professors. The provincial centers proved short-lived, but the schools in and around Lima enjoyed sustained success.[36]

Known widely as *el maestro* or *el compañero rector*, Haya threw himself into the UPGP's day-to-day operations. In addition to instruction, he hired staff, assembled the roster of courses, signed students' identifica-tion cards, and scheduled extracurricular activities. No detail was too small; Haya even "diagnosed (his students') illnesses and prescribed rem-edies."[37] In addition to his responsibilities as professor and administrator, a paternalistic Haya advised workers on their personal problems. Accord-ing to the historian Steve Stein, "he became a kind of mentor and settled disputes between father and son, husband and wife, and friend and enemy."[38] Haya also created and edited a journal for the Popular Univer-sity, *Claridad*, patterned after Henri Barbusse's *Clarté*, which was widely disseminated throughout Latin America. Barbusse's 1927 *Manifeste aux intellectuals* became a call to action for literati to transform society's ills.[39]

On a fellowship to Europe, compliments of the Peruvian government, Mariátegui encountered Barbusse in Paris in the early 1920s. To the bud-ding Marxist, Barbusse represented a new type of intellectual, someone who eschewed individualism in order to better society. Mariátegui became an important contributor to *Claridad*, and later, under his editorial direc-tion, the literary magazine's content became increasingly more political.[40] In his masterwork, *Los siete ensayos de interpretación de la realidad peruana* (1928), he criticized the restrictive, discriminatory nature of the Peruvian university system, demanding that the elitist institution be opened up to the entire population, including the country's impoverished Indigenous.[41]

It soon became apparent that Peru's student leadership had their sights set on more than just the reform of higher education. As in Argen-tina, higher education's purpose had been to train the next generation to

serve the political establishment. Now progressive faculty and students
questioned the morality of serving and sustaining corrupt and repressive
governments. In two short years the Universidad Popular boasted five
thousand adult students and would be an excellent recruiting tool for
Haya's fledgling political movement, APRA. Much of the future Aprista
union leadership studied at the UPGP in the early 1920s.[42]

With his reputation preceding him, Haya went on a four-month,
well-publicized speaking tour of the Southern Cone in 1922. His goal
was to develop closer ties with fellow student federations. In the Argentine capital, he lectured at the University of Buenos Aires; met with
prominent public intellectuals Ricardo Rojas and Ingenieros, as well as
del Mazo and Yrigoyen; and in Montevideo, spoke with Uruguay's reformist president José Batlle y Ordoñez. In Santiago, Chile, he visited the
Universidad Popular José Victorino Lastarria and laid a wreath on the
tombs of students and workers who had lost their lives to government repression. The trip confirmed Haya's status as one of the leaders of the
student movement.[43] He returned to Peru heartened by the potential for
collaboration and intent on bringing about meaningful change at home.

Lima was growing dramatically during the 1920s, its population increasing from two hundred twenty thousand in 1920 to a half-million
twenty years later. More than 60 percent of *Limeños* were of migrant origin. As historian Alberto Flores Galindo notes, greater educational opportunities, expanded transportation and communication networks, the
opening of the Panama Canal, and new journals and newspapers made it
possible for students from the provinces like Haya and many of his chief
lieutenants to expand their intellectual horizons and come into contact
with like-minded colleagues in the capital. Improvements in the publishing industry meant that students and their peers now had access to inexpensive editions of works of political theory, social criticism, and
literature by international writers.[44]

Haya characterized this larger, society-wide transformation as generational, pitting students against their elders. "In reality the young are following no master—for they have denied all," he contended.[45] In another column
he criticized the Arielista generation, which "fell into intellectualism, lost itself in literature and forgot about reality," contrasting them with students
who "agitate, think and act ... Because of this, with pride, I ought to call
them revolutionary."[46] While certainly there were intellectual elders who opposed the reforms, as we have seen, there also were prominent intellectuals
who embraced the youngsters' values and fought alongside them.

Then-student and later distinguished historian Jorge Basadre penned a thoughtful memoir of his participation in the student movement, noting the confluence of momentous changes occurring abroad with the students' resolve to bring about change at home. In addition to the revolutions in Mexico and Russia, he cited such topics as the failure of liberal democracy in Europe, the rise of totalitarianisms of the right and the left, and the end of the Spanish monarchy and the early promise of the republic, all of which provoked considerable debate. Coupled with the students' growing frustration with the Leguía dictatorship, Basadre's account characterized the time as one of relentless ferment: "Events occurring around us enveloped and oppressed us; in such a milieu, many reacted with enthusiasm or violence, and much later with anxiety and displeasure."[47]

Matters came to a head in May 1923. To legitimize his efforts to extend his term in office and to solidify the support of Peru's conservatives, the dictator declared that his administration would sponsor a religious ceremony dedicating the nation to the "Sacred Heart of Jesus." Emboldened students and professors took exception, fearing that the president intended to reestablish Catholicism as the official state religion.[48]

Haya seized the opportunity to further his political ambitions. He led five thousand protestors from the San Marcos campus to the Plaza San Martín in downtown Lima. Before they reached their destination, they were met by soldiers dispatched by Leguía to subdue the protest. In the ensuing fracas, one student and one tram worker were killed and dozens injured. The next day Haya and some of his supporters marched to the morgue, where they seized the bodies of the two victims and carried them back to campus. There Haya presided over a moving memorial service in a university auditorium. The following day, he led a procession of some thirty thousand mourners to the cemetery where the bodies were interred.[49]

Student demonstrations erupted all over Peru in solidarity with the San Marcos students. In response, the archbishop was forced to cancel the ceremony, embarrassing the regime and angering conservatives.[50] The campaign against the consecration cemented Haya's status as the leader of the opposition against the dictatorship. Mariátegui believed that the events of May 1923 marked a turning point for the nation: They revealed how closely "the working class and the student vanguard ... had become allied socially and ideologically. On that date, in exceptionally favorable circumstances, the new generation played a historical role when it advanced from student unrest to collective and social protest."[51] Haya went into hiding to avoid arrest, but before he did he spoke in prophetic terms. "I do not know what will happen to me. . . . If I have to go into exile, someday I shall return. I shall return in my own time, when the hour of the great transformation has arrived."[52]

The close working relationship between students and workers alarmed Leguía, and the mainstream press lambasted the UPGP, denouncing it as an incubator of Bolshevism. In the fall of 1923, Leguía once again cracked down on the protests. Enrique Cornejo Koster, then a student and later a chronicler of the movement, described what ensued: "During eight days Lima lived in a state of siege. Student assemblies, which came on the heels of tumultuous demonstrations that were broken up by the police, occurred incessantly. The government shut down the university, . . . schools, the student federations, and the offices of workers' unions. Not having anyplace to meet, students and workers invaded the offices and clubs of scientific societies . . . that were then immediately padlocked by government agents. . . . The leadership of the unions and the professors at the popular universities were arrested and taken to prison."[53]

As far as the students were concerned, personalistic caudillos, plutocrats, the military, and the church were all worthy of their scorn and derision. Corruption was endemic, much of it benefiting Leguía and his cabinet, family members, and cronies.[54] Haya repeatedly denounced what he called the forces of reaction. He was especially critical of the regime's and the oligarchy's complicity with *yanqui* capital, which had expanded considerably during the first decades of the century.

Haya also bashed what he called faux nationalism, stirred up by the powers that be, which distracted his countrymen from addressing the serious socioeconomic problems besetting their nation. Niggling border clashes stoked by self-serving oligarchical interests, like the Tacna-Arica dispute between his native Peru and Chile, sowed xenophobia, and to what end, he asked. "From the day I was born, from the day every Peruvian is born, he is taught to hate Chile. That's patriotism. . . . It doesn't matter that the dominant classes of both countries are friends. What is important is to sow divisions among the peoples [of Latin America], all the while inculcating senseless hatred between the two countries." Such mindless demagoguery, Haya added, had killed the dream of Central American union and contributed to Panama's secession from Colombia.[55]

Later that fall, the regime rounded up and incarcerated Haya, union leaders, and UPGP teachers.[56] Imprisoned on the island of San Lorenzo, Haya began a hunger strike. It was cut short, however, by Leguía's decision to deport him and a number of other student activists to Panama in October 1923.[57] Over the next six months, the regime shuttered most of the branch campuses of the Popular University, save those in Lima, where workers managed to turn back the soldiers. Mariátegui kept some of the branches open until 1927, when the regime closed the doors of the UPGP for good.[58] Repression against students and workers, however, continued unabated until the end of Leguía's rule in 1930.[59]

The repression prompted a fierce reaction across the continent. The celebrated Bengali poet Tagore's visit to Peru in the fall of 1924 was cancelled in part because of Latin American students' outrage over the repression. Tagore had been invited to visit Ayacucho for celebrations commemorating the centenary of Peru's victory against Spanish colonial rule. While in Buenos Aires, he received a letter from the Centro de Estudiantes Ariel in Montevideo, which warned him of the political consequences of such a visit: "President Leguía imprisons and banishes the students ... Our colleagues Haya de la Torre and Manuel Seoane, ex-presidents of the Student Federation, were banished after being prosecuted and imprisoned. ... The ideal of America as a sole and fraternal community speaks through the voice of youth. ... We feel it is necessary that you as a master of love must be aware of these facts." Tagore heeded the Uruguayan students' warning and cancelled his trip.[60]

Owing to the repression and fissures within the movement, opposition to the dictatorship dissipated after Haya's deportation. Some students pursued a liberal-democratic path, while leftist activists joined either Haya's movement or the communists. Mariátegui lamented that the students had been their own worst enemy. All too often succumbing to "superficial enthusiasms," the rebellious students had failed to sufficiently articulate their agenda. Instead, they were satisfied to "accept token efforts or vague promises that melted away once they relaxed their vigilance."[61]

Undeterred, Haya and his colleagues wandered for the next eight years throughout Latin America, the United States, and Europe, delivering lectures wherever they went and writing numerous columns that were syndicated in the Latin American press. Haya called for solidarity against dictatorships, imperialism, the church, and the oligarchy. The Peruvian continued to preach the gospel of the popular university in Cuba in November 1923 and Mexico throughout the winter and spring of 1924. The Universidad Popular José Martí (UPJP) in Havana and the Universidad Emiliano Zapata in Mexico City opened their doors either contemporaneously to or just after his visits. Soon, popular universities opened in Quito, Bogotá, Havana, Montevideo, Panama City, Caracas, Guatemala City, San Salvador, and Tegucigalpa. Vasconcelos's Ministry of Education donated reading materials to worker and artisan libraries as far away as Honduras and Nicaragua.[62]

One of the defining qualities of the university reform movement was its interconnectedness: student organizations throughout Latin America corresponded with each other and often acted in solidarity with peers abroad, especially those who were experiencing repression. As Mariátegui noted in his incisive 1928 essay "La reforma universitaria," "students throughout Latin America, although moved to protest by local problems, seek to speak the same language."[63]

Literary magazines like Mariátegui's *Amauta*, which, like *Repertorio Americano* and *Ariel*, published the works of prominent Latin American and European writers, acted as a vehicle to transmit avant-garde cultural and political ideas to students and workers.[64] Inspiration came from Europe as well. The Spanish philosopher Ortega y Gasset's *El tema de nuestro tiempo* had popularized the theory of historical generations—that individuals born roughly during the same period share a set of customs, traditions, and beliefs. This widely discussed book provided a heuristic framework that helped make sense of the proliferation of student activism on a global scale during the 1910s and 1920s.[65] Whereas some generations felt comfortable with the status quo, others, Ortega y Gasset argued, exercised a "constructive belligerence" in relation to their elders. Intent on discarding rather than conserving the past, youthful generations were, by definition, polemical and combative. As a result, "this minority lives condemned to not being well understood."[66] He insisted that disciplines or professors should not dictate or limit what was taught; instead, "the university must be the institutional projection of the student."[67] While Marxists dismissed his ideas because they failed to account for the proletariat's centrality in bringing about revolution, *El tema de nuestro tiempo* resonated with many students who felt a commitment to something greater, a hemispheric movement committed to significant reform that transcended their institutions of learning and the nation-state.[68]

Some students situated their critiques within *au courant* leftist ideologies, such as anarchism, anarcho-syndicalism, socialism, and communism, which lent form and an analytical framework to their rhetoric.[69] Indeed, during the early 1920s, it was the anarchists and the anarcho-syndicalists who were the most numerous and best organized of all leftist groups, especially in Chile, Argentina, and Cuba. The infighting among these groups was ferocious, but their commonalities were considerable. Students on the left agreed on "the cruel fictions of representative democracy and party politics" and held up the political class to public ridicule. Although all envisioned systemic change, rather than resort to revolutionary violence, most were willing to seek reform within their country's political structures. This capacious left knew full well who their enemies were: a repressive state, the oligarchy, and an emergent bourgeoisie. With some exceptions, they eschewed orthodoxy and sought to build multiclass coalitions with the urban and rural poor, white collar employees, and professionals. Such inclusive pluralism remained the policy of the Communist International (or Comintern) until 1928.

Not all students of this generation were men and women of the left. Conservative and moderate students, many of them matriculating at Catholic universities throughout the region, were opposed to much of their peers' emancipatory agenda. But the presence of a raucous left in the streets and in the press drowned out their more conservative rivals.[70]

The student movement quickly gained momentum across the hemisphere, in some cases out of proportion to its numbers and modest achievements. A knowledgeable observer, the Protestant minister Samuel Guy Inman, who had spent ten years as a missionary in Mexico, believed that, excepting newspapers, the generation of the reform was "more responsible for creating what there is of 'public opinion' in their countries than any other force." As early as 1921, he contended, students had already exercised considerable control over their universities.[71] As historian Eric Hobsbawm notes, the student movement also "inspired new populist-democratic and nationalist movements" and ultimately led to the establishment of mass-based political parties like APRA, the MNR, AD, and the Partido Revolucionario Institucional (PRI) in Mexico.[72]

More than their deeds, the students' insolence infuriated the powers that be. The initial surge to reform the university and create parallel popular universities would be either co-opted or repressed by authorities. Governments, according to Miller, "simply traded direct channels of control for more indirect methods of manipulation."[73] The popular universities, because they facilitated collaboration between the working class and the students, proved to be the most threatening to the establishment, and were ruthlessly suppressed in Peru, Colombia, Chile, Venezuela, and Argentina.

The fluid movement of radicals across porous national borders greatly concerned authorities, who concluded that the collective sharing of intelligence among law enforcement organizations was essential in countering the threat of subversion. The historian Raymond Craib documented a February 1920 meeting between representatives of law enforcement of seven South American countries "to facilitate policing across and within borders of the various signatories and encourage them to coordinate their police efforts to suppress subversion."[74] Efforts to monitor the movement of student militants became accepted practice throughout the hemisphere in the 1920s. The exile who attracted the most attention was Haya de la Torre.

Twenty of Us Can Move Latin America

Over the course of his exile, Haya spent much of his time delivering lectures and attending conferences throughout the Old World and the New, where he established Aprista cells and wrote countless columns that were disseminated in newspapers and magazines throughout Latin America. In the spoken and written word Haya preached his gospel of anti-imperialism, "Indo-Americanism," economic nationalism, the internationalization of the canal, social justice, and educational reform. He also never missed an opportunity to repudiate dictatorship in all of its guises and decried what he perceived to be the pernicious collaboration between regional elites and North American politicians and investors.[75]

Haya's arrival in the Mexican capital in late 1927 represented a homecoming of sorts. After brief stays in Panama and Cuba, he found safe harbor in Mexico in early 1924, thanks to Vasconcelos, who found a post for the diminutive Peruvian in his department. By the time Haya returned to the Mexican capital three years later, APRA chapters had been established in Paris, London, Buenos Aires, Santiago, Lima, La Paz, San Salvador, Guatemala City, Havana, San Juan, and Santo Domingo. His transnational movement appeared to be gaining momentum.[76]

Aprista cells abroad featured a small, dedicated cadre of followers, who formed study groups, disseminated the movement's publications, contributed columns to local newspapers, and proselytized to the uninitiated. His followers were encouraged to continue their education abroad.[77] Haya acknowledged early on the impact that anarchist notions of sowing working-class consciousness through education and culture had on his thinking.[78] APRA's Parisian cell, the first and probably its most active, established a Center for Anti-Imperialist Studies, which held lectures and workshops and disseminated publications, thanks to the purchase of a mimeograph machine.[79]

From the start, the movement evinced a spiritual sensibility. Calling themselves a communion of true believers, Aprista leaders felt strongly that theirs was a sacred undertaking, intent on rooting out "the evil political Pharisees that had ruled in the past." Meetings included the singing of the movement's hymn, the "Marsellesa Aprista," and when militants met each other they greeted each other with the phrase "only Aprismo will save Peru."[80]

Haya's aphorism "exile is the best school of rebellion" speaks to how his relatively small cadre of followers approached the years they spent away from Peru. It was viewed not as a punishment but as an opportunity for propagandizing and agitation. APRA scholar Martín Bergel notes that militants wore their displacement as "a badge of honor. It conferred on the few a visibility and a reputation that distinguished them. . . ."[81] Not unlike an army, discipline was expected, and once policy was set, dissent was frowned upon. Haya's "penchant for order" only intensified during his exile.[82]

He argued that revolutionary change required action, not endless ideological discussions. "A lucid intelligentsia capable of leading the way" would bring about transformational change."[83] The significance of a cohort of committed revolutionaries probably came from his familiarity with the Russian Revolution. After he arrived in Mexico, Haya befriended North American communists Ella and Bertram Wolfe and Jay Lovestone, who persuaded him to travel to the USSR to experience the revolution firsthand.[84] In the Soviet Union, Haya was impressed by the ideologically motivated militants, whose task it was to raise the political consciousness of proletarians. Haya patterned his movement's cell-like structure on the Soviet model. Membership cards were dispensed only after careful consideration of a novice's commitment and aptitude. In a letter sent to coreligionists, he noted, "what's essential at this time is to form proletarian cells, to constitute, in a word, a red army." Even after his rancorous break with the communists in 1928, APRA continued to employ Leninist organizational principles.[85]

Seoane confirmed the significance of committed "agents of change," since Peru's small industrial proletariat and its peasantry lacked political awareness.[86] While a revolutionary vanguard was valued, Aprismo's appeal ultimately was dependent on its leader. Haya's charisma and personal warmth proved contagious. He was the undisputed paterfamilias of what took on the trappings of a messianic movement. As the not-so-humble leader phrased it, "the hero interprets, intuits and directs the vague and imprecise aspirations of the multitude." Equal parts opportunist, demagogue, and mystical visionary, Haya would remain chameleonlike for the rest of his political career.[87]

Depending on circumstances and conditions, Haya's movement took different forms in different countries. From Oxford, England in 1926, he explained his thinking to Seoane: "APRA is above all a partnership; not only a political party, but an alliance or coalition of forces. . . . In Peru it will be a political party like the Kuomintang, designed to conquer power and overthrow the imperialists. That same thing could take place in Bolivia, Venezuela, Colombia, Central America, etc. In Argentina and Chile, it [APRA] could simply be an alliance of the people's forces, a focal point of action and support."[88]

Given the great distance between the cells, it is not surprising that variations in emphasis and tactics emerged. Some groups employed Marxist terminology in their literature, while others studiously steered away from it so as to distinguish themselves from their rivals. Sometimes praxis and theory came into conflict. For instance, the Havana cell consistently praised the Soviet Union, even as its magazine *Atuey* dismissed the idea of class struggle.[89]

Although the movement was established in exile, clandestine meetings of the Peruvian Universidad Popular continued to be held in the homes of APRA leaders in Lima while Haya's extended exile continued. During a yearlong lecture tour of Mexico and Central America (November 1927–December 1928), Haya declared that he intended to return to his homeland to run for the presidency in 1929 against the incumbent Leguía, who, after ten years in power, had announced that he intended to run yet again for office. Haya was convinced that the dictator would never permit him to stand for election. His actual purpose was to lay the groundwork for a nationwide rebellion. His followers in Peru were instructed to forge alliances among peasants, workers, and the middle class while they dutifully awaited his return.[90]

No longer an idealistic student seeking to reform antiquated educational institutions, Haya was now an internationally known public intellectual and activist. Often those roles conflicted, a tension that came with a significant political cost to his movement. As an Aprista scholar has noted, "Haya the activist has all too often had to compromise the highsounding theories expounded by Haya the *pensador*, and the result in the public mind has often been confusion and indeed disappointment."[91]

In addition to conspiring to overthrow Leguía, Haya envisioned himself as *the* leader of a continentwide anti-imperialist groundswell. Increasingly at odds with the CI, the indefatigable self-promoter needed progressive allies across the region, like the ULA, to burnish his revolutionary credentials. His lieutenant Seoane, then heading up an Aprista cell in Buenos Aires, insinuated himself so successfully into ULA that he soon replaced Palacios as the group's general secretary from 1928 to 1930.[92]

Haya's lecture tour began in the relative tranquility of Mexico City, where, during a span of six months, enthusiastic audiences turned out for a series of eight lectures at the National Preparatory School and the University of Mexico.[93] Local press coverage of his lectures was abundant. Haya's anti-imperialist message struck an especially resonant chord among many young Mexicans who were opposed to U.S. intervention in Nicaragua. As we shall see, Washington's frustration with the Mexican government's meddling in Central America and the revolutionary government's passage of laws targeting U.S. investments roiled relations between the two countries. In addition, Haya's hostility toward dictatorship had earned him the admiration of most, but not all, of a boisterous exile community in the capital, some of whom, like Haya, had fled repression and were themselves hatching plots from a distance against caudillos in their homelands. At the same time that he presented his ideas publicly, the Peruvian was completing a book manuscript called *Antiimperialismo en América Latina* and, with the assistance of other Apristas, putting the final touches on "Plan México"—the name given to the plot to stage an anti-Leguista rebellion in the oil fields of northern Peru.[94]

Haya's second exile in Mexico was not met with universal approval. Unlike in 1924, when he was accorded a hero's welcome by the revolutionary regime and given political asylum and a sinecure in the Ministry of Education, now Calles, anxious to mend fences with the U.S., was not as hospitable. Yet the Mexican president only reined in Haya so far. As the leader of a revolutionary state, it would not be politic to actively harass an activist espousing such anti-imperialist views.

Central American diplomats in Mexico, however, had no compunction whatsoever about openly voicing their displeasure. They insisted that Haya stay put in Mexico, lest he move down the isthmus and incite unrest among dissidents in their countries. Meanwhile, the Peruvian secret police had their agents in Mexico tracking his every move.

Perhaps the most venomous criticism that Haya received came from the left. In April 1928, his former colleague Mariátegui sent a cutting letter to APRA's Mexican cell, questioning Haya's tactics, his recourse to "bluff and lies," and the movement's similarities to Italian fascism. Haya

responded in kind a month later, chiding the Peruvian communist for
not having embraced the anti-imperialist revolution, "the only possible
and immediate revolution of this era."[95]

In that vein, communist militants, including Mella and Gustavo
Machado, discredited Haya at every turn, painting him as a misguided,
petty bourgeois reformer who was doomed to failure because he stood in
the way of an authentic proletarian revolution. Mella even turned up at a
lecture Haya gave at the National Preparatory School in October 1928
and, in the question and answer period, criticized several of Haya's positions.[96] Mella was especially upset that the self-styled Peruvian revolutionary had never lent any material support to Sandino's rebellion,
certainly not to the extent that MAFUENIC and LADLA had. In addition, Haya's call for the internationalization of the Panama Canal, the
Cuban remarked, was a faux issue. In the unlikely case that the U.S. ever
ceded control of the canal, he mused, who but other imperialist powers
would step into the breach and ensure that Latin Americans would never
share oversight of the waterway.[97]

It was at this moment that Mella published his withering attack
against Haya, "¿Qué es el ARPA?" which denounced the Peruvian's
movement as fascist, a defender of British imperial interests, and pseudo-
revolutionary. Mella intentionally misspelled APRA in the title, comparing Aprismo to a harp (*arpa* in Spanish). The pamphlet was, in some
respects, a reprise of a debate that the two darlings of the left had had at
the Congress of Oppressed Nationalities at the Egmont Palace in Brussels in 1927. The conference brought together many of the leading lights
of the global left—Barbusse, Gorky, Sun Yat-Sen's widow, Jawaharlal
Nehru, Albert Einstein, and Roman Rolland, among others. Young fire-
brands like Mella, Machado, and Haya came, but also on hand were
members of the older generation of anti-imperialists, such as Vasconcelos
and Ugarte. Optimism ran high that the conference had the potential to
bring about a unified global movement dedicated to redressing the twin
evils of colonialism and imperialism.[98]

If the conference's goal was to unify a fractious global left, the results
failed to measure up. Mella and Haya and other ideologues squared off,
debating the Aprista contention that the struggle against Western imperialism necessitated the forging of a multiclass coalition. Haya staked out
an independent position for his movement and presented Aprismo as *the*
leader of Latin American anti-imperialism. This position was totally unacceptable to the communists; as Haya put it after the congress, "For

Communism there could not exist another party of the left which was not the official one of the Third International of Moscow, of Stalinist orthodoxy. Every political organization that Moscow doesn't command must be execrated and combated."[99] Haya later related that he first became disenchanted with communism during his three-month visit to the Soviet Union in 1925, where he had been an observer at the Communist International's Fifth Congress. He was disheartened that the delegates were so ignorant of conditions in Latin America.

Calling his nascent political party the Kuomintang of Latin America, after the party that initially forged a popular front coalition before turning against the Chinese Communist Party in 1927, Haya sought to differentiate his movement from the CI by emphasizing its uniquely Latin American character. He argued that the rise of the proletariat would unfold differently in Latin America than it had elsewhere. Lenin's notion that imperialism was the last stage of capitalism might fit a European reality where countries were, by comparison, highly capitalized, but in underdeveloped countries, Haya contended, imperialism was the first stage of capitalism.[100]

His time spent in exile in Europe had led him to conclude that the Old World had little to teach Latin Americans about how to bring about meaningful change. Well before Brussels, he told a colleague, "every day I'm more convinced that the revolution of American workers must be 'the work of themselves' without intervention or mentoring of Europe. It would be admirable if the proletarians of Europe and Latin America would march side by side, but that is not realistic at this point. Here [in Europe] not only do they ignore our problems, but they don't give them much importance."[101]

The mean-spirited polemics eventually cost Haya the backing of a number of radical supporters in Peru, including his righthand man, Pavletich.[102] Communists were upset that the Peruvian so cavalierly appropriated Marxian concepts. Concerned with Haya's growing popularity throughout Latin America and his independent streak, the CI sought to discredit and undermine him at every turn.[103]

A year later, in 1928, the Sixth Communist International adopted a sectarian position concerning revolutionary movements worldwide. Predicting correctly that a worldwide economic crisis was looming and that the global capitalist order was on the verge of a collapse, the International changed its earlier policy of supporting popular movements and forbade collaborations with peasants and petty bourgeois elements. Reformists were now "to be unmasked" and labeled "social fascists" and poseurs. The CI turned its energies to building a base of support among the proletariat, in its mind the only true revolutionary class. In practice, this new line meant greater uniformity and ideological consistency for Latin America's Communist parties.[104]

The CI believed that Latin America had been held back by feudal modes of production and a dependent relationship with imperial powers. As a result, they treated the region's fledgling communist parties paternalistically, viewing the region as a laboratory where theory and praxis could be applied and tested and, when needed, discipline could be enforced. As Stalin consolidated his power over the party, discordant voices in Asia, Africa, and Latin America were increasingly stifled. Those who joined the party understood that absolute loyalty was required; dissent meant expulsion or worse. That degree of conformity cost the party adherents, but those who remained were highly disciplined and devoted.[105]

To critics, the CI painted the region with too broad a brush. Even Mariátegui, who continued to support Stalin and the party until his early death in 1930, felt that the CI had misjudged Peru's distinctive Indigenous peasantry. While there were "striking parallels" between Russia's and Peru's agrarian character, the Quechuas' and Aymaras' communal heritage, he believed, made them excellent candidates for a socialist revolution. "Our socialism thus would not be Peruvian—neither would it even be socialism—if it did not show solidarity, first and foremost with indigenous demands."[106] He also disagreed with the CI about Peru's economic mode of production. His country's mid-nineteenth-century guano boom and subsequent economic integration into the global economy meant that it was only partially feudal; tradition-bound haciendas, he reminded his readers, coexisted alongside capitalist mining enterprises and communal villages. He also raised eyebrows among his more dogmatic peers by insisting that Marxism was as much a faith as it was an ideology: "revolutionary movements embody a mystical, religious, spiritual force" akin to early Christianity.[107]

Haya shared with Mariátegui an appreciation for the Russian Revolution, but he was convinced that given Latin America's social, cultural, and economic diversity, a "one-size-fits-all" socialism imposed from without was a prescription for disaster. As he aptly noted, "a political party composed only of the proletariat is a party without any possibilities of success in Latin America."[108] The struggle for socialism, Haya believed, must be incremental, given how rudimentary and weak the proletariat was throughout Latin America.

More impatient than Mariátegui, Haya thought it unnecessary to wait for a proletarian-led revolution; a multiclass popular front could be forged to overthrow Leguía, the oligarchy, and their foreign collaborators, thereby hastening the arrival of socialism. Mariátegui countered that a popular front was a fool's errand. Lacking in political awareness, peasants, workers, and the petty bourgeoisie required further education before a truly revolutionary party could take hold in Peru.[109] The break between the two came in 1928 when Haya, then in exile in Mexico, created a national political party. An incensed Mariátegui felt that Haya had shown his true colors.[110]

The change in strategy by the CI not only posed a problem for APRA, but it also had ominous implications for Sandino's movement, which up to that point had enjoyed logistical, financial, and moral support from the communists. To be sure, the left's penchant for internecine warfare proved to be a godsend for authorities in Peru and elsewhere, which painted these movements with a broad red brush. When Haya made his break with Marxism final in his essay "Aprismo y marxismo," the fault lines were clear; activists had to choose one path or the other.[111]

Central American Sojourn

After his well-received lectures in Mexico, in June 1928 Haya left for Central America, where he continued his speaking engagements over the next six months in much more hostile territory. Authorities in several countries appear either to have acceded to pressure from North American diplomats to hound the fiery activist or they did so of their own accord, Haya contended, because they felt it would please their patrons. As a result, the Peruvian enjoyed the dubious distinction of deportation from one country (Guatemala), escape from another just before he was about to be expelled (El Salvador), and prohibition of entry to two others (Honduras and Nicaragua).

Wherever he went, Haya stirred the pot. His five-week stay in Guatemala, sponsored by Guatemala City's Popular University and the National Federation of Labor, was turbulent, to say the least. At the former venue he was critical of both the United Fruit and Cuyamel Companies for provoking a confrontation between Honduran and Guatemalan troops along their shared border, an issue he would return to in print. Haya also repeatedly denounced the nation's former dictator, Manuel Estrada Cabrera, and his successors. This elicited a favorable response from his youthful audience, since the Association of University Students played a significant role in the dictator's overthrow in 1920. Now, eight years later, owing to Estrada's aides and followers, who replicated the caudillo's brutal methods, Haya lamented that "Cabrerismo lives on." Drawing a parallel between what happened to Turcios's *Ariel* and the government's recent censorship of the Guatemala City daily *El Nuevo Diario*, he claimed that the latter was shuttered solely because its editor had had the courage to invite him to come to Guatemala to speak. This, Haya inveighed, was the "price of *yanqui* favor."[112]

He also gave a number of lectures in the largely Indigenous highland city of Quetzaltenango, where he energized students, workers, professionals, and progressive elements of the Liberal Party. His call for a unified *indoamérica* was well received in this Indigenous stronghold. When his deportation order was issued, he castigated authorities for prostituting themselves to *yanqui* imperialism, telling several reporters, "I won't be scared away; on the contrary, this will make me stronger. I will continue to fight for the unification of our America." University students in the capital denounced Haya's deportation in an open letter and scrawled images of the Peruvian activist on the walls of city streets. Haya's time in Guatemala may have roused Liberal Party adherents. Soon after he departed, they rose up in rebellion against the government. It took six thousand troops to quell the uprising, and more than three hundred rebels were killed.[113]

In San Salvador, Haya's lectures and newspaper columns sparked "vigorous debates in the press, with significant reformist and anti-imperialist editorializing." His impact was felt in the provinces as well. Writing in his memoirs, Reynaldo Galindo Pohl recalled that Haya's visit resonated with many: "In Sonsonate, it would have been hard to find a person who did not express anti-imperialist ideas."[114] Haya was even more provocative in his critique of El Salvador's repressive and sycophantic political class. In "Una rectificación y una denuncia" (A Rectification and an Accusation), written afterward from the relative safety of Costa Rica, he lamented that El Salvador, which he dubbed the Prussia of Central America for its repressive past, had functioned for many years under a permanent state of siege, where the rule of law gave way to the whim of the U.S. minister. He also lashed out against corrupt politicians who mortgaged the nation to foreign bondholders by taking out seventy million dollars' worth of "immoral" loans—monies that lined the pockets of avaricious officials. In addition, he opined that the chief of police, a

Honduran by birth, was but a poorly disguised mercenary in the pay of the North American legation. Detailing how authorities dispatched spies to infiltrate his five lectures, including one he delivered at San Salvador's Popular University, he described in some detail his eleventh-hour escape to the Mexican embassy, which had saved him from certain imprisonment and deportation.[115]

Nicaraguan authorities made clear their reasons for denying Haya permission to visit: they were adamant that Haya not be allowed to travel to the Segovias to confer with Sandino. Yet even democratic Costa Rica—a country that heretofore had prided itself on an established tradition of welcoming political refugees—bowed to pressure from its neighbors and Washington and denied the Peruvian permission to speak at public venues. The U.S. minister in San José even took the unusual step of actively discouraging private institutions from allowing Haya to speak.

Despite the harassment, Haya's three-month stay in Costa Rica paid considerable dividends. Thanks to a tolerant immigration policy, a critical mass of political exiles resettled there. And unlike many nations in the region, freedom of the press was not just practiced in the breach. As a result, the capital, San José, was a hotbed of dissent. Haya gave well-received lectures at the Instituto Bíblico and the Colegio de Abogados, where he spoke about university reform, economic sovereignty, the need for pan-Latin American solidarity, and the ills of banana monoculture.[116]

Like *pensadores* elsewhere, Costa Rican intellectuals were drawn to his message. Activist Lucia González recalled, "for me, [Haya's visit] was a revelation . . . [and] we have reached out and our enthusiasm . . . has been put at the service of our America." Her colleague Carmen Lyra added that the Peruvian had made her reevaluate her priorities: "I know that listening to Haya de la Torre I was ashamed of my comfortable skepticism and pessimism, which represented little more than ignorance of the reality confronting us and my country's future and that of all of Central America."[117]

Such an enthusiastic response contributed to concrete outcomes: an APRA chapter was created in San José; and an institute, the Centro de Estudios e Investigaciones Económicas, which conducted research on foreign economic penetration in Latin America and sought to forge ties between activists and peasants and workers, was established. In addition, Haya found time to celebrate and encourage the work of the Popular University in the Costa Rican capital. Reports of his various lectures and the harassment they engendered from local authorities were covered in full in *Repertorio Americano.*[118]

Why did authorities consider Haya so dangerous? He certainly was not a military threat to Leguía, let alone to the governments of the countries he visited. His APRA movement was conspicuously small, had no military capability to speak of, and was largely focused on consciousness-raising. Yet the U.S. government, Central American authorities, the Communist International, and Leguía all regarded him as either a demagogue or a subversive.

Haya's determination to differentiate his movement from the Bolshevik and Mexican Revolutions did not diminish in the least his steady reportorial barrage against international capital and its collaborators. In *Repertorio Americano* he contributed a column criticizing regional governments, the banana companies, and Washington for inflaming passions along the border between Honduras and Guatemala. Sensing conspiracy in the words and actions of Paz Barahona and Summerlin—the two who had just colluded to silence Turcios's *Ariel* that same summer—Haya was convinced that the border dustup over a disputed two-thousand-square-mile tract was intentionally blown out of proportion to diminish support for Sandino and to drown out protests of North American intervention. According to Haya, Summerlin was the "viceroy of the new empire," and the "servile" and "pliable" Honduran puppet president had prompted the conflict. How rich, he contended, that Kellogg was now insisting on a hearing on the border dispute before the Central American Court of Justice, a regional judicial body the U.S. government had either treated cavalierly or ignored in the past when it suited its purposes.[119] Elite propagating of regionalism and localism, "tears at the fabric of Latin American unity."

Elsewhere, he lamented the so-called patriotic causes that pitted Peru against Chile, Brazil against Argentina, and Colombia against Ecuador. Dictators and oligarchical regimes stoked such mindless chauvinism in order to obscure more pressing socioeconomic concerns.[120] Guatemalans, in principle, did not hate Hondurans, so efforts by authorities and agents of imperialism to sow discord and pit these neighbors against each other were as divisive as they were fruitless. In fact, what Haya sensed from his travels across the region was that there was strong sentiment to reestablish the Central American Union, because isthmian youth, a number of whom were now fighting in the mountains of Nicaragua with the EDSNN, saw through their political classes' complicity with the forces of imperialism. "The day is coming when the Central American people will throw out the imperialists. The world will be surprised. But I won't be, because if Central America has given the world monsters like Chamorro and [Adolfo] Díaz, Paz Barahona and Moncada, it has also given the world Sandino, a glorious and immortal figure, and behind him are thousands of anonymous heroes acting behind the scenes."[121]

Companies like *el pulpo*, Haya contended, exercised undue influence on Central American governments. In "Imperialism in Central America," Haya blamed U.S. investors for practicing "the most violent, most unconditional and piratical form of monopoly." They meddle in elections, influence the press, and "incite ... a misleading, petty, local patriotism, which only favors imperialism."[122]

Haya's calls for regional unity resonated among politicized expatriates in Europe. Paris's Aprista cell organized demonstrations in support of Sandino and against U.S. intervention in the region. At an APRA meeting, Ugarte echoed Haya's talking points when he explained that the U.S. was not solely to blame for Latin America's predicament: "We must also be critical of the lack of expertise and the complicity of our improvident and corrupt governments, [of] tyrants and oligarchies, and the cynical political parties which bring our republics to the abyss. ... If Latin America finds itself in this situation it is because of those who handed over mines, trains, monopolies and loans to foreign companies. ... This situation is the result of a lack of foresight by those that made our countries cripples that can only walk with foreign crutches. This failing on the part of the governing classes must be punished."[123] Ugarte's polemic, which enjoyed wide dissemination abroad, ended with a call to Latin American youth to root out their "unpopular governments."

Also residing in Paris at the time was the young Guatemalan writer Asturias, who was quite taken with Haya's teachings. As a student at the Guatemalan National University, Asturias led a strike against Estrada in 1920, attended the International Student Congress in Mexico City a year later, and in 1922 answered the Peruvian's call to establish popular universities across the region.[124] During Asturias's stay in Europe, he penned more than four hundred columns on cultural, social, and political topics of the day for the Guatemalan newspaper *El Imparcial*. In one piece, he praised Gandhi's tactics in India against the British Empire and issued a call to action that resonated with Haya's advocacy of economic nationalism: "the best way to oppose imperialism is to deny them our lands, to keep them for ourselves."[125]

Asturias also helped establish an anti-imperialist student group and compared notes with other youthful Latin American exiles in cafes in

Montparnasse. Years later he recalled: "during the conversation what we might call a competition emerged amongst the Venezuelans, Guatemalans and Mexicans, repeating anecdotes about our respective dictators— don Porfirio Díaz, Estrada Cabrera and the dictator of Venezuela [Gómez]—everyone told stories."[126]

It is instructive that the most transcendent Latin American novels of the era, those that gained an international audience—including Asturias's *El Señor Presidente*, the Venezuelan Rómulo Gallegos's *Doña Bárbara*, the Ecuadorian Jorge Icaza's *Huasipungo*, the Mexican Gregorio López y Fuentes's *El indio*, and the Argentine Ricardo Güiraldes's *Don Segundo Sombra*—all repudiated dictatorships, regional oligarchies, and rapacious foreign investors. Their novels either implicitly or explicitly called for alliances between progressive elements of the middle and upper classes and the Indigenous and other marginalized sectors of their societies. That was precisely the message Haya hammered home in his writings and lectures.[127]

Haya's barbs, however, provided his enemies on the right and the left with ample grist for their polemics. Long after his well-publicized split with the communists, he and his acolytes continued to unnerve the CI, especially when he employed Marxist terminology and conceptual categories of analysis in his writings and speeches.[128]

Another point of contention between Haya and his leftist critics was his admiration for the Mexican Revolution. At a moment when Mexican communists were attacking their own government for abandoning its revolutionary principles—and experiencing withering repression for their stance—Haya was more measured in his assessment of the one nation that had opened its doors to him. As early as 1924, he had heaped praise on the revolution's agrarianism, *indigenismo*, and economic nationalism.

Vasconcelos's cultural ideas about *mestizaje* and Indo-America had a profound influence on Haya.[129] The Peruvian was particularly taken with the life and work of the peasant revolutionary Emiliano Zapata. Although much had been accomplished in Mexico, Haya reflected, its distinctive path could not be considered a blueprint for the rest of Latin America. "In Mexico, we find a spontaneous revolution, with scarcely any program, an instinctive revolution lacking in scientific principles." Mexico's revolution may have been as important for Latin America as Russia's had been for Europe, Haya noted, but it was bereft of theorists and leaders. "It is a marvelous succession of improvisations, guesswork, blunders, saved by the popular will, energetic instincts, and the almost indomitable will of the revolutionary peasantry." As effervescent as such spontaneity was, he concluded, ultimately it ran the risk of stagnation.[130]

Moreover, Haya left himself open to criticism by frequently making improbable claims. In a letter to Turcios in February 1928 that enjoyed wide circulation in the regional press, he wildly overstated his movement's capabilities to assist Sandino. "Our [APRA's] services unconditionally place ourselves at the orders of the Nicaraguan Liberation Army so as to fight in their ranks."[131] Mella rightfully derided Haya's commitment to the rebel's cause as hollow and a "phantasm." It appears that only one Aprista had actually fought in Sandino's army.[132]

Even if Haya's support for the Nicaraguan rebel was largely rhetorical, however, it drew the attention of Nicaraguan and North American officials and angered the CI, which had its own reasons for keeping the Peruvian activist from reaching the Segovias. Given how weak national communist parties were throughout Latin America at that time, an APRA-EDSNN alliance with ties to like-minded progressives in Latin America, Europe, and North America could not be taken lightly.

This is why both Haya *and* Sandino became objects of vicious smear campaigns throughout 1928 and 1929. Typical was a statement by an Argentine delegate at the VI Congress of the CI in Moscow in 1928: "We must fight tooth and nail against APRA, which is a type of Kuomintang in Latin America, and against all groups that seek to impede the hegemony of the proletariat in the struggle against imperialism."[133] Mella and his colleagues may have been right about Haya's toothless offer to assist Sandino, but their relief was palpable when the Peruvian was expelled from Central America. Of the two, Sandino was more difficult for the communists to discredit, simply because of his heroic David versus Goliath struggle against the U.S. But Haya's steadfast refusal to relinquish the mantle of leadership of the anti-imperialist movement in his ideological battles with Mella and his countryman Mariátegui did earn him the admiration of many progressives leery of the CI.

Haya's steady drumbeat of anti-American rhetoric was the subject of correspondence between the U.S. legations in Central American countries and the State Department. Unhappy with what U.S. officials interpreted as a Bolshevik-sounding call for the "nationalization of wealth," the State Department began accumulating a file on the agitator and asked its consular and diplomatic agents throughout Latin America to forward any information they obtained about Haya and APRA to Washington. Convinced that Haya was "operating under the orders and at the expense of Mexican agents," the Department was determined to isolate him.[134]

Haya's persistent call for the internationalization of the Panama Canal was particularly worrisome to Washington, especially when, after finishing up his Costa Rican engagements, he booked passage to Panama City. It had been Haya's intention to change to a different ship in Panama City so he could return to Mexico. But Canal Zone authorities were concerned that if they allowed him onshore he would egg on nationalistic Panamanians. U.S. officials decided to seize Haya in the harbor, even though his ship was in Panamanian waters, where the U.S. did not have jurisdiction. He then was "literally shanghaied" and taken across the isthmus to Panama's Atlantic coast, where he was detained until he was placed on another ship destined for Bremen, Germany. Haya even had to pay a ninety-dollar fare for a passage he had not booked, to a destination that complicated in no small way his plans to oust Leguía. Since he did not possess a German visa, it was conceivable that if that government turned down his request for entry, he would be placed right back on board and returned to Panama. Thankfully for Haya, an unlikely coalition, consisting of U.S. officials anxious to maroon Haya in Europe, German progressives, and sympathetic Peruvians living in Germany, interceded on his behalf, successfully lobbying the German government to grant him a visa.[135]

The heavy-handed treatment accorded to Haya turned out to be a public relations blow for Washington, as accounts of his harassment in Panama and Central America flooded the Latin American and European press. Only a month after his ouster from Guatemala, Deambrosis Martins published a column in the Parisian press, relaying Haya's account of his mistreatment and his charge that local officials were complicit with Washington in denying him the right to express his views.[136] Haya later gloated about his misfortune, telling his supporters in Europe, "My expulsion from Panama raised up a wave of protest throughout America that has been for me the best indication that we throughout the Americas are not far apart from one another."[137]

His years spent in exile and the harassment he was subjected to helped foster the legend of Haya's eternal persecution, something he seemed all too willing to cultivate. From this point on, he presented himself as a martyr for the causes he and his movement espoused. In his and his lieutenants' speeches and writings, terms like *apostle, crusade, mission,* and *faith* were repeatedly invoked. Spiritual invocations gave his movement a

Haya addressing a crowd in Peru, 1931. Courtesy The History Collection /
Alamy Stock Photos.

veneer that stoked both fanatical support and a sense of victimization. But
Haya gave off mixed signals about the desirability of armed revolt in his
speeches and writings, sowing confusion among the faithful and enemies
alike.[138]

After 1930 Haya lent his energies to building a viable political party in
Peru. APRA was not averse to employing political violence to achieve its
ends. Its militants carried out a series of high-profile political assassinations,

topped off by the murder of Peruvian president Luis Sánchez Cerro in 1933. Repression of the party ensued as Haya spent much of the next twenty years either in prison, underground, or in exile. Some of his key lieutenants also were forced to flee. Chile was the destination of choice for many, owing to its proximity and to more tolerant governments after 1932. Under Luis Sánchez's determined leadership, APRA's Chilean cell and the Santiago publishing house Ercilla kept the movement's transnational message alive. In his writings, Haya continued to emphasize the importance of building an Indo-American, anti-imperialistic movement, but his refusal to leave Peru diminished his visibility and his stature as a voice for progressive change elsewhere. Ironically, Haya himself became more critical of exile during his time in hiding. He criticized party members who had left Peru for becoming soft and undisciplined.[139]

Conclusions

Under attack from the Latin American right and the left as well as the United States, Haya battled to carve out an ideological position to win over those demanding change. But his agenda was not as sweeping as the transformations called for by the communists. Rhetorically, reformers like Haya had to walk an even finer line. To demonstrate that they were serious about reform, it was incumbent on them, lest they lose the support of their base, to attack North American intervention in all its forms and to portray themselves as staunch economic nationalists. When Washington took umbrage at such rhetoric, it only buttressed red-baiting hawks in the U.S. and Latin America, a Greek chorus that painted the reformers as wolves in sheep's clothing.

North American officials treated Haya as if he were a contagion. The great pains they took to harass and expel him from the region speak to a number of salient themes in U.S.-Latin American relations during the 1920s and 1930s, which historians have mistakenly pigeonholed as products of the Cold War. It was evident in Washington's pervasive, almost knee-jerk fear of revolution, an anxiety that contributed to an often self-defeating disinclination to distinguish reformers from revolutionaries. Such an indiscriminate lumping together of such disparate agents of change as Aprismo and communism painted the U.S. into a corner of its own making, leaving it little choice, or so it presumed, but to continue backing reactionary forces. This, in turn, drew acrimonious responses from reformers and fueled widespread anti-American sentiment.

Profiles of the political awakening of two Venezuelan student activists offer a glimpse of this process of politicization, as well as the different ideological paths that students and activists took during the 1920s. Rómulo Betancourt and Gustavo Machado would be archenemies for much of their adult lives, but they shared common goals during the 1920s; most notably to end Juan Vicente Gómez's two-decade-long stranglehold over Venezuela and to create a more just and egalitarian society.

CHAPTER THREE

The Generation of 1928

He organizes a union in the morning, instructs peasants in the afternoon, scrawls slogans in the city at night, [and] distributes propaganda at dawn.

—RAÚL ROA ON RÓMULO BETANCOURT, 1949

A DIVERSE GROUP OF Venezuelan students—some quite dogmatic, others idealistic neophytes—experienced a political coming of age during the late 1920s. "The Generation of '28," so named because it was the year that student protests against the dictatorship first pricked the public's consciousness, decades later became the nation's political establishment. Rómulo Betancourt, a twenty-year-old law student at the University of Caracas, who hailed from the state of Miranda east of the capital, gave up his studies to join the struggle to overthrow the dictator. Years later, he recalled how what transpired all across the region had inspired students to protest against the dictatorship. "In some chance magazine, we would read—our youthful eyes shining with the emotion of one who suddenly surveys an unknown world—of the student fights in Córdoba, Argentina; of the street demonstrations in Lima, Peru; and of the battle beginning in Cuba against the *machadato*—the dictatorship of Machado. Moved by the growing insurgence of youth throughout America we organized 'The Week of the Student.'"[1]

In early February 1928, during the annual Student Week festivities that coincided with Carnival, members of the Federación Estudiantil Venezolano (FEV) delivered incendiary speeches demanding an end to the dictatorship and political reform. One of Betancourt's classmates, Jóvito Villalba, speaking at the National Pantheon beside Bolívar's sarcophagus, reminded those in attendance that December would mark the twentieth anniversary of Gómez's dictatorship. "Only in the University, where the true Venezuela has been in hiding for years, can the rebel cries of freedom be heard again."[2] Student protestors in Caracas's Plaza Bolívar openly mocked Gómez's motto, "Union, Peace and Work," by chanting "Union in the jails, peace in the cemetery, and work in the road gangs," and threw rocks at a plaque with Gómez's name on it.[3] Later that week, Betancourt took the stage at the Rivoli movie house across from the Capitol to denounce the dictatorship. At the culminating event, the coronation of the festival queen, protest poetry was read aloud.[4]

This was not the first time that student agitation had roiled the regime—opposition had briefly surfaced in 1908, 1914, 1918, and 1921. Each time the protests were met with repression. After the 1921 demonstrations, Gómez proscribed the FEV. Then, in 1927, he lifted the ban, permitting students to organize once again. The scope and duration of the protests throughout 1928, however, were far and away the most significant repudiation of Gómez's rule to date. The students' call for democratic governance, according to Venezuelan anthropologist Fernando Coronil, struck a nerve in civil society and "redefined the terms of public discourse."[5]

As in Argentina and Peru, Venezuelan students were disgusted with their professors' servile posture toward Gomecismo. Many members of the professoriate obtained sinecures from the regime in return for their drafting of six different constitutions during the dictator's twenty-seven years in power. The exiled writer Blanco Fombona was infuriated that intellectuals had sold out: "Who has groveled at the feet of the monster? Who have prostituted themselves in the service and adulation of the assassin, never protesting against imprisonments, banishments, persecutions, torments, poisonings, and larcenies? Against the surrendering of the country and its sources of wealth to foreigners and to the family of Gómez? Who have sullied themselves for a miserable pittance?"[6]

The students were particularly incensed by sweetheart deals the dictator signed with foreign oil companies. Anti-imperialist sentiment also was stoked by Ugarte's visit. One activist recalled protesting with fellow students in front of the U.S. consulate in the capital shouting "Down with the Yankees! Long Live Sandino! Long Live Nicaragua!"[7]

Gómez responded by jailing the ringleaders of the protests, including Betancourt and Villalba. That impelled more than two hundred students to cable the dictator that he should jail them as well, since they bore equal responsibility. He promptly complied. Those arrests, in turn, sparked spontaneous demonstrations in Caracas, La Guaira, and Maracaibo—one estimate put the crowds at 135,000. A general strike ensued in late February, shutting down commerce throughout Caracas and paralyzing transport and communications as tram workers, telephone operators, and chauffeurs walked out of their jobs, demanding that they, too, be imprisoned. Temporarily on his heels, Gómez released the students, who were then given a hero's welcome by Caracas residents.

Then, in early April, cadets at the military academy, with assistance from some university students, briefly seized the unoccupied presidential palace. El Cuartelazo, as the brief takeover came to be called, was quelled by troops loyal to the dictator. The regime again rounded up hundreds of protestors and sentenced them to six months of hard labor. Luckily, Betancourt avoided imprisonment for a second time, fleeing the country. Villalba and others were not so fortunate.[8]

Past uprisings against the dictatorship, Villalba noted, were little more than circumscribed coups led by self-serving caudillos who treated the poor like cannon fodder. But this marked the first time that students, military cadets, and workers had collectively taken to the streets.[9] Moreover, a significant number of women "organized support groups, produced and distributed publicity, and performed clandestine activities."[10]

Another round of demonstrations erupted that fall under different leadership, but with the same results. The FEV again sparked the protests, sending a letter to the dictator demanding the release of those still imprisoned. Thirty-five of the signatories were promptly arrested, and when more students came forward in solidarity asking that they too be jailed, they were apprehended by authorities and made to perform hard labor. In response to this latest round of arrests, a massive demonstration rocked the capital on October 12.[11]

The political divide largely fell along generational lines. In his memoirs, the prominent newspaper publisher Miguel Ángel Capriles recalled arguments with his father, who had lived through decades of political upheaval and civil war. Many of his father's generation viewed Gómez's iron hand as a much-needed antidote for decades of unrest, while impatient youngsters called for an end to caudillo rule.[12]

To be sure, idealism trumped organization, and inexperience overrode a well-defined political agenda. Twenty-year-old student activist Miguel Otero began work on a novel about the student movement. In *La Fiebre* (The Fever), the protagonist, Vidal, has few illusions about the students' inchoate motivations: "Our political ideology—to be an enemy to tyranny—is not exactly a political ideology; it's an expression of our human condition." The novel also sheds light on the students' relationship with workers, who, after some initial concerns about the formers' privileged position, are won over by their commitment to ousting the dictator.[13]

A recent biographer characterized Betancourt and his peers' political coming of age as romanticized Garibaldism, a reference to the Italian general's ill-fated rebellions. The implication was that rather than take the time and spadework required to build sustainable political coalitions, the students opportunistically hitched their political fortunes to a series of stillborn uprisings led by disgruntled caudillos and military officers.[14] While students participated in three unsuccessful caudillo-led revolts between 1928 and 1931, the movement broadened their political calculus. Whereas in the past, armed uprisings led by regional strongmen originated in the provinces and moved to the cities, the protests of 1928 were a nonviolent movement that began in the capital and were decidedly socially heterogeneous.[15]

Betancourt already was thinking of next steps. What preoccupied him was that his countrymen's predilection for strongman rule would outlive Gómez's removal. He had no interest in exchanging authoritarianism for democratic personalism. Discouraged by the wave of coups throughout Latin America in the early 1930s, he told a peer, "We make no commitments with caudillos, whether military men or civilians."[16]

The students, however, were quickly disabused of their idealism when they learned firsthand of the repressive reality of Gomecista jails. "A new dimension of human suffering was revealed in the dungeon," Betancourt recalled. "Those of us who had figured most prominently in the demonstration were thrown into prison, where two pairs of leg irons . . . were placed on our ankles (the classic type . . . weighed sixty pounds . . .). It was in this penitentiary cell that I celebrated my twentieth birthday."[17]

Villalba remained incarcerated in two appalling prisons, La Rotunda in Caracas and El Libertador castle in Puerto Cabello, until 1934. Journalist (and poet) Andrés Eloy Blanco spent six years in the latter. His crime was editing a clandestine newspaper, *El Imparcial,* copies of which were smuggled inside the jail.[18] But the time student leaders spent imprisoned enabled them to forge ties with like-minded inmates, who remained trusted collaborators in the struggles to come.[19] In some cases, the inmates were forced to labor in penal camps situated in "malaria-infested regions." When asked about the deplorable conditions in the camps, Gómez dismissed the criticism: "Since they don't want to study I am teaching them how to work."[20]

Meanwhile, the dictator's backers, including regime apologist Laureano Vallenilla Lanz, whipped up a smear campaign in the government press, calling the student movement a "red terror" that would bring "Soviet horrors" to Venezuela and undermine "the sacred institution of the family."[21] Betancourt and Otero later responded from the safety of exile, hotly contesting the red baiting in a pamphlet, *En las huellas de la pezuña* (In the Wake of the Wounded Animal). It cast the students as patriotic idealists committed to social democracy, intent on rooting out corruption and bad government. The authors decried how Gómez had enlisted state governors and military officers in his monopolistic business schemes and had made a fortune from the acquisition of ranches, livestock, and slaughterhouses. One study found that the dictator owned 1,631 properties in six states totaling almost 40,000 hectares.[22] Corruption was endemic; the regime had doled out lucrative tax-farming concessions to loyal political operatives in the provinces, who then "abused their authority to monopolize the production and sale of liquor in their jurisdictions ... imposed unauthorized fines ... [and] appropriated public lands cultivated by squatters." Most damning, Gómez granted oil concessions to cronies, who turned a tidy profit by selling off the rights to foreign oil companies. The students also criticized the Catholic Church for its support of the regime and bemoaned that the working poor, lacking in education and political awareness, were resigned to their plight and appeared unwilling to mobilize.[23]

In exile Betancourt wrote prolifically about the evils of authoritarianism and the need for a social revolution—and not just in Venezuela. The political situation in his country, he argued, was being replicated all over Latin America, where "local *caciques* [political bosses], in shameless collaboration with foreign invaders, held forth in Lima, in Havana, in Central America, regimes organized along fascist lines." He excoriated dictators like Leguía, Machado, and others, who not only shut down independent presses in their own countries but shamelessly ran stories in their own government-controlled newspapers praising other strongmen. The result was a "vast complicit network" that was determined to undermine democracies.[24]

Eradicating dictatorship in Latin America became for the young Betancourt a moral crusade that consumed much of his adult life. In this struggle, he received assistance from prominent reformers, such as the exiled Peruvians Haya and Sánchez and Eduardo Santos and Germán Arciniegas in Colombia. Those students fortunate enough to flee Venezuela found sanctuary in the region's democracies.[25] Betancourt and his compatriots also attracted ample moral (and, in one case, material) support from Mexico, whose intellectuals thought of themselves as the progressive voices of Latin America. In a three-part series, "El terror en Venezuela," published in *Repertorio Americano* in the fall of 1928, the Mexican diplomat and jurist Isidro Fabela documented Gomecista atrocities in detail.[26] Fabela's muckraking account prompted outrage throughout Europe and Latin America, where solidarity campaigns were organized against Gómez.[27]

Support from *pensadores* abroad, while comforting, did little to insulate the exiles from the fear of retribution. The dictator's long arm of repression was every bit as transnational as his opponents' protests. Gómez's spies, often members of his secret police posing as diplomats, kept tabs on political enemies abroad. His foreign ministry lobbied authoritarian regimes throughout the greater Caribbean, seeking their assistance in harassing exiled dissidents. According to one contemporary account, "every consul and minister was responsible for the activities of the Venezuelan exiles in his area and he maintained his own staff of informers to keep them under surveillance."[28] In fact, Gómez's surveillance methods were so successful that such practices would become *de rigueur* among Caribbean dictators.

A young, idealistic Puerto Rican, Luis Muñoz Marín, who befriended Venezuelan exiles in both San Juan and New York City, documented, in his article published in the *Nation*, "Tyranny and Torture in Venezuela," how the dictator cowed the opposition even from afar: "Gómez rules by terror and corruption, the terror being so effective that the corruption must be accounted a luxury. . . . In his kindly moments Gómez exiles his enemies and retains their families as hostages against the possibility of propaganda in foreign countries." The tactic of holding loved ones against their will was emulated by aspiring strongmen across the region.[29]

Exile became a way of life for young Venezuelan dissidents. A cantankerous diaspora, labeling itself "the orphanhood of exile," extended from nearby Trinidad, Curaçao, and Colombia throughout the Caribbean and to Central America, Mexico, the United States, Spain, and France.[30] During the spring and summer of 1929, for instance, Betancourt made the most of his time in Colombia, Haiti, and the Dominican Republic, raising funds to purchase arms with the intention of joining an expeditionary force led by a disaffected Venezuelan general, Román Delgado Chalbaud.

In the Dominican Republic, Betancourt delivered a number of speeches about the evils of caudillo rule. The twenty-one-year-old was the featured speaker at a conference sponsored by a Dominican student organization. During his four-month stay on the island, he crossed paths with the Peruvian poet and fervent Aprista Magda Portal and befriended the young writer Juan Bosch, who later led the fight against a Dominican version of Gómez, General Rafael Trujillo. Betancourt's lectures attracted the attention of the Venezuelan consul general, who alerted authorities that the upstart and his peers were anything but innocents abroad. In fact, fifty Dominican volunteers signed on to Delgado Chalbaud's uprising. Years later, Betancourt recalled with gratitude how Dominicans generously donated "antiquated rifles and revolvers" to their cause. With local authorities closing in, Betancourt and his confederates set off on a boat that proved not up to the task. When *La Gisela* immediately started taking on water, the rebels crawled back to the shoreline. Undeterred, the youngsters set out again and made their way to Trinidad, only to learn when they arrived that troops loyal to Gómez had already put down Delgado Chalbaud's uprising.[31]

It was during his visit to the Dominican Republic that Betancourt first articulated an idea that became central to his thinking about the threat that dictatorships posed to democratic rule in Latin America. Removing Gómez from power, although necessary, was not an end in itself. It was part and parcel of a larger transnational struggle to eliminate the scourge of strongman rule. To accomplish this, democratic governments needed to band together. In a column published in the Dominican newspaper *La Opinión*, the precocious twenty-one-year-old wondered, "why do upstanding leaders of free peoples exchange messages of courtesy and friendship with the criminal outlaw who arbitrarily holds political power in my country? Why do governments that still believe in international democracy not agree to declare a collective boycott of Juan Vicente

Gómez, until such time as his regime is considered a pariah state?" The seeds of what was later called the Betancourt Doctrine are found in his early columns. Dictatorships, he argued, needed to be first quarantined and then excised. The only way to accomplish that worthy goal was for democratic governments to collectively take it upon themselves to correct the problem.[32]

After all, did not caudillos across the region work closely together to monitor their own dissidents and those of their allies? Exiles were quick to point out that Gómez and Machado, for instance, shared information and that on occasion, rather than returning troublesome exiles to their homeland, they simply did their colleague a favor and eliminated the problem. A perfect example of such an "assisted" execution was the disappearance off the coast of Cuba of Venezuelan communist Francisco Laguado Jaime in March 1929. Laguado Jaime had published an incendiary pamphlet titled *Tiranicidio o revolución: Venezolano, mata a Gómez* (Tyrannicide or Revolution: Venezuelan, Kill Gómez) documenting many of the dictatorship's most heinous crimes. Shortly after Cuban authorities arrested the dissident, put him on a warship filled with political prisoners, and then took him to a military prison from which he never emerged. Laguado Jaime's compatriots in exile in Panama City claimed to have proof that authorities later fed him to the sharks in Havana Bay. Referring to Gómez as Machado's mentor, militants contended that this was far from an isolated case, because "tyrants were assassins without borders."[33]

Flirting with Marxism

In his memoirs, Betancourt acknowledged his early infatuation with Marxism, taking pains to emphasize his growing displeasure with the party's dogmatism and its insistence on "blind obeisance" to the CI. This, however, was a selective reading back and conflation of his intellectual transformation. His actual path is much more instructive for what it tells us about how young activists squared the daunting political realities they faced with the ideological models presented to them.[34]

In exile, Betancourt's journalistic output was, by any measure, prodigious. In a piece published in Barranquilla, Colombia's *La Nación* in May 1930, he burnished his leftist credentials, lamenting that Venezuela was a creature of U.S. interests: "For the new conquerors, captains of *yanqui* industry, all options are on the table and all tactics are honest, as long as it leads toward their ultimate goal—to transform our autonomous economy and our sovereign policy into one determined by the *yanqui* dollar and bayonet. In a nutshell, they want to take us back to colonial rule from which we were freed by the efforts of the liberators. Behind our giddy jingoism, our call for an independent country, lies the rough, rude, bleak truth about our political and economic tutelage. Wall Street produces presidents of the republics and without its say-so the best governments falter and the most public-minded men are excluded from power."[35]

An early convert to the Partido Revolucionario Venezolano (PRV), a forerunner of the Venezuelan Communist Party, Betancourt soon had a falling out with its leadership, then in exile in Mexico. Taking their cue from Moscow, party heads believed that the PRV's focus needed to be on raising consciousness among Venezuela's proletariat. Betancourt de-murred, insisting that the most effective way to depose the dictator was to build a broad, multiclass coalition à la Haya de la Torre. He fired back at dogmatists attending the first Latin American Conference of Commu-nists held in Buenos Aires in 1929, who had tarred intellectuals like Haya as hopelessly misguided demagogues and insisted that only their meth-ods would create the conditions necessary for an authentic workers' rev-olution. Echoing Haya, Betancourt retorted that dogmatists had little understanding of Latin America's reality: "Blinded by their desire for or-thodoxy . . . the 'Reds' of the continent . . . dismissively characterized our struggle as a 'petty bourgeois movement led by intellectuals.' If these colleagues were less willing to meekly and uncritically accept arguments issued in Europe which lack even the most obvious knowledge of socio-political conditions on our continent, they would not dismiss out of hand our struggle to bring about revolutionary change."[36]

His objective was "to overthrow creole dictatorships . . . allied with foreign imperialism." The young Venezuelan not only articulated his cri-tique in print, but had acted on his beliefs, forging ties with other dissi-dents, no matter their social class. Although he never rejoined the PRV or its successor, the Partido Comunista Venezolano (PCV), the budding intellectual found much in Marx's critique of capitalism to consider and debate.

Parsing Betancourt's fidelity to communism during this period is complicated by his frequently contradictory writings. In one column he might appropriate Marxist terminology to bash capitalism, while at other times excoriating the CI for its disinterest in the region in private corre-spondence with fellow exiles. Whether the combative Venezuelan did this intentionally is difficult to gauge. As a noted scholar of the history of communism in Latin America has argued, given the potential for reprisals and repression from within the party *and* from dictatorial regimes, it was not uncommon for militants to employ dissimulation to mask their views.[37]

In 1931, Betancourt and other like-minded expatriates reconnected in Barranquilla. There, in the back of the store owned by the father of his friend Raúl Leoni, the dissidents ate, drank, and dreamed of bringing about meaningful change to their homeland. The biographer Manuel Caballero recreates these youthful activists in their element: "Perhaps in the backroom of the fruit shop, they get together to drink a *tinto*, the Colombians' bitter coffee, to smoke like chimneys, and, late in the afternoons, open up a bottle of Caribbean rum. Of this last, it can be inferred that they are young and Venezuelan, but these boys are austere, virtuous, Jacobins. Their only vice, practiced as if possessed, is politics. Of this, they talk twenty-four hours a day, because even when they dream, that is what they dream about."[38]

Taken with the aspirations of the Mexican Revolution, the exiles decided to copy the practice of Mexican rebels, who first set out their agendas in a plan. The Venezuelans penned their own manifesto, "The Plan de Barranquilla." Of the twelve signatories, five would go on to play significant roles in AD—Betancourt, Leoni, Valmore Rodríguez, Ricardo Montilla, and César Camejo.[39] The plan itself was composed of two parts. The first section, a long historical preamble, traced the roots of Venezuela's backwardness, placing blame for the country's current plight on the dictator and the nation's elites. Marxist categories of analysis and jargon shaped their assessment of Gómez's corrupt ties to rural oligarchs and foreign oil companies. A modernizing state not in the hip pocket of the petroleum industry and its local collaborators, they insisted, could be a true engine of growth for the nation.

Leftist invective gave way to a pragmatic agenda in the plan's second part. It called for Gómez's ouster, the confiscation of his properties, the retraction of special laws that gave the dictator and his cronies privileged status, the convening of a special Tribunal of Public Health to bring to justice civil servants accused of appropriating public funds, a bill of rights, the renegotiation of concessions for foreign oil companies, and the removal of the military from political positions.[40] It also explicitly rejected future caudillo-led rebellions, a promise the activists did not keep when they assumed power for the first time in 1945 as the result of a military coup.

Calling themselves the *Agrupación Revolucionaria de Izquierda* (the Revolutionary Leftist Group, or ARDI), the exiles distinguished themselves from traditional personalistic political parties that fought unsuccessfully to remove Gómez from power.[41] ARDI drew a clear distinction between Gómez and Gomecismo. In a hard-hitting 1932 pamphlet, *Con quien estamos y contra quien estamos* (Whom We Are For and Whom We Are Against), which sparked a lively debate within the exile community, the authors emphasized that the problem was not solely the dictator but "the tyranny of the landholding, industrial, commercial CLASS [caps in original]—in a word, capitalist ... [which benefits] from the collaboration of Gómez and his gang of cronies and relatives." Unless meaningful change came about, the bourgeoisie and their foreign allies would outlive the dictatorship and continue to dominate national politics.[42]

Although the rhetoric was unquestionably Marxist, Betancourt and his peers in ARDI were, at that moment, closer philosophically to APRA than the communists, especially concerning the movement's need for a mass-based, multiclass movement. The popular classes were not cast as passive victims and politically ineffectual; instead, they were to be the backbone of a disciplined, unified organization. Students were no longer viewed as a vanguard but rather as integral cogs in a larger political project intent on bringing about revolutionary change.[43]

ARDI's pronouncements were at odds with the communist agenda of the destruction of the capitalist order, the working class's seizure of power, and the *desiderata* of a dictatorship of the proletariat. Petroleum was not to be nationalized, but certainly the self-serving contracts that Gómez had dispensed to foreign oil companies demanded revision. Since Venezuela was not an industrialized nation, the group contended, its reality was distinct from what Marx and Lenin had envisaged, and so the strategies employed to bring about an end to dictatorship must reflect Venezuelan reality.[44] ARDI's chief failing, however, was its insularity; with few contacts inside of Venezuela and few resources, the young upstarts could only impatiently await the end of the dictatorship.

Additional proof of the youthful Betancourt's eclecticism is found during his Costa Rican exile, where he first became an Aprista while teaching at the Popular University in the capital. He taught courses on political economy at the Aprista Centro de Estudios de Investigación Económica. He later wrote about the impact that Haya's ideas had on him, musing that although there was much that he found philosophically compatible, he ultimately felt that the Peruvian's movement was reform-

ist, not revolutionary; too personalistic; and better suited to a predomi-
nantly Indigenous country like Peru than to Venezuela. Like Mariátegui,
he also was suspicious of the cultlike aura surrounding the movement's
leader. Not until he and his colleagues began political organizing in Venezuela in the late 1930s did Betancourt pivot back to Haya's conception
of the need for a broad-based party that incorporated the middle class,
peasants, and workers, precisely the position that the CI rejected outright between 1928 and 1935.[45]

His brief infatuation with APRA came to an end in 1931, when he
again declared himself a communist, joining the Costa Rican Communist
Party (*Partido Comunista de Costa Rica*, PCCR). Betancourt became a key
ideological architect of that party; the editor of its newspaper, *Trabajo;*
and an instructor of classes for party leaders on such topics as *Das Kapital*
and anti-imperialism.[46]

One of Betancourt's biographers contends that during this formative
period, the young rebel developed an affinity for Leon Trotsky. The Russian revolutionary's ideas, Germán Carrera Damas suggests, were appealing, precisely because they were inherently less dogmatic than the
International's line. This is what initially encouraged him to gravitate towards Aprismo and social democracy, not as an end in itself, but as way of
preparing the masses for communism in the future.[47] At a 1988 sympo-
sium honoring his career, Betancourt confirmed that during his Costa
Rican exile he had "studied Marxism systematically" in the National Library and was an avid reader of Trotsky. While he never became a devo-
tee of the revolutionary, Betancourt admitted in jest that reading Trotsky
certainly delivered him from "Stalinist temptation."[48]

However tempting it may be to see such a well-thought-out evolution in Betancourt's thinking before and during his exile, there is little
evidence (other than an early squabble with the PRV) that he took exception to the CI's line until the late 1930s. For example, he, like Farabundo Martí and other party members, denounced Sandino as a petty
bourgeois traitor after the PCM had irrevocably severed ties with the
rebel in 1930.[49] Writing from exile in Chile in 1933, cultural critic Mariano Picón Salas unsuccessfully tried to persuade his compatriot that
Marxism was not the answer for what ailed Latin America: "In South
America, we can't jump over stages of historical process ... in politics,
one cannot proceed by abstractions or ideologies. ... Our problem, dear
Betancourt, if we want to be men of action, is not to deliver ourselves to
the first romantic impulse before verifying it in reality."[50]

Since Betancourt's exile status in Costa Rica meant that he was legally prohibited from participating in domestic politics, he never was officially named a member of the PCCR's central executive committee. But according to a recent, well-documented study, "he assiduously attended its meetings" and represented the party at a major Latin American student conference held in San José in May 1933.[51] While it was true that during the early 1930s the PCCR was so small that its strategic value to Moscow paled in comparison to other communist parties in the hemisphere, during its early years it did adhere to the CI's sectarian line. Beginning in 1932, however, the PCCR was permitted to participate in municipal and national elections. In fact, Costa Rica was the only country in the isthmus that did not proscribe the Communist Party. Thanks to some modest success at the polls, the PCCR subsequently toned down its rhetoric.[52]

The PCCR's political organizing among banana workers on the Atlantic coast, however, raised significant concerns with authorities. President Ricardo Jiménez Oreamuno signed a decree expelling Betancourt and four other "undesirable foreigners" deemed "a danger to state security." Betancourt denied the charge in a letter to the editor of *La Hora* in September 1934: "I am and I always will be a communist. But I took no active part in the political struggles in Costa Rica."[53] Yet as late as 1934, his actions belied his words, as he helped organize banana workers employed by UFCO on the Atlantic coast.[54]

It was not until late 1935 that Betancourt openly disagreed with the PCCR's decision to join the Comintern, arguing that Latin Americans should find their own path. He subsequently resigned from the party. His Cuban colleague Roa attributed the break to the CI's inflexibility: "Violent was [Betancourt's] rupture and the principal cause of his repudiation was the stereotypical formulas of the . . . International and the autocratic orders of the [Party's] Caribbean Bureau."[55]

Years later, reflecting on this period of political experimentation, Betancourt wrote, "the experience of Costa Rica, much study, and serious thought led me to the conviction that neither the communist thesis nor the Communist Party was appropriate for reaching my revolutionary goals: the achievement of national liberation, of effective political democracy, and of social justice of my Venezuelan homeland." Like many of his generation, he had dabbled in the hothouse of leftist student politics. It was only after he became disillusioned with Stalinism and "resisted the temptation to submit our political independence to Soviet leadership" that he became a fervent anticommunist.[56]

The Mad Dogs

Other Venezuelan student activists—never numerous, yet always intensely dedicated—were consumed with replicating the Russian Revolution in the tropics. At first glance, Gustavo Machado's upper-class upbringing made him an unlikely disciple of Marx, Lenin, and Stalin. His radicalization intensified after he fled Venezuela and went into exile and after he had gravitated toward peers who had found their political calling.

Machado joined the student movement at the age of fourteen, and two years later he was jailed for participating in some of the first protests against the Gómez regime. After serving ten months in prison, he was released and enrolled in law school, where he continued his plotting. When an uprising failed, Machado's affluent family helped Gustavo and his brother flee to New York City, where they joined a vibrant, politically engaged Hispanic diaspora. There they came into contact with the Cuban intellectual Jorge Mañach and the founder of the Puerto Rican independence movement, Pedro Albizu Campos, among others. As his biographers put it, "this brief contact . . . was Gustavo Machado's political birth certificate."[57]

After his stay in New York, he went to Paris in 1920 to pursue a law degree at the Sorbonne. Machado's political education progressed when he heard Trotsky speak at an Anti-Imperialist Congress in Paris. After completing his degree, torn between his growing politicization and his family's aspirations for him, Machado decided to take an unlikely position in Havana, working as an attorney for the North American–owned Cuban American Sugar Corporation.[58]

In Havana, Machado witnessed a student movement in open rebellion against his eponym's dictatorship. No country in Latin America had such a radical and politically engaged student-labor partnership as Cuba, and few experienced such repression. The young attorney saw parallels between Gómez's cozy relationship with foreign oil companies and Gerardo Machado's ties to North American sugar interests. In response, Cuban students had forged ties with tobacco, railway, and dockworker unions. In those activities the Venezuelan militant befriended the student leader Mella. Soon thereafter he quit his job, joined the Cuban Communist Party (PCC) in 1925, and later followed Mella into exile to Mexico City.[59]

In the Mexican capital, the restless Machado helped organize the Sandino solidarity organization MAFUENIC. As historian Barry Carr relates, Mexico's revolutionary state afforded the young Venezuelan radicals in the 1920s "unique opportunities to acquire arms for the fight back home as well as the chance to enlist support from sympathetic Mexican military officers and high political officials who were prepared to support uprisings against dictatorial and reactionary regimes in the Americas."[60] In a speech soon after he was sworn in as president in 1924, Calles explained why the revolution felt compelled to support the exiles. "The time has come for tyrants to disappear from the face of the earth." If anything, his predecessor, Obregón, was even more committed to the cause; he not only supported the Venezuelans materially while president but continued to do so as a private citizen.[61]

Machado and like-minded Venezuelan refugees in Mexico City—a group of angry young men whom Betancourt later nicknamed *los perros rabiosos* (the mad dogs)—cofounded the Partido Revolucionario Venezolana (PRV) in 1926. Cells staffed by expatriates soon opened in New York, Paris, Panama City, and Barranquilla.[62]

From afar, Machado was of two minds about the 1928 Student Week uprising in Caracas and the role that university students ought to play in Venezuelan politics. In an editorial, "Los estudiantes venezolanos y la revolución," written for the PRV newspaper *Libertad*, he applauded the "honest" and "sincere" students for their determination and courage and recognized them as a "revolutionary force capable of putting in motion all the oppressed classes." But the PRV stopped short of viewing middle-class students as capable of bringing about an authentic revolution. Any alliance between the working class and the middle class was, in the party's mind, illusory; when push came to shove, the benefits promised to the workers were invariably denied. Most, but not all, of the students, acting in their own class interest, instead allied with other caudillos and betrayed the workers. Machado's views were shaped by what he had learned in Mexico, where conservative students, who had fought alongside workers and peasants to overthrow the dictator Porfirio Díaz in 1911, had, after the fighting subsided, betrayed the working class when it sought to make the revolutionary state fulfill its promises.[63]

In March 1928, Machado and fellow communist Aponte made the trek to Turcios's bookstore in Tegucigalpa, carrying funds and medical supplies for Sandino's army from the U.S. Section of the All-American Anti-Imperialist League and MAFUENIC.[64] For Machado, Sandino's war was not only a struggle against imperialism, but it recalled Bolívar's pan-Latin American conference in 1826. "The people of America recognize the spirit of the Venezuelan revolutionaries and know that their struggle is not circumscribed by the narrow frontiers of their native land; that spirit is the same one that animated the sacrifice of the liberators ... in the first war for independence."[65]

Machado and Aponte became members of Sandino's general staff. But Machado's ideological rigidity and the military leader's eclectic ideas did not make for a good match. On the one hand, he understood that Sandino's movement represented something more than the "simple Arielism" of decades past. In addition, he was pleased that the struggle against the occupation pushed Sandino to promote a more progressive agenda and to break with traditional Nicaraguan Liberals.[66] But he scoffed at what he called "the political confusion" between the general's brain trust and his peasant fighting force. "They [the intellectuals surrounding Sandino] defend national sovereignty in the name of the [Indo-Hispanic] race and the Hispanic American spirit and totally ignore the country's economic plight and the nature of the forces that oppress them."[67]

Yet if he was ideologically at odds with Sandino's movement, Machado was well aware of the outpouring of support throughout Latin America for the freedom fighter. After four months in the Segovias, he returned to Mexico City, carrying with him a U.S. flag captured from the Marines in a skirmish in May 1928. The Venezuelan Marxist never missed an opportunity to show it off at political rallies in Mexico City, and he even brought it with him when he spoke before Mexico's Chamber of Deputies, where he whipped up opposition to the North American intervention in Nicaragua.[68]

After breaking with Sandino, Machado hustled off to Moscow to plead for a boat to launch an invasion of his homeland. In 1929, he joined a poorly planned assault from Curaçao, just off the coast of Venezuela. He somehow eluded capture and spent the next five years in exile in Bogotá. Machado worked to build the PCV into a national workers' party until well into the 1960s. Meanwhile, his comrade Aponte continued to pursue the life of an itinerant internationalist, eventually moving to Cuba, where he joined the leftist rebel Guiteras in his unsuccessful battle to topple Batista.[69]

An Abbreviated Return

Venezuela's exiles returned home soon after Gómez's death in 1935. His successor, General José Eleazar López Contreras (1936–41), promised sweeping reforms, including the lifting of censorship, tolerance of political and labor organizing, and a reduction in the presidential term from seven to five years. He was tested on his promises early and often. When Caracas police shot and killed several protesters at a demonstration at the Plaza Bolívar protesting press censorship in the capital on February 14, 1936—the eighth anniversary of the student uprising against Gómez—a crowd estimated at forty thousand gathered spontaneously later that day at the Central University to protest the repression. With young female demonstrators leading the way, the crowd marched to the presidential palace, where, in the words of the historian Miguel Tinker Salas, "in a scene unimaginable one year earlier ... López Contreras actually received the protestors."[70] The march then ended at the Panteón Nacional, where the former student leaders Betancourt and Villalba called for the establishment of democratic rule.[71]

To young students like Carlos Andrés Pérez, who later became Betancourt's personal secretary, López Contreras represented nothing more than the continuation of Gomecismo.[72] Proof of this assertion, he pointed out, could be found in the congress and the military, both stocked with the former dictator's supporters. Additional evidence manifested itself in López Contreras's repression of a forty-two-day strike by twenty thousand petroleum workers in 1936. Then, a year later he pushed a measure through the congress that severely restricted the right of assembly. Former and current students called for the law's repeal, the dissolution of Congress, and new elections. They kept the pressure on the regime by calling for a general strike. But even though protests bubbled up in a number of cities, the government held firm, and the strike never gained traction.[73]

The post-Gómez era also witnessed the emergence of an energetic women's movement. Led by middle- and upper-class professional women and feminist, civic, charitable, and cultural organizations—not all in Caracas—the movement advocated for an array of reforms, including suffrage, greater access to education, and health care for mother and child. Similar to pioneering feminist associations elsewhere, many of the groups refrained from challenging existing gender norms. Interestingly, López Contreras had presided over a progressive-for-its-time revision of the existing labor code, which provided for pre- and postmaternity leave, nurseries at places of employment, and equal pay for equal work. But its provisions were not enforced. Implementation of the law thus became a rallying cry for the budding women's movement.[74]

Both Betancourt and Machado had to tread carefully, lest they run afoul of the regime. Anarchist and communist ideas had been proscribed

by the 1928 Constitution, and López Contreras retained the authority
"to expel or imprison anyone suspected of leftist tendencies." Machado
also faced a changing dynamic within his own party. When the PCV was
established in 1931, it was so small that the CI classified it as a "sympathetic" party and deferred granting it full status until 1935. In that same
year, the CI yet again altered its policy, reverting back to a popular front
strategy, wherein national parties were now encouraged to seek common
ground with precisely the classes they had been forbidden to ally with
during the seven preceding years. To broaden its base, for a brief time
the PCV renamed itself the Partido Revolucionario Progresista.[75]

While the communists underwent this transition, Betancourt, Picón
Salas, and their peers founded ORVE (Movimiento de Organización
Venezolano). Its platform resembled ARDI's reformist agenda, calling for
an end to dictatorship, a pluralistic party system, universal suffrage and
direct elections for the president and the legislature, the reworking of
one-sided concessions to foreign oil companies, an end to nepotism and
corruption, and the confiscation of the dictator's properties. The FEV,
led by Villalba, threw its support to the fledgling organization. Years
later, Mercedes Fermín, a feminist activist, recalled that what attracted
her to ORVE was its inclusivity: "I can't say that I preferred one party to
another because I liked the ideology or because I had thought over the
program. . . . On the other hand, ORVE was a movement which wanted
to incorporate all citizens; it was what I would consider a front of classes,
with a broad platform, where there was room for intellectuals, manual
workers, students, employees. There was room for me."[76] Indeed, ORVE
adopted the demands of the women's movement as its own. Its leadership
established a big tent political party, the Partido Democrático Nacional
(PDN), which for a time even included the communists.

In reality, the PDN started out as a collection of disparate groups,
foreshadowing competing leftist and reformist factions inside AD. Betancourt sent young militants all across the country to establish Pedenista
chapters. Among those who got their first taste of political organizing
were Alberto Carnevali, Luis Lander, and Valmore Rodríguez, who all
went on to play key roles in AD during the 1940s and 1950s.

Competition for leadership of the party was keen between Villalba and
Betancourt, with the communists secretly supporting the charismatic Villalba, who they believed was more willing to work with them. Betancourt,
who wanted to create a unified, centralized political party, was understandably upset when he discovered that the communists were backing the FEV

head. He never forgave the PCV for what he felt were backdoor efforts to divide and conquer.[77]

López Contreras's government sought to discredit the PDN, publishing a clumsily edited collection of documents that smeared its leaders as unrepentant Marxists. The *Libro rojo* (Red Book) included correspondence between Betancourt and his cohort during their years abroad.[78] Citing *Libro rojo* as incontrovertible evidence of treasonous actions, López Contreras refused to legalize the new party and in March 1937 ordered the deportation of forty-seven dissidents, including Betancourt and Machado. Just as he did in Costa Rica, Betancourt went into hiding, while Machado and others were deported to Mexico. Over the next three years, Betancourt freelanced to help pay the bills, pounding out six hundred columns on a range of topics that he published anonymously in the Caracas daily *Ahora*. He evaded authorities by moving repeatedly from one safe house to another. His uncanny ability to keep one step ahead of his pursuers earned him the admiration of many.[79]

The communists' decision to first join and then leave the PDN portended what became a convulsive, on-again, off-again relationship with Pedenistas and their party's successor, Acción Democrática.[80] Perhaps with only a modicum of exaggeration, Pérez characterized the infighting between the PCV and AD in union halls and on campuses as "a death struggle," as opinions differed widely on both sides about the relative wisdom of collaboration.[81] As early as June 1938, the PCV would publicly disavow Betancourt in its paper *El Martillo*.

With the regime closing in, Betancourt went into exile again, this time a brief fourteen-month stay in Chile in 1939–40, a time that left a lasting imprint on his intellectual formation. After years of clandestine activity in Costa Rica and Venezuela, he relished having the freedom of movement and expression to present his ideas and forge relationships with like-minded progressives. His time there overlapped with Pedro Aguirre's short-lived Popular Front government, whose agenda, in many respects, was comparable to Roosevelt's New Deal. It was also during this exile when the young Venezuelan forged ties with members of that nation's sizable Socialist Party, including the young doctor Salvador Allende. Owing to the country's commitment to democratic governance, the Chilean Socialist Party was the strongest of its kind in Latin America. At that party's Sixth Congress, Betancourt, representing the PDN, declared that his party was "a true part of the democratic left, socialist, but not communist." He also threw himself into organizing the First

Congress of Latin America's Democratic and Popular Political Parties, which was held in Santiago in 1940.[82]

Before leaving Chile, he persuaded his party to publicly declare its opposition to the 1939 nonaggression pact between Germany and the Soviet Union. By siding with the Allies against the Axis during World War II, the PDN (and its successor, AD) not only presented itself as *the* antifascist party in Venezuela, but it drew a bright line between itself and Machado's PCV, which continued to follow Moscow's line.[83]

On his return to Venezuela in 1941, he made the first of many statements confirming his break with the communists in *Ahora*. "I consider a Venezuelan Communist Party unnecessary. ... I reject the Communist Party, with all of my Venezuelan intransigence, because its dependence on Moscow would convert it into a simple bureaucratic appendage of the Soviet state. And if we reject Nazism, which follows the dictates of Hitler, then we must reject the Communist Party, which follows Stalin's dictates."[84]

Refreshed and recommitted to the task of building a national political party, what Betancourt observed on his return was a capital-intensive petroleum sector, whose rapid growth had the paradoxical effect of increasing the size of the middle class, the number of white collar workers, and the service sector while failing to generate a corresponding increase in the number of blue collar jobs. Moreover, the surge in oil exports brought with it overvalued exchange rates, making it difficult for two traditional mainstays of the national economy—coffee and cacao—to compete. As oil monoculture gained ascendancy, agricultural production declined, and those rural workers who could not find employment in the petroleum sector left the countryside for the cities. While the nation's twenty-six thousand petroleum workers were militant and drawn to the PCV, the oil camps were relatively few in number and isolated from urban centers. Nor was there much of a manufacturing sector in Venezuela until the 1950s. This economic landscape posed significant challenges for AD's leadership as it went about the task of constructing a sustainable national political party.[85]

Thanks to improved roads, Betancourt and his lieutenants took their reformist agenda to the farthest reaches of the country. As Caballero relates, "riding in a little-to-recommend-it 1938 Chevrolet, he set out on this pilgrimage, usually accompanied by some of his most reliable companions. ... Wherever the car could not go, he used other means of transport, or he went on foot."[86] In each pueblo, Betancourt and his peers tried to win over respected, influential individuals—"a doctor, a lawyer, a teacher, a pharmacist"—who could present AD's message on its behalf.[87] The party organized itself both vertically and horizontally; on the one hand, patronage helped tie urban barrios and rural communities to the national party organization, while corporate entities, such as labor unions, peasant federations, and professional and student organizations, became party affiliates. Acción Democrática, Betancourt's proudest achievement, became, in the first half of the 1940s, the country's first modern political party. Leadership may have been a collective enterprise and debates were invariably contentious, but the wily Betancourt was always the "determining influence."[88]

Despite AD's growing presence, Betancourt was well aware that many people perceived him as a lightning rod. Equal parts tenacious and obstinate, he appeared Machiavellian to his critics. His followers, on the other hand, demonstrated a blind faith in his actions that he did not always deserve. As a result of his polarizing reputation, AD decided to run less-confrontational candidates in the 1941 presidential and vice presidential elections—the novelist Gallegos and the poet Eloy Blanco. The congress, which selected the president, chose yet another military general, López Contreras's minister of war, Isaías Medina Angarita. When asked to explain why the party selected Gallegos to run even though the outcome was a foregone conclusion, Betancourt explained the party's rationale: "We accomplished what we wanted to: dispute the idea of *continuismo* and stir public opinion, which until then had been suppressed."[89]

Conclusions

Betancourt and Machado's politicization during the turbulent 1920s and 1930s defined their future as politicians and revolutionaries. Energized by the university reform movement and the injustice they witnessed, they both plotted to overthrow a despot and failed. According to the students' mentor, Gallegos, however, Venezuela's Generation of '28 played an essential role in awakening a new political consciousness. "National transformation could not be realized without a commotion directed against the benumbed political conscience, and it had to be our uncontaminated youth that would form the ranks of the opposition."[90]

Betancourt, Machado, and their peers all experienced prison, repression, and exile. The years abroad, in particular, served as political workshops, a time and space where they could reflect on the changes that their country underwent. The Generation of 1928 may have failed to overthrow

Gómez, but their political education would prepare them for the leadership roles they played in their respective political parties in the coming decades. Their extensive time in exile also exposed them to new ideas and gave them an appreciation for the fact that the problem of fighting dictatorships was something they shared with other Latin Americans.[91]

Both acted on their internationalist convictions, Machado in Mexico, Cuba, and Nicaragua and Betancourt in the Dominican Republic, Haiti, Colombia, Costa Rica, and Chile. Initially, both found Marxism appealing. For Betancourt, leftist radicalization was formative but not defining. Machado, however, remained a true believer as the party underwent periodic shifts in praxis.

The political currents emanating from the Latin American student movements had many "tributaries" over the course of the twentieth century. As one student of these movements noted, it was "the best ideological school for the most progressive elements ... and the richest site for recruitment" for those youngsters on the front line in the ongoing battle against regional oligarchies and dictators. Over the course of the next half-century, leaders of the student movement gravitated to important leadership positions in virtually every major political party throughout Latin America.[92]

The students' greatest success story would be Cuba, where activists allied with urban workers and members of the middle class to overthrow Gerardo Machado in 1933. The Cuban case succeeded because of a unique conjuncture of domestic and external factors that collectively undercut the pillars of the regime. But Machado also had himself to blame. A series of miscalculations galvanized a sustained, multiclass opposition. All of Latin America would take notice of what transpired in Cuba; ousting a dictator who enjoyed Washington's economic and military backing proved instructive for those who came of age during the early 1930s.

CHAPTER FOUR

Polestar

The universities seem useless, but out of there come martyrs
and apostles.

—JOSÉ MARTÍ, 1885

WHAT WAS DISTINCTIVE ABOUT the Cuban student movement was the island's unique neocolonial relationship with the United States. Although
U.S. involvement in the island's economy predated the War of 1898, the
first two decades of the twentieth century witnessed a significant spike in
investment, especially in the expanding sugar industry. During the early
1920s, more than four hundred U.S. banks funneled over one hundred
million dollars into the sugar sector, and North American investors
owned half the mills. Thanks to a 20 percent reduction in U.S. tariffs, the
island's share of the North American sugar market climbed to 65 percent
by 1922. Sugar processed in mills owned by U.S. investors increased
from a 15 percent share in 1906 to 75 percent in 1928. In effect, the island became an appendage of the U.S. economy.[1]

Cubans who owed their livelihood to commerce between the two
countries were exposed to North American values and culture. But the
more Cubans were drawn to the trappings of "the American way of life,"
the more resentment it engendered, especially among nationalistic students. Newspapers, such as *El Heraldo de Cuba* and *El Mundo*, regularly decried the loss of sovereignty, launching an islandwide debate about the

costs and benefits of North American patronage. Even moderate, young intellectuals, like Jorge Mañach, were upset with Cuba's "semi-subjection," which tarnished "the joy and pride of liberation."[2]

More so than anywhere else in Latin America, anticolonialism and anti-imperialism were imbricated in demands to reform the university. The widely shared perception was that the Platt Amendment (1903), which effectively transformed Cuba into a U.S. protectorate, had compromised the nation's sovereignty. Yet Cuban politicians had little choice but to collaborate with their neighbor. As a British diplomat stationed in Havana noted in 1919, "The Government has been made to understand that they retain power only by the consent of Washington, and the Government is accordingly duly obedient."[3] North American officials did not disagree. U.S. governor-general Leonard Wood, who oversaw the military occupation from 1906 to 1909, acknowledged, "There is, of course, little or no independence left in Cuba under the Platt Amendment. It is quite apparent that she is absolutely in our hands."[4]

Cuban students were quick to point out that it was the political class who repeatedly invoked the amendment, calling on Washington to meddle in domestic affairs whenever it suited their political designs. Just as vexing to students, the first presidential administrations of the First Republic gave new meaning to the word *venal*. Alfredo Zayas's term (1921–25) was especially egregious, as the president and his minions reportedly defrauded the treasury of millions of dollars.[5]

Student martyrs, who gave their lives during the first struggle against Spanish colonialism, were invoked each year in solemn commemorations held at the University of Havana. The symbolism cut two ways: students were memorialized for their sacrifice while current politicians were taunted for their subservience to the island's new masters.[6] Literary critic Ana María Dopico aptly captured the frustration that many students felt during the early republic: "As Cuban revolutionary victory turned into American occupation, the anger and frustration of at least three generations were both internalized and institutionalized: internalized as national shame and resentment and institutionalized in the form of cynicism and corruption."[7]

Unlike Argentina and Peru, where students focused on reforming higher education first before turning their attention to national politics, the reverse was true in Cuba. In November 1921, students at the University of Havana Law School signed a petition protesting the university's decision to confer an honorary degree on U.S. envoy Enoch Crowder.

They considered the punctilious Crowder *the* architect of U.S. intervention in Cuban affairs.[8] After serving in the Philippines and then in Cuba as a legal advisor during the 1906–1909 occupation, Crowder was sent back to the island by the Wilson administration in March 1919 to revise the country's electoral code. In an effort to circumvent the blatant machinations, oversight over the electoral process was given to the judiciary.[9] But when claims of electoral fraud surfaced two years later, Crowder advised his superiors that revisions of the code were insufficient and that additional measures were needed. He was then elevated to special representative, a post that gave him "sweeping authority" to reform the bloated bureaucracy, prune budget overruns, and manage debt negotiations between the Cuban government and New York banks. As a Brookings Institution study indicated, Crowder held the "whip hand" in talks with Zayas because the latter "knew that without aid from outside the country would go bankrupt and thereafter Cuban credit would be ruined or seriously impaired."[10] One biting political cartoon depicted the North American proconsul placing his hand over Zayas's hand, just as the latter was about to sign a bill into law. The puzzled president asks himself, "Which name shall I sign? Crowder's or mine?"[11]

Fittingly holding forth from a U.S. battleship in Havana harbor, Crowder issued fifteen ultimatums to Zayas so as to bring about, in his words, "a moral readjustment in the national administrative life of the Cuban government." This would be accomplished, the envoy explained, through "insistent advice, recommendations and finally the virtual demands of the United States through my Special Mission."[12] He then cleaned house by sacking Zayas's ministers and appointing a new "honest cabinet." A caustic Beals wrote that Crowder "had the penchant of a zealous reformer, plus the cold appraisal of a bank emissary—efficient but imaginationless."[13] J. P. Morgan banker Dwight Morrow concurred, although he phrased it somewhat more tactfully: "With some Americans, Cuba is a governmental problem; with others it is a business problem; with Crowder it is a religion."[14] Successive secretaries of state, Charles Evans Hughes and Kellogg, however, thought highly enough of his service that he would stay on, serving as ambassador from 1923 to 1927. The more that Cubans learned of Crowder's outsized influence, however, the more outspoken they became.[15]

Not surprisingly, anti-Americanism ran hot; a double-page headline in a Havana newspaper declared: "Hatred of North Americans Will Be the Religion of Cubans."[16] What especially angered University of Havana students was that the legislature had to authorize the university to award the honorary degree, since its charter prohibited it. Offended students and professors read the congressional mandate as incontrovertible proof of how servile and emasculated officials were, and how they politicized and used *their* university to legitimize the government's relationship with Washington.[17] Seeking to mollify the students, Zayas met with student leaders, but to no avail. Not willing to risk an embarrassing incident, Zayas walked back the decision to confer the degree.[18]

There were several parallels between the Cuban movement and its counterparts. As in Argentina and Peru, Cuban students campaigned to modernize the university. Initial demands of the Federación de Estudiantil Universitaria (FEU) were comparable to those of students elsewhere. Like the Peruvian movement, they were spurred on by a visit from a luminary from Argentina, the rector of the University of Buenos Aires, José Arce, who delivered a riveting lecture on the impact of the Córdoban movement. It is revealing that Arce, who went to Havana to participate in a medical conference, was then named honorary rector by the students, a slap in the government's face after the Crowder fiasco.[19] The same exogenous forces that had spurred reform elsewhere—the Mexican and Russian Revolutions—impelled militancy at the University of Havana as well. And just as other governments initially acceded to demands, Cuban authorities agreed to many of the reforms, but they drew the line at university autonomy.[20]

Enrollment at the University of Havana had increased steadily during the first decades of the twentieth century, from six hundred in 1904 to three thousand in 1921, reaching five thousand a decade later.[21] Of note was the considerable number of female students matriculating in the mid-to-late 1920s. Approximately a fifth of the graduating classes were women, slightly less than the percentage of those attending universities in the United States at the same time. Some female students joined feminist organizations and demanded the vote. They would figure prominently in protests against Zayas's successor, Machado.[22]

Contemporaneously with the university reform, writers and artists began to speak out against corruption. Led by the poet Rubén Martínez Villena, who later became head of the PCC, the protest prompted the formation of an avant-garde literary movement that encouraged artists and intellectuals to incorporate social and political criticism in their oeuvre. The movement's output reflected a host of themes then in vogue, including opposition to North American intervention in Latin America, cultural nationalism, and pan-Latin solidarity.

The island's preeminent literary organization was the Grupo Minorista, which scoured the island's past for clues to its current lamentable predicament, discussed its most pressing social problems, and expressed solidarity with other Latin American countries in their struggle against dictatorships. Among its most prominent members were Martínez Villena, Emilio Roig de Leuchsenring, and the young writer Alejo Carpentier, who later initiated a midcentury boom in Latin American literature. The Minoristas never numbered more than forty, but their impact was galvanizing. When Martínez Villena and twelve others disrupted an official ceremony in 1923 to signal their opposition to widespread corruption, the "Protest of the Thirteen" garnered national attention. The cohort exemplified what the Mexican *pensador* Vasconcelos called "the whole generous heart of Cuba . . . the purest, most patriotic, the hope of Cuba."[23]

Such enthusiasm was tempered by the frustrations that faculty and students felt during the early 1920s. Roa, then a young student, captured the sense of malaise that he and his peers felt, while at the same time lashing out against crooked officials who had helped Cuba forfeit its sovereignty for their private gain: "A frustrated republic, a university in decline, a world shaken by subterranean earthquakes. This was the disturbing and gloomy panorama that our generation confronted. . . . We were not to blame for this hideous debacle. It certainly had not been our generation that had handed over the national wealth to foreigners, that had gutted the content of democratic institutions . . . that had converted the national treasury into a private patrimony, that had mortgaged the republic, that had corrupted the administration . . . that had fomented impunity."[24]

The students' muse for leftists and moderates alike was, of course, Martí, whose martyrdom for the cause of independence inspired an almost cultlike reading of his literary and political works. Another mentor was the students' beloved professor Varona. The republic's first minister of education in 1902, a philosopher and a poet, and a contemporary and colleague of Rodó and the Arielistas, Varona, who fought valiantly during his tenure to modernize higher education, was not above goading his charges. In a piece that appeared in *El País*, Varona lamented that students seemed to have more interest in (the baseball star) Adolfo Luque's curveball and (the boxer) Kid Chocolate's fists.[25] Literary critic Carlos Ripoll believes that Varona enjoyed such cachet because he had been a vital "geologic witness" of the republic's founding transgressions. "If Martí is the prophet, Varona is the high priest who officiates at the temple of this generation [of students]."[26] Even a leftist like Roa admired the professor's single-minded commitment to bringing about an end to dictatorship. At Varona's memorial service in 1933, he delivered the eulogy, noting that the maestro's "pen did not rest. . . . Nobody analyzed the reasons for the general failure of democracy in our America with greater depth and fairness. . . . Nobody criticized [despotism] with his passion and vigor."[27]

Impassioned students pressed their demands in two publications, *Alma Mater* and *Juventud*, and eventually obtained the removal of more than a hundred professors who rarely taught and who had obtained their sinecures as political payoffs. Through their dedication to reforming higher education and their concerted opposition to strongman rule, students took on the mantle of the moral conscience of the country.[28]

The Making of a Professional Revolutionary

Mella, the young, charismatic, and forceful student leader whom Gustavo Machado fell in with, was Cuba's Haya. Of Irish and Dominican descent, Julio Antonio Mella came from the middle class. Rebelliousness, evident at an early age when he was expelled from a Catholic secondary school for criticizing his teachers, was also a part of his inheritance. His grandfather, Ramón Mella Castillo, had been one of the founding fathers of Dominican independence, fighting first against the Haitian occupation of his country and then against Spain.

Mella attended a private secondary school in Havana, Academia Newton, where his teacher, an exiled Mexican poet and a friend of Martí, Salvador Díaz Mirón, imparted stories about "his" revolution and stressed the importance of working for social justice and meaningful political change. The poet, just as Mella would do in the years to come, had fought against and fled from dictatorship in his native country. Díaz Mirón's mentoring led to Mella's four-month trip to Mexico in 1920, where the impressionable seventeen-year-old witnessed firsthand the promise and the devastation wrought by the revolution. By the time he enrolled at the University of Havana's law school, Mella already had a well-deserved reputation as an advocate for reform and a spellbinding orator.[29]

He helped organize a National Student Congress in October 1923, which brought together 138 students from 49 secondary schools and institutions of higher education across the island.[30] Participants set forth a Declaration of Rights and Duties of the Student, which pledged to fight

Julio Antonio Mella. Courtesy Chim Harno / Alamy Photos.

imperialism, work toward "Bolívar's dream of a united Latin American republic," establish diplomatic relations with the USSR, and forge ties with the working class.[31] Speaking before the student body, Mella denounced the Platt Amendment and the Monroe Doctrine and delivered an impassioned call to reform the university: "My words are a torrent of blood and my spirit is gravely wounded at the sight of the University as it is today. . . . I come to demand the reform of the university, proclaiming hereby that I shall not be silent in the face of coercion or of threats, that I shall not waver, and that I shall lay bare all the defects that exist in this University."[32]

The young firebrand could be a polarizing figure, inspiring many but also eliciting criticism. Students from parochial schools were particularly

incensed by the student congress's anticlerical resolutions, and they succeeded in defeating several of Mella's more controversial motions. As a
result, the chastened radical stepped down from the FEU's presidency
and created, with limited success, an alternative student organization
more in keeping with his revolutionary aspirations. This established a re-
curring pattern for the ambitious upstart: enlisting in groups that later
expelled him or resigning from organizations that he founded either because of philosophical differences or disputes over methods and tactics.[33]

Like student activists elsewhere, Mella and his peers sought to root
out the dead wood. Deriding the faculty as a "museum of fossils," Mella
cast the struggle as one between bosses and workers and urged his peers
to demand a system of education that benefited all Cubans, not just the
privileged. One abuse in particular that rankled students was when faculty
sold students poorly reproduced materials for classes that were needed to
pass the examinations and then offered private tutoring sessions for the
exams for a fee. To combat such abuses, students boycotted classes by professors who they believed were unfit. In the face of persistent student protests, administrators asked the government to shut down the university.
The students responded by declaring a free university and naming Mella
its rector. After months of protracted negotiations between the students
and the Zayas administration, a hundred professors were cashiered, and
the president agreed to establish a university assembly, composed of professors, students, and alumni.[34]

Seeking to emulate Haya's Popular University, on November 3, 1923,
students and faculty established a popular university, naming it after Martí
(Universidad Popular José Martí, or UPJM).[35] A founding statement of
principles declared that "a well-educated and informed proletariat will assume leadership of the movement" and that it was incumbent upon students to set aside their petty bourgeois roots and join the ranks of the
working class.[36] At its peak, the UPJM boasted five hundred students,
drawing largely from the capital's urban working class. Evening classes offered by professors and students included primers on the Russian and
Mexican Revolutions, anticolonial struggles in China and Ireland, and
U.S.–Latin American relations. Prominent veterans of the war of independence, who were frustrated by the venality of the political class, were
invited to give lectures. The UPJM also offered a film series, classical
music concerts, experimental theater, and a variety of nontraditional lectures and courses. Mella, for instance, gave a lecture on how the French
Revolution's Declaration of the Rights of Man and of the Citizen was a

"dead letter" in Cuba thanks to the capitalist order, while another lecturer weighed in on the systematic oppression of the Catholic Church.[37]

Despite its evident success, one of the Popular University's limitations was that organizers had no contact with the rural poor in the countryside.[38] Some students balked at the leftist content of the classes and lectures, pointing out that what the workers wanted were fewer remonstrations about the ills of the capitalism and a greater emphasis on math, grammar, literacy, and geography.[39] Still, according to Miller, the Martí Popular University was "probably the most sustained and effective attempt ... made by intellectuals anywhere in Spanish America to make contact with working people."[40]

Present for its inauguration in late 1923 was none other than Haya de la Torre. In an address delivered in the university's main assembly hall, Haya discussed how Peru's popular university educated workers. He then detailed his nation's socioeconomic problems and blasted its reactionary political class and the church hierarchy. According to Haya, four million Peruvians (out of a total population of six million) were illiterate. He movingly captured the shameful plight of his country's Indigenous: "Whoever has visited our solitary Andean landscape has witnessed the multitude of miserable peasants covered in rags, crestfallen with the burden of four centuries of sinister slavery weighing down their shoulders."[41] The popular university's principal task, the Peruvian added, was to remedy this situation. He urged his audience to make it their sacred duty to work for social justice.[42] In a subsequent lecture at the UPJM, Haya attacked dictatorships and North American businessmen and policymakers for supporting tyrants such as Leguía and Gómez.[43]

Mella, who later became the Peruvian's chief ideological rival, described Haya's twelve-day visit to Cuba in rapturous tones, calling him a messiah and comparing him to Martí and the French revolutionary leader Mirabeau. Peru's consul had another opinion, demanding that authorities deport the troublemaker.[44]

Soon after Haya's visit, one of the leaders of the Argentine student movement Del Mazo wrote an open letter to Cuban students, which Mella later published in *Juventud*, pointing to the commonality of interests among Latin American students.[45] Another example of hemispheric cross-fertilization was Ingenieros's brief stopover in Havana harbor just before his death in 1925, where he met with and congratulated student leaders for their work with the Popular University. Since he was too ill to disembark, a group of admiring youngsters—writers, poets, journalists, and students—took a launch out to the *pensador*'s steamer to pay their respects.[46] A familiarity with the struggle of their peers elsewhere could also be gleaned in the pages of *Juventud*, founded and edited by the indefatigable Mella. Comparable to *Ariel* (Honduras), *Repertorio Americano* (Costa Rica), and *Amauta* (Peru), *Juventud* was chock-full of essays by the leading lights of European and American progressivism.[47]

Another factor contributing to Cuban students' militancy was their familiarity with the aspirations of their peers throughout the Caribbean Basin. During the 1920s, Havana had become a safe haven for exiles fleeing dictatorships. Leftist Venezuelan refugees and Cubans sympathetic to their cause started a magazine in 1921, *Venezuela Libre*, which issued broadsides against the Gómez regime and foreign oil companies. The magazine's editorial board, which included Mella and Martínez Villena and the Venezuelans Salvador de la Plaza and Gustavo and Eduardo Machado, called for Latin American unity to resist such plunder. *Venezuela Libre* quickly added correspondents in ten Latin American countries. The exiles also worked alongside their Cuban colleagues at the UPJM and opened an aptly nicknamed office, The Red Cave, in Havana, where meetings were held and propaganda dispensed. In their writings, they urged other Latin American governments to follow Mexico's and Argentina's example and sever diplomatic relations with Venezuela.[48]

The Peruvian Pavletich and several other Apristas, fresh from Mexico City opened a cell in the Cuban capital. Led by another exile, Luis Bustamante, the Havana APRA chapter preached its ideas in two new magazines, *Atuei* and *Indoamérika*. Bustamante reached out to local intellectuals, such as Martínez Villena, Roig de Leuchsenring, and Mañach, who added their names to an Aprista broadside condemning North American intervention in Nicaragua.[49]

Roa, who later served as Fidel Castro's first foreign minister in 1959, recalled how Venezuelan and Peruvian exiles energized his peers. "The arrival of various students deported from Venezuela and Peru by Juan Vicente Gómez and Leguía strengthened the group's activities considerably. . . . The Cuban revolutionary struggle was at once turned into a continental fight."[50]

With encouragement from these exiles, the CI and the PCM, Mella, Martínez Villena, and others established the PCC in August 1925. The student leadership's leftist inclinations, however, were far from dogmatic. As one student of the history of Cuban communism noted, Mella, Martínez Villena, and their cohort were best described as "impatient voluntarists."[51]

Mella's impulse to build as broad a coalition as possible against Machado was in keeping with party praxis. Until 1928, when the CI abruptly changed course, assembling alliances with different classes, even the middle class, was something to be encouraged. A perfect example of Mella's reaching across class and ideological lines was the well-attended protests he organized in Havana harbor and in front of the Italian legation to disrupt the arrival of the frigate *Italia*, sent to the island by Mussolini for a commercial exposition in September 1924. Among the three thousand protestors were rank and file from the anarchist labor union, the Federación Obrera de Havana, and members of Mella's newly created student organization.[52]

His speeches and writings increasingly took on a more incendiary tone. Labeling Cuba a "castrated" republic, he reminded his peers that the movement was about more than university reform. Just as Betancourt had praised the spirit of sacrifice among his fellow Venezuelan students, Mella called on his peers to reject half-measures and mobilize, "no matter what happens, whatever the cost." He denounced Machado, who had succeeded Zayas in the presidency in 1924, as a "tropical Mussolini" and mocked the politician's close working relationship with North American investors.[53] Invoking the storied past, he demanded that Cubans take action: "The cry of six generations of Cubans ... has been *Cuba libre.* What does it mean? A great desire to secure liberty: yesterday from the Spanish regime; today from machadista despotism and American imperialism."[54]

The Butcher of Las Villas

Privately, U.S. diplomats agreed with Mella's characterization of Machado. He was nicknamed the Butcher of Las Villas, and not just because he had been a butcher (and a cattle thief) in his hometown before turning to politics.[55] The dictator's secret police (*la porra*) terrorized any and all opposition. It boasted a dedicated department, La Sección de Expertos, which "specialized" in targeted assassinations, disappearances, and torture. So brazen was the *porra* that it published its own scientific and methodological journal, *Policía Secreta Nacional.*[56] Owing to the considerable number of female students participating in the protests, the *porra* created a separate subsection that included female *porristas* who roughed up women demonstrators. In one notorious case, female *porristas* beat and scratched with metal fingernails two female protestors and then humiliated them by forcing them to strip in public.[57]

Cuban dictator Gerardo Machado, April 15, 1925. Library of Congress, Prints & Photographs Division, National Photo Company Collection, C-F81-35174.

A U.S. envoy concluded that the dictator's "pathological obsession [was] that only repressive measures, culminating in acts of hideous cruelty could stifle the opposition." Stimson would later offer a more tactful, if patronizing, assessment in his diary: this "was not the government that we would care for in America, but ... it seemed to be in full control in Cuba ... it was popular with the army, and that was the main thing in Latin American countries."[58] Beals was less politic. Comparing the regime's methods to a "Balkan dictatorship," he denounced Machado for "happily doing American bidding" while "slaughtering his people."[59]

Mella and his peers reached out to those who shared their frustrations with Machado. When Afro-Cuban students at the University of Havana protested the segregation of public space at Santa Clara's Parque Vidal in 1925, Mella urged Black students to demand equal treatment. "Justice is to be conquered," he declared, "otherwise, slavery is deserved." He also was the first to publish the poetry of the young Afro-Cuban Nicolás Guillén in *Alma Mater.*[60] In addition, Mella supported feminist causes, inviting a young lawyer, Ofelia Domínguez Navarro, to speak to the Cuban Students' Federation about the need to ensure the rights of illegitimate children.[61]

Students also threw their support behind moral renovation campaigns led by several newly created groups, such as the Cuban Committee of National and Civic Renovation and the Veterans' and Patriots' Association. Both organizations called for an end to corruption, and the latter protested a reduction in government pension payments. Representing more than one hundred thousand veterans of the War for Independence, the Veterans' Association broadened its demands to include an end to the notoriously rigged national lottery, equal treatment for women under the law, and a prohibition against the reelection of the president. Authorities declared both groups "seditious and rebellious," which only encouraged some of their members to seek more radical solutions.[62] With assistance from Mella and Martínez Villena, the Veterans' and Patriots' organization hatched plans in September 1923 to acquire arms and airplanes in the United States to overthrow the Zayas government. The plot failed, in part because the Cuban president prevailed upon the Harding administration to prohibit the sale and shipment of arms to the island (unless purchased by the government). Martínez Villena was arrested and imprisoned by federal authorities in South Florida for violating the arms embargo.[63]

To defuse simmering nationalist discontent during his electoral campaign, Machado's Liberal Party platform called for greater autonomy for the Cuban state, a more favorable revision of the 1903 Reciprocal Trade Treaty, and the eventual elimination of the reviled Platt Amendment.[64] Taken in by Machado's promises, the FEU's leadership, minus Mella, publicly came out in support of his election.[65] But Machado's nationalist platform turned out to be just so much political grandstanding; he catered to U.S. business interests first and foremost and never seriously pressed Washington to revoke the Platt Amendment. His 1927 Customs-Tariff Law, while protectionist in certain respects, failed to break sugar's stranglehold over the island's economy.[66]

Nor did he shy away from letting North Americans and Cubans know where he stood. A month before his inauguration, the president of American Sugar Refining, one of the largest investors in the island's sugar industry, held a lunch in Machado's honor at the Astor Hotel in New York. Five days later, Machado assured the president of the National City Bank of New York, which also owned a number of sugar mills, that under his administration "there will be an absolute guarantee for all businesses and there is no reason to fear that disorder will occur because I have sufficient material forces to repress them."[67] Additional evidence of his close ties to foreign capital, his critics pointed out, were the eighty million dollars his administration borrowed from the Chase National Bank for massive public works projects. Most of those funds were funneled to his or his cronies' construction companies.[68] For aggrieved students preoccupied with the close working relationship between foreign investors and local authorities, Machado's rhetoric and policies were cause for alarm.

The president was convinced that he needed to rein in student dissent. A month after he took power, he told his predecessor that he intended to overhaul higher education and "to put an end to [the protests] . . . whatever the cost. If I need to close the university and the institutes I will. I will be uncompromising."[69] Years later, Roa placed the Cuban dictator in dubious company: "If someone personified the patrimonial concept of power in our unfortunate land, it would be Gerardo Machado. His use, abuse and Roman enjoyment of power exceeded Porfirio Díaz, Manuel Estrada Cabrera, Juan Vicente Gómez, and Augusto B. Leguía. Only Rafael Leónidas Trujillo, the leper of America . . . outdid him."[70]

Recognizing that Mella and his cohort were far more radical than their peers, Machado deftly exploited divisions within the student body, banned the publication of *Juventud*, and then had Mella expelled from school, jailed, and held without bail for inciting a riot. Defying a directive from the PCC, Mella went on a well-publicized hunger strike in prison, perhaps emulating Irish prisoners of war who had employed the same tactic in their struggle against British colonial rule.[71]

Although the FEU's leadership distanced itself from Mella, other students and Venezuelan and Peruvian exiles who worked with him in the UPJM quickly formed a Free Mella Committee. Students and workers took to the streets demanding his release from prison. Among them was Domínguez Navarro, who organized demonstrations in Santa Clara. She and other members of the Club Femenino led a march of students and workers to the home of the dictator's parents. After the protestors explained the circumstances surrounding the arrest and Mella's perilous condition, Machado's mother cabled her son, imploring him to release the rabblerouser.[72] The campaign also picked up support from an unlikely quarter when the conservative newspaper *El Día*, whose editor had been an early victim of state repression, championed Mella's release, carrying daily articles of his medical condition along with distressing images documenting his deteriorating health.[73] Student leader Carlos Franqui recalled in his memoirs that Mella's hunger strike "shook the nation."[74]

The eighteen-day hunger strike captured the imagination of much of Latin America and the Hispanic community of New York. LADLA organized demonstrations in front of Cuban consulates in Mexico City and Buenos Aires, and in New York more than two thousand demonstrators turned out to show their solidarity. Mella's plight also elicited support from foreign governments. The Mexican and Argentine Senates and the Buenos Aires municipal government all implored the Cuban government to release him.[75]

Indeed, hunger strikes have the potential to invert "the moral calculus of causation." By stipulating that he would not eat until Machado acceded to his demands, Mella implicitly transferred responsibility for his life or death to the dictator. Bowing to pressure, Machado relented, dropped the charges, and ordered the militant's release in December 1925. One Cuban scholar deemed it "the first great popular victory against Machado's tyranny."[76]

Interestingly, Mella was thrown out of the PCC for two years for, in the inimitable language of the party's internal tribunal, "tactical opportunism," insubordination, and insufficient solidarity with other detainees who were arrested at the same time. He rejoined the party in May 1927 (while in exile) thanks to the intervention of the CI.[77]

After his release from prison, Mella learned that the university's rector was ready to press charges because he had violated the terms of his expulsion from the school by appearing on campus. Sensing that his days in Cuba were numbered, and thanks to an offer of political asylum from Calles, Mella left his homeland. The PCM welcomed him with open arms in February 1926, even as its Cuban counterpart denounced him as a traitor and an opportunist, a self-aggrandizer interested only in "mellismo."[78]

By 1926, Machado felt secure enough to revoke many of the students' hard-won victories, including abolishing the university assembly that his predecessor had established.[79] His handpicked administrators at the university awarded him an honorary degree that May, the first one granted in 198 years of the university's existence.[80] In his acceptance speech, Machado invoked the dictators Mussolini and Spain's Primo de Rivera to make the larger point that adhering to democratic principles was not as important as accomplishments. So what if such rulers were called dictators, he asked rhetorically: "The nation's will provides the head of state with limitless power. The people do not mind if the exercise of this power is called a dictatorship. They only ask that he [the ruler] strive to protect them."[81]

Machado's repressive tactics initially succeeded in demobilizing the student movement. He was assisted by some faculty and administrators who, according to Roig de Leuchsenring, conspired with the regime to undermine the movement: "By banishing student leaders from the university for several years, the professors, working in cahoots with the Government, succeeded in demobilizing the movement. About a hundred young men had to quit their studies or leave the country, because they were either brought up on charges or harassed by authorities."[82]

Bereft of its charismatic leader and internally divided, the movement appeared to have run its course, as it had elsewhere in Latin America. But a confluence of internal and external forces during the late 1920s reignited the movement and enabled its leadership to play a decisive role in ousting the dictator. In this they were aided by Machado, whose refusal to relinquish power sparked widespread protest.[83]

After receiving a green light from Crowder and Coolidge, Machado coerced and bribed members of Congress to amend the constitution and extend his term of office by two years. A year later, he handpicked delegates to a constitutional convention, which adopted a single six-year term for the presidency. Running unopposed, Machado was reelected to a second term in November 1928.[84] After three decades of repeated meddling in the island's internal affairs, Washington's acquiescence to such maneuvers was read by Cuba's political class as "approval and endorsement" of Machado's reelection.[85] Other dictators in the region took notice; Machado's methods to remain in power became accepted practice. Virtually every dictator from the Somozas to Trujillo to Carías amended their respective national constitutions to accomplish the same goal.[86]

Students and faculty saw through the chicanery and denounced the ruler's upcoming reelection as a bald-faced ploy and a perversion of democracy. After meeting in the university's Great Hall, students composed a manifesto objecting to the machinations and walked to Varona's home to obtain their mentor's blessing. The police broke up the march and then forcibly entered his residence. Present was Roa, who dramatically recounted what transpired next:[87] "We barely started to read our petition aloud when the police, led by its chief, suddenly entered, verbally and physically abused Varona, and then lashed out (at us) indiscriminately and destroyed the furniture in the room. A few of us, who were defenseless, stayed with Varona trying to protect him. The chief of police . . . addressed him threateningly. And then this tiny, frail, sick old man, pointed to the door and said, with an anger that awaited no reply, 'get out of here despicable man! You have done to this republic what no Captain General of the colony ever dared to.' "

Outraged by the attack against their aging *maestro*, students stormed the Senate building—only to be beaten back by the police.[88] Machado responded by having sixty student leaders deported, dissolving the FEU, temporarily shutting down the university, and ordering the arrest of leftist journalists.[89] In remarks he made before his reelection, Machado defended his actions. "We have suffered some difficulties in our highest institution of learning; my government found itself caught between the opinion of the faculty and that of a rebellious group of students, between maintaining the university as a center of learning or allowing a few irresponsible youths to take possession of it. . . . I could not hesitate, I was obliged to reestablish the rule of law."[90]

Students then established a new organization, the Directorio Estudiantil Universitario (DEU), in 1927, committed to the removal of the dictator from power. The leadership was chosen by their peers in each of the university's graduate schools. Many in the DEU's Student Directorate would later become prominent political actors during the 1940s and 1950s, including Roa, Chibás, Carlos Prío Socarrás, and Sánchez Arango.[91]

The DEU issued a manifesto denouncing Machado's blatant efforts to remain in power, couching its demand for the strongman's removal as part of a larger critique of Cuba's neocolonial relationship with the United States. The students contended that in return for Washington's acquiescence to his second term, the dictator had become a hapless shill. By making the island "the unconditional advance guard for Dollar Diplomacy and imperialism," the dictator had sullied efforts by the people to pressure Washington to grant Cuba its sovereignty. They also categorically rejected Machado's red-baiting of the opposition: "You [Machado] accuse us of being political, Bolsheviks, impulsive, immature, etc. If to oppose the dictatorship is to be a Bolshevik, then we are Bolsheviks. If by opposing the prolongation of powers we are being impulsive, then we are impulsive. And, if we are being immature by demanding a truly sovereign and free republic, then, we are immature."[92]

Silent Cal and Lucky Lindy

Machado poisoned the well even further by his actions in and around his hosting of the Sixth International Conference of American States during the winter of 1928. Facing criticism at home, he viewed the monthlong meetings as a vehicle to showcase his administration's material accomplishments and to legitimize his rule. He also persuaded the Coolidge administration to announce a lowering of the sugar tariff and to renegotiate the nation's sizable debt to North American lending institutions.[93] In addition, the journalist Ruby Hart Phillips reported that the dictator "ordered a hasty whitewashing of the city." What she neglected to mention was that the president had called out the police to paint over the graffiti scrawled on the city's walls denouncing U.S. intervention in Nicaragua. (Indeed, Sandino's rebellion was very much on the minds of many of the delegates in attendance, a subject that will be addressed in chapter 6).[94]

Except for the conference's opening session, which was held at the 2,500-seat National Theater on the Parque Central, committee and plenary sessions took place under armed guard at the recently shuttered University of Havana. Three new campus buildings were built expressly for the meetings, and the *New York Times* reported that during the last few days before the opening of the meetings "hundreds of workmen" were putting the finishing touches on "decoration work" for the university's Great Hall.[95]

Anxious to inoculate the delegates against popular unrest, Machado declared the proceedings closed to the public. He had three prominent Haitian nationalists intercepted at the port of Santiago to prevent them from staging a protest at the meetings against the North American occupation of their country. The dictator also had students and leftist activists rounded up and detained, and he pressured the Havana press corps to refrain from reporting on topics that might embarrass his patrons in Washington.[96] Cuba would be one of the few nations to obsequiously defend U.S. policy during the proceedings, recompense, Roig de Leuchsenring believed, for Coolidge's acquiescence to Machado's reelection.[97]

Machado had one more reason to dampen demonstrations. During his last visit to Washington in 1927 he had extended an invitation to the

U.S. president to speak at the conference. On the advice of Kellogg, who thought an appearance would allay the criticism of the U.S. occupation of Nicaragua, Coolidge reluctantly agreed. Years later, freed from the tact required of diplomats, Undersecretary of State Sumner Welles wrote that Coolidge "lacked both knowledge of and interest in inter-American affairs. The question, in his [the president's] opinion, was one that involved relations with insignificant peoples whose good will was of no real importance to the United States."[98]

Coolidge did not help matters by arriving on the battleship U.S.S. *Texas*, escorted by a flotilla of destroyers and cruisers. *The Nation's* reporter covering the conference thought it a "suggestive way of opening a Pan-American conference. More than one observer wondered whether the Washington officials deliberately chose the *Texas*, named after the state we stole from Mexico."[99] Machado welcomed his invited guest at the harbor, and amid much pomp and circumstance, including an elaborately-staged, hourlong procession by car through the streets of the city, they arrived at the presidential palace, where a dinner was held in Coolidge's honor.[100]

When Machado took to the podium at the opening session at Havana's National Theater on the morning of January 16, he welcomed the delegates while fawning over his special guest: "gazing over this hall, adding brilliancy to this transcendental occasion, we behold the illustrious person of his excellency, Calvin Coolidge, chief executive of the greatest of all democracies, head of the great people whom Cuba had the honor of seeing at her side in her bloody struggle for independence."[101]

"Silent Cal" turned positively loquacious during his keynote address. It was a classic example of how a foreign dignitary, trying to appear diplomatic, could so unknowingly misrepresent reality and infuriate so many. Although Coolidge never uttered Machado's name, the dictator certainly came in for high praise.[102]

> The very place where we are meeting is a complete demonstration of the progress we are making. Thirty years ago, Cuba ranked as a foreign possession, torn by revolution and devastated by hostile forces. Such government that existed rested on military forces. Today Cuba is her own sovereign. Her people are independent, free, prosperous, peaceful, and enjoying the advantages of self-government. Our fair host has raised herself to a high and honorable position among the nations of the earth ... they [the

Cuban people] have reached a position in the stability of their Government, in the genuine expression of their public opinion at the ballot box, and in the recognized soundness of their public credit that has commanded universal respect and admiration.

The disjuncture between a North American president praising a despot for commanding "universal respect and admiration" abroad while students and workers were brutalized at home could not have been more apparent to dissidents. In the minds of the opposition, Coolidge's description of Cuba as "independent, free, prosperous, peaceful," and self-governing was vacuous at best. Where most Cubans saw a strong-man making a mockery of democratic norms and ramming through constitutional amendments that ensured that he could remain in power for a minimum of ten years—an incumbent about to run unopposed for reelection—here was his patron extolling the "genuine expression of their [public] opinion at the ballot box." *The Nation's* editor, Oswald Garrison Villard, blasted the president's "shameless hypocrisy" and wondered if Coolidge thought he was speaking to the American Legion.[103]

Heading up the U.S. delegation was Hughes, who followed his president's lead, telling a journalist "the American delegation considers it a privilege to be able to participate in the noble vision of President Machado."[104] After the address, members of the presidential party were shepherded to Machado's *finca* Nenita for lunch, a tour of his sugar mill, and dinner.[105]

Coolidge and Crowder also participated in an ostentatious inauguration of a plaza surrounding the U.S.S. *Maine* Memorial in the capital. The opening coincided with the thirtieth anniversary of the ship's explosion in Havana harbor. In his remarks, Machado expressed his gratitude to his patrons in Washington. At a cost of one hundred ten thousand dollars, Machado's administration had contracted with a French architect and landscapist and a North American sculptor to beautify the plaza. The unveiling of busts of William McKinley, Theodore Roosevelt, and Wood at the plaza was viewed in some quarters as "an insult to the memory of nationalist patriots."[106] After the ceremony, Coolidge quickly slipped away and returned home, missing the rest of the proceedings.

The regime did all it could to distract delegates and the press from the conference itself. In addition to excursions to the port of Mariel, the government trumpeted the upcoming visit of probably the most popular figure in the world at that time, Colonel Charles Lindbergh. Then in the midst of a Caribbean goodwill tour arranged by the State Department to deflect disapproval of its Nicaraguan intervention, the flier's arrival in the Cuban capital in the *Spirit of St. Louis* on February 8 electrified the island and completely overshadowed the proceedings.

Nine months after his epic flight across the Atlantic, Lindbergh's brief stopover in Havana toward the end of a nine-thousand-mile trip throughout the region included time enough for the flier to take the Cuban president up for a spin over the capital. Lindbergh, who kept a journal of his trip for the *New York Times,* reported: "I believe the President was well pleased with his ride." In fact, Lindbergh's entire visit was choreographed by the regime to maximize the dictator's exposure to the celebrity. At a lavish banquet in his honor for the diplomatic corps and conference participants at the National Theater, which, according to press reports, even outdid the extravagant feast given for Coolidge, Machado bestowed Lindbergh with the Grand Cross of the Order of Carlos Manuel Céspedes. In addition, five hundred thousand postage stamps commemorating his visit to Cuba were issued and put on sale.[107]

Machado certainly viewed the conference as an unqualified success. But external criticism, largely from political exiles, began to mount. Hundreds of critics who had left the island during the late 1920s for Mexico City, Miami, Washington, New York, and several European capitals ran an aggressive campaign—lobbying the State Department, disseminating propaganda, and raising money and arms to support a burgeoning underground on the island.

Machado Is My Assassin

No one was more hard-hitting in his criticism than the twenty-three-year-old Mella, who arrived in Mexico City and immediately went to work. He founded ANERC and contributed columns for the association's paper, *Cuba Libre.* He also wrote opinion pieces for the PCM's newspaper *El Machete* and LADLA's *El Libertador.* The goal of columns like "El terror de Cuba" and "El grito de los mártires" (The Cry of Martyrs) was to maintain pressure on the dictator while keeping the exile community informed about resistance to the regime on and off the island.[108]

His organizing also had an internationalist dimension. As secretary-general of LADLA, he raised funds for both Sandino's EDSNN and Gustavo Machado's PRV. He somehow found time to lend his energies to a Pro Sacco and Vanzetti United Front group, a cause that had captured the imagination of Mexico's working classes. Throughout the summer of 1927, Mella spearheaded protests on behalf of the anarchists at the U.S. embassy in Mexico City. Agitators like Mella spoke the language of proletarian internationalism, tying the case of the two anarchist workers to broader critiques of capitalism and imperialism. As one student of the global response to the cause célèbre has noted, the CI deftly used Sacco and Vanzetti's trial and execution not only to bash the United States but to undermine the International's anarchist and socialist rivals and to seize control of the global left.[109]

In addition, Mella directed the PCM's department of agitation and propaganda. Here his work paid dividends. Although the party had only six hundred members, *El Machete* boasted a circulation of 11,500 in November 1928.[110] Mella and his confederates employed "radical print culture" to communicate with and keep abreast of like-minded peers throughout the Caribbean, the United States, and Europe. Peripatetic intellectuals like Mella, Carr relates, "practiced a mobile form of contentious politics in which they slid or, more often, were pushed, across national boundaries, driven by economic need, ideological fervor, the desire for revolutionary adventure and, usually, the repressive actions of police and armies."[111]

Mella kept up the attacks in Brussels in 1927, where he presented a searing indictment of Cuban-U.S. economic ties. He reprised that presentation in Moscow at the tenth anniversary celebrations of the Russian Revolution.[112] His oratory and writings energized ANERC chapters in Paris, Madrid, New York, and Bogotá. The Paris chapter was particularly motivated. Spearheaded by 160 Cuban medical students who transferred to the Sorbonne after Machado shut down the university, the exile group staged protests and put up posters denouncing the dictator throughout the French capital. Exiles did face consequences for their actions. Carpentier spent six weeks in a French jail for protesting against Machado, and upon his release he was kept under surveillance by authorities.[113]

Attacking the Cuban educational establishment as a corrupt, bourgeois institution, Mella labeled those who earned a living from it self-interested and "allies of reactionary capitalism." The faculty came in for withering scrutiny. "Those who debase their thinking by becoming slaves to conventional wisdom or to ignominious tyranny should never be called intellectuals."[114]

He never once wavered in his determination to oust the strongman. In a column published in *Cuba Libre*, "Hacia dónde va Cuba" (Where is Cuba Heading), Mella declared that the only way to rid the country of dictatorship was through armed struggle.[115] To that end, ANERC secured arms from its Venezuelan compatriots. Just as the PRV was hatching plans to launch an expedition against Gómez from Mexico, the Cuban exile organization planned a similar operation against Machado.[116]

ANERC's plotting was demeaned in PCM circles as adventurist, however. The party's central committee considered ANERC a side project for Mella. Nor were they pleased that at a moment when the CI was dictating a rigid sectarian line, ANERC was, *pace* Haya de la Torre, pursuing a broad, multiclass coalition, even reaching out to disaffected members of the island's political class. In other words, Mella practiced what he criticized Haya de la Torre for advocating in "¿Qué es el ARPA?"[117]

When the Cuban traveled secretly to New York to raise funds for the expedition, he did so in defiance of the PCM's orders, just as he had defied the PCC during his hunger strike. Internal party documents now carried a dangerous descriptor for him—Trotskyite. To compound the problem, he was actively discouraged from further planning by the CI, which, at a meeting in Havana in 1928, sent orders via a trusted agent to inform Mella "to subordinate (himself) to the cc [Central Committee] of the Mexican Communist Party."[118] Again unwilling to accept discipline, the professional revolutionary voluntarily resigned from the party in December 1928, just one month before his assassination.[119]

Machado kept close tabs on Mella. As early as April 1926 the Cuban government lodged a protest with the Mexican Foreign Ministry, demanding that Mella and other Cuban exiles be returned to the island, and if not, be prohibited "from publicly denigrating" Machado. Cuban diplomats warned that if nothing were done they would take matters into their own hands.[120] At the same time, the cagey Machado sought to persuade Mexican authorities to monitor the professional revolutionary's activities. According to Beals, "Machado invited high Mexican officials, one after another to Cuba, wined, dined, fêted and decorated them, in hopes of eventually getting the government to harass the Cubans who had fled to Mexico."[121] Calles, however, refused to muzzle Mella or his coreligionists. Nor did he make public the dictator's threats against the exiles. According to Mella's biographer, the two governments did agree to a quid pro quo, however. In return for the Mexican government's surveillance of ANERC's activities, the Cuban regime promised to do the same for Mexican Catholic refugees of the Cristero War who had recently settled on the island.[122]

In fact, the Cuban secret police had Mella and other ANERC members under surveillance in Mexico City. When he learned about preparations for the invasion of the island, Machado had his agents spread disinformation and leaked false documents about a communist plot to assassinate Calles, as well as the defense minister and the chief of police.[123]

The last straw for Machado may have been an excoriating column Mella published in *Cuba Libre* in November 1928. In "Ante la farsa electoral" (Confronting the Electoral Farce), Mella mocked the one-candidate slate, reiterated that Machado was a fascist, and described in detail the climate of fear enveloping his staged reelection: "Freedom of expression has been abolished. Various journalists have been assassinated for expressing ideas contrary to the regime. Workers' organizations persecuted and many of their leaders have disappeared. The university and other institutions of learning have been militarized. A large number of Cuban citizens have had to emigrate to save themselves."[124]

Machado made good on his threat. With the apparent complicity of Mexico City's chief of police, whom Machado had entertained in Havana, the dictator hired *pistoleros* to travel to the Mexican capital, where they gunned down Mella on January 10, 1929. His last words were said to be, "Machado is my assassin. I die for the revolution."[125] His lover, the Italian photographer Tina Modotti, who was present at the time he was murdered, was furious that Mexican authorities, seeking to conceal their connivance, subsequently tried to frame her as the architect of a crime of passion. At a protest held a month to the day after Mella's assassination, she laid the blame where it deserved to go: "In Mella they killed not only the enemy of the dictatorship in Cuba, but the enemy of all dictatorships. Everywhere there are people who sell themselves for money, and one of these has tried here to conceal the motive for the assassination of Mella by presenting it as a crime of passion. I affirm that the assassin of Mella is the president of Cuba, Gerardo Machado."[126]

Mella became a martyr to students back home. On the second anniversary of his assassination, students imprisoned by the regime held a daylong homage. The memorial included a moment of silence, a poem read in his honor, and a reflection composed by Sánchez Arango, who had worked alongside Mella in the UPJM.[127] Roa felt the best way to honor Mella's memory would be to "attack the dictatorship's strongholds, gun in hand." The communist writer Pablo de la Torriente Brau, who would write a poignant essay on his one hundred five days in a Machadista prison, likened Mella to "a polestar for Cuban youth ... the quintessential example of a revolutionary."[128]

Heirs of Martí

Varona continued to egg on the students. In an interview in *El País*, he chided them for their apathy and implored them to bring about change.[129] As a result, a reconfigured DEU, calling itself the 1930 Student Directorate so as to differentiate it from its predecessor, organized a demonstration to coincide with the opening of classes on September 30.[130] After authorities learned of the new Directorio's intentions, they occupied the university. When a confrontation ensued, the student president of the law school, Rafael Trejo González, was shot six times and killed and a policeman was seriously injured. Machado ordered that only family members escort Trejo's casket to the cemetery, threatening to use force against protestors who resisted the order. In defiance, six thousand turned out for the student leader's funeral procession. Domínguez Navarro and other feminist leaders led the march, carrying "the casket on their shoulders from the chapel to the gravesite." Historian Luis Aguilar marks that bloody encounter and the protests that followed as "the turning point in the struggle against Machado."[131]

The dictator immediately declared martial law, denounced the university as a bastion of communism and closed it indefinitely. It remained shuttered until 1933. In response, Varona blasted the dictator, declaring, "the shots were aimed not at Trejo, but at our liberty!" The Directorio issued a manifesto, decrying the repression and berating some of their conservative professors as "intellectual props of the dictatorship." The students added that they would not return to the classroom until Machado stepped down from power.[132]

The embattled students received support from an unexpected source. Frank wrote an open letter to the Directorate in late December 1930 encouraging students to stand firm against the dictatorship and to lead by example. Criticizing the nefarious partnership between the Machado regime and U.S. corporate interests, he praised the students for their courage and principled tenacity: "What can a citizen of the United States urge you to do? You are alone in your fight, alone with the student bodies and the intellectuals of other Hispano-American communities who, for the most part, are as dispossessed as you. . . . Even if you are imprisoned, even if you are shot down (as some of you have been) you must have the satisfaction of knowing that you are living the sole way that makes life tolerable. . . . The enemies who have sold themselves for dollars are not happy. . . . And that is why they hate you: because you, in your purity, are the constant revealers to themselves of their own nullity."[133]

Roa, who spent two years in several Machadista prisons, captured how much had changed for his peers. "The student was turned into a combatant. He had exchanged the book and his personal interests for jail, activism, the bomb and the rifle. ... His life acquired a feverish rhythm. ... To become a prisoner was the best thing that could happen to one."[134] A case in point was Domínguez Navarro, who was arrested on several occasions during the early 1930s. That experience radicalized her. In her memoir, she provided harrowing descriptions of the sights, sounds, and smells of Cuban prisons, and of the unspeakable abuse and humiliations young female militants suffered while incarcerated.[135]

Falling world market sugar prices and an ill-conceived valorization scheme that Machado implemented to curtail cane production during the late 1920s had disastrous consequences. Unemployment and underemployment spiked in the countryside, and related sectors of the sugar industry contracted. The onset of the Great Depression would bring with it rock-bottom sugar prices and the U.S. Congress's passage of the highly restrictive Smoot-Hawley Tariff. As a result, the Cuban share of the U.S. sugar market nosedived from 49.4 percent in 1930 to 24.3 percent in three years. During the same period the annual sugar harvest plummeted from five million to less than two million tons, and the total value of the harvest shrank from $200 million before the stock market crash to $42 million in 1932.[136] That precipitous decline cost thousands of jobs as the length of the harvest was reduced to sixty-two days, a little over two months' pay for cane cutters. Those workers fortunate enough to keep their jobs saw their wages fall to ten cents a day, generally half paid in cash, half in credit. The Depression's impact in the United States also contributed to a significant drop-off in tourism (as well as gambling and prostitution), all of which had grown significantly during the 1920s.[137]

The beleaguered dictator relied on the military to keep the peace. As many on the island struggled to make ends meet, the despot bestowed lavish sums on a politicized institution that turned into his chief instrument of repression. Officers replaced civilian provincial governors, mayors, and police chiefs across the island. Most government agencies were placed "under some form of military jurisdiction or review." Moreover, the Military Penal Code was amended to give tribunals the authority to prosecute "cases involving explosives, crimes against the military, destruction of sugar or cane machinery, and disruption of transportation and communication facilities." As a result, the military acted with impunity. A district judge in Santiago de Cuba accused it of committing forty-four murders in his district over a ninety-day span in 1931.[138]

By late 1930, public opinion had moved decidedly against Machado. In response, he feigned conciliation with the students, offering autonomy and the resignation of the rector of the university. Refusing to accept what it interpreted as half-measures, the Directorio demanded Machado's resignation. The dictator then reverted to form, and on January 3, 1931, he imprisoned twenty-two students, including several members of the Student Directorate. Six weeks later the government indicted eighty-five professors on charges of sedition and conspiracy to overthrow the regime.[139]

Beals painted a bleak picture of the shuttered university campus during the early 1930s: "the gardens are overrun with weeds. Armed soldiers guard the various entrances, lifting gun and bayonet against everyone who approaches too close. Since September 1930, the main patio has been converted into an encampment of tents."[140] Ruby Hart Phillips opined that the dictatorship rued the day that it turned against the students and their professors: "Machado's greatest mistake was his attempt to suppress radical student elements by violence and assassinations. Despite the graft and excessive expenditures of his administration, Cubans would have overlooked these, had he not turned to bloodshed."[141]

A consensus emerged that the student leadership was in the vanguard of the opposition. In a lecture delivered at New York City's Town Hall in November 1931, the noted scholar Fernando Ortiz characterized the opposition as primarily urban, "chiefly made up of professors and students from the University." He added that young secondary students and women also played a prominent role in the resistance. "Even the most distinguished women in society have signed a manifesto proclaiming their solidarity with the students' actions. Many of those adding their names are the wives of well-known men from the professional and wealthy classes. All of this is new in Cuba."[142]

Imprisoned student leaders split into radical and moderate factions, a rift that was never fully healed. The former, calling itself the Ala Izquierda Estudiantil (Leftist Student Wing, AIE), was founded in January 1931. It paid homage to Mella and criticized its moderate compatriots as opportunistic petty bourgeois who were solely focused on ousting Machado, rather than coming to terms with the real culprit, imperialism. Aligned philosophically yet independent of the PCC, the AIE denounced moderates for their insistence on forging a multiclass coalition and called on students to build consciousness among the urban and rural proletariats. They also criticized (but never distanced themselves from) the PCC for imposing a simplistic foreign model on a much more complex reality and for its slavish obedience to the CI. Several of their leaders, most notably Roa, would become influential writers and activists during the 1940s and 1950s. Others, like de la Torriente Brau, would join the International Brigades during the Spanish Civil War. Between 1931 and 1933, working in tandem with the PCC, the AIE and leftist labor unions encouraged cane cutters to occupy mills, hold hunger marches, and stage land seizures.[143]

Several unsuccessful uprisings crystallized in 1931. Some were aided and abetted by exiles, who sent arms and funding; others were at the behest of opportunistic elements of the traditional political class, who enlisted students into their ranks only to capitulate when the regime brutally responded.[144] Putting trust in old guard leaders uncommitted to meaningful structural change entailed significant risks for student participants because it often led to betrayals when those leaders compromised and cut deals with the regime. A brash former student, Antonio Guiteras, read this most recent round of defeats as an indication of a generational changing of the guard; at a meeting of opposition leaders in eastern Cuba, he bristled, "you have finished the struggle, while I am just starting."[145]

Divisions within the student movement mirrored rifts in the body politic. Adding to the opposition's disarray, the ABC, a clandestine and ideologically eclectic group of students, former students, faculty, and professionals, came into existence in 1931. Borrowing a page from the tactics of nineteenth-century Italian and Russian secret societies, the five thousand members of ABC formed discrete, pyramidlike cells to facilitate urban terrorism. Members were required to swear an oath to liberate Cuba. Targeted bombings and selective assassinations of the chief of police and the president of the Senate were justified as a necessary evil to prove to Cubans that the dictatorship was not impregnable.[146]

From the outset there were close ties between the leadership of the DEU and the ABC. Phillips, who befriended members of the group, had this to say about their tactics: "The members of the terroristic gang ... were pleasant mannered, well-educated youths, despite the fact that they were certainly actual murderers. ... The actual terrorists or 'action squads' were composed of not more than 150 youths, the majority of them university students who were willing to sacrifice their lives and often did so in fighting Machado."[147]

Political propaganda published clandestinely in the ABC's paper, *Denuncia*, proclaimed, "ni comunistas, ni fascistas: cubanos!"[148] At the same time, the ABC's political platform was reformist, not revolutionary, in part to elicit broad-based support. While it criticized the island's dependence on the Colossus of the North and deplored the unequal distribution of wealth in society, its broadsides made clear that private property was inviolable. Large landholdings, instead, should be broken up and distributed to smallholders. Not surprisingly, the communists denounced the ABC as demagogues.[149]

Emblematic of the brutal methods employed against students to eliminate dissent was the regime's use of the nefarious *ley de fuga*, the practice of ordering suspects to run away before shooting them in the back while they putatively attempted to escape. Hart Phillips's husband, *New York Times* correspondent James Phillips, was an eyewitness to the *porra's* murder in broad daylight of two students thought to be connected to the ABC in mid-April 1933. The night before, police reported that students had set off seventeen bombs throughout the city. Angered by this spate of lawless violence, authorities began a crackdown the next day, raiding possible hideouts and detaining suspects. Two brothers, Solano and Juan Antonio Valdés Daussá, aged fourteen and fifteen, respectively, were picked up at their home and taken to a police station in the capital. Members of the *porra* drove the students to a populated area in the center of the city, pushed them out of the car and ordered them to start running. From his apartment's balcony, Phillips witnessed snipers in plain clothes firing from the rooftops at the students. He put the murders in a broader context, remarking that the streets of Havana were a daily battleground between authorities and students, with casualties aplenty on both sides.[150] This incident, although commonplace during the last years of the Machadato, was unusual if only because it was reported by the *Times*, not in the Cuban press. Years of censorship (and self-censorship) and targeted assassinations of local journalists who had the audacity to write about the regime's daily brutalities had had their desired effect. As Phillips soon learned, however, even foreign journalists were not immune to intimidation. He began to receive death threats from the *porra*. Refusing to back down, he continued to file stories about the regime's atrocities.[151]

Welles's Mediation

In late spring 1933, reenergized exile committees in the United States mounted a concerted propaganda campaign to depose Machado, raising funds, holding meetings, and lobbying Congress and U.S. businesses with investments on the island to withdraw their support for the dictator. Five exile groups formed a revolutionary junta in New York City. Sensing that change was imminent, two thousand exiles returned to Cuba from the United States during May and June alone.[152] The Cuban ambassador in Washington implored the Roosevelt administration to show its support for the regime, "otherwise chaos would result, the sort of chaos that might easily require the United States to intervene in a military way."[153]

Cognizant of the implications of a revolutionary uprising, the State Department sent its chief troubleshooter, (then) Undersecretary of State Welles, to the island to mediate a settlement in May 1933. In his marching orders to Welles, Secretary of State Cordell Hull admitted that students were instigating the rebellion. Even though institutions of higher learning and secondary schools had been closed by the dictator for the last three years, and while a fair number of students had taken flight to Europe and the United States, he noted that "a large percentage of them are actively engaged in subversive activities, notably through such organizations as the ABC." Despite being the target of assassination and imprisonment by authorities, the student activists used methods that raised concerns that violence had poisoned the body politic. "It is apparent that the younger generation from whom the leaders of Cuba of tomorrow must spring, are being brought by experience to the conviction that changes in government in Cuba must be effected not by the orderly processes of constitutional government, but by the resort to measures of violence and revolution."[154]

Initially, the Directorate, professors, the ABC, and members of the old guard political establishment agreed to participate in mediation talks.[155] Welles then enticed Machado to join the talks by proposing revisions to the existing bilateral commercial treaty and adjustments to the sugar quota. He thought the long-term benefits of such a revised treaty would redound to Cuba's benefit by helping the island's economy recover from depressed sugar prices, while at the same time giving "us [the United States] practical control of a market we have been steadily losing for the past ten years not only for our manufactured products but for our agricultural sector."[156]

Welles sounded pleased that the Student Directorate agreed to participate, since their influence "will be very great because the university carries greater weight with public opinion in Cuba than can be realized outside of the Republic."[157] Such a willingness to acquiesce to North American intervention and again work with the political class, however, was simply unacceptable to some students. As student leader Justo Carrillo explained, the prevailing sentiment was that "Machado's got to be toppled! By whatever means! No matter who comes afterward!" Years later he conceded that the Directorate had made a strategic blunder, borne out of political naiveté, to initially agree to participate in the mediation.[158]

But for other students, trust in Washington was in short supply. Student leaders asked that two Latin American governments send diplomats to participate in the negotiations. Although Welles did not reject the request out of hand, he thought it "remote" that other opposition groups would agree because they knew that other governments in the region held little sway over the dictator. Machado, Welles felt certain, would "only be willing to agree to the tender of good offices by the representatives of Latin American governments such as those of Venezuela or the Dominican Republic, which are dictatorial in their nature like his own."[159] Left unsaid was that students would not have countenanced the participation of diplomats from autocratic regimes in the talks.

Just as soon as it voiced its support for mediation, however, the Student Directorate did an about-face. Dismayed that it was at the same table as the dictator's sycophants, it abruptly pulled out of the negotiations, stating that it would not accept mediation by a foreigner. By taking such an uncompromising position, the students broke ranks not only with the traditional political establishment but also with the ABC, a rupture that had significant ramifications.[160]

After only five days of talks, Welles was convinced that it was a question of when, not if, Machado stepped down. He pressured the dictator to gradually restore civil liberties, allow political parties the freedom to operate, promise that he would not stand for reelection, and reestablish the office of the vice presidency, which had been eliminated in the controversial electoral reform that had extended the dictator's term in office. Welles's intention was that whoever was elected to the vice presidency in November 1934 would replace Machado to ensure an orderly transition of power. To his way of thinking, this was simply a question of teaching Cubans best practices. Just as his mentor Crowder had, he pushed for a reform of the electoral code.

Machado continued to insist that he stay in power until the end of his term. But Welles was not someone to be easily put off. Described by one of his deputies as condescending and possessed of an "occasional frosty formality," Welles was known to have dressed down the dictator privately. Frustrated with the despot's public posturing, Welles wrote FDR that he fully intended to shorten Machado's term by one year.[161]

Adding to the unsettled situation was the stunning eleventh-hour decision by the PCC to cut a deal with the dictator. He agreed to restore legal recognition to the party and to its labor confederation if both agreed not to participate in a general strike then paralyzing transportation and commerce across the island. The party's public appeals to end the strike fell on deaf ears, however, and the last-minute agreement with the discredited despot would cost it dearly.[162]

At first glance, collaboration between communist parties and right-wing dictatorships appeared to unite ideologically incompatible elements. Indeed, these alliances were, more often than not, short-lived marriages of convenience. The PCC in Cuba and Communist parties throughout Latin America that engaged in similar tactics often drew harsh criticism from moderate reformers, and there was a price to pay in terms of popular support.

A tumultuous summer, marred by the general strike, the massacre of 20 demonstrators (with 160 wounded) near the presidential palace, an anti-Machado conspiracy within the armed forces, and Welles's backroom politicking, collectively backed the dictator into a corner.[163] Mobs attacked symbols of the regime, tearing down street signs that read President Machado Avenue and replacing them with signs carrying the name of a student who had been a victim of the repression.[164]

Complicating matters was that Welles's arrival in Havana took place at a moment when the Roosevelt administration had announced a new direction in U.S.–Latin American relations. Henceforth, FDR declared that he would pursue a Good Neighbor Policy, which eschewed military intervention while completing his predecessor's troop withdrawals from Nicaragua and Haiti. It was clear that the new president was anxious to rehabilitate Washington's reputation in the region. In reflecting years later on his mission, Welles spoke of reconciling the paternalistic role that the U.S. had played in Cuba since 1898 with this new noninterventionist pledge. "To President Roosevelt two facts were clear. First, that while the existing treaty with Cuba gave this country the right to intervene, any such intervention would be contrary to the general line of inter-American policy which he had set for himself. Second, that a state of affairs where governmental murder and clandestine assassination had become matters of daily occurrence must be ended."[165]

Welles, who championed the new policy within the administration, may have felt constrained in the abstract, but it was not apparent to those on the island. He manipulated interest groups to ensure that a caretaker government friendly to U.S. interests took power. He first offered the presidency to Army Chief of Staff General Alberto Herrera in the hope that the military would impose a political settlement among the warring factions. He informed Herrera that he had permission from Roosevelt to send in the Marines if needed.[166]

Machado tried to play the nationalist card, encouraging Cubans to close ranks and defend their sovereignty against North American intervention. If that occurred, however, the military would be called upon to defend against the invasion, which was not a prospect that Herrera relished. Moreover, he and the other members of the high command had ample reason to fear that the military would be blamed for its past loyalty to the dictatorship. Acceding to Welles's wishes, Herrera consented to push Machado out in return for a promise that the armed forces would be "maintained without any alteration" until May 1935.

Machado finally went into exile on August 12, 1933. His departure triggered a wholesale settling of scores, as members of the despised *porra* and the dictator's business cronies and political associates met their fate in sometimes hideous fashion. One estimate put the number killed at more than a thousand, while several hundred homes of politicians were ransacked and looted. Among those killed: the man reputed to be one of Mella's assassins, José Magriñat.[167]

Along with Welles and the military, students were responsible for Machado's ouster. No other Latin American student movement was as engaged or as involved in the political arena as this generation of students. They paid dearly for their principles, but in the process earned the abiding respect of the Cuban people. As historian Lillian Guerra noted, the martyrdom of so many became deeply imbricated in the national political consciousness. But as the Student Directorate came to realize, theirs was only a partial victory.[168]

Conclusions

In several important respects, the Cuban student movement was distinct from its counterparts. The year 1898 and its aftermath was a bitter pill for nationalistic students to swallow, and from the outset they remained committed to reducing North American influence. Their goals for reforming the university, however, were comparable to those of their peers throughout Latin America. Notable leaders of the Latin American student movement came to Havana to tell their stories, a popular university brought students and workers closer together, and charismatic Cuban faculty and student leaders rallied support for their objectives—goals that expanded over time to include challenging the early republic's corrupt political class and its dictator. Furthermore, political refugees seeking safe haven from repression in their home countries came to Havana and lent energy and experienced hands to the movement.

An increasingly repressive Machado, perceived by militants as little more than a pawn of Washington, proved himself increasingly incapable of containing unrest. By brazenly subverting the democratic process and failing to make good on his campaign promise to annul the Platt Amendment, Machado indirectly united disparate elements of society against his regime, groups that otherwise would have had little to do with each other.

Over the course of a decade, students learned valuable lessons about the benefits of forging multiclass coalitions to bring down a dictator. Even so, in the rough-and-tumble theater that was Cuban politics, such alliances proved fleeting at best. Throughout his first term, Machado adroitly exploited ideological cleavages among students and faculty, employing both the carrot and the stick to sow divisions and co-opt his opponents. As elsewhere, some students became radicalized during the 1920s and invested much of their energies in raising the consciousness of the working class, rather than allying with fellow students and other members of the middle class. Others experimented with leftist politics, but eventually moved to the center and focused on removing Machado and charting a more modest path. Such fissures undermined solidarity and sowed distrust in the ranks of the opposition, which was never more in evidence than when the PCC and its allies in the labor movement struck a deal with Machado in 1933 and pulled out of a general strike.

Like Gómez in Venezuela, a cornered Machado lashed out against opponents abroad. The lengths to which he coaxed, cajoled, and threatened the Mexican government to silence his enemies indicate just how threatened he felt. His targeted assassination of Mella sent an unmistakable message to exiles that no place was safe. Other tyrants throughout the Caribbean adopted Gómez's and Machado's war-without-borders foreign policy. Trujillo later let the practice devolve into a macabre art form. As the practice of selective assassination became more commonplace, dictators tapped strongmen elsewhere for intelligence and for assistance with the surveillance of exiled dissidents. At other times, dictators meddled in the internal affairs of their neighbors, violating their sovereignty and, in the process, inflaming relations between countries that on the face of it should have been allies. In 1930, for instance, Machado earned the enmity of a young Trujillo by sending arms to his political rival, President Horacio Vásquez, who was then seeking to extend his own term in office.[169] Such spats among despots were generally short-lived because there was much more to be gained through cooperation. Indeed, only a year later, the Dominican general agreed to a Machado request to intercept a boat carrying forty Cuban rebels and arms bound for the Cuban coast.[170] Border conflicts, in fact, became de rigueur throughout the greater Caribbean by the mid-twentieth century, practiced by democracies and dictatorships alike. While Latin American governments were quick to decry U.S. intervention in their domestic affairs, they rarely practiced what they preached.

The decadelong struggle to unseat Machado had additional transnational implications. Cuban political refugees in the U.S. linked up with leaders of the U.S. labor movement, journalists, academics, and progressives, and together they lobbied politicians in Washington, urging them to withdraw their support for the dictator. Other exiles, like Mella, who viewed imperialism as the heart of the problem, sought alliances with leftists in Europe and in the Americas.

Although anti-imperialism was a common rallying cry for student activists throughout the hemisphere, nowhere did it have greater resonance than in Cuba. The island's protectorate status stoked a nationalistic backlash that galvanized the opposition, leftists and moderates alike. Well aware of the sensitivities, the State Department employed a variety of methods to cope with unrest—boots on the ground, jawboning diplomats, meddlesome proconsuls like Crowder and Welles, periodic redbaiting, and Coolidge's hands-off decision to let Cubans decide for themselves whether they wanted Machado to stand for a second term.

What transpired in Cuba was not an isolated instance. As Washington withdrew its troops from the Caribbean theater and declared its Good Neighbor Policy, it ensured that well-provisioned and trained militaries could contain unrest while protecting U.S. nationals and their properties. Student militants across the region also took notice of stormy relations between Mexico and the Colossus of the North. Controversies over oil, land, and Mexican support for Central American liberals would bring the neighbors to the brink of war.

CHAPTER FIVE

Mexican Impasse

All of the Central American area including the isthmus of
Panama constitutes a legitimate sphere of influence for the
United States. . . . Our ministers . . . have been advisors whose
advice has been accepted as law. . . . Call it a sphere of influence
or whatever you want to call it, yes, we do control the destinies
of Central America, and we do so for the simple reason that the
national interest absolutely dictates such a course.

—ROBERT OLDS, Assistant Secretary of State, 1926

TRANSNATIONAL TIES BETWEEN LATIN AMERICAN reformers and North
American progressives during the twenties and thirties did bear fruit on
occasion. Small battles were won, even if the "peace progressives" in the
U.S. Congress, as they came to be known, never had the numbers to cut
funding for the military occupations of, first, the Dominican Republic
and later Haiti and Nicaragua. Although their lobbying kept the pressure
on, the Republican administrations of the 1920s dug in their heels. Employing both carrot and stick, the Harding, Coolidge, and Hoover administrations delayed withdrawing the Marines from the region for
years. Probing the strategies employed by activists and their foes within
the foreign policy establishment helps us understand the lessons learned

from these battles and how they shaped future efforts by Latin American reformers to win over policymakers in Washington.

Essential to unraveling the dynamics of U.S. policy and how it responded to Latin American reformers was its often prickly relations with its southern neighbor. Since the Mexican Revolution enjoyed considerable legitimacy among progressives, the nationalistic Calles administration's diplomatic brinksmanship with Washington during the 1920s drew considerable attention. In addition, Mexico's passage of a series of laws intended to set limits on foreign investments heartened economic nationalists. Calles's policies were at first an inspiration and then a cautionary tale for young activists, who contemplated similar measures in their homelands.

When U.S. oil companies and the Coolidge administration responded by fighting Calles's measures tooth and nail, however, a nasty diplomatic standoff brought the two countries to the brink of hostilities in 1927. Only a face-saving compromise brought an end to the impasse. It proved to be an object lesson to reformers in just how difficult it was for a Latin American state to carve out even partial autonomy within a North American sphere of influence.

Just as disconcerting to the State Department as the Mexican president's policies was his unexpected decision, in the summer of 1926, to send arms and monies to Nicaraguan Liberals. This muscular foreign policy inflamed tensions among neighboring countries in the isthmus and prompted a bellicose response from Washington. State Department officials believed, with ample justification, that until relations with Mexico were resolved satisfactorily—and by that they meant that Mexico must back away from its provocative posturing at home and abroad— there would be little peace in the region.

The impasse was averted when the two sides set aside the heated rhetoric, made concessions, and reached a compromise. By the late 1920s, Calles's conciliatory efforts with his neighbor and his repression of the PCM signaled a fundamental change in the revolution's direction. For Latin America's youthful progressives, many of them now in exile, the revolution's reorientation was a teachable moment, one that left them with the realization that no model, whether it be the Soviet Union, Mexico, or Western liberal democracy, meshed with their political sensibilities.

The Limits of Autonomy in the Isthmus

In certain respects, Calles's determination to contest North American influence in Central America represented a continuation of the foreign policies of two of his predecessors: the dictator Porfirio Díaz, who had aided Nicaragua's Liberal president José Santos Zelaya in 1909–1910, and Venustiano Carranza, the nationalistic leader who proved to be a thorn in Washington's side during the violent first decade of the revolution. Not only was Carranza an outspoken critic of Wilson's occupation of Veracruz in 1913, but after he assumed leadership of the revolutionary government he repeatedly voiced opposition to U.S. interventions throughout Central America and the Caribbean.

In September 1918, the nationalistic Carranza issued a statement of internationalist principles that repudiated all forms of foreign intervention. In an ironic twist, the Carranza Doctrine invoked Wilson's universal call for the right of national self-determination. Given the U.S. president's occupations of the Dominican Republic and Haiti, Carranza must have relished tweaking Wilsonian idealism. The Carranza Doctrine represented a thinly disguised call for an anti-imperialist alliance of likeminded liberal regimes to counter U.S. hegemony in the region.[1]

There were glaring contradictions, however, between Carrancista rhetoric and actions. In a shameless violation of his nation's sovereignty, he permitted General "Black Jack" Pershing's ten-thousand-man expeditionary force to enter northern Mexico in 1916. Pershing's army spent the better part of the ensuing year roaming throughout the northern desert in a futile search for Carranza's nemesis, Pancho Villa, who infuriated North Americans by crossing the border and shooting up Columbus, New Mexico, in February 1916.[2]

Carranza also failed to practice what he preached in Central America when in 1917 he intruded in Nicaraguan politics, aiding Liberals in their fight against the Conservatives. He and Central American Liberals were especially upset with the Bryan-Chamorro Treaty, which, they argued, made Nicaragua little more than a North American protectorate on a par with Cuba and Puerto Rico. To promote his diplomatic initiative, Carranza's agents fanned out across the isthmus, delivering incendiary speeches about the perils of U.S. policy.[3]

The Carranza Doctrine's emphasis on nonintervention struck a chord among anti-imperialist critics and raised concerns with Washington policymakers, who, according to diplomatic historian Lorenzo Meyer, saw the doctrine "as a direct threat to their interests in Mexico and as a potentially dangerous precedent."[4] In fact, Sandino invoked the Doctrine some ten years later when, in a letter to Latin American presidents, he warned that *yanqui* designs on the isthmus would isolate Mexico and interfere with its rightful role as "the advance guard of Hispanism in America."[5]

Carranza's successor, Obregón, had to be more circumspect because he had not yet gained U.S. recognition of his government. Washington made recognition contingent on the settlement of claims filed by U.S. companies and individuals who had experienced property losses during the revolution. Knowing that his country needed foreign investment to rebuild after a devastating ten years of civil war, Obregón concluded that interfering in Central American politics paled in comparison to encouraging U.S. companies to invest.[6]

Once the two nations settled the outstanding claims in 1923 by signing the Bucareli Accords, the U.S. finally recognized Obregón's government, and the diplomatic restraints were removed. A year later, his successor, a resolute Calles, followed in Carranza's footsteps, criticizing U.S. intervention and staking out an aggressive, independent foreign policy. Much to Washington's chagrin, Mexico became one of the first nations in Latin America to recognize the Soviet Union in 1924, and Calles became a strong proponent of Central American union, viewing it as a bulwark against North American encroachment. Soon after he was sworn in as president in 1924, Calles began to disperse funds and arms to Nicaraguan Liberals, while the Confederación Regional Obrera Mexicana (CROM) aided Nicaragua's nascent labor movement.[7]

The Mexican government also offered, at no cost, radio stations to all of its neighbors. A North American correspondent for the *New Republic* related that much of the programming filling the airwaves of the Central American countries that availed themselves of the equipment originated in the Mexican capital and carried a decidedly anti-imperialist slant. As a result, "an American in Costa Rica," the reporter noted, "is about as popular as the Pope would be at a Ku Klux Klan Konklave [*sic*]." Calles employed more traditional diplomatic methods as well to advance his agenda, successfully persuading both the Guatemalan and Costa Rican governments to refrain from recognizing the Coolidge administration's preferred option for the Nicaraguan presidency, the Conservative Adolfo Díaz.[8]

Then in April 1925 the usually reticent Coolidge, in a move that surprised his own State Department, told the *Associated Press* that his administration was ready and willing to take on a more expansive role in the backyard. "The person and property of a citizen are part of the general domain of the national even abroad," and it was incumbent upon his administration to "afford protection in the persons and property of their citizens, wherever they may be."[9]

Calles quickly responded to those remarks, and not just rhetorically. More so than his predecessors, he lent substantial support to Nicaragua's Liberals against the U.S.-backed Conservatives, signing a remarkably comprehensive pact with Juan Sacasa in 1926.[10] Mexico agreed to send arms, several hundred thousand dollars, and military advisors to the Nicaraguan Liberal Party. Calles's minister of industry (and the head of CROM), Luis Morones, was put in charge of supplying arms for the rebels, while his minister of war, Joaquín Amaro, coordinated the arms shipments. Over a four-month period beginning in August 1926, the Mexican government dispatched seven commercial ships filled with arms. Calles also provided transport for Nicaraguan exiles then living in Mexico and for a small contingent of Mexican volunteers, largely former military personnel.[11] The Liberal-led Guatemalan government permitted Mexican ships to use its Atlantic port of Puerto Barrios as a conduit, while Costa Rican officials winked and nodded as Mexican arms shipments destined for Nicaragua's Liberals arrived at Costa Rican ports before the cargos were then transported overland across its northern border.[12]

One of Calles's principal reasons for supporting Sacasa was that they saw eye to eye on Bryan-Chamorro, sharing the belief that the treaty was at the root of the region's chronic instability. Article 5 of the Calles-Sacasa pact expressly called on Nicaragua to abrogate the treaty because it constituted a "menace to the sovereignty and national integrity of Nicaragua." Such treaties, Calles and his foreign minister, Aarón Sáenz, believed, were "harmful to Latin American hegemony."[13] The Mexican president also pledged that his nation would promptly recognize Sacasa's government once he obtained a foothold in Nicaragua and agreed to help the Liberals secure recognition from neighboring governments. Finally, Calles backed Sacasa's intention to initiate a "campaign for the unification and independence of Central America," the long sought-after goal of Liberals like Sandino and Turcios.[14]

Although it knew of the Mexican arms shipments, the U.S. initially chose not to make an issue of them. By the fall of 1926, when Mexican armaments turned the tide of battle in Nicaragua and the Conservatives were on the verge of defeat, the administration responded. Coolidge, who sixteen months earlier had pulled the Marines out of Nicaragua after a thirteen-year occupation, did an about-face and ordered the immediate return of three thousand Marines, and dispatched eleven cruisers and destroyers to

Nicaraguan ports.[15] In addition, the State Department attacked Mexico publicly for attempting to engineer "Bolshevist control in Nicaragua and thus drive a wedge between the United States and the Panama Canal."[16]

In this posturing, the Department received support from Hughes. In a speech to a Minneapolis audience, he noted that public opinion "is practically unanimous that in the interest of our national safety we could not yield to any foreign power in the control of the Panama Canal or the approaches to it, or the obtaining of any position which would interfere with our right of protection or would menace the freedom of our communications."[17]

Coolidge's claim that troops were needed to protect U.S. citizens and property in Nicaragua, however, rang hollow to critics, who were quick to point out that private sector investment in the small country was miniscule in comparison to the rest of Latin America. Meanwhile, the international response to the U.S. intervention, galvanized by an increasingly vocal anti-imperialist movement, was unequivocal in its condemnation. Even before Sandino had picked up a rifle, the return of the Marines to Nicaragua sparked "worldwide outrage."[18]

Even though investment was modest, there was considerable pressure on the administration from special interests to construct a second canal through Nicaragua. Senator Walter Edge (Republican–New Jersey), the chair of the Interoceanic Canals Subcommittee, had sponsored a joint resolution for a new survey of a Nicaraguan canal route on behalf of shippers, the construction industry, civil engineers, and retired naval and army officers.[19]

Complicating matters further for Mexican-U.S. relations was the Calles administration's contemporaneous passage of a new petroleum law and an "Alien Land" statute. The new legislation referenced the Calvo Doctrine, which stipulated that foreigners involved in commerce abroad were to follow the laws of those nations and "could not appeal to their government until they had exhausted legal remedies in the host country."[20] The State Department and the oil companies criticized the new legislation because it went against the spirit of the Bucareli accords. As part of those deliberations, the Obregón administration informally had agreed to respect existing oil concessions and refrain from implementing Article 27 of the 1917 Constitution, which had given the Mexican state ownership of subsoil deposits. Mexican nationalists, however, were outraged at Obregón's side agreement, which they viewed as capitulation pure and simple.[21]

Calles's new petroleum decree required that foreign oil companies exchange their deeds of ownership for fifty-year concessions, dating from the company's first operations or "positive act." Encouraged by an abrasive U.S. ambassador, James Sheffield, and by Kellogg, attorneys for the larger U.S. oil companies cried foul, arguing that Article 14 of the Constitution had laid down the principle that legislation could not be retroactive. That principle, they pointed out, had since been upheld in the courts. Confident they were on firm legal ground, the companies refused to relinquish their titles of ownership, as the new law stipulated.[22]

Calles countered that foreign investment was welcome as long as it was beneficial to both parties, and Saénz accused the Coolidge administration of a double standard. After all, the U.S. regulated the property rights of foreigners in its country. To drive home his point, the foreign minister quoted former Supreme Court Justice John Marshall: "the jurisdiction of the nation within its own territory is necessarily exclusive and absolute. It is susceptible of no limitation not imposed by itself. Any restriction upon it, deriving validity from an external source, would imply a diminution of its sovereignty."[23]

Calles was upset that representatives of the combative oil companies had "boasted all over Mexico that they did not need to obey the laws of Mexico."[24] When, as the new law mandated, the holdout companies refused to rework their preexisting contracts, the Calles administration denied them drilling permits and declared their concessions null and void.[25] He also began a concerted public relations campaign in the United States, seeking to justify the new law. In a piece published by *Foreign Affairs* in October 1926 titled "The Politics of Mexico Today," Calles sought to reassure his U.S. audience that his legislation was not an assault on foreign investment; rather, it was an effort to stop privileging powerful special interests like the oil lobby.[26]

Angered by Calles's efforts to circumvent Bucareli, Kellogg made, in his biographer's words, a series of "gratuitously belligerent remarks."[27] First, the secretary of state leaked unsubstantiated rumors of an imminent rebellion against the Mexican president, and then aggravated matters further by declaring that the U.S. would back the Calles regime only so long "as it lived up to its international obligations." Warning that "the government of Mexico is now on trial before the world," Kellogg, who, his staffers admitted, had a "hasty and explosive temper," tactlessly threatened Mexican sovereignty and dared Calles to do something about it. Not surprisingly, the Mexican president responded by playing the nationalist card. The U.S. had crossed a line and was recklessly interfering in his country's affairs. Without offering proof, the Mexican leader declared that Washington was plotting against his government.[28]

Policymakers in Washington were convinced that the Mexican initiative in the region must be countered. A State Department staffer in the Latin American Division, Stokely Morgan, counseled Olds that "there is good reason to believe that the Mexican government now hopes to set up Governments in the five Central American countries which will be not only friendly but subservient to Mexico and completely under Mexican domination."[29] Olds relayed Morgan's concerns to Kellogg, warning that U.S. "prestige" in the region was on the line: "We must decide whether we shall tolerate the interference of any other power (that is, Mexico) in Central American affairs, or insist upon our own dominant position. If this Mexican maneuver succeeds, it will take many years to recover the ground we have lost."[30]

The dispute turned nastier when, in a fit of pique, the impolitic Sheffield insulted the Mexican president by insensitively alluding to him as an "Indian" and then more confusingly as someone who was of an "Oriental-Indian-Latin nature." He then further incurred Calles's wrath by hobnobbing with out-of-favor, disgruntled conservatives, who were still fighting a war that had long since been decided. A Republican fundraiser with no diplomatic experience prior to his appointment, Sheffield did not hide his contempt for the revolutionary government and informed his superiors that he would not be averse to using force to bring obstinate governments to heel.[31] The tactless diplomat went further, claiming that Morones was a communist, despite evidence to the contrary, and that the president himself was a fellow traveler. A "trusted informant" had overheard that Mexican authorities intended to destroy U.S. properties and "implant the doctrines of Lenin." For proof that Calles was a dupe of Moscow, one had to look no further, he told Kellogg, then his arming of Nicaraguan Liberals.[32]

In addition, the U.S. consul general in the Mexican capital, Alexander Weddel, recklessly claimed that a "radical Jewish trinity" residing in the Mexican capital, composed of a young historian, Frank Tannenbaum, the journalist Ernest Gruening, and AFL labor leader Robert Haberman, who all had written favorable accounts of the revolution, were actually propagandists on the Mexican government's payroll. For good measure, Weddel then went after Beals, who he claimed was "in charge of Bolshevist propaganda in Mexico." All such assertions were later proven to be false. While Tannenbaum did enjoy close ties to members of Calles's inner circle, he was not averse to working his contacts to promote dialogue between the two sides. To that end, he arranged a confidential meeting in February 1926 between Sheffield and three cabinet ministers, the ambassador's first such meeting with anyone of rank in the Mexican government.[33]

The *Associated Press* ran with State Department insinuations about the leftist threat in a provocatively titled story, "US Acts to Halt Mexico in Nicaragua Intrigue, Specter of Bolshevist State in Isthmus Seen in Washington," and the *Washington Post* claimed that specially trained Soviet agents were undermining the Nicaraguan regime. The *New York Times* picked up the theme, editorializing that Mexico was seeking "to drive a Bolshevist wedge between the continental United States and the Panama Canal."[34]

Sheffield's smear campaign reminded nationalistic Mexicans of his predecessor Henry Lane Wilson, who in 1913 engineered the ouster of the democratically elected Francisco Madero, a palace coup that set off years of civil war. An indignant Mexican press countered that the stories in the U.S. press were fabrications and that charges of communist influence in Central America were an ill-considered ploy by the State Department to win domestic support for Coolidge's get-tough policy. Response to U.S. saber rattling from leftist critics in Latin America was swift and bracing. As early as July 1925, the Centro Ariel in Montevideo and the Buenos Aires–based ULA had issued a joint protest against the State Department's arrogant comportment toward Mexico.[35]

The mudslinging continued during the last months of 1926 and the first months of the next year. In mid-November, Olds painted for the press an alarmist picture of the proliferation of communist activities in Mexico, which, he contended, were gradually filtering south down through the isthmus. Mexican expansionism, Olds insisted, was now a very real threat to the canal. The timing of his media briefing was not accidental. Eleven days later, the State Department announced its support for Díaz, who dutifully promised to uphold Bryan-Chamorro and to defeat the Mexican-backed Liberals. Kellogg added fuel to the fire in late December by leaking to the press an unsubstantiated claim that the Soviet Union was behind Mexican meddling in Nicaragua.[36]

A defensive U.S. president echoed Olds's and Kellogg's comments in an address to Congress on January 10, 1927. Present unrest in Nicaragua "connived at by Mexico," Coolidge claimed, jeopardized "actual and potential canal rights" while endangering foreign investment. He declared that his administration had conclusive proof that Mexico was shipping "arms and munitions in large quantities ... to the revolutionists in Nicaragua." Under the circumstances, Coolidge told lawmakers he was compelled to act: "I have deemed it my duty to use the powers committed to me to insure the adequate protection of all American interests in Nicaragua, whether they be endangered by internal strife or by outside interference in the affairs of that republic."[37]

Of course, the president may have been alluding to Mexican interference, but as his detractors were quick to point out, Mexico was not the only nation that could be accused of "outside interference." A day after Coolidge's speech, Saénz dismissed Washington's allegation that Mexico had territorial or economic designs in Nicaragua, but never denied that his nation was running guns to the Liberals. In a column published in the Mexico City daily *Excélsior,* he drew attention to the Coolidge administration's double standard: "Can only the United States legitimately lend aid to the government of another nation? Is Mexico forbidden from doing the same thing? Why should Mr. Coolidge be amazed at the attitude adopted by the government of Mexico and not at the attitude his own government has adopted when the two are essentially identical?"[38]

After Coolidge's speech, the State Department kept up the pressure on Calles. In the clearest declaration yet of U.S. prerogatives in the isthmus, Olds issued a statement that invoked the inflammatory rhetoric of the Roosevelt Corollary: "Geographic factors cannot be ignored. ... There is no room for any outside influence other than ours in the region. We could not tolerate such a thing without incurring grave risks. At this moment a deliberate attempt to undermine our position and set aside our special relationship in Central America is being made."[39] Olds finished his broadside by calling Mexican interference "a direct challenge to the United States." Kellogg followed up with an incendiary report of his own, titled "Bolshevik Aims and Policies in Mexico and Central America."[40] When he appeared before a secret session of the Senate Foreign Relations Committee two days later, Kellogg repeated his fears of a communist threat and charged Mexico with playing a provocative role in spreading revolution across the isthmus: "They have set up as one of their fundamental tasks the destruction of what they term American imperialism as a necessary prerequisite to the successful development of the international revolutionary movement in the New World. Thus, Latin America and Mexico are conceived as a base for activity against the US."[41]

Conservative Central American politicians, who conflated agrarian reform with communism, needed little prodding from Washington to express their fears of leftist penetration. The Mexican minister to El Salvador reported to his superiors that "panic is so intense and so firm in this government's belief that all Mexicans are Bolshevists" that an official at the Salvadoran Interior Ministry claimed to have proof that issues of the leftist Mexico City newspaper *El Libertador* were arriving in "diplomatic pouches this legation receives." The minister lamented that "we do not have adequate means at our disposal [to] counteract" the concerted campaign launched by North American diplomats and journalists.[42]

Kellogg intimated, not too subtly, that domestic opposition to the Calles regime would receive a sympathetic ear in Washington. Calles was persuaded that there was more to the administration's campaign than idle rhetoric; in fact, he had reason to believe that the U.S. was laying the groundwork for an invasion of Mexico's Gulf Coast oil fields. Mexican diplomats in the United States also were apprehensive that Calles's domestic opponents would, in the case of an uprising, receive material assistance from the U.S. government and the oil companies. Meyer suggested that there was some truth to these rumors, since General Arnulfo Gómez, who was purportedly plotting against Calles, was a close friend and ally of North American oil interests.[43]

Adding to the intrigue, due to a well-placed spy in the U.S. embassy, the Mexican president had in his possession confidential government documents revealing not only that the War Department had drawn up contingency plans, but that Coolidge was prepared to "suspend its Neutrality Laws, which forbade export of weapons and ammunition to Mexican opposition groups." That was precisely what Coolidge did in March 1927, terminating the recently agreed-to antismuggling convention, making it easier for Calles's opponents to secure arms across the border.[44]

Calles quietly moved five thousand troops from western Mexico to Tampico on the Gulf Coast and gave orders to Lázaro Cárdenas, the commander of military operations in that port, that in the event of a U.S. invasion he was to burn all the oil fields owned by North American companies—"making a light which they will be able to see in New Orleans." He also informed U.S. diplomats that unless Washington stood down, he would embarrass it before the court of international opinion by sharing the documents with the press.[45]

Facing a glut in production and low prices, the oil companies had little incentive to capitulate and decided to play for time. The general manager of the British-owned El Aguila Oil Company told the British ambassador in 1927 that "the oil companies have nothing to gain by an early settlement. There was at present an extremely bad market for oil owing to over-production. The companies accordingly stood to gain more by menacing the Mexican government with closing down, than by making concessions at the moment with a view to the immediate un-shackled resumption of productivity."[46] Standard Oil took precisely that stance, threatening to abandon its holdings.

As it turned out, Calles had unexpected allies. A diverse domestic opposition to intervention in the circum-Caribbean was cresting in the United States by the late 1920s. An eclectic coalition of lawmakers, pastors, labor leaders, journalists, and academics demanded that Coolidge bring the troops home from Nicaragua and reach a diplomatic solution to the Mexican crisis. Coupled with a steady barrage of criticism from the Mexican government and anti-imperialist critics throughout the region and in Europe, the Coolidge administration found itself increasingly on the defensive.

Opposition to Intervention

Senators William Borah (Republican-Idaho) and Burton Wheeler (Democrat-Montana) found the Coolidge administration's handling of Mexico and Nicaragua morally repugnant and counterproductive and pressured the administration to reconsider. Leery of foreign entanglements in the aftermath of World War I and insistent on transparency in policymaking, these combative, independent-minded Western progressives forged alliances with Senate colleagues on both sides of the aisle, such as George Norris (Democrat-Nebraska), Robert La Follette, Jr. (Republican-Wisconsin), Henrik Shipstead (Farmer-Laborer-Minnesota), John Blaine (Republican-Wisconsin), and Joseph Robinson (Democrat-Arkansas), who all shared a distrust for "big business, armament manufacturers and other special interests."[47]

As historian Emily Rosenberg noted, anti-imperialist congressmen during the 1920s were not at all isolationist; in fact, they cared deeply about America's place in the world. Even though they did not always speak with one voice, they were strongly opposed to Dollar Diplomacy and Washington's predisposition to intervene in the internal affairs of other countries when asked to do so by corporate interests.[48] These feisty peace progressives held no brief for U.S. empire-building in the

Caribbean and recoiled at what they perceived as a much too cozy relationship between U.S. companies with investments in the region and the Harding and Coolidge administrations.

They also were put off by Kellogg's red-baiting. Wheeler, whom *Life* called "one of the wiliest and toughest operators in American politics," called for the secretary of state's resignation, deriding Kellogg's "fevered imagination" of "seeing a red behind every bush."[49] Representative George Huddleston (Democrat-Alabama) emphatically stated his opposition to sending Americans to fight in Mexico, just "so that oil companies could reap dividends."[50]

Moreover, the peace progressives and their anti-imperialist allies at home and abroad surmised that the administration's decision to return the Marines to Nicaragua in late 1926 had everything to do with sending Mexico an unequivocal message that Washington would not tolerate its neighbor extending its influence down the isthmus, and little if anything to do with national security or protecting corporate investments in Nicaragua, which, they were quick to point out, were meager at best. Was it a surprise that so many Latin Americans were contemptuous of Washington, they wondered aloud?

Congressional outspokenness about the Mexican imbroglio did not come out of the blue. Borah, in fact, had been a critic of the occupation of Veracruz and Wilson's interventions in the Dominican Republic and Haiti. The Monroe Doctrine, which was designed to deter European aggression in the Americas, was now, according to Borah, invoked seemingly at will "to dominate the Western States or dictate their course." We had no right "to invade territory, to tear down governments and to set up other governments."[51] The Nicaraguan intervention, he argued, violated the principle of self-government while protecting our investors, men who "hoped to exploit another nation's peoples." Washington should only do what was absolutely necessary to protect our citizens and their property abroad. Borah, who for nine years occupied the influential post of Chair of the Senate Foreign Relations Committee, was especially concerned that the Nicaraguan occupation could trigger a far more hazardous conflict with Mexico. He warned of the folly of a second Veracruz, telling reporters, "the truth is, that an effort is being made to get this country in a shameless, cowardly, little war with Mexico."[52] He mused aloud, how was it that British oil companies had little problem reaching an accommodation with the Mexican government, while their North American counterparts repeatedly requested that the administration intercede on their behalf? He elaborated in a piece that was later picked up by the Buenos Aires daily *La Prensa:* "The United States public ought to understand that all of these claims about 'communism' and the destruction of property are deliberate efforts to justify a war against Mexico. . . . It [the administration] speaks of 'communism' and 'bolshevikism' [*sic*] but what it means is simply war. I believe the owners of the oil refineries have every right to have their investments and properties guaranteed by every reasonable means, but I also believe that the most irrational, brutal and fruitless means would be a war against Mexico."[53]

To be clear, Borah and other peace progressives never questioned the administration's ends. To their way of thinking, Mexico and Central America were firmly within the U.S. orbit. Furthermore, they acknowledged that under international law, Washington had an obligation to protect the property of U.S. citizens and companies abroad. But they strenuously objected to Kellogg's and Coolidge's methods.[54]

Labeled Saint Borah and The Great Opposer by his critics, the eloquent, if self-aggrandizing, Idahoan surprised some observers when he announced that he was ready and willing to undertake a fact-finding mission to Mexico to get to the bottom of the dispute. Borah also seconded Calles's call to submit the matter to arbitration at the Hague. Perhaps the most nuanced contemporary analysis of Borah's persona was offered by a caustic Lippmann, who thought the senator, at heart, a contrarian: "the career of Borah is built upon opposition, the League [of Nations], the Court, the Caribbean policy, against Coolidge Republicanism . . . his passion is to expose, to ventilate, to protest, to prevent and destroy."[55]

Thanks to the unexpected support of corporate lenders, who were increasingly troubled about the potential fallout from the war of words between Washington and Mexico City, Borah secured the passage of a resolution, by a vote of 79–0, to submit the dispute to arbitration—an ominous setback for Kellogg and Coolidge.[56] Several like-minded colleagues in the Senate kept up the pressure, passing a number of resolutions during the month of February 1927, each meant to embarrass both the administration and the oil companies.[57] When Kellogg only partially satisfied a congressional resolution's request for data on which U.S. oil companies complied with the new petroleum law, the Mexican Foreign Ministry was only too happy to provide a complete list to the Senate Foreign Relations Committee.[58]

Also nicknamed the Watchdog on the Potomac, Borah kept up the pressure by holding daily news conferences about Mexico and Nicaragua throughout the first few months of 1927, and continued to do so even after Congress adjourned. As Coolidge quipped, "Senator Borah is always in session."[59] Kellogg opted for a more solicitous approach; by plying the bombastic senator with "numerous communications, phone calls and invitations to department functions," he hoped Borah would be less likely to embarrass the Department. The strategy rarely succeeded.[60]

The senator and his colleagues on the Hill were not alone in their fight. A slew of activist organizations were relentless in their efforts to pressure the administration to reverse course. Since the standoff with Mexico occurred at the same time that Marines were on their way back to Nicaragua, opponents not infrequently conflated the two issues.

Several factors contributed to the peace progressives' critique of the administration's foreign policy. Progressive religious groups were especially vocal. Typical was the Committee on Cultural Relations with Latin America (CCRLA), composed of members drawn from a number of Protestant missionary organizations. Hubert Herring, executive secretary of the Social Relations Department of the Congregational Church (and later a prominent historian of Latin America), headed the CCRLA. During the height of tensions with Mexico in late 1926 and early 1927, his committee led a high-profile, thirty-member fact-finding mission across the border in the hope that this group could "exert wide influence on American public opinion." That trip to Mexico City turned into an annual affair, the largest of which brought two hundred influential Americans to Mexico. The CCRLA seminars incorporated both lectures and field trips, including presentations by Tannenbaum, Gruening, and Beals, no less. When those returning from Mexico voiced their objections to U.S. policy, however, Kellogg dismissed them as "cranks . . . [who are] never in favor of their own country."[61]

Herring's predecessor as executive secretary, Inman, was an especially outspoken opponent of the administration. A lay minister and teacher with the Disciples of Christ, he had worked as a missionary in rural Mexico between 1905 and 1915, and he wrote columns denouncing the pernicious impact of U.S. companies in the country. Inman contended that missionaries, not marines, were the proper agents of change in Latin America.[62] Even before the Mexican crisis came to a head, his 1924 *Atlantic Monthly* article "Imperialistic America" mocked the intimate ties between Wall Street and Washington and took jibes at proponents of American exceptionalism. The U.S was just as imperialistic as its counterparts in the Old World, he argued. "Central and South America are a game preserve from which poachers are excluded but where the proprietor (the North American businessman) may hunt as he pleases." A corporate tycoon like Rockefeller not only kept poachers out but opposed "game laws that would interfere with his own hunt." He also criticized the fruit companies for encouraging revolutions. Moreover, Inman was furious that the administration was inviting Latin American governments to send their military officers to West Point for additional training. U.S. foreign policy, he concluded, was morally bankrupt.[63]

The piece was quoted liberally in the European and Latin American press and sparked a lively debate about U.S. policy at home. Both houses of Congress discussed the article's claims, and it even led to the creation of a special subcommittee of the Senate Foreign Relations Committee charged with examining the government's role in monitoring relations between U.S. companies and foreign governments.[64]

Inman's broadside elicited a forceful response from the State Department, which thought the religious leader "a parlor Bolshevist type" at best and a "demagogue" and a "subversive" at worst.[65] In "Is America Imperialistic?" Welles, who had just negotiated an end to the Dominican occupation in 1924, insisted that trade between the United States and the region was mutually beneficial and that the United States "meant to substitute civilization for the cycles of self-serving revolutions and the anarchy that long prevailed." He did allow that in the past, companies had exploited countries in the "most shameless manner," plied officials with bribes and kickbacks, and even on occasion provided arms and funding to encourage uprisings. But other, more respectful companies had gone out of their way to foster harmonious relationships. Writing before Coolidge decided to send the Marines back to Nicaragua, Welles claimed that the U.S. was becoming less imperialistic and that Dollar Diplomacy was a remnant of the past. The United Fruit Company also took offense at Inman's broadside; its attorneys threatened to sue the magazine if a retraction was not made. Two months later, the *Atlantic Monthly*'s editors issued an apology. As Rosenberg has perceptively noted, the debate between Inman and Welles cast the two in "a morality play over the fate of the nation."[66]

Other articulate advocates emerged during the 1920s, such as the socialist and pacifist Norman Thomas and the founder of the American Civil Liberties Union, Roger Baldwin. The former, a Presbyterian minister and later the head of the League for Industrial Democracy, became a tireless critic of North American adventurism abroad. In addition, the

National Council for the Prevention of War (NCPW) called on the administration to stand down and submit the dispute to arbitration. The pacifist organization sent telegrams to "hundreds of prominent people," asking them to lobby the administration, and it circulated a statement to political scientists and experts in international law. After more than one hundred academics signed on, the NCPW forwarded the petition to Coolidge. The Federal Council of Churches joined the campaign and urged its clergy to do the same.[67] William Green, the president of the AFL-CIO, added the voice of organized labor to the anti-imperialist movement, insisting that U.S. workers were displeased with the administration's warmongering and its support for regional dictatorships. He also refuted the charge that Morones's and his union had "Bolshevik tendencies." Green and other U.S. union leaders made it possible for representatives of the Mexican labor movement to appear before the press and the public.[68]

The mainstream media were of two minds about the administration's handling of the Mexican and Nicaraguan conflicts. While Lippmann, Mencken, Lincoln Steffens, and Heywood Broun were critical of Kellogg and Coolidge, the *Wall Street Journal* thought Calles "a thief and an assassin" and echoed the administration line that Mexican policy in the isthmus would result in the entire region falling into the hands of the Bolsheviks. A *Washington Post* editorial concurred: "with communist control in Nicaragua, the United States would have an enemy at the very doors of the Panama Canal."[69] It claimed that Calles's anticlerical laws had led "the outside world to suspect that communists have a firm hold on the Mexican government and have led it into the folly of imitating the Russian Soviets in attempting to destroy religion."[70]

The Hearst newspapers and the Catholic press also rallied around the White House, as did the Knights of Columbus, which announced it was spending a million dollars to inform the American public about Calles's anticlerical policies.[71] A Hearst paper, the *New York American*, scurrilously claimed that Herring, Gruening, the *Nation*'s editor, Villard, Borah, and three other congressional critics of the administration's policy were on the Mexican government's payroll.[72] The Senate subsequently investigated that allegation and discovered that Hearst paid a well-known Mexican document forger twenty thousand dollars for papers without verifying their authenticity. One of the senators, Norris, alleged to have taken monies, denounced the Hearst chain as "the sewage system of American journalism."[73]

On the other hand, the *New York World* called for the removal of Sheffield and belittled Kellogg, calling him a "poorly informed and incompetent old-timer." The paper criticized the State Department more generally, claiming that it had "adulterated the news to sway public opinion against Calles."[74] Writing in his journal, the *American Mercury*, Mencken cautioned Mexico that if it were not vigilant, "it would find itself dismembered in fragments."[75] A number of other major newspapers also came out against administration policy, including the *Baltimore Sun*, the *St. Louis Post Dispatch*, and the *New York Times*.

Even Lippmann was taken aback by Kellogg's expansive argument that the protection of private property of nationals abroad deserved a higher standing "under international law than the right of sovereignty." As he rightly noted, the implications of this stance were enormous, and not just for the parties involved. If the administration had its way, Mexico or any other nation would not have the right to alter preexisting contracts. "Such a doctrine, applied so absolutely, means an irreconcilable collision between the power of this country and the will of its neighbors."[76]

By the summer of 1927, cooler heads prevailed, as Mexico and the United States stepped back from the precipice. Domestic pressures forced Calles's hand. Peasant supporters of the Catholic Church, upset with the regime's anticlerical measures, had taken up arms to defend their faith. The Cristero Rebellion would drag on for three inconclusive years at a significant human and material cost. In addition, oil revenues had plummeted because of the standoff between the Mexican state and the foreign oil companies. According to one press report, "no new wells were drilled and thousands of oil workers" were idled.[77] With a fiscal crisis looming and his administration in dire need of revenues, Calles sought a way out of the standoff. Harder to gauge was whether Washington's lobbying of Central American politicians—already displeased with the Mexican government's support for the Nicaraguan Liberals—was paying dividends. Certainly, the Salvadoran government had made its dissatisfaction with Calles's meddling clear when it detained a Mexican ship filled with weapons destined for Nicaraguan Liberals.[78]

Agreeing to suspend assistance to his Nicaraguan clients was a small price to pay to Calles. Encouraged by the Mexican government's gesture, the U.S. backed off as well. Kellogg subsequently toned down the rhetoric and first reprimanded and then recalled Sheffield, replacing him with a more conciliatory diplomat, Dwight Morrow. Highly recommended by his colleague at J. P. Morgan, Thomas Lamont, and by Machado, the

Spanish-speaking Morrow had experience troubleshooting fiscal matters in Cuba during the early 1920s. Unusual for a U.S. diplomat, he believed that governments should refrain from using military force to collect debts—an explicit repudiation of the Roosevelt Corollary. He also was opposed to U.S. military intervention. When asked what his charge was before setting off for the Mexican capital, the banker-turned-diplomat deadpanned: "My only instructions are to keep us out of war with Mexico."[79] In this matter, Morrow and Calles had a useful ally in Lamont. Representing the interests of two hundred thousand bondholders who had been waiting patiently for repayment of Mexican debts, Lamont was convinced that the oil companies' belligerence threatened to jeopardize sensitive ongoing debt negotiations with Calles's administration.[80]

Morrow suggested to the Mexican president that more could be gained by compromise. Given the regime's fiscal situation, perhaps sorely needed development loans might be floated in exchange for concessions.[81] In addition, fresh eyes on the problem found a solution. J. Reuben Clark, a recent addition to Morrow's staff, was surprised to learn upon his arrival in Mexico that his colleagues at the embassy had done little research into the oil question; instead, they had accepted the views of the oil companies at face value. "We had come to the point where in effect we were saying that the Executive of Mexico did not know the law of Mexico, neither did the Legislature of Mexico, neither did the Courts, and that the only people who knew what the law of Mexico was, were the oil attorneys."[82]

Morrow conceded that the subsoil was the property of the Mexican nation and that Mexico had the sovereign right to legislate property rights, so long as new legislation was "neither retroactive nor confiscatory." In return, he persuaded Calles to ask the Supreme Court to rule the relevant articles of the new petroleum law unconstitutional. After the Supreme Court did so, a revised law was passed which made no reference to the fifty-year window on concessions given out before 1917 and which did not require that oil companies exchange their original titles.[83]

Morrow also understood the value of public relations; he invited his future son-in-law, Lindbergh, and comedian Will Rogers to pay visits to Mexico City. A crowd of 125,000 turned out to welcome the celebrated flier, who overcame fog, navigational errors, inaccurate maps, and malfunctioning radio and radar to fly his *Spirit of St. Louis* from Washington to the Mexican capital.[84] Writing in *El Machete*, Mella contended that the Lindbergh visit was much more than a public relations stunt; it represented a

duplicitous change in strategy designed to conceal Washington's true intent in the region: "In recent times, *yanqui* imperialism has changed its tactics. It has traded violence for intrigue. While it offers peace with a gloved
hand, its other iron hand strikes with the sword. Now we have Morrow instead of Sheffield. Instead of the airplanes that dropped bombs over our
defenseless cities, we now fear the *Spirit of St. Louis* and its kind greetings;
however, the objective remains the same—conquer Latin America to exploit it even more."[85]

   Leftists were not the only ones unhappy with the more conciliatory
policy. The oil companies dug in—that is, until the State Department
made it clear that it supported this compromise. The companies then reluctantly turned in their titles.[86] Olds apparently had a change of heart as
well. The oil companies, he wrote in a memorandum, would like for "us
to use the club on Mexico" but that always "made the whole situation
worse ... if anything is plain from our experience with Mexico ... an
ideal solution is not to be expected."[87]

   As historian Alan Knight contends, increasingly, at home and abroad,
oil interests, especially in the wake of the Teapot Dome scandal, seemed
not only high-handed but out of step with other special interests, like
bankers, bondholders, landowners, and exporters, who all had little problem coexisting "profitably with the Revolution." Morrow's final words on
the subject were certainly music to the ears of nationalists. "A Mexico
which was allowed peacefully to develop its reform program was a far
better proposition for [North American] business than a Mexico subjected to the iron rod of the oilmen."[88]

Conclusions

Mexican-U.S. relations during the mid-1920s proved significant not only
because of the former's newfound assertiveness. The diplomatic showdown made it very apparent that Washington, even when it faced widespread criticism of its policies at home and abroad, would not tolerate
interference in its backyard. In fact, by the end of those three tumultuous
years, a chastened Mexico, facing nettlesome problems at home and a
concerted U.S. diplomatic and economic offensive, was forced to end its
support for Nicaragua's Liberals and reach an accommodation with U.S.
oil companies and the State Department.

   Indeed, the Mexican Revolution, once considered the darling of regional progressives, would take an unexpectedly sharp turn to the right

after 1928, as Calles and his successors not only unleashed a brutal wave of repression against the PCM but cracked down on Latin American political exiles to whom they had given safe harbor. They also treated Sandino as a contagion when he came to Mexico in search of arms in June 1929.

In fact, the Hoover administration, overextended in Latin America and anxious to mend fences with its neighbor, came to Calles's aid when a domestic rebellion erupted in 1929. The rebellion was easily put down.[89] In short, the contentious episode between the two countries became an instructive chapter for Latin American student activists. By 1929 the revolution not only had lost its luster, but Calles was exposed as just another heavy-handed caudillo. Many became increasingly disillusioned with the direction of the Mexican Revolution and its capitulation to the Colossus of the North.

CHAPTER SIX

Something New in American History

The attitude which we have assumed in Nicaragua, viz., that we
will support by force the government which we deem
constitutional, goes farther than the minimum necessary to
protect the lives and property of aliens. Followed to its logical
conclusion it would lead to armed intervention in every Central
American revolution.

—HAROLD DODDS, electoral consultant, 1927

ON SPECIAL ASSIGNMENT IN April 1927, the former secretary of war,
Henry Stimson, brokered an agreement among Nicaraguan Liberal and
Conservative leaders at Tipitapa, just north of the capital, Managua.
Three days before he met with the belligerents, he delivered an ultimatum. Both sides were to accept a ceasefire, recognize the U.S.-backed
Conservative candidate Díaz as president, and turn in their arms for
cash. On this last point, little was left to the imagination. "The forces of
the United States," he admonished, "will be authorized to accept the custody of the arms of those willing to lay them down including the government and to disarm forcibly those who will not do so."[1] Faced with such
stern prodding, the two sides turned in a combined 6,200 rifles, 262 machine guns, and five million rounds of ammunition. In return, the U.S.

consented to supervise presidential elections in 1928 and 1932 and to offer the Liberals amnesty and government positions.[2]

Even though the Liberals were awarded six governorships, the party leadership was displeased that Stimson refused one of its key demands: the removal of Díaz from power. But they felt that they had little choice but to consent, especially when the mediator threatened military force if their party declined to accept his terms.[3]

Stimson's offer to supervise the upcoming elections was not unfamiliar to Nicaraguans. In fact, the U.S. had overseen every presidential election since 1912. In that year and then again four years later, Liberals were proscribed from participating, providing Moncada additional proof, if he needed any, that Stimson's threat was not an idle one.

All too aware that supervision of Nicaraguan elections had been problematic in the past, the State Department had urged Stimson to refrain from making such a promise. But the colonel knew that the Liberals would not come to the table without that assurance, so convinced were they that without monitoring, the Conservatives would fix the results. The United States, he insisted, should serve as an honest broker in the elections.[4]

Díaz was successful in turning down a recommendation from Stimson to have other Central American governments help monitor the voting. "Not one of the Central American governments would be a disinterested and impartial party," Díaz remarked. "Honduras would favor the Conservatives, Guatemala and Costa Rica the Liberals, and Salvador while doubtful at present would certainly not be neutral." The U.S. minister in Managua, Charles Eberhardt, concurred, adding presumptuously: "It is self-evident that the details could only be handled by a first-class world power enjoying a free hand, acting alone, and having at its command the competent, official personnel, administration machinery and other resources necessary for the ... supervision of the national elections of a country in which conditions of chronic disorder and bad administration prevail."[5]

The Coolidge administration rehired Dodds to revise the existing electoral code that he had crafted for Nicaragua several years before and appointed a brigadier general who had worked with Stimson in the Philippines, Frank McCoy, to supervise the elections. The Nicaraguan Supreme Court appointed McCoy to chair its national board of elections. The Nicaraguans on the board were, in the words of one historian, "largely decorative."[6] More than nine hundred U.S. monitors, many of them military personnel, flooded the country to ensure that the 1928 elections were free of fraud.[7]

Stimson and the Coolidge administration's desire to inculcate best practices in governance was not only futile, it had pernicious consequences. Intended to maintain order, protect U.S. investments, and permit the gradual withdrawal of troops, the U.S. military's training and arming of constabularies in Nicaragua, the Dominican Republic, and Haiti, quashed internal dissent and further politicized the role of the region's militaries. New professional tools, including the use of fingerprinting and mug shots, gave militaries and police forces additional tools to monitor and track dissidents.[8] While the United States did not invent strongman rule, it gave commanders like Somoza and Trujillo the means to defeat rivals and consolidate their power. What was envisioned as a defensive mechanism by Washington became, by the early 1950s—due to bilateral military assistance treaties—a finely tuned instrument of repression.

This chapter explores the ramifications of, and resistance to, U.S. policy during the late 1920s and early 1930s. Peace progressives in the U.S. Congress and their allies in the media, the labor movement, academia, and women's organizations raised their collective voices in opposition to the Coolidge administration's Latin American policy. Their outspokenness dovetailed with public weariness with extended occupations. Domestic critics were emboldened by growing transnational opposition to the Nicaraguan and Haitian interventions.

It was not surprising, then, that the 1928 inter-American meetings in Havana became a referendum on U.S. policy. The proceedings permitted a hometown dictator like Machado to legitimate his rule, but they also became a showdown between the United States and upstart Latin American delegations. Only the latter's disunity enabled the U.S. delegation and its allies to table a nonintervention resolution. The acrimonious debate in Havana, however, led to a reappraisal of U.S. policy by the Hoover and Roosevelt administrations.

Following Hoover's goodwill tour of Latin America in early 1929, he (and now–Secretary of State) Stimson pledged to gradually recall the Marines from Nicaragua and Haiti, refrain from future interventions, and no longer use the U.S. military to enforce repayment of debts. The administration also attempted to resolve once and for all the prickly matter of the recognition of new governments. By reverting back to the pre-Wilsonian practice of recognizing de facto governments no matter how they came to power, the United States made it easier for regional dictators to seize and remain in power.

Squabbling about how best to bring about change, Latin American progressives proved to be their own worst enemies. Sectarian disputes undermined Sandino and Haya just as opposition to gunboat and dollar diplomacy reached a crescendo. As Washington's efforts to bring about regime change gave way to a selective hands-off policy, activists increasingly found themselves losing ground to despots.

He Flies Around Like a Mosquito

Stimson's parting words before returning home—"I believe this marks definitively the end of the insurrection"—would come back to haunt him.[9] Alone among Liberal chieftains, Sandino refused to accept the Tipitapa agreement. He denounced Moncada in the Managua press as a Conservative-turned-Liberal, a traitor to the cause. "Nobody ever authorized him to leave the Constitutionalist [Liberal] ranks in order to enter into any secret treaties ... with the enemy, and, more particularly with the invaders of our country. His high position demanded of him to die like a man rather than tamely to permit the humiliation of our country. Moncada has made himself responsible for a crime which calls for vengeance."[10]

In an open letter to Hoover in March 1929, the rebel warned that not every Nicaraguan could be bought off so easily. He cautioned that "as long as you continue the policies of Coolidge and Kellogg, you will continue encountering Sandinos."[11] He and his followers refused to turn in their arms. Surrendering weapons to the Marines was also a sore point for one of the Mexican soldiers who had first traveled to fight with the Liberals in 1926. In fact, Captain José Paredes decided to join Sandino's international brigade because he was upset that Liberals were making a profit by selling arms that he had helped transport from Mexico to Nicaragua.[12]

Initially, Stimson underestimated the Segovian's resolve, but continued clashes between the rebels and the Marines soon persuaded him that three thousand troops were insufficient to contain the rebellion. By early 1928 the numbers of Marines stationed in Nicaragua had almost doubled, even as the rebellion remained localized in the rugged northern mountains. Stimson realized that the presence of the Marines and the supervision of two elections were but short-term solutions. The linchpin of a more lasting solution was the professionalization of the Guardia Nacional, a national police force created several years earlier at the behest of the Harding administration. Stimson believed that with additional arms, outfitting, and training, the constabulary could put down Sandino's rebellion and keep the peace.[13]

The professionalization of the Guard, however, remained a work in progress for quite some time. Abuses abounded, discipline was in short supply, accountability was lacking, desertions were abundant, and civilians were more often victimized than aided. To address these shortcomings, former U.S. soldiers became officers in the Guard. Moncada even brought in a brigade of mercenaries, under the command of a particularly brutal Mexican, which only led to greater dissension in the ranks. As late as 1930, Buell reported that recruits even tried to blackmail their superiors that "if certain concessions were not made they would join Sandino."[14]

To rectify matters and defeat the rebellion, Stimson restored the U.S. military's authority for the Guard's training, recruited more carefully, and improved court-martial procedures to curb desertions.[15] Given proper preparation, he reasoned, the Guard would be able to maintain order, pacify the interior, and bring nettlesome caudillos like Sandino to heel. The Munro-Cuadro Pasas agreement of December 1928 set the Guardia's budget at $700,000 per year for 93 officers and 1,136 enlisted men with provisions for expansion in the future.[16] As Munro put it: "The establishment of non-partisan constabularies in the Caribbean states was one of the chief objectives of our policy. ... The old armies were or seemed to be one of the principal causes of disorder and financial disorganization. They consumed most of the government's revenue, chiefly in graft, and they gave nothing, but disorder and repression in return. We thought that a disciplined force, trained by Americans would do away with the petty local oppression ... that occurred and would be an important step toward better financial administration and economic progress generally."[17] Establishing a professional institution that was divorced from partisan politics, it was felt, would build legitimacy for democratic institutions. At the same time, it was understood that the Guardia would protect the property of foreign investors and maintain cordial relations with the United States.

The costs of establishing the Guardia, however, far outweighed its benefits. Yes, regional caudillos were defeated, eliminated, or co-opted, but the countryside became ever more militarized, and it did not take long for the force to devolve into a crass instrument of political manipulation. After he was elected president, Moncada quickly recruited Liberal

Party members into the force. Buell was disappointed at how repressive Moncada was. He not only censored the press, but "imprisoned political offenders to a greater extent than any other president now in office in Central America." Sadly, Buell added, the 150 Marines who now served as officers in the Guard were complicit in the repression.[18]

Moncada's successor, Sacasa, continued to populate the officer corps with party stalwarts. Three years on, Stimson's effort to improve the Guard's standing in the eyes of Nicaraguans was still a work in progress. Buell zeroed in on how many residents felt about their new peacekeeping force. "Even today, a number of Nicaraguans claim that the Guardia is a law unto itself. They declare that Congress and the Cabinet have no control over their body."[19] State Department officials were concerned about the Guard's efficacy as well. As early as 1931, a precocious staffer named Laurence Duggan, who would rise quickly through the ranks to become chief of the Department's Division of Latin American Affairs during the Roosevelt administration, could not understand why others thought that the constabulary would ever fulfill its responsibilities. It was patently obvious that it was hamstrung by the "vitriolic animosity of the two parties, which is as bitter today as it was two hundred years ago. Therefore, it is difficult to understand why hope was ever entertained that a non-political force could ever be established."[20]

Democracy never materialized in Nicaragua, and the National Guard became the nation's most formidable institution. Authoritarian rule in Nicaragua remained in the iron grip of its commander, Anastasio "Tacho" Somoza García, who had served as Stimson's translator during the Tipitapa talks and who employed the force as his Praetorian Guard. Tacho and his two sons, Luis and Anastasio, Jr., established a family dynasty that governed Nicaragua for the better part of the next fifty years.

But in the spring of 1927, there was cautious optimism in Washington that the Tipitapa agreement and a more skilled constabulary would bring about an end to hostilities and allow the Marines to return home. McCoy was named Envoy Extraordinary, and in addition to supervising the elections, he oversaw the training of the Guard.

The general did not take Sandino lightly. In his reports, McCoy praised the rebel's mobility, knowledge of the terrain, and instincts for guerrilla warfare. "He flies around like a mosquito," he told Stimson. He also was impressed by the "undeniable popular support" for the rebel. McCoy realized that until Sandino "had been killed, captured or been run out of the country, the Marines had failed their mission."[21]

Sandino's rebels remained a potent threat, so much so that the Moncada administration floated a one-million-dollar loan in 1931 to again increase the size of the Guard by five hundred men. The Guard now was costing the budget 50 percent more than it had four years earlier, forcing the government to address a budget shortfall by closing schools and slashing funds for public education. Despite the additional funds apportioned, the Guardia failed to put down the rebellion. Five years after their return to Nicaragua, 1,400 Marines were still giving chase to the rebel army.[22]

Compared to the U.S.-Mexican conflict, the global response to the Nicaraguan intervention was vitriolic. Newspapers in Europe and Latin America mocked Washington's assertion that its methods differed from Old World imperialism, each citing chapter and verse of how Washington's actions failed to live up to its rhetoric. The *Boston Globe* lamented America's loss of prestige abroad: "in Europe, our nation is being pilloried from the Baltic to the Straits of Gibraltar, from London to Angora (Ankara). The painfully developed prestige, the tradition of American disinterestedness toward and support of small nations in their right to sovereign independence, has received a blow from which it will require years to recover."[23]

Nicaragua consumed the U.S. press. The *New York Times* ran 269 stories on the intervention during the first three months of 1928 alone.[24] Beals's series about his time spent with Sandino succeeded in personalizing the rebel for a North American audience while raising questions about the administration's characterization of him as a bandit. Still, the mainstream press remained divided about the uprising and the administration's motivations.[25] Broun was disappointed that much of the reporting by the "big news agencies" accepted the administration's characterization of Sandino at face value and seemed resigned to the inevitable—a continued North American presence. The *Cleveland Plain Dealer* agreed: "The Government dispatches describe Sandino as a 'rebel,' also as an outlaw and a brigand. In his own eyes, of course, Sandino is no rebel. He is opposing what he considers an extra-constitutional regime, which would not last ten days without United States support."[26]

But the *New York World*, which up to that point had attacked the administration's policy "with considerable vigor," now changed its tune; while sending in the Marines had been a mistake in the first place, "pulling out," the editors contended, "would only make a bad matter worse."[27] The *Pittsburgh Courier* and the *Chicago Defender*, both newspapers that

served the African American community in their respective cities, also
took aim at the Coolidge Administration's policy in Nicaragua, but in the
same breath wondered why press coverage of the occupation of the small
Central American country dwarfed that of Haiti.[28] Meanwhile, Marcus
Garvey's *Negro World* and the NAACP's *Crisis*, edited by W. E. B. Du
Bois, opposed intervention and voiced their support for Sandino.[29]

To be sure, there were resolute supporters of the occupation. In a
disquisition on the vagaries of international law published in 1929, John
Foster Dulles, a young corporate attorney employed by the New York
firm Sullivan & Cromwell, which provided legal representation for
UFCO, claimed that occupying other nations was par for the course for
"highly developed nations." After all, he acknowledged, the U.S. had,
over the last century, "used its military forces abroad over one hundred
times."[30] Given the relative disparities between nations, diplomatic relations could not always be conducted on a level footing. Military interventions were justified because smaller states, in his words, "failed to
grow up." Although the attorney, who years later presided over controversial interventions in Iran and Guatemala while serving as secretary of
state during the Eisenhower administration, did not mention
Nicaragua or Haiti by name in the essay, the inference was clear. Indicative of how little the future Cold Warrior's views evolved over time can
be found in the essay's enigmatic conclusion: "I suppose that it is inevitable that nations interfere with one another and influence each other. If
so, I submit, there may well be situations where intervention by military
force is the most humane procedure."[31]

It is perhaps understandable that Sullivan & Cromwell's legal responsibility to protect the interests of its corporate clients abroad influenced
the twenty-six-year-old senior partner's views on interventionism. Between 1924 and 1931 his firm handled 250 million dollars in loans to
Latin America. But it was the young attorney's diplomatic experience
during the Wilson administration that had persuaded him that U.S. interests abroad were better served by working with dictators. Just as the U.S.
prepared to enter World War I in 1917, Dulles's uncle and Wilson's secretary of state, Robert Lansing, sent him "on a confidential mission" to
persuade the governments of Costa Rica, Nicaragua, and Panama to declare war on Germany as soon as the U.S. announced its intentions. The
goal, Dulles noted, was to "bring the Central American states into align-
ment with us against Germany . . . so that we could effectively protect
the Panama Canal." Costa Rica, however, presented a challenge. A coup

had just brought to power Federico Tinoco, a brutal autocrat whom the administration had been reluctant to recognize. After meeting with the dictator, Dulles counseled his superiors in Washington that the exigencies of the moment required that the administration overlook the repression and assure the dictator's loyalty by recognizing his government.[32] The administration did not take the young attorney's counsel, and when Tinoco fell in 1919, it was, in the words of one historian of Central America, "a rare example of United States destabilization ... directed against a dictator."[33] Dulles, however, remained resolute in his affinity for strongmen.

Although the Coolidge administration had its supporters, just as with the Mexican imbroglio, a concerted campaign by congressional doves put the State Department on the defensive. Critics demanded that the administration be more forthcoming about the occupation and called for investigations into alleged atrocities. Wheeler cheekily suggested that if U.S. troops were going to fight bandits, they should be sent to Chicago. Norris went further, comparing Sandino to George Washington and rebuking the president for using the Marines to "destroy human life, to burn villages, and to bomb innocent women and children."[34]

Sandino appealed to progressives for several reasons: he had publicly distanced his movement from communism; he was critical of U.S. investment; and a number of western and midwestern lawmakers identified with the agrarian roots of the rebellion. One congressional resolution questioned whether the executive branch had the right to undertake hostile operations abroad when the legislative branch had not declared a state of war. Another hotly contested rider to an appropriations bill sought to cut off funding entirely for the occupation. At first the Senate approved that measure, but then, under administration pressure, wilted and recanted—in part because Borah, who had originally spoken against the return of the Marines to Nicaragua, reconsidered and changed his vote at a crucial moment.[35]

The chair of the Senate Foreign Relations Committee never warmed to Sandino, in large part because he had befriended old guard Liberal Party politicians who influenced his views of the conflict. Heartened by Stimson's plan to bring about an end to hostilities, Borah was convinced that boots on the ground were needed to protect the electoral process. Unlike other congressional critics, who believed that the Liberals had shamelessly capitulated to Stimson, it was his opinion that Moncada, Sacasa, and their partisans deserved an opportunity to govern the country. A North American presence, Borah reasoned, was also needed to monitor the actions of the incumbent Conservatives. *Sans* supervision of the elections, the untrustworthy Conservatives would do what they had done repeatedly in past elections—use fraudulent tactics to steal the vote. But despite his opposition, the rider received 22 votes in the Senate, the largest number of votes to cut off funds for an overseas military intervention up to that time. Although Borah's defection did not bring an end to opposition to administration policy, it presaged future disagreements among progressives that diminished their effectiveness as a voting bloc.[36]

Although Nicaragua drew the most attention, the peace progressives' criticisms were part of their larger critique aimed at the administration's uncritical support for the private sector abroad. Wheeler authored a resolution calling for a Senate investigation into the "often unjustifiable" concessions given to U.S. companies in the Caribbean. Shipstead demanded that the executive branch cease any assistance, direct or indirect, to U.S. citizens abroad. Although they realized that they did not have the votes to roll back the administration's policy, the peace progressives convinced themselves that the sum total of their hearings and resolutions raised public awareness about the costs of intervention and kept the administration on the defensive.[37]

Richard Grossman, a student of progressive solidarity movements during the 1920s, has identified two types of public opposition to the Nicaraguan intervention: those individuals and groups who opposed U.S. policy but did not necessarily support Sandino; and others, who found common cause with the rebel's anti-imperialist stance and raised funds and lent moral support to the insurgency. Among the most vocal of the anti-imperialist groups was the People's Lobby, led by John Dewey. The organization published a tough-minded pamphlet, *Why United States Marines Are in Nicaragua: Why the Marines Should Come Out*, which denounced U.S. imperialism while glossing over Sandino's motivations.[38]

The principal solidarity group in the United States was a communist front organization, the All-American Anti-Imperialist League, which disseminated propaganda about Sandino's struggle, held antiwar rallies, sent medical supplies and funds to the rebels, and leafleted Marine bases to discourage troops about to ship out to Nicaragua. Solidarity committees sprang up in New York, Chicago, Los Angeles, and Detroit. Sandino's half-brother, Sócrates, spoke at a number of rallies organized by the league. The executive secretary of the Workers' Party (the Communist Party of the United States) boasted that by "rendering direct aid to the

Nicaraguan forces fighting American imperialism" the league's campaign constituted "something new in American history."[39] In addition, leftist Hispanic exiles in New York City—a mélange of anarchists, anarcho-syndicalists, and communists from a variety of Spanish-speaking countries—showed their support for the rebellion, taking to the streets and shouting "Viva el General Sandino!" In the nation's capital, one hundred pro-Sandino activists were jailed for demonstrating "without a parade permit outside the White House," a number that "far exceeded" those imprisoned during the suffragist movement a decade earlier.[40]

Munro later acknowledged that "domestic criticism probably actually had more effect on American policy" than the collective outrage pouring out of Latin America.[41] But that was not to say that the administration was entirely tone-deaf to criticism in the Latin American press. In Colombia, for instance, the Liberal and the Conservative press, which rarely agreed on much, both came out in support of the rebel.[42] LADLA kept the pressure on with pamphlets imploring the youth of Latin America to enlist with Sandino and defeat the imperialists.[43]

Opposition from Latin American critics would crystallize at the VI International Conference of American States, held in Havana in January and February of 1928. The site and timing of the meetings were a nightmare scenario for the Coolidge administration. At a moment when the U.S. was preaching disarmament and nonaggression in Europe, when Latin American hostility to U.S. intervention in Nicaragua was at "a fever pitch," the inter-American meetings were to be held in a country ruled by a despot who served at the pleasure of Washington.[44]

Havana Turbulence

Ever since Martí's accounts of the inaugural Pan American Conference in Washington in 1889–1890, Latin American intellectuals had viewed these regional meetings with disdain, for two reasons: their governments rarely appeared willing or able to contest U.S. interests lest they jeopardize their access to loans and military and economic assistance; and the results obtained were meager, since matters of substance were rarely discussed.[45]

But the atmosphere had turned contentious at the meetings in Santiago, Chile, in 1923, when fifteen Latin American nations expressed vocal opposition to U.S. intervention in the Dominican Republic, Haiti, and Nicaragua. The rump caucus advanced a resolution that nations should have the right to settle disputes with foreign investors conducting business within their borders and that individuals and companies were subject to the laws and constitutions of the countries where their investments resided. The U.S. countered that international law afforded governments the right to defend the interests of its citizens abroad. After several stormy sessions, the U.S. managed to table the resolution.[46]

Some Latin American delegations went further, questioning the legitimacy of the Monroe Doctrine. Again, the U.S. delegation protested, arguing that the 1823 doctrine was a statement of its foreign policy, which should not be subject to debate.[47] Welles, a member of the delegation, was taken aback by the vitriol expressed during the thirty-nine-day conference: "In the long history of Pan American conferences, the United States was never more completely at odds with its American neighbors than during those sessions."[48]

Four years after the Santiago meetings an Inter-American Commission of Jurists conference in Rio de Janeiro unanimously passed a resolution condemning intervention of any kind while affirming the inviolability of national sovereignty. That set the stage for the Havana conference.[49] Kellogg, who had experienced firsthand Latin American belligerence in Santiago, counseled his delegation on its way to the summit to be prepared for diplomatic fireworks: "The past year has seen the development of a vigorous anti-American propaganda throughout Latin America based on charges of 'imperialism' and characterized by violent criticism of the relations existing between the United States and Mexico and the American policy in Nicaragua. . . . An effort may be made by some delegates . . . to bring up controversial matters which the United States would not consider appropriate for a gathering of this nature."[50]

No matter; it was the diminutive rebel—in absentia—who dominated the proceedings. Sandino sent a blistering letter to the conference urging the delegates to "protest the presence of illegal delegates of so-called President Adolfo Díaz; [and] protest against the hypocrisy of Coolidge, who speaks of good will and sends an army to murder Nicaraguans." Embarrassed by "the indifference and servility" that some Latin American delegations had demonstrated in the past, he implored delegates to demand the immediate withdrawal of the Marines.[51] In fact, the Havana newspaper *El Heraldo de Cuba* published dispatches from Sandino—relayed by the media hound Turcios—for the duration of the conference.[52] And when the flags of the each of the nations were hoisted, Nicaragua's received an ovation.[53]

Aware of the undercurrent of animus, Hughes went on the offensive in a speech delivered to the Havana Chamber of Commerce a few days after the proceedings had begun. The architect of the Dominican and Haitian interventions defended the continued occupation of the latter until such time as "we had reasonable expectations of stability." He justified the Marines' presence in Nicaragua as "an imperative but temporary emergency" from which "we shall retire as soon as it is possible."[54]

Cuba, Nicaragua, and Peru were the only delegations that came to Hughes's defense. The Cuban Ambassador to the United States, Orestes Ferrara Marino, protested that the word *intervention* held a very different connotation to Cubans: "We cannot join in the general chorus of 'no intervention,' because the word *intervention* in my country has been a word of glory, of honor, of triumph, of freedom—it has meant autonomy" (italicized in the original).[55]

The Argentine delegate Honorio Pueyrredón made a forceful case for nonintervention: "The sovereignty of the states lies in the absolute right to full domestic autonomy and external independence. This right in the stronger nations is guaranteed by their strength, and in the case of the weaker ones, by the respect given by those strong nations. If this right is not firmly established and exercised . . . international legal harmony does not exist."[56] He added that the usual North American justification for its overseas deployment of troops to protect the persons and property of its nationals abroad was insufficient to override a nation's right to defend its sovereignty: "Intervention—diplomatic or armed, permanent or temporary . . . cannot be justified on the plea of . . . protecting the interests of citizens. For the weaker nations cannot exercise such a right when their citizens suffer damage during convulsions in strong states."[57]

The U.S. delegation did its best to quash any discussion of the Commission of Jurists' resolution on nonintervention. Much to its relief, an agreement was reached in subcommittee that postponed discussion of the resolution until the next Inter-American Conference, set for Montevideo in 1933. But that was not the end of it. In the plenary session, the Argentines again expressed misgivings that the matter had not been given the attention it deserved. That triggered similar speeches by delegates from Haiti, the Dominican Republic, Guatemala, and Colombia. After some discussion, the Salvadoran foreign minister, Gustavo Guerrero, formulated a resolution that drew on the jurists' language.[58]

What ensued was far from the usually staid speechifying. Some delegates shouted that Guerrero's nonintervention resolution was out of

order, while others spoke out strongly against North American intervention. Some of the remarks were so incendiary that presiding officers of
the conference later expunged them from the official record.[59]

Hughes then took to the rostrum and dismissed the idea that the
U.S. wished to avoid any discussion of the issue. It was just that more
time was needed to work through all the ramifications of a broad nonintervention pledge, he insisted. "There was nothing to conceal. There are
no hidden motives." Hughes then categorically rejected that the United
States had acted as a hegemon in the Caribbean: "We do not wish the
territory of any American republic. We do not wish to govern any American republic. We do not wish to intervene in the affairs of any American
republic. We simply wish peace and order and stability and recognition
of honest rights properly acquired."[60] He shifted the blame squarely onto
the shoulders of Latin American governments. The allusion to Nicaragua was not lost on the delegates: "What are we to do when government
breaks down and American citizens are in danger of their lives? Are we to
stand by and see them butchered in the jungle because a government, in
circumstances which it cannot control and for which it may not be responsible, can no longer afford reasonable protection?" U.S. occupations,
he averred, were of a "temporary character—for the purpose of protecting the lives and property of its nationals." At one point, Hughes pointed
to Nicaragua's foreign minister and suggested that the assembled take up
the matter directly with him: "he can tell you the situation in Nicaragua
. . . we are there simply to aid them in obtaining free elections."[61]

By all accounts, Hughes was persuasive, eliciting cheers from some delegates.[62] But he also was disingenuous. With the exception of a few months
in 1925, the Marines had been stationed in Nicaragua since 1912. The U.S.
presence in Haiti was in its thirteenth year. Nor was there the slightest indication that troops would be leaving either country anytime soon.

Despite support from the Mexican, Colombian, Haitian, and Argentine delegates, Guerrero realized that he did not have enough votes to secure passage of his resolution. Nor was compromise possible. Ultimately,
he withdrew the resolution. According to most contemporary assessments of the conference—and scholars of U.S. foreign policy since—
Hughes's stirring speech had saved the day for the United States.[63] But a
few others concluded otherwise, noting that the only countries that had
supported the United States were dictatorships. Duggan characterized
the set-to as one of the "worst diplomatic defeats ever suffered by the
United States."[64]

Lippmann, in attendance at the meetings, could have been speaking for many observers when he wrote, "our delegation wanted to avoid a scolding and did so." While conceding that Latin America had good reason to loathe Washington—"our policy only produces more interventions, constantly drawing us into a situation which can't be fixed"—Latin American governments, he thought, were congenitally incapable of standing up to their northern neighbor. Sadly, "the enormous unpopularity of our policy finds no effective political expression." He chided the Latin American delegates for their disunity; while there was an "intellectual intelligentsia, which could become militant," by and large, the delegates opted for the "course of prudence" and held their tongues. Mexico, he noted, certainly could not afford to "rock the boat"; otherwise it might have thwarted prospects for a settlement between Washington and Mexico City. As for the other countries, he understood why they were so restrained; they were in need of assistance and could not risk alienating their benefactor.[65] Inman echoed those sentiments. "Latin America still holds her protest meetings, and prints her virulent editorials and organizes her anti-imperialistic societies to condemn the Yankees, while her officials float loans in New York." The proceedings were proof positive "that anything like a concert of Latin American states to oppose the United States was a fiction."[66] Leftists, like Argentine journalist Máximo Soto-Hall, agreed that "with all that was happening in Nicaragua, 'the silence' out of Havana, only signified an inexplicable complicity."[67]

The debate that started in Havana caught a second wind in *Foreign Affairs* a few months later when the Democrat Franklin Roosevelt and the Republican Ogden Mills offered contrasting assessments. Drafted with Welles's assistance, Roosevelt's contribution steered clear of Nicaragua but was critical of the other occupations. While the interventions were not, in principle, in error, Roosevelt contended, the methods employed left much to be desired. Notwithstanding the material improvements accomplished, "we seem to have paid too little attention to making the citizens of these states more capable of reassuming the control of their own governments." Was it any surprise, he added, that Washington had alienated many of its neighbors? "[Our policy] has allowed a dislike and mistrust of long standing to grow into something like positive hate and fear." Roosevelt, who had been assistant secretary of the Navy during the Wilson administration and had had a hand in writing Haiti's 1920 Constitution, had since concluded that there were unintended consequences of extended interventions. In what became a preview of his administration's Good Neighbor

Policy, he argued that in the future the U.S. must act more collaboratively with Latin American governments. "Single-handed intervention by us in the internal affairs of our nations must end; with the cooperation of others we shall have more order in this hemisphere and less dislike."[68]

Undersecretary of the Treasury Ogden Mills rebutted Roosevelt, praising Hughes to the hilt, quoting early and often from the former secretary's speech. Addressing Nicaragua specifically, Mills reiterated the administration's position that "we could not do less than to send troops there when American lives were in danger and the situation had gotten beyond the control of the local authorities." It was incumbent on the U.S. to stay the course and oversee the elections.[69]

The pundits were correct that by delaying discussion of a nonintervention pledge, Hughes had scored a tactical victory. Discussions would be put off until the next conference in Montevideo in 1933, when a new administration was less likely to reject such a pledge. But the implications for U.S.–Latin American relations of what occurred in Havana would reverberate for decades to come. The unpleasantness exhibited in the final plenary exposed the gulf between reformers, their authoritarian governments, and their allies in Washington. Coupled with what had transpired in Santiago five years before and the cresting opposition to interventionism at home and abroad, it was not surprising that in the aftermath of Havana, the Hoover administration would undertake a reappraisal of U.S.–Latin American relations.

By definition, the attendees at Pan American conferences were drawn invariably from the political class of their countries. In that respect, the warm response to Hughes's speech by the majority was unsurprising. What was striking was that a handful of delegates would take Washington to task in such a public setting, making pronouncements that often were at odds with their government's policy. Criticizing the United States at such a proceeding was not just a diplomatic faux pas committed by a boisterous few, but for delegates representing those nations it amounted to biting the hand that fed their governments with assistance and loans.

Some delegates, in fact, paid dearly for their principles on their return home. Guerrero, for one, was called on the carpet by his superiors and had to defend his actions. At the National University, where he found a receptive audience, he said that as long as he was foreign minister, "he would impose upon the foreign policy of El Salvador the line of conduct that the dignity of the nation demanded." But President Pío Romero Bosque was displeased, and from his perspective, with good reason. He had cabled Guerrero during the meetings, urging him to "moderate" his remarks, instructions that his minister chose to ignore. Shortly thereafter, the newfound darling of the anti-imperialists found himself effectively consigned to diplomatic oblivion, reassigned to a minor post at the League of Nations.[70]

After Havana, the Coolidge administration was given a gift from an unexpected source. Once powerful advocates, communists now turned against Sandino, and proved more successful in undermining support for his rebellion than Stimson's constabulary.

Sectarian Disputes

At a moment when Washington was set back on its heels, rancorous disputes fractured the left's unity, gifting the Hoover administration a welcome reprieve. The two darlings of international activists, Sandino and Haya, were the principal casualties of the infighting. In 1930 Haya returned to Peru, where he put his energies into transforming APRA into a bona fide political party. He ran for the presidency in 1931, losing by a substantial margin. Although Haya remained a formidable political actor in his native Peru and continued to be an advocate for anti-imperialism and economic nationalism, he never again commanded the hemispheric stage the way he had in the 1920s.

A stubborn, principled Sandino did himself no favors at home and abroad. When the leadership of the Liberal Party consented to Stimson's proposed settlement, Sandino was left on a political island in his own country. Even as Conservative newspapers in Managua and Granada called for an end to the U.S. occupation, he refused to reach out to them. Similarly, he never acknowledged the propaganda work of Conservative activists who supported his cause. His reticence is best explained by his distrust of traditional politicians. His struggle always had as much to do with breaking the stranglehold that local oligarchs held in the countryside as it did with the North American presence.

Since patronage was so deeply embedded in Nicaraguan society, most campesinos were already linked vertically to a powerful scion of either the Liberal or Conservative Party in their respective *patrias chicas*. Sandino's determination to keep fighting until the Marines had left the country may have galvanized support abroad, but cutting his ties with the Liberal Party at home cost him the backing of many of the country's working poor, who were tied either to wealthy elites of the two principal political parties or to regional warlords. As a result, he attracted little support from his countrymen outside of the Segovias. At one point, he mused to a journalist that the only segment of Nicaraguan society that had consistently demonstrated a commitment to his cause was students.[71]

Sandino posed a special problem for the CI. While Haya questioned Marxist dogma (even as he gleaned insights from it), the Peruvian never posed a credible threat to the International's self-proclaimed identity as the chief architect of hemispheric revolution. Sandino was another matter. His ongoing struggle not only garnered headlines worldwide but also attracted young, idealistic foot soldiers from all across Latin America. As far as the CI was concerned, Sandino was guilty of muddled political thinking and of acting like any other self-serving caudillo. They demanded that he sever ties with bourgeois and petit bourgeois elements.[72] As Marxists, they also were uncomfortable with Sandino's burgeoning spirituality. Left unstated was that if his rebellion succeeded, it had the potential to spawn like-minded multiclass movements.[73]

The rebel may well have been a regional strongman in the literal sense of the word, but he was one with uncommon traits. Charismatic, he believed that his cause was an inherently moral one. To be labeled a caudillo was especially insulting; in his opinion, the prototypical strongman preyed on the poor, was corrupt, and was part and parcel of the political establishment—everything he repudiated.[74]

Isolated at home and abroad, bereft of funds and arms, in 1929 Sandino sought assistance from the only country in Latin America that had undergone a broad-based revolution, one that only a few years before had given generous assistance to Nicaraguan Liberals. But Sandino's ten-month stay in Mexico proved to be an unmitigated disaster. The Mexico the rebel encountered was dramatically different from the radical political laboratory he had first experienced in the Tampico oilfields in the mid-1920s. At a time when the revolutionary state was tacking strongly to the right and as Mexico City aligned itself ever more closely to the U.S., the regime's "revolutionary" credentials were in question.

But to Sandino, outside of the communists, the Mexican government represented his only potential source of assistance for his rebellion. So he heaped praise on the revolution's accomplishments and cast his movement as its rightful offspring.[75] He also naively believed that he could repair his relationship with MAFUENIC, whose headquarters were in Mexico. Caught in a political vise between satisfying the communists and not alienating his hosts, he wound up pleasing neither.[76]

After consulting with U.S. diplomats, President Emilio Portes Gil decided to treat the popular revolutionary as an unwanted guest. The regime provided the rebel with asylum, a modest stipend, and security, but it effectively quarantined Sandino and his small band of supporters a thousand miles away from the capital, in Mérida, for much of his stay. The government also forbade him from engaging in any political activity and politely ignored his repeated requests for arms and funding.[77]

In a last-gasp effort to repair the rift with the communists, Sandino attended a meeting in Veracruz in February 1930 with the leadership of MAFUENIC and the Mexican Communist Party, where he was asked to embark on a speaking tour of Latin America and Europe to enlist support for the CI and to speak out against U.S. imperialism. But a prerequisite before making the trip was that he publicly criticize his host for its repression of the PCM. A diffident Sandino first agreed to this but then thought better of it, probably convinced that if he did so, authorities might prevent him from returning to Nicaragua. Instead, he met with Portes Gil and, in return for additional funding, he agreed to return to Nicaragua to continue the fight.[78]

The break with the communists was now irreparable. Sandino was someone who could no longer be trusted. As one biographer noted, "Sandino was in Mexico as a guest of the Mexican government, Sandino was taking money from the Mexican government, and Sandino despite his promise to attack it, had not only failed to do so, but continued to meet with its agents behind their [the communists'] back. The conclusion was easily drawn. Sandino was a traitor."[79]

The one-time Aprista, now communist Pavletich belittled the Nicaraguan, calling him a cross between St. Francis and Trotsky, while Farabundo Martí denounced him as a petty bourgeois caudillo.[80] Gustavo Machado ignored a request from the general to serve as the EDSNN's official representative abroad, the post originally held by Turcios.[81]

The CI's fierce campaign against Sandino proved costly to the rebel. Coupled with the loss of Turcios's formidable promotional skills, it denied the rebel both a platform and access to funds. But to young students across Latin America he remained a potent symbol of anti-imperialism and opposition to caudillo rule.

With Sandino weakened, the United States had a golden opportunity to extricate itself from an unpopular occupation. Hoover may have promised a fresh and more empathetic policy toward Latin America, but he soon found himself in a predicament partly of his own making. Wishing to steer clear of future entanglements that might necessitate intervention, his administration declared that henceforth it would recognize de facto governments no matter how ruthlessly they came to power. Nor were its diplomats to meddle in domestic politics. The transition was anything but smooth, and the results proved catastrophic for those fighting for a democratic future.

Recognition

Whether U.S. policy substantively changed after Havana is a matter of some debate. On the one hand, despite increasing opposition at home, troops remained in Haiti and Nicaragua until 1934. If not for fiscal constraints resulting from the Depression, the occupations might have lasted even longer. As noted, constabularies continued to be trained, equipped, and funded, assuming the role of national police forces that kept U.S.-backed dictatorships in power for decades to come. The United States provided much the same materiel and training to other militaries in the region, obviating the need to send Marines to new trouble spots. What was of utmost concern for the dictators and their North American ally was order, political stability, and the protection of foreign properties.

Some scholars contend, however, that the Hoover and Roosevelt administrations fundamentally altered the gunboat policy of their predecessors. The Good Neighbor Policy signaled the start of a different kind of relationship between the United States and its neighbors—one based on mutual reciprocity, respect, and bilateral trade agreements. In announcing his new policy initiative soon after he was sworn in, Roosevelt assured the public *and* Latin America that his administration would no longer send in troops to assure stability and security for U.S. investors in the circum-Caribbean. Fulfilling that pledge became a challenge, though, especially in Cuba, where a reformist movement gained headwind during the first year of FDR's presidency.[82]

In certain respects, the Good Neighbor Policy did not reflect a significant change in policy. Instead, it built on incremental changes already put in place by Roosevelt's predecessors. Cognizant of growing dissent, the Republican administrations had initiated a process of gradual disengagement from Nicaragua and Haiti, moderated their rhetoric, and, when facing stiff opposition at home and abroad, had backed away from confrontation and appointed, with some exceptions, less abrasive diplomats to work in trouble spots.

The first indication that such a change was in the works was a memorandum written during the last months of the Coolidge administration by Undersecretary of State Clark. Fearful that European criticism of interventionism abroad might scuttle ongoing negotiations of what became the quixotic Kellogg-Briand Pact, Kellogg asked Morrow's former aide to research whether the Monroe Doctrine justified U.S. intervention. Clark had ample experience in this regard; during his early years at the State Department he had worked on U.S. relations with Haiti, Panama, and Cuba.

Clark's memo drew a bright line between the doctrine, which sought to prevent European powers from reestablishing colonial rule and expanding their influence and territorial designs in the hemisphere, and military occupations and the creation of protectorates. Borrowing from an argument made by Hughes in 1923, Clark contended that the recent interventions did not fall within the doctrine's purview. Like the Roosevelt Corollary, the occupations and inter-American relations more generally were instead "an expression of a national policy, which ... originates in the necessities of security or self-preservation." Each case, he insisted, was idiosyncratic and deserved to be justified on its own merits. Moreover, military action to secure the safety of nationals and their properties was legal and accepted under international law.[83]

In retrospect, it is understandable how such a statement led some contemporary observers to conclude that Roosevelt's big stick no longer guided U.S. actions in the backyard. But Clark's memo was narrowly drawn, neglecting the legal and policy implications of the occupations. Its tone was at once haughty and defensive. It is hard to imagine that critics like Haya and Sandino (let alone Mella) could have taken much solace from statements like the following, which dismissed Latin American claims of sovereignty out of hand: "The Doctrine makes the United States a guarantor ... of the independence of Latin American states, though without the obligations of a guarantor to those states, for the United States itself determines by its sovereign will when, where and concerning what aggressions it will invoke the Doctrine, and by what measures, if any, it will apply a sanction. In none of these has any other state any voice whatever."[84]

Perhaps surmising that the memo's contents would be deemed controversial in Latin America and with peace progressives at home, Kellogg sent it first to the embassies and consular posts to gauge what his diplomats thought the reaction might be. Interestingly, Hoover delayed its

publication until 1932 because he thought it would unnecessarily alienate European—not Latin American—allies.[85]

Hoover did take steps to ease tensions by undertaking a two-month,
ten-nation "Mission of Good Will" while president-elect. Even before he
left his native California, he was met by protesters carrying banners condemning U.S. intervention in Nicaragua. The *New York Times* reported
that the Quaker and pacifist was "considerably troubled by the incident."
As early as 1922, he expressed reservations about occupations. Police
actions, he contended, were ineffective and costly and did little to advance national interests.[86]

He knew what he was up against as he made his way south. His goal
was "for the purpose of dissipating the fears and antagonisms . . . as to the
intentions and policies of our Government."[87] His message during the trip
echoed Hughes's earlier pledge that the U.S. had no territorial designs,
and he promised increased trade and cultural exchanges. In Nicaragua, he
brought longtime political foes Chamorro, Díaz, and Moncada together
for a meeting. He also walked back Coolidge's unconditional support for
U.S. business interests abroad when he stated, "It ought not to be the policy of the US to intervene by force to secure or maintain contracts between our citizens and foreign states or their citizens. Confidence in that
attitude is the only basis upon which the economic cooperation of our citizens can be welcomed abroad."[88] In fact, it was Hoover who first coined
the term *good neighbor*, a term that Roosevelt later adopted as his own.

Hoover's mission was, for the most part, reassuring to U.S. allies, but
in Buenos Aires, street demonstrators chanted the Nicaraguan rebel's
name and carried banners reading "Long Live Sandino! Long Live Nicaragua! Down with North American Imperialism!" Two days prior to that
demonstration the police broke up a plot by anarchists to bomb a train
carrying the president-elect.[89] In an open letter to Hoover, Palacios dismissed the president-elect's nonintervention pledge; it meant nothing as
long as troops remained in Nicaragua.[90]

Whether Hoover was chastened by the mixed reception he received
is unclear, but upon his return, he indicated that his administration was
prepared to turn over a new leaf. He established a commission to study
the merits of pulling troops out of Haiti and reduced the number of Marines stationed in Nicaragua. To be sure, the burgeoning cost of the two
interventions—nearly nine million dollars by 1931—weighed heavily on
policymakers. Still, when asked by the press about a timetable for the
withdrawal of troops from either country, he hedged.[91]

When eight Marines were killed in Nicaragua on the last day of 1930, the debate about the merits of the occupation flared up again in Congress. To defuse criticism, Stimson declared that U.S. investors should not assume that it would automatically step in and defend their interests abroad. The administration "will hesitate long before becoming involved in any general campaign of protecting with our forces American property throughout Nicaragua," the secretary of state cautioned.[92] Also weighing on his mind was the Japanese invasion of Manchuria. Stimson knew that administration critics would be quick to draw parallels between the Japanese occupation and the U.S. occupying force. In a nationwide radio broadcast in May 1931, Stimson, in the clearest repudiation of the Roosevelt Corollary to date, stated that the U.S. military would no longer be employed to collect debts in the region. U.S. citizens who did not feel safe abroad should either leave the country or move near the coastline, where they could be safely evacuated should unrest occur. He pledged to withdraw all troops from Nicaragua after its 1932 presidential elections, an assurance that for the moment took the winds out of the sails of congressional critics.[93]

U.S. policy, however, remained rife with inconsistency. While, in the main, Hoover made efforts to scale back involvement, policy toward a given country varied, depending on a host of variables. A decidedly partisan Welles later dismissed Hoover's goodwill message as so much public relations. Proof of this, he argued, was the administration's excessively discriminatory Smoot-Hawley tariff bill: "No country can make it impossible for its neighbors to sell to it their products and expect to retain their good will . . . what is equally important, no nation can refuse to buy the products of its neighbors and expect for any length of time to continue to sell them its own products. And it is exactly the dual result which was the logical outcome of the Smoot-Hawley Tariff Act. As a result of that misguided policy, our exports to Latin America have consistently dwindled."[94]

The Hoover administration did, however, think twice about intervening elsewhere as a slew of military revolts toppled civilian governments across the region. Less than two years after Havana, noninterventionism as a policy was now selectively proclaimed by the administration. But whether the U.S. should recognize military governments that came to power by force was a thorny issue. The administration did not help matters by recognizing some military dictators immediately while delaying recognition of others.

The expedited recognition of strongmen drew fire from former undersecretary of state Norman Davis, who contended that the administration's rush to judgment did not give the inhabitants of those countries time to express their support or acquiescence "by ballot or other constitutional means." With recognition, he added, came the possibility of acquiring loans from other governments and banks, and "these may be all that it [the dictatorship] needs to maintain itself in power through force or corruption." That, he contended, only encouraged greater instability and coups. Davis, who served under Wilson and Harding, much preferred Wilson's approach to the recognition of new governments, which stipulated that the U.S. not recognize governments that came to power by force until there was sufficient evidence of popular approval of the new regime.[95]

The root of the problem was that the incessant coup plotting and uprisings not only disrupted the stability of the country experiencing the unrest but, owing to porous borders, violations of neutrality, and entangling alliances, often destabilized neighboring countries. To begin with, the orderly transition of power from one political party to another was rare. Elections were often considered by a given political party or caudillo as a device to legitimate their remaining in power. Eberhardt stated the obvious in a memo to Kellogg: "Owing to government-controlled elections, the only way to accomplish change in party control or Government is by revolution or coup d'état."[96] Then when governments tottered, Washington invariably was asked or felt compelled to step in and broker disputes between adversaries. Yet negotiated settlements often proved short-lived; within months or a year, another rebellion would break out and the cycle began anew.

In an effort to promote regional stability and diminish the seemingly endless carousel of coups and "revolutions" in the isthmus, the Harding administration had made a good faith effort to solve the problem. Hughes brought together diplomatic representatives of each Central American country to Washington in late 1922 to hammer out a set of agreements. The key provision of the General Treaty of Peace and Amity was the treaty's second article, which required the "nonrecognition" of regimes that came to power by force, even if the regimes were subsequently "legitimized" by elections. The treaty drew on an international legal principle first espoused by Ecuadorian foreign minister Carlos Tobar in 1907, which stipulated that Latin American states could intervene indirectly in disputes among their neighbors by denying recognition to de facto

governments that came to power by force. While Mexico (which cospon-
sored the conference) and the United States did not sign the General
Treaty, it was implicit that both countries would use their influence on the
weaker Central American signatories to enforce its provisions.[97]

Even so, implementation did not have the desired effect; the coups
and rebellions continued apace, because by seeking to end rebellions, the
treaty could not ensure free elections or guarantee an orderly transition
of power. Duggan lamented that rather than encouraging democratic
governance, the treaty instead fostered a "mutual protection association
of the dictators then in power. Since free elections were unknown in
Central America outside of Costa Rica, it excluded the only practicable
means, revolution, of bringing about a change of government."[98]

Costa Rican president Jiménez, a well-respected international lawyer, came to believe that the treaty invited precisely the kind of interference that many in the region abhorred.[99] In 1924, for instance, Welles, as
he had during the Dominican occupation, acted as a proconsul in Honduras, standing in the way of certain aspirants to the presidency and having a say in those who did come to power.[100] In Honduras and Nicaragua
especially, Buell noted, "the American legation has been besieged in past
election campaigns by candidates asking whether or not, if elected, they
would be recognized by the United States."[101]

Nor was there universal support from the signatories of the General
Treaty. El Salvador's legislature never approved Article 2, arguing that it
was a violation of its sovereignty. Jiménez declared that Costa Rica reserved "the right to determine the constitutionality" of changes in power
in the isthmus. A test case was the Coolidge administration's preference
for president of Nicaragua in 1926. Deploring the underhanded manner
in which the Conservatives kept the Liberals from the presidency, Jiménez refused to recognize Díaz.[102]

Debt-ridden Central American governments, however, rarely had
the luxury of autonomy in such matters. Leverage came in the form of
"loan control." In 1922 the Harding administration had implemented a
new policy requiring bankers and investors to submit foreign loans on
offer to the public to the State Department for review. Although lenders
did not have to abide by the decision, according to one student of the period, "the failure to comply and receive the State Department's imprima-
tur would hamper efforts to float a loan."[103]

The implications of this new policy were evident to lenders and bor-
rowers alike. As one critic of the new policy predicted, approval of a loan

now implied that the administration was obliged to muscle in should the borrower default. In certain cases, Central American governments fell so far in arrears that receiverships were established, wherein customs revenues were garnished to pay off the debt service. To discourage the plotting, the State Department banned loans to governments that it had not recognized. More than ever, Central American governments understood that debts accrued significant political interest charges.[104] When Washington hounded Central American governments to adhere to the treaty provisions, the response was akin to "a feeling of dazed helplessness and a desire to know what the United States will do next."[105]

A case in point was the *autogolpe* that brought Vice President and Minister of War General Maximiliano Hernández Martínez to power in El Salvador in December 1931.[106] Junior officers conspired to overthrow the constitutionally elected government, with the intention of naming Martínez president.[107] This was, of course, a clear violation of the General Treaty, and the State Department asked its recently named minister, Charles Curtis, to inform the officers that it had no intention of recognizing the general. Curtis, who felt that withholding recognition would be a mistake, later admitted to his superiors that he "did not bring it up to the attention of the revolutionary leaders until the success of the revolution was already certain."[108]

This was not what Stimson wanted to hear. A timely opportunity to dissuade the plotters, he believed, had been squandered. This was the not the first time that Curtis and Stimson did not see eye to eye. Just a year before, while serving as ambassador to the Dominican Republic, Curtis's legation had politicked openly to prevent Trujillo from ousting a democratically elected government. Like Somoza in Nicaragua, Trujillo gained a reputation for brutality and corruption as commander of the U.S.-trained National Police. But the dictator enjoyed the backing of his former Marine handlers in the War Department. When Curtis's lieutenant in the embassy, a young John Moors Cabot, tried to persuade Trujillo to step down, the general fired back: "On whose authority do you make such a demand? Do you think that the American government can dictate to another government ... who commands and doesn't command its forces? It's none of your business, nor the United States'."[109]

The difficulties associated with political engineering in Nicaragua left an impression on policymakers in Washington. After a paramilitary group loyal to Trujillo went on a rampage, Curtis requested, to no avail, that warships be sent to the island as a show of force. He warned his superiors

that if the strongman became president, "it seems likely that the Dominican Republic will have to endure a prolonged military dictatorship."[110]

With Trujillo poised to win what proved to be a fraudulent election,
the Department cabled Curtis that while that it agreed with his conclusion "that it was most unfortunate that the head of the Army should use
the position for his own political advancement and as a means of obtaining the presidency," the minister was to refrain from meddling in domestic politics.[111] "You are not authorized to suggest any United States
participation in or even supervision of the elections. The last thing we
want is to get in [a] situation where that would result."[112] Indeed, the Department's response to the embassy's alarming reports left little room for
ambiguity. Curtis was informed that the administration "expects to recognize Trujillo" when he triumphed at the polls and "will maintain the
most friendly relations with him and his government and will desire to
cooperate with him in every proper way."[113] Cabot was beside himself.
Here was a man, he bristled, who had seized power through "gross
treachery," repeatedly walked back promises he made to the legation, and
was "intensely hated by the great majority of the Dominican people."
Under such circumstances, he asked, why would the Department "show
what appears to be marked favor to a thoroughly unpopular, unscrupulous, and perhaps unstable government, or even to bolster it?"[114]

Stimson's answer to Cabot's question was that the United States was
not beholden to the same treaty obligations in the Dominican Republic
as it was with the Central American republics. If a government demonstrated that it could maintain order, if there was "no active resistance" to
it, and if it could pay its debts, it met the secretary of state's criteria for
recognition. Just two months after Trujillo came to power, he confided in
his diary that the general "is panning out to be a very good man."[115]

But such was not the case in El Salvador, where the General Treaty
prevailed—or so it seemed.[116] Complicating matters was that Curtis appears to have played a role in the coup itself. He consulted with junior
officers in order to reach consensus on the composition of a transitional
junta, which governed for three days before turning over the reins of
government to Martínez. Curtis's contravention of the Department's
instructions about recognition of the new regime and his meddling angered Stimson.[117]

In mid-December, the Department replaced the ambassador with a
"special representative" to San Salvador, Jefferson Caffery, who had
earned a reputation as a risk-taking troubleshooter in Colombia. He also

was tapped because he had a greater familiarity with the political landscape than his predecessor, having served as minister to El Salvador from 1926 to 1928. Stimson's faith in Caffery to do what Curtis had not been able to accomplish was evident in his open-ended instructions: "you should be given entire freedom of action to make such recommendations after your arrival in Salvador as you judge advisable, and without having your hands tied in respect to any particular aspect of the situation."[118]

Caffery was far more assertive than Curtis, informing the general that "under no circumstances would we (the United States) recognize him." He also met with the junior officers who had engineered the *golpe* in the hope that fellow officers would pressure Martínez to step down. He informed them that the State Department would be willing to recognize anyone not otherwise precluded by the treaty.[119] Despite assurances from the officers that they intended to replace Martínez, they refused to act. As one scholar wryly put it, "they told Caffery what he wanted to hear, not what they intended to do."[120]

The general dug in, notifying Caffery that El Salvador had never ratified the specific article of the General Treaty pertaining to recognition; that in any case, he had not played any role in the coup; and that as vice president of the deposed government, he was, as the Salvadoran Constitution stipulated, serving out the former president's term.[121] Moreover, the Salvadoran public agreed with the general, Caffery confided to Stimson. He was concerned that if he pushed any harder it could prompt a backlash because of a generalized perception that "we are forcing our will on them."[122]

Perhaps Martínez also surmised that the moment was propitious to hold firm; the U.S. Congress and the public were certainly weary of interventions. He also received assistance from an unlikely source. *Diario Latino*, a liberal Salvadoran paper, although unhappy with how Martínez had seized power, nevertheless called on its readers to take to the streets to show their displeasure with the heavy-handed North American diplomat who was acting, in its words, as an "international policeman." The ensuing demonstrations convinced the Department that Caffery, like his predecessor, could not fulfill his mission. Two weeks after he arrived in San Salvador, he was promptly sent back to his post in Bogotá. Further efforts by the legation to persuade Martínez to leave office were unsuccessful.[123]

The diplomat was under no illusions of what kind of government was in store for El Salvador under Martínez's leadership. Ultimately, Caffery came to the same conclusion that Curtis had reached: the

general enjoyed the backing of the local elite and the army, and that
withholding recognition any longer was counterproductive.[124]

Six weeks after Martínez assumed the presidency, the western highlands were beset by peasant unrest. A catalyst for the walkouts was the
Salvadoran Communist Party's victories at the polls in several municipalities. When the army refused to permit the victors to take office, peasants
seized a half-dozen townships.[125] The regime's response, *La Matanza*
(the massacre), was one of the most heinous atrocities in modern Latin
American history, costing the lives of more than twenty-five thousand
peasants. Whether Farabundo Martí and other members of the Partido
Comunista de El Salvador and its affiliated organizations, the Socorro
Rojo Internacional and the Federación Regional de Trabajadores Salva-
doreños, instigated this uprising or whether it was the result of internal
conflict among peasant communities, it certainly was perceived as communist by the authorities, diplomats, and the local and foreign press.[126]

Martínez seized upon this agitation as a justification for the regime's
two-week reign of terror in the western highlands. The army received
assistance in its pacification of the countryside from civilian vigilantes, or
paramilitaries, in the parlance of the Cold War. The historian James
Dunkerley argues that these so-called brotherhoods should be considered forerunners of El Salvador's odious death squads of the 1970s and
1980s.[127] Within weeks of the massacre, Martínez rounded up suspected
dissidents, including Martí, who was court-martialed and shot.[128]

A number of factors contributed to the regime's excessive response
to the uprising, including the appearance of five U.S., British, and Canadian warships off the coast of El Salvador, sent to put down a revolt believed to be "backed by Moscow." In fact, U.S. military preparations for
an invasion of the country were well advanced. Acting on an urgent request from the U.S. chargé d'affaires in San Salvador, the Navy sent
cruisers and destroyers from Panama, and "arrangements were being
made for the rapid transfer of U.S. marine units in Nicaragua." Just three
days after the rebellion began, the U.S. Navy sent orders to its forces to
"be prepared any time after daylight tomorrow Sunday to send maximum available force of aircraft to Salvador on same mission carrying
such infantry as practicable."[129]

Given that Washington refused to recognize the regime, Martínez
had reason to anticipate a U.S. occupation. To his way of thinking, the
complete pacification of the countryside by his military was imperative.
Only after the massacre, when he was able to provide assurance to

foreign diplomats that the rebellion had been crushed, did the U.S. Navy stand down.[130]

After the decisive defeat of the insurgency, it was even more difficult for U.S. diplomats to dislodge the dictator. The State Department considered closing its legation but thought better of it, realizing that if it did so and Martínez refused to step down, the only option remaining was military intervention, something that not only would have been inconsistent with Hoover's pronouncements but probably would have precipitated both foreign backlash and domestic criticism.[131]

There is little question that if not for the General Treaty, recognition would not have been an issue for the secretary. He certainly felt differently about Martínez after La Matanza. By the summer of 1932, Stimson had accepted the inevitable, although formal recognition took some diplomatic maneuvering and time. Caffery's replacement never investigated the massacre and the administration never condemned it.[132] In his diary, Stimson later praised the general, calling him "a pillar against the success of what seems to be a nasty proletarian revolution."[133]

When it became clear that Washington had no intention of removing Martínez from power, Central American governments, pleased that the general had eliminated a nascent workers' movement that threatened to spill over and stir up unrest in their own nations, quietly recognized his government. For a time, the Guatemalan dictator Jorge Ubico remained the lone holdout. It took diplomatic arm twisting from the State Department to convince him to change his mind.[134]

When the General Treaty came up for renewal in 1934, all of the principals convened a conference in the Guatemalan capital, which concluded that this noble experiment in diplomatic engineering had been an abject failure. The Roosevelt administration formally recognized the Martínez regime, and he remained in power until 1944. For much of the next five decades El Salvador would be governed by repressive military governments.

Conclusions

In 1930, seven governments in the region came to power in undemocratic fashion. When facing the decision of whether to recognize the new regimes, the Hoover administration returned to the longstanding policy, dating back to Jefferson, of recognizing de facto changes in power, no matter how that government assumed power.

This was an auspicious moment for such a dramatic policy pivot. Unlike in the past, where the existence of a countervailing threat from European and Asian powers influenced North American policy responses in the region, the onset of the Great Depression now meant that the United States' traditional competitors were far less likely to risk involvement and expend precious resources far from home.[135]

Central Americans, no matter their political inclinations, had quite enough of Washington's inconsistency simply because it begat what many considered needless meddling. To be sure, Latin American critics of the United States wanted it both ways. They were upset when Washington interfered in the internal affairs of a particular nation when the result was a regime inimical to their interests. But they also were angry when the U.S. either selectively recognized coups or, in the case of El Salvador, stood idly by while a general overthrew a democratically elected government and committed a despicable atrocity, and then recognized his regime.

The U.S. decision to recognize de facto regimes in Central America no matter how they came to power, and the corollary of refraining from meddling in domestic matters, had lasting repercussions. The reason for the change in policy was understandable. Years of efforts to inculcate best practices in the region had proven an unqualified disaster.

Dictators in the isthmus were quick to make the most of the new policy. Martínez, Somoza, Ubico, and Carías moved expeditiously to alter constitutions and rig elections, ensuring that each remained firmly ensconced in power for years to come. A fitting epitaph to Washington's hands-off policy would be written by the Nicaraguan National Guard commander. In the span of twenty-nine months between February 1934 and June 1936, Somoza had Sandino murdered (violating his own promise of safe conduct to the rebel), ousted the democratically elected president, Sacasa, and staged fraudulent elections that put him in power. Several years later, FDR rewarded Somoza with an official state visit and a parade down Pennsylvania Avenue.

In an April 1936 memo to his diplomatic missions in Central America, Hull emphasized that the new policy of "noninterference" was in line with the administration's Good Neighbor Policy. Moving forward, foreign service officers were to refrain from "offering advice on any domestic question, and, if requested to give such advice, they should decline to do so." His ambassador to El Salvador, Frank Corrigan, aptly labeled the change a "sin of omission" and predicted it would give strongmen fewer incentives to observe constitutional niceties. Or as Haya put it, Roosevelt was now "the good neighbor of tyrants."[136]

"Now, in this case, we recognize the government but we don't see the machine gun," March 16, 1957. A 1957 Herblock Cartoon, © The Herb Block Foundation, and Library of Congress, Prints & Photographs Division, LC-DIG-hlb-04324.

As historian Max Friedman noted, a paradox underlay Washington's determination to lend support to dictators. Owing to their acceptance of "the racial hierarchy of peoples," policymakers were convinced that "strongmen were the appropriate governors for immature Latins." The region's democrats, on the other hand, were viewed a priori as anti-American, weak, and unreliable. That thinking did not change appreciably until the Cuban Revolution forced a reconsideration in policy.[137]

Despite frequent setbacks, reformers gradually came to the realization that policymakers in Washington were, in fact, susceptible to reproach, especially when their hard-hitting broadsides illustrated the gulf between U.S. rhetoric and actions. Moderates concluded that it was in their enlightened self-interest to invest their energies in attempting to win over public opinion in the U.S. in the hope that a chastened executive branch might gradually distance itself from the forces of reaction and align itself with agents of democratic reform. The best way to do this, they reasoned, was to establish alliances with progressives in the U.S. Congress, the labor movement, the press, women's organizations, and academia, who, it was hoped, would then collectively pressure the administration to alter U.S. policy.

The recognition conundrum raised broader questions about U.S.–Latin American relations that continued to bedevil administrations in future decades. Given that the United States' military might and economic clout were so great, whatever policymakers elected to do or not do, the decision was sure to be parsed, debated, and felt in the region. Years later, the journalist Herbert Matthews posed a number of salient questions about interventionism's slippery slope: "In a practical sense we were always going to intervene, The questions ... therefore became: What was deliberate and what unavoidable intervention? What was acceptable and what unacceptable? When were trade and fiscal policies a means of intervention? When did the sale of arms keep a government in power against the will of the people? Was recognition—or non-recognition—of new governments being used as an instrument of policy?"[138]

When he wrote these words in 1959, Matthews had in mind not just the New World but his experience as a correspondent for the *New York Times* during the defining moment of his distinguished career, the Spanish Civil War. He was convinced that the United States' insistence on neutrality during that fratricidal conflict, the failure of the Roosevelt administration to assist the Republic against the forces of fascism, was a grievous and morally indefensible error. By not standing up for what was right in Spain, another war with far greater casualties had to be fought. To Matthews, if the United States abdicated its responsibility with respect to Latin America, by turning the other cheek when strongmen ousted civilian governments, by showering military and economic aid on despots, by going it alone and neglecting to collaborate with other governments in the region in a principled, purposeful way, and by repeatedly invoking the mantra of nonintervention and refusing to draw a bright line between authoritarianism and democratic rule, it risked making the very same mistake it made in Spain.[139]

CHAPTER SEVEN

Tony Guiteras

The most empathetic figure . . . the most indomitable will, the most energetic arm and the purest spirit of the national revolutionary movement was lost.

—RAÚL ROA, referring to Antonio Guiteras's death

Batistas have to be bribed. Sandinos have to be machine-gunned.

—CARLOS RAFAEL RODRÍGUEZ

ANTONIO "TONY" GUITERAS BECAME an outspoken opponent of Machado after Mella's assassination. His rebelliousness was inherited. An uncle fought and was later executed during the unsuccessful first struggle for Cuban independence, the Ten Years' War (1868–1878), while his father fought in the 1895 War for Independence. His maternal uncle languished in British prisons for espousing the cause of Irish independence, and his mother, who was a formative influence, was never shy about voicing her anticolonial and anti-imperialist beliefs.

Growing up in Pinar del Río in western Cuba, Tony participated in student demonstrations during his high school years and later joined the university reform movement at the University of Havana in the mid-1920s.[1] Unlike many students who became part of an urban underground,

Guiteras took the fight to the countryside. His graduate degree in pharmacy not only proved helpful in the making of explosives, it provided employment as a sales representative for pharmaceutical companies in eastern Cuba. The mobility the job afforded him made it possible for Tony almost singlehandedly to fashion a multiclass movement against the dictator in the early 1930s. Employing hit-and-run tactics, Guiteras and his followers burned cane fields, robbed banks, and broke into armories. After he led an attack on a barracks in Oriente Province in 1931, he fled to the foothills of the Sierra Maestra. He and his small band held off soldiers for weeks before he was eventually captured, imprisoned, and tried and sentenced to eight years in prison. Thanks to a general amnesty four months later, he was released. Twenty years later, Fidel Castro burst into national prominence, replicating Guiteras's strategy and tactics to a tee in eastern Cuba. He, too, would be captured, imprisoned, and amnestied as a result of his failed attack on the Moncada Barracks in July 1953.[2]

It is not surprising that Guiteras felt nothing but contempt for Welles's mediation.[3] After Machado's ouster, the twenty-seven-year-old became the most influential cabinet member of a junta that, for one hundred days between September and January of 1933–34, sought to bring about meaningful change to the island.

What set Guiteras apart from many of his youthful contemporaries was his scorched-earth brand of politics. His call for an autonomous, egalitarian revolution free of external influence, whether from Washington or Moscow, earned him the admiration of many. At the same time, his dogged unwillingness to compromise unnerved and discomfited elements of the left, the center and the right, and ultimately contributed to his death in May 1935.

Guiteras also exhibited an internationalist worldview, forging linkages with anti-imperialist organizations throughout the greater Caribbean.[4] One of his biographers noted that the young man was especially taken with Sandino's struggle. His internationalism was not just rhetorical; when Guiteras was in a position of influence, he aided Dominican exiles in their efforts to overthrow Trujillo. He came to believe that armed struggle was the only way to remove tyrants.[5]

Like Martí before him, Guiteras left a legacy that both reformers and revolutionaries later appropriated. To better understand his meteoric rise and fall, we need first to understand the political vacuum Guiteras and the DEU sought to fill after Machado fled the island in mid-August 1933.

The Proconsul and the Junta

After Machado's ouster, Welles offered the provisional presidency to a grizzled holdover from Crowder's "honest" cabinet, someone he was quite familiar with, the former ambassador to the United States, Carlos Manuel de Céspedes y Quesada. As early as 1921, Welles told Crowder that de Céspedes would be an excellent candidate for the presidency because of his "amenability to suggestions or advice which might be made to him by the American Legation."[6] With the benefit of hindsight, a future ambassador to Cuba, Spruille Braden, however, remarked that this aristocratic son of one of Cuba's liberators was the wrong man for the job. Educated abroad, much of Céspedes's career up to that point had been in the foreign service. "He had a beautiful house in Paris, entertained lavishly, was a boulevardier and a gourmet, and knew no more of his native land and how to cope with its politicians (and they took coping) than any European. But Sumner liked him."[7]

Welles predicted that the majority of Cubans would welcome de Céspedes with open arms. He was in for a rude awakening. First, the DEU took exception, reminding the public that de Céspedes had served as foreign minister in Machado's first cabinet. Others carped when the provisional president included in his cabinet prominent members of the ABC, and the Conservative and (Machado's) Liberal Parties.[8]

On August 22, the DEU issued a manifesto, calling for a new provisional government committed to reform, the purging from the government of "all political groups and forces that had helped Machado's tyranny," university autonomy, women's suffrage, a new constitution unmoored from U.S. influence, and sweeping political, social, and economic reforms. What resonated with many Cubans was the students' demand to purge the army's high command, a number of whom had blood on their hands from the darkest days of the Machadato.[9]

Since the dictator's legislature and the military remained in place, Machado's ouster, as one historian noted, "resembled more of a palace coup than revolutionary change."[10] As a result, Cubans took matters into their own hands. Anyone associated with the dictatorship became a target of retribution. Fearful for their lives, congressmen dared not meet in session, and provincial authorities went into hiding.[11] The ABC, Beals reported, was "the leading undertaker at the funeral ... meting out summary death to hated Machadistas." But to survive in the new political landscape the organization was "obliged to widen its membership overnight to include anyone and everyone who would affiliate. Machado elements, scurrying for cover, flocked" to Cuba's version of the brown shirts, as did former members of the *porra*.[12]

Welles believed that the students were an especially disruptive force in the political arena. He hoped the ABC's presence in the new government would serve as a counterweight to the "utterly lawless student groups" that constituted "the most pernicious element in Cuban public life." At first glance, Welles's preference for the ABC seems puzzling. Both groups were committed to the violent overthrow of Machado, and, as noted, there was considerable overlap between the two organizations. But Welles had greater familiarity with the ABC, owing to its participation in the mediation and the provisional government. Moreover, he perceived the students to be more leftist in orientation, and their stridently anti-imperialist rhetoric appeared to confirm this. The Student Directorate, he told Hull, was provocatively obstructionist, "constantly issuing inflammatory proclamations and making speeches of the same character on the radio."[13]

De Céspedes's chief problem was the public's perception of him. At a moment when Cubans felt emboldened by their participation in the overthrow of a despot who, up until his last months in power, enjoyed Washington's favor, de Céspedes never emerged from Welles's shadow. The proconsul handpicked several members of the cabinet and "weighed in on decisions big and small." Many Cubans understood the difference between Washington's meddling in local politics, which they deplored, and anti-Americanism. Most realized that North American influence was too pervasive to reject outright. Yet it was the denial of sovereignty that rankled even those most closely connected to U.S. investors.[14]

Welles's choice barely lasted three weeks in power before he was ousted by a clique of young noncommissioned officers on September 4, who, hearing rumors of budget cuts, demanded that their pay and positions be protected.[15] Among those spearheading the Sergeants' Revolt was the young stenographer-sergeant Fulgencio Batista y Zaldívar, who hastily promoted himself to colonel and soon after to chief of staff. But as Pérez makes clear, it was the DEU, which rushed to Camp Columbia, the largest military base on the island, to ally itself with the rebels and which insisted that the junior officers adopt its political platform, that "invested the sergeants' mutiny with a political dimension transcending the limited objectives inherent initially in the protest." Students and professors legitimated the "sergeants' sedition ... converting an act of insubordination into the midwife of the new government."[16] In return, the non-commissioned officers pledged their support for the DEU's August manifesto.

Why did the Student Directorate, which had been harshly critical of the military's complicity with the dictatorship, reverse course and support the mutiny? In a statement issued soon after September 4, it justified its actions. "The Directorio is against . . . the inanimate government named by the U.S. Ambassador. . . . With this chaotic state in the country, without principle of authority and with many Machado-stained men still in the armed forces, the Directorio decided to launch its revolutionary action, with the relatively untarnished section of the armed forces."[17]

The Sergeants' Revolt paved the way for the creation of a reformist government, led by Dr. Ramón Grau San Martín, a professor of physiology who had gained national attention by opposing Machado's decision to extend his term in office.[18] Subsequently, Grau had been imprisoned for protesting the arrests of student dissidents. Upon his release from prison, he fled the country, settling in Miami, where he worked with other exiles until he returned to the island after Machado fled.

Acting on its own authority, the Directorio appointed Grau to lead a provisional "revolutionary" government. No longer mobilizing in the streets to demand change, Cuba's student leadership was now, if not "the," then "a" determinant of political power in the provisional government.[19] Heralding a "Cuba for Cubans," Grau's reformist agenda emphasized economic nationalism, social justice, and an end to corruption. Welles straightaway conveyed his displeasure with the new leadership to Hull. In a telephone call just one day after the uprising. He informed the secretary that the new government "is composed of the most extreme radicals in Cuba." He requested that two warships be sent to Havana and one to Santiago. The proconsul was especially wary of how much influence student and former student radicals like Guiteras had over the president of the junta. He informed Grau that the political opposition believed that the present government was illegitimate precisely because it "had been selected by the students and that the members of his Cabinet were subservient to (their) every whim."[20] Scarcely two weeks after the government had been formed, Welles predicted that Batista would "either seek an understanding with the political parties to oust Grau or, failing that, seek to install himself in control of the government." If that were the case, he mused in a telegram to Hull, "the student groups will be definitely eliminated by the army and that in this manner this disturbing element will be removed from the scene."[21]

His pejorative portrayal of the Directorate's influence was either an exaggeration or a serious misjudgment of the junta's aims. Other North American diplomats felt that Welles was taken in by quarrelsome Cuban elites. In a cable to Hull, Ambassador to Mexico Josephus Daniels, a confidant of Roosevelt, countered Welles's alarmist rhetoric. Suggesting that "the rich and powerful in Cuba, and their allies in the United States" were behind such overstated claims, he urged restraint and advised that if and when the U.S. acted, it should do so collaboratively with other Latin American states to bring about a peaceful solution to the crisis.[22]

Welles countered that restraint would be construed as weakness. He told Roosevelt that the "psychology of the peoples of the Caribbean Republics" had to be given due consideration. "The impression is fast growing that our attitude is due to fear of public opinion of Latin America. . . . Respect for us is diminishing and the belief is rising, sedulously fostered by the radicals, that the United States can be flouted with complete impunity."[23] He asked for "a strictly limited intervention," including "the landing of a considerable force at Habana and lesser forces in certain of the most important ports of the Republic." His request for such a military presence was rationalized as "policing power" and "would most decidedly be construed as well within the limits of a policy of the 'good neighbor.' "[24]

The Mexican chargé d'affaires, Luis Padilla Nervo, told Acting Secretary of State Caffery that students elsewhere in Latin America, inspired and in solidarity with their Cuban peers, were staging protests against their own governments' support for "American intervention" in Cuba. Padilla Nervo was concerned that Welles's meddling was undermining the goodwill engendered by the new policy, and he urged the United States to recognize Grau's government. Padilla Nervo concluded that "it is almost miraculous how President Roosevelt has been able to change Latin American feeling towards the United States in a few months. We do not want to see that good feeling fade away."[25]

After consulting several Latin American governments, Hull turned down the proconsul's request to land troops on the island because it "would be regarded by the whole world, and especially throughout Latin America, as a creation and creature of the American Government" and "would have disastrous effects.[26] He surely had his upcoming trip to Montevideo for the VII Inter-American Conference that December on his mind, where the controversial nonintervention pledge tabled in Havana five years earlier was sure to be reintroduced. Waiting until Hull was on his way to Uruguay, Welles then went over the secretary's head and asked Roosevelt to send warships and to authorize the landing of troops.[27] The president agreed to the former, sending twenty-nine warships to ring the island, but stopped short of authorizing the landing of troops.[28] Roosevelt told diplomats that the ships were sent to Cuba to ensure the orderly evacuation of U.S. citizens in case of hostilities, but, given the United States' history of intervention in Cuban affairs, the presence of that many ships was read quite differently on the island.[29]

The arrival of the fleet, ostensibly to protect the 5,500 North Americans living on the island, appeared to many as a prelude to a military intervention.[30] According to Beals, the ships' presence precipitated a "frenzy of hatred for the United States. In the dead of night, the side of one cruiser was daubed with huge letters, 'Down with American Imperialism!'"[31] Grau counseled restraint: "It's true that North American warships surround the island," he declared, "but Roosevelt will not inaugurate his Good Neighbor policy on the eve of the Pan American Conference in Montevideo by militarily occupying Cuba."[32]

While Welles and Hull debated how best to respond to the provisional government, Guiteras accepted the invitation of his former professor to join his cabinet. Before beginning work for the new administration, however, Tony undertook a triumphal procession of sorts from his base in the eastern end of the island to the capital, attracting huge crowds and delivering fiery speeches at each stop along the way. In Holguín, for example, five thousand came out to hear him speak.[33] (Fidel would mimic Guiteras's trek when, in early January 1959 after Batista had fled the island, he and his followers were fêted by enthusiastic crowds as they gradually made their way from the Sierra Maestra to Havana.)

Tony Guiteras held three portfolios in the cabinet: Interior, War and the Navy, and Public Works. His supporters, including Beals, thought him "utterly fearless" and "incorruptibly honest," someone "who was utterly indifferent to his personal fate."[34] Critics, however, labeled him an *enfant terrible* because he went out of his way to alienate elements of the armed forces, the police, the communists, foreign companies, and the proconsul. *Time* magazine declared Guiteras "the most anti-American and the most anti-imperialist of all of the Cuban leaders."[35]

Depictions of Guiteras while a member of Grau's cabinet paint him as a whirling dervish. Sporting reddish-brown hair and freckles inherited from the Irish side of his family—an unusual look by Cuban standards—the hard-driving Guiteras worked all hours, rarely eating and only occasionally sleeping, and when he did, nodding off on a couch in his office. With little concern for the trappings of power, the chain-smoking, *cafecito*-drinking, disheveled young bureaucrat reportedly wore only white or gray suits, only adding to the mystique of an unconventional politician. In her diary, Hart Phillips joked that Guiteras was a man of few words, a "decidedly . . . unCuban characteristic."[36]

As a confirmed economic nationalist, perhaps Guiteras's most significant initiative was the enactment of a sweeping national agrarian reform law. Under the law's provisions, the government would distribute all untitled lands to the rural poor—estimated at 600,000 acres—and purchase an additional 250,000 acres from the private sector for the same purpose. Significantly, the decree guaranteed that cane farmers would not be evicted from lands under cultivation, even if (as many did) they rented lands from North American sugar companies. A new agricultural bank would be created to manage the reform. Expectations were raised among the rural poor, even as U.S. sugar companies and conservatives denounced the decree out of hand.

His ministry also enacted a comprehensive labor reform that guaranteed cane cutters a minimum wage, an eight-hour workday, a six-day workweek, and workmen's compensation. The new labor code also outlawed child labor, eliminated payment in scrip, and gave a newly created Labor Ministry the authority to arbitrate strikes. In addition, a Nationalization of Labor Decree mandated that henceforth 50 percent of all employees had to be Cuban in the manufacturing, mercantile, and agricultural sectors; that half of all salaries in those enterprises be earmarked for nationals; and that foreign agricultural workers be repatriated. At a time when un- and underemployment were high and nativism was on the rise, the Nationalization of Labor Decree enjoyed widespread popular support.[37] In addition, he mediated disputes between telephone and railway workers and their employers, and when U.S.-owned utilities and sugar mills dug in their heels, he nationalized their properties. At Guiteras's behest, the provisional government also outlawed political parties that had collaborated with the dictator, seizing Machado's holdings and those of his cronies, and it set up special tribunals to try those in the past administration accused of corruption.[38]

The new government also announced the termination of the despised Platt Amendment—though the U.S. did not recognize its repeal—and it enacted a bevy of additional reforms, including women's suffrage, the reduction of postage and electric rates, the legalization of trade

President Ramón Grau San Martín's cabinet; Tony Guiteras, back row, second from right; and Grau, first row, middle, 9/13/33. Courtesy of New York Times, Redux Pictures, and the Cuban Heritage Collection, University of Miami Libraries, Coral Gables, Florida.

unions, the creation of a social security system, and university autonomy. While passage of the new laws heightened expectations, implementation moved more slowly, frustrating rural and urban workers alike.[39]

From the outset, Guiteras understood that he could not take on Batista alone. To counter the chief of staff's base of support in the army, he courted leftist unions, the DEU, and an ABC splinter group called the Radicals. What especially alarmed Batista, however, was Guiteras's repeated efforts to enlist allies among progressive officers in the navy and the police and his decision to establish a marine corps that would be loyal to him, not to Batista.[40]

Guiteras's outsized role in Grau's cabinet was emblematic of current and former student participation in the new government. So pervasive was Student Directorate involvement that one journalist mockingly called it "a student oligarchy."[41] It was not only operating outside the confines of the university—the University of Havana had not reopened since Machado closed its doors in the late 1920s—for the first time the student leadership had a voice in the making of policy.

But the Directorio was as discordant and divided as the rest of society. Some members were more conciliatory to Washington and Batista than others, and Welles set to work playing one off against the other.[42] The proconsul warned Hull that if not nipped in the bud, the students' anti-imperialist rhetoric would undercut Washington's legitimacy.[43] After all, significant economic interests were at stake, he declared. "Our own commercial and export interests in Cuba cannot be revived under this government."[44]

Despite Welles's desire to paint the leadership with a broad brush, some student leaders turned on Grau almost as quickly as he did. The more radical among them were especially upset with Grau's pandering to Washington and the slow pace of reform. Roa's criticisms of Grau's administration recalled Mella's of Haya; the physician-turned-politician was just another two-faced political hack who tried to please all sides: "The apolitical, technocratic and academic government did not know where to begin, nor what to do, nor where to go. Bewildered, it twisted and turned. . . . He [Grau] graciously flirted with the left and winked conspicuously at the intimidated bourgeoisie. He uttered affronts to Welles and paid the foreign debt. He was anxious to be recognized by Washington and permitted anti-imperialist meetings. He launched a violent manifesto against business and corporations and secretly sent emissaries to seek their support."[45]

Roa unfairly derided the Student Directorate as collaborators "but never leaders," who neglected to represent the interests of their constituents, the student body. While most students called for reforms of the university—reopening the university, free tuition for those in need, curriculum revision—he belittled the leadership for letting their lofty position in Grau's provisional government go to their heads.[46]

The PCC, which had been excluded from participating in the Sergeants' Revolt, did all that it could to undermine the junta's legitimacy. Party militants actively promoted unrest in the countryside and in the streets of the capital as sugar workers took over mills and unions staged demonstrations and went out on strike. The provocations incited fears of a leftist revolution among conservatives, the middle class, the State Department, North American companies, and the military.[47]

Then on September 29, a massive demonstration took place in the capital to memorialize the return of Mella's remains from Mexico. The exhumation, cremation, and transfer of his ashes from a gravesite in Mexico to the island had been a complex affair, undertaken by a Pro-Mella United Front Committee in consultation with Mexican authorities. Writing for *Bohemia* twelve days before Mella's ashes arrived in Havana harbor, an emotive Roa was struck by the irony of the avowed anti-imperialist's remains returning to the *patria* at a time when U.S. warships ringed the island "threatening to spew desolation and death."[48]

Ten thousand turned out for a silent march from Havana's city center to Fraternity Park, where there was to be a provisional internment of the martyr's ashes until a more permanent site could be found. A temporary funeral mound adorned with flowers and an obelisk commemorating Mella were constructed for the occasion by the city's public works employees. Such a ceremony, however, was in violation of a municipal regulation that mandated that burials take place in cemeteries. At the last minute the government rescinded the permit for the demonstration, but the organizers, defying the authorities, went ahead with the memorial. The result was a violent confrontation between authorities and demonstrators that left six dead and twenty-seven wounded.[49] Soldiers destroyed the obelisk and then raided the offices of one of the country's largest leftist labor unions.[50]

The attack on the PCC's staging of the ceremony was not an isolated instance. To reassure Washington and U.S. sugar interests on the island, Grau's provisional government called on the army to repress the left. Even the DEU's *Alma Mater* issued a statement that the left be reined in and that unrest in the countryside brought to an end.[51] Guiteras took another tack, pleading with the rank and file of communist-affiliated labor unions not to go out on strike and to give this administration a chance to satisfy their demands. He warned that "the [communist] National Confederation of Labor will be responsible before history for the setback that the masses will suffer if we give the Americans a pretext to intervene."[52]

Even though the Directorate made its opposition to the communists clear, Welles continued to lump it together with the PCC. So long as radical elements held sway over the junta, the administration must withhold recognition. He explained his reasoning to Hull: "The [State] Department will understand that Grau San Martín is entirely under their [the DEU's] orders and whatever decision they reached he will be forced to abide to. ... The general impression I gained [of the student leadership] was one of complete immaturity, a failure to grasp even in a rudimentary sense the grave dangers which the republic confronts and a feeling of almost impermeable self-satisfaction."[53]

This marked the first time since 1898 that a government had come to power in Cuba without Washington's consent.[54] As we have seen, the Hoover administration overlooked a massacre of peasants in El Salvador and recognized Martínez. Yet immediately after Grau's inauguration, Welles imposed four preconditions before granting recognition: the junta must demonstrate a capability to govern; order must be maintained; popular support exhibited; and the government must comply with its obligations (that is, repayment of debts accrued by Machado's government). Such a litmus test broke new ground. Yet the absence of recognition surely made meeting the demands that much more difficult. According to journalist Charles Thomson: "without recognition, it [the junta] could not fulfill the conditions of recognition. The hostility of Washington encouraged the opposition elements, thus demonstrating its inability to maintain order and consolidate its political position."[55] Welles was certainly cognizant of the implications of his recommendation. In a cable he wrote Hull, "no government here can survive for a protracted period without recognition by the United States."[56] Indeed, the delay was interpreted by opponents of the junta as an open invitation to conspire.

The State Department went further, privately pressuring other Latin American governments to withhold recognition. Only five nations bucked Washington and recognized Grau's government. Incensed, Grau told a reporter from the *New York Times* that Washington's refusal to recognize his government was a new species of meddling: "non-recognition in our case signals a new type of intervention—intervention by inertia, if nothing else in our internal affairs."[57]

The proconsul also "consorted with enemies of that [Grau's]s government ... [and] sought to encourage further military treachery by encouraging Army elements within the Grau government to bring about its destruction."[58] He then explained the political facts of life to a reticent Batista: In a "protracted and very frank discussion" Welles coached up the inexperienced chief of staff, assuring him that he was the "only individual in Cuba today who represented authority" and that U.S. companies needed protection. The principal obstacle "was the unpatriotic and futile obstinacy of small groups of young men who should be studying in

The "only individual in Cuba today who represents authority": Col. Fulgencio Batista and Sumner Welles, Washington, DC, November 10, 1938. Library of Congress, Prints & Photographs Division, photograph by Harris & Ewing, LC-H22-D-4913.

the university instead of playing politics and of a few individuals who had joined with them for selfish motives."[59] He viewed the relationship between the chief of staff and the students as a zero-sum game. As "Batista becomes more influential," he wrote the Department, "the power of the students and Grau San Martín diminishes."[60]

With Welles's encouragement, Batista conspired to oust the junta. Rather than take power himself, he approached Carlos Mendieta, the head of one of the mainstream political parties, to explore his willingness to assume power should the army remove Grau. Interestingly, Mendieta insisted first on approaching the Directorate to get its support. When student leaders rebuffed him, he begged off, convinced that without the DEU's backing there would a recrudescence of bombings and unrest. When Welles pressed Mendieta to explain his reluctance to participate in the conspiracy, his response was revealing: "several students might be killed and the government would then have to confront the concerted antagonism of all of the student body because of the death of these 'martyrs.' "[61]

When the student leadership brought Batista's treasonous plotting to Grau's attention in early November, Guiteras and the DEU demanded that he be arrested and stripped of his position. Grau refused, instead choosing to confront his chief of staff and demand an apology. Why Grau did not cashier Batista has been the subject of much debate. His supporters contended that the provisional president believed that Batista was a known commodity and whoever replaced him as head of the army would probably have been worse. Others argued that by backing the chief of staff, he was asserting his independence from the Directorate in the hope of mending his relationship with Washington.[62]

Furious with what it viewed as Grau's capitulation to Batista and Washington, the student leadership, at a very contentious meeting, concluded that it would not in good faith continue to support the junta. Surprisingly, the Directorate decided to dissolve itself, issuing a perplexing statement that the "duty of the students is to return to the University." The Directorate, however, left it up to individual student leaders to determine if they wanted to continue working for Grau's government.[63]

In retrospect, the actions of the inexperienced student leadership during the fall of 1933 appear confounding. Initially, it boldly participated in a military coup that deposed a government that enjoyed Washington's blessing. It then named Grau president of the junta and played a major role in shaping the new government's sweeping agenda. Finally, it demanded that Grau stand up to Batista (and Welles). After all these proactive steps, at a moment of crisis, the DEU walked out on the junta, abdicating its role in national politics and, at the same time, undermining the legitimacy of a government that it had helped establish and a leader it had backed in the face of repeated calls for his removal. While key members of the Directorate remained in the government, in the eyes of one key principal, "it was probably, in all the history of the DEU, its most grave error."[64]

In December, the junta's delegates to the Seventh Inter-American Conference in Montevideo denounced the Platt Amendment. The head of its delegation, Dr. Angel Giraudy, mocked the Good Neighbor Policy: "If Ambassador Welles' propagating the revolution . . . is not intervention, if surrounding the island with warships is not intervention—then the United States has never intervened in Cuba."[65] The delegation also supported passage of a resolution opposing intervention by one state in the affairs of another. Given that many in Cuba felt that Washington was determined to remove Grau at any moment, the resolution took on greater significance than if it had been an abstract statement of principle.

Heading the U.S. delegation to Montevideo, Hull, like his predecessors, was stung by the vehemence of the criticism leveled against the U.S. Since the administration was championing its Good Neighbor Policy, he felt that he had no choice but to back the nonintervention resolution. With the United States no longer standing in the way, the resolution that had engendered so much controversy in Santiago and Havana now passed without a whimper.[66] Even so, the U.S. continued to view Cuba and Puerto Rico as special cases in comparison to the rest of the hemisphere. In Cuba's case, the Platt Amendment, policymakers argued, gave it oversight over the island's affairs.

Shouldn't We Wait at Least a Week?

Hull concluded that Welles had outstayed his welcome. Welles was recalled that December, much to the satisfaction of the students. In their eyes, the diplomat personified all that was wrong with the U.S.-Cuban relationship. The marching orders given to his replacement, Caffery, did not change one iota, however. In his unpublished memoir, Caffery vividly recounted Roosevelt's terse admonition before he left for Havana in late December 1933: "get rid of Grau," but "remember, no Marines."[67] Such were the parameters of the Good Neighbor Policy in Cuba.

Upon arrival in Havana the envoy quashed any hopes that Welles's departure might signal a change of direction in the administration's policy.[68] His welcome to the island was tumultuous, punctuated by "the resounding boom of at least a hundred bombs ... heard every night, as well as the sound of street and housetop fighting" and an "organized parade" of twenty-five thousand in front of the embassy "meant to impress me."[69]

His fastidious persona was more reserved than that of his pompous predecessor, but the goal remained the same—persuade Batista to remove Grau from power.[70] One Cuban observer thought the pragmatic Caffery had "fewer Machiavellian fumes in his head" than Welles, but "more practical feelings for 'business.' "[71] Not all accounts were so kind. One critic characterized the Louisianan aristocrat as "a somewhat frostbitten diplomat of the old school, [who] holds to the Hamiltonian belief that those who have should rule."[72]

"Get rid of Grau . . . remember, no Marines": Ambassador
to Cuba Jefferson Caffery. Courtesy of Philip F. Dur
Papers, Coll. 288, Box 8, Folder 13, Edith Garland Dupré
Library, University of Louisiana at Lafayette.

The tall, slender, soft-spoken Caffery and Batista hit it off surprisingly well. An unlikely pair, given their respective backgrounds, they realized that they shared common passions, such as horseback riding and cockfights. Caffery took his massive bloodhound Miguelito on their rides through the countryside. Batista, he appraised, had a "keen native intelligence, and a keen desire to learn." Following in Crowder's and Welles's footsteps, he was only too happy to serve as Batista's mentor.[73]

Caffery's instant assessment was that the provisional government could only count on the backing of the military and the "ignorant masses," who had been "misled by [Grau's] utopian promises."[74] His prodding of Batista paid dividends. The chief of staff confronted Grau, stating the obvious—that the U.S. would never recognize his government—and asked him to step down.

When opposition groups refused to support his call for elections, Grau realized that his position was no longer tenable. He reluctantly agreed to resign in mid-January 1934. Grau later contended that what had sealed his fate was "the handiwork of Mr. Caffery."[75]

Managing the transition proved complicated. Batista's and Caffery's preference to succeed Grau was Mendieta, but Guiteras and his allies in the navy balked. Their choice was Carlos Hevia, Grau's minister of agriculture, who initially prevailed. But the special envoy felt it essential that the more conservative Mendieta fill the vacuum left by Grau's departure. "The situation is very serious," Caffery wrote the Department. If Mendieta cannot be persuaded, "Batista might turn towards the left," which would be a serious blow "to our interests here."[76] The envoy may have been exaggerating about the likelihood of the chief of staff tilting leftward, but the potential for unrest was apparent. Guiteras denounced both Caffery and Batista and called for a strike of U.S.-owned utility companies. But Batista won over recalcitrant elements in the navy and the strike never materialized. After only thirty-nine hours in office, Hevia was forced out.[77]

Well aware of the consequences of Washington's refusal to recognize the provisional government, Mendieta made his acceptance conditional on an assurance that recognition would be forthcoming. But when Caffery requested "immediate authorization to recognize" Mendieta's government, Acting Secretary of State William Phillips, wary of the precedent that such a pledge might set, demurred.[78] Mendieta reconsidered and accepted the presidency without an explicit assurance.

Caffery was ecstatic. On a stopover in Havana on his way back to the States, Gruening laughed when the ambassador asked whether he thought the U.S. should recognize the colonel as soon as possible. Gruening's reply was priceless: "Wouldn't it look pretty crude if we gave Mendieta instant approval when we had denied it to Grau San Martín for months? Shouldn't we wait at least a week and be apparently going through the motions of determining his qualifications?"[79]

Five days was apparently sufficient. Caffery accomplished what he was unable to do in El Salvador, the removal of a recalcitrant head of state. The relief was palpable in Washington. The administration recalled ten of the sixteen warships.[80]

That spring and summer the administration announced a series of measures designed to prop up the new government. First it abrogated the despised Platt Amendment, and then the U.S. Congress passed the Jones-Costigan Act. The latter, which had been in the works for more than a year, revised the Reciprocity Treaty, guaranteeing the island a regular portion of the U.S. sugar market. The administration also agreed to provide substantial funding for Mendieta's government, including an emergency two-million-dollar credit to purchase food from the U.S. Surplus Relief Corporation, a measure that had the added benefit of providing relief for struggling North American farmers hard hit by the Depression. Then the Export-Import Bank provided a 4.4-million-dollar loan, the first installment on 14 million dollars in loans to Cuba over the course of the next two years. All of these initiatives, Cuban critics claimed, never would have come to pass as long as Grau governed.[81] Grau did not dispute that assertion. In August 1935, he told reporters in Panama that the Platt Amendment may have been repealed, but it lived on "in the presence of Caffery."[82]

Despite the chaos and upheaval, Grau retained his popularity. A British diplomat, who was at the pier when he left for Mexico, painted a picture of a "head-in-the-clouds" politician, who, by charting an ambitious agenda and raising expectations, had energized many of his followers: "A crowd of his adherents gathered at the wharf and, as the vessel steamed down the harbor, they ran along the sides. They belonged to the poorer classes and were very enthusiastic. They regarded the impractical, consumptive doctor as their champion . . . he made reforms, some of which will last. Students of Cuban history will remember his term because a great change came over Cuba."[83]

Guiteras penned a no-holds-barred analysis of the failed "September" revolution that had removed de Céspedes from power. Many, who now claimed to be *Septembristas* had in fact undermined it out of self-interest. All that stitched together the many groups that first supported Grau was their shared hatred of Machado and his cronies. An absence of ideological unity contributed, in Guiteras's opinion, to a rudderless, incoherent movement. Defeatists warned the government, " 'this way we will never be recognized by the Americans' or 'the Americans will land, we won't be able to sell our sugar.' " As a result, efforts to transform the Sergeants' Revolt "into an anti-interventionist revolution—and, above all—to take this anti-interventionism to its logical conclusion" were stymied.[84]

He formed a revolutionary organization with the apt name of TNT, because setting off incendiary devices became its preferred modus operandi. A year later, he changed its name to *Joven Cuba* (Young Cuba), but his goal remained the same: an insurrection against Mendieta, Batista's reluctant frontman. He fumed when Washington, which had withheld recognition from Grau for months, took only days to recognize the new president. Joven Cuba committed itself to ousting the regime, ending the island's neocolonial relationship with the United States, and establishing a democratic socialist (not a communist) society.[85]

Any government that allied itself with the United States was unacceptable to Guiteras. *Pace* Martí, he told Beals, "We must have economic independence. Political independence means nothing." He believed that Cuba would not achieve its true objective until it became "a producing society with the means of production in the hands of the Cuban people, not held by absentee foreign capital and protected by a servile government based on military tyranny."[86] Issued in August 1934, Joven Cuba's platform bore considerable similarity to the aspirations of the Mexican Revolution: property should have a social function, the nationalization of subsoil rights and public utilities, an agrarian reform, repudiation of the foreign debt, improvements to health and education, and a national campaign to combat illiteracy.[87]

The State Department may have thought the firebrand a communist, but the PCC considered him a demagogue and a loose cannon. After Grau stepped down, the party again opted to remain on the sidelines, refusing to endorse Joven Cuba or participate in the growing civic unrest. Their passivity drew criticism from many in the struggle against Batista's puppet government. At a student meeting, Eddie Chibás expressed his frustration with the Communist Party's intransigence: "These so-called revolutionary leaders, who . . . ordered the proletariat to go back to work, are today claiming to speak in the name of the revolution. (Yet) they are employing their same old tactic of attacking revolutionaries more violently than they do reactionaries. The more revolutionary a person is, the more strongly the communists attack him. They attack the ABC more strongly than they do the Conservatives, and the *Auténticos* (Grau's party) more strongly than the ABC—and as for Guiteras, they would love to eat him alive. Just because I am so much attacked by these little leaders of tropical communism, I am sure that I am a good revolutionary."[88]

Guiteras sought allies on and off the island, even reaching out to Aponte, who had fought in the Segovias for twenty months and had been an integral part of two uprisings against Gómez. When Aponte was asked about his reasons for joining Guiteras, he gave high praise: "This one is another Sandino."[89]

Joven Cuba engaged in urban terrorism throughout 1934 and the first part of 1935, "exploding hundreds of bombs in Havana and other cities," confronting the army in the streets, robbing banks, exacting forced loans, staging prison breaks, and kidnapping and ransoming government officials and businessmen. One high-profile kidnapping of a former Machadista alone netted Joven Cuba three hundred thousand dollars. Authorities viewed Guiteras as public enemy number 1.

But the rebel had a knack for wriggling out of repeated attempts to bring him to justice. After several near misses, he was finally captured by authorities in August 1934. Charged with conspiring to overthrow the government, he was brought before a special court established to prosecute terrorists. When the court absolved him of the charge, the police kept Guiteras in custody on a firearms violation, but even that charge did not stick, and soon the revolutionary walked free to the cheers of his supporters. An irate Caffery blasted the judiciary, nothing that he was not aware of a single judge who had convicted "any terrorist of an important political faction."[90]

The Right Man for the Job

Guiteras's militants tried unsuccessfully to assassinate Mendieta and Caffery. Indeed, Caffery was the target of multiple attempts on his life during his three years in Cuba. In May 1934, just as he was getting ready to exit the embassy, assailants driving by in a vehicle opened fire, missing the ambassador but seriously injuring a guard. After that near miss, authorities stationed soldiers in front of the embassy and assigned a detachment to serve as his bodyguard.[91]

Perhaps the closest call came just over a year to the day after the embassy shooting, when six assailants, familiar with his routine, staged an armed attack at his residence. Caffery's "sumptuous" thirty-room mansion, located in the posh Alturas de Miramar district some six miles from the downtown, was replete with tennis courts, a swimming pool, and a state dining room that seated eighty. It must have been an inviting target for dissidents who despised North American influence.

Like clockwork, every Sunday just before 10 a.m., the ambassador left his residence to attend mass before spending the rest of the day at the Havana Yacht Club, where he hobnobbed with the local elite and the diplomatic corps. "On this particular Sunday," he related in his memoirs, "I forgot something and went back to the room to get it." While he was

still inside, the assailants opened fire on the thirty police assigned to protect his home. Caffery escaped injury, but one of his bodyguards died in
the shootout.[92] Speaking to reporters, the diplomat dismissed the attack
as "Cuban terrorism, a racket nothing else. They are mere gangsters."
Even if he publicly dismissed the attempts on his life, the U.S. and
Cuban governments made certain from that point on that the ambassador's Diana touring car always had a two-automobile escort, "one loaded
with civilian machine gunners and the other with native troops."[93]

Either by chance or, in the case of Cuba, by design, Caffery, who later
served as chief of mission in six countries over a span of three decades,
had been present at or complicit in some of the most brutal acts of repression in modern Latin American history. Previous postings in Colombia
and El Salvador had prepared him well for the Cuban political cauldron.

In 1928 while serving as minister plenipotentiary to Colombia, a
massacre of hundreds of banana workers occurred, an episode memora-
bly recounted in Gabriel García Márquez's *One Hundred Years of Solitude*.
Contentious labor relations dated back to 1918, when railway workers
for UFCO first went out on strike. The company's representatives took a
hard line in its negotiations.[94]

The appearance of anarchist and communist labor organizers in the banana zone along the Caribbean coast stoked militancy. Matters came to a
head in 1928, when the union representing the banana workers sent a petition with nine demands to *el pulpo*, including the recognition of the status
of contract workers, a wage increase, and the closure of company stores.
The fruit company again held firm, claiming that since many of the twenty-
five thousand workers were employed by either labor contractors or Colombian growers, it should not have to adhere to provisions in the National
Labor Code pertaining to medical attention, sanitation, and workmen's
compensation. In response, seven thousand workers went out on strike.[95]

At first Caffery's legation tried to persuade the company to reach a
compromise with the workers. While the fruit company did make minor
concessions, they were insufficient to resolve the impasse. Adding to
what soon became a combustible mix, Liberal Party politicians critical of
the Conservative government then in power and local banana growers
unhappy with the company's monopolistic practices sided with the workers. The strikers also received support from local merchants, who were
losing business to the United's commissaries.

When negotiations faltered, the legation requested a warship with a
"small armed force" to send a message to the strikers and the Colombian

government that Washington was prepared to defend UFCO's interests. Wary of yet another intervention, the outgoing Coolidge administration denied Caffery's request. The legation then pivoted and seconded *el pulpo*'s urgent appeal to authorities to suppress the strike. Even though North American "boots on the ground" were never likely, Colombian officials remained unconvinced.[96]

The military commander sent to pacify the region, General Carlos Cortés Vargas, felt certain that if his troops did not restore order to the banana zone, North American soldiers would. Such a violation of his nation's sovereignty, he later wrote in defense of his actions, was simply unacceptable. He declared a state of siege, jailing the *bananeros* and protecting strikebreakers. Workers responded by staging a series of disruptive actions and destroying company property. Then on December 6, 1928, the army mowed down the workers in the town of Ciénaga. Estimates of casualties varied from dozens to more than a thousand.[97]

The massacre, however, did not bring an end to the repression. For some months afterward, fatalities continued to mount. An upstart Liberal Party legislator named Jorge Eliécer Gaitán, who had spent ten days interviewing survivors, called for a national investigation into the tragedy. Comparing the martyred *bananeros*' struggle to improve their lot to Sandino's rebellion, Gaitán denounced the collusion between the army, the fruit company, and the U.S. government. Not surprisingly, Caffery lauded the authorities' response to the strike and dismissed the young politician as an "opportunist."[98] Cuban observers were not unaware of the diplomat's role in Colombia. At the height of *batistiano* repression against workers and students, De La Torriente Brau reminded readers of Caffery's tenure in Colombia.[99]

Three years later in El Salvador, Caffery tried unsuccessfully to remove General Martínez; right after Caffery left, Martínez oversaw La Matanza. In El Salvador and Colombia, the diplomat and his superiors in Washington had opted to side with the status quo. In each case, the lingering legacy of political violence would be rekindled on Cold War killing fields. As Caffery's biographer noted, "The day of the CIA had not yet dawned, but, in a sense, Caffery anticipated it."[100]

He was decidedly hands-on in Cuba, but with a lighter touch. Years later, Ellis Briggs, second secretary in the embassy during Caffery's tenure, framed the ambassador's job description best: "to mobilize men, money and ideas, and do so without creating the impression that the American government was manipulating the actors, or the embassy was pulling the strings." A pedestrian public speaker and surprisingly tactless for a diplomat, he nevertheless possessed "a rare ability to size up men and their motives. . . . Popularity he regarded as an overrated tool in diplomacy."[101]

After acting behind the scenes to remove Grau, Caffery continued to serve, in the words of one Cuban scholar, as the "hegemonic guarantor of legitimacy." When a new electoral law was needed, it was the ambassador who hired Dodds to rewrite the existing statute. The academic, who had revised Nicaragua's electoral code in the 1920s, now did the same for the Cuban government. As Briggs admitted in his memoirs, "with Ambassador Caffery in the background, such a statute was speedily confected in the embassy."[102]

And when Batista's relationship with then-president Miguel Mariano Gómez soured, it was Caffery who recommended that he not stage a coup, but instead employ "legal and constitutional" means to impeach the president. To ensure the desired result, Batista instructed his lieutenants to harass and intimidate "lawmakers known to be hostile to impeachment." After threats proved insufficient, Caffery reported, Batista let it be known that a coup could be in the offing. The military attaché in the embassy thought Caffery's relationship with Batista was on such firm footing that the latter "listened willingly to and almost invariably followed the sound advice of the American ambassador in such matters as were of sufficient importance to justify the ambassador's interest."[103]

Batista's and Caffery's mettle was sorely tested over the next three years. Three separate strikes threatened to upend the new government, two of them led by students and their professors. Knowing full well where resistance to the new regime was centered, one of the first pieces of legislation passed by the new government rolled back Grau's university autonomy decree. That prompted an April 1934 march by students to the presidential palace. Batista responded sternly, sending troops in to occupy the university. Then on May Day, thousands of demonstrating workers and students were met with force. Subsequent confrontations over the next few days at the Instituto de Habana left one dead and several gravely injured.[104]

Batista was quick to blame student militants and the professors who "had misled them." If matters persisted, he mused to a journalist, higher educational institutions might be put under the control of "private educational centers under government supervision. Perhaps this plan would remove the youth somewhat from the malignant influences which have been at work in these schools for the past few years."[105]

The year 1935 witnessed a series of work stoppages. It was ushered in with yet another student strike, and when authorities responded with repression, university students, with the support of faculty, called for an "indefinite strike."[106] Then in February, thirty thousand tobacco workers walked out. This was followed by primary and secondary teachers and their students, who called their own work stoppage, demanding back pay and improvements to substandard working conditions. In solidarity, professors and university students joined their walkout, and in so doing, broadened the strikers' demands. The strikers now called for an end to military influence in politics, the restoration of democratic governance, and the release of all political prisoners.[107] By February 23, the strikes had spread across the island, with three hundred thousand students, teachers, and workers publicly voicing their frustrations with the new government.[108]

It all culminated in mid-March, when a general strike, considered the largest in Cuban history, brought half a million into the streets. Students again made their presence felt. Former DEU leader and strike organizer Sánchez Arango perceptively assessed the students' organizing efforts: "the only call for a general strike after the downfall of Machado which received a unanimous echo was sent out by the students of the university, who have an amorphous social composition, and who ... do not constitute a social class, though psychologically and economically they come in an immense majority from the ranks of the petit bourgeoisie. ... The students ... knew how to interpret exactly the objective and subjective circumstances of the moment."[109]

Interestingly, neither the PCC nor Joven Cuba instigated the protests. They were late to join and then did so only reluctantly. Both were convinced that the strikers needed to be armed and better organized to withstand the anticipated repression.[110] Their assessment proved correct; the strikers were no match for the army. Batista "ordered troops to drive the buses, occupy postal stations, take over the university and protect strike breakers. All constitutional rights were suspended." An estimated one hundred workers were killed and many more were wounded in the ensuing violence. The unions that had participated in the strike were declared illegal and dissolved, their headquarters ransacked, and funds garnished.[111]

Writing later from exile in Mexico, Sánchez Arango contended that the repression "exceeded in ferocity the most acute and critical period of the struggle against Machado." Hundreds of student and union activists were imprisoned, and professors, teachers, and civil servants were summarily fired. Estimates of death attributed to the violence ranged from a dozen to several hundred. Authorities closed the recently re-opened university for the next two years.

Recent scholarship on Batista has emphasized both his populist demeanor and the repressive character of his final years in power, but there was ample evidence of what he was capable of early on. A byproduct of the upheaval was the military's wresting "of power from nearly every branch of the government." According to Caffery, civil servants lost legitimacy, owing to their "procrastination." He praised Batista and the army for taking charge of the situation.[112] The results were there in plain sight for all to see. "Cuba today," a *Times* dispatch noted, "is an armed camp."[113]

Batista took full advantage of provisions in Guiteras's labor code to stifle unions. The code mandated that strikes were legal only after a compulsory five-day cooling-off period and after eight days' notice had been given to the Ministry of Labor. Disputes were then to be submitted to a special commission, a cumbersome process that included provisions for negotiations and appeal. Only after these procedures were exhausted could workers legally strike. The Ministry of Labor's enforcement of these provisions not only curtailed the number of strikes but effectively undermined any autonomy unions possessed.[114]

As the repression intensified, Guiteras, constantly on the move, hiding often in plain sight, hatched detailed plans for an invasion of Cuba from Mexico. The scheme included purchasing a ranch in Mexico, which would be used as a training base for the revolutionary organization. Once his militants received tactical training in urban and guerrilla warfare, an armed expedition would then set off from Mexico to eastern Cuba, where its arrival would be coordinated with uprisings across the island. Guiteras rented a yacht for the expedition. The revolutionary viewed the overthrow of Batista and his puppets as a necessary first step. His and Aponte's ultimate goal was to assemble a group of revolutionaries from all across the region who would fight to eliminate dictators. Joven Cuba would, by extension, become Joven América. But Batista's forces learned of Guiteras's plans before he could leave for Mexico and in a shootout in early May 1935 outside of Matanzas, several hundred troops gunned down Guiteras, Aponte and twenty-five members of Joven Cuba. Guiteras's death broke the back of the resistance.[115]

Beals, who befriended him when he was in Grau's cabinet, wrote a moving eulogy of the revolutionary, responding to those who had labeled him a bandit and a terrorist. He compared Guiteras to John Brown, who

The journalist and author who tracked down Sandino and
befriended Mella and Guiteras: Carleton Beals, 1941.
Photograph appeared in the *Minnesota Morning Tribune*.
Courtesy of the Hennepin County Library.

also fought and died to help bring an end to a morally indefensible regime.
Indeed, Beals was experiencing a morbid sense of déjà vu; he had been
present at his friend Mella's bedside in a Mexico City hospital during his
last hours. Nor was the symbolism of Aponte's death by Guiteras's side lost
on the journalist. Recalling that he had first encountered the Venezuelan
in the Segovias, he reminded readers that the Nicaraguan rebel, too, had
been contemptuously referred to as a bandit. "Guiteras," Beals penned, "is
the Sandino of Cuba. Aponte knew this. That's why he was by his side."[116]

 Guiteras's sacrifice was not forgotten. When Castro informed his
lieutenant Huber Matos during the final offensive against Batista in 1958

that he was naming Matos's column after Martí, the former teacher asked that it be named instead after Guiteras. After all, Matos reminded Fidel, so much in Cuba already bore the apostle's name. Guiteras "is one of the greatest men of Republican Cuba . . . the author of the only social democratic and nationalist legislation of that period. . . . It seems just that a column of the rebel army, in a decisive moment of the struggle, carry his name."[117]

Batista drew a very different lesson. Cognizant of how the site in Matanzas where Guiteras was killed had become a shrine for rebellious youth, he had this to say to one of his officers: if Fidel Castro should be taken alive, it would be preferable to "burn him, let the wind carry his ashes away, and no one will know where he is buried. I don't want another Guiteras."[118]

Conclusions

As students soon realized, theirs was only a partial victory. Between Machado's ouster and Batista's election to the presidency in 1940, Batista stepped in and removed seven civilian presidents from power. Corporatist in style and substance, Batista was no Machado, but like his predecessor, he turned increasingly more autocratic and corrupt. Much to the chagrin of those who fought against the strongman, he permitted two hundred former Machadista civil servants to reenter the bureaucracy.[119]

Batista harbored delusions of grandeur. Just ten months after removing Grau from power, the 34-year-old colonel told *New York Times* correspondent James Phillips: "I believe that I have been appointed by destiny to do my utmost for the republic. To me, all figures of history who have emerged from the masses to change the course of a nation are guided for a predestined purpose."[120]

Batista revamped an increasingly politicized military to ensure its loyalty, increasing its size by one-third and its share of the budget from 15 percent to 22 percent and completely modernizing and overhauling its operations.[121] Commanders were appointed to govern each of the island's six provinces while officers ruled each district. Local police forces were placed under the military's jurisdiction. In the wake of the unsuccessful general strike, such was its purview over governance that, in the words of the North American consul in the island's second-largest city, "the military commander is, in reality, governor, mayor and police chief of Santiago. The army's tentacles have grown until they reach out in the control of insignificant municipal jobs." It also became much more cognizant of its prerogatives. Another embassy staffer compared Batista's regional commanders' penchant for self-enrichment to "American gang-leaders." Indeed, it was incumbent upon the chief of staff to make sure that his officers received "certain emoluments, financial, political and military," and to assure their "immunity to punishment. Only in this way can he command their loyalty and obedience as a body."[122]

Corruption and impunity of the military aside, Batista now cast himself as a populist. Thanks to student and worker protest during the mid-1930s, many of the improvements that Grau, Guiteras, and the DEU had worked for during their one hundred days in power, including a progressive labor code, the nationalization of labor decree, a modest agrarian reform, an increase in funding for rural schools, and a social security system, were codified in Batista's Three-Year Plan and the 1940 Constitution. It is one of the ironies of modern Cuban history that the man who had Guiteras murdered saw fit to preserve his legacy.[123]

To make the transition from the barracks to the presidential palace, Batista needed to persuade the urban and rural poor that he now had their interests at heart. In addition to appropriating Grau's reforms, he reached out to the communists, who also had been targets of the repression. Rather than settle its differences with Grau and his supporters, the PCC did an about-face and joined the strongman's coalition, just as it had during the waning days of Machado's regime. In return for its loyalty, Batista restored the party's legality in September 1938 and gave it control over the island's largest labor union. And the party, which later renamed itself the Partido Socialista Populista (PSP), came through for the candidate, delivering the votes that sealed Batista's victory at the polls in 1940.

With its own daily newspaper and radio station, the party grew impressively from 5,000 members to 122,000 between 1937 and 1944, making it one of the largest in the hemisphere. Batista even incorporated two communists in his cabinet, the first government to do so in the hemisphere.[124] The party's willingness to work with the strongman was symptomatic of similar tactical collaborations with despots. The fight against fascism during World War II allowed dictators to lend their names to a noble cause, allaying any stigma associated with the partnership.[125]

Meaningful change, however, had to wait until 1959. As a disillusioned De la Torriente Brau put it, "Cuba was a graveyard of illusions and revolutionary plans. There was not even a faint hope of fighting successfully for its liberation."[126] Even in defeat, students, significantly weakened by divisions within their ranks, imprisonment, and the murder or exile of their leaders, nevertheless secured modest improvements.[127] Mendieta awarded the university partial autonomy, but only in return for a proscription of student involvement in politics.[128]

Meanwhile, a debilitated and fractured student movement, bereft of leadership, fell prey to *bonchismo* (literally, bunches), or armed gangs who employed selective violence, intimidation, and extortion to cow their peers, the faculty, and the administration. These loosely run student groups first appeared in secondary schools and then spread to the university. Often led by professional students, who appeared on the university's matriculation rolls for up to ten years without ever completing a degree, the *bonches* had little interest in ideology or in pursuing radical change. The student-manned *bonches* of the 1930s would turn into the lawless, violent political action groups of the 1940s and 1950s. Guiteras would have been appalled to learn that former militants in Joven Cuba, who created the fearsome Unión Insurreccional Revolucionario (UIR), did so little to carry on his legacy. The UIR's deadly rival, the MSR (*Movimiento Socialista Revolucionario*, Revolutionary Socialist Movement), which dominated university politics in the early to mid-1940s, may have espoused anti-imperialism and anticommunism, but it was far more interested in establishing protection rackets and pursuing political influence.[129] When autonomy was restored to the university in 1937, the police were prohibited from entering the campus, thereby providing armed thugs a wide berth for their mayhem. Castro, who entered the university in 1945 and soon joined the UIR, would later joke that it was a more dangerous place than the Sierra Maestra.[130]

Batista co-opted the *bonches* by plying their leadership with sinecures. Some used their civil servant positions as a springboard to public office, while others, according to the historian Jaime Suchlicki, "acted on their own, [and] still others sold their services to the highest bidder."[131] During the 1940s and 1950s, successive presidential administrations gave out subsidies to these groups, under the assumption that it was better to have them beholden than left to their own devices.[132]

While some students descended into wanton criminality, Grau and Directorio of 1930 leaders reorganized themselves politically, establishing the Partido Revolucionario Cubano, or the Auténtico Party (PRC-A) in February 1934. The new party demanded Grau's return to power and sought to build an APRA-like multiclass coalition made up of workers, peasants, and the middle class. Economic nationalism remained one of the Auténticos' core principles. Angered by Washington's complicity in the coup, Grau called for a reduction in North American economic influence, and the curtailment of cheap foreign labor. He briefly returned to the island from his Mexican exile in May 1934, and one hundred thousand supporters turned out to welcome him back. Batista, who had always viewed the indecisive Grau and his followers as his most potent rivals, harassed party stalwarts mercilessly and forced Grau and other party leaders to once again take flight.[133]

Still, the Auténticos remained a force to be reckoned with in the legislature, and after ten years in the political wilderness, Grau was president once again, defeating Batista's hand-picked candidate at the polls in 1944. His first order of business was to clean house. Hundreds of corrupt politicians and businessmen were jailed, "thousands of holders of sinecures ... lost their jobs," and two dozen military officers and five hundred police officers were fired. But the second coming of the physician-turned-politician as president from 1944 to 1948 fell far short of expectations. Prío, who succeeded Grau as president in 1948, proved to be just as ineffective. Graft and corruption were just as flagrant and widespread under Auténtico presidents as they had been during the Batista era.[134]

An Auténtico splinter group made up of former students and professionals founded the Ortodoxo Party in 1947. Led by a former Directorio stalwart, Chibás, the Ortodoxos were disillusioned by Auténtico graft. Castro began his political ascent as a member of the Ortodoxos. Chibás's movement was as much about the past as the present. As Guerra noted, the tumultuous events of the 1920s and 1930s had left a deep imprint on national politics: "heroism, martyrdom, and messianism were deeply inscribed in the political consciousness of Cubans, born of the ideological sense of national identity resulting from decades of national struggle and multiple U.S. betrayals."[135]

There were lessons that Washington might have taken if it had been so inclined. In a speech given scarcely six months after his departure from Cuba to the Young Democratic Clubs of America, Welles reflected on Washington's past history of intervention in Cuban affairs. Yes, the Platt Amendment was the original sin that led to repeated meddling, but local politicians deserved their fair share of criticism:[136]

Occasionally the threat of intervention has been utilized to forestall revolution; at other times, to dictate financial policy. It has included landing and retention for protracted periods of American troops on Cuban soil. No greater impediment to the free exercise by the Cuban people of their inherent right to sovereignty could have well been devised. It has operated as means of deterring the Cubans for exercising the muscles of self-reliance essential for self-government. Whenever conditions arose in Cuba which required correction, the Cuban people became accustomed to look to Washington for such correction instead of undertaking the task themselves. You cannot keep a child in braces until it reaches the age of maturity and expect it to walk successfully alone.

Indeed, the self-serving diplomat was quick to place blame on everyone but himself. He unfairly castigated Grau—he "had no program or policy to pursue" and resorted to "an artificial anti-American campaign." He also mischaracterized the junta's broad base of support: "The Grau regime not only lacked the support of, but was violently opposed by every one of the groups that had opposed Machado . . . with the exception of a small percentage of the university students." But he saved his harshest criticism for the students. "The Grau San Martín regime was to all intents and purposes run and administered by a group of some twenty students. Decree after decree was issued, some of them excellent in intent but impossible of fulfillment; others, destructive of the most elementary rights universally recognized by the constitutions of the continent."

Finally, he had the temerity to call his decision not to withhold recognition of Grau's government "unassailable." One wonders how he squared his initial critique of past U.S. meddling in Cuba with his blatant efforts to enlist Batista to force Grau out. Little changed when he was relieved by Caffery. In a space of six months, the two envoys conspired to oust Machado and Grau while at the same time encouraging and then legitimizing the rise to power of a little-known, opportunistic sergeant, who ruled Cuba either indirectly or directly for much of the next quarter-century. What continued to remain nonnegotiable for Washington was a truly sovereign state. Even the abrogation of the Platt Amendment in 1934 did not change that.

PART II

Democratic Effervescence and Authoritarian Retrenchment

CHAPTER EIGHT

Your Words Inspired

Our ideals and way of life must be nurtured in Latin America to
the eventual exclusion of totalitarianism and other foreign
ideologies. . . . In Latin America, we must lock the stable door
before danger ever arises. Prevention is relatively cheap; crises
are exorbitantly expensive in money, in time, and often in blood.

—SECRETARY OF WAR ROBERT PATTERSON, March 1947

SCHOLARS OF POSTWAR LATIN American history characterize its first five
years as fitful, a short-lived democratic moment beginning in 1944, when
popular risings led by broad multiclass movements toppled dictators in
nine countries. Demographic growth, rural to urban migration, import
substitution industrialization, and the rise of populism upended the status
quo as the urban middle class and organized labor became political actors
to be reckoned with for the first time.[1] Once in power, reformist political
parties sought to address income equality, to legalize labor unions and
peasant federations, and to expand the franchise to women and people
who were illiterate. But the democratic wave did not jell, giving way by
the end of the decade to a resurgence of authoritarianism.[2] This is the tale
that is told about this half-decade. While accurate in the main, this synopsis fails to do justice to what was for the contemporaries who experienced
it a vexing moment in regional geopolitics.

Ironically, two avatars of democracy destined to have a profound impact during the next two decades—Betancourt and Figueres—came to power, not through the ballot box, but the barrel of a gun. In fact, Venezuela's brief three-year experiment in democracy between 1945 and 1948 was not the result of a bottom-up popular mobilization but of a bloodless military coup. In Peru, Haya never gave up the idea of employing violence to seize power. During his years in hiding and imprisonment in the 1930s and 1940s, Aprista militants recruited dissident junior military officers, took to the streets, and targeted opponents. The movement's failure to seize power extralegally in the late 1940s was not for lack of trying.[3]

In contrast, the Argentine military officer Juan Perón, whose grandiose designs and diplomatic machinations galvanized autocrats across the region, breezed to victory at the polls in 1946 and 1952. The charismatic Perón built a formidable political base among the urban working class, and, unlike his predecessors, he delivered on his promises. Working conditions improved, labor laws were enforced, a state retirement system was underwritten, and workers for the first time were guaranteed (unheard-of) vacation time. He may have been an admirer of Mussolini, but he recognized that with fascism in disgrace worldwide, he needed the legitimacy that elections and democratic institutions afforded.[4]

The Truman administration viewed the nationalistic Argentine leader with suspicion, and not just because Argentina harbored Nazis during his presidency. Perón's state-centered corporatist model was directly at odds with the liberal postwar economic order that Washington championed. Peronist efforts to promote a regional trade bloc in the Southern Cone free from foreign tutelage also were concerning. Furthermore, by insisting that he was not beholden to any particular ideology, he unnerved policymakers in Washington. "We are not sectarian," he declared. "If there is something in communism that we can take, we take it. Names don't scare us. If fascism, anarchism or communism have something good, we take it."[5]

No friend of the Argentine's autocratic disposition, Betancourt understood Perón's appeal to Latin Americans, who had been schooled to distrust "dollar imperialism" and were willing to "give [Argentina] the benefit of the doubt, as a sister Hispanic country." He counseled restraint to a North American diplomat and warned that if the Truman administration made its reservations about Perón public, it should anticipate a strong backlash.[6]

While Perón evinced populist tendencies, the region's small communist parties uncharacteristically remained on their best behavior during World War II, working hand in glove with dictatorships while counseling their labor unions to adopt "no-strike" pledges for industries considered vital to the war effort. Although the Hitler-Stalin pact had cost local communist parties adherents during the first years of the war, Germany's invasion of the Soviet Union reversed that trend. After the USSR sided with the allies, local communist parties were legalized in almost every Latin American country, and in several—Chile, Cuba, Costa Rica, Peru, and Brazil—party membership and voter support spiked. In 1948, the State Department estimated that party membership in Latin America totaled 360,000, but some estimates put the figure at closer to half a million. The Chilean Communist Party, for instance, polled 17 percent of the vote, and three Communists served in President Gabriel González Videla's cabinet. Another success story was Brazil, where the Communists, boasting 180,000 members, elected 14 deputies and 1 senator to the National Congress. Well into the following decade, the region's parties, in return for concessions, chose cooperation and accommodation over resistance.[7]

Initially, Washington did not appear overly concerned about the gains made by leftist political parties, in large part because Soviet expansionism was not the imminent threat that it was perceived to be just a few years later. And while communists did make inroads with organized labor, by the end of the 1940s their regional labor confederation, the Confederación de Trabajadores de América (CTAL), everywhere ceded ground to the AFL-CIO affiliate, the Confederación Interamericana de Trabajadores (CIT). By the end of the decade, however, tolerance of communist parties had diminished significantly.[8]

Complicating matters further were precipitous shifts in U.S. policy and personnel between 1944 and 1948, which only served to muddy the diplomatic waters for democrats and tyrants alike. Four secretaries of state in that period were accompanied by a comparable number of changes at the Latin American desk. It was not just a change in personnel. For a brief twenty-month period between 1945 and 1947, the State Department expressed a decided preference for democratic rule, while distancing itself from the Trujillos and Somozas of the hemisphere. What signaled the change was a controversial memorandum, "Policy Re Dictatorships and Disreputable Governments," written by now Assistant Secretary of State Spruille Braden. It argued that the U.S. should no

Assistant Secretary of State for Western Hemisphere
Affairs Spruille Braden. Library of Congress, Prints &
Photographs Division, photograph by Harris & Ewing,
LC-H25-65832-A.

longer coddle autocrats, nor should it arm their armed forces if there was
reason to suspect that the military in question would use the arms to harass neighboring countries or stifle internal dissent.[9]

It was Braden's tour of duty in Cuba during the war years that crystallized his thinking about the jarring disconnect between fighting
against fascism while working closely with dictatorships. At a moment
when the Good Neighbor's nostrum of nonintervention became an
article of faith at Foggy Bottom, the diplomat was determined to do all
he could to wheedle and coax Batista not to stand for reelection in 1944.
"To permit Batista to establish himself as the Trujillo of Cuba," he

warned his superiors, "would be a negation of everything for which we are fighting this war and would constitute an appeasement for which we would pay dearly in the future." Although other factors contributed to the Cuban's decision not to run again, Braden was elated when Grau defeated Batista's choice in 1944.[10]

Braden and his backers in the Department also were convinced that the four hundred million dollars in wartime Lend-Lease sales had boosted the stature and firepower of Latin American militaries and fed their appetites for political power.[11] And they could point to a bevy of recent examples. In 1944 and 1945 in El Salvador, Guatemala, Venezuela, Bolivia, and Paraguay, military officers utilized Lend-Lease tanks and planes in their not always successful attempts to bring down existing governments. Duggan, who thought Braden's prodemocracy initiative counterproductive, nevertheless concurred that arm sales "inflated the confidence of the officer caste in its ability to make and break governments" and ignited a regionwide arms race. "Each country began eyeing its neighbors' armaments acquisitions to see who was getting the most."[12] What must have given Trujillo pause was that Braden and his chief lieutenant, Briggs, were well acquainted with the exiled opposition as a result of their recent postings in Havana. They were aware that his exiled opponents were scheming to launch an invasion of their homeland to overthrow him.

Now given a free hand by Secretary of State James Byrnes, Braden singled out Trujillo, sending a scathing aide-mémoire to the Dominican Foreign Ministry that explained in no uncertain terms why the U.S. would no longer pander to the general.[13]

> The Government and people of the United States necessarily have a warmer friendship for and a greater desire to cooperate with those governments which rest upon periodically and freely expressed consent of the governed. This Government has over the past years observed the situation in the Dominican Republic and has been unable to perceive that democratic principles have been observed there in theory or in practice.

Byrnes was firmly in Braden's corner. In a no-holds-barred assessment to President Truman, he articulated why a decisive change in policy was needed. "President Trujillo is the most ruthless, unprincipled, and efficient dictator in the hemisphere. He holds the country in an iron grip, rules by fear, and extracts an annual tribute estimated at five million dollars from the economy of the country and the Dominican people. . . . His regime is completely unsavory and we should scrupulously avoid even the appearance of lending him any support."[14]

Braden explained why business as usual was no longer acceptable in an address to the American Geographical Society. The adherence to nonintervention—a cornerstone of the Good Neighbor Policy—should, in light of the democratic uptick throughout the hemisphere, be revisited. In addition, it was not just a question of refraining from interfering in the internal affairs of neighbors, because by not moving proactively to promote democratic norms, Washington implicitly was sending a message. "Not to use our power may be, in actuality, to misuse our power. . . . The conclusion is inescapable; that if a nation has great power, as we have in abundance, it cannot shun its obligation to exercise commensurate leadership."[15]

Even before Braden enunciated the new approach, foreign service officers in the trenches were clamoring for a new direction in foreign policy. U.S. ambassador to El Salvador Walter Thurston reported that Salvadorans found it difficult to reconcile the Atlantic Charter and the Four Freedoms "with the fact that the United States tolerates and apparently is gratified to enter into association with governments in America which cannot be described as other than totalitarian." Claude Bowers, who had served in the foreign service in Spain during the Civil War, contended that the imminent Allied triumph afforded the United States a singular opportunity. "We do not have to compromise on principle. Not only are we in a position now to take a strong stand against nondemocratic regimes . . . but millions in South America expect our leadership." Furthermore, it was not lost on prodemocracy proponents that at a moment when the Allies were pressuring the Soviet Union to permit political pluralism in Eastern Europe, it was hypocritical of the United States if it did not do the same next door. But the new policy did not sit well with all foreign service officers. In response to a circular, five of the fourteen missions in the region were unenthusiastic. The Ambassador to Paraguay, Willard Beaulac, wondered, perhaps tongue in cheek, "what wise man or wise group of men is going to decide which governments are reputable and which are disreputable?"[16]

Braden put arms sales on hold or significantly cut back on the amounts of weaponry sold to the Dominican Republic and seven other authoritarian regimes, while encouraging other governments to do the same. The cold shoulder was extended to the economic sphere as well. Henceforth, U.S.

aid would be forthcoming only if it benefited the people, not just the regime.[17] He rubbed additional salt in the dictators' wounds by approving the
establishment of two military missions and the outfitting of infantry and
artillery battalions to newly democratic Venezuela. His office also advised
U.S. companies with investments in the region to steer clear of domestic
politics and to refrain from giving bribes.[18]

Withholding military and economic aid were not the only ways the
Truman administration expressed its reservations with strongman rule.
For more than a year, the State Department withheld recognition of a
puppet government Somoza had placed in power, after the strongman
had ousted a president who had proved insufficiently pliant. Since Somoza had staked his legitimacy on his close working relationship with
Washington, this came as quite a shock to the dictator. Ambassador
Fletcher Warren, who relayed the decision personally to Somoza, reported that he took the news especially hard. It was "one of the most unpleasant conversations I shall ever have. There is something terrifying in
seeing disintegrate the confidence of an egotist in himself." The administration also turned down a Nicaraguan request for a three-million-dollar
Export-Import Bank loan on "political grounds, Somoza is a dictator."
And when the despot inquired if a state visit might be arranged to coincide with an upcoming trip to the States to attend his son's graduation
from West Point, Byrnes's response left little to the imagination. Somoza
was welcome, of course, but an official visit at this time "might prove
embarrassing."[19] The slight must have been especially disconcerting because the red carpet had been rolled out for the dictator in 1939.[20]

Now Braden was adding insult to Byrnes's slight by discouraging
U.S. companies from investing in authoritarian states like Nicaragua.
"Disreputable governments ... and dictators," he cautioned, "do not
make good investments." Such diplomatic cold-shouldering did, according to the historian Jeffrey Gould, limit "the regime's dictatorial excesses."[21] While Washington pressured Somoza not to run for reelection,
however, it never forced the issue; nor did it insist that he step down as
head of the National Guard, always the basis of his power. Nonrecognition may have been uncomfortable, but as with Martínez in El Salvador
in the early 1930s, it was not enough to force Tacho out.[22]

Support for Braden's prodemocracy initiative came from Uruguay's
chancellor, Eduardo Rodríguez Larreta, at a November 1945 conference
of Pan American nations at Chapultepec Castle in Mexico City. Arguing
that peace was sustainable only where democratic governance prevailed,

General Anastasio Somoza rides up Pennsylvania Avenue
with FDR at his side during an official state visit, May 5,
1939. Library of Congress, Prints & Photographs Division,
photograph by Harris & Ewing, LC-H21-C-998.

Larreta presented a resolution that called on the hemisphere's nations
to take multilateral action against any state that violated democratic
principles and basic human rights. Uruguay's motivation was close to
home, since Perón's rise posed a threat. The region's democracies and
the United States supported the resolution. Expressing "unqualified adherence" for what came to be called the Larreta Doctrine, Byrnes called
on Latin American governments to act collectively against despotism. "If
they are to preserve peace, the American republics cannot permit oppres-
sive regimes to exist in their midst."

But the resolution attracted little support from other states, which
feared it might precipitate a return to gunboat diplomacy. Even some civilian governments objected, arguing that multilateral interventions

could easily become a stalking horse for Washington's designs. By a vote of 13–8, Larreta's resolution was defeated.[23]

Opponents of dictatorships, however, took Braden's and Larreta's initiatives to heart. After an NBC interview with Braden and Briggs was broadcast throughout the region, the U.S. embassy in Managua reported that the program "has acted like a shot in the arm to the opposition." A few weeks later Warren wrote to the Department that anti-Somoza demonstrators in the streets of the capital were shouting their approval of the Larreta Doctrine. One of the leading lights of the Dominican diaspora, Ángel Morales Córdova, showed his appreciation for the policy by writing Braden a letter of gratitude. "Your words inspired. . . . The people of my country, cruelly humiliated, exploited, trampled over, for more than fifteen years by the action of a despotic power that has no parallel among the common run of American dictatorships will turn with faith to principles once more . . . the decline of despots is on."

While it drew praise from the region's democrats, Braden's campaign understandably left the dictators perplexed and angry. After all, they had been reliable allies during the war years, and now it appeared that they were being shown the door. Nicaragua, for instance, had permitted the U.S. military to build airbases in Managua and Puerto Cabezas, as well as a naval base at Corinto. In addition, a strategically important antisubmarine base was erected at Samaná Bay in the Dominican Republic. The autocrats, who never lost their advocates in the War Department and retained retired U.S. military officers on their payrolls as advisors and lobbyists, may have professed their astonishment publicly at the new policy, but they were determined to wait out this abrupt sea change. As an insulted Trujillo pouted to a U.S. diplomat, "We are still your friends, even if we are your mistreated friends."[24] In the interim, the strongmen ramped up propaganda campaigns that red-baited Braden and his lieutenants in the State Department.[25]

In Washington, the dictators' supporters were quick to point out that Braden's proactive measures were at odds with the Good Neighbor Policy. A longtime friend of the Dominican ruler (and Somoza), General George Brett, who headed the Caribbean Defense Command in Panama, explained why abandoning the Dominican military at this juncture flew in the face of long-term U.S. interests: "The bases of the Dominican army were established by the U.S. Marine Corps during the years of the occupation, 1916–1924. . . . Almost without exception, the National Army's high command, including President Trujillo, are products of the

National Guard established by the Marines. The same army is modeled in accord with U.S. norms, especially the Marine Corps."[26] Thanks to the War Department's creation of a military mission program in 1938, ties between Latin American military establishments and the United States had grown considerably closer. In three short years, the U.S. had army, air force, and naval advisors on the ground in nearly every major country in the hemisphere.[27]

Early on, Briggs realized that one of the most serious threats to the promotion of democracy came from within. In September 1944, while serving as ambassador to the Dominican Republic, he cautioned Hull that "certain officers of our military establishments in the Caribbean do not share my estimate of the situation or my views concerning policy. What is more, they are apparently prepared to undertake on their own initiative steps which run counter to that policy." Brett's visits to the Dominican Republic in particular were "directly contrary" to the Department's aims. Brett was so taken with the "footloose General . . . and by the attentions of El Benefactor to himself, that he could scarcely contain the sawdust stuffing beneath his bemedaled tunic." The Department, Briggs concluded, needed to "reassert its authority over the conduct of foreign relations." Such mixed messaging only encouraged both democrats and despots to marshal their arguments for why they deserved Washington's support.[28]

Trujillo and other despots made the most of well-paid lobbyists who worked the corridors of power in Washington. When longtime advisor and Washington insider Joseph Davies retired in 1947, the dictator replaced him with Roosevelt's former attorney general, Homer Cummings, a well-known physician who cared for Truman. If needed, these influence peddlers made end runs around the State Department, in some cases reaching out to more amenable agencies. At other times the lobbyists took their case directly to the president.[29]

The one sphere where dictators responded aggressively to the new policy was arms procurement. Shut out from the United States during the Braden interregnum and not sure for how long, they sought armaments elsewhere. Trujillo, in particular, took advantage of a lively postwar international arms market, obtaining weaponry from the Brazilian military dictator Eurico Gaspar Dutra and ships from Canada.[30] Nor was he averse to smuggling war materiel from the States or surreptitiously purchasing equipment from members of the Cuban high command interested in turning a profit. By 1948, the Dominican air force boasted 140 planes.[31]

In a twist of irony, the dictators received unexpected assistance from none other than Welles, who lit into Braden's policies in *Foreign Affairs*. "Intervention and Interventions" argued that the foundation of FDR's Good Neighbor Policy was indeed nonintervention, and that Braden's criticism of Perón in particular, and the censure of dictators more generally, was guaranteed to diminish "the moral standing and the great prestige which this country had derived from Roosevelt's policy." Intervention in the past, according to the retired statesman, had only engendered "hatred and suspicion" for the United States.[32] Cubans, who remembered Welles's heavy-handed interference in 1933, could only nod their assent.

Welles's column undercut Braden, but it was the onset of the Cold War and the resulting changes in the geopolitical landscape that sealed the latter's fate. When a more security-conscious George Marshall replaced Byrnes as secretary of state, Braden, realizing that his human rights initiative was now out of step with the Department's position, resigned in June 1947, never to work in government again. Meanwhile, Briggs was demoted to an ambassadorship in Uruguay. In one fell swoop, three key advocates of the policy were removed from their positions.

Without fanfare, arms sales to dictatorships resumed.[33] This policy reversal coincided with a heightening of global tensions. Recent communist inroads in Poland and Hungary and in the eastern Mediterranean were foremost in the minds of policymakers, as the United States rushed to fill the vacuum left by Great Britain's departure from the Balkans. In fact, the core principles of U.S. foreign policy during the Cold War were first tested out during the Greek civil war of the late 1940s: the provision of significant military assistance to a foreign government during peacetime, the strategic use of advisors and trainers, an affinity for counterinsurgency operations, and involvement in hostilities "without the commitment of maximum resources."[34] Each of these principles would be employed in the proxy wars fought in Latin America.

In a March 1947 speech, the president painted a dire picture of an existential struggle between two ways of life. In what would be called the Truman Doctrine, he emphasized that the United States had a moral imperative to contain the Soviet and the international communist movement's aggression wherever it posed a threat.[35]

A February 1948 coup in Czechoslovakia, which brought to power communists loyal to Moscow, and a leftist coalition's credible showing in Italy two months afterward heightened fears in Washington of Soviet expansionism. Later that year the signing of the Inter-American Treaty of

Reciprocal Assistance (the Rio Treaty) laid the basis for greater hemispheric military cooperation between the United States and the region. Administration officials and U.S. defense contractors hoped that this mutual defense pact would enable Latin American nations now to rely exclusively on U.S.-made weapons. The dictators had outlasted Braden.[36]

The region's democrats took solace from the fact that the onset of the Cold War did not precipitate an arms rush. The War Department's campaign to arm Latin American militaries with weaponry after World War II failed to gain traction for a number of reasons: the prohibitive cost of standardizing the armaments of the region's militaries, bureaucratic wrangling, concerns that sales would set off an arms race, and simply because other hotspots were given a much higher priority than Latin America. The 1949 Mutual Defense Assistance Act, for instance, authorized $1.3 billion in military aid abroad, none of it earmarked for Latin America. As the best scholarship on the topic reveals, the Cold War had a paradoxical effect. On the one hand, the Truman Doctrine relegated Latin America to the end of the arms supply chain, but at the same time, growing fears of Soviet penetration into the hemisphere brought an abrupt end to Braden's initiative. Even though bilateral arms agreements and the establishment of additional military missions were not inked until the final year of the Truman administration, Marshall's decision to lift Braden's ban on arms sales to dictatorships represented a symbolic defeat for democrats.[37]

Whether the region's political actors applauded or disparaged the prodemocracy initiative, they found such pendular shifts in the Truman administration's policy inherently destabilizing. As one synthesis of the first five years after the war noted, "it is important to stress the degree to which United States policy [toward Latin America] was marked by hesitancy, confusion and division."[38] Secretary of State Dean Acheson did his best to allay concerns. In a speech before the Pan American Society in September 1949, he told his audience that the days of gunboat diplomacy were over and that the U.S. remained steadfast in its commitment to the principle of nonintervention. On the one hand, the administration encouraged "the growth of representative and honest government by all suitable means," but it would not undertake "unilateral intervention in the affairs of another country."[39] Such hedging did little to dispel the concerns of democrats.

U.S. policy also whipsawed after the war when it came to the perceived threat of Soviet infiltration. Initially, Washington's national security establishment acted as if it were not overly concerned. As late as 1947, a CIA memorandum reported that there was little possibility of a communist takeover anywhere in the hemisphere. In fact, compared to the attention and resources the administration showered on the Far East, the Middle East, and Europe, Latin America appeared very much an afterthought. Proof of this could be found in the very modest sums of foreign economic aid the administration dispensed to the region. Western Europe, thanks to the Marshall Plan, received nearly fifty times more aid between 1945 and 1950, with Belgium and Luxembourg receiving more funds than all of Latin America.

In response to Washington's reluctance to disperse aid, Latin American economies turned inward. A progressive group of economists headquartered in Santiago, the United Nations Economic Commission for Latin America (ECLA or its Spanish acronym, CEPAL) championed import substitution industrialization (ISI) and protectionism, neither of which was music to Washington's ears. ECLA argued that European and North American states had become increasingly autarkic during the interwar period and that the terms of trade had turned decidedly against primary producers. As a result, Latin America's wealth was siphoned out of the hemisphere, because manufactured goods imported to the region cost significantly more than the primary products produced there. In short, the game was rigged in favor of the richer nations. ECLA economists noted that the Depression only confirmed that the export-led model was a vestige of the past and that Latin American states had to create and sustain internal markets and industrialize. The fault of the late-nineteenth- and early-twentieth-century export boom was not too much state interference, as classical economists insisted, but too little; not that Latin American countries failed to export enough, but that they failed to pay sufficient attention to the home market and domestic industry.[40]

Although the administration did not have much success in discouraging ISI, the anticommunist messaging it emphatically conveyed at the Ninth Inter-American Conference in Bogotá in April 1948 did have the desired effect. One after another, Latin American governments, whether democratic or autocratic, proscribed local communist parties and harassed leftist unions.[41] Gould's observation about Somoza applied to all dictatorial regimes at that time: "The regime's internal necessities—to clamp down on all 'subversion'—meshed nicely with the international imperative to combat communism in the new geopolitical world of the late 1940s."[42]

Amid such policy shifts, an untidy assemblage of political refugees, adventurers, and mercenaries of diverse political inclinations, and their allies in a handful of democracies joined together, declaring their intention to eliminate the scourge of dictatorship root and branch. The Liberation Army of the Caribbean, or the Caribbean Legion, as it came to be called, inflamed the region in a manner that drew comparisons to the unsettled 1920s. Not since Sandino's Latin American Legion had such transnational solidarity been in evidence. This "nuclei of exiled leaders" proved instrumental in Figueres's successful rise to power in 1948.

The Legionnaires had their supporters. Arévalo generously offered his country as a safe haven. In December 1947, he and the exiled leadership of Nicaragua, Honduras, the Dominican Republic and Costa Rica met in Guatemala City and agreed to the Caribbean Pact. The accord's objectives were to eliminate dictatorial regimes from the region, liberate the remaining European colonies in the Caribbean basin, and establish the long-sought-after Central American union. To drive home the point, the Guatemalan president severed diplomatic relations with five dictatorships. As Arévalo bluntly affirmed in a speech in November 1945, "governments that machine-gun their people have lost their right to exist."[43]

An understated feature of the fight against authoritarianism was the participation of Spanish Civil War veterans. After the fall of the Republic in 1939, upward of half a million refugees fled Franco's dictatorship. A significant number relocated to Latin America, with substantial concentrations in Mexico and the Southern Cone. In some cases, Republican veterans were peripatetic Latin Americans, like the Cuban airman Bayo, who fought for eleven years for the Spanish monarchy against Rif tribesmen in Morocco and later lent his services to the Republic. Although they downplayed or disguised their contributions for pragmatic or ideological reasons, Spanish republicans were a critical component in the fight to oust the dictators. As Bayo put it so eloquently in his memoir: "In Spain, humanity lost a battle, but it didn't lose the war."[44]

Dictators learned the hard way that Spanish republicans were an obstreperous lot. To "improve the race," Trujillo had permitted several thousand Civil War veterans then living in detention camps in France to emigrate in 1939. When asked why the racist general welcomed such a mélange of anarchists, socialists, and communists, one Spanish émigré cracked, "we are white and we can breed."[45] Many took the first opportunity to leave the country for more ideologically compatible destinations, such as Mexico. But those who remained on the island posed a challenge. In 1942, Dominican authorities rounded up and deported forty Spaniards who had been identified as ringleaders of a strike at a sugar plantation.[46]

And when émigrés were not displaying their martial prowess, they offered their business establishments, resources, and good intentions to the democratic cause. Havana's seven-story Hotel San Luis, owned and operated by the unassuming Canary Islander Cruz Alonso Rodríguez, became, according to Bayo, the "safe harbor of every Caribbean conspiracy." Exiles stopped by the hotel lobby regularly to map out strategy and to glean the latest news and rumors from their homeland. There they encountered displaced refugees from other countries. The well-connected Cruz Alonso may have been a longtime supporter of Cuba's Auténtico Party, but his generous spirit knew no ideological bounds. Impeccably turned out in his trademark white guayabera and bowtie, the affable innkeeper was "always disposed to assist the revolutionary cause." Bayo's fond recollections were confirmed by Dominican exile Juan Ducoudray, who joked years later that the Hotel San Luis may have merited only one-and-a-half stars, but when it came to solidarity and hospitality, it was clearly a five-star establishment. For the typical cash-strapped exile, the centrally located San Luis, close by the Malecón, was a godsend, providing "a roof and meals until he could pay."[47]

Just as the Hotel San Luis was a safe space, so too was Mexico City. Cárdenas welcomed those fleeing Franco with open arms. As a result, during and immediately after World War II, Mexico City was an active nexus of cross-pollination. The Canadian journalist William Krehm, who had fought for the Republic himself and who was based in the Mexican capital during the early 1940s, recalled how Spanish exiles encountered a "constant stream of refugees from Central America."[48]

Much of the unrest came to a head in March 1948, when the Caribbean Legion played a significant role in Pepe Figueres's armed rebellion in usually quiescent Costa Rica. Nineteen flights filled with weapons were transported from Guatemala to Costa Rica over the course of a forty-day civil war that cost an estimated four thousand lives.[49] Eighteen members of the Legion fought alongside the Costa Ricans, with the Dominican Miguel Ángel Ramírez serving as Figueres's chief of staff and several others playing significant supporting roles in his small army. Their presence in Costa Rica during and immediately after the conflict heightened tensions throughout the isthmus and brought neighboring Nicaragua and Costa Rica to the brink of war.[50] To the lasting disappointment of Dominican exiles, who were the Legion's most dynamic and consistent presence, however, their efforts to overthrow the dictator Trujillo met with failure.[51]

A month later in Colombia, on the eve of the inter-American meetings scheduled to begin in that nation's capital, three thousand were killed during an incendiary urban riot, the *Bogotazo*. The razing and looting of the downtown were triggered by the assassination of the charismatic Gaitán. He had built a massive following in his speeches and his popular Friday radio addresses, in which he excoriated oligarchical elements of both his own Liberal Party and the rival Conservatives. A strong proponent of workers' rights, Gaitán, like Perón, used his position as minister of labor to build a powerful political base among the urban working class. In his speeches, "The Tribune of the People," gestured toward the Argentine's nationalistic third way (neither capitalism nor communism). Judgments by contemporaries and scholars about Gaitán vary significantly. While the leadership of his own party viewed him as a dangerous demagogue who excited the passions of the mob, others pigeonholed this product of the university reform movement as a democratic socialist, who channeled the aspirations of the progressive wing of the Liberal Party.[52]

In the months leading up to his murder, the country was wracked by political violence. On February 7, 1948, Gaitán organized a silent march against the bloodshed in downtown Bogotá. One hundred thousand of his followers, dressed in black, turned out for a "Prayer for Peace" at the Plaza de Bolívar. Two months later, his assassination and the *Bogotazo* detonated *La Violencia*, a twenty-five-year civil war that took the lives of an estimated 250,000 Colombians and displaced countless more. It also brought to power one of the most reactionary politicians in modern Latin American history, Laureano Gómez Castro. The drift rightward following Gaitán's assassination presaged an end to the region's short-lived democratic wave.

Golpes in Peru and Venezuela a month apart in late 1948 continued that trend. In the former, General Manuel Odría ousted a nominally democratic government and, as did his predecessors, immediately turned his wrath on Haya's APRA. Even though the Peruvian agitator had spent much of the past twenty-five years either in exile, in prison, or in hiding, Haya's movement was viewed with trepidation by the left, the oligarchy, and civilian and military rulers.[53] The party's evolving policy prescriptions, now a reasonable facsimile of the New Deal, were a far cry from its earlier progressive platform. Rather than seize and redistribute the wealth of the oligarchy, the party now stressed that it would focus its energies on generating wealth for the underserved.[54] Support for Aprismo remained stubbornly discrete, however; it flourished in certain regions and among certain sectors of society (that is, urban unions and white-collar employees), but the few times APRA was allowed to participate in electoral politics, it never surpassed 40 percent of the vote, and that high-water mark was achieved only once, in 1945.

As a result, APRA's leadership assumed the role of power broker, too often obstructionist, infrequently constructive. It blocked political rivals, yet it was unable to take power itself, at least not until 1985. Too often the party's leadership was at war with itself, with militant and accommodationist wings working at cross-purposes. Curiously for a movement that had such clearly defined goals during its early years, the few times it found itself with political leverage—between 1945 and 1948 and then again between 1956 and 1962—its representatives in the legislature failed to advance concrete policy proposals.[55]

Despite Haya's repeated repudiation of fascism during the war years and communism thereafter, Odría's junta considered him nonetheless a demagogue and Aprismo a contaminant deserving of eradication. What was especially alarming to Odría was that the movement had considerable success in winning over ambitious junior officers, who, according to a military historian, were disillusioned with the tradition-bound personalism of the high command and appreciated Aprismo's characteristic discipline.[56]

After assuming control, Odría purged the military of Aprista sympathizers; rounded up, jailed, and deported hundreds of the party faithful; imposed a draconian internal security law; and forced Haya to seek refuge in the Colombian embassy in January 1949. The junta refused to recognize his request for political asylum, and it denied the Colombian government a safe conduct pass to let him leave the country. Haya de la Torre remained locked up in the embassy for the next five years, surrounded by soldiers in machine gun nests, searchlights, and tanks. Proscribed from giving interviews, his writings censored in the national press, Haya was suspended in a legal limbo.[57]

Odría's former student at Chorrillos Military Academy, the Venezuelan colonel Pérez Jiménez, emulated his instructor, staging a coup of his own a month later, abruptly ending Venezuela's three-year experiment in representative democracy. This was not the first time that the colonel and other nationalistic officers intent on modernizing the armed forces had interjected themselves into politics. Three years earlier, they had formed a secret military lodge, the Unión Patriótica Militar (UPM), and conspired with the leadership of Acción Democrática to overthrow Medina Angarita. AD agreed to lend its support to Pérez Jiménez's cabal with the understanding that the party and the military would govern until elections were held. In October 1945, the coup succeeded and a civilian-led junta took charge.

Five of the seven members of the junta were members of AD, including junta president Betancourt. As brief as it was, the *trienio* government brought with it long-overdue changes, including the extension of the franchise to women and people who were illiterate, expanded access to public education, and the country's first untainted elections. In three short years the number of children attending school jumped from 300,000 to 500,000, and 287 pueblos received electricity for the first time.[58] One of the provisional government's first decrees was to prohibit members of the junta from running in the upcoming presidential elections. This law was intended as a shot across the bow against *continuismo*.[59]

The provisional government also raised taxes on oil exports and mandated greater controls over foreign investment, but stopped short of nationalizing the industry. In fact, the once-fervent anti-imperialist Betancourt went to great lengths to nurture a friendship with the head of Creole Petroleum (a Standard Oil subsidiary), Nelson Rockefeller. The relationship paid dividends as the oil magnate and the junta partnered on a number of economic development projects. Betancourt also improved Venezuela's relationship with the Truman administration. As the historian Judith Ewell noted, the one-time communist "had concluded that democracy and social reform in a major oil producing country could only be achieved with Washington's consent."[60]

Acción Democrática's explosive growth—from an estimated eighty thousand adherents in 1941, the year the party was founded, to a half-million seven years later—gave it a singular advantage over its rivals. While AD won three national elections by convincing margins, the endless electioneering that accompanied those contests ginned up tensions, however. The party's cardinal sin was its reluctance to reach across the aisle and work with the opposition.[61]

AD's haughtiness triggered a backlash from powerful elements of civil society, which found themselves unable to defend their interests in the new political environment. Given that this was Venezuela's first experiment with civilian governance, it was not surprising that support for the new order, especially among elites, was tenuous. By excluding their opponents from legislative coalitions and senior appointments in the bureaucracy and neglecting to consult on policy matters with rival parties, the *trienio* leaders cost themselves dearly in the court of public opinion. In the brief time they held power, they managed to alienate members of the oligarchy, the Catholic Church, and the military high command.[62] Indicative of the ill will was the pejorative label foisted on AD members by the opposition: "Adeco"—a contraction of AD and Communist. Although initially it was meant as an epithet, the term later became a badge of honor to party militants.[63]

Examples of the junta's overreach included a new law that challenged the church's traditional preserve, private education, and its decision to send a message that corruption, long the coin of the realm in a country awash in oil revenues, was no longer tolerated in the new democratic Venezuela. Betancourt, who always set a scrupulous example of probity, established a Tribunal of Civil and Administrative Responsibilities, which brought charges against more than 150 former public officials, including two former presidents, López Contreras and Medina Angarita. Those found culpable were fined and had their properties confiscated, angering many who believed the process was politically motivated and arbitrary. Concerns that the junta's governance amounted to rule by fiat were given additional credence when overzealous Adeco militants sabotaged the rallies of opposition parties. Moreover, the party's candidate, Gallegos, who won the presidential election handily in 1947, tactlessly declared in his inaugural address that his decisive victory was a mandate and that he fully intended to carry out AD's agenda.[64]

Initially, the high command was pleased with the performance of the provisional government. In a public rebuke of its former commanders-in-chief, the coup leaders lavished praise on the junta. "In only eight months, the Revolution has done more for the army than your government, in which we of the Armed Forces had so many hopes, hopes that were ultimately disappointed."[65] That honeymoon, however, was short-lived. Even though Gomecista-era holdovers were removed from active service and the armed forces' budget tripled during the *trienio*, the high command, which had made this experiment in democratic rule possible, was plainly upset that it was relegated to a subordinate role in the new government. Nor was it pleased with political interference in military appointments.[66] It became alarmed at AD's efforts to win over dissident officers and with rumors that the party was arming its partisans. The result was incessant conspiratorial activities within the armed forces. As one officer recalled, the military could be its own worst enemy: "the organization of conspiracies was the order of the day during those three long years; the lack of confidence within the armed institution was constantly manifested by the unfaithfulness, disloyalty and suspiciousness that was shown for superiors, comrades in arms and subordinates."[67]

Factionalism within the ruling party mirrored the military's dysfunction. Disputes within AD's leadership concerning tactics and direction sent mixed signals at a time when unity of purpose was required. Despite its mandate at the polls and strong support from organized labor, the peasantry, and professionals, the party's hold on power was never secure because democratic institutions were so weak. Finally, AD's decision to name Gallegos as its standard bearer was a mistake; the novelist lacked the requisite political skills to navigate such a fraught moment.[68]

The November 1948 coup—undertaken by the very same military officers who had installed AD in power three years earlier—was not as unexpected and (initially, at least) as unpopular as it might have looked. The high command was regarded in some quarters as national heroes, since it had stepped away from the political fray in 1945 and handed over power to civilians. Whether or not the reports that AD was arming its militants were overblown, what the military wanted to prevent at all costs was another *Bogotazo*. Pérez Jiménez presented Gallegos with an ominous ultimatum, which would have significantly reconfigured his cabinet, circumscribing AD's influence by incorporating additional members of the military and the political opposition in the government. When the president refused to consider these "requests," the coup became a foregone conclusion.

When the *junta militar* promised to return Venezuela to democratic rule in the near future, many took it at its word. While some political parties took a wait-and-see approach, AD's leadership never believed for a moment that the military junta would relinquish power without a fight, and it initiated a bitter, decadelong battle to restore democracy. Years of organizing had paid dividends. Its political base in the countryside, and to a lesser extent in the country's burgeoning urban centers, became the backbone of the resistance against the dictatorship. During the 1950s a resolute AD operated clandestinely inside the country and abroad.[69]

Prior to the Venezuelan coup, at the inter-American meetings in Bogotá, Betancourt warned of the perils of remaining indifferent to the authoritarian resurgence. Dictatorships anywhere, he cautioned, imperiled democrats everywhere. What was especially disconcerting was the emergence of an informal coalition of dictatorships, which he labeled La Internacional de la Espada. The tyrants not only shared intelligence and assisted each other in rooting out dissidents in their own countries, but they insidiously backed "revanchist groups of regressive political forces" in the region's remaining democracies.[70] He could have been referring to the *trienio*'s having to squelch several right-wing plots that were aided and abetted by Trujillo and Somoza.

In fact, he also had tiny Costa Rica in mind, which had just fended off an incursion from Somoza's National Guard. Shouldn't the newly established OAS take as its first order of business to collectively condemn and penalize Somoza's flagrant violation of the principle of nonintervention, he asked the delegates. Interestingly, the final order of business at the inter-American meetings was not an injunction against the Nicaraguan despot but a consolation prize of sorts—awarding Venezuela the honor of hosting the next meetings in 1954. If it was given to validate his nation's democratic turn, it felt all the more ironic when participants assembled in Caracas six years later. By then Betancourt and many of his confederates were in exile, and their homeland was once again under the thumb of dictatorship.[71]

The notable exception to the authoritarian resurgence took place, surprisingly enough, in Guatemala, a country with no track record of democratic governance. The 1944 October Revolution survived numerous coup attempts to implement a number of ambitious reforms, including the abolition of forced labor, the legalization of unions, a progressive labor code, and the extension of voting rights to women and the indigenous. The "Guatemalan Spring" managed to buck the region's authoritarian trend until 1954.[72]

Conclusions

For reformers, the last years of the decade had profound consequences. An Aprista leader put it best. "The year 1948 was terrible for everyone. Some sinister hand had decided to crush our hearts, not only mine, not only those of the Apristas, but the hearts of all Latin Americans. Every day brought the announcement of another calamity."[73] Those fortunate enough to escape the repression gravitated to the few remaining democratic states. As they had during an earlier wave of repression in the late 1920s and early 1930s, they rededicated themselves to ousting dictatorships and retaking power.

It is perhaps understandable why the onset of the Cold War is the factor that scholars privilege when they analyze the brief rise and precipitous fall of democracies during the first five years of the postwar period. As indicated, that observation obscures a more complex reality. While the Truman administration's desire for a reprise of Fortress America in the hemisphere—this time against international communism—did emerging reformers no favor, it does not explain why the democratic surge ended so abruptly.

As the Venezuelan, Peruvian, and Nicaraguan cases illustrate, endogenous forces were of far greater import than the Cold War's arrival. Nor can the region's militaries be easily pigeonholed as defenders of the traditional order. In a number of cases, the armed forces deposed strongmen, making it possible for democracies to take root in the first place. That they changed their minds a few years later had little to do with the fear of Soviet penetration. Indeed, the hemisphere's communist parties were everywhere on the defensive. The reasons that military establishments reversed course varied and had far more to do with their suspicions about reformers' intentions and their perception that their institutional prerogatives were under attack. If they rhetorically invoked anticommunism, they did so because they knew that it played well in Washington and that it opened the spigot ever wider to armaments and training.

What also preoccupied the region's armed forces was the undeclared war without borders between democrats and dictators. That long-running conflict was given new life by the postwar democratic surge. In this struggle, the fledgling democracies gave succor, to the extent that they could, to a motley constellation of exiles. While some political refugees were of a leftist persuasion, their overriding objective was to build a democratic future in their homelands. In that respect, the Caribbean Legion should be understood as a quixotic, misbegotten effort by an inchoate group of rebels who had banded together to defeat a common enemy. The only site where they contributed in a meaningful way was Costa Rica. Ironically, the government that Figueres's army vanquished was not a dictatorship. It certainly was corrupt, and its electoral practices were suspect, but policywise Figueres's "revolution" simply took up where his predecessors left off.

To be sure, the exiles who launched attacks against dictatorships often were their own worst enemies. Ideological disagreements, factionalism, and leadership squabbles inhibited repeated attempts to forge unified fronts. To make sense of how the Legion's different constituencies emerged when and why they did, we turn to the Dominican opposition to Trujillo.

CHAPTER NINE

Give the Canary Birdseed and
Listen to It Sing

Trujillo's dictatorship doesn't just imprison, kill and rob, it
also degrades.

—LUIS MUÑOZ MARÍN TO CHARLES PORTER, April 23, 1957

JUAN ISIDRO JIMENES GRULLÓN, one of the founders of the Partido Revolucionario Democrático (PRD), spent twenty-six years in exile, splitting
time between Cuba, Puerto Rico, Venezuela, and the States. He was not
alone. Whether lodged in Havana, Caracas, Port-au-Prince, Mexico City,
San José, San Juan, Guatemala City, Bogotá, Panama City, Santiago,
Miami, or New York, stateless bands of Dominican exiles knew that their
stays would be brief. Given how vulnerable and short-lived democracies
were during this period, and how susceptible civilian governments were
to domestic and external pressures, an exile's only certainty was that the
welcome sign, often without warning, would soon be switched off.

Navigating the political eddies of each of their new homes was an education in itself. Fortunately, they benefited from the generous assistance of
like-minded hosts, who not only lent a hand or provided shelter or funding, but in some cases, risked their lives for the cause of Dominican liberty.
As the exiles learned to their lasting regret, however, such altruism, no
matter how well-intentioned, often came with political strings attached. As

we shall see, in 1934 and then again in 1947, Cuban politicians, who empathized with the Dominican exiles' aims and who invested considerable resources into plotting, managed to sink promising expeditions.

Resistance to Trujillo's dictatorship came not only from without. Especially during the first few years of the regime, conspiracies bubbled up from within the military establishment and from civil society. Too often, scholarship on the regime has given short shrift to the opposition's persistent plotting, uprisings, and assassination attempts, which only serves to magnify the trope of Trujillo's omnipotence. It is remarkable how committed and imaginative the dictator's opponents were—both on and off the island—especially considering the daunting obstacles and their repeated failures. What remained elusive was how to cultivate and sustain linkages between the internal and external opposition.

Trujillo's regime went after dissidents at home and abroad and was a constant thorn in the side of democratic governments that lent them assistance. Moderates, such as Grau, Betancourt, and Figueres, were hectored and their administrations undermined. The general's aggressive foreign policy succeeded in keeping his adversaries off-balance. Efforts by his patrons in Washington to persuade his regime to stand down were, with some notable exceptions, unsuccessful. For three decades, a small country with limited resources pursued an astonishingly aggressive foreign policy, which destabilized the entire Caribbean Basin.

Trujillo not only disrupted democratic governments, he also subverted dictatorial regimes, especially if they were considered threats. Less frequently and more idiosyncratically, regional despots experienced his wrath because they were insufficiently compliant or outwardly appreciative for gifts or loans he had bestowed. What follows examines the regime's brutal methods to establish its authority and cow the domestic opposition, and how rebels within Trujillo's own army and among the civilian population resisted. Then I turn to the threat posed to the dictatorship from the diaspora, focusing on two different nodes of resistance—Haiti and Cuba. It should be emphasized, though, that the despot utilized the same strategies wherever dissidents resided. In each instance, Trujillo responded as if the very survival of his regime depended on it.

Repression

Early on, Dominicans knew what to expect from Trujillo. In the first few chaotic months of 1930, the general not only betrayed the president he served, Horacio Vásquez (1924–1930), but he deceived a popular politician, Rafael Estrella Ureña, and a budding Civic Movement composed of intellectuals and professionals.[1] After forcing the president to step down, Trujillo employed ruthless repression and a rigged election to seize control of the government.[2] Well before he entered the political fray, it was apparent to the U.S. legation that the general was "vain," "autocratic," and "lacking in scruples." His actions during the winter and spring of 1930 did nothing to disabuse diplomats of that assessment.[3]

Unlike Machado, who waited three months after being sworn in as president before ordering his first political assassination, Trujillo went after his enemies even before he took office.[4] His paramilitary thugs, "La 42," unleashed a wave of terror in the run-up to the May elections. According to historian Frank Moya Pons, wherever La 42 went, they left "a trail of corpses behind."[5]

The notorious hoodlums, who received salaries, arms, and "military honors," also became a proving ground for future assassins. One of the regime's most feared *pistoleros*, Félix Bernardino, got his start in the paramilitary organization. Thanks to an elaborate network of informants and spies that Trujillo created with the assistance of his former Marine handlers during the U.S. occupation, meetings of the opposition were routinely disrupted. Disappearances, a term usually associated with the latter stages of the Cold War, were commonplace. Among the reported missing were former members of the cabinet, reporters, landowners, businessmen, and students.[6] In the first year of Trujillo's rule alone, conservative estimates of the dead or disappeared numbered in the hundreds.[7]

In Andrés Requena's didactic, polemical novel, *Cementerio sin cruces* (Cemetery without Crosses), at a certain point, authorities decide that the sight of so many victims' bodies lying in the streets in plain sight is counterproductive. From that point on, the dead are dumped in the sea and fed to the sharks. Questions about the missing are strongly discouraged, lest they draw attention to the perpetrators. Still, news of the disappeared circulates by word of mouth. In fact, the novel's title, its *dedicatoria* to the "thousands murdered," and its plot line illustrate how the entire island becomes a peculiar kind of graveyard, one where Dominicans cannot even pay their respects to their loved ones.[8]

Requena, who served in Trujillo's foreign service before becoming one of the regime's most dogged critics, was assassinated in New York by a hitman hired by Bernardino three years after the novel's publication.

His account is corroborated by another insider-turned-outsider, Carmen "Carmita" Landestoy Félix, who lamented that the dictator "takes pleasure in denying them [families of victims] the only recourse of their heart," knowing full well that the "sacred custom" of mourning the dead was "so deeply rooted" among her countrymen.[9]

To be sure, Trujillo was not without popular support. As historian Richard Turits has described so well, by bestowing land parcels and other gifts, he purchased the loyalty of the peasantry.[10] The dictator's patronage also extended to the needs of the soldiers, who received periodic bonuses and were eligible for inexpensive housing and access to a club, a theater, and a military hospital considered to be one of the best in the country.[11] But his clientele paled in comparison to the devoted following that a Perón or a Cárdenas enjoyed.

Spearheading the democratic resistance was the politician and diplomat Ángel Morales, whose 1930 vice presidential bid was a casualty of Trujillo's shady electoral maneuvers. In fact, Morales and other members of his Alianza Nacional Progresista Party were fortunate to survive the campaign. After soldiers broke up their political rally in Monte Cristi on the north coast, Morales and other Alianza politicians returned to the capital in a three-car convoy. On the outskirts of the country's second-largest city, Santiago de los Caballeros, soldiers opened fire, spraying bullets scattershot at the automobiles.[12]

Facing such intimidation, the party withdrew its candidates, urged its adherents to abstain from voting, and then sued to have the count invalidated. Before the Appeals Court could render its decision, however, La 42 paid a visit to the courthouse, persuaded the judges that it was not in their best interest to rule on the case, and confiscated the ballots. Under the circumstances, the judges acted prudently; some went into hiding, while others walked into foreign legations and requested asylum.[13] From that point on, to be an Alianzista was to be a target. Even those lucky to flee the island continued to be harassed, their lives at risk.[14]

Fearing for his own safety, Morales left the island, never to return. For the next three decades, he remained a well-respected and influential figure in the exile community, in part because of his friendship with another inveterate opponent of the dictator, Welles.[15] Even before he left the island, Morales had urged Welles to use his influence to prevail upon the Hoover administration to "adopt an attitude of open opposition to Trujillo." If not, he predicted, the general "will be master of his own destiny until he is defeated by force." On hiatus from the State Department,

Welles advised Morales that the opposition should take matters into its own hands before the dictator consolidated his rule.[16]

Like his mentor, Vásquez, Morales believed that his country should maintain amicable relations with the United States. Others in the opposition, however, were wary of the United States, especially since the Hoover administration had recognized the dictator and helped prop him up by dispensing economic and military assistance.

Welles knew the Dominican Republic and its history well, having spent two years there as a special commissioner in the early 1920s. He was persuaded that democracy in the Dominican Republic depended on the "absolute impartiality" of a newly trained military. Marine officers stayed on after the occupation in an advisory capacity, ostensibly to ensure the professionalism of the National Police and to reinforce its nonpolitical character. As proved to be the case in Nicaragua and Haiti, however, Welles's hopes for an apolitical constabulary were naïve. It was Trujillo who became the chief beneficiary of the U.S. withdrawal, earning a string of promotions during the early 1920s that placed him in a position of leadership.[17]

As he had in Cuba, Welles plotted behind the scenes to undermine the new regime. Openly aiding and abetting exiles like Morales, he leaked their inflammatory broadsides to columnists such as Drew Pearson, who wrote a series of scathing articles about the dictatorship. After his mission in Cuba, Welles was appointed assistant secretary of state for inter-American affairs by Franklin Roosevelt, a promotion that, on the face of it, augured well for those, like Morales's Alianzistas, desirous of removing Trujillo from power.[18]

During the Roosevelt years, however, the State Department did not speak with one voice. A second group, led by Hull, thought about U.S.–Latin American relations pragmatically. Unlike previous North American diplomats, who were often arrogant and patronizing, the humble and folksy Hull appeared to be the very embodiment of the Good Neighbor. Like his predecessor Stimson, Hull preferred strong rulers, especially when they proved loyal. Working with the Trujillos of the world was far preferable, in his estimation, to chronic instability or revolution.[19]

That Welles kept in close contact with Morales and other Dominican exiles remained an abiding concern to Trujillo. It was axiomatic that Washington's support was critical to the dictator's survival, and he was determined to maintain favorable relations. Even though he was impressed by what European fascist leaders had accomplished, Trujillo was acutely aware of his nation's client status in a U.S. sphere of influence, and understood how the State Department perceived possible ties with the Nazi regime.

The despot was not without influential supporters. The U.S. War Department (renamed the Department of Defense in 1947) viewed him as a dependable ally. In fact, he hired North American officers, who knew him from the time of the occupation, as consultants. They never missed an opportunity to praise him publicly, while working behind the scenes on his behalf.[20]

Occasionally, he defied or contested diplomatic pressure, and during his tenure relations between the two countries were far from tranquil. But the State Department never seriously entertained altering relations with Trujillo until the last months of his thirty-one-year rule. Confirmation of this is found in a remarkably forthright CIA report filed in 1957: "Trujillo ... is fully aware ... that there is a definite limit to how far he can go in irritating the United States government. He is aware of the fates of some past Caribbean heads of state who defied the United States. He will make every effort to cooperate, providing cooperation does not destroy his family, his authority or his intelligence network, upon which he bases his defensive system."[21]

During his first term in office, Trujillo's hold on power was never assured. In 1933 the regime declared Morales and other prominent exiles "traitors to the nation." Their letters to loved ones on the island were intercepted and their properties confiscated, condemning them to a hand-to-mouth existence abroad. For the elitist Morales, this must have been quite an adjustment. When he was not plotting against the regime, he worked for a lumber business in Puerto Rico owned by a similarly displaced countryman. Historian Robert Cassá has described Morales as scrupulously honest, someone taken up with the biases of his social class—"appearances, race and culture ... although not so much money."[22]

Family and friends who remained behind paid the price for his outspokenness. In what would become a staple of trujillista spite, relatives of those deemed "enemies of the state" could not obtain passports. In fact, Morales's wife was never permitted to leave the island.[23] And when holding the relations of notable exile leaders under house arrest did not cow an opposition leader, then harassment and blackmail of family members was sure to follow. Juan Bosch's and Pericles Franco's fathers, for instance, were arrested on trumped-up charges and remained imprisoned until protests lodged in the international press were brought to bear.[24]

Even efforts to assist the Morales family were repeatedly punished. A family friend, Dr. Ramón de Lara, was arrested for helping Morales's wife send money to her husband. Just as he had opposed Vásquez's bid for re-election, de Lara, who was a prominent physician, hospital director, and former rector of the Universidad de Santo Domingo, had come out publicly in early 1934 against Trujillo's bid for a second term in office. His candor resulted in a twenty-year prison sentence, which included a regimen of forced labor. Despondent, he tried to take his life in prison. With De Lara's health failing, Trujillo decided to release him in December 1936. The physician promptly left the country, settling in Caracas, a hotbed of anti-Trujillo discontent, where he became one of the leaders of the opposition.[25]

Morales's friendship with Welles was of great concern to the dictator. So much so that in April 1935, Trujillo hired a hitman to assassinate his rival, then residing in New York City. In a case of mistaken identity, the man killed in his apartment was fellow exile Sergio Bencosme, who had been tasked by the opposition with acquiring arms for a rebellion.[26] A New York City grand jury indicted a Dominican purportedly in the pay of Trujillo for Bencosme's murder. Efforts to extradite Luis "Chichi" de la Fuente Rubirosa from the Dominican Republic, however, proved fruitless.[27]

This case of mistaken identity had far-reaching implications. Police believed Chichi's first cousin Porfirio Rubirosa, then a diplomat in Trujillo's foreign service, had tapped his kinsman for the hit, and was in New York the night before the murder. But when detectives tried to question him, the Dominican government refused to make him available, citing diplomatic immunity. From that point on, several of the regime's most dangerous *pistoleros* had sinecures in the foreign ministry.[28]

It is also unclear why Morales was targeted at that particular moment. Like other critics, he used his pen to great effect, publishing numerous columns in the U.S. and Latin American press.[29] Perhaps Trujillo's spies learned of Morales's involvement in the making of an upcoming *March of Time* newsreel. "An American Dictator" appeared in theaters in the United States just over a year after Bencosme's murder. Its impact was far greater than a one-and-done column. *March of Time* newsreels typically ran for ninety days in more than five thousand theaters in three thousand cities across the United States. The audience for such films was estimated at twelve million viewers. The short films, akin to contemporary docudramas, combined authentic footage with staged scenes. The newsreels presented themselves as even-handed, but often were one-sided polemics on controversial topics. At that moment, the evils of fascism were a theme of special interest to *Time*, the *March of Time's* parent company, which may explain why the filmmakers were drawn to an exposé on Trujillo.[30]

The six-minute film portrayed the dictator in a decidedly unflattering light. Making comparisons to Mussolini, Hitler, and Stalin, the newsreel emphasized his brutality and venality while mocking him for renaming the capital, streets, buildings, statues, parks, and even his yacht after himself.[31] Morales's fingerprints were everywhere. Not only was he interviewed on camera, but he probably provided content, including the names of prominent members of the opposition whom the dictator had assassinated. The film's most dramatic recreation, the mistaken murder of Bencosme in Morales's Manhattan apartment, was interspersed with cutaways to a staged recreation of Trujillo toasting the victim's health at a banquet.[32]

If Trujillo entertained thoughts about eliminating the dissident before "An American Dictator's" screening, he had ample motivation to do so afterward. On July 22, the regime staged a massive demonstration in the Parque Colón in the capital to denounce the film. The dictator and his acolytes also campaigned vigorously to shut down showings in the States, lobbying the filmmakers, theaters, and the State Department. Hull was prevailed upon to issue a generic statement of regret and to lobby the filmmakers. New York's Radio City Music Hall did suspend its screenings, but the effort to censor it nationwide only served to attract attention. The regime also pressured governments in the Caribbean, Central America, and England against screening the newsreel.[33]

Morales was troublesome because he made it a point to share his opinions with both North American and Latin American journalists. Albert Hicks, who wrote a searing exposé of the regime in 1946, *Blood in the Streets*, met with Morales in New York on several occasions and "through him met many Dominicans."[34] Morales and other exiles also befriended a Puerto Rican newspaper editor, Francisco Girona Pérez, who in 1937 published a screed documenting the regime's many abuses. Exiles considered *Las fechorías del bandolero Trujillo* to be "the best work of anti-Trujillo propaganda written to date." The author claimed that he had "received hundreds of letters from Puerto Rico and abroad" requesting copies of his book. There was even interest in translating the muckraking account into English.

But Trujillo had his diplomats pressure Puerto Rican authorities to charge the author with libel. A Puerto Rican court found Girona guilty and copies of *Las fechorías* were confiscated. The author appealed the conviction and four years later, in 1941, Puerto Rico's Tribunal Superior overturned the lower court's decision. Although he eventually lost the case, Trujillo's ploy proved successful. Not only were copies of the book removed from circulation, it never was translated into English.[35]

The dictatorship was averse to negative publicity of any kind. The highest priority was given to controlling the content and the flow of information at home and abroad. To that end, his brother Petán ran the government's radio network, La Voz Dominicana. By the end of the dictatorship, government-owned media dominated the airwaves, with thirty-one radio and two television stations reaching fifty thousand Dominicans daily.[36] Any news that might reflect poorly was kept from the public. So acute was the general's sensitivity to unfavorable coverage that reports of the ousters of neighboring dictators in 1944—the Salvadoran Martínez and Guatemala's Ubico—were censored.[37] Thanks to monitoring equipment provided by the War Department to track clandestine German radio stations in the Caribbean, the Dominican military listened in on Cuban, Venezuelan, and Haitian radio stations that lent airtime to exiles. Dissidents, however, came up with creative ways to reach Dominicans back home. A Guatemalan radio station with sufficient power to reach island listeners, for instance, played merengues that were critical of the regime.[38]

The political theorist Juan Linz has singled out Trujillo as the archetype of the sultanistic ruler—a hybrid head of state who melded characteristics of both authoritarianism and totalitarianism. Conversations with Spanish exiles, especially Jesús de Galíndez, another regime insider who later turned against the dictatorship and paid for his outspokenness with his life, convinced Linz that while Trujillo embodied many traits characteristic of traditional autocrats—the absence of charisma, the cultivation of an extravagant personality cult, the customary practice of patronage and institutionalized gift-giving, an unquenchable thirst for venality, a hollow embrace of the trappings of constitutional rule, the arbitrary utilization of terror, the reliance on trusted family members and business associates, and the expectation of unquestioned loyalty—his methods nonetheless reflected a distinctive blend of the traditional and the modern.

What set his rule apart was his absolute dominion over his subjects, "unencumbered by rules or any commitment to an ideology," and the adoption of modern technologies. This not only facilitated the tracking down and elimination of suspected enemies of the state but enabled the regime to scrutinize and control the lives of everyday Dominicans.[39]

Linz's assessment was corroborated by an admiring contemporary of Trujillo, the Venezuelan minister of the interior Laurenano Vallenilla Lanz Planchart. "Trujillo is a special case, a rare persona." Other dictators operate under constraints, he added, but Trujillo's fiat is law. Even exiles cannot elude him. He either "tracks them down wherever they are or bends them to his will."[40]

Telephone eavesdropping, jamming of foreign radio broadcasts, and surveillance of foreign diplomats and journalists all contributed to a claustrophobic atmosphere on the island. Every important societal institution, from the armed forces to the police, from Trujillo's political party to the bureaucracy to bootblacks, barbers, and lottery ticket vendors, was expected to watch, listen, and report on their communities. The regime even enlisted domestic servants to spy on their employers.[41]

Informants fared no better. Should an individual disappear, it was better to "forget that name, don't ask about him anymore," Landestoy explained. Bolito, the snitch in Requena's nightmarish account, whose eyes and ears led to the brutal death of an alleged political enemy, could be anyone and everyone. While given an impressive title, Special Agent of Political Investigations, Bolito drew a meager salary from the country's only sanctioned political party, Trujillo's Dominican Party, and engendered precious little respect from his neighbors.[42]

Surveillance was not a state secret. In fact, the general made a personal appeal in a 1946 government circular that it was incumbent upon civil servants to remain vigilant. "I want to know if you have had conversations with persons who are enemies, unfriendly or neutral toward the government and what efforts you made to influence those persons in its favor. If you did not, what was your reason?"[43] As historian Robin Derby has illustrated so elegantly, over the course of his three decades in power, the dictator and his inner circle cunningly utilized secrecy, rumors, leaks, denunciations, and praise-speech to cultivate a "culture of compliance."[44]

Another factor that diminished outright resistance was the Trujillos' stranglehold on the labor market. A U.S. government report written several months after Trujillo's assassination in May 1961 estimated that 45 percent of the labor force owed their livelihood to businesses either directly or indirectly linked to Trujillo, family members, or business associates. This included the lucrative sugar sector; an estimated four-fifths of that industry was in family hands by 1961. An additional 35 percent of the population was employed by numerous government-controlled enterprises, such as banks, utilities, hotels, and the armed forces. To be sure, the Trujillos' economic dominion increased over time, but even during the dictatorship's first decade there is ample evidence that the monopolization of entire sectors of the national economy was well underway.[45]

In most respects, Trujillo followed in lockstep the path taken and the practices employed by his mentor, Gómez. Nowhere was this more apparent than the ways their obsessive preoccupation with their regime's survival assumed almost supernatural proportions. What Coronil ascribed to the Venezuelan tyrant applies equally well to his apprentice: "his ability to defuse his enemies' plans added to the mysterious aura constructed around his public persona and enhanced his image as a powerful caudillo."[46]

At times, the regime literally buried its unspeakable brutalities, but on occasion it displayed them "to highlight their theatrical effect." After Sergeant Enrique Blanco took to the hills to launch a rebellion, he fought an extremely effective guerrilla campaign for the better part of a year. So admired was Blanco that he became the subject of a popular merengue. But after months of fighting, rather than turn himself in, the exhausted and now cornered sergeant took his own life. Trujillo's men, upset that they were deprived of their prey, decided to send a message to the rebel's campesino followers anyway: they placed Blanco's remains in a chair and paraded it around Santiago and surrounding pueblos in a wagon, stopping long enough in each locale to force residents to sing and dance with the corpse.[47]

The dictator utilized multiple, overlapping paramilitary groups to eliminate regime opponents. Composed of current and former soldiers and policemen, former convicts, and civilians, groups such as Los Jinetes del Este, Los Cuarteleros, and La Reserva Cívica reported directly to Trujillo. Each had specific responsibilities. Los Cuarteleros, for instance, were charged with rooting out sedition within the military. Other groups turned out to be proving grounds for those who demonstrated proficiency. Bernardino, the head of Los Jinetes, was the dictator's childhood friend. He swore fealty to his *jefe* because Trujillo had granted him an early release from prison and clemency for a murder he had committed. He proved so adept that the general later brought him into his inner circle and tasked him with special assignments abroad. One critic claimed that the dictator had a policy of periodically even ordering the death of his thugs, in part because they knew too much, but also to send a message to other members of a paramilitary group. Only three of La 42, for instance, survived. One of those select few was Bernardino. As one student

General Rafael Trujillo during an official state visit,
Washington, DC, July 6, 1939. Library of Congress,
Prints & Photographs Division, photograph
by Harris & Ewing, LC-H22-D-6917.

of the Latin American military notes, Trujillo's deployment of state-
sponsored "gangsterism" was more akin to the traditional *caudillismo* of
Cabrera Estrada and Gómez than the professional constabularies that
policymakers in Washington had in mind.[48]

On the island, no fewer than ten homegrown conspiracies—many
led by disaffected members of Trujillo's army—emerged in the first four
years of his rule. All were brutally suppressed by troops loyal to the regime. But the plotting left the despot on edge. Given how much dissension there was within the ranks, Trujillo understandably harbored a
healthy distrust of the high command. As an insider put it: "The Dominican Army, far from being a Praetorian Guard, was kept in a state of
frightened subjection. Trujillo took every precaution to guard himself

against a military coup. Officers were shifted constantly from post to post, and were ruthlessly purged at the slightest provocation."[49]

The reliance on the security apparatus to undermine the military's esprit de corps was one of the dictatorship's most durable features. In his memoirs, the last chief of Trujillo's Servicio de Inteligencia Militar (SIM), Johnny Abbes García, confirmed his agency's autonomy, although he did admit that members of the armed forces were tapped from time to time to carry out "repressive functions" after hours.[50] The regime's overriding goals were to isolate and humiliate dissenting members of the high command while promoting factionalism within the institution.[51]

Resistance

Despite such impediments, civil society, working in tandem with disgruntled officers, refused to be cowed. Between 1932 and 1935, no fewer than four attempts on the dictator's life were foiled. Materials for the bomb for the initial plot in 1932, an attempt by the student group Asociación Nacional de Estudiantes Universitarios, were smuggled in from Puerto Rico. This drove home the need for a sophisticated counterintelligence apparatus, one beholden only to Trujillo, which could effectively harass, penetrate, and neutralize the opposition on and off the island.[52]

In the first months of 1934, significant resistance emerged in the Cibao region. The central highlands had long been an autonomous stronghold, apprehensive of the capital's political clout.[53] Secondary students, former military officers, and local intellectuals banded together to eliminate Trujillo.[54] Organizers were determined to stop him from staging another fraudulent presidential election later that spring. A young normal school teacher, Ángel Miolán, recalled that faculty and students were "inspired" by the actions of Cuban students, who had just "waged a heroic battle against the dictator Gerardo Machado, forcing him to flee the country."[55] Throughout early 1934, the resistance in Santiago bombed public buildings, set private residences to the torch, plastered the walls of the city with broadsheets, and tried to assassinate both the dictator and the governor of the province during Trujillo's visit to the city in March. But the regime's security apparatus infiltrated the movement and successfully thwarted the plot.[56] The rebels were arrested, tortured, and those fortunate to survive the mistreatment were tried and convicted. Of the forty-one participants who were later arrested, half were students and professionals. Somehow, over the next few months,

the imprisoned organizers of the uprising were able to coordinate a series of bombings in different parts of the city.[57] One of the movement's
leaders, Jimenes Grullón, who later spearheaded exile opposition to the
dictatorship, was sentenced to twenty years in prison. In a move that he
would come to regret, Trujillo released Jimenes Grullón from prison
eighteen months later, and the leftist fled the island.[58]

The Santiago uprising unraveled, and the reasons for its failure continued to plague the homegrown opposition. Dissension within the
ranks, insufficient firepower (largely because the Marines had disarmed
the populace during the occupation), the logistical difficulties of coordinated uprisings, and the regime's sophisticated surveillance methods all
were contributing factors. While a 1946 State Department report noted
that crackdowns became more selective over time and that "open acts of
repression are less necessary," internal opposition persisted throughout
the late 1930s and 1940s. Ninety were killed, for example, after a plot led
by a military officer was exposed in 1940. Similar numbers were put to
death quelling significant civic and labor unrest in 1945–1946, and in
1946 a disaffected officer plotting against the regime was arrested and
tortured for months before being hanged in prison, while twenty-nine
alleged coconspirators were rounded up and murdered.[59] In fact, the sporadic protests that took place in 1945–1946 were by far the largest of
Trujillo's three-decade-long rule. As late as October 1946 several thousand protesters took to the streets of the capital, with smaller demonstrations occurring in Santiago, La Vega, San Pedro de Macorís, and
Barahona. Each time the protests met with fierce repression and could
not be sustained.[60]

Resistance to the dictatorship came from without as well. Here
again, the regime's best defense was a relentless offense. Foreign Minister Manuel Peña Batlle captured the prevailing siege mentality best: "It
is time for the Dominican people to realize that they are surrounded by
enemies, that there exists, concerted and unveiled, constant activity
aimed at damaging them, destroying their most intimate connections,
dragging them along the darkest paths of disorder and anarchy."[61]

The Haitian Dilemma

Having political exiles plotting in Haiti was especially worrisome to the
dictator. So too was the sparsely populated frontier between the two
countries, which could be used as a staging ground for an invasion. As a

member of the U.S. legation to Haiti noted, Trujillo "not only wants a friendly government in power (here)," but one "that won't permit the presence of Dominican exiles."[62] When Trujillo learned in early 1932 that former general Daniel Ariza, then residing in Haiti's second-largest city, Cap Haïtien, was plotting, he hired hitmen to assassinate him. Thanks to the timely intervention of the Haitian National Police, Trujillo's "spies" were arrested before they could strike.[63] Ariza and his followers subsequently crossed the frontier and attacked an armory in Mao, more than fifty miles inland from the border. Two soldiers were injured, but the attack was repulsed. In response, Trujillo's diplomats lodged vigorous protests with both Haitian and North American authorities. U.S. Marines, who occupied Haiti until mid-1934, were given orders "to inform all Dominican refugees residing in their districts" to desist from taking any action against their government.[64]

To keep the pressure on, Trujillo used carrots and sticks, sometimes menacing his neighbor by massing troops along the border, while at other times extending an olive branch to Haitian officials to enlist their cooperation. During a meeting with Haitian president Stenío Vincent, the Dominican leader agreed to cede approximately 100,000 acres of land along the disputed border in exchange for Vincent's pledge to rein in the exiles.[65] When Vincent's administration dawdled on its part of the bargain, a well-placed bribe to Interior Minister Elie Lescot expedited the exiles' forced relocation from Cap-Haïtien and Port-au-Prince to Jérémie in southwestern Haiti, far from the border.[66]

Several exiles residing in Haiti protested to Vincent and the Haitian Senate that their countrymen were "jailed without justification," on the basis of unsubstantiated claims by Dominican diplomats. Labeling them "agitators," they added, made it impossible to hold on to jobs. So destitute were some of the dissidents that at one point a collection was taken up by sympathetic merchants in Cap-Haïtien. Trujillo's agents' true purpose, the exiles claimed, was to force Vincent's hand and return them to the Dominican Republic, where they faced certain death. Comparing their predicament to Napoleon's exile on St. Helena, they strenuously objected to their relocation to Jérémie.[67]

Miolán's odyssey testifies to how purposefully Trujillo undermined Haitian sovereignty to harass his opponents. As one of the leaders of the Santiago uprising, in May 1934 he crossed the border to evade the regime's clutches. Unlike many who settled there, he was familiar with the culture and spoke Kreyòl, having grown up in Dajabón, a border town where many Dominicans of Haitian descent resided. When he was an adolescent his family had moved to Quartier Morín in northern Haiti, where he helped manage his father's tobacco plantation. Now on the run from Dominican authorities, he decided to move back in with his family. At first, Trujillo tried unsuccessfully to have Miolán extradited. But authorities eventually succumbed to diplomatic pressure and arrested him.[68]

During the three months he spent in Haitian prisons, Miolán attracted a great deal of notoriety. Not only did the local press run with his story, but nationalistic youths, deploring what they viewed as their government's unseemly capitulation to the Dominican strongman, showed their solidarity by sending him parcels of cigarettes and sweets. Even Dominican women working in the cabarets, he recalled, were kind enough to drop off a bed cover and a pillow "to make his captivity more bearable." Meanwhile, his father and several friends camped outside the prison every night to guard against his being spirited back to the Dominican Republic.

Miolán's support system was exceptional. More often surveillance abroad resulted in the exile community's policing of itself. So great was the anxiety that many, fearful of spies, took great pains to avoid coming in contact with known dissidents. Landestoy's commentary is telling in this regard: "When one goes abroad one has to be careful not to stumble across any exile, even if he or she is familiar to you." If an activist stayed at your hotel, she counseled, better to move to a different place, or if you caught a glance of certain individuals coming around the corner, walk the other way. Greeting them in public was risky, Landstoy warned, because "everyone knows what will happen to you when you return home."[69]

After Miolán was released from prison, he joined other expatriates in Jéremie. There, he had to withstand efforts by the Dominican minister to Haiti, Arístedes García Mella, to have authorities deport him to Jamaica. Infamous among exiles, the minister earned the nickname "Trujillo's Torquemada," a reference to the repressive Dominican monk who oversaw the Mexican Inquisition. García Mella was said to dispense safe conduct passes to dissidents, "almost all of whom were murdered when they crossed the [Dominican] border." His objective was to prevent Miolán from settling in Cuba, where dozens of dissidents were congregating. (At the same time, the diplomat pressed Haitian authorities to prohibit the entry of Dominican exiles coming from Cuba). But the rebel stubbornly held out, informing Haitian authorities that he would only consider a move to Cuba.[70]

Machado's ouster meant that for the moment Cuba was now a safe haven for Dominican refugees. In fact, Grau San Martín's provisional government went out of its way to assist the dissidents. In the fall of 1933, Guiteras dispatched a naval vessel to Jéremie to pick up exiles and bring them back to Cuba.[71] Although Miolán arrived at that remote outpost months after Guiteras and Grau had been forced out, the Dominican fondly remembered the Cuban minister of the interior's generosity some sixty years later. Jimenes Grullón seconded those thoughts: Guiteras's willingness to rescue his countrymen was an "unforgettable gesture."[72]

Another factor that prompted the exiles to leave Haiti was the withdrawal of the last contingent of U.S. Marines in August 1934. Absent a North American presence, the exiles believed that whatever restraints Trujillo was operating under were lifted. In fact, Miolán departed from Haiti a few days after the North American occupation came to an end.[73]

Trujillo's fears of subversion from without were not unfounded. In fact, he postponed his October 1934 visit to Port-au-Prince to meet with Vincent because of a purported attempt to assassinate him by members of the Cuban paramilitary organization ABC. The plot was detected before the armed assailants disembarked at the Haitian capital. Adding to the intrigue is that it was unclear whether their mark was actually Trujillo or Machado, since after its stopover in Port-au-Prince the ship was bound for Ciudad Trujillo, where the former Cuban dictator resided. Interrogation of those apprehended revealed that the plot was prompted by Trujillo's willingness to give asylum to Machado and his denial of the Cuban government's extradition request to return him to Cuba.[74]

A 1936 treaty between the Dominican Republic and Haiti that clarified the border zone failed to allay Trujillo's concerns.[75] The general was convinced that he needed to secure, militarize, and populate the frontier with "loyal" Dominicans, not Dominicans of Haitian birth who had lived in that fluid bilingual and bicultural border zone for generations. Vincent's willingness to cooperate was made more palatable by the general's promise to crack down on the Haitian president's political enemies, who at that moment were assembling in the Dominican capital.[76]

Trujillo repeatedly suborned Haitian politicians and members of its high command. According to a 1946 FBI report, even the Haitian secret police did his bidding.[77] Nor did he stand for criticism in the local press. Haitian leaders either accepted his blandishments and served his interests or were harassed. One all-too-conspicuous example was future president

Lescot, who by one estimate was gifted $160,000. His obsequious thank you note to the Dominican ruler speaks volumes about the asymmetrical nature of such transactions: "My family and I are slaves of your generosity and of your insurmountable kindness." Lescot's choice of words came back to haunt him when relations between the two leaders soured in 1942. When the once compliant Lescot turned against the Dominican ruler, the regime leaked his compromising letters to the press, with devastating consequences for the Haitian president.[78] The noted public intellectual Jean Price-Mars, then serving as ambassador to the Dominican Republic, captured the outrage felt by his countrymen: Lescot's letters, he remarked, "demonstrate ... to what extent the government of our country has been put up for auction."[79]

Even after most dissidents left Haiti, Dominican authorities remained vigilant about a potential invasion. It is unclear how much this factor played a role in the army's unprovoked massacre of six thousand unarmed Haitians living in the Dominican Republic during a ten-day rampage in October 1937, but a considerable number of the dead resided along the nation's northern frontier with Haiti.[80] Roosevelt and his advisors knew who was responsible for the killing spree: this gruesome operation was despicably labeled *El Corte* (the cutting down) because Dominican troops used machetes and clubs to murder their defenseless victims.

Haitians blamed both heads of state for the massacre—Vincent for acquiescing to a modest payoff from the Dominican government and Trujillo for conducting, in the words of the highly regarded writer Jacques Roumain, "a massive lynching." Roumain criticized the Dominican head of state from the apparent safety of Paris. But Dominican officials sued him in French courts on the charge of uttering an "outrage against a foreign head of state." Although arrested and put on trial, Roumain was never convicted.[81]

What aggravated exiles no end was the United States' kid glove treatment of Trujillo. It was not just Washington's recognition of his regime in 1930, or its muted response to El Corte, but the Roosevelt administration's willingness to hand Trujillo public relations victories, in the form of state visits, treaties, Export-Import Bank loans, and Lend-Lease sales of military equipment, that legitimized his rule and fed his megalomania.

The emoluments had everything to do with the Roosevelt administration's efforts to build a Fortress America in the hemisphere against Axis aggression. As diplomatic historian Eric Roorda has noted, the slew of agreements constituted "a new kind of Good Neighbor Policy" for Washington and Ciudad Trujillo: "This version cut through the long-standing moral tension between nonintervention and approval of dictatorships, a tension that nurtured State Department opposition to ties with Trujillo, and instead fully embraced his regime for the sake of national defense."[82]

Realizing that Washington refused to use its influence to unseat the regime, the exile community took up the challenge. Initially, Havana and Santiago de Cuba were hubs of conspiratorial activity, but over the course of the first fifteen years of the dictatorship, the diaspora spread throughout the Caribbean basin, Mexico City, and New York. There is no small irony to the fact that the exile organizations were better known outside the Dominican Republic than they were on the island. In fact, some Dominicans were resentful of the émigrés, who they believed lived in comparative safety abroad while they remained to endure the repression.[83]

Trujillo's response was to wage an unrelenting campaign on multiple fronts. In virtually every respect, the tactics he employed against the exiles were a mirror image of his domestic campaign against the opposition. And given its proximity to the Dominican Republic and the presence of Cuban governments that at times tolerated and at other times generously aided the exiles, it is not surprising that Trujillo directed so much attention to the neighboring island.

Dominican Imperialism

In the summer of 1933, with the connivance of Cuban authorities, Estrella Ureña hatched plans for an expedition to overthrow the dictator.[84] Morales, who traveled from New York to Havana in December to participate, met with Batista, who boasted that if necessary he was prepared to lead the invasion himself in boats provided by his navy.[85] Batista also promised to deliver Morales five hundred rifles, thirty machine guns, and a detachment of soldiers. The rebels trained at the Marina de la Guerra Navy Base, located at the port of Mariel, thirty kilometers from Havana. That the training occurred there suggests Guiteras's (and Grau's) approval of the scheme. Dominican exiles in New York and in Santiago and Guantánamo in eastern Cuba were primed to join the expedition as well.

Why did Grau, Batista, and Guiteras back the plot? They were upset with Trujillo, who, through his representative, Porfirio Rubirosa, had extended an invitation to Machado to settle in the Dominican Republic.

There were said to be discussions of the former dictator investing in cattle ranches in the Dominican Republic. The Cuban provisional government was not concerned about the prospects of Machado pursuing a gentleman's retirement. Rather, they were convinced that he would use the Dominican Republic as a base of operations to plot a return to power. To preempt that scheme, Cuban authorities informed the Dominican Foreign Ministry that if Machado came to the Dominican Republic, they would file an extradition request so that he could be returned to Cuba to stand trial for embezzlement.[86]

For his part, Trujillo viewed Grau's provisional government as much more than an irritant. Welles's presence in Cuba as special envoy that summer and fall worried the dictator. So too did the actions of Cuban students in Santiago de Cuba. who, when they learned of Dominican efforts to lure Machado, voiced their displeasure. The Dominican consul reported to Trujillo that his life was in danger and that "over the last few days the radio stations . . . are flinging all kinds of lies and abuse against you, the country, and me."[87]

The Dominican courtship of Machado persisted throughout the fall and winter of 1933–1934. In January Trujillo promised the Cuban that "I will make all efforts to ensure that you will feel surrounded with affection and with the attentions of a brother." Later that spring, Machado accepted Rubirosa's invitation to attend the inauguration of a new bridge, and in August, he and his family moved to the Dominican Republic. There were unconfirmed reports that he paid authorities a tidy sum to settle there.[88] Machado's presence certainly galled Cuban authorities. He came replete with a retinue, including former members of the *porra*, who soon found employment in Trujillo's security service.[89]

The two despots had a history of collaboration. In 1931 the Dominican ruler agreed to a Machado request to intercept a boat carrying forty rebels and arms bound for the Cuban coast. A year later, when Trujillo asked the Cuban leader for assistance in training his fledgling air force, Machado was happy to oblige. The Cuban military not only trained Dominican pilots but also sold its military arms and munitions. Then Trujillo proposed and Machado agreed to a "secret mutual aid pact," which included the sharing of intelligence and harassment of political enemies.[90] Machado told the Dominican minister in Havana, Osvaldo Bazil Leiva, that he had set up "something similar with . . . President Gómez of Venezuela, and he had the opportunity to assist Gómez more than Gómez had [helped] him." Should an "enemy of yours appear," Machado boasted to the diplomat, his police would have the troublemaker picked up, jailed, and "finished off." The Cuban leader even offered the younger Trujillo unsolicited fatherly advice. Years of experience had taught him of the importance of keeping the army disciplined and out of politics, and to "take care of your relationship with Washington; be sure to maintain cordial relations."[91]

Estrella Ureña's expedition became a casualty of domestic politics. As early as December 1933, Morales, in a letter to a colleague in San Juan, forecast storm clouds on the horizon. Welles's recent recall to Washington may have been cause for celebration in Santo Domingo, but Morales realized he had lost an influential ally in Havana. Moreover, even though Grau San Martín "was with us body and soul," what really gave Morales pause was the provisional president's unpopularity and his staying power. Should he be forced to step down (which, in fact, occurred three weeks after Morales expressed his reservations), the exiles would lose a useful partner.[92]

While the fall of Grau in January 1934 did not dent the Dominican exiles' ambitions, whether Batista continued to support the rebels bore watching. As late as June 1934, a colleague of Morales on the island indicated that the Cuban chief of staff was still on board.[93] Thanks to the continuing assistance of certain elements within the Cuban Navy allied with Guiteras, a multinational contingent of rebels grew in size and ambition. By December 1934, Morales wrote Welles that there were still between four hundred and five hundred rebels at the base, more than half of them Cubans. Morales came away impressed with the rebels' training and firepower. The expedition was "ready," he added, "to leave at a moment's notice."[94] Venezuelan exiles, who remembered fondly Dominican support for their efforts to overthrow Gómez, also enlisted.[95] There was even heady talk among the rebels that once they had ousted Trujillo, they would take the fight to Gómez. Moreover, for one of the few times during the dictatorship, there appeared to have been some degree of coordination between the Dominican domestic opposition and the exiles.[96]

But the rebels were far from united. Morales had little use for Estrella Ureña, who was suspect because he initially had conspired with Trujillo to depose Morales's mentor, Vásquez. He "was not anyone's idea of a reformer," Morales wrote a colleague, "he only wants to replace Trujillo, and his sole aspiration is his ambition to rule."[97] That same month, a colonel reported to Batista that the rebels ran the gamut, from communists and Auténticos to members of ABC and Joven Cuba. It is revealing that the officer paid such close attention to the Cubans at the base; no such political or ideological distinctions were made of the Dominicans there. Joven Cuba militants were of special concern to Batista because there were officers in the navy who remained loyal to Guiteras. The report even raised the worrisome prospect of the rebels' first deciding to enlist in Joven Cuba's revolutionary movement before launching an invasion of the Dominican Republic.[98]

Cognizant of how critical Batista's backing was to the expedition's success, a colleague urged Morales to bribe the strongman (and, if necessary, Guiteras and Grau) with "concessions and some monopolies in the Dominican Republic." What must have been unsettling to the dissidents were the rumors that Trujillo already had bought off Batista for a half a million dollars.[99]

It is also conceivable that the Dominican president's decision to cede territory to Haiti when he did was in part predicated on the expectation that Vincent and the Haitian National Police would not permit Estrella Ureña's expeditionary force to launch their invasion from Haitian territory. Similarly, the timing and wording of the decree declaring Morales, Estrella Ureña, and other dissidents "traitors to the nation" was meant to be a warning to any government that aided and abetted the exiles. The decree's wording made that clear: "All foreign governments that in any way lend assistance or encourage the activities of the persons included in this law are considered enemies of the Dominican people."[100]

While exiles were grateful for Cuban support, they were all too aware that their neighbors' participation was contingent and could quickly change. After Grau and Guiteras were removed from power, Batista's interest waned. Perhaps this was the result of pressure from Welles's replacement, Caffery, who was said to be "displeased" with the operation.[101] What Batista and the proconsul wanted to prevent at all costs was Machado's return, fearing that it might plunge the country back into chaos.

By 1935 Batista and Trujillo had reconciled their differences, and Estrella Ureña shelved his plans. In a letter to his ambassador in Washington, the Cuban secretary of state, Cosme de la Torriente, asked his diplomat to meet with his Dominican counterpart to express their government's gratitude to Trujillo not only for keeping Machado in the Dominican Republic, but for neutralizing Cuban "revolutionary elements" that were "developing plans against the present [Cuban] government."

Exiles knew they had lost a key ally when Guiteras was assassinated in March 1935. An elated Dominican diplomat stationed in Santiago de

Cuba predicted that the revolutionary's death was sure to put a damper on future adventurism: "with Dr. Guiteras's death the hopes of all these people [exiles] acquiring resources to arm their fantastic expeditions are gone."[102]

The tantalizing rumors that Trujillo bought off his counterpart were later lent additional credence because it would not be the last time the tyrant suborned a Cuban army chief to shut down a plot to overthrow him. Thirteen years later, a much more ambitious effort to remove Trujillo from power was undertaken, this time from Cayo Confites, a spit of land off Cuba's north coast. Grau (now president of Cuba) would once again give his initial blessing to the operation and once more, hundreds of Cubans signed up to fight alongside their Dominican brethren. His administration channeled a million dollars to expedition organizers. Trujillo tried to quash that plot by having his agents bribe the Cuban chief of staff, Genovevo Pérez Damerá.[103]

What the documentary record makes abundantly clear is that Dominican diplomats, just as they had in Haiti, showered bribes on Cuban bureaucrats, the military, and the media to advance their objectives. Indeed, wherever exiles resided, payoffs became a staple of the regime's foreign policy. Or as Trujillo's secretary of state, Arturo Logroño, so quaintly put it: "give the canary birdseed, and listen to it sing."[104]

Batista continued to view his relationship with his Dominican counterpart instrumentally. The Dominican minister to Cuba, Roberto Despradel, warned Trujillo that the Cuban was not someone to be trusted. Writing in February 1938, he characterized Batista's modus operandi as "totally pragmatic"; he was someone who could "turn against us" if circumstances warranted. When Welles "governed the destinies of Cuba [in 1933]," he reminded Trujillo, Batista "thought of us [the Dominican government] as bad company." Years later, Trujillo received a comparable assessment of the Cuban strongman from Vallenilla Lanz. Here was a puzzling man, someone willing to "risk a coup" at one moment and then pivot to welcome communists into his cabinet (which Batista did twice, in 1940 and again in 1954). This was proof positive, as far as the Venezuelan minister was concerned, that the Cuban head of state "lacked firm convictions." Trujillo concurred: "In all respects, we agree in our respective assessment of the Cuban leader."

Vallenilla Lanz's and Trujillo's pejorative characterizations of Batista are corroborated by Cuban scholars. The head of state's *raison d'être* was to remain in power by any means. To accomplish this, he tacked from repression to liberalization, often within the span of a few months. As Bonachea and Valdés note, "It was the irreconcilable paradox of an illegitimate ruler dreaming of legitimacy. Thus, on some occasions, he used repression against militant adversaries and then suddenly relaxed it, hoping to create a liberal environment in which his flexibility would win him support." Such fickleness meant that Batista found himself caught up in a disruptive cycle of his own making. Easing up on political opponents only engendered greater challenges to his rule, which led, in turn, to periodic bouts of repression.[105]

A pattern was established that characterized relations between the two strongmen over the next twenty-five years: periods of extended cooperation, which included the sharing of intelligence about dissidents, followed by intervals of friction. Neither trusted the other, and Batista especially had ample reason for alarm about how invasive Dominican diplomats were in the domestic sphere. Whether bribing politicians, offering monthly subventions to foreign newspapers and radio stations (and, in a few cases, acquiring newspapers outright), or contracting local *pistoleros* to eliminate dissidents on Cuban soil, Trujillo never spared any expense. An insider who subsequently broke with the regime hinted that the Dominican ruler employed tactics eerily similar to those employed by Franco during the siege of Madrid and later perfected by the Nazis—"methodically establishing fifth columns" as a means of continuously stirring the pot.[106]

A December 1949 confidential memo from a special consultant to the Cuban Ministry of State identified two objectives of the Dominican's "clearly aggressive" foreign policy—a defense of the dictatorship, and more ominously from the Cuban perspective, expansionist aspirations. The Dominican regime's strategic use of legations, embassies, and consulates to spew hostile propaganda "against governments it considers its enemies," and an excessive military buildup, all out of proportion to the needs of the state, were telltale signs of "Dominican imperialism." So concerned was the Cuban high command about the Dominican threat that, as Colonel Ramón Barquín explained, a "light infantry battalion" was established to guard expressly against an invasion. In addition, he was asked to draft a report addressing "the military potential of the neighboring regime."[107]

Given the degree to which the Dominican government invested in winning the hearts and minds of the Cuban public, it is striking how supportive many were of their Dominican brethren. Over the course of two decades, exiles benefited from their neighbors' generosity and material assistance in their ongoing campaign to restore democracy to their homeland. Cuban students, workers, the media, and especially Auténtico Party leaders adopted the cause of anti-trujillismo as their own. Nationalistic Cubans reminded their peers that support for their Dominican brethren was repayment in kind for a debt incurred. The Dominican Máximo Gómez, who rose in the ranks to become one of the most distinguished generals in the Cuban War of Independence, had generously lent his services to the cause of *Cuba libre*.

Senator Eddie Chibás was especially committed, meeting with the leadership of exile organizations, forming the Comité Pro-Democracia Dominicana and spearheading a drive to pass a congressional resolution condemning the Trujillo regime. The young university student Fidel Castro also showed his support for the exiles by playing a leadership role in the University of Havana's Dominican solidarity committee. Cuban historian Eliades Acosta Matos speculates that a column published in *La República* highly critical of Trujillo was probably Castro's handiwork, although, curiously, he substituted his father's name, Ángel, for his own in the byline.

No Cuban journalist gave Trujillo more bad press than *Bohemia*'s owner and director, Miguel Ángel Quevedo. A steady stream of damaging articles about the regime filled the magazine's pages. Quevedo, who managed the magazine from 1926 to 1960, made it his mission to document corruption of all kinds. At various times, *Bohemia* went after Batista, the Auténtico administrations, and Trujillo. As a result, Quevedo's magazine, which enjoyed a wide readership on and off the island, was repeatedly censored, he himself was jailed and tortured, and his contributors sometimes paid a hefty price for their columns. Despite the harassment, the magazine, which boasted a readership of a half a million Cubans, gave voice to the writings of prominent exiles residing in Havana, like Betancourt and Bosch.[108]

A case in point was Galíndez's sensationalistic "Opereta bufa de Trujillolandia," which appeared in July 1952. In what amounted to a précis of his forthcoming doctoral dissertation, sans scholarly analysis and citations, the Basque did not hold back: "For the Dominicans that suffer, the Trujillo regime is a daily drama that silences lips and oppresses hearts. For foreigners with open eyes, the Benefactor and his megalomanias are a treasure trove of incredible surprises."[109]

In addition to airing the regime's dirty laundry, including its pervasive nepotism, "La opereta bufa" mocked the general's endless accumulation of laudatory titles and military promotions even though Trujillo had never set foot on a battlefield. He also documented how ridiculed and marginalized the dictator was throughout the Caribbean. Last but not least, he indiscreetly discussed the paternity of Trujillo's son, Ramfis. The likely heir apparent, the professor revealed, actually was not the generalissimo's offspring but the product of his third wife's prior marriage to a Cuban.[110] The article hit a nerve with the dictator; in March 1956, his acolytes abducted the professor in Manhattan and flew him back to the island, where he was subsequently tortured and murdered.

Exiles were convinced that Galíndez's attack on Trujillo's manhood sealed his fate. By casting "doubt upon the purity of the Trujillo bloodlines," he had signed his own death warrant. In fact, the Basque had reiterated his claims in a PRD pamphlet, published in English- and Spanish-language versions. "A study of the Trujillo family tree reveals a thick-sprouting underbrush of illegitimacy," he mocked. An exile later theorized to a journalist that if Galíndez had just stuck to politics like Requena or Bencosme, he would have been murdered in New York. By casting aspersions on the dictator's heir apparent, "the affront became a personal one," requiring that he be brought back to the island, to face special treatment before being put to death.[111]

Trujillo's sensitivity to bad press presented problems for Batista because exiles enjoyed broad support in Cuba. As a result, the Cuban ruler never clamped down on the press and radio stations enough to satisfy the Dominican head of state, nor did he ever do enough to shorten the exiles' leashes. Unlike Cuba, where even during the darkest days of Machadista repression independent newspapers and magazines, such as *Bohemia, Carteles,* and even the conservative-minded *Diario de la Marina,* continued to document abuses, Trujillo never tolerated any criticism from the Dominican press.[112]

In fact, it was under Batista's not-so-watchful eye that one of the most important Dominican exile organizations, the PRD, was established (1939), and it was where the first general congress of exiles was convened at the University of Havana (1943). Even so, Trujillo greatly preferred Batista to the Auténtico governments of Grau and Prío (1944–1952). The Dominican ruler especially fixated on the threat that Grau and fellow democrats in Guatemala, Venezuela, and Costa Rica posed. He repeatedly tried to destabilize Grau's presidency (1944–1948), greasing the wheels of the opposition press, undermining unions loyal to the Auténtico Party, initiating plots to overthrow the president, besieging authorities with complaints, and wooing the Cuban high command and security apparatus.

In the Dominican Republic, rifles and bayonets were the weapons of choice, Landestoy related, but everywhere else, gold sufficed.[113]

Indeed, bribes became the coin of the realm for hand-to-mouth exiles who were amenable to Trujillo's blandishments. Carlos Durán, whose code name was GFANS, became a reliable mole, obtaining information for Dominican diplomats in Havana about the ties between Acción Democrática and the PRD. In one notable case, he passed along intelligence in 1950 that the two organizations had agreed to a pact wherein the PRD agreed to assist AD in its efforts to retake power in Venezuela, with the understanding that AD would later return the favor. It will become apparent that both sides kept their promises, although it took a decade for their efforts to bear fruit.[114]

In the case of the Cuban military, the objective was not just to suborn officers but to send an unequivocal message about their neighbor's burgeoning military strength. Lavish all-expense-paid junkets to the Dominican Republic for Cuban officers generally included a tour of La Fundación, the national armament factory located in Trujillo's hometown of San Cristóbal. They came back alternately impressed by and concerned with the threat posed by the Dominican armed forces. An offhand Trujillo remark that he now had sufficient armaments "to destroy Havana in three hours" was not idle chatter.

When Grau purged the military of loyal batistiano officers soon after he became president, the dictator next door jumped at the chance to foment unrest. In Grau's first year in office, Trujillo backed the pretentions of a rogue colonel intent on ousting the democratically elected president.[115] Then, in late 1946, according to the general's former personal secretary, José Almoina Matos, Trujillo agreed (through his intermediaries) to loan several of the sacked officers (now residing in Miami) five million pesos and to provide them with arms. The elaborate scheme called for the camouflaging of Dominican planes with Cuban air force markings. The planes were to fly over Camp Columbia at the same time that plotters there were rising up in revolt.[116]

Not surprisingly, the assistance came with several strings attached. If the plot succeeded, Trujillo insisted that the conspirators imprison Grau and his relatives and employ torture if need be to get them to reveal information about Trujillo's enemies. In addition to repayment of the monies, the rebels were to appoint Machado's former aide and longtime Trujillo sympathizer Orestes Ferrara Marino as minister of state in the new government. Henceforth, Dominican exiles were to be detained by

Cuban authorities and then deported to the Dominican Republic, and all anti-Trujillo publications, meetings, and demonstrations were to be proscribed. One account contends that the plot fell apart because Trujillo insisted that the conspirators also eliminate Batista.[117] Even though the plot was stillborn, Trujillo's minions continued to wreak havoc during the eight years of Auténtico rule. Is it any wonder that Grau San Martín was so willing to aid the 1947 Cayo Confites expedition?

If ever there was a time when such a bold amphibious invasion might succeed, this was it. Owing to the peculiar conjuncture of international and domestic factors, Cayo Confites represented the most serious threat to the regime's survival up to that point.[118] Thanks to Braden's prodemocracy initiative, the despot was on the defensive in Washington. At home, unrest was making its presence felt, and away, four civilian governments— Cuba, Venezuela, Guatemala, and Haiti—were united in their desire to rid themselves of the troublesome tyrant and had pledged significant resources to that end.

The brinksmanship began in earnest after Venezuela's junta severed relations with the Dominican Republic in November 1945. The matter that provoked the rupture was the war of words that began after the publication by a Venezuelan publisher of *De Lilís a Trujillo*, a scorching denunciation of the Trujillo regime by Luis Mejía, an exile residing in Caracas who had close ties to AD's leadership.[119] Later that summer, Betancourt, now a head of state, toured Mexico, Colombia, Central America, and the Caribbean, making the case at each stop that democratic governments should implement a *cordon sanitaire* against dictatorships. The Betancourt Doctrine called for civilian governments to withhold recognition from de facto regimes that came to power by force.[120] That Latin American democracies needed to band together to isolate one of their neighbors was novel, and in some quarters debatable, as the Dominican foreign minister Peña Batlle noted a few years later. At least from the Dominican government's perspective, Betancourt was regarded as an unwelcome meddler, far more concerned with internationalism than with Venezuelan affairs.[121]

In July 1947 prominent Dominican exile leaders met in Havana to form a steering committee and to sign an Act of Acceptance, committing themselves to an armed invasion of their homeland. Unlike the Mariel expedition, this operation boasted significant firepower—seven ships, a dozen airplanes, bazookas, machine guns, and a thousand rifles.[122] As the diplomatic offensive against La Internacional de la Espada continued,

Grau, just as he had in 1933, greenlighted the expedition and provided the exiles with funds and a training site.

Recruitment committees were established in Havana, Matanzas, and Santiago de Cuba. Signing up in plain sight at the Parque José Martí, Cruz Alonso's Hotel San Luis, and the Palacio de Deportes in the capital were secondary and university students, workers, and professionals. Typical of the well-intentioned, if green, participants who enlisted was Castro. When Fidel's mother attempted to dissuade her son from participating, he replied, "I can't pull out. ... To overthrow Trujillo is a democratic mission, and if the price is life, then all of us here are ready to pay it."[123]

As they had in 1934, Dominican exiles residing in New York, San Juan, and Caracas packed their bags, traveled to Cuba, and joined the expedition. Displaced Spanish Republicans and militants from Venezuela, Nicaragua, Honduras, Puerto Rico, and the United States offered their services. Twelve hundred enlistees were placed in three battalions and whipped into shape at the Instituto Politécnico in Holguín. According to one press account, residents of Holguín turned out to watch the preparations as if it were a theatrical production.[124]

Trujillo made the mistake of allowing a prominent domestic critic, one of the island's wealthiest landowners, to leave the island. "Juancito" Rodríguez García's monies would be used to bankroll Cayo Confites and future operations against the dictatorship. Exile leaders fully expected the U.S. to remain neutral and to wink and nod at the purchase and shipment of arms from the mainland to Cuba.

On his heels, Trujillo's multipronged response was impressive. To secure the home front, he first lured the domestic opposition out into the open by promising political and labor reforms he had no intention of honoring. Tied to the disingenuous opening was a brilliantly conceived ploy that had his emissaries offer the Cuban Communist Party (PSP) a tempting opportunity to organize the island's sugar workers. The PSP took the bait, despite dire warnings from exile leaders in Cuba. Bosch penned two such admonishments, "Cuidado, comunistas!" (Beware, communists!) and "Así es Trujillo, comunistas" (That's how Trujillo is, communists"), which predicted what eventually came to pass. The PSP was permitted for a brief time to organize in the Dominican Republic, enabling authorities to flush out opposition. How ironic that in a society where repression was the rule, Galíndez perceptively noted, it was the communists who were for a time given free rein to organize workers.

"But when the jig was up, Trujillo cast himself as the champion of anti-Communism."[125]

The maneuver resulted in an added layer of intrigue, which redounded to Trujillo's benefit. It pitted the exiles against each other along ideological lines. Leftist defenders of the PSP branded Morales and his supporters "reactionary adventurers" for their involvement in the expedition and went out of their way to sow dissent.[126]

Just as had occurred in 1934, the combination of U.S. diplomatic muscle and Cuban political infighting undercut the multinational force, which spent two months on the mosquito-plagued key training for an invasion that never happened. As they had during Mariel, Cubans wrested control of preparations from their Dominican partners. Horacio Ornes Coiscou, one of the Dominican leaders of the expedition, admitted years later that he and his countrymen made the mistake of ceding control to the far more numerous Cubans, who were themselves far from unified.[127]

If Grau needed additional reason to shut down the operation, it came in the form of rumors that the expeditionary force was intent on overthrowing his own government.[128] In retrospect, however, it is easy to see how Braden's resignation in June 1947 effectively sealed the force's fate. Recognizing that a shift in Washington's policy was in the offing, Trujillo implored Marshall to pressure Grau to shut down the operation. The secretary of state acceded to the despot's plea for assistance by lifting Braden's ban on arms sales to the Dominican Republic. Marshall's decision to pressure Grau was made in spite of unsettling intelligence that at that moment Trujillo was targeting the overthrow of the Venezuelan junta. Betancourt had presented the State Department with details of Trujillo and Somoza's financial and material involvement in a plot to restore former dictator López Contreras to power.[129]

What factored into Marshall's decision to pressure Grau to stand down was that preparations were under way that summer for the upcoming Rio Pact conference. The prospect of a regional conflagration erupting just as the nations of the hemisphere were about to sign a historic mutual defense treaty could not have been an appealing prospect for the secretary of state.[130] The United States' demand also may have been influenced by apprehensions about the ideological affinities of some of the key participants. The Cuban PSP's support for the expedition was particularly worrisome. In addition, a significant number of the Cubans who joined the expedition were, if not leftist, decidedly anti-U.S.[131]

Trujillo's campaign to unseat the Auténticos persisted. In the summer of 1951, he coaxed Batista, then residing in Florida, to overthrow Grau's successor, Prío. The following year's presidential elections offered uninviting possibilities to the Dominican head of state—a Prío handpicked Auténtico candidate or the virulently anti-Trujillo Chibás (who was considered a strong contender before he died of a self-inflicted gunshot wound later that year). Facing such unattractive prospects, the general took matters into his own hands.

Prío's foreign minister, Miguel Suárez Fernández, warned that Miami was a viper's nest. A "well-heeled" plot was afoot there that had the active backing of Trujillo and Pérez Jiménez. Coordinating the plot were Petán and the Dominican consul in Miami, Augusto Ferrando Gómez. The consul was well known in Cuba; while serving in the same post in Santiago de Cuba, he had been implicated in a plot to assassinate Grau in 1944. (That same year he also was linked to an attempt on the life of Haitian president Lescot).

Disgruntled Cubans on and off the island were drawn to this scheme, Suárez Fernández continued, including former Machadistas, pseudorevolutionaries, Marxists, and Spanish Civil War veterans. Even members of the so-called action groups—armed gangs that were a cancer preying on the body politic—had been approached by Trujillo's diplomats. These gangs, the foreign minister reported, were unscrupulous enough "to ally themselves with Dominican spies, some for the money, others out of resentment [of our government]."[132] Alas, he concluded, there were many Cubans all too willing to serve foreign dictatorships. While this particular conspiracy was no more successful than so many others, it suggests the lengths to which Trujillo was willing to go to remove political enemies in neighboring countries.

Although hard evidence is lacking that Trujillo was of assistance to Batista when the latter staged his own coup in March 1952, a letter two months later from Bernardino to the Cuban head of state indicates that the general felt that Batista still was not doing enough to rein in dissidents. "I have no doubt of your good faith ... but since the change of government ... nothing concrete has happened to change the systematic aggression to which we are subjected."[133]

Batista's coup did little to patch up relations between the two strongmen. In February 1955 Trujillo's chief of state security, Arturo Espaillat, conferred with Batista while attending his presidential inauguration. He was instructed by Trujillo to extend an olive branch to the Cuban ruler in the hope of securing greater collaboration between their two countries. Espaillat related Batista's transparent response: he "was as enthusiastic about an alliance with Trujillo as he would have been [about] exposure to leprosy. He said he would welcome any secret assistance Trujillo might give him, but for heaven's sake, don't let anyone know about it."[134]

If Batista did not rein in the exiles, Trujillo would take it upon himself to do so. In August 1955, two *pistoleros* hired by Bernardino murdered Dominican activist Manuel de Jesús "Pipí" Hernández Santana on the streets of Havana. His death was the second time in five years that the man that Trujillo called "el gángster" had employed Cuban thugs to eliminate a troublesome dissident in Havana.[135] The murder and the subsequent trial of the perpetrators was played up in the local press, while Batista's political opponents demanded that he respond to such an obvious provocation against national sovereignty.

José Antonio Echeverría Bianchi, the president of the Cuban Federación Estudiantil Universitario (FEU), gave a rousing speech alleging complicity between the Cuban chief of police, Rafael Salas Cañizares, and the Dominicans in Hernández's murder. In an interview with a journalist from *Bohemia*, Echeverría denounced "trujillista infiltration into Cuba. . . . The Cuban people cannot imagine the web of espionage carried out by Mr. Trujillo's embassy." Later that fall, the president of the student organization traveled to Mexico City to meet with Castro, the exiled leader of the 26th of July movement. The two leaders signed a unity pact on behalf of their organizations. An astonishing nine of the nineteen clauses of "The Mexican Letter" dealt with Trujillo's nefarious actions. Article 5, for instance, listed the Cuban officers he allegedly bribed who had participated in Batista's 1952 coup, while Article 9 declared that the FEU and the 26th of July movement would, unlike "the hypocrite and coward" Batista, salvage the nation's honor by "settling its account" with the Dominican dictator. In fact, the pact was far more critical of Trujillo than it was of the United States.[136]

Rumors were rife throughout the fall and winter of 1955–1956 of dissension within the Cuban military. Two discordant factions were plotting to overthrow the despot. Inconclusive evidence exists that Trujillo allied himself with both groups of plotters. Muddying the waters were sweeping claims made by Batista that all his political enemies, including rivals within the military, Castro's 26th of July movement, and Prío's supporters, were in league with the Dominican president.

Moreover, there were startling claims that the Dominican government was providing arms and training to Prío's supporters. The former president had just returned to the island for the first time since the coup. His October 1, 1955, rally in Havana attracted fifty thousand supporters, and he was said to be in cahoots with dissident officers, as well as two other resistance organizations dedicated to the overthrow of the dictator—Sánchez Arango's clandestine Triple A (Acción Armada Auténtica) and the 26th of July movement.[137]

An alliance between the former Cuban president and the Dominican dictator, on the face of it, seemed preposterous. The two had been at loggerheads from the outset of Prío's presidency and, as noted, the dictator had enlisted Batista in a plot to oust the Auténtico head of state in 1951. Yet the U.S. embassy had it on good authority that *sub rosa* Trujillo was backing a diverse group of anti-batistianos. Espaillat confirms as much, noting that trujillista agents had met Prío's lieutenants to coordinate an uprising in eastern Cuba.[138] The Dominican head of security personally oversaw the smuggling of "munitions and explosives into Oriente for the use of Prío's partisans." Moreover, "key military and naval officers" were paid to look the other way. Espaillat's recollections were corroborated by the Cuban army's chief of staff, who informed Batista that several ships had been seen dropping off armaments near Santiago. A subsequent memorandum reported that the Dominican military was training two hundred Cubans. But the conspiracy sputtered when Prío's supporters failed to collect the arms. Batista was able to flush out the conspirators, and Prío was put on a plane bound for Miami. Those arms, Espaillat recalled, eventually found their way to the 26th of July movement.[139]

Prío's involvement in gun running already had come to the attention of North American authorities. In 1954 he and a number of his supporters were indicted and convicted for violating U.S. neutrality laws. After receiving a slap on the wrist for this, his first offense, Prío went back to the drawing board, this time with more ambitious plans. According to charges filed in 1958 by the Southern District Court of New York, this second conspiracy could be traced back to the spring of 1956, precisely when Prío, with assistance from Trujillo, was hatching plans to invade the island. Not only did the ex-president conspire to launch expeditions against Batista, but he set up training camps for this purpose in the Dominican Republic, Mexico, Haiti, *and* the United States. Pilots were trained on airplanes purchased "for the purpose of bombing and strafing the Republic of Cuba from bases within the United States and elsewhere." According to the indictment, acts of sabotage were planned and specific Cuban politicians were targeted for assassination.[140]

Meanwhile, Castro rejected out of hand Batista's claim that he was receiving assistance from Trujillo. In a long, rambling letter sent from Mexico to Quevedo in late August 1956 (and subsequently published in *Bohemia*), he said there was little to distinguish between the two dictators. "The same ideological and moral abyss that sets us apart from Batista, separates us from Trujillo." Both autocrats detained, tortured, and then disappeared their opponents "without leaving any traces."[141] Yes, Trujillo's "bloodhounds" were dispatched throughout the diaspora to eliminate his political rivals, but the same was true of Batista. As proof, he quoted from a Mexican newspaper, *Últimas Noticias*, which had just reported that two members of the Cuban dictator's security apparatus were sent to Mexico to investigate exiles plotting against Batista. "The presence of these Antillean policemen has sown alarm among the Cuban residents in our country." Castro did not need to remind readers that an earlier dictator, Machado, had ordered his thugs to travel to Mexico to assassinate Mella in 1929. Batista either should deny that he was in cahoots with the Dominicans or defend Cuba's sovereignty by declaring war on its neighbor, Castro insisted. He finished his tirade by once again repudiating the charge that he benefited from trujillista largesse. "The stand I took when I was a student, I take today and it will always be my stand against Trujillo."[142] The Cuban rebel protested too much, since other sources tell a different story. Up until late 1956, his movement did indeed receive arms and monies from the despot.[143]

The Dominican head of state continued to meddle in Cuban politics. Senator Rolando Masferrer Rojas, a longtime Trujillo critic, accused the Dominican ambassador, Federico Llaverías, of trying to buy his support. The diplomat apparently thought enlisting Masferrer, who commanded a two-thousand-man paramilitary force nicknamed "Los Tigres de Masferrer," was worth the trouble. The ambassador wrote Trujillo that this was "a brilliant opportunity. . . . He is a man of action, determined, and one that everyone fears. I believe he is capable." More to the point, Masferrer had keen political aspirations, and Llaverías believed he was "someone who is interested in overthrowing Batista with your assistance."[144]

Banking on Masferrer was a mistake foretold, a serious lapse in judgment by the usually shrewd Dominican ruler. As a teenager, Masferrer had joined the PSP and Joven Cuba before leaving for Spain to fight in the Abraham Lincoln Brigade. Upon his return he formed the MSR, which was given a wide berth for its criminal activities during the Auténtico years. Masferrer's intimate involvement in the planning of Cayo

Confites should have given the Dominican ruler pause, but nine years later his ambassador took the risk of bribing him because he knew that the Cuban had long since traded in what remained of his leftist ideals for the pursuit of ill-gotten gains.[145]

The diplomat's ploy backfired when Masferrer published an exposé in his newspaper, *Tiempo de Cuba*, which included an incriminating transcript of a recording of his telephone conversation with the ambassador. A strike force of twenty-four planes and five hundred men, including members of the 26th of July movement and Prío's Auténticos, Masferrer averred, were preparing to invade Cuba. The story set off a firestorm, resulting in the ambassador's recall. Presenting himself as a patriot, Masferrer pushed a bill through the Senate calling for a special commission to document the full range of hostile trujillista activities. The commission called thirty-five witnesses in all, including the heads of Cuban National Security and the National Police and the foreign minister. As a result of its findings, the Senate issued a resolution condemning Trujillo's actions and recommending that the Cuban head of state sever relations with the Dominican Republic when he saw fit to do so. The leader of the country's largest labor union subsequently called for a national boycott of Dominican goods.[146]

Backed into a corner, an irate and embarrassed Batista had his military draft plans to invade the Dominican Republic. Although there is no evidence that he intended to act on those plans, he tried to turn the marriage of convenience between Prío and Trujillo to his advantage by playing the nationalist card. In fact, U.S. Ambassador Arthur Gardner cabled the Department that Batista believed that the "situation" had handed him "added pretext for limits and controls on opposition activities."[147]

In sum, over an eighteen-month period from mid-1955 to early 1957, a series of imprudent moves by the petulant Dominican head of state—Pipí Hernández's murder, his complicity in a plot to overthrow Batista, and efforts to bribe Masferrer—had brought the two countries to the brink of hostilities. Cooler heads prevailed, however, and relations between the two dictators were patched up in 1957, but only because a weakened Batista had little choice but to turn his full attention to a growing insurrection against his regime. From that point on, La Voz Dominicana curtailed its attacks against Batista, and in return, the Cuban strongman agreed to censor criticism of Trujillo and other members of La Internacional.[148]

A year later, the Cuban regime, saddled with a temporary weapons ban from the United States, turned to Trujillo for assistance. The Cuban military placed an order for San Cristóbal automatic rifles, replicas of weapons once produced for Hitler by Hungary's Skoda factory and now reproduced by refugees welcomed to the island by the Dominican ruler after the 1956 uprising. Along with the rifles the Dominicans sent a "more fearsome weapon": napalm. Knowing how despised Trujillo was in Cuba, Batista denied making the purchases. This was "a brazen lie," according to the CBS News correspondent Robert Taber, who noted that eleven Cuban airmen opted to flee the island rather than transport arms that would be used against their own countrymen.[149]

Betancourt took heart from Trujillo's disruptiveness. In a letter to Sergio Romauldi, an AFL-CIO labor diplomat, he mused that the dictator's actions were proof that he was going through a bout of criminal neurosis similar to what the Soviet leadership went through during Stalin's last years. The tyrant's actions in Cuba were explosive enough, but coupled with the kidnapping of Galíndez in New York in March 1956, were proof that dictatorships "do not just terrorize their people, but are active foci of international disturbances."[150]

Betancourt had it right: the policies that Trujillo pursued in Cuba were not unusual. An extraordinary report, written in September 1947 by the former Spanish Republican Almoina, who had served as the dictator's personal secretary and his son's tutor before fleeing to Mexico City in late 1946, shows a similar no-holds-barred foreign policy toward Colombia, Mexico, Venezuela, and Central America. The detailed report, copies of which were sent to the foreign ministries of democratic countries throughout the region, the United States, and Dominican exile leaders, urged reformist governments to take collective action against a bellicose regime.[151]

Targeting Dissidents

What Trujillo could not control was the exiles' determination to repeatedly air the regime's belligerent actions in the media. He countered such sensationalistic stories by investing millions of dollars to foster a more edifying view of his regime. He bought airtime and print space everywhere exiles resided. In fact, the regime spent six million dollars alone parrying the fallout from the abduction and assassination of Galíndez.

Trujillo also bankrolled newspaper publisher Stanley Ross in his 1955 purchase of a failing Spanish-language New York paper, *El Diario de Nueva York*. The two had a history of collaboration. In 1947 they purchased the Dominican paper *El Caribe*. Eight years later, Ross wrote to Trujillo proposing a similar arrangement regarding *El Diario de Nueva York*. In a memorandum that left little to the imagination, he not only promised "to follow a political line in accordance with the desires of your Excellency," but to publish favorable columns about the dictator's rule. Ross explained why it would be better to keep their arrangement "a well-guarded secret: "Thus, we could act with even more force in your favor. If Trujillo's papers say something good of the Dominican Republic, that is to be expected. But if an independent periodical does so, that would carry more force. The periodical must avoid, in every way whatever, evidence of contact between us, even though we must maintain constant contact."[152]

El Diario de Nueva York advanced Trujillo's agenda by spinning out puff pieces about the regime's accomplishments and those of his allies in La Internacional while denigrating prominent democrats like Muñoz Marín. Ross did not lack for ambition. "From here we can exercise much influence in Latin America," he promised the dictator. He pitched a Special Editions feature that would be subsidized by despots anxious to receive favorable publicity. *El Diario de Nueva York* would confect special edition issues dedicated to Trujillo, Pérez Jiménez, Somoza, Batista, and Franco. The title on the cover of the Venezuelan issue, "Venezuela: Country of Peace and Progress," left little doubt about its slant.[153] Ross even afforded Galíndez space for columns in *El Diario de Nueva York*, but his contributions never touched on Dominican topics.[154]

A September 1959 *Washington Post* story found that sixteen firms or individuals had registered in the United States as agents of the Dominican government. "These range from large public relations setups to one man who manages a baseball team in New York City." (Trujillo knew that his countrymen were passionate about baseball and had subsidized a Dominican entrepreneur from East Harlem who had established a baseball team in 1948.) The *Post* piece estimated the sums paid to agents at a million dollars a year.[155]

When Trujillo was not responding to the exiles with self-serving pap placed by his retainers in the media, he took a page from Gómez, requiring that his foreign service officers keep close tabs on the dissidents' activities. Diplomats not only eyed the exile community but repeatedly lodged complaints with local authorities about their activities. Eight months before the Dominican labor organizer Mauricio Báez was "disappeared" in December 1950 by Cuban *pistoleros* in Trujillo's employ,

Bernardino, then serving as a consul in Havana, complained to the Cuban foreign minister that the exiled union leader was plotting with other refugees at the Hotel San Luis to commit "terroristic acts" against the legation. *El gángster*'s mere presence on the island was enough to send shivers through the exile community; a *Bohemia* piece, "Assassin Without Borders," recounting his ghastly exploits, only drove home that point.[156] When a police investigation into Bernardino's specious claim failed to uncover anything untoward, the emboldened Báez made the lethal error of incurring the one-time member of La 42's wrath. In an interview given to a radio station in June he declared that Bernardino was a cold-blooded assassin.[157]

The elimination of troublesome opponents was a conscious strategy employed by the dictator for the duration of his rule. Why were certain dissidents in the diaspora murdered while others were harassed or bought off? The common denominator among the six high-profile murders was that in each case the detractors had employed different forms of media to embarrass and humiliate the dictator. Whether it was a newsreel (Bencosme and Morales), print journalism (Morales, Requena, Galíndez, Hernández), radio interviews (Báez), or books (Requena, Galíndez, Almoina), the methods utilized were selected to assure the widest possible dissemination (see table 1). Báez, who kept up a steady barrage of attacks on the regime on Cuban radio stations, had been warned by other exiles that such public denunciations were sure to elicit a response.[158] In Requena's case, he not only edited his own anti-Trujillo paper, *Patria*, and authored a fictional indictment, but he passed along incriminating diplomatic correspondence to the PRD allegedly documenting the dictator's ties to the Third Reich. The papers came into his possession while serving in Trujillo's foreign service in Chile.[159]

Table 1. Assassinations of regime critics

Name	Date	Location
Sergio Bencosme	April 28, 1935	New York
Mauricio Báez	December 10, 1950	Havana
Andrés Requena	October 2, 1952	New York
Manuel de Jesús "Pipi" Hernández	August 8, 1955	Havana
Jesús Galíndez	March 12, 1956	New York
José Almoina	May 4, 1960	Mexico City

A master at stirring the pot: Trujillo at the microphone; his brother, President Héctor Trujillo, to his left; Felix Bernardino (aka *el gángster*) to his right; with Johnny Abbes García in the back, c. 1956. Instituciones Estatales #0388, Archivo General de la Nación.

Each of the murders was an act of retaliation, the brutish hallmark of vengeance apparent to all who opposed the regime. Pipí Hernández's death came soon after the longtime exile led a campaign to discourage Cuban businesses from taking part in the Dominican Republic's International Fair for Peace and Brotherhood of the Free World, a lavish exposition celebrating Trujillo's silver anniversary in power. The fair was intended to flaunt the nation's civic improvements and remind Washington that the despot was a reliable ally in the struggle against communism.[160]

Hernández's outspokenness was not appreciated in Ciudad Trujillo. Filing a report with Frances Grant at the Inter-American Association of

Democracy and Freedom (IADF), a liberal human rights organization, just before his own abduction in March 1956, Galíndez mused aloud about the circumstances surrounding Pipí's death. He shared with Grant details revealed in an investigative report published by *Bohemia* two weeks after the journalist's death. The Cuban police reported that the murder was politically motivated and that its methods invited comparison to previous assassinations attributed to the generalissimo's hired thugs.[161] What stood out about this case was that the culprits were apprehended, interrogated, and charged with murder after the police recovered passports linking the crime directly to the Dominican government. A letter to Trujillo from an unnamed Dominican diplomat in the embassy in Havana six months later admitted that embassy personnel had acted "imprudently and clumsily" by allowing "suspicious people linked to the assailants" to drop into the embassy in plain view. Clinching the investigation for the authorities was that after questioning, the perpetrators admitted that they had been paid off by Dominican officials. The Hernández murder, then, was exceptional. When it came to bothersome dissenters, Trujillo usually covered his tracks.[162]

More often than not, the despot was successful because he was patient in meting out retribution. Rarely did he exact revenge right away; in fact, in several instances—Almoina, Requena, and Galíndez—the murders came well after the perceived offense occurred. In Almoina's case, the murder occurred more than a decade later. Once again, his henchman of choice was Bernardino, whose official title, Inspector of Embassies, Legations, and Consulates in Latin America, conferred immunity from prosecution while he carried out "special assignments." Bernardino also would be implicated in the deaths of Báez, Requena, Hernández, and Galíndez.

For the dissidents, there was an air of inevitability about their impending deaths. Both Galíndez and Almoina shared their disquiet in writing with friends and colleagues.

Considering Almoina's close working relationship with Trujillo for so many years, his reflections were especially poignant: "I know that Trujillo has sentenced me to death, and with his immense economic and political power, with that group of *pistoleros*—some with diplomatic passports—that he has at his disposal . . . I will not be able to escape death."[163]

Indeed, it is remarkable that Almoina lived as long as he did. Not only had he authored and distributed the damning report that provided Trujillo's enemies with a significant body of intelligence, but two years later, he wrote a tell-all book, *Una satrapía en el Caribe*, admittedly under a pseudonym, which, like Galíndez's "La opereta bufa," openly mocked the tendentious despot. Trujillo was well aware that Gregorio Bustamante and Almoina were one and the same. What probably spared his life in the short run was that the Spaniard had a powerful patron close to the seat of power: Trujillo's third wife, María de los Ángeles Martínez. According to the former personal secretary's biographer, she prevailed upon Almoina to set himself right with her husband by spinning out a hagiographic account. While *Yo fui secretario de Trujillo* (published just a year after *Una satrapía*) did buy him ten more years, it effectively silenced him from that point on, while doing little to ease the dread he felt that at any moment he could be murdered.[164]

In Galíndez's case, he did little to hide his disgust for Trujillo, delivering talks and writing articles for *Bohemia* (Havana), *Élite* (Caracas), *Cuadernos Americanos* (Mexico City), and publications of Dominican exile organizations, such as *Quisqueya Libre* and the *Boletín del PRD*.[165] Especially galling to the Basque nationalist was the Dominican dictator's campaigning for Spain's inclusion in the United Nations.[166]

Devout Catholic, public intellectual, political analyst, legal scholar, widely read journalist, outspoken critic of authoritarianism, a political refugee twice over, passionate about Hispanic culture, Galíndez's zest for life was boundless. That, coupled with a penchant for flirting with danger, won him many admirers in New York and throughout Latin America. Among them was a pacifist, James Peck, who had the opportunity to observe him at a number of events: "At meetings he was often the most fiery speaker. He rarely missed a picket demonstration." Peck vividly recalled the first time he heard Galíndez speak. It was at a memorial on the first anniversary of Requena's death in front of the Manhattan tenement where the dissident was gunned down. "Galíndez was the main speaker. He warned that if the police continued to be apathetic about the Requena case, one of the people present at the meeting might well be the next victim."[167]

If Galíndez's days were not full enough, for the better part of fifteen years he was a paid informant for the FBI and the CIA (and its predecessor, the OSS). That meant keeping tabs on New York's Hispanic community. A detailed report that he filed with the FBI documents his attendance at a bundle of progressive and leftist events. During one five-month period alone in the early 1950s he attended meetings of the Puerto Rican Nationalist Party, the Labor Youth League, the Joint

Anti-Fascist Refugee Committee's protest of the Rosenberg case, and a commemoration of the 1935 Ponce (Puerto Rico) massacre. Five days before his kidnapping, he attended a fundraiser for Castro's 26th of July movement.[168]

Assisting Washington during the height of McCarthyism was not unusual for exiles like Galíndez. For some it was a way of demonstrating their ideological opposition to totalitarianism or, perhaps in his case, a measure of gratitude for the United States government's moral and financial support for Basque nationalism; for still others, it was a means to supplement their income or obtain or renew residency. To be sure, Galíndez's compromising position as an informant complicated in no small way federal and local investigations of his kidnapping and murder.[169] The CIA, in particular, would be a constant thorn in the side of investigators, fearful that too much digging into Galíndez's activities would shed light on the agency's ties to and financial support for a "Basque espionage network." The agency was reputed to have funneled millions of dollars through Galíndez, who handled financial matters for the New York headquarters of the Basque government-in-exile.[170]

In addition to filing reports for U.S. intelligence agencies, he pursued a doctoral degree at Columbia. By all reports, he became consumed by his thesis topic on the inner workings of the Trujillo regime. As his mentor at Columbia, the noted historian Frank Tannenbaum, related, "Galíndez came to resemble nothing so much as a walking one-man intelligence bureau. He knew more about Trujillo than anyone else in the whole wide world."[171]

As early as 1952 Bernardino's sister, Minerva, who worked in the Dominican consulate in New York, had learned about Galíndez's thesis topic. Trujillo's agents responded by trying to buy him out, reputedly offering fifty thousand dollars for the manuscript. Galíndez's handlers at the FBI strongly discouraged him from pursuing the thesis, warning him of the likelihood of reprisals and making it clear that the bureau could not guarantee his safety. When Galíndez refused to heed their advice, his handlers threatened to terminate his services should he become enmeshed in public controversy.[172]

In a ghastly twist, the Dominican regime enlisted the assistance of the FBI to do its dirty work. In November 1955, the dictator's agents concocted a document, "Alleged Plot to Assassinate General Rafael Trujillo by Jesús de Galíndez and Nicolás Silfa," which they then shared with the bureau. The story was a complete fabrication, but it had the desired effect,

"He knew more about Trujillo than anyone else in the whole wide world":
Jesús de Galíndez, c. 1939–1943. Photographer Kurt Schnitzer (Conrado),
1.5.6/1597.5, Archivo General de la Nación.

as the law enforcement agency was now more willing to part with intelligence it had on the activities of exiles with the Dominican government.[173]

Well before he was kidnapped in March 1956, Galíndez had ample
warning that the general's men were closing in on him. He told his FBI
contact that he was certain that his phone was tapped and his mail
rifled.[174] In January 1955, he wrote Morales, "I continue smelling the
Trujillo pressure."[175] Silfa was certain that the stress was getting to his
good friend. Evidence of this was Galíndez's application to carry a handgun—a request the New York City police refused. This may explain why
he left an unsigned will and testament in his apartment, which the police
found after he went missing. Dated October 1952, immediately after
Requena's death, the will explicitly fingered Bernardino for his good
friend's murder. If something were to happen to him as well, he added,

the police should focus its investigation on the Dominican consulate in New York.[176] A year after Galíndez disappeared, the FBI came to much the same conclusion. In a letter to the State Department's director of security, J. Edgar Hoover admitted that the bureau's investigation pointed to Bernardino as the mastermind and Espaillat, who earned the nickname "Navajita" because of the small-clasp knife he always carried with him to slit the throats of the regime's enemies, were the men who had directed the abduction.[177]

Galíndez had been open about his predicament with his students at Columbia, informing them that he had received anonymous notes on five separate occasions, each asking him to meet with the letter writer somewhere. He assured his students that he would never do so because "he feared the Dominican government would kill him." The harassment extended to blatant efforts to disrupt his teaching. A student later told the FBI that two unidentified men came to class on multiple occasions, sometimes together or by themselves. Jerome Kessler recalled that they "did not dress like college students nor did they take notes during the lecture." He was "slightly amazed" that his professor "made derogatory statements about the Dominican Republic" with the visitors present. While there was at least one visitor in attendance in every class up to the night he went missing, Kessler never saw them after that. Another student, Evelyn Lang, corroborated that account, describing one of the mysterious visitors as a "Latin gangster type" who came to class "dressed in flashy clothes."[178]

The Basque wrote Morales in late November that he was certain that the regime was closing in on him. "I have reinforced the locks of my apartment. I . . . advise you to do the same for all yours." He added that he had put copies of the almost completed thesis "outside of my home. IN CASE" (caps in original).[179] Tannenbaum later told Chilean editor Alfonso Naranjo that in the days before he was declared missing, his student was feeling especially anxious. "I know that Galíndez was apprehensive about what might happen to him and to his work, so that the final tragedy which has occurred justifies his fears. . . . I myself have given up all hope of his return. It is a great tragedy because Galíndez was an unusual person; a loyal friend, an excellent scholar and an individual of unusual integrity devoted to the cause of freedom . . . his career as a scholar within the University lay just ahead of him. He was looking forward to it with great enthusiasm. . . . I agree with you that if what we assume is actually the case, that Galíndez is the most recent martyr to political freedom in Latin America."[180]

Galíndez had the foresight, his advisor recalled several years later, to "deposit a copy of each chapter as it was being written with a friend— just in case he should be the victim of foul play."[181] In fact, just three days before he was kidnapped, he turned over an edited version of his seven-hundred-page thesis to Naranjo.[182] Tannenbaum warned Naranjo to be on his guard: "Now about his book, you may have the only available copy of the dissertation. . . . Therefore you must be very careful with it and keep it under lock and key because those interested in preventing its publication will probably not stop at anything if they know how to find out where such a copy exists. . . . I think that it is important, as you your-self indicate, that the book be rushed to the press as quickly as possible. I am sure that it will have very wide acceptance throughout Latin America. [It] is a unique volume, the likes of which does not exist in the political literature of Latin America. It will remain a monument to scholarship."[183]

La era de Trujillo made his advisor a prophet in more ways than one. A searing indictment, it remains to this day the most cogent political analysis of the dictatorship. It also became an instant bestseller through-out Latin America, fueled by the sensational circumstances of his disap-pearance. Naranjo could not keep up with the demand as the book went through seven printings in six weeks.

Tannenbaum's warning, however, could not prevent Naranjo's wife from being roughed up in Davis, California, presumably by Trujillo's thugs. When he learned of the attack, the professor expressed his heart-felt sympathy to Naranjo and attempted to explain why the news of his student's disappearance resonated so differently in the United States and Latin America: "The real difficulty with the Galíndez matter . . . is that [North] Americans have found it impossible to believe that this kind of crime could be committed by agents of a foreign government in the United States. Most Latin Americans, when they heard about the case automatically reacted as if they knew exactly where the responsibility lay, and who had committed the crime. Most North Americans, when they are [sic] told about it, and told about the accusations reacted with incre-dulity. They would say 'you don't really mean it.' Or 'how was it possi-ble?' or 'what evidence have you?' It is so unusual a matter that most Americans are psychologically unprepared to accept it."[184]

Legal wrangling stalled publication of the thesis in English. Dr. Vic-toria Kent, the editor of *Ibérica*, asked Naranjo for permission to print several English-language excerpts. As portions of the book began appear-ing in *Ibérica*, so too did anonymous death threats against the magazine's staff. Soon thereafter, U.S. immigration authorities interrogated Kent, a prominent Spanish Republican attorney. The line of questioning led her to believe that she had been denounced by the Dominican government and that North American officials were probing for a reason to initiate deportation proceedings.[185]

Perhaps Galíndez's impact is best measured by the simultaneous memorials held in his honor on the fifteen-month anniversary of his disappearance. On June 12, 1957, tributes were held in eleven Latin American countries and in Paris and New York. The event in Manhattan, held at the Community Church on 35th Street and Park Avenue, brought together members of twenty organizations, reflecting the astonishingly broad range of his interests. Among the speakers were Juan Díaz, Requena's co-editor of *La Patria;* Felipe Arana, the president of the Ibero-American Confederation of Writers and Poets; Sabi Nehama, a member of Local 22 of the International Ladies Garment Workers Union; Alberto Urriarte, the president of the Centro Vasco Americano; General José Asensio, a representative of the Spanish Republican government-in-exile; Ian Adamson, one of Galíndez's Columbia students; and Frances Grant, representing the IADF.[186]

Outspoken dissidents like Almoina and Galíndez were not the regime's only targets. Trujillista aggression extended even to heads of state—democrats and dictators alike. Leaving aside numerous attempts on the lives of political enemies who subsequently rose to power, and ongoing efforts to destabilize or overthrow unfriendly governments, Trujillo was implicated in the attempted assassinations of the heads of state of Haiti (1937, 1944, 1949), Cuba (1944, 1956, 1959), Costa Rica (1957), Guatemala (1957), and Venezuela (1950, 1960). If there was a common denominator in all these attacks, it was that each of these rulers had crossed him in some way, shape, or form. Venezuela's Carlos Delgado Chalbaud and Guatemala's Carlos Castillo Armas—both military men—appear to have been the tyrant's only "successes."

Conclusions

With Washington's energies channeled toward greater threats in Europe, the eastern Mediterranean, and the Far East, tyrants like Trujillo and, to a lesser extent, supporters of democracy had more room to maneuver. As a result, political turmoil was unleashed in ways not seen in the region since the mid-1920s.

Peripatetic Dominican exiles were remarkably tenacious in their efforts to overthrow Trujillo. They sought ties with dissidents on the island, and when that proved impossible, thanks to the support of democratic states, they launched expeditions. They also became the backbone of the Caribbean Legion, if not in numbers then in the leadership roles they played. Expressing solidarity with the cause of democracy, Dominicans selflessly put their lives on the line, helping Figueres seize power in the spring of 1948 and then immediately joining their Nicaraguan brethren in their unsuccessful efforts to oust Somoza.

Trujillo's regime took the threat seriously, employing tactics that his security apparatus had refined from its ongoing battles against the internal opposition. The general not only built one of the most powerful militaries in the Caribbean Basin, but assembled an assertive foreign service that repeatedly violated the sovereignty of its neighbors by wooing and winning over politicians, high commands, and the media. More often than not, pliant (that is, well-paid) Cuban and Haitian officials acted as an extension of the Dominican regime.

Yet Trujillo destabilized dictatorships as well as civilian governments. And as we saw in the case of Prío, if he perceived it as in his self-interest, he was only too willing to set aside past resentments and work with a reviled enemy to achieve a goal—in this case, Batista's ouster—that served both of their interests.

Owing to proximity and the size and vitality of the exile communities residing there, the dictatorship closely monitored Cuba and Haiti. But as recent scholarship on Dominican imperialism in Venezuela and Central America illustrates, the despot used a comparable modus operandi to harass dissidents and their hosts in Caracas, Guatemala City, or San José as well. To cite but one example, he clashed with successive Venezuelan rulers—López Contreras and Medina Angarita—because he felt that each allowed Dominican exiles too much freedom to operate. And all of this occurred well before the man he referred to as his "mortal enemy," Betancourt, ascended to power in 1945.[187]

In response, reformers—some in power, others in exile—mounted a fulsome challenge to La Internacional in the early 1950s. Rolling back the authoritarian tide became their principal objective.

CHAPTER TEN

In Defense of Democracy

In the Caribbean and in general Latin American opinion the
issue of "democracy" versus "dictatorship" . . . is a matter of
far greater importance than the question of communism or
anti-communism.

—DIRECTOR OF THE OFFICE OF SOUTH AMERICAN
AFFAIRS, 1946

If I were to blame the United States for something in the
twentieth century in Latin America, it would be for connivance
with corrupt dictatorships. This has been the worst sin. . . . It
went on all the time.

—JOSÉ FIGUERES, July 8, 1970

DURING THE EARLY 1950s, thirteen of twenty countries in the region were
ruled by autocrats. This ominous trend galvanized reformers. In January
1949, Roger Baldwin and Frances Grant of the International League for
the Rights of Man asked Eleanor Roosevelt to have the UN's Human
Rights Commission open an investigation into the recent rash of coups

d'état, which, they argued, were clear violations of both the Universal Declaration of Human Rights and the OAS charter.[1] Latin American reformers collaborated with international human rights advocates to voice their objections. But the State Department stymied efforts to take up the matter before the UN, because it was concerned that it would shift attention away from Soviet abuses.[2]

Moderates decided to hold a three-day meeting at Havana's Hotel Nacional in May 1950 to advance their agenda and to frame their commitment to promoting democratic principles and eradicating authoritarianism. A more pragmatic goal of the organizers was to create a hemispheric network of reformist leaders "which could be called upon when crises in human rights occurred."[3] With funding provided by the conference host, the Cuban president Prío, two hundred of the leading lights of North and Latin American liberalism from seventeen countries came to Havana. Among the participants were one former and ten future presidents: Figueres (Costa Rica); Frei and Allende (Chile); Santos, Lleras Camargo, and Carlos Lleras Restrepo (Colombia); Villeda Morales (Honduras); Bosch (Dominican Republic); and Betancourt, Leoni, and Pérez (Venezuela).

A distinguished North American contingent attended as well. Among the participants were Waldo Frank, Norman Thomas, NAACP head Walter White, AFL president George Meany, four U.S. congressmen, a bevy of academics, and three members of the liberal advocacy organization Americans for Democratic Action—Charles La Follete, James Loeb, and Arthur Schlesinger, Jr. In addition, several well-respected, progressive journalists who reported on Latin American matters were in the audience, including Galíndez and three Cubans, Mañach, Roa, and Quevedo.

The organizing committee's initial press release mapped out the conference's charge, rejecting dictatorships on both the right and the left. Speaking of a dual danger in Latin America, rightist "neo-fascist and military" dictatorships and communists who "are quick to take advantage of the confusion," the two sides "have united in an unholy alliance" that "represses freedoms." The conference promised to "consider the democratic crisis in the hemisphere, recommend direct action, and establish a permanent organization to promote democracy and freedom in all the American republics."[4]

Prío welcomed the participants in the Capitol's parliamentary chambers. Under discussion during the three days were whether democracies should recognize governments that seized power by force, how to ensure that U.S. assistance did not entrench despots in power, and how best to undermine communist infiltration. Also addressed was Franco's troubling influence on the region. His reactionary ideas, some delegates argued, were too eagerly embraced by the region's dictators.

While some delegates were unsparing in their criticism of autocrats, most news reports described the conference's tone as moderate. One resolution that challenged the characterization called on democratic states to permit arms sales to other democracies threatened by authoritarian regimes. U.S. support for dictatorships also was a common refrain. When the local press and the *New York Times* drew attention to that criticism, North American delegates felt compelled to issue a defensive-sounding statement that "although memories of Yankee imperialism have not altogether died," most Latin American participants offered "warm understandings and cordial support of the role of the United States in helping rally the free world against the menace of communist aggression."[5]

The conference's most lasting accomplishment was the establishment of the IADF, which became in the years ahead equal parts advocacy group, lobbyist, and human rights organization. Led by the indefatigable Grant, the IADF became the flagship of reformers. From a small office in Freedom House on 44th and Lexington in New York City, the organization published a monthly newsletter, *Hemispherica*, held periodic conferences, gave countless press briefings, cultivated the liberal media, denounced repression, highlighted the accomplishments of human rights advocates and reformist governments, and served as a liaison to progressive organizations and political parties in the U.S.

Absent from the proceedings, but present in spirit, was Haya de la Torre, whose asylum case had become a cause célèbre. A number of the speakers publicized his plight. Conference organizers named him in absentia to the IADF's Executive Council. Eventually, his case wound its way to the International Court of Justice in the Hague, one of the first asylum cases of its kind to reach that court. In a curious sense, Haya's moral standing, diminished of late by what his critics viewed as his crass opportunism and the contradictory statements he had given about his movement's willingness to employ violence, was rehabilitated during his five-year captivity in the Colombian embassy in Lima.[6]

In the conference's valedictory, Betancourt invoked the Larreta Doctrine in responding to critics who argued that the democratic nations' fight against La Internacional amounted to the same kind of interventionism that Latin Americans had repudiated at Montevideo in 1933. "At this conference no one has proposed that a certain State Department on this continent should intervene in the internal affairs of another country." Nonintervention is inviolate, Betancourt allowed, but that principle was not inconsistent with nations collectively acting in defense of the "rights of man" articulated in the UN's San Francisco Charter. If western democracies condemn communist regimes for human rights violations, should not members of the OAS, he asked rhetorically, show consistency and criticize dictators who govern without the consent of the people and who repress their citizens? How is it that the same countries that censure Iron Curtain states for repressing their citizens then argue that the OAS "should indifferently keep silence over the muzzled press, mass exile, the hundreds and even thousands of unwarranted prisoners thrown into dark dungeons, the daily violations of the rights of labor"? Indeed, international organizations like the OAS, the UN, and the International Labor Organization must pressure dictators to respect human rights. If member states stand idly by, another iron curtain will descend over this hemisphere, Betancourt warned.[7]

Figueres delivered the most stirring speech during the sessions, declaring that Latin America's democracies had a moral obligation to assist those living under the thumb of the region's dictatorships. The "displaced persons of America," he remarked, were a symptom, not the cause of the problem. Dictators were on the wrong side of history. "Within a generation," Don Pepe predicted, "there will be no more tyrants. The citizens of America have the right to live freely in their own house. And when this right is denied them, they are under the obligation to regain it." But they cannot do so alone, Figueres insisted. "To say to the people of Santo Domingo or Nicaragua that their political situation is an internal matter and that they are the only ones responsible for its solution" is morally unacceptable. How does this current generation "secure the civic culture, the energy and the physical means" to confront these police states? Only with the assistance of the region's democracies, was Figueres's response. In the interim, he concluded, with more than a hint of self-righteousness, countries like his own, which had been providing a safe harbor for these exiles, deserve "the gratitude of history."[8]

Figueres's speech was not just a rhetorical flourish; over the course of the preceding two years, tiny Costa Rica had repulsed Nicaraguan incursions across the border. In fact, in December 1948, when Somoza's National Guard had spilled across the Costa Rican border in support of Figueres's political rivals, Nicaraguan and Dominican "displaced persons" had fought heroically alongside his own forces to turn back the invaders.

His critics contended that his lofty rhetoric in defense of the refugees who made up the Caribbean Legion was always more talk than action. Nicaraguan exile organizations, in particular, had every right to feel aggrieved. Once in power, Figueres welshed on a promise he made to help them unseat Somoza after they had done the same for him against his political rivals. Were it not for the repurposed Cayo Confites weapons that Arévalo forwarded to Figueres and the martial prowess of Dominican and Nicaraguan exiles, it is likely that Figueres's small army would have been defeated. But after the victory, in the face of mounting pressure at home and abroad, Figueres returned the weapons to the Guatemalan president and expelled the Legionnaires from Costa Rica.[9] Perhaps out of guilt or to defend himself against his critics, Pepe would spend the better part of the next decade atoning for his failure to honor his pledge.[10]

Figueres, of course, earned plaudits for abolishing his country's armed forces, but the circumstances surrounding that momentous decision had little to do with any pacifist impulse. It was an accommodation agreed to by Don Pepe and his political rivals, who concluded that it was in each of their interests to dismantle a largely discredited and ineffectual military and leave in its stead a reconfigured national police force. His opponents felt that eliminating the army was the best way to disarm Figueres's followers, while he and his supporters sought to forestall a future coup. The apparent symmetry between the two sides was more apparent than real, because the reconfigured police force was composed largely of PLN loyalists.[11]

Reformers staked their ideological ground in Havana. This chapter delineates the reformers' brief, their aspirations, and the daunting challenges they faced during the early 1950s. Especially problematic was Washington's cozying up to dictatorships. As long as the U.S. and La Internacional continued to hide behind the shield of nonintervention, democrats insisted, Latin America would never defeat the authoritarian scourge. Not to intervene, while providing aid to dictatorships, was not only hypocritical, but was instead a not-so-subtle form of intervention.

Policymakers in Washington protested that they were honoring the time-tested principles of the Good Neighbor policy, reminding their critics that Bradenism—an explicit repudiation of dictatorial regimes as antithetical to American values—had only exacerbated regional instability.

The State Department contended that it was safer to eschew favoritism and recognize all de facto governments, no matter how they came to power. As this chapter argues, postwar administrations were uncertain about the wisdom of supporting civilian rule in Latin America. Not only were some reformers considered ideologically suspect, but hawks in both the State and Defense Departments were convinced that they would shrink before the communist challenge. Doves in the State Department, on the other hand, countered that autocratic regimes would force opponents leftward and that reformers represented the United States' best hope in an increasingly bipolar world. While reformers did not agree with Washington's Cold Warriors that communist subversion was an imminent threat, they understood that they needed to assure policymakers in Washington that they would not collaborate with leftists.

Push came to shove when the Eisenhower administration assessed how reformist or revolutionary certain governments were. Projecting how progressive regimes in Bolivia and Guatemala would turn out was not an exact science. Rather, a number of variables had to be assessed, especially the role of the armed forces in their respective countries. In the Bolivian case, Washington eventually sided with the reformers, not without some hand-wringing and hesitation. In Guatemala, it concluded that President Jacobo Árbenz was beholden to the Guatemalan Communist Party (*Partido Guatemalteco del Trabajo*, PGT). Contrary to the accepted wisdom, the decisionmaking process that went into these momentous decisions suggests that even during the height of the McCarthy era, a measured cost-benefit analysis took precedence over knee-jerk reactions.

Each Country Is Being Occupied by Its Own Army

Regional democrats insisted that Washington withhold recognition from dictators or military regimes that seized power extralegally. A few years before, Acheson had sought to explain why this was such a complicated issue. In a speech on the state of U.S.-Latin American relations before the Pan American Society in New York in September 1949, Truman's secretary of state noted that "Washington's dilemma" was that while supporting democratic institutions might be "desirable in practice, withholding recognition" was often counterproductive. Sounding very much like a latter-day Stimson, he added: "We may have the gravest reservation as to the manner in which a [a new government] has come into power. We may deplore its attitude towards civil liberties. Yet our long-range objectives in the promotion of democratic institutions may, in fact, be best served by recognizing it and thus maintaining a channel of communications with the country involved." Since military force must be avoided at all costs, nonintervention should remain a central tenet of U.S. policy. "There should be no insistence upon 'model USA.' Latin Americans must solve their own political problems."[12]

Acheson was especially reluctant to criticize dictators. One could hear a pin drop at Foggy Bottom after Pérez Jiménez annulled elections in December 1952. The colonel, who openly acknowledged his defeat at the polls, nevertheless repudiated the vote on the grounds that his principal electoral rivals were said to have conspired with AD and the communists.[13] The administration's subdued response was revealing. Warren met with the strongman privately to express his support. His missive to his superiors pulled no punches: He could not "recommend too strongly" that the United States "ignore the question of the [annulled] election" and continue to support Pérez Jiménez. Several years later, a *New York Times* editorial rebuked the Truman administration for its failure to speak out against such fraudulent practices: "It is an open secret that if the United States had expressed its displeasure at the robbery of the Venezuelan election by partisans of Colonel Pérez Jiménez in November 1952, the latter would have retreated, or at least would have come to an agreement with the opposition. By keeping ourselves strictly outside the conflict, and quickly recognizing the Pérez Jiménez regime, we, in a certain sense, intervened."[14]

To those who worked the Latin American desk in the Department, however, nonintervention had become "something big and immovable," a bedrock principle of inter-American relations. According to U.S. Ambassador to Costa Rica Robert Woodward: "It [nonintervention] was just there. You took it for granted. . . . Charles Evans Hughes had taken a big step in Havana, by almost committing the United States. Then, in Montevideo, [Cordell]) Hull had added to it. . . . The big test came when the Mexicans seized the oil properties [in 1938]—and nonintervention prevailed."[15]

When officials were queried about Washington's support for despots, they invariably brought up the lessons learned from Braden's criticism of Perón. The savvy Argentine had played the nationalist card during his successful run for the presidency, portraying Braden's attacks as uncalled-for meddling in his nation's domestic affairs. The latter's falling out of favor within the Department became an object lesson to foreign service officers. As Holland put it, denouncing dictators would be "going back to Bradenism."[16]

Adolf Berle, Jr., former assistant secretary of state for Latin American affairs and now a valued consultant to the Department, zeroed in on his government's double standard. On the one hand, the Department believed that if it exhibited "sympathy for a Betancourt during the dictatorship of Pérez Jiménez . . . [it] would spoil or embitter inter-relationships." In contrast, "courtesy, even decorations, given to dictatorial officials were thought to assist in maintaining good relations. One no more questioned the popular implications of such moves than eighteenth century ambassadors in Europe questioned the right of the reigning prince, however unpopular, to his throne." Sadly, he contended, nonintervention only reinforced the status quo, often with pernicious consequences. "The only certainty was that at some point the status quo will change" and the dictator will be deposed, with the United States saddled with an outsized share of the blame.[17]

Reformers readily agreed with Berle and were quick to point out that the region's communist parties were historically weak and that more than a few had, in the recent past, discredited themselves by collaborating with dictators. They rightfully viewed these partnerships as cynical marriages of convenience. As a result, they, not the communists, were the ones who bore the brunt of a dictator's *mano dura*.

Yet part of the problem was the manner in which reformers presented themselves. In its propaganda, AD, for instance, proudly called itself "a party of the revolutionary left" and "anti-imperialist," descriptors that were far from accurate. In part, this was a rhetorical effort by the party to appropriate the left's talking points, but it invariably elicited questions at home and abroad about what it really stood for, while at the same time raising expectations it had little intention of fulfilling.

Even a Marxist like the Venezuelan Domingo Alberto Rangel agreed that it was the struggle between democracies and dictatorships, not the conflict between Moscow and Washington, that best defined Latin America's political reality during the 1950s. In a thoughtful essay, Rangel contrasted the earlier era of traditional caudillos to contemporary military regimes that had prodigious "machineries of domination" at their disposal. The earlier phase of personalistic dictatorships, and some that enjoyed an extended lease on life, like Trujillo or Somoza, employed their militaries as if they were their own personal armies.[18]

Resistance against dictatorships had reached a critical mass only in the universities in the 1920s, Rangel reminded his readers. Up until that time, the caudillos' principal competitors for power were rival strong-men. Workers and peasants, with some exceptions, were sidelined. While occasional violent episodes occurred in which the masses took to the streets, there was little constructive change to show for it.

By 1950, however, Latin American societies were undergoing momentous changes—massive rural to urban migration, industrialization, a spike in the size of the middle class, growing land hunger in the countryside, and since the end of World War II, an inflationary spiral that had increased the cost of basic goods while depressing real wages. Seeking to persuade the masses of the benefits of modernization, military regimes, according to Rangel, made the argument that opening up their countries to foreign investment would pay dividends in the future. But the once-docile peasantry and proletariat were now becoming increasingly politicized. While some joined leftist parties and labor unions, the great majority of the popular classes gravitated toward broad-based, reformist political parties.[19] In fact, AD's political tent initially was expansive enough to incorporate "a brilliant, opinionated, vociferous" leftist like the outspoken Rangel.[20]

A thoughtful State Department memo echoed the thrust of his analysis, even as it betrayed apprehension over the reformers' unruly methods: "During the last thirty years the traditional ruling elements in the Caribbean republics have been faced by steadily increasing demands for social, economic and political change. These demands come ... from urban elements, students and intellectuals, business and professional men, labor leaders and junior army officers. ... They have no common program, but all desire recognition and a share in political power. In seeking to arouse mass support they have tended to adopt extremist doctrines and demagogic tactics."[21]

The memo may have been accurate in its appraisal of which groups were behind the impetus for reform, but it was off base about the absence of a cohesive agenda. Boasting adherents in virtually every country, social democratic parties shared a common set of principles. In addition to promoting elections and democratic rule, the parties were committed economic nationalists, wary of foreign penetration. In addition, they advocated industrialization, diversification, and agrarian reform and pushed for the nationalization of companies that had a track record of monopolization, such as banks and utilities. By investing in social welfare programs, such as public housing, education, public health, and social security, social democrats promised to ameliorate the quotidian existence of the urban and rural poor. They were convinced that the state alone had the clout and resources to bring about meaningful change. By and large, their socioeconomic blueprint was comparable in scope to Roosevelt's New Deal.[22]

To stem communist penetration in the hemisphere, successive Democratic and Republican administrations felt compelled to arm their neighbors. Overcoming congressional opposition, the Truman administration pushed through $38 million in direct military aid to Latin American states in 1951 and $51 million the following year, and bilateral military pacts were signed with every country in the region except Mexico and Argentina. Under the terms of the agreements, Latin American militaries were to permit the United States to establish a military mission in their country, provide access to its strategic raw materials, make their military installations available to its forces, and promise to use the arms solely for hemispheric defense. Eight hundred U.S. military personnel were assigned to the eighteen military missions, and ten thousand Latin American officers and enlisted men received training in the Canal Zone during the 1950s. In addition to providing training, the Southern Command served as a regional distribution center and maintenance service for Latin American militaries and a hub for intelligence gathering and sharing.[23]

In addition, a U.S. program dedicated to arming and professionalizing the hemisphere's police and secret police forces was created in 1954. Three years later the program's purview was broadened to better integrate military and police assistance with judicial reform. The lynchpin of the new Overseas Internal Security Program was the training of police officers either in country, the Canal Zone, or the United States. By 1958 the program had police advisors in twenty-four countries worldwide and a budget of $35 million.[24] The CIA obtained permission from the administration to insinuate its agents "under the guise of police advisers" into the new program.[25]

Latin America's military establishments willingly accepted the Eisenhower administration's assistance and training, but some did so with a jaundiced eye. Course instruction at Peru's Center for Higher Military Studies during the 1950s and 1960s, for instance, agreed with Washington about the communist threat, but it also warned that Peru's economic dependence was predicated on an unholy alliance between the country's oligarchy, international bankers, and North American companies.[26]

Still, rather than protect the hemisphere from external aggression, dictatorships invariably used the arms and training they received to crush domestic opposition. As a student of the U.S. military assistance programs has noted, to the extent that the pacts maintained "internal stability," from the Pentagon's perspective, they diminished the need to divert military assets to the region, while awarding "a virtual monopoly" to North American arms suppliers.[27] It was "the unique political position of military groups in Latin America," a 1956 NSC policy paper noted, which helps explain why it was "important to the United States to maintain influence with these groups." In some cases," the paper concluded, "it is in the United States' interest to provide such equipment primarily for *political* reasons" (emphasis added).[28] The paper's inference was clear: both geopolitical and economic interests necessitated cozying up to dictators and lavishing resources and attention on the armies that sustained them in power, since these institutions played such an outsized role in domestic political affairs. According to a scholar of the Latin American military, "The quantity of arms provided is probably less important than the psychological effect. Where the civilian and military are vying for power, United States military aid could unwittingly tip the balance in favor of the armed forces."[29]

Reformers were frustrated by Washington's reluctance to criticize or cut off military aid to authoritarian regimes. At a forum held at Columbia University, Santos bemoaned the region's burgeoning militarization. "Against whom are we Latin Americans arming ourselves? Why are our countries ruining themselves buying arms which they will never use? ... What we are doing is building up armies which weigh nothing in the international scale but which are juggernauts in the internal life of each country. Each country is being occupied by its own army."[30] What especially concerned reformers was that U.S. arms and planes were, in some cases, employed against neighboring democracies. Foster Dulles noted that he had received reports from the field "that much of the military equipment maintained by Latin American countries is obtained in an effort to counter equipment which they fear might be used against them by some rival country." Even though Eisenhower doubted that the region's militaries could really contribute in a meaningful way to hemispheric defense, his administration nevertheless pushed ahead with its plans to forge a regional alliance comparable to FDR's Fortress America. Dulles, who appeared to have initial reservations, was won over by the argument that the dictators would simply acquire arms from another country if the U.S. did not make them available. As a result, Pérez Jiménez received $180 million in military equipment over the course of his ten-year dictatorship, and thanks to U.S. armaments and training, Trujillo's armed forces became the envy of fellow tyrants in the Caribbean.[31] Matthews may have exaggerated when he wrote that "selling arms to a

Latin American general is like selling narcotics to a drug addict," but few knowledgeable observers quibbled with the sentiment.[32]

Washington, Betancourt contended, played right into the hands of the despots. By hiding behind the cloak of nonintervention, both Democratic and Republican administrations not only enabled and legitimized tyrants but undermined their oft-stated commitment to promote democratic ideals abroad. When Assistant Secretary of State for Latin American Affairs John Mears Cabot maintained that putting preconditions, such as the release of political prisoners, on the Venezuelan dictator amounted to "intervention," Betancourt, in a letter to Muñoz Marín, fumed at the apparent hypocrisy. "Of course, it [the U.S.] has no problems criticizing Russia [for human rights violations] in the United Nations ... but [it is] complacent when it encounters repression closer to home."[33]

From the Eisenhower administration's perspective, however, the United States was in a no-win situation. A 1954 National Intelligence Estimate sized up the democracy versus dictatorship quandary confronting its policymakers.[34]

> The conflict between "democracy" and "dictatorship" in the Caribbean confronts the United States with a dilemma, for both sides feel entitled to active U.S. support. The "dictators" present themselves as guarantors of stability and order and of cooperation with the United States. The reformists, by definition, are an unsettling influence, but they contend that the United States, as a progressive democracy dominant in the area, has a moral obligation to foster social and political development, and they attribute the denial of positive support to the sinister influence of the "dictators" and the United Fruit Company on United States policy. Conversely, "the dictators" resent any indication of United States support for reformist regimes as a betrayal of the "true friends" of the United States. (Quotations in original)

In reality, hardliners in the administration had a low regard for the region's democrats. A March 1953 NSC policy paper concluded that reformist political parties were "often controlled by immature idealists, who not only are inadequately trained to conduct government business efficiently, but also lack the disposition to combat extremists in their ranks, including communists." Inexperienced politicians, the report continued, felt pressured to address rising expectations "to produce results which are both immediate and tangible." Given the pent-up demand for change, reformers had "a tendency to court popular favor by sensational, irresponsible acts." Also worrisome was their propensity to criticize U.S. policy. To be fair, the report then listed reasons why the United States was such an easy target: "lingering resentment over the loss of half of Mexico and the Panama Canal and the US military occupation of several other American states; paternalistic, disdainful and arrogant attitudes sometimes assumed by North Americans; [and] the fact that, for reasons of our own, we have not extended economic aid to them on a scale remotely comparable to that of other areas."[35]

Cold Warriors considered reformers naïve. As Assistant Secretary of State for Latin American Affairs Roy Rubottom noted: "Latin Americans were inexperienced with communist dictatorship, so they were willing to allow things to go much too far before they were willing to accept the lesson that [a] dictatorship of the left can be just as onerous, if not more so, than the dictatorship of the right."[36]

There were a few voices in the State Department who believed that working with moderates was the right thing to do, however. A 1951 Department policy statement, for instance, characterized Costa Rica's opposition to communism "genuine and sincere ... the Government has given every indication of being alert to the threat of infiltration by the agents of international Communism."[37] Three years later, Holland expressed similar sentiments in a letter to U.S. Ambassador to the United Nations Henry Cabot Lodge. There was a marked difference in Latin America between progressive nationalists and communists: "we should exercise caution against judging leftist leaders such as Betancourt and Figueres as communists."[38] A young Che Guevara, coming from a very different ideological perspective, agreed with Holland's assessment of Betancourt when the Argentine and the Venezuelan crossed paths in San José in 1953. "My impression is that he's a politician with some firm social ideas in his head, but otherwise he sways toward whatever is to his best advantage. In principle, he is solidly with the United States. He spoke lies about the Rio Pact and spent most of the time raging about the communists."[39]

A Probing Analysis

Galíndez enjoyed a wide readership in Latin America during the early 1950s. Well versed in the history, politics, and culture of the Hispanic diaspora, the Basque was, in certain respects, his generation's José Martí.

Like the Cuban, Galíndez spent a significant portion of his exile working as a journalist in New York City. Both actively contributed to numerous cultural and civic organizations in the city's lively Hispanic community.[40] Galíndez also shared Martí's aversion to extremism and a preoccupation with the United States' impact on the region. When he wrote about such topics as dictatorial regimes, anticommunism, the Caracas conference, and the Guatemalan intervention, Latin Americans took heed.

Galíndez's liminal status as an independent-minded Basque made it possible for him to steer clear of the highly factionalized world of exile politics, all the while befriending disparate members of that community no matter their ideological persuasion. As willing to criticize a Trujillo as he was Foster Dulles, he was as welcome a presence at meetings of communist front organizations as he was at gatherings of the Puerto Rican Nationalist Party. A combination of a rootless, stateless existence and his Basque identity made it possible for him to identify with the plight of similarly displaced émigrés. As he admitted, "we are Basque, we can hold another citizenship, we can love the country we live in; we can have compassion for the problem of others. . . . Some people think it strange that I should share the problems of Puerto Ricans in New York . . . attack Latin American dictators . . . take part in the International League of Human Rights; that I should be moved when I hear the patriotic hymn of a Mexican *charro* or the drumbeat of a black Caribbean."[41]

In "Anticomunismo negativo y positivo," a column written just before the 1954 Inter-American Conference opened in Caracas, Galíndez categorically rejected both fascism and communism. Having fought on the side of the Republic during the Spanish Civil War, he had witnessed firsthand the barbarism unleashed by extremist ideologies. He then had spent six years toiling in Trujillo's Santo Domingo, an eye-opening experience that left him with few illusions about the daily indignities of life under authoritarian rule. But the buffeting of the Cold War, with its unanticipated "ideological changes of direction," was disorienting for the public intellectual. If in the United States, Galíndez noted, anticommunism signified protecting an American way of life, to Latin American dictators it meant repressing basic human liberties. To the region's tradition-bound creole oligarchs, Galíndez explained, anticommunism denoted something altogether different—the maintenance at all costs of a socioeconomic status quo they had inherited from the colonial era and considered their birthright.[42]

Reformers were on the defensive everywhere, he noted, yet the fault was partly of their own making. While it was evident they were opposed to communism, they had failed to clearly articulate what their vision for the future was. "We may be anticommunists, but what is our final goal, for what are we fighting?" Latin Americans may be yearning for change, he added, but they have not yet lived through "the torture of a communist dictatorship." What they had all too much experience with, however, were the miseries of authoritarianism and creole oligarchy. It should not be a surprise, then, that Latin America was propitious soil for future communist expansion, Galíndez added. In the face of such a stark reality, social democrats harbored a "grave" responsibility: "We need a positive anticommunist agenda. Problems need to be tackled with deeds not words; we need better solutions than the communists. Only with liberty and social justice will communism be repudiated." He urged the democratic delegations in Caracas to present bold proposals that set forth a constructive agenda.[43]

As anticommunist as he was, Galíndez continued to reject the simplistic bromides voiced by Washington's Cold Warriors. "The true cancer in Hispanic America," he noted, "continues to be personal dictatorships and egotistical oligarchies." What had always defined democratic reformers was their steadfast commitment to the elimination of dictatorships, whether on the right or the left.[44]

Reformers also had to remain alert to the threat of reprisals from La Internacional, which pooled its resources and shared intelligence whenever its loosely affiliated members felt threatened or it wanted to send a message to democratic governments. While dictators had their occasional differences with each other, whether they acted alone or in concert with other strongmen, they were seldom averse to disrupting the internal affairs of their democratic neighbors. Outnumbered and often outmanned militarily, democracies throughout the circum-Caribbean were engaged in a rearguard battle, even as they sought to prove to Washington that they were committed to turning back the communist threat.

Still, proponents of democratization were never reluctant to air their misgivings about U.S. policy in the press. As a result, they proved to be a persistent thorn in the side of the Eisenhower administration. Despite reformers' admiration for the United States' system of government and its way of life, they were quick to criticize North American economic penetration and to question the unequal terms of trade for Latin American exports and the pernicious impact of U.S. tariffs. Nor were they shy about expressing their frustrations with Washington's meddling in their internal affairs.

To Intervene or Not to Intervene

Differentiating between social democrats, who confusingly proclaimed themselves "revolutionaries," and dogmatic leftists perplexed analysts in the State Department. Why, for instance, did the Eisenhower administration tint Guatemala's Árbenz red but opt to work with and provide economic and military assistance for Bolivia's revolutionary government? Why did the Guatemalan agrarian reform law raise hackles, while the Bolivian MNR's much more expansive redistribution program *and* its nationalization of the tin and tungsten sector—commodities of much greater strategic import to the United States than bananas—did not? As one scholar has noted, in Guatemala, the Eisenhower administration ascribed "attacks on private property and fits of anti-American pique to the dispositional manipulation of communist infiltrators and the predisposition of Árbenz toward unfriendliness; in Bolivia they attributed those same disturbing features to constraints imposed by Bolivia's poverty, underdevelopment, and the political mobilization that accompanied a revolution that threatened constantly to lurch out of control."[45]

Both regimes may have called for economic nationalism, agrarian reform, a social safety net, and democratization, but of the two, it was the MNR that operated during the first four years of its existence without recourse to a legislature or municipal governments and was not reluctant to mete out repression against its opponents.[46] It was the military officer Árbenz who came to power via the ballot box while the MNR, which saw its electoral victory annulled by the Bolivian military in 1951, seized power by force. Mineworker and peasant militias loyal to the party rose up in rebellion and, with the assistance of the National Police, defeated the Bolivian army.

Predicting the MNR's future direction was chancy, given its unusual ideological trajectory. For much of the 1940s it resembled a fascist political party. Influenced by the rise of Peronism next door, it was defiantly nationalistic and anti-Semitic. Indeed, Peronist diplomats kept a high profile in the Bolivian capital. A propaganda blitz in the press and on the radio spewed Argentine propaganda, and its legation was rumored to have had its hand in the 1943 coup that brought General Gualberto Villarroel to power and the MNR into his cabinet. Perón even boasted that he would help the landlocked country recover its outlet to the sea, which it had lost to Chile in the War of the Pacific (1879–1884).[47] Concerned with the cozy relationship between the Peronists and the MNR, the

State Department forced the removal of MNR ministers from Villarro-el's cabinet in 1944. As late as 1946, the U.S. embassy characterized the party as a "typically totalitarian [party] of the Nazi-fascist type."[48] The party's later nationalization of the mines or agrarian reform could have been the farthest policies from its mind.

Over the next five years—a period during which an estimated five thousand militants (including much of the party's leadership) were exiled to Argentina—the MNR underwent a striking transformation. North American liberals were confident that the party had changed its political stripes. Rutgers economist Robert Alexander and Romauldi both urged the State Department to work with Paz's reform-minded government. The former pleaded with Assistant Secretary of State for Inter-American Affairs Edward Miller in April 1952: "This revolution is not something we can stop. We can ride with it and try to guide it, but we will be fool-hardy indeed if we try to brake it or break it." He reminded Miller that just the month before, the administration had not delayed in the slightest to recognize Batista, even though he had staged a coup that annulled elections in which he had run a distant third.[49]

What was troubling to the Truman administration was that leftist mineworkers, members of one of the largest Trotskyite parties in the world, and the Bolivian Communist Party all had backed the MNR in the 1951 elections. But the party's urban, middle-class leadership, including Paz, Foreign Minister Walter Guevara Arze, and the ambassador to the United States, Victor Andrade Urquiano, waged a highly effective public relations blitz to convince the Eisenhower administration that the party was anticommunist, pro-U.S., and committed to protecting private property. Paz also took steps to distance his government from Buenos Aires, promising U.S officials that he would curtail Peronist labor organizing.[50]

After the Bolivian president decreed the nationalization of the tin mines, the administration initially took a hard line, a moratorium on future tin contracts with the Bolivian government. But over the course of the spring of 1953, it had a change of heart, agreeing to recognize the revolutionary government and floating an aid package, a tin contract, and a promise of future economic and food assistance if Paz agreed to negotiate compensation with the processors and if the regime toned down its anti-American rhetoric. That he consulted U.S. officials on the details of the ongoing negotiations between the processors and the mineworkers' union also helped allay suspicions.[51] In truth, the U.S. had Bolivia over a barrel. Famine was setting in, food stocks were in short supply, and government coffers were empty. Since North American tin processors were the only ones that could process its low-grade ores, Bolivia had nowhere else to turn for its primary source of foreign exchange.

The Eisenhower administration's decision to work with the Bolivian government was politically driven. As a *New York Times* editorial explained, "The United States has already stockpiled enough tin for a long siege and we do not need more." Still, the reformist government deserved the administration's support, the paper recommended. It had "resisted the blandishments of Perón, held the Reds in check, and somehow managed to hold itself together."[52] The administration justified its decision by drawing a distinction between communist regimes like Guatemala and reformist ones like Bolivia. In doing so, its embassy in La Paz appeared to split ideological hairs, characterizing Paz as someone with "Marxist inclinations" that "are of a personal nature and used as intellectual tools in an attempt to grapple with problems related to the development of Bolivia." Cabot's lieutenant, Rollin Atwood, counseled restraint, telling the House Subcommittees on Foreign Economic Policy and Inter-American Affairs that "if Bolivia was really driven to the wall on this tin situation and the present Government did fall, I think we could expect to have another Guatemala situation."[53]

Over the course of the 1950s, Bolivia received more foreign aid per capita than any other country in Latin America.[54] Other democracies in the region took notice. Figueres, for one, was elated: "I wish the Bolivian Revolution and ... U.S. policy towards it were better known. Here is proof ... the U.S is sympathetic to political and social progress."[55]

For answers to why the administration elected to employ different strategies in the two countries, we need to consider additional variables: the relative proximity of the two countries to the United States, the prospects for success of an attempted coup, the political leaders' willingness to work alongside endogenous leftist elements, the relative strength of their oligarchies, and whether U.S. officials and North American investors felt they could do business with Paz Estenssoro and Árbenz.

First, organizing and carrying out a successful coup in remote Bolivia would have been far more challenging than in Guatemala. Dating back to 1898, the United States had overturned governments in the Caribbean theater with relative ease. According to historian John Coatsworth, in its sphere of influence policymakers "expected a particularly high degree of conformity to U.S. policy preferences."[56] Moreover, in

Guatemala the U.S. could also count on allies nearby willing to provide logistical support. It would have been more difficult to secure cooperation from Bolivia's neighbors.

In addition, Árbenz felt he needed the assistance of the PGT and its affiliated labor organizations to carry out the agrarian reform, in part because his high command opposed the new law. To implement Decree 900, he enlisted the members of the PGT, agricultural extension agents, forestry guards, teachers, and loyal junior officers to carry out the land reform.[57]

It was far easier for the administration to accept the MNR's nationalization of the tin mines and its agrarian reform because the stakes were not as great for U.S. investors in Bolivia. Decree 900, on the other hand, targeted 15 percent of *el pulpo*'s extensive holdings. Nor did North American stakeholders in the Bolivian tin industry undertake anything comparable to the United Fruit Company's aggressive anti-Árbenz public relations and lobbying campaign. Six months after the passage of the agrarian reform decree, Árbenz legalized the PGT. Domestic and foreign opponents seized on the announcement as confirmation that the president was either in league with the communists or their dupe.[58]

Another striking difference was the divergent roles played by the two military establishments. Árbenz's efforts to professionalize the armed forces at Guatemala's West Point, the Escuela Politécnica, had produced a cadre of younger officers, or "officers of the school," who, up until the coup, remained loyal to him rather than to their superiors. By contrast, many of the more senior officers, or "officers of the line," who had come up through the ranks during the Ubico dictatorship, were plainly uncomfortable with Árbenz's progressive agenda.[59]

Since the late nineteenth century, the Guatemalan army had held carte blanche in the countryside, where it directed the rural militias and oversaw conscription. With the military's prerogatives over the means of coercion in rural areas now undermined by the agrarian reform, a generational rift within the officer corps widened. Árbenz did move loyal officers into key posts and "highly prized" civil servant positions, but that only served to diminish their influence within the armed forces.[60]

Although philosophical and generational differences persisted, to its credit, the Guatemalan military repeatedly turned back coup attempts against Arévalo and Árbenz up until it refused to do so in 1954. Perhaps its willingness to defend civilian rule is best explained by the popular support it garnered for its actions during the October 1944 revolt that

ousted Ubico. For one of the few times in its history, the military was regarded as heroes by many Guatemaltecos. Whatever reservations it had
about Arévalo's and Árbenz's policies, the officer corps warmed to its role
as an independent arbiter of the body politic, a task it embraced with increasing regularity in the future, with often devastating consequences for
the nation.[61]

Árbenz had only recently won a power struggle with his principal
rival, the chief of staff, Colonel Francisco Arana. The latter's death in a
shootout in July 1949 triggered an uprising among his loyalists that left
150 dead and 300 wounded.[62] That rebellion was quashed only after
labor confederations declared a general strike and Árbenz had taken the
extraordinary step of arming civilians. When he triumphed at the polls a
year later, Árbenz pursued a two-pronged strategy to ensure the high
command's loyalty. He purged the army of a number of Arana loyalists
and attempted to "buy" the allegiance of others by promoting his own
loyalists. He raised salaries and offered perks to officers, including pen-
sions, travel allowances, study overseas, insurance, mortgage loans, access
to military hospitals, and commissaries, where officers could buy imported goods tax-free and then sell them for a profit. According to a U.S.
military attaché, Árbenz also rewarded officers who came forward with
information about conspiratorial activities.[63]

The day after Arana's unexpected death, the U.S. ambassador to
Guatemala, Richard Patterson, cabled his first impressions of the political lay of the land. His cryptic remarks were remarkably prescient: "regardless of responsibility [for the] assassination, end result eliminates
important moderate elements [in the] government and strengthens [the]
Left materially."[64]

Some officers, such as eventual coup plotter Colonel Carlos Castillo
Armas, an Arana man, harbored resentment for what transpired and
knew where to place the blame. The forty-year-old son of a wealthy
hacendado and a graduate of the U.S. Army Command and General Staff
College at Fort Leavenworth, Kansas, Castillo Armas and several fellow
army officers, who were demoted or dismissed after Árbenz cleaned
house, conspired to attack a military base in the capital. In fact, Castillo
Armas had first cast his net widely, discussing plans for a coup with representatives from the Dominican Republic, Nicaragua, and El Salvador.
The dictators, who already had backed several unsuccessful efforts to
oust Arévalo, were unconvinced that he had sufficient backing within the
high command and refused to provide any funds.[65]

Undeterred, in November 1950 Castillo Armas and seventy loyalists launched their rebellion, which was easily put down. Injured in the fighting, he was taken to a military hospital. He was subsequently expelled from the army and a military tribunal sentenced him to death. While awaiting his fate in the Central Penitentiary, he and eight others managed an escape. The rebel then sought and obtained asylum at the Colombian embassy before eventually reaching Honduras. There, while employed as a furniture salesman, Castillo Armas and other like-minded exiles once again waxed conspiratorial.[66]

The Guatemalan public intellectual Luis Cardoza y Aragón, who had served as a diplomat under Arévalo, later claimed that Árbenz lacked his predecessor's finesse at playing off the different factions within the armed forces.[67] To be sure, Castillo Armas's and his peers' disaffection posed a problem for the president and an opportunity for the United States. As we shall see, the CIA and the U.S. ambassador to Guatemala, John Peurifoy, played upon the fissures within the military with some success, offering substantial bribes to senior officers in the hope of turning the military against the president.[68]

The same was not true in Bolivia, where a discredited military and a weakened oligarchy meant that the MNR did not need a militant left to carry out its reforms. Learning from prior setbacks, the party carefully laid the groundwork for the April 1952 insurrection, cultivating junior officers in the military and the leadership of the National Police. After two days of intense fighting in and around the capital, La Paz, between the army and "hastily formed units of factory workers, MNR militants, townsfolk and miners" and two thousand *carabineros*, the military capitulated.[69]

To diminish the potential of a counterrevolution, the Bolivian president and his successor, Hernán Siles Zuazo, elected to reform but not abolish the armed forces. Military funding was cut back significantly, from just under a quarter of the national budget before the revolution to 6.7 percent in 1957. The two MNR administrations (1952–1964) also purged 155 members of the officer corps and slashed the number of troops from eighteen thousand to five thousand. Peasant and worker militias and the National Police were rewarded for their loyalty to the revolution and deployed to counter the armed forces' traditional monopoly of power. The regime never divorced itself entirely from the military, but the institution's role was substantially reconfigured. The high command even agreed to send in advisors to train the militias, and soldiers were assigned to development projects. Owing to ample military assistance and training from the Eisenhower administration, which never fully trusted the militias, by the end of the decade, the armed forces. according to historian Elizabeth Shesko, had reclaimed their position as "the main arbiter of high politics."[70]

The idiosyncrasies of the Bolivian and Guatemalan cases argued against a uniform policy response from the United States. NSC reports sometimes drew speculative conclusions about whether prodemocratic elements within a given Latin American military might be a positive force for change or how a retrograde element within another armed force "renders likely the eventual outbreak of revolutionary violence."[71] But as this comparison of two incipient revolutionary moments makes clear, each case was distinct, shaped by endogenous and exogenous forces. Washington's assessment of the role that militaries might play in a "revolutionary" situation often was an imperfect calculus.

Ultimately, the Eisenhower administration concluded that it could negotiate with Paz, his foreign minister, and ambassador; the same could not be said for Árbenz and his aides. Even though Washington could not prevent the MNR from nationalizing its tin sector, since ownership of the smelters remained in the hands of North American and European companies, the Bolivian president was more willing to negotiate with Washington than his Guatemalan counterpart.

Two other differences in the Bolivian case are more difficult to assess. First, President Eisenhower was directly involved in the negotiations with the MNR, whereas he left negotiating with the Árbenz regime to his hawkish ambassador. Perhaps it did not hurt that Andrade was an occasional golf partner of the president. And the president's brother Milton, who agreed with the administration's assessment on Guatemala, had counseled the president that negotiating with Paz was worth the candle.[72]

Conclusions

Eisenhower's decision to support the Bolivian Revolution buoyed reformers. It was a sign that under the right conditions Washington was willing to tolerate progressive reform. The same could not be said for the decision to intervene in Guatemala. Figueres, Betancourt, and their peers agreed with Washington that Árbenz had to go but, cognizant of how toxic the issue of U.S. intervention was in the region, they kept their counsel.

Instead of prying Washington from its resolute support for dictator-ships, the Inter-American Conference in Caracas in March 1954 and the overthrow of Árbenz three months later placed reformers on the defen-sive. If they did not express support for the CIA-assisted coup, they risked alienating the Eisenhower administration. If they voiced support for the coup publicly, they angered their political base, which equated in-tervention with the return of the Big Stick. Social democrats found themselves hemmed in, with few good options. In contrast, dictators were crystal-clear where they stood. If anything, the Caracas Conference and the Guatemalan intervention reinforced the administration's convic-tion that it was dictators, not democrats, who really understood what was at stake during the Cold War.

CHAPTER ELEVEN

We Are Fighting in Difficult Circumstances

What will become of this Caribbean world, which, due to its
geographic peculiarity and its proximity to the United States and
Europe, seems one of the epicenters of Latin American tension?
Will it continue to be a site of dictatorships like that of Rafael
Trujillo or of chaotic communist subversion, a world of
revolutions . . . or of democracies, as Betancourt heralded?

—MARIANO PICÓN SALAS

IN EARLY 1954, FIGUERES announced that his nation would not send a delegation to the upcoming Tenth Inter-American Conference in Caracas.
Costa Rica could not in good faith attend meetings held in a country
where repression was commonplace. Praised by proponents of democratization across the region, Figueres's stance was seen as a stinging rebuke
of Pérez Jiménez. Under his dictatorship, Venezuela's domestic opposition had been viciously repressed and the country's prisons were filled
with political prisoners.

Casting himself as an apostle of democracy, Figueres hoped that his
decision to boycott the Caracas meetings would serve as "an eloquent cry,

calling attention to the long-abandoned problem of ... democracy in Latin America."[1] His administration outlined its rationale in a column that appeared in the press ten days before the conference began. "Democracy and Caracas Cannot Be Reconciled" assured constituents that although Latin America stood "staunchly with the West" in the Cold War, "America is fighting two struggles simultaneously, a global war against external aggression and an internal battle between democracy and dictatorship." Figueres lamented that the former appeared to take precedence over the latter: "During the last half century, only the global struggle has been addressed. The peoples of the Americas have been asked to be patient with internal oppression and to maintain our faith in democracy until external threats have been eliminated. We can wait no longer while thousands of law-abiding citizens languish in jail for years without coming to trial or are forced into exile." He recognized that other governments might decide to attend the meetings, but felt—with more than a hint of self-righteousness—that it was necessary "that one country bear witness to the sufferings of the American people at the hands of totalitarian regimes."[2]

The Caracas Conference has been cast in the scholarly literature as a precursor to intervention in Guatemala, where Latin American governments acquiesced to a North American resolution that cleared the diplomatic decks for the overthrow of Árbenz. To be sure, Foster Dulles accomplished his objective in Caracas, but what was readily apparent from the debate during the meetings was that only Washington actually believed that international communism represented a threat to the region's security. As we shall see, many Latin American states reluctantly went along with the resolution, but felt that it violated the principle of nonintervention enshrined in Montevideo in 1933. While the resolution provided the United States with diplomatic cover for the coup—by stipulating that the nations of the hemisphere would act in concert against the threat of Soviet penetration—Operation PBSUCCESS was far from the unified response that the secretary of state desired.

Reformers came to the Caracas Conference with a very different agenda. They viewed the meetings as an opportunity to move forward on two interrelated fronts. To strengthen the region's fragile democracies, they argued, their languishing economies required immediate attention. Stuck in their collective craw was that the United States had invested millions of dollars to rebuild Western Europe after the Second World War while offering little in the way of assistance to loyal Latin American allies who had aided the U.S. in the fight against fascism.

Economic development was a long-term fix, however. Of more pressing concern was the proliferation of authoritarian regimes. Costa Rica's refusal to attend the conference had nothing to do with Guatemala or the Cold War. Encouraged by his good friend Betancourt, who since 1952 had been a guest of his government, Figueres's decision to boycott the meetings was meant to draw attention to heinous human rights violations in Venezuela, to publicly embarrass its dictator, and to deny the regime the legitimacy it expected to reap from hosting the meetings. If the boycott campaign gained adherents, a case could be made that repressive regimes should no longer be tolerated in the hemisphere.

Since Venezuela was not only a site of repression but the locale for the meetings, it was only natural that Betancourt and Figueres made that regime their focus during the run-up to the conference. By early 1954, AD's struggle to defeat Pérez Jiménez had reached an inflection point. The underground's leadership was decimated and the lines of communication between it and AD-in-exile were frayed. At a desperate moment, Betancourt and his colleagues used the boycott to demand the release of its militants from prison and to make a broader case for a return to democracy before the court of international public opinion. This chapter discusses Betancourt's and Figueres's motivations, their efforts to build a sustainable transnational coalition of democratic partners, and their unsuccessful efforts to win over the United States to their cause.

Until the meetings in Caracas, Latin American governments parsed dissonant messages within a bifurcated U.S. foreign policy establishment. Now the State Department and a burgeoning national security establishment spoke with one voice, however. Foster Dulles and his brother (and CIA director) Allen were convinced that autocratic regimes were far better equipped to defeat the threat of leftist subversion. Their rhetoric and actions did little to hide their doubts about the reliability and métier of civilian governments. What became painfully obvious to reformers after Caracas was that the Cold Warriors in Washington would greatly complicate their crusade to eradicate authoritarianism.

To Live Freely in Their Own House

Figueres's decision was influenced not just by the alarming drift toward authoritarianism in the hemisphere but by matters much closer to home. La Internacional had its sights set on destabilizing Costa Rica. In May 1953, Raymond Leddy, the Central American desk officer, told the

House Subcommittee on Inter-American Affairs that " 'conservative countries' have ganged up and gotten together $300,000, which is a good wad of dough in Costa Rican terms," to prevent a Figueres victory at the polls in the upcoming presidential election. Despite the threat, Figueres won easily that fall, but he knew that not sending a delegation to the upcoming conference would embarrass and anger Pérez Jiménez and other members of La Internacional.[3]

He did, however, qualify his decision. If Pérez Jiménez agreed to a general amnesty for political prisoners and to restore civil liberties before the conference began, Costa Rica would reconsider. In making such demands, Pepe was following the lead of the Venezuelan exile, who for the better part of the past year had traveled the length and breadth of the region, pleading with "the democratic countries of the hemisphere [to] bring pressure to bear on the Venezuelan government."[4] During his trip, Betancourt talked up a boycott with the democratic presidents of Chile, Uruguay, and Bolivia.[5]

In a widely disseminated essay published in *Cuadernos Americanos* in the fall of 1953, Betancourt presented a compelling brief as to why governments must abstain from the proceedings. Portraying the Venezuelan capital as a South American Budapest and his *patria* a place "where systematically, day-by-day, the fundamental rights of man and citizen are violated," he called upon the Latin American republics to send an unambiguous message to the dictator, and by extension to other regional strongmen, that conducting business as usual in Caracas was not acceptable.[6] The regime outlawed its principal foe, AD, less than a month after the 1948 coup, and shut down several of the party's newspapers and its labor federations. Even though the PCV condemned the coup and the suspension of civil guarantees, and its paper, *Tribuna Popular*, was suspended on several occasions, the junta saved its most savage repression for AD, in part because its underground had carried out several high-profile assassinations and bombings during the first few years of the dictatorship.[7]

Pérez Jiménez's voluble security chief, Pedro Estrada, who had earned a notorious reputation as a sadistic butcher, did not help the dictator's image during the run-up to the conference. In a *New York Times* interview he promised that there would be no repeat of the 1948 *Bogotazo* riot that had taken place during the last Inter-American Conference, "even if we have to round up every suspicious character in the country and jail them throughout the conference."[8]

Betancourt estimated that Venezuela's jails held four thousand political prisoners, some of whom had been imprisoned for more than three years without having charges brought against them. Conditions in the prisons and penal colonies were appalling. Guasina, a prison camp situated on a muddy key seventy miles from the mouth of the Orinoco River, drew comparisons to Devil's Island. Even the Catholic Church, which had hailed the coup that brought the military junta to power, deplored the treatment of prisoners in the penal colonies.[9] Moreover, targeted political assassinations by the regime had become routine. Thanks to its militant underground, which kept AD's leadership abroad well informed, Betancourt did not just speak in generalities, he named names, listing the latest party members who had become victims of the dictatorship.[10] The party compiled a detailed compendium of the regime's atrocities. Published in 1952, *El libro negro de una dictadura* (A Dictatorship's Black Book) was a gruesome recounting of the brutalities of a dictatorship that years later garnered the puzzling descriptor *dictablanda*.[11]

Betancourt gave Estrada his due when he grudgingly admitted, "it cannot be denied that he had a nose for knowing who were the most dangerous enemies of the regime."[12] Estrada's Secret Police were relentless in dismantling the underground. Two of Betancourt's closest collaborators, Leonardo Ruíz Pineda and Antonio Pinto Salinas, were assassinated, while a third, Alberto Carnevali, died in prison because he failed to receive proper medical attention.[13]

Betancourt's harrowing descriptions did not exaggerate. One of the most persuasive treatments of the period, written by a Marxist critical of Betancourt, characterized Venezuela as a hellish police state. Juan Bautista Fuenmayor, the historian and one of the founders of the PCV, had a basis for comparison. Like many of the Generation of 1928, he had experienced Gomecista repression. The uptick in state terror, he noted, coincided with Estrada's elevation to director of Seguridad Nacional (SN) in late August 1951.[14]

A former policeman, Estrada moved to the United States during the short-lived experiment with democracy from 1945 to 1948. There he fell in with right-wing exiles scheming to topple the *trienio* government. He then gained valuable training for his future line of work in the Dominican Republic, where he was hired by Trujillo's Secret Police to undertake "special assignments." With money, weapons, and planes provided by the Dominican despot and Somoza, Estrada and like-minded exiles unsuccessfully tried to overthrow Venezuela's constitutional government in January 1948.[15]

Ten months later another coup accomplished what Estrada and his co-conspirators could not. The new ruling junta dispatched Estrada to its embassy in Washington, where he was assigned the task of cultivating ties with the CIA and creating a nest of spies whose responsibility it was to monitor the movement of AD's exiled leadership.[16] As he recalled in his memoirs, "Washington was for me an enormous source of knowledge. Everything I knew about subversion, I learned there."[17]

He must have acquitted himself well, because he was called home in the summer of 1951 and appointed director of the SN. Rewarded with autonomy and seemingly unlimited resources, Estrada beefed up the size of the agency significantly. The SN now boasted five thousand agents and an undisclosed number of part-time informants believed to number in the thousands. The agency now rivalled the size of the army.[18] Not surprisingly, given Estrada's ties to the U.S. national security establishment, the SN's leadership received counterinsurgency training in the States.[19]

Estrada's nickname, "The Jackal from Güiria," was fitting. Operating out of a gray, five-story building on Avenida México in downtown Caracas, his operatives compiled massive dossiers on thousands of Venezuelans and spun elaborate conspiracies and collected political gossip in order to heighten fear and immobilize dissidents.[20] According to Silfa, the Jackal shared "many of the methods of inquisitional torture" with his colleagues in La Internacional. The pupil now was the teacher, as his heinous methods would be adopted as standard operating procedure by Trujillo's Secret Police.[21]

One might presume that the SN's purview was restricted to civil society, but surveillance reached into the barracks. The junta had ample reason to be suspicious of its own. Between May 1950 and October 1952, the AD underground and disgruntled junior officers unsuccessfully conspired on five occasions either to assassinate junta leaders or to seize armories. Whether at home or abroad, SN agents identified, tracked, and eliminated conspirators within the armed forces. Some dissident soldiers paid for their purported sins with time spent in the penal camps.[22]

Pérez Jiménez may have been a career officer, but the preoccupation that his colleagues might turn against him loomed so large that he implemented the humiliating practice of having every senior military officer searched by the SN before meeting with him. As one student of the Venezuelan military noted, "Professional military men resented the practice . . . it symbolized the growing separation between the Commander-in-Chief and his uniformed subordinates."[23] In one high-profile case, the well-respected military officer and classmate of Pérez Jiménez at Los

Chorrillos Military Academy in Lima, Lieutenant Colonel Martín Márquez Añez, made the mistake of lodging a complaint. Too much, he told the junta chief, was being spent on the "vast security apparatus against the officer corps and . . . citizens of estimable reputation"; greater attention ought to be paid to how public funds were administered. Márquez Añez's reproach certainly had merit; a journalist noted that it was common knowledge that "certain individuals connected to the regime are disproportionally enriching themselves." Pérez Jiménez, in particular, amassed a massive fortune by the time he was driven from power in 1958. In return for concessions for infrastructural projects, he and his cabinet received kickbacks from industrialists amounting to as much as 30 percent of the total cost of the project. The complaint must have hit a nerve, because after his meeting with the strongman, Estrada's agents escorted Márquez Añez to prison.[24]

So great was the regime's animosity toward AD that automobile license plates beginning with those first two letters were banned. While the party's underground always was Estrada's principal target, no individual, no matter his or her social class or ideological disposition, felt safe. Even the wives and daughters of AD militants were tortured and violated in the regime's prisons. The *Libro negro* compiled a list of 110 women known to have been imprisoned or exiled during the dictatorship's first four years. Betancourt's outrage with the practice was visceral. "What surpassed all previous limits in Venezuela and probably in all of Latin America for savagery was the imprisonment, indignity, and torture inflicted upon numerous women. . . . Even Juan Gómez respected the female sex."[25]

The press needed to be careful about what it printed about the regime's allies. Newspaper publisher Miguel Ángel Capriles ran afoul of authorities when the editor of his paper *Últimas Noticias* chose what turned out to be a not-so-clever byline to hide the identity of a journalist who had written "a true anatomy of the Trujillo regime." The byline "W. Krem" was chosen to remind knowledgeable readers of the Canadian journalist William Krehm, who had published a pejorative account of the region's dictators. Seething Dominican diplomats immediately lodged a complaint with authorities and Capriles was dressed down by Vallenilla Lanz. who warned the publisher "not to play with fire."[26]

The publishing business during the Pérez Jiménez era had its challenges, Capriles recalled in his memoir. He already was on thin ice because his newspapers hired foreign correspondents who, on occasion, submitted columns containing veiled criticism of the regime. Between the fines, censorship, and harassment, he and his editors were "walking a tightrope," not always sure what was permissible to the censors. His decision to carry on with what he called "a minimum of dignity" drew fire from all sides. Some detractors accused him of either being insufficiently critical or playing by the dictatorship's rules. On the other hand, he and his editors repeatedly had to defend their papers' content to the Secret Police. Visits to SN headquarters were nerve-racking, he admitted, but even more intimidating was the "insolent" Estrada's recurrent visits to his editorial offices. Small wonder that the Secret Police earned the moniker *la* Gestapo *criolla*.[27]

Meanwhile, Adeco exiles in Buenos Aires, Santiago, Mexico City, Madrid, Paris, New York, San José, San Juan, Guatemala City, La Paz, and Havana kept up a steady drumbeat of criticism of Pérez Jiménez and Estrada in their publications, in the local press, and where permitted, at public rallies.[28] Just as they had in the 1920s, like-minded exiles from different countries sought each other out in their new homes. In his memoir, the Cuban Huber Matos captured the spirit of solidarity among those fleeing oppression. He recalled that during his time in exile in San José, Costa Rica, Cuban exiles regularly met refugees from Venezuela and the Dominican Republic for coffee at the Soda Palace, a cafeteria near the Parque Central. He was quick to identify distinctions among the refugees: the Dominicans were the smallest contingent and not as well organized as the Venezuelans, while his countrymen were balkanized into competing political organizations. Yet the common experience of repression and displacement brought them closer. "Much more unites us than separates us. . . . In the Caribbean region . . . we speak an almost identical political language. The tyrannies have much in common. The suffering of oppressed peoples may vary in its intensity and details, but the drama is the same."[29]

Many refugees commented on how welcome they were made to feel in their temporary homes. Pérez was heartened by the expressions of support he and his fellow Adecos received in Havana in the early 1950s. "To say you were a Venezuelan exile was a marker of enduring solidarity."[30] But that camaraderie only went so far. They lived a hand-to-mouth existence, unsure if and when they would ever return home. Pérez remembered that there were times when he and his wife did not have enough money to buy milk for their two children. Getting work in another country also was difficult, and some had to rely on contributions from family members still in Venezuela. Betancourt, however, wore his poverty proudly. A spartan existence abroad, he believed, helped differentiate his party from others.[31]

Bickering and cliquishness were pervasive. Although this afflicted all exile organizations, AD's situation was unique. Unlike Dominican or Nicaraguan exiles, who had never once reached the political summit, AD had governed for three heady years and then had seen its power taken away. As Betancourt put it, "Exile is a foolproof breeding ground for all the quarrels and resentment, and even more so when one has left your country with the weight of defeat on your shoulders."[32]

No place was safe. Taking a page out of the tyrant Gómez's manual, SN agents closely monitored dissidents abroad.[33] No less an authority than Trujillo's intelligence chief, Abbes García, had high praise for Estrada's dragnet. While stationed in the Mexican capital during the mid-1950s, Abbes was impressed with the SN's network of well-paid agents and informers, which had infiltrated not just the AD underground but exile organizations from other Latin American countries. On the SN's payroll were the staff of various embassies, journalists, and members of the Mexican police. Moreover, Abbes boasted of how seamlessly the SN and the Dominican SIM collaborated. "A [security] matter affecting Venezuela had the same importance to me as one that affected the Dominican Republic." Abbes and his staff traveled to Caracas frequently for consultations, and the same was true for Estrada's agents, who visited SIM offices in Ciudad Trujillo.[34]

Betancourt was targeted on multiple occasions. Hitmen hired by Pérez Jiménez and Trujillo pursued him doggedly during his nine-year exile (1949–1958). When the AD leader was lodged in the Colombian embassy in Caracas right after the 1948 coup while awaiting approval of his request for political asylum, *pistoleros* hatched plans to storm the embassy and assassinate him. Betancourt escaped harm only after the junta squelched the plot, reasoning that an assassination in the embassy might precipitate an international incident and disrupt its efforts to secure recognition from the United States.[35]

He was very fortunate to survive a botched attempt on his life in Havana in April 1951. A "hired thug" tried to inject Betancourt with what chemical analysis later determined was a lethal cobra serum. Just as he was opening the door to his car in the Cuban capital, "a tall, badly dressed mulatto came up behind him, threw his arms around him and tried (unsuccessfully) to force the point of a syringe into his arm. In the struggle the syringe fell to the ground and the assassin fled." Betancourt took out his pistol and took aim at the assailant, but a mother walking with her child blocked his line of vision and he held his fire. He went to a nearby clinic where the wound was cauterized, while his aide took the syringe to the Cuban Secret Police's crime lab. When the technician administered some of what remained of the serum to a guinea pig, it keeled over and expired.[36]

Betancourt was certain that the attempt was "planned, organized, and financed" by the SN. The Cuban Secret Police investigation, however, concluded that the perpetrator was a Dominican. Authorities later determined that three assailants had been paid $150,000 to eliminate the AD chief. Given how closely the two agencies worked together, it is certainly plausible that this was a joint operation.[37] Additional clues pointed to collaboration. The Venezuelan military attaché in Havana reported to the Foreign Ministry that Betancourt recently had given an inflammatory radio interview in the studios of Santiago's Radio Oriental, the Cuban radio station with the largest listening audience in Venezuela.[38] Pérez Jiménez also was upset about Prío's unabashed support for AD-in-exile. An Adeco militant recalled in her memoir that the Cuban foreign minister provided Cuban passports to members of the Venezuelan underground, facilitating their movements to and from their homeland. For their part, Dominican authorities had reason to be concerned about how Prío and Dominican exiles were smuggling arms and monies. Bosch bragged years later that just months before the attempted assassination of the Venezuelan leader, he and Figueres were enlisted by the Cuban president to serve as couriers, and they successfully delivered $250,000 to Betancourt's home in Havana for the underground.[39]

Indeed, Betancourt lived a charmed, if harrowing, existence. Wherever he roamed during this, his third, extended exile, attempts were made on his life. The plots—in Havana (1951), San José (1953, 1954, 1955), Mexico City (1955), and San Juan (1956)—were often the work of the SN, but on other occasions, attacks were carried out with the assistance of Trujillo's hired guns. The attempts came with such regularity that the garrulous Venezuelan, with a penchant for invoking "Venezuelanisms," began to poke fun at the near misses, labeling each foiled attack after recent assassinations. For example, he declared after the 1953 attempt in the Costa Rican capital that the SN had tried to "delgadochalbonear" him, playfully recalling the 1950 kidnapping and murder of the former Venezuelan junta leader Carlos Delgado Chalbaud. "Degalindear" was how he described the junta's 1956 attempt to murder him in San Juan, invoking Galíndez's recent disappearance. Between 1948 and 1960 Betancourt survived at least eight attempts on his life.[40]

His situation was *sui generis* among exiles because he was in the crosshairs of not one but two vengeful despots. The constant harassment, coupled with Betancourt's willingness to provide material and moral support for Dominican exiles, was too much for Trujillo to tolerate. In his memoirs, Vallenilla Lanz recalled a conversation at a state dinner that illuminated the depth of the dictator's animus. "And what's with Rómulo Betancourt," Trujillo asked. "I know he's planning uprisings in the Caribbean. He is my mortal enemy."[41]

The Port Where It Was Convenient to Drop Anchor

Betancourt was certain that Perón was the puppet master pulling the strings of La Internacional. He claimed that the Argentine ambassador to Venezuela had been involved in the conspiracy to overthrow Gallegos and that the Argentine ruler and Peru's General Odría had served as mentors to Pérez Jiménez.[42] Nor had he forgiven Perón for his hasty recognition of the military junta.[43] With their well-stocked money bags, Peronista diplomats were seemingly everywhere, Betancourt complained, "conspiring, whispering, encouraging" fellow members of the coalition while financing schemes against any regime with which they did not agree. In a tough-minded column titled "La amenaza del totalitarismo derechista," (The Threat of Rightist Totalitarianism), which appeared in Mexico City's *La Jornada* in August 1949, the AD chief characterized La Internacional as "a family of Siamese twins born of a single womb, the Argentine government of Juan Perón."[44]

Betancourt's complaint about Perón's deep pockets was not far from the mark. The Argentine populist set up a school to train labor diplomats and then placed its graduates in the nation's embassies and legations. In 1952 he created a regional labor confederation, ATLAS (Agrupación de Trabajadores Latinoamericanos Sindicalizados), meant to be independent of the communists' CTAL and the AFL's affiliate, ORIT (Organización Regional Interamericana de Trabajadores). The rollout for the new confederation was characteristically "Peronesque": one hundred delegates from eighteen countries were given all-expenses-paid trips to Mexico City, where they listened to speeches deriding both capitalist and socialist unionism.[45]

His labor attachés disseminated propaganda lauding the general's accomplishments and met with and provided funds and stipends to a diverse group of student federations, political organizations, and labor unions. The regime also engaged in "labor tourism"—junkets to Buenos Aires awarded to the leadership of organizations that the Peronists were keen to court.[46]

Argentine diplomats were especially busy in Cuba, subsidizing a Havana newspaper and investing in radio stations. When Fidel Castro needed funds to attend a student conference in Bogotá on the eve of the inter-American meetings in 1948, he applied for and obtained a stipend from Peronist diplomats. Host governments, however, viewed Peronist envoys as *agents provocateurs*. Some were sent packing for their "rude interventions."[47] In his memoir, Franqui recalled how impressed he and his peers were by the Argentine populist. But the young leftist also expressed misgivings: "The hostility of the United States toward the Peronist movement in Argentina made us instinctively see Perón and his followers in a favorable light. Many pamphlets with Perón's speeches to the workers, his nationalist declarations, his appeals to the masses, and his attacks on oligarchies were circulating among the students around that time. We were impressed by those speeches, but had qualms about them because they leaned toward concentration of power in one man supported by the military ... this clashed with the fervent constitutionalism and democratic feeling that we students had."[48]

Nevertheless, ATLAS organizers were instrumental in securing gains for Venezuelan oil workers, Nicaraguan miners, Costa Rican banana workers, and Chilean copper miners. The new labor federation also posed a serious challenge to reformist political parties, such as AD and APRA, which had spent years organizing peasants and factory workers in their respective countries. Alexander and Romualdi believed that the Peronists were better organized and represented a greater threat to ORIT than the communists did. Indeed, dictators like Pérez Jiménez and Colombia's Gustavo Rojas Pinilla were more welcoming to ATLAS's labor attachés than were democracies.[49]

Another Peronist export that spread throughout the region was military lodges, secret societies composed of relatively small groups of officers with political aspirations. Peronist dogma held that the military had a sacred obligation to defend the fatherland. The military's directive was to root out contaminating elements in society.

The Peronist lodge Grupo Obra de Unificación (GOU) harbored transnational ambitions. Its manifesto left nothing to the imagination: "Alliances will be our next step. Paraguay is already with us. We will get

Bolivia and Chile. Together and united with these countries, it will be easy to exert pressure on Uruguay. These five nations can easily attract Brazil, due to its type of government and its important groups of Germans. Once Brazil has fallen, the South American continent will be ours."[50] GOU's nativistic membership railed against communists, Jews, masons, and the United States government.[51] The Argentine lodge made an impact on neighboring military establishments, as secret societies soon proliferated across the region. As we have seen, the Venezuelan equivalent of the GOU, the UPM, made up of 150 army officers, overthrew one of its own in 1945.[52] That autocrats held Perón in such high esteem and valued his counsel only heightened the perception among reformers that the Argentine was the godfather of La Internacional. Trujillo, for instance, went out of his way to insinuate himself into Perón's good graces as the mutual exchange of honorific titles followed from diplomatic contacts.[53]

Betancourt and Alexander claimed that Perón had had a hand in the overthrow of three democracies during the 1940s—Bolivia in 1943 and Peru and Venezuela in 1948. Their suspicions—at least for Peru—were confirmed by a Peruvian intelligence chief; Argentine diplomats did indeed work behind the scenes to incite the *golpe*. In fact, Peronist machinations were not limited to those three countries. The goal effectively was to "Peronize" the continent. To this end, Argentine envoys also were complicit in coup plots in Uruguay in 1946, Chile in 1948 and 1951, and Paraguay in 1949. His diplomats were especially meddlesome in neighboring Chile, where he funded first the senatorial and then the presidential aspirations of the former despot Carlos de Ibáñez, who Perón's ambassador to Chile was confident would "apply the Peronist doctrine in all its economic and social content." When the Chilean president Gabriel González Videla learned of Argentine plotting with officers in his army, he was incensed and threatened to sever diplomatic relations. Perón, however, did not stop interfering, and his involvement paid off when Ibáñez was elected president in September 1951.[54]

Often, perception masked reality. Italian diplomatic historian Loris Zanatta argues that despite the considerable time, energy, and resources invested, Peronism's ambitious imperial designs failed to persuade. This was in part because its messaging was too often unclear and contradictory. Peronism's exaggerated nationalism too often conflicted with its pan-Hispanic internationalism. Not infrequently, its agencies worked at cross-purposes. Labor organizers, for instance, attempted to woo Guatemalan unions while military attachés denounced Árbenz. Moreover, Argentina's courting of specific regimes, such as Bolivia, Paraguay, and Peru, prompted anxious neighbors to band together to undermine Peronist designs.

Attempts to cultivate relations with one government could unnerve even Peronist allies in La Internacional. A glaring example occurred in 1947, when Argentina, in need of oil for its industrialization program, sought to barter grains for petroleum with the *trienio* government. Trujillo, who at that very moment was conspiring with reactionary Venezuelan exiles to install a more favorable regime in Caracas, communicated his displeasure to the Argentines, and Perón backed away from the negotiating table. Finally, Peronism's Third Way—neither capitalism nor socialism—while rhetorically appealing, failed to account for the unshakable geopolitical reality that many Latin American countries were beholden to the United States for investment and aid. When Perón attempted to engineer trade pacts that abolished tariffs with Argentina's neighbors, the U.S. quietly sent foodstuffs to scuttle the pacts.[55] In addition, admiration and emulation went only so far; dictators such as Somoza and Trujillo may have repeatedly sung Perón's praises, but they could not or would not sever ties with their benefactors in Washington. To many in the region, Perón was an important interlocutor, but Buenos Aires never would be, in Zanatta's evocative phrasing, "the port where it was convenient to drop anchor."[56]

If Perón's counsel was not always welcomed, the opposite held true for another authoritarian, Francisco Franco. The idea of a transnational "Hispanic bloc" of nations that was proudly Catholic and celebrated a shared Iberian heritage was immensely appealing to conservatives. Betancourt was convinced that there was more to this than a meeting of the minds—the Spanish caudillo also was complicit in the 1948 coup that abruptly ended the *trienio*.[57]

Facing diplomatic isolation and slow to recover from the devastating economic impact of the Civil War, the Spanish dictator understood the import of collegial relationships for his regime's survival. As the historian Raanan Rein relates, pan-Hispanism became a "central component of its [the Franco regime's] self-identity and its foreign policy," especially after World War II, when it took on heightened significance in the wake of the Axis defeat.[58] Just as Mussolini cultivated loyal "Little Italies" abroad, the Franco regime invested in cultural programming, such as theater troupes, art exhibitions, and academic conferences, as well as reciprocal educational exchanges wherever Spanish emigrants congregated.[59]

Again, Perón led the way. Dubbing his administration *"franquismo a la criolla"* (Francoism, creole-style), in October 1946 he signed a bilateral trade treaty with the Spanish regime that provided badly needed grains and cooking oils to a destitute population. The Spaniard also counted on Perón plying his influence not only with neighboring Southern Cone countries, but in the words of the Spanish ambassador to Argentina, "to extend his efforts . . . to other American states."[60]

An enthusiastic Trujillo elevated his nation's diplomatic presence in Spain from a legation to an embassy, and Franco responded in kind. In addition, Franco hosted lavish state visits of Latin American dictators, which included receptions where pillars of his regime, such as the Catholic Church, the military, prominent Falangists, regime-friendly intellectuals, and economic elites, were in attendance. Trujillo's 1954 state visit even included side trips to see the sights in Barcelona, Ávila, and Toledo.[61]

By the early 1950s authoritarianism was ascendant. The few remaining democracies had to defend themselves against rightist attempts to unseat them. In Chile, a civilian government denounced and quashed a fascist cell patterned on the Peronist model, and in Guatemala, Arévalo survived an astonishing thirty-two *golpes*.[62] He later claimed that all but two of the conspiracies had received foreign assistance of one kind or another. Arévalo did not have to specify where the funds and arms originated; his strident opposition to dictators and his support for exiled opponents of those regimes made him an outsized target of La Internacional. That he completed his term as president was frankly surprising to many observers.[63] Roa, who had his finger on the pulse of geopolitics in the Caribbean, reported that Perón's and Franco's goal was to establish a network of like-minded authoritarian regimes, extending from the Southern Cone to the Caribbean.[64]

Military dictatorships were a study in contrasts, since each was tethered to its distinctive political culture. Venezuela's regime, for instance, lacked Perón's populist working-class base of support, nor did it have its own political apparatus. Unlike Argentina, Venezuelan labor unions were persistent critics of the dictatorship. It also was far easier for Perón to inveigh against North American imperialism; Venezuela's oil sector relied heavily on North American capital and technological inputs. In the mid-1950s, petroleum accounted for 95 percent of the nation's exports and 97 percent of its foreign exchange. As a result, Pérez Jiménez was much less likely to play the nationalist card than his counterpart.[65]

A comparison of the dictators came from someone who spoke with consummate authority on the subject. During a visit to Ciudad Trujillo,

Vallenilla Lanz met with Trujillo, who offered a blunt assessment of his peers. Tacho Somoza was "good for nothing"; he had done little to improve his country. Although Trujillo admired Gómez, compared to what he himself had accomplished without access to a seemingly inexhaustible supply of petroleum, the former Venezuelan head of state had failed to modernize his country. He regarded Vallenilla Lanz's chief, Pérez Jiménez, as feeble at best. While Trujillo gave him credit for investing in infrastructural improvements, his position was far from secure. He warned Pérez Jiménez's minister of the interior to remain vigilant. Given the country's wealth, "there is not a lack of those who aspire to govern it, even at the cost of treason."[66]

Trujillo's impressions were seconded by an unlikely source. From his jail cell, AD's Carnevali scoffed, "what good is a dictatorship if it cannot even guarantee its own victory at the polls." He was alluding to the bungled 1952 elections, when Pérez Jiménez's party came in a distant third and then the militarist awkwardly annulled the results and declared himself dictator. Echoing Trujillo, Carnevali told his jailer, "your government is very weak." Quite unlike Perón, "the timid, indifferent" Venezuelan possesses precious few of the traits required of a strong leader.[67] But Pérez Jiménez was a serial conspirator. In addition to invalidating the 1952 elections, he was the ringleader of coups d'état in 1945 and 1948, and in 1950 he was reputed to have been involved in the kidnapping and murder of Delgado Chalbaud.[68]

The Boycott

Rather than just draw attention to the evils of the Venezuelan police state, Betancourt cast his boycott campaign in broader terms in order to win the backing of the other reformist governments. He framed it as a test of the political and moral resolve of the fledgling OAS. The regional organization's charter, which had been approved at the last Inter-American Conference, not only guaranteed the security of its member states but promised to defend their sovereignty and to promote peace and justice. Dictators emphasized that nonintervention was a central tenet of the OAS Charter, but Betancourt reminded his readers that democratic governance and the protection of individual liberties also were hallmarks of the inter-American system. He drew attention to Article 5 of the charter, which held that "any state that attacks the public liberties and civil rights of its citizens or proscribes its workers from their enjoyment of ample and just social guarantees [was] in violation of the spirit and letter of the [Bogotá] Pact."⁶⁹ Democratic nations, he told an audience in Panama City in 1946, should establish a "prophylactic cordon," to ward off dictatorships so that they would not infect civilian governments.⁷⁰

Betancourt practiced what he preached. When he was president of the junta that governed Venezuela, his administration severed diplomatic relations with Spain, the Dominican Republic, and Nicaragua.⁷¹ (Despite well-founded suspicions of Perón's involvement in La Internacional, the *trienio* government never broke off relations with Argentina, because he was voted into office). Betancourt felt that he had more than sufficient reason for putting these dictatorships on notice. The Dominican strongman, for instance, made his capital a second home for dissident reactionary Venezuelans seeking the junta's overthrow. For both Trujillo and Betancourt, the severing of ties amounted to an undeclared declaration of war, one that had lasting consequences for the region.⁷²

Isn't it ironic, Betancourt mused, how dictatorships played the sovereignty card and repeatedly cried anticommunism, and then disingenuously invoked nonintervention whenever critics drew attention to human rights violations in their countries? Dictators were quick to employ "a strident anticommunism as a burnished shield and the doctrine of nonintervention as a barricade."⁷³ The principle of nonintervention had become a double-edged sword, a political talking point cynically employed by tyrants to deflect criticism. The Uruguayan senator Dardo Regules noted that the original rationale for nonintervention—to protect small countries in the region from North American interference—was manipulated by tyrants in such a way that it now served as "the perfect defense for military regimes"; if something was not done about this, "it could turn the international protection of human rights into the international protection of the despots' 'rights.' "⁷⁴

In the months leading up to the Caracas Conference, reformers were on the offensive, seeking to embarrass La Internacional. Seizing the moral high ground, social democrats pressed their case to boycott the meetings in the hopes of driving a wedge between the dictators and the hegemon. But Betancourt's campaign and Costa Rica's principled decision not to send a delegation to Caracas only angered the Eisenhower administration and emboldened Pérez Jiménez and his allies, who were targeting the elimination of the troublesome Costa Rican president.

Despite recent trends, the ever-optimistic Betancourt believed that there were signs that the fraternal ties among dictators in the hemisphere were fraying. Perón was now on the defensive in his native Argentina. A military regime was removed in Bolivia, and democracy had taken root in Brazil.[75] In a letter to a colleague, Betancourt observed that a siege mentality was palpable within La Internacional. "We are getting closer, in my opinion, to what happened during the 1930s ... when a number of strongmen fell."[76]

Betancourt's message struck a responsive chord, and not just among moderates. The PCV decried the hypocrisy of holding such an august assemblage of 483 delegates from twenty countries in the midst of a police state. In late 1953 the Communist Party's *Tribuna Popular* declared: "In a country filled with prisons and concentration camps, with more than three thousand political prisoners, where fascist methods of terror, assassinations and repression have gained a new legitimacy, it was not possible to choose a more sinister, tragic and antidemocratic setting than the 'hospitality' of the pérezjimenista military dictatorship."[77]

Betancourt and Figueres also found ample support from their peers on the continent. In the Chilean Congress, the moderate Frei and the socialist Allende both denounced the Venezuelan dictatorship. The former, who turned down an invitation to serve in his country's delegation, said holding the meetings in Caracas would be a farce: "It is patently ludicrous that the meeting is being held at the very moment when all political parties ... have been dismantled, when citizens are incarcerated without trial, and none of the fundamental rights are guaranteed. ... It is true that the nonintervention principle is a great safeguard for weaker nations, but it has its limits when there is an ethical and moral imperative."[78]

Even Chile's center-right Radical Party insisted that its government not send a delegation to Caracas. Senator Luis Bossay called for a change of venue and demanded that the OAS investigate the repression. The boycott also was debated in the Mexican and Ecuadorian legislatures.[79] A Uruguayan senator opined that meeting in the Venezuelan capital would make "a bloody mockery of Pan American ideals."[80] The national legislatures of Chile and Uruguay subsequently passed resolutions calling on their governments to join the boycott unless Pérez Jiménez released political prisoners and enacted reforms. Upon learning what the Uruguayan Congress had done, Figueres sent a special plea to its president asking if his nation would stand with Costa Rica in making attendance conditional upon the release of prisoners. This, he wrote, would send a powerful message that would rescue "Pan-Americanism from the certain risk of discredit."[81]

Indeed, the mainstream press throughout the hemisphere seconded Betancourt's initiative and demanded that its governments boycott the proceedings.[82] Support appeared in the editorial pages of liberal and centrist papers such as *El Sol* and *La Tierra* (Quito), *La Hora* and *La Nación* (Panama City), *El Espectador* (Bogotá), *El País* (Montevideo), *Última Hora* and *El Diario* (La Paz), *El Universo* (Guayaquil), *El Imparcial* (Santiago), and *La Prensa Gráfica* (San Salvador).[83]

Betancourt was pleased with the favorable response. He wrote Alexander that the reaction to Figueres's gesture sent a clear signal to dictators and to local communist parties that democrats were willing to stand up and be counted. "Tiny Costa Rica and its magnificent leader has provided a great service to [Latin] America and to [the cause of] liberty." He also was happy to see that some North American union leaders, journalists, and professors were praising the Costa Rican president in the press. Latin Americans, especially those living under the heel of tyrants, were taking heed. "This will reap dividends in the future," he predicted.[84]

His allies in the United States were less sanguine. According to Grant, the response to the IADF petition drive calling for the release of political prisoners had fallen short of expectations. She attributed the tepid response to the climate of fear in the U.S.: "People here are reluctant to sign . . . in view of the present atmosphere created here by Senator McCarthy." A few weeks later, Grant lamented to Betancourt that "some of our good friends did not want to sign . . . it is discouraging, dear friend, but I have long ago realized that this is a struggle in which only a *very few* are willing to expose themselves to the end. . . . Now, as always, we work very much alone" (italicized in the original).[85]

In his reply to Grant, Betancourt expressed disappointment but promised to keep the faith: "We are fighting in difficult circumstances. On one side you have the McCarthyites and on the other, the communists. Between the two equally aggressive totalitarian currents, we will work with those who demand social justice, but also liberty; those who desire security, but also democracy. The popular majorities in Latin America are with us, and not with 'them.' Every time when the people are presented with the opportunity, they show their hatred for totalitarianism."[86]

Betancourt and his allies in the States already had read the tea leaves. Supporters of Adlai Stevenson in the 1952 elections, reformers realized that an Eisenhower administration would favor the dictators. On the eve of the elections, Romualdi warned Betancourt that "if Eisenhower wins we will be completely bereft of any influence and the [U.S.] alliance with the military regimes will intensify." Betancourt could only agree: "Eisenhower's victory will have unfavorable repercussions in every respect. It will stimulate Latin American militarism and put the direction of United States foreign policy in the hands of large companies."[87]

Betancourt knew he had to reassure the incoming administration of his anticommunist bona fides. Witch hunts in the United States meant that former members of the Communist Party at home and abroad were met with suspicion. As historian Steven Ellner noted, Betancourt realized that Washington "would never tolerate a forcefully anti-imperialist government in the hemisphere."[88] Even though his actions as head of the junta during the *trienio* should have reassured U.S officials on that score, his membership in the Costa Rican Communist Party dating back to the early 1930s was invariably brought up by Cold Warriors who questioned his trustworthiness. This is why he never missed an opportunity in his writings, interviews, and on the lecture tour to remind his audience of where he and AD stood. For AD "to have much more than pragmatic and limited understandings with the communists would be suicide," Betancourt mused. It would mean not just "cutting the jugular, but all of the arteries."[89]

He and others of his generation had reason to question the wisdom of allying with the communists. Betancourt reminded his supporters that the PDN's short-lived alliance with the communists in 1936 had backfired, precisely because it gave their political enemies on the right the ammunition they needed to discredit their party. Nor could he and other stalwarts forgive the PCV for taking up arms against the October 1945 coup that brought AD to power. Still, the *trienio* government never outlawed the Communist Party, as its peers in the region did in the late 1940s, nor did it move against PCV-affiliated labor unions. And when it was apparent that a *golpe* was imminent in the fall of 1948, the leadership overlooked any misgivings it had and asked the PCV to mobilize militants to defend the *trienio* government.[90]

But what Betancourt said for public consumption belied a more complex reality inside the party. While most of AD's *guardia vieja* (old guard), whether in exile or not, agreed with the hard line toward the communists, the underground's leadership and youngsters immersed in the quotidian struggle against the regime, those who often paid dearly for their commitment, were much more willing to collaborate with Gustavo Machado's PCV.[91]

Indeed, youthful militants often had more in common with their peers in the PCV's cadres than they did with the *guardia vieja*. Those who remained and resisted the dictatorship were radicalized by their experience in the underground, while those in exile, Rangel surmised, gravitated toward ever more centrist positions the longer they remained abroad.[92]

Betancourt fretted about the duration and the nature of this exile. Societies are not static, and the longer the exiles stayed away, the more difficult it was to remain in touch with what was occurring back home. He sought to offset this by poring over the Venezuelan newspapers he could get his hands on. À la Haya, he counseled militants abroad to do as he did; that is, to read, study, and write. He also was concerned that with Adeco cells littered all over the hemisphere, the potential was heightened for individuals to embrace new ideas (namely, Marxism).[93]

In theory, the underground's leaders, the Comité Ejecutivo Nacional (CEN), dictated strategy, while its allied arm abroad, the Comité Coordinador de las Actividades de AD en el Exterior (CC), raised funds, procured arms, and through its publications and advocacy in the foreign press, raised awareness about the struggle. But the reality was far more problematic. Communication between the CEN and the CC was often disrupted, which meant that coordination was difficult. Furthermore, the regime's targeting of successive heads of the CEN meant that at certain moments, the CC had to make tactical or policy decisions in a vacuum.[94]

The elimination of party leaders resulted in young militants' filling the vacuum left by their seniors. A female party activist who was imprisoned and interrogated several times by Estrada claimed that thousands of young women joined the ranks of the underground.[95] Turnover translated into a yawning gap between the underground and the exiles. Upon his return from exile in 1958, Betancourt had to introduce himself to the AD's new secretary-general, Simón Sáez Mérida.[96]

The toll taken also meant that the militants were not as familiar with party orthodoxy. When confronted with fluid circumstances on the ground, they occasionally freelanced. This was anathema to Betancourt, who preached that party discipline was paramount. There is much to be said for Caballero's observation that AD's top-down command structure was in large part a byproduct of Betancourt's formative years as a Communist Party militant. In true Leninist fashion, he believed that the party's largely all-male leadership should act as a revolutionary vanguard. Youngsters and women in the underground understandably chafed at such rigidity.[97]

Reflecting on his growing disenchantment with Betancourt and the old guard leadership-in-exile, Rangel posited that until they met their demise, the heart and soul of the resistance was Ruíz Pineda and Carnevali. Both were committed to a big-tent coalition, and that meant working with the communists, even as the CC repeatedly issued denials. This disjuncture fed ongoing debates about tactics and strategy between the CEN and the CC.[98]

Betancourt blamed the communists for sowing discord in AD's ranks. In a letter to Romauldi, he bemoaned that they were pitting "Betancourtists" against "anti-Betancourtists." AD's heterogenous character, its "mixture of political Jacobinism and of social and nationalist demands," made the distillation of a coherent and consistent message by the leadership challenging at best, while providing ready-made ammunition to its critics.[99]

Pérez Jiménez took advantage of AD's fissures. He went on the offensive, dismissing the boycott as little more than a publicity stunt conjured up by Betancourt and Figueres. He retorted that he already had released four hundred political prisoners in a New Year's Day amnesty and warned that Venezuela would not stand idly by and permit other heads of state to meddle in its internal affairs.[100]

Don Pepe Holds Firm

In the interim, Figueres faced criticism for his refusal to send a delegation to the meetings. La Internacional and Figueres's domestic rivals were quick to point out that Pepe was not the honest broker he presented himself to be. During his brief eighteen-month tenure as head of Costa Rica's governing junta (1948–49), there was ample evidence that he had employed *la mano dura* (harsh treatment) against his domestic enemies, making a mockery of commitments agreed to during the negotiations between the communists and his forces that brought an end to hostilities. He implemented martial law, limited press freedoms, and dissolved leftist labor unions and imprisoned their leadership. In the junta's first twelve months in power, three thousand members of the Partido Vanguardia Popular (PVP, formerly the PCCR) were exiled and fourteen were executed. The junta declared the PVP illegal and dissolved its affiliated organizations, and when workers in the sixty proscribed unions tried to reconstitute their organizations, "they were harassed, their meetings broken up, their leaders arrested."[101] Communists were not the junta's sole targets. Followers of Figueres' chief political rival Rafael Calderón Guardia also faced persecution.[102]

With some justification, his adversaries insisted that no head of state had done more to promote regional instability. Indeed, Pepe had spent the better part of the previous five years pursuing—covertly and overtly—the defeat of his archenemy, Somoza. He also irked La Internacional and domestic critics by providing moral and material assistance to Nicaraguan exiles. By embroiling their tiny country in conflicts abroad, his domestic rivals complained—battles that Costa Rica had no business involving itself in—Figueres put his countrymen at risk.

Figueres's supporters rallied to his defense. When the opposition newspaper *La Nación* pointed out that earlier Pan American conferences had been held in countries governed by dictators (for example, Cuba under Machado in 1928), a prominent deputy from Figueres's PLN countered that what made this conference different was that it was the first one to take place under the aegis of the OAS Charter, which included language that explicitly guaranteed the protection of political freedoms.[103]

Another political rival, former president Otilio Ulate, disagreed with the decision not to send a delegation. The president, he declared, was under the "Svengali-like influence" of Betancourt, who was then ensconced in the Costa Rican capital. But as he himself acknowledged, the right of political asylum was enshrined in Costa Rica's constitution and had become an article of faith for all Costa Ricans. Ulate may have not have been pleased with the Venezuelan's presence, but it was he, not Figueres, who had granted Betancourt political asylum in 1952 during the first months of his presidency.[104]

AD's chief took exception to Ulate's charge that he was exercising undue influence on Figueres in a letter to the editor that appeared in Ulate's newspaper, *El Diario de Costa Rica*. "This untruth is as massive as the Himalayas." It is abundantly clear to everyone, he continued, that Figueres thinks for himself. "I am his friend, just as I am a friend of ex-President Ulate and of so many other Costa Ricans of all ideological stripes." As a political refugee, Betancourt said, he was indebted to Costa Rica for providing sanctuary and insisted that he never had abused that privilege by meddling in domestic politics.[105] While Betancourt was grateful for Figueres's "heroic" act of solidarity, he did not think it advisable that he go it alone and had told Don Pepe so. In fact, he never felt that an actual boycott was essential. The threat alone, he hoped, would bring about the release of compatriots wasting away in prisons and forced-labor camps. Figueres, however, refused to reconsider his decision.[106]

The boycott announcement came just as Figueres was in the midst of protracted negotiations with UFCO on revisions to an existing contract. Like many social democrats, Pepe believed that foreign companies conducting business in their countries should pay an equitable share of taxes and a living wage to their workers. The size and scope of *el pulpo*'s operations in a country as small as Costa Rica made it "a country within a country."[107] In an essay he contributed to the *New Leader*, he repudiated what he called "discriminatory concessions. ... I know what it feels to have a state within a state; to play host to a privileged business that does not abide by the law of the land, but by the terms of its 'own' concession." He also felt that foreign investment should not continue indefinitely in his country. After receiving fair market value for their properties, foreign companies should gradually phase out operations. While some in the U.S. cried communist, Figueres's supporters answered that, unlike leftists, Figueres had no intention of nationalizing the company's holdings or restricting foreign investment.[108]

El pulpo, however, understood that whatever concessions it made at the bargaining table would be used as a benchmark for other governments in the isthmus.[109] Owing to the acrimonious manner in which negotiations had unfolded between UFCO and Guatemala, the State Department encouraged both sides in the Costa Rican talks to seek common ground. To Figueres, Cabot emphasized the Department's "strong belief in the sanctity of contracts." But in a confidential memo to his aide, the assistant secretary of state related that he had met with the company's chairman of the board and its vice president and advised "that it is better that they bend before they are broken."[110] The Department was acutely aware that United Fruit had a lot to live down. As one memorandum put it: "The Company's over-all financial strength (estimated at $580 million dollars) and its dominant position in several national economies are regarded as a threat to national sovereignty. This sense of an implicit threat is strengthened by the recollection of former times when the Company bought-up [*sic*] venal politicians to facilitate the negotiation of favorable concessions and was commonly understood to have also procured revolutions whenever its interests would be furthered."[111] In the Costa Rican case, the problem was exacerbated by the fruit company's separate school system for the children of its workers. Nationalistic Ticos took pride in their public schools and considered UFCO's schools tantamount "to an affront to national dignity."[112]

After nine months of hard bargaining between three cabinet ministers and three company representatives, the fruit company and Figueres's administration settled. *El pulpo* agreed to a doubling of the tax rate on its net earnings from 15 to 30 percent and accepted a new minimum wage, which would be adjusted for inflation in the future. One estimate concluded that Costa Rica would reap an additional ten million dollars a year in revenues for the duration of the thirty-four-year contract.[113] The *frutera* agreed to turn over to the government 3 hospitals, 45 dispensaries, and 68 schools, and it committed to purchasing goods in-country to the extent possible. In return, Figueres consented to clamping down on leftist organizing in the banana zone.[114]

UFCO's willingness to renegotiate with Costa Rica "battens down one hatch," Don Pepe confided to a North American friend. It not only opened the door to comparable agreements with Honduras and El Salvador, but it had the effect of turning up the heat on Árbenz, where negotiations between the fruit company and his administration had stalled.[115]

Over the next few years Figueres was positively bullish about the benefits of his administration's collaboration with *el pulpo*. Woodward, who accompanied the president on a tour of the Pacific banana zone in October 1955, was stunned by his about-face: "those on the tour . . . witnessed the remarkable spectacle of Figueres asserting to large groups of workers that they have an important stake in the stability of the Company's operation, because the Government is a 'partner' of the Company to the extent of thirty percent of the profits, and because this tax yield is the source of eventual social and economic benefits to the workers."[116]

The successfully concluded negotiations were not enough to win over Figueres's critics in Washington. Hardliners in the State Department questioned his reliability and pressed him to reconsider his decision not to attend the Caracas meetings. The absence of such a prominent spokesman for democracy would be interpreted, in the words of one State Department official, as "an embarrassment." It did not help his cause when the *New York Times* declared, in the wake of his electoral victory, "Socialists Sweep Costa Rica Voting."[117] Others warned that he was soft on communism, an ominous tag at that political moment.[118]

Figueres sought to reassure North American audiences, in print and at speaking engagements stateside, that Latin Americans not only valued U.S. leadership in global affairs, but that partnering with Washington was the best way forward for the region's economic development.[119] Just as dictators retained public relations representatives in the United States, so too did Figueres. Former undersecretary of state during the Truman administration Mark Leva's responsibility was to make sure that Figueres received favorable press. One of his political opponents marveled at what Leva accomplished in terms of coverage.[120]

Pepe's staff, many of whom were educated in the United States, actively cultivated key players in the State Department, members of Congress on both sides of the aisle, the labor movement, progressive advocacy groups like Americans for Democratic Action, the liberal press, and academics. The loquacious Figueres made himself a known quantity in the U.S., writing columns, giving interviews, and delivering lectures at universities. In addition, he also enjoyed the backing of two well-regarded interlocutors: Berle and the president's brother, who sought to allay concerns about Pepe's anticommunist credentials in the executive branch.

A friendly voice was Schlesinger. In his weekly syndicated column, he called on the administration "to support anti-communist and pro-democratic leadership." To Schlesinger, Pepe resembled a cross between Fiorello La Guardia and Adlai Stevenson, two liberal standard bearers with whom his audience was familiar. In a wide-ranging interview in San José in the fall of 1954, Figueres let on how he had dispatched aides to warn democrats in Guatemala to beware "of falling into the communist trap." He then went on to promote his vision of a hemispheric democratic project, in which he, Muñoz Marín, Paz Estenssoro, and Betancourt all "will play a leading part."[121]

Given that Somoza's National Guard had violated Costa Rican sovereignty three times over the last ten years and that Figueres's tiny nation now lacked a standing army to repel subsequent incursions, the Costa Rican statesman was well aware that there could be a price to pay for his principles. In a 1997 oral history, he acknowledged that his country's collective back was against the wall. "We knew that we had a permanent enemy in John Foster Dulles. And we knew Foster Dulles was a friend of Pérez Jiménez, a friend of Somoza, a friend of Batista, and a friend of Trujillo."[122]

That Dulles had a decided preference for siding with dictators was confirmed in a conversation between Berle and Woodward. Upset with what he perceived as the Department's mistreatment of Figueres, the ambassador told the Department's troubleshooter that he was seriously considering tendering his letter of resignation. "John Foster Dulles has a skunk against Figueres for his refusal to attend the Caribbean [Caracas] Conference." He recalled that at one staff meeting when he served as Deputy Assistant Secretary of State under Cabot, Dulles did not equivocate: "do nothing to offend the dictators; they are the only people we can depend on."[123] Dulles's colleague, Secretary of Treasury George Humphrey, cast the matter as a zero-sum game at an NSC meeting: "wherever a dictator was replaced, communists gained."[124] As Berle realized, speaking one's mind about such matters in Dulles's Department came at some cost. Cabot's successor, Holland, "had gone as far as he can bucking this to the point of getting himself in the doghouse; Jack Cabot suffered the same fate."[125]

Dulles's predilection for dictatorships coincided with the apex of McCarthyism. With anticommunism and national security as major talking points during the 1952 electoral campaign, Republicans made hay about security lapses within the Truman administration's State Department. When coupled with the House Un-American Activities Committee hearings, Truman's Federal Employee Loyalty Program, and the Alger Hiss case, the transition from a Democratic to a Republican administration in early 1953 was especially problematic for those who failed to toe the line.[126]

In an especially frank note to Warren, Berle relayed his concerns about the impact that McCarthy and the zealots surrounding him had on departmental morale. While "extremists like McCarthy make life impossible by continued attacks of one sort and another," what was especially unfortunate was that the administration remained silent in the face of withering attacks against specific individuals. "The Administration should immediately have gone to bat to stop this sort of thing." But apparently the executive branch did not feel it could speak out, Berle added. He was apprehensive about how this would affect foreign policy moving forward. "If McCarthy and his small group shift into open opposition, they can hamstring the Administration at every point."[127] For a staunch anticommunist like Berle, who did not suffer fools gladly and had zero tolerance for milquetoast liberals, to express such profound misgivings spoke volumes about the Red Scare's impact.[128]

Dulles's words and actions were anathema to resolute opponents of dictatorships. When in 1954 the administration reconsidered its long-standing refusal to recognize Franco's dictatorship—in exchange for the carrot of placing U.S. military bases on Spanish soil—the usually circumspect Galíndez was stung by the policy reversal. The staunch defender of Basque autonomy considered Washington's actions as a bald-faced betrayal of democratic principles. He lamented the sheer transactional nature of the decision, which he feared would buoy autocrats everywhere.

The Basque, who moonlighted as an informant, openly expressed his reservations in the strongest possible terms to his FBI handler: "Since John Foster Dulles entered the picture, the United States has started to write the blackest pages of its international relations. Never before in the history of the world has one single government more effectively supported dictatorial powers."[129]

The administration's pressure campaign against the boycott had the desired effect. Not one other democracy in the region joined Costa Rica. Were they fearful that there would be a price to pay for staying home? Did the Eisenhower administration's hints that failing to attend might result in cutbacks in assistance have the desired effect?[130]

Almost a Pyrrhic Victory

Just as Machado did in the run-up to the 1928 conference, Pérez Jiménez went on a massive spending spree to ready the capital for the conference. Two major highway projects were completed just before the start of the meetings. The first, between Maiquetía Airport and the capital, was completed in time to transport delegates to the city center. The second, an east-west highway, connected the downtown with the city's more upscale districts. In addition, streets were paved, two hospitals were built, and hotels to house the delegates were readied. The *pièce de résistance* was the inauguration of a nine-story library at the Central University, which included a lavish main auditorium where plenary sessions were held, "equipped for simultaneous conversion of speeches into any of the four official languages of the hemisphere."[131]

Still, the resistance found innovative ways to shame the regime. Women's groups collected five thousand signatures on a petition criticizing the dictatorship and somehow managed to smuggle copies of the *Libro negro* into the conference proceedings, placing them on the desks of delegates.[132]

Latin American delegates were poised for an earnest discussion in Caracas. As late as August 1953, Cabot had predicted that the conference's likely focus would be on "problems of an economic nature."[133] This made perfect sense because Eisenhower's brother Milton had just returned from a monthlong, ten-country fact-finding mission in late July. His report considered the region's social and economic problems and offered policy recommendations. It noted that trade between the United States and the region was significant; in 1952 alone, it had climbed to 3.5 billion dollars, more than U.S. trade with Asia, Africa, and Oceania combined. As a destination for U.S. imports, Latin America even outpaced Europe. Moreover, almost 30 percent of U.S. long-term, private sector investment went to the region. Aside from Canada, more corporate dollars were invested there than anywhere else. Development and democracy, the report concluded, went hand in hand. Their absence had pernicious consequences for U.S. geopolitical interests.[134]

Milton Eisenhower's recommendations were relatively modest: technical assistance, the sale of surplus food stocks, and support for commodity price stability. Those suggestions, however, ran counter to the administration's "trade not aid" maxim. Its tonic for economic growth was private capital. The tight-fisted Humphrey, who had been given a seat on a restructured NSC, had what amounted to veto power of any foreign assistance program that "violated sound fiscal policy." While the president's brother was not successful in changing the thinking of the president or his treasury secretary, his high-profile trip raised expectations among Latin American leaders that the administration was willing to address their economic concerns.[135]

Unfortunately for Latin American governments, Dulles had little interest in discussing economic matters. His unhappiness with the proposed boycott had everything to do with Guatemala. He believed that Árbenz's agrarian reform and the political lieutenants who had his ear were proof enough that he was intent on taking his country communist. If reformers saw the conference as an occasion to present their vision of a democratic Latin America, Dulles viewed it as an opportunity for the OAS to stand united in the struggle against international Communism.

The geopolitical context in 1953 appeared ominous to Washington's Cold Warriors. Eastern Europe was firmly ensconced behind the Iron Curtain, China had gone communist, and Korea and Indochina were moving in that direction. Berlin was now subjected to a Soviet blockade. Under the circumstances, adding a communist beachhead in the backyard was patently unacceptable. As a result, maintaining diplomatic unity in the hemisphere took on heightened significance for policymakers. Taken together, the Latin American republics constituted 20 percent of the United Nations General Assembly. A March 1953 NSC policy statement emphasized that "hemispheric solidarity in support of our world policies, particularly in the United Nations and other international organizations," should be a cornerstone of U.S. foreign policy.[136] The State Department's goal of persuading other Latin American nations to support an anticommunist resolution in Caracas was defensible, officials insisted, precisely because multilateralism and unanimity had been such points of emphasis at recent inter-American meetings.[137] More than any other factor, it was the State Department's desire for a united front, comparable to FDR's Fortress America during World War II, that best explains why Foster Dulles was so incensed with Figueres's decision.

The secretary may have considered the passage of an anticommunist resolution essential, but his team was of mixed minds about the threat of Soviet penetration in the hemisphere. After initial objections, Cabot came around and supported the decision to oust Árbenz, but appeared less concerned about a potential communist threat in the hemisphere. In a speech to students at the Canadian War College in October 1953, the diplomat admitted: "no South American government is today much influenced by communists; on the contrary, on the government level communists have unquestionably tended to lose ground in recent years. Whether they have lost popular support is a more difficult question; but it seems probable on the whole they have. The internal problem of Communism as the fifth column of the Kremlin's imperial ambitions is therefore latent rather than acute."[138]

Sentiments like this explain why he fell out of favor with hardliners. But his views were in line with the findings of George Kennan, who had toured South America a few years earlier. The architect of containment found that the linkages between the Soviet Union and the region's communist parties were indirect and tenuous at best. Although fanatical and rabidly anti-American, local communists were anything but dogmatic. Kennan's ten-thousand-word report about Latin Americans and their governments was extremely patronizing and condescending—so much so that Acheson refused to publish it—but the architect of containment did recommend a flexible approach to deterrence, depending on the political situation in each country. If that meant working with regimes that "would not stand the test of American concepts of democratic procedure ... such regimes may be preferable alternatives, and indeed the only alternatives, to further combat communist successes."[139]

The administration did itself no favors when word leaked out about its plans to oust the Guatemalan president. In late January 1954 Árbenz announced that he had incontrovertible proof that Somoza and a "northern government," in cahoots with the turncoat Castillo Armas, were behind a "counterrevolutionary plot." Apparently, the evidence came to the president's attention when a CIA agent left incriminating materials in his hotel room in the Guatemalan capital. The following day Árbenz's accusation was front-page news all over Latin America.[140]

Cabot thought Dulles had minimal interest in the region and that if it were not for Guatemala he would not even have attended the conference.[141] In fact, Dulles had little regard for Latin Americans at all. In a February 1953 telephone conversation with the president, he did not hide his condescension; all that was needed with "tropical people" was to "pat them a little bit and make them think that you are fond of them."[142]

In the run-up to the meetings, the taciturn secretary showed himself to be especially tone-deaf to criticisms about the venue or the dictator. Speaking on Capitol Hill before he left for the conference, he side-stepped human rights concerns and focused instead on how welcoming Pérez Jiménez was to U.S. oil companies: "I am glad we are meeting in Venezuela. Venezuela is a country which has adopted the kind of policies which we think that the other countries of South America should adopt. Namely, they have adopted policies which provide in Venezuela a climate which is attractive to foreign capital to come in. If all of Latin America followed suit, the danger of communism and social disorder would disappear."[143] Indeed, Venezuela was open for business. Between 1951 and 1957 foreign investment tripled, with nearly three-quarters of the total coming from U.S. firms. Furthermore, the FBI and the CIA were given carte blanche to conduct surveillance of labor unions, while U.S. oil companies provided the FBI with their employees' fingerprints "to determine if they were communists or 'fellow-travelers.' "[144]

When Dulles arrived at Maiquetía Airport, it was Estrada who met the secretary and escorted him in the dictator's automobile to the U.S. ambassador's residence in Caracas.[145] Indifferent to the appearance of having the exiles' bête noire provide protection, Dulles went further to demonstrate his support for the dictator. First he announced a three-year exemption on oil import taxes for Venezuela, a perk amounting to one hundred million dollars annually, and then the administration fast-tracked ten million dollars in high tech arms sales to its military.[146]

In his speech at the conference, Dulles contended that ever since the Soviet Union had disbanded the Comintern in 1943, Moscow had secretly overseen all national communist parties. In Dulles's mind, it was simply inconceivable that a country would accept communism of its own volition; therefore, the impetus for such a change must originate "outside this hemisphere." Guatemala's policies thus were a product of exogenous subversion, not the result of an authentic indigenous desire for reform.[147]

Although he was publicly hawkish about Moscow's role in Guatemala, in private he admitted to the president, "there was no firm evidence tying the Guatemala regime to the Soviets."[148] As late as early 1954, an internal State Department memo could only agree with that assessment, suggesting that the evidence of Soviet influence was "largely circumstantial."[149] In fact, the USSR's economic footprint in the region was miniscule. As one study indicated, trade with Latin America during the 1950s was "highly sporadic, unstable, and confined to only a few countries." Guatemala was not one of them.[150]

Dulles's resolution, "The Declaration of Solidarity for the Preservation of the Political Integrity of the American States against International Communism," held that if the international communist movement took over the political institutions of any country in the region, it would pose an existential threat "to the sovereignty and political independence of us all, endangering the peace of America" and justifying "appropriate action in accordance with existing treaties." The relevant treaty obligation was the Rio Pact, which held that an attack on one member state was regarded as an attack on all. Dulles's resolution may have intentionally omitted Guatemala's name, but there was little doubt to those in attendance about its purpose.

What the resolution signified was that an exception to the principle of nonintervention was warranted in the case of external subversion. It was ironic that during the two weeks of debate in Caracas, the declaration's principal enthusiasts were the dictatorial delegations, the same regimes that had staunchly defended nonintervention. Dulles later admitted to a congressional committee that "the support of the so-called dictator countries"—Nicaragua, the Dominican Republic, Peru, Colombia, Paraguay, Cuba, and Venezuela—was "sometimes a bit embarrassing."[151]

Anxious to showcase hemispheric unity, Dulles and his aides took measures to ensure the resolution's passage. As Rubottom recalled, the secretary "spared no effort and spared no blandishment to get this Caracas resolution through. . . . I'm sure there must have been a lot of arm twisting—very severe arm twisting."[152] A year after Dulles instructed Cabot to "devise an imaginative policy for Latin America—but don't spend any money," he now persuaded the parsimonious Humphrey to open the purse strings.[153] Besides softening restrictions on Export-Import Bank long-term loans, Dulles convinced the Cabinet to approve a treasure trove of sweeteners: loans, economic aid, arms shipments, tariff overrides, debt forgiveness, and, by consenting to pay higher-than-market prices for certain commodities, outright subsidies. When inducements failed, threats to withhold assistance sufficed. The vote buying to secure passage of the resolution came with a high price tag, as hundreds of millions of dollars were lavished on Latin American governments "at the expense of American producers, taxpayers and consumers."[154]

The resolution passed by a vote of 17–1 (Guatemala, the lone dissent) with two abstentions (Mexico and Argentina). Even though eight of the votes came from reliable dictatorships, the final tally was deceiving. Substantive opposition surfaced from the democracies that saw the maneuver for what it was: a justification for intervention in Guatemala. Padilla Nervo gently defended Guatemala during the proceedings, drawing a parallel between present claims of communist subversion and the 1920s, when the Coolidge administration engaged in similar redbaiting. "I remember the time when Mexico stood alone and we were going through an economic and social reform, a revolution, and if at that moment you had called a meeting of the American States to judge us, probably we would have been found guilty of some subjection to foreign influences."[155]

Delegates were plainly uncomfortable with the precedent the resolution set and the wide latitude afforded Washington in the future. An astonishing fifty-one amendments were proposed, seeking to dilute the singular focus on anticommunism. The amendments drew attention to the root causes of external subversion—the systematic violation of individual rights, the undermining of democratic institutions, and the pressing need for social and economic reforms. Although virtually all the amendments failed to secure the two-thirds majority required for passage, the U.S. delegation did agree to add a final paragraph that the declaration was not intended "to impair the inalienable right of each American state freely to choose its own form of government and economic system . . .," a bewildering clause that undermined the thrust of Dulles's resolution.[156] A patronizing U.S. delegate afterwards dismissed the amendment as "Latin American window dressing—somehow they have to stress their independence."[157] A recent revisionist interpretation of the conference posits that by adding this amendment, "Latin American diplomats had seized the initiative" and transformed Dulles's resolution "from a license to intervene into a warning to the United States not to interfere in Guatemala." Even if the clause helped assuage any remorse delegates felt about voting for the resolution, it is difficult to read what transpired as Latin American governments' winning the day. Dulles now had the diplomatic cover he wanted.[158]

Dwight Eisenhower meets with John Foster Dulles upon the latter's return from the Inter-American Conference in Caracas, March 15, 1954. National Park Service Photo. Courtesy of the USNA, Eisenhower Presidential Library, Abilene, Kansas.

The secretary left the conference right after the vote, midway through the monthlong proceedings—a hasty exit that recalled Coolidge's early departure from Havana in 1928—and gave the appearance that the U.S. had little interest in other items on the agenda.[159] Fretting that Dulles's early departure was insulting to the other delegations, Cabot later confided: "I feared that we were losing Latin America."[160]

Conclusions

There were eerie parallels between the Caracas proceedings and the conference held in Havana twenty-six years earlier. Then, the Cuban capital was placed under armed guard; dissidents were rounded up; North American dignitaries (Coolidge and Lindbergh), by their presence, helped to legitimize a repressive dictator; and delegates vocally expressed their dissatisfaction with U.S. aggression in Nicaragua. There was a fundamental difference, however. If in 1928 the United States tabled a resolution calling for nonintervention, in 1954 that principle was now considered a cornerstone of inter-American relations, and it was now the United States asking that an exception be made.

Indeed, a longtime critic of North American intervention, Fabela aptly characterized what transpired in Caracas as an inversion of what he had witnessed in Havana. In a column in *Excélsior* he reminded readers that a U.S. delegation led by Hughes had tabled a Latin American resolution proscribing intervention. In contrast, by securing passage of his "Declaration," Dulles gave Washington the authority to depose a democratically elected government. The secretary's "imperial and intransigent" attitude signified not only the export of McCarthyism to the rest of the hemisphere, but an ignominious end to the era of the Good Neighbor. "No, Mr. Dulles did not come to negotiate, he came to impose his will," Fabela lamented.[161]

Upon his return from Caracas, Dulles once again demonstrated a lack of sensitivity about the conference venue. During a debriefing of his trip with the House Committee on Foreign Affairs, he pointed out that members of the other delegations had taken notice of the salutary impact of U.S. corporate investment in Caracas. He hoped this would be an object lesson to other states in the region: after all, "American private capital . . . is available in amounts infinitely greater than anything you can get out of an Export-Import Bank loan." What the secretary failed to mention, however, was that it was the country's oil reserves that lured U.S. investors to Venezuela. Delegates were well aware that attracting remotely comparable levels of corporate investment to their countries was hardly a realistic possibility.[162]

The secretary was at least honest about the deliberations. At an NSC briefing, he admitted that his resolution "was not adopted with genuine enthusiasm." Rubottom, who had to cope with the diplomatic fallout from the conference and its aftermath when he became assistant secretary of state for inter-American affairs in 1957, thought the declaration so toxic to moderates that it was effectively dead on arrival and had ominous implications for U.S.-Latin American relations: "One of the great disillusionments I suffered, and one of the great problems that I had to deal with, was the fact that this Caracas Resolution simply was not tolerable to Latin American liberals." As a result, it could not "be used against the threat of Communism under Castro. It was almost a Pyrrhic victory, in the sense that even though the Secretary [Dulles] did work hard and got this through, we were never able to invoke that resolution."[163]

Rubottom, who was privy to Dulles's reasoning, was dubious that the resolution was worth the cost. Hemispheric agreements already existed, he noted, such as the Rio Pact, the OAS Charter, and the Chapultepec Agreement, that "might have obviated the need for the Caracas resolution." But it was important to Dulles, the future assistant secretary allowed, to "name Communism as a target." It was not just the resolution that rankled Latin American attendees, however. Rubottom understood, in a way that Dulles never could fathom, what the political repercussions were of staging the conference at a site roundly detested by the delegates. "Because that resolution was passed during a conference hosted by the Pérez Jiménez government, it has been untouchable and almost unmentionable."[164]

Six months after the Caracas meetings, the administration further infuriated regional democrats when Warren awarded the dictator the Legion of Merit for "special meritorious conduct in the fulfillment of his high function, and anti-communistic attitudes."[165] That the ambassador presented the medal on behalf of the President of the United States at his Caracas residence before 250 invited guests and a fawning press corps could only be construed as a slap in the face to reformers.[166] As will become apparent, the motivation for and the timing of the award had more to do with a gathering political storm in the isthmus in late 1954 and early 1955, pitting La Internacional against defenseless Costa Rica.[167]

In a letter to the editor of the *Times*, Alexander opined that Ike ought to reconsider singing the praises of the dictator's commitment to anticommunism. Referring to Venezuelan communists who were collaborating with the dictator, he noted that the pérezjimenista regime was "larded with ex-communists, whose status as 'ex' is highly doubtful."[168] As for Guatemala, in the short term Dulles's resolution bolstered Árbenz's popularity at home. Alexander, who was in Guatemala during the meetings, reported that "Caracas strengthened, rather than weakened the communists" by prompting a nationalist backlash among moderate elements opposed to Árbenz's reforms.[169]

After the conference ended, Figueres endorsed the U.S. resolution. His critics concluded that his decision was driven by political expedience. They contended that he had put his country on a diplomatic island and now needed to make amends with Washington. But that missed the larger point. Refusing to succumb to State Department pressure was never about whether Árbenz was a fellow traveler or a communist. Nor was it solely a byproduct of Figueres's friendship with Betancourt. If the conference venue had been Santo Domingo, Managua, or Buenos Aires, his determination to stay home probably would have been the same. He simply had no interest in taking part in a conference that legitimized Pérez Jiménez or any other brutish thug, for that matter.

CHAPTER TWELVE

La Lucha sin Fin
(The Never-Ending Struggle)

From these small countries fenced in by tyranny, come and go
conspiracies, labyrinthine dictatorial intrigues. An advisor in the
pay of Trujillo is, at the same time, an official in the Chilean
Secret Service. Who advises whom?

—PABLO NERUDA, 1946

A FULL YEAR BEFORE the coup, Pepe Figueres expressed serious misgivings
about Árbenz, agreeing with Washington that something had to be done.
The Guatemalan leader may not have been a communist, but as far as
Figueres was concerned, he was a dupe. By censoring the opposition press,
rounding up dissidents, heeding the counsel of the PGT, and cultivating
ties with the leftist CTAL labor confederation, Árbenz was, in the eyes of
social democrats like the Costa Rican president, demonstrating unmistakable signs of creeping totalitarianism.[1] He "had no capable friends, no intellectuals" to rely on, Figueres mused to Berle during the latter's visit to
Costa Rica. So it did not come as a surprise when communists filled the
void. "By now," he wrote Berle, "Árbenz was very nearly their prisoner."[2]

Alexander tendered a comparable assessment of the influential role
played by "Stalinists" in Árbenz's government. Guatemalan unions affili-

ated with CTAL had made significant inroads dating back to the president's predecessor, Arévalo. Militants in the PGT, Alexander noted, although few in number, controlled the national radio station, the Social Security Institute, peasant organizations, and the student movement.[3]

Still, Figueres was opposed to a U.S. military intervention, preferring instead "a type of moral intervention in which the United States as a democratic power stood with [regional] democratic forces ... against communist totalitarianism." Failing that, it made sense either to sit tight until "elements in Guatemala were prepared to deal with the communists by force," or he would be happy to assemble a group of "Central American countries together to pressure Árbenz to throw out the communists." But there were limits to how far he would go. Working with Somoza to remove Árbenz from power was simply out of the question.[4]

Berle also had no illusions about Árbenz. He submitted a well-thought-out, sixteen-page memo to the State Department about a way forward in Guatemala. He recommended that Figueres "take leadership" of a Central American initiative to oust Árbenz. At first glance, he reasoned, working with Somoza looked like the attractive option. The general would be only too willing to do so, for "a price," and his National Guard "has the greatest degree of immediately available strength" to defeat the Guatemalan military. But it was a monumental mistake, in his estimation, to rely on the Nicaraguan strongman. Somoza was a "symbol of corruption." He had plundered his country—estimates of his wealth ranged from $40 to $60 million—and he made sure that one of his sons or a reliable puppet would succeed him. Working with the dictator, Berle concluded, would be a "dangerous course of action."[5]

His suggestion was that the United States assemble a coalition of Guatemala's neighbors to pressure Árbenz to "jettison his communist friends." As the region's best-regarded democrat, Figueres should lead that effort. If Árbenz refused, Berle thought, it would at the very least encourage the internal opposition that already existed to rise up against him. It might take a year to a year and a half. "But if done that way, it would stay done."[6]

Berle's recommendations, however, fell on deaf ears at Foggy Bottom, for one reason. Dulles informed Eisenhower that other governments in the region, Nicaragua especially, "loathed" the Costa Rican head of state and would never work with him.[7] Berle thought Dulles was getting bad advice from his diplomats in Managua. During his March 1953 visit to the Nicaraguan capital, he was appalled to learn that no one in the embassy spoke Spanish. Nor was Berle enamored with Ambassador

Thomas Whelan, one of Somoza's biggest boosters. Instead, "they rely on their Nicaraguan clerks. . . . We might as well have been in Fargo," he added, a snide reference to Whelan's hometown.[8]

Betancourt agreed with Berle and Pepe about Árbenz. The Venezuelan was miffed that Pérez Jiménez had restored diplomatic relations with Guatemala and that Árbenz, unlike Arévalo, was now giving the cold shoulder to AD exiles.[9] Less than two months before the overthrow, Betancourt, writing on behalf of the party's executive committee, justified AD's position on Guatemala to its rank and file: "The Guatemalan government has never backed us in our antidictatorial efforts, nor have they been welcoming to AD exiles, and one by one [our] exiles (living) there have been leaving the country. The evident influence of the communists in the government and their absolute control of the workers' movement has influenced how the government feels about AD. . . . We have never received any assistance from the Guatemalan government in the past, nor is there any possibility of obtaining any in the future. . . . We have no intention of joining the chorus of those supporting Mr. Dulles in his attacks on that government, nor will we adopt a simple-minded attitude and convert ourselves into its [Guatemala's] defenders."[10]

For Betancourt to say that the Guatemalan government had never backed reformers was a blatant misrepresentation of the recent past. Arévalo had championed their cause. Under enormous pressure from within and without, Árbenz did not have that luxury. As Figueres did, Betancourt suspected that the Guatemalan president's days were numbered. Wary that criticism of Guatemala might be read as implicit support for North American intervention, he urged the party faithful to use discretion in speaking about Árbenz and his government—"don't attack or defend them!"[11] But members of an AD cell in Mexico City, including Gallegos and Rangel, were upset with Betancourt's reluctance to criticize the United States and threatened to go public with a statement on their own. To preserve party unity, he relented and agreed to release a brief statement criticizing the intervention.[12]

Just before the coup in early June, several members of the Mexican cell issued their own statement declaring their opposition to the intervention. Betancourt went out of his way to reassure a North American diplomat of his party's stance. He informed the first secretary of the U.S. embassy in San José that those who had spoken out were now facing expulsion from the party. He also qualified his support for Árbenz's removal, cautioning that "a military regime or a reactionary type of government . . . would not represent an improvement."[13]

If Dulles held out hope that the region's democracies might condemn Árbenz after the Caracas meetings, he was sorely disappointed. Although he noted in a memorandum that he was relieved to have the Brazilian government's backing, "since we needed support from other than the Somozas in the hemisphere," the Uruguayan and Mexican governments, mindful of how much opposition existed in their own countries to U.S. intervention, kept their counsel.[14] The French Ambassador to Mexico, Gabriel Bonneau, remarked that there was widespread support for Árbenz in Mexico, where the Guatemalan's agrarian reform law was viewed as comparable to its own. He also noted that Mexicans remembered all too well how in the 1920s their "revolution had been denounced as Marxist too."[15]

In the summer of 1953, when Figueres concluded that Guatemala was no longer salvageable, he offered the Eisenhower administration Costa Rica's assistance in deposing Árbenz. As had other governments in the isthmus, Costa Rica severed diplomatic relations with Guatemala.[16] Later he admitted, "I had no moral compunction. In fact, I was all for overthrowing Árbenz, who was a communist."[17] But for all Pepe's tough talk afterward and despite intense pressure from the State Department, which asked United Fruit to withhold a promised million-dollar loan to the Costa Rican government until Figueres went public with his opposition to Árbenz, he soft-pedaled his objections to the Guatemalan president in the months prior to Operation PBSUCCESS.[18] In fact, a month before the coup Figueres did not mince words about how Latin Americans would interpret a U.S. intervention. If Washington "cracks down, it could do more harm than good," he told a reporter. "The United Fruit Company, powerful in Central America, is a symbol of colonialism. If a revolution more or less sponsored by the United States were to occur, who would make the 160 million Latin Americans believe that it was not an act of economic support for the fruit company? Surely it is interpreted as a sign that once again, the stick is imposed."[19]

Moderate politicians recognized early on that they were in a no-win position. If they spoke out publicly against Árbenz, they would be assailed by many in the region opposed to North American meddling. If, on the other hand, they condemned the United States, they risked losing Washington's support. Better not to take a public stand either way.

A sober Galíndez predicted that North American intervention would be an unmitigated disaster for social democrats. In a prescient piece, "La tragedia de Guatemala," written forty-eight hours after Castillo Armas's invasion began and with the outcome still in doubt, he dismissed as simplistic, ahistorical, and misleading Washington's "red versus anti-red" characterization.

Interestingly, Galíndez learned of the impending coup a year earlier from his student at Columbia. The Korean War veteran mentioned that he had been offered a significant sum of money by Guatemalan elites to train soldiers preparing for an invasion. In fact, Operation PBSUCCESS had all the markings of a rightist Caribbean Legion: the CIA supplemented Castillo Armas's small army of Guatemalans with mercenaries from the Dominican and Nicaraguan National Guards, the Honduran army, and Colombian veterans of the Korean conflict. Washington, which had put the brakes on the Legion five years earlier because it considered it a source of regional instability, had no problem helping Castillo Armas recruit combatants from the ranks of La Internacional.[20]

Galíndez reminded his readers that Guatemala's revolutionary spring, 1944–1954, had implemented badly needed land and labor reforms, changes that "merited the support of all men of good will." Unfortunately, a small, dedicated group of communists had now hijacked the reforms. Although few in number, "everyone was aware of their activity and discipline." He was frustrated that Árbenz had rejected counsel from "sincere friends" like Betancourt and Figueres, who both had pleaded with him to "clarify his situation" and disavow ties to the communists. But what saddened him even more was the key role reactionary elements of the Guatemalan oligarchy were playing in the plotting, and that Castillo Armas had the blessing and backing of neighboring dictatorships. Of this he was certain: the conspirators and their "egotistical" Guatemalan oligarchical allies would exact their revenge.[21]

Galíndez pictured two possible outcomes, neither hopeful for Guatemala's future and both posing ominous consequences for democrats everywhere. Should Árbenz somehow prevail, it was a foregone conclusion that "communist influence will increase and Guatemala will lose its democracy and liberty." But if the "invaders win"—a more likely outcome, because he had it on good authority that the United States had its fingerprints all over this operation— "I fear much more that reactionary elements [in Guatemala] will annul the reforms of the last ten years . . . and the liberal elements fighting with them will have little hope of leading the new regime." He also was certain that the likely reversal of Árbenz's agrarian reform would be a boon to communist propagandists. Galíndez predicted that U.S. support for the plotters would prompt a significant backlash against the United States all across the region and that anti-Americanism would fester for years to come.[22]

"I confess I am more pessimistic than ever," he concluded. Indeed, Galíndez's forecast proved prophetic. Within a half-year of the coup, Castillo Armas dismantled leftist labor unions; jailed, exiled, and in a few cases, executed their leadership; returned nationalized lands to hacendados and the United Fruit Company; and ended Guatemala's ten-year democratic experiment.[23]

Even though Pepe, Betancourt, and other reformers never publicly condemned Árbenz, they did not join the chorus of criticism of the coup. They accurately predicted that the intervention would conjure up memories of gunboat diplomacy. They paid dearly for their silence, however; young leftists, more than a few in Betancourt's political party, never forgave them.[24]

Scholars of U.S.–Latin American relations during the 1950s treat the Guatemalan coup as a fulcrum of the Cold War. Viewing the coup through that lens, however, belies a far more complex reality. The region's reformers, and many other Latin Americans for that matter, found the Eisenhower administration's actions in Guatemala far more problematic than the fear of communist penetration. In their eyes, La Internacional was a much greater threat to regional stability. It was disheartening, but perhaps unsurprising, that the CIA preferred to collaborate with Somoza, Trujillo, and Pérez Jiménez rather than to seek their assistance.

After the coup, La Internacional immediately turned its attention to removing Figueres from power. His support for Nicaraguan, Dominican, and Venezuelan exiles had become intolerable. The dictators also believed that since they had assisted the United States in Árbenz's overthrow, Washington would look the other way when they went after Figueres. While the administration agreed that the Costa Rican leader's adventurism was a prime source of regional instability, it was stung by the intense criticism of its intervention. As a result, it played a double game when, in January 1955, a La Internacional–backed proxy army invaded Costa Rica. Working with the OAS, the State Department publicly backed and aided Costa Rica, while the CIA greenlighted the invasion. The ambiguity pleased no one. After Somoza withdrew his forces from Costa Rica, Figueres declared victory, but the undeclared war between La Internacional and reformers only grew hotter.

A Small Price to Pay

The CIA enjoyed its first covert success in the Middle East in 1953, engineering the overthrow of the Iranian prime minister, Mohammad Mosaddegh. Emboldened by this victory, the agency drew up plans to remove Árbenz.[25] Interestingly, preliminary discussions about a coup in Guatemala

had originated with a joint pitch to the Truman administration from Somoza and an attorney for the United Fruit Company in the summer of
1951, well before Árbenz's agrarian reform law was enacted. The Nicaraguan ruler bragged to a U.S. military advisor that he would "clean up Guatemala for you in no time."[26]

Somoza received initial support for the idea from fellow members of
La Internacional, including Trujillo, Pérez Jiménez, Batista, and Odría, as
well as disgruntled officers in the Guatemalan army. Estrada was said to
have asked Pérez Jiménez how much he would be willing to contribute
to such an undertaking. Initially, the dictator offered fifty thousand dollars, but when the security chief related that that was the amount Trujillo
had promised, he doubled Venezuela's contribution.[27]

The Dominican dictator was not to be outdone. According to a CIA
briefing, in September 1952, his representatives ponied up arms, airplanes, and sixty thousand dollars for Castillo Armas at a meeting in Tegucigalpa. As always with Trujillo, there were strings attached. Once
Árbenz was removed from power, Castillo Armas was to extradite Dominican dissidents then residing in the Guatemalan capital. Reneging on
Trujillo's request would come back to haunt the Guatemalan colonel.[28]

The Truman administration reconsidered its involvement after Somoza's aides indiscreetly let word leak out about the plot. Acheson feared
that the operation, code-named PBFORTUNE, would set back relations
with the entire region. In October 1952, he met with CIA director Walter Bedell Smith and pressed him to shut it down. Unbeknownst to the
secretary, Smith continued to solicit support in the region to oust Árbenz.
The agency approached disgruntled Guatemalan army officers, promising arms and funds. The arms were subsequently smuggled from the Dominican Republic into Guatemala, with the United Fruit Company
contributing a reported sixty-four thousand dollars toward the scheme.
"Neither dead nor alive," the plot limped along as the CIA awaited the
upcoming transition in the White House. Not until the summer of 1953
did Eisenhower approve preparations for Operation PBSUCCESS.[29]

In fact, the governments of Nicaragua, the Dominican Republic, El
Salvador, Honduras, and Venezuela continued to conspire about how
best to oust Árbenz right up until the coup. In July 1953, Somoza's son
and the head of the National Guard, Anastasio Somoza Debayle, procured weapons and ammunition for Castillo Armas from an arms dealer
in Hamburg, Germany. As a staff historian of the CIA relates, as late as
three months before the coup the agency was considering a scheme to

hire "Trujillo's trained *pistoleros*" to murder "fifteen to twenty of Guatemala's top leaders."[30]

Figueres offered to serve as an honest broker with Árbenz, but the CIA did not want or need his assistance, preferring instead to work with the likes of Somoza, Trujillo, and Honduran president Juan Manuel Gálvez. In February 1954, the agency, with Somoza's approval, established two training camps in Nicaragua and its base of operations in Managua. One hundred fifty recruits received training in sabotage and demolitions at the dictator's estate, El Tamarindo.[31]

Scholarship on Operation PBSUCCESS portrays the intervention as the quintessential CIA covert operation. But from the outset, La Internacional was intimately involved. Castillo Armas and the CIA received assistance from regional dictators and Guatemala's neighbors, who were concerned that leftist agitating would spill over into their countries. In fact, just a week before the coup, Estrada offered the Guatemalan three P-51 Mustangs and an additional two hundred thousand dollars.[32] Then on the eve of the outbreak of hostilities, a Dominican schooner, "La siesta de Trujillo," carrying arms for Castillo Armas's Liberation Army, was intercepted by the Guatemalan military.[33]

The State Department was generally cautious when it came to military interventions, and the CIA had little tolerance for foreign service officers, but the hard-nosed envoy that Foster Dulles chose for Guatemala was a notable exception. Peurifoy's experience collaborating with the CIA in Greece to consolidate "anti-Communist elements" within the military had prepared him well for this posting.[34] To keep the communists out of the political arena, he weighed in on a dispute over how Greeks should choose their representatives and threatened to cut off U.S. aid if the government did not accede to his preference. He had no concern about criticizing the government; he urged the reinstatement of a military hero as commander-in-chief of the Greek armed forces; and he openly expressed support for a rightist party. As an otherwise flattering write-up noted about his unctuous meddling, "he intervened so brazenly in the country's internal affairs that even the meek Greek government felt compelled, on one occasion to complain publicly."[35]

He did precisely the same in Guatemala. From the moment he assumed his post in late 1953, "Smiling Jack" Peurifoy cajoled, bribed, and exploited divisions within Árbenz's high command in order to facilitate an institutional coup d'état. One colonel grudgingly gave the ambassador his due: he was "an abusive, arrogant ambassador—but this was very effective:

he scared a lot of officers." Sporting "a shoulder holster slung over his arm," he may not have looked and acted the part of the typical proconsul, but his title, Ambassador Extraordinary and Plenipotentiary, and marching orders were identical to the ones given to Welles in Cuba—persuade the armed forces to turn against a regime considered inimical to U.S. interests.[36]

While Peurifoy schemed from within, Castillo Armas's tiny fighting force attacked from neighboring Honduras and El Salvador. Four initial incursions in mid-June were easily turned back by forces loyal to Árbenz. When two of the three F-47 Thunderbolt fighter-bombers that made up Castillo Armas's air force were quickly put out of commission, it was Somoza and a wealthy consultant who came to the rebels' and the agency's rescue. To give the administration plausible deniability, the dictator ostensibly paid $150,000 for the purchase of three surplus Thunderbolts from the Department of Defense. But the funds did not come from the Nicaraguan government; instead, the monies were advanced by a rabid anticommunist millionaire, William Pawley, then serving as a consultant to the CIA. Pawley delivered the money to the Nicaraguan ambassador to the United States, Guillermo Sevilla Sacasa, who in turn purchased the planes on behalf of his government from the Defense Department.[37] The dictator promptly leased the fighters to Castillo Armas with the understanding that the planes would be replaced at a later date by the administration. The renewed bombing runs over the Guatemalan capital and a CIA-coordinated disinformation campaign that spread rumors of "nonexistent civilian uprisings, military defections, and bogus incidents of sabotage" helped persuade the Guatemalan military to abandon their president.[38] One of several lessons that Fidel Castro and Che Guevara gleaned from this intervention was that a nation's military carried within it the seeds of the counterrevolution. Unlike Árbenz, Castro systematically dismantled Batista's army during his first months in power.

As Dunkerley has pinpointed so well, the tactics employed in Operation PBSUCCESS became a template for the duration of the Cold War. Among the methods the U.S. first employed in the coup were "the interdiction of arms, real or imagined, from the Soviet bloc; the funding of counter-revolutionary forces operating across borders; a concerted campaign of diplomatic isolation . . .; a condemnation of basic social reforms as communist in character; an economic boycott; the manipulation of the relative liberty permitted to local media as well as the use of clandestine broadcasts; aerial and maritime sabotage; assertion of an underlying Soviet 'imperialistic' conspiracy and mortal danger to the hemispheric order; and agitation of the religious question."[39]

Ten days after hostilities commenced Árbenz resigned, driven out by former loyalists in the army. Like the Cuban military, which forced Machado to relinquish power in 1933, the high command reasoned that even if it defeated Castillo Armas, something far worse was in the offing—a U.S. military invasion. Abandoning Árbenz was a small price to pay for its own self-preservation.

After the coup, Peurifoy's unseemly imposition of Castillo Armas to govern Guatemala, despite strenuous objections from the high command, ensured that the colonel would be a dead man walking. He did not endear himself to his former colleagues when he incorporated his so-called Liberation Army into the ranks of the armed forces.[40] Taunted mercilessly by Guatemalans for failing to defend the nation, a humiliated high command now had to accept the integration of an invading army and a commander-in chief whom it considered to be a traitorous renegade and a rank opportunist who had conspired with a foreign power. Castillo Armas, who assumed power on September 1, 1954, did exactly what Washington desired. He implemented a sweeping campaign against communist subversion, as perhaps as many as five thousand workers, peasants, and politicians were "jailed, tortured, exiled, or killed" by the military, police, and paramilitaries.[41] For the moment, the oligarchy was relieved, but as Dunkerley noted, "so thorough was the counterrevolution that the Guatemalan left subsequently remained deeply suspicious of legalist and electoral strategies." As a result, Guatemala became one of the first countries in the Caribbean Basin to follow Cuba's insurrectionary path.[42]

Invoking Past Interventions

Spontaneous protests against the intervention erupted in Buenos Aires, Mexico City, Havana, Rio de Janeiro, Montevideo, Quito, Bogotá, Tegucigalpa, and Santiago.[43] Just as Sandino had been the darling of youthful anti-imperialists in the 1920s, the far less charismatic Árbenz now became a living martyr for this generation of Latin American students.

The Chilean response to the intervention was emblematic. Just three days after Castillo Armas crossed into Guatemala, Santiago's central square, the Plaza de Armas, was filled with thousands of student protestors, who denounced North American imperialism by burning a U.S. flag. Allende spoke at the demonstration and argued that the coup was proof that Washington's two-decade-old Good Neighbor Policy was a dead letter. By his bellicose actions, Eisenhower signaled his willingness to return to the gunboat methods of the past. The Chamber of Deputies passed a resolution protesting the intervention.[44]

A State Department memo zeroed in on the reasons for Latin Americans' heightened "sensitivity." U.S. intervention "is a matter of far more urgent importance than that of an indirect and long-term communist threat."[45] It did not help matters when Castillo Armas, grateful for Venezuela's assistance in deposing Árbenz, made public his appreciation by decorating its notorious security chief, Estrada.[46]

An intriguing suggestion for damage control came from Muñoz Marín, who, a few days after Árbenz resigned, cabled Foster Dulles, recommending that the administration be proactive in response to Latin American criticism. The governor suggested that much of the misunderstanding swirling around the intervention might be resolved if the administration issued a statement clarifying that its opposition to communism did not preclude Guatemalans' legitimate right to implement land reform or other social reforms by democratic means. No doubt the Puerto Rican governor had in mind Figueres's successful negotiations with *el pulpo*. But Muñoz Marín's plea fell on deaf ears; no statement along these lines was ever issued by Dulles or his subordinates. Land reform was not something the State Department was interested in encouraging.[47]

In fact, the administration showed itself to be remarkably tone-deaf to Latin American public opinion when it took a victory lap by inviting Castillo Armas for a state visit in late 1955. Arriving in the nation's capital, the colonel and his spouse were greeted on the airport tarmac by Vice President Nixon and his wife, where the guests of honor received a twenty-one-gun salute and a full military review. Later that evening the Nixons hosted a state dinner in their honor. Following his three-day stay in Washington, New York rolled out the red carpet. In addition to a reception at the Council on Foreign Relations, Castillo Armas held forth with newspaper publishers and television and radio moguls at a dinner, met with Mayor Robert Wagner, attended a high mass in his honor at St. Patrick's Cathedral, and then lunched with Cardinal Francis Spellman. Columbia and Fordham did their share by bestowing honorary degrees on the Guatemalan president. After New York the triumphal tour continued with stops in Detroit, St Louis, Houston, and New Orleans. The colonel concluded his trip by meeting privately with Eisenhower at an army hospital in Denver, where the president was convalescing from a coronary thrombosis.[48]

The optics of the state visit did not sit well with reformers. When Tannenbaum bestowed his university's honorary degree on Castillo Armas the reaction was swift. Gallegos, who had received the same honor from Columbia in 1948, publicly renounced his degree, while forty-eight Mexican intellectuals sent a letter of protest to Columbia's president. How could an esteemed institution of public learning, the letter asked, confer such an honor on a dictator who "burns and bans books, persecutes universities, and attacks and closes cultural centers"?[49]

Figueres's response to the intervention, brimming with cynicism, was illuminating. He wrote Berle of how PBSUCCESS had altered the political landscape. "As you know, the reaction throughout Latin America has been bad. Intervention is considered a worse evil than communism. Especially since intervention is never applied to foster a democratic cause. The south (Latin America) is not aware of the imminence of world conflict, while the north is practically hysterical about it." A sea change in U.S. policy was in order, Pepe argued: "On the moral field, we shall not go anywhere until the United States, as a leader, upholds an ideology. This ideology has to be democracy. Unfortunately, at this moment, the opposite is true, in the minds of Latin Americans. The United States appears as the ally of tyranny and political vandalism. This situation has been 'temporary' for the last forty years." Such pronouncements did not deter him in the least from recognizing Castillo Armas's government—a week before Washington did.[50]

Berle's characterization of Figueres is only partially satisfying. When it came to anticommunism, the two men certainly spoke the same language. But Berle fretted about Pepe's lack of political savvy. "I'm becoming inordinately fond of Pepe, a philosopher rather than a politician, a man of delicate sensibility, struggling with the fact that politics is not all saving your soul, but of getting viable arrangements—even if your soul suffers as a result."[51] Berle's sketch of a man with his head in the clouds, however, was at odds with the rough-and-tumble maneuvers Pepe employed against his domestic opposition and his repeated deployment of covert and overt measures to destabilize his neighbors.

In truth, Figueres was a complicated individual. He could be alternately disarming and infuriating, idealistic and cynical. In a revealing letter to the leftist Guatemalan intellectual Edelberto Torres Rivas, written just after his triumph in the 1948 Civil War, he illustrated a politician's facility to tell his audience—in this case, a Marxist sociologist—what he wanted to hear: "It is necessary to destroy the capitalist order in order to

destroy the reactionary. Our first great battle must consist of the liquida-
tion of the capitalist forces of Central America since these are the enemies of the Central American Union and have been what props up all the
dictatorships." Speaking in a lexicon familiar to Torres Rivas, he then
drew a distinction between dogmatic ideologues and a pragmatist like
himself, who was willing to "face the Yankees and capitalism head-on"
and get what he wanted. "I will make friends with the capitalists and the
Yankee State Department and win the battle from inside, and I don't care
what label I have to wear as I gain their confidence. Once they trust me,
then I'll know what to do. . . . You ought to use any politician who is useful to you, without telling them what your true purpose is until after the
victory. . . . I not only sympathize with the ideology you support but I am
infinitely more radical than you."[52]

Is it any wonder that he incensed as many as he charmed? In addition
to absorbing punishing criticism from leftists for his self-imposed silence
about Guatemala, Figueres waged an uphill battle to win over policymakers in Washington, who had lingering concerns about his trustworthiness.
One unflattering State Department memorandum bemoaned Figueres's
"Messiah complex and volatile personality." U.S. Ambassador to Costa
Rica Robert Hill also shared a jaundiced view of the Costa Rican president with the House Subcommittee on Inter-American Affairs. Pepe was
"an extreme socialist . . . a very strange personality . . . who is supposed to
be anti-communist, but is probably as dangerous a man as there is in all
of the Latin American countries." He recommended taking a hard line.
"The only language they understand is the big stick . . . we can't let these
countries near the United States have too much rope, because they are
going to . . . kick U.S. industries out of the country. That is Mr. Figueres's
objective."[53]

What eased the concerns of others in the Department were Figueres's closest advisors. Unlike Árbenz, who relied heavily on the leadership
of the PGT, Pepe had a brain trust, according to an embassy memo titled
"The Men Around Figueres," who were not ideologues: "none carries
the reputation of an extremist. . . . All profess pro-US sentiments or, at
least, are not reputed as unfriendly to the United States."[54]

Within the State Department, opinions on Figueres remained mixed.
As late as March 1959, a biographical sketch prepared for a briefing in
Washington between the Costa Rican and Acting Secretary of State
Christian Herter characterized Pepe as "a colorful, but very complex, de-
vious and controversial individual with Messianic tendencies." Even so,

he is "pro U.S. and on several occasions has gone out of his way to praise the United States while speaking in other Latin American countries."[55]

Still, some Costa Ricans were convinced that after the coup the U.S. might well turn on them, especially after the manner in which Don Pepe embarrassed the Eisenhower administration over its Caracas boycott. But Figueres doggedly remained faithful to his core principles—support for democratization abroad, animus toward communists, and an activist foreign policy that sought to build alliances with democrats while providing asylum for moderate reformers who had been forced to flee their homelands. A month after the intervention, his administration once again brandished its anticommunist credentials, prohibiting the "publication, importation, sale, exhibition, and circulation of pamphlets, magazines, books and other writings of a communist ideology or tendency."[56]

His stance on the Caracas Conference and Guatemala, however, stirred up a hemispheric hornet's nest that put his political survival in jeopardy. As a State Department staffer phrased it: "Figueres's anti-communist record and the fact that he has made his peace with the United Fruit Company will not stay the hand of Somoza and Pérez Jiménez against him. Pérez Jiménez has made it plain that, from his point of view, the elimination of Figueres is a matter of more urgent importance than was the elimination of Árbenz."[57]

For the Dominican dictator, before dealing with Figueres, first there must be, in Silfa's words, "a settling of accounts." The arms and funds Trujillo provided to Castillo Armas did not just contribute to Árbenz's ouster but also made it possible for the rebel to become his country's next president. Gifts required reciprocation, and Dominican diplomats made clear what the terms of repayment were to be: the extradition of Figueres's former chief of staff and former Legionnaire Ramírez, who was then residing in Guatemala; a state visit, when Trujillo would receive the country's highest honor, the Order of the Quetzal; the return of unused arms or their equivalent paid in cash; the reestablishment of diplomatic relations between the two countries; and repayment of Trujillo's "loan"—rumored to be in the hundreds of thousands of dollars. The Guatemalan foreign minister apparently rejected the first three "requests" while presumably making good on the others.[58] In April 1957, Tachito Somoza stepped in to try to persuade Castillo Armas to "openly and fully collaborate with the *Generalísimo*," but his request fell on deaf ears.[59] Bernardino came to Guatemala City to deliver the same message, but the impolitic Guatemalan ruler reportedly told *el gángster* that "he was not in the mood to tarnish his actions by associating with tyrants." The Guatemalan head of state not only reneged on his promise to deport Ramírez and other former leaders of the Legion, but also failed to stop them and two dozen more exiles from receiving asylum at the Costa Rican, Mexican, and Argentine embassies.[60]

Trujillo never forgave Castillo Armas for his tepid response to his "settling of accounts." The Guatemalan colonel, who outlasted multiple coup attempts during his three years in office, must have thought he was invincible. However, his luck ran out in July 1957 when he was murdered in the presidential palace. The prime suspect was a twenty-four-year-old member of the presidential guard, who, it was reported, then walked upstairs and killed himself. But a five-month-long investigation by a congressional commission concluded that the Dominican military attaché Abbes, the ambassador Ernesto Sánchez Rubirosa, and an embassy secretary had masterminded the plot. Sánchez Rubirosa's reputation preceded him. Known as a "crass butcher," he moonlighted for Trujillo's security apparatus when he was not attending to his diplomatic tasks. Just as in the Galíndez affair, this cover-up entailed a slew of murders to silence those who otherwise might come forward with information—seven in all. Few put stock in the suicide story because the exact same tale was spun in the Galíndez cover-up. In that case the Dominican copilot who flew Galíndez on the final leg of his journey to Ciudad Trujillo, Tavito de la Maza, was said to have hung himself in his prison cell, victim of an apparent suicide. In both cases, implausible notes were left behind to explain why they took their own lives.[61]

The commission recommended that Castillo Armas's successor Miguel Ydígoras Fuentes break off diplomatic relations with the Dominican Republic. There were indications, according to the minutes of an NSC meeting, that right-wing elements within the Guatemalan government, cultivated by Dominican agents, were involved in the magnicide as well. A State Department official expressed frustration with the Dominican regime's "radio attacks on Guatemalan political figures [that] have gone far beyond the bounds of propriety and truth and have tended to sow confusion, distrust and division."[62] Although the member of the presidential guard later was charged and found guilty of the crime, it still remains an open question if Trujillo was complicit in what came to be called The Crimes of Mirador.[63] As one of the dictator's cronies noted, "the Castillo Armas affair is one of those mysteries that Trujillo took to the grave."[64]

The Dominican strongman seemed impervious to diplomatic pressure. Within months of the assassination, he was at it again, this time backing the candidacy of the Guatemalan chief of police, said to be implicated in Castillo Armas's murder. The State Department thought that if the reactionary Colonel Enrique Trinidad Oliva became president, it would "turn back the clock" to the dark days of the Ubico dictatorship. They warned the Guatemalan foreign minister that Dominican interference in the political arena "might well result in the undoing of all that has been accomplished in Guatemala since 1954."[65]

Never one to miss an opportunity to twist the knife, the fiendish Dominican ruler moved Sánchez Rubirosa from his post in Guatemala, where he had been declared persona non grata by the Guatemalan government, to the same position in Costa Rica. Figueres never would have accepted Sánchez Rubirosa's credentials, but his successor, Mario Echandi Jiménez, did. A PLN deputy, Luis Alberto Monge, expressed outrage at Echandi for accepting the Dominican diplomat's credentials. In a column titled "The Dominican Republic's Ambassador is a Hitman who Insults Costa Rica's Dignity," Monge denounced Sánchez Rubirosa for his role in the magnicide. Dominican embassies, like those of the Soviet Union, he added, were centers of espionage and bases of operations for assassins. In a follow-up piece, Monge reminded his readers that the ambassador did not have to look far for mentors—his relatives Porfirio and Chichi Rubirosa were both linked to the murder of Bencosme in New York in 1935. "We don't want Costa Rica to be the next site of mysterious crimes, kidnappings, and diplomatic intrigues. We don't want Trujillo to interfere in our domestic politics, like he did in Guatemala." The PLN then passed a resolution in Congress that declared the ambassador persona non grata.[66]

Requiring "Direct Action"

If Trujillo was upset with Castillo Armas, Somoza and Pérez Jiménez reserved their hatred for Figueres and Betancourt. The latter was the public face of the Venezuelan resistance *and* a tireless advocate for democratic rule. During his exile Betancourt used every means at his disposal to attack the dictatorship. He was seemingly everywhere at once, delivering addresses, lobbying politicians, granting radio interviews, and writing countless columns that were syndicated across the region and in the States.

Well before Operation PBSUCCESS the Nicaraguan government had identified the partnership between the Costa Rican president and the Venezuelan exile as a threat to its survival. In September 1952, Sevilla

Sacasa warned the veteran State Department hand Thomas Mann that "Rómulo Betancourt was the guiding hand behind Figueres" and predicted that a Figueres victory in the upcoming presidential election (which came to pass in the fall of 1953) "would contribute greatly in the resurgence of Betancourt's power in Venezuela."[67]

The dictators had reason to be concerned about the presence of the AD leadership in San José. Although Figueres and the exiles vehemently denied it at the time, the kind of logistical support the leadership received from the Costa Ricans went well beyond rhetorical expressions of solidarity. Pérez admitted years later that the party operated openly and without constraints. Figueres's hacienda, Lucha sin fin, about an hour south of the capital, served as a CC command center. Employing clandestine radios, the exiles sent and received coded messages to and from their compatriots in Venezuela several times a day, while maintaining close contact with Adeco cells throughout the diaspora.[68]

AD's brain trust abroad never envisioned that a guerrilla campaign could be successfully waged against Venezuela's formidable military. Instead, they felt that a coordinated effort was needed, wherein the CEN, working in tandem with disaffected military officers, would be bolstered by small numbers of well-trained exiles transporting weaponry from abroad. Arms were obtained from a number of democratic presidents. Arévalo, Figueres, and Grau and Prío drew La Internacional's attention, but as documents in Betancourt's personal archive attest, Paz Estenssoro provided assistance after he came to power in 1952, and Lázaro Cárdenas persuaded Mexico's president, Miguel Alemán Valdés, to contribute to the cause as well. Prío's commitment to AD was impressive: he continued to aid the Venezuelan insurgents even after he was ousted from power in March 1952.[69]

The needs of the underground were compelling. In a March 1952 letter, CEN chief Ruíz Pineda asked Betancourt if an operation codenamed Berta was still on. "Can we count on Berta? When will it happen?" He stressed how desperate their plight was. "We are going through a difficult situation due to the repression. The last few weeks we have been hit extremely hard. Tortures in Caracas and Maracaibo have reached inconceivable extremes."[70]

With Figueres's blessing, arms and ammunition were stockpiled in Costa Rica and a boat was secured from Honduras in preparation for Operation Berta—a scheme by which five hundred exiles and arms would be dropped off in eastern Venezuela, where the exiles would rendezvous with members of the underground. Despite their best efforts, however, Berta proved to be a logistical nightmare. The final nail in its coffin was that the boat the CC had procured proved unseaworthy. Much to the chagrin of Ruíz Pineda and the underground, the badly needed reinforcements and armaments never arrived.[71]

The arms did not go to waste, however. What happened to those weapons illustrates how intertwined the different exile organizations were. The armaments were repurposed and sent to Cuban rebels seeking to unseat Batista, including the 26th of July movement. In reality, this squared the circle, because it was Prío who had originally financed AD's arms purchases. With Berta shelved, Pérez was put in charge of delivering everything from automatic rifles and 50-caliber machine guns to mortars to Prío's supporters and the AAA. "We made several shipments to Cuba," he recalled, including arms for another group of urban activists, the Directorio Revolucionario Estudiantil (DRE). Those arms were put to use in an audacious attack on the presidential palace in 1957. Although Batista was unharmed, the attack galvanized the urban underground.[72] As for the 26th of July movement, in addition to weapons, its propaganda arm, Radio Rebelde, beamed its first broadcasts from Costa Rica.[73]

The CC warned the Costa Rican president about "the risks he was taking with this open-door policy," but it took full advantage. Betancourt and his aides repaid the favor by assisting Costa Rican authorities whenever called upon. Pérez remarked that he "would enter the presidential palace at all hours" to tackle jobs for Figueres's administration. In return, the president generously helped him find employment at the editorial desk of the PLN newspaper, *La República*.[74]

To La Internacional, Costa Rica was a viper's den, one that needed to be shut down. The dictators expected that Washington would at the very least turn a blind eye to their efforts to disrupt the Figueres-Betancourt tandem because of their assistance with Árbenz. Mann, however, made it clear to Sevilla Sacasa that the Department thought differently of Figueres. He dismissed the likelihood of Costa Rican aggression; should Costa Rica invade Nicaragua, he tried to reassure the Nicaraguan diplomat, the Rio Treaty would be invoked.[75]

Constraining Betancourt's freedom of movement and his access to the underground in Venezuela were paramount to Pérez Jiménez and Estrada. A State Department staffer on the Latin American desk in Washington warned Hill: "I can assure you that Venezuela is definitely out to make life miserable for him [Betancourt]. Of course, that is no secret, but in making life difficult for Betancourt, they are also making life difficult for Figueres and for Costa Rica."[76] Estrada bluntly told a U.S. diplomat that he was certain that "the Figueres problem . . . required direct action."[77]

La Internacional's conflation of Betancourt and Figueres was driven home in the months leading up to the Guatemalan coup, when the long-simmering Somoza-Figueres feud reignited. In April 1954 Tacho learned that Figueres had been behind an abortive assassination attempt on him launched by Nicaraguan exiles from Costa Rican territory. After the National Guard snuffed out the plot, the ringleaders revealed under torture that they had received assistance from Figueres and the Costa Rican Civil Guard. Most of the conspirators were Nicaraguan exiles based in Guatemala and Costa Rica, but a few were former members of the Caribbean Legion who had relocated to Costa Rica just five months before.[78] "If the criminal attack had succeeded," Somoza claimed, "Nicaragua would have served as a base of operations against Cuba, Venezuela and the Dominican Republic." Offering no proof, he charged that Betancourt had devised the plot and therefore should be deported from Costa Rica immediately.[79]

Somoza was partially correct; Pepe's fingerprints were all over the plot to assassinate him. The Costa Rican leader permitted two dozen (mostly) Nicaraguan exiles to stage the operation in country. Arms, which had been purchased in Mexico, were flown to Costa Rica and then trucks from Figueres's hacienda transported the armaments to the border.[80] Costa Rican authorities even provided an escort from La Lucha to the frontier. The conspirators planned to contact opponents of Somoza in the Nicaraguan capital and then assassinate the dictator. Money for the plot came from both conventional and unconventional sources: Prío, now living in Miami, gave generously, but also contributing was the Mexican comedian and film star Mario Moreno (Cantinflas), who reportedly gave ten thousand dollars.[81]

Pepe initially sought to deflect criticism of his involvement. Consider the source, he retorted. The Nicaraguan National Guard had violated Costa Rica's sovereignty on three occasions over the last decade. He reminded Costa Ricans of how Somoza's troops had armed and trained a Calderonista force that launched an unsuccessful invasion of their nation from Nicaraguan territory in December 1948. Figueres joked that since Somoza only raised concerns about two dozen out of the four thousand Nicaraguans residing in Costa Rica, our "surveillance must be adequate."[82] When his chief domestic rival, Ulate, called him out for his involvement in the assassination attempt, he fired back: his opponent was guilty of colluding with the dictator and was using the incident to further his own political fortunes.[83] A headline in the San José daily *La Nación*, "Ulate Allies with [former president and now exile Rafael] Calderón Guardia," lent credence to Pepe's complaint that the domestic opposition was in cahoots with the exiled leader. Ulate dispelled any doubt during a visit to Washington, when he declared that "nondemocratic means should be employed to get rid of Figueres."[84]

Then in June 1954, just days before Figueres's inauguration, a Venezuelan military plane flew over San José and Alajuela in broad daylight, dumping thousands of leaflets with pornographic caricatures portraying Figueres and Betancourt as homosexual lovers and perverts. Costa Ricans of all political stripes were outraged at the tawdry stunt.

In the months after the overthrow of Árbenz, Pérez Jiménez, Somoza, and Trujillo hatched a plan to assassinate the Costa Rican president.[85] According to a July 14, 1954, top secret NSC Briefing titled "Possible Costa Rica Coup," Estrada met with peers in Nicaragua, Panama, the Dominican Republic, Cuba, and Honduras to discuss plans. Panamanian President José Remón Cantera's support was considered critical; coupled with Somoza's backing, it meant that Costa Rica, with only a 1,400-man Civil Guard to protect itself, would have to defend its northern and southern flanks. Venezuelan arms were, in fact, moved into position along Panama's frontier with Costa Rica. Dulles noted reports "that equipment and personnel used by Castillo Armas in Guatemala would now be turned against Costa Rica."[86] In fact, Betancourt had received intelligence as early as January from the AD underground that a sergeant in the Venezuelan military had been sent to Managua with orders to train one thousand Costa Rican exiles intent on ousting Figueres. A shipment of arms was on its way as well.[87]

In addition to the preparations, a prickly war of words festered. The way each leader cast the conflict was telling. As Figueres told a reporter for the *New York Times*, "This is simply part of the long struggle between democracy and dictatorships." He contended that the Venezuelan regime had thrown in with Somoza and former Costa Rican presidents Calderón Guardia and Teodoro Picado Michalski.[88] The two, in exile in Nicaragua, were yet again poised to lead their supporters across the border.[89]

In contrast, the Nicaraguan dictator painted his rival as a godless communist. Rightfully upset about the attempt to assassinate him, Somoza insisted that Figueres expel Nicaraguan exiles and any remnants of the Legion and fire five members of his cabinet allegedly involved in the conspiracy. To please Trujillo, he also demanded that Figueres expel Bosch, and at the behest of Pérez Jiménez, he reiterated his call for Pepe to deport Betancourt, whom he accused of heading up a reconstituted Legion.[90]

No one defended Figueres with greater resolve than Muñoz Marín. The governor first met with Holland at the end of July 1954, asking him to get Somoza to stop harassing his southern neighbor.[91] Later that fall, after Muñoz Marín had attended Figueres's inauguration, he made a special plea to Eisenhower in a cable: "I am familiar with Costa Rica. It undoubtedly is one of the few countries in Latin America that measures up to the standards of a genuine democracy and Figueres is among the best friends of the United States in that region because his friendship arises from common ideals of freedom. His government is now being seriously threatened by so-called revolutionaries aided by his neighbor to the north. I do not think the Free World can let this model democracy go into the dictatorship camp. I know the State Department is alert to the situation, but feel it my duty to bespeak your personal interest so that all possible legitimate measures might be taken before it is too late." The governor also sent out cables to democratically elected heads of state, such as Paz, that Figueres was in grave difficulty. He asked that these leaders announce their public support for the Costa Rican.[92]

Betancourt lashed out at Somoza in the Costa Rican press. The dictator should beware of casting stones. Somoza had a well-documented history of attempting to destabilize democracies. Indeed, Betancourt had intimate knowledge of one such thwarted coup against his own government in late January 1948. Somoza and Trujillo had aided and abetted dissident Venezuelan exiles, including Estrada and former dictator López Contreras, in an audacious transnational conspiracy to prevent Gallegos from being sworn in. At a critical moment, U.S. Ambassador Walter Donnelly shared with Betancourt a cable decoded by US intelligence, which explained that four airplanes obtained in the United States had stopped to pick up "mercenaries" and arms in Ciudad Trujillo and Puerto Cabezas, Nicaragua. The conspirators, Betancourt explained, had every intention of flying on to Caracas to bomb the capital and launch their *golpe*. Only timely diplomatic pressure from the Truman administration dissuaded the plotters from leaving Nicaragua.[93]

The State Department's assessment of and response to the growing tensions between Costa Rica and Nicaragua went through several stages.

Early on, it wanted the dispute to disappear, lest it complicate plans to remove Árbenz. Dulles's telegram to the embassy in San José a month before the coup recommended that the matter be handled "dispassionately," otherwise it "would distract our mutual efforts [to] rid hemisphere especially Central America area of international communist threat."[94] As a result, the Department first dismissed Figueres's claims that Somoza's National Guard was preparing an expeditionary force of exiles.

The CIA, however, was well aware of Somoza's ongoing efforts to train the exiles. In a 1987 interview, Woodward admitted that he had spoken to Allen Dulles before taking his post in San José in the spring of 1954. The CIA director's cryptic comment only made sense to Woodward in hindsight: "He made the very odd remark to me: 'I want to assure you that the CIA is not going to attempt to overthrow the Figueres Government.' I didn't know quite what to make of that remark (laughter). But I later discovered that what he really meant was the CIA was not reporting on this subject, but was aware of it. The reason that the CIA was apparently turning a deaf ear to this was that Somoza had been of assistance in the overthrow of Árbenz."[95]

It is hard to imagine that the State Department was also unaware of Somoza's intentions. But it presented itself as reluctant to take sides. Its perspective changed after the adverse criticism it received for the intervention, however. It quietly acceded to Figueres's request for assistance by selling Costa Rica fifteen tons of light arms and some outdated planes. That token shipment came a few months after the administration had concluded a bilateral military agreement with Nicaragua.[96]

Was this an attempt to level the playing field? It may have been meant as a message to Somoza and his allies in La Internacional that the Department would not tolerate an invasion of Costa Rica. The reasons for helping Figueres were twofold. Policymakers concluded that the removal of such a prominent democrat so soon after the intervention would be "strongly adverse to U.S. interests." More importantly, the administration felt, with good reason, that it "would be held responsible [for] Figueres's overthrow," one of the region's sole remaining democrats.[97] Ulate, with some justification, felt that the administration was playing a dangerous game; by arming both parties, it was sowing the seeds of a violent confrontation.[98]

Still, the Department had every right to be exasperated with Pepe's persistent adventurism. A wistful embassy memo captured the frustrations of reining in Figueres (and Somoza): "If only he could be prevailed upon to devote himself to his domestic problems and remain mum about other countries and their governments, it might be possible to establish at least a wary but peaceful status quo. The background of both men, unfortunately, mitigates against the attainment of this highly desirable achievement."⁹⁹ In early August 1954 Ambassador Hill asked for permission from his superiors to issue a stern warning to the Costa Rican president "to restrict his verbal and written attacks" on Somoza and have him keep "a close watch on Nicaraguan exiles to prevent a recurrence of the April assassination plot."¹⁰⁰

The State Department's tacit support for Figueres had residual effects. Estrada warned Maurice Bernbaum, an embassy staffer, that Washington's "insistence upon protecting Costa Rica ... could result in serious damaged [*sic*] relations with our real friends." Perhaps those "friends," he intimated, would not be quite as reliable in the future as they had been with Guatemala. In a memo to Holland, Atwood noted that "Venezuela had reacted strongly" to the modest assistance the U.S. provided for Costa Rica, "since it indicated that Venezuela could not successfully treat Figueres as another Árbenz."¹⁰¹ Estrada's warning was not just idle talk. Figueres's foe Calderón Guardia had flown to Venezuela on four occasions during the second half of 1954, raising fears in San José that an invasion was imminent.¹⁰²

Foster Dulles confirmed reports of the plotting. He cabled the embassy in Guatemala that "although reports of invasion plan [were] not yet substantiated," there certainly were sufficient "circumstantial developments" that a scheme was afoot, headed by Costa Rican exiles with Venezuela and Nicaragua implicated. He added: "Firm US policy ... is to ameliorate political tensions. ... We [are] also concerned [about] adverse world reaction from overthrow legitimately elected liberal democratic Costa Rican Government, for which US would be censured because of our predominant position in area and alleged role in recent change of government in Guatemala."¹⁰³

Then there was the knotty problem of what to do about Betancourt. Estrada was adamant that it would be "unacceptable" for Washington to grant him a visa because of the legitimacy it would confer. Concerned that relations between Caracas and Washington were deteriorating, Atwood recommended "arranging for a destination other than the US for Betancourt."¹⁰⁴

Whether to grant Betancourt a visa was no simple matter for immigration authorities and the Department. An appraisal of the applicant's political views by the State Department had concluded that Betancourt's "political orientation may best be described as nationalistic, leftist, non-communist, and frequently outspokenly anti-communist." On the one hand, it was noted approvingly that as head of Venezuela's *trienio* government, he had "cooperated with the U.S." But Betancourt's past membership in the Costa Rican Communist Party meant that he was technically inadmissible under the Immigration and Nationality Act. Still, his continued presence in Costa Rica "would be contrary to the national interests of the United States," Dulles informed Attorney General Herbert Brownell. He recommended in a note (marked secret) that it was "urgent and important" that the Department of Justice exercise its discretionary authority and grant Betancourt a temporary visa.[105]

It is unclear whether other destinations were under consideration for the Venezuelan exile, but Dulles, aware that he needed to appease Somoza and Pérez Jiménez, ultimately prevailed upon Brownell, who approved a ninety-day visa. Figueres objected strenuously. Having the Venezuelan forced out in this manner, he insisted, violated Costa Rica's longstanding commitment to political asylum.

It was Betancourt himself who decided that his presence in Costa Rica had become a liability. As much as it must have rankled him to cave in to the dictators' demands, he thought it best to accept Muñoz Marín's offer and move to San Juan. Before leaving Costa Rica on July 26, however, he sent off a letter to the editor of *La República*, in which he insisted that he was leaving on his own volition, and that he had never meddled in domestic politics. Nor would he ever do anything to compromise Costa Rica's foreign policy.[106]

Betancourt's and Bosch's exit did little to mollify Somoza. He insisted that the Venezuelan, in particular, should not be permitted to return to Costa Rica.[107] But it was the dictator's animosity toward Figueres that had observers concerned. An NSC briefing about the fallout from the botched assassination attempt could not have been more chilling: "President Somoza bitterly hates Figueres—would personally kill him if [he] could."[108]

The Department's message to Somoza was the same as it had been to Figueres. In late July 1954 Holland asked Whelan to inform the general to put a stop to the battle of nerves because it was "creating serious problems" for the secretary of state. Dulles, Holland continued, "would be grateful, if our good friend, and we know he is our good friend, President Somoza, would take those steps that will be effective to bring about a rapid dissipation of this tension."[109]

As for Venezuela, the United States realized that relations needed to be mended. An NSC report agreed with Bernbaum's assessment that relations with Venezuela "had deteriorated because of our support of Costa Rica and our action in granting a visa to Rómulo Betancourt." Dulles cabled the embassy in Caracas that the Department was "working to eliminate the number of miscellaneous exiles generally believed to be intriguing in Costa Rica."[110] Sensing that this was insufficient, the administration decided to award the Legion of Merit to Pérez Jiménez. The impetus for the decoration actually came from Venezuela's ambassador to the United States, César González, who, in an unusually forthcoming conversation with Holland, went into some detail about his government's apprehensive state of mind: "The President [Pérez Jiménez] is always fearful of its [government's] stability. Pedro Estrada has the mentality of a policeman and has to preserve an atmosphere of suspicion and vigilance in order to justify his own position in the Government. The President's naturally suspicious nature makes him accept Estrada's interpretation of events." González added that it was his hope that Venezuela "will outgrow its military dictatorship," a startling admission from a diplomat whose government he was obliged to present in the best possible light. A decoration, González was convinced, would make the "current resentments and suspicions . . . disappear."[111]

This helps make sense of the reasoning behind, and the timing of, the award so many months after the Caracas meetings. Even though the Department knew that there would be strident criticism about the decoration from Betancourt and his allies across the region, it felt it needed to make a public display of its support for the dictatorship. As to be expected in honorary citations of this kind, the wording enumerated the dictator's accomplishments—among them, his hosting of the Inter-American Conference, his cooperation with the United States, his military's contribution to the defense of the Western hemisphere, and "his continuing awareness of the subtleness of communist infiltration."[112] The discussions and the award had the desired effect, the end-of-the-year NSC report concluded, "because United States relations with Venezuela promptly took a turn for the better."[113] Additional proof of improved relations came in the form of the U.S. Air Force's sale of twenty-two F86F Sabre jet fighters to the Venezuelan military in 1955.[114]

The administration went further in its efforts to appease the Venezuelan regime. As a thank-you for maintaining order during the meetings and to assuage any ruffled feathers, the State Department invited Estrada for an extraordinary red-carpet visit, the likes of which were generally reserved for heads of state. In addition to being wined and dined, he met with the Dulles brothers and J. Edgar Hoover. Boasting that Estrada was the first intelligence chief to be accorded an official visit, a duplicitous Gónzalez confided to Pérez Jiménez "our Seguridad Nacional . . . has received the backing and praise of the United States government." Romauldi was disgusted. Such cynicism, he fumed to Betancourt, had not been on display "since the times of Goebbels."[115]

Despite its best efforts, the administration failed to reduce tensions in the isthmus. Throughout the fall of 1954, Costa Rican authorities became increasingly convinced that Calderón Guardia loyalists were, with the assistance of Somoza, Pérez Jiménez, and Trujillo, preparing to invade Costa Rica. A story ran in late November in the conservative San José paper *La Nación* that four hundred Costa Ricans had crossed the Nicaraguan border to join Calderón's band of rebels, reigniting fears that the domestic opposition had made common cause with the former president.[116]

When Whelan seemingly gave his nation's blessing to the rebels by reviewing the troops at their training camp in Coyotepe, Nicaragua, Costa Rican officials lodged a vigorous protest. Critics pointed out that Whelan, a political appointee with no experience in the region, had become, over the course of a decade at his post, little more than a "propagandist for the regime." According to one scholar, the ambassador went so far as to criticize his superiors "for not returning Somoza's friendliness and support in equal measure." That he was never recalled during his tenure in Managua makes clear that Foster Dulles believed that the ambassador's cozy friendship with Somoza was of significant value.[117]

That fall, Costa Rica's Foreign Ministry quietly went on the offensive. Diplomats were dispatched to Latin American and Caribbean governments to deliver the message that an invasion was imminent and when it happened, Costa Rica was prepared to invoke the Rio Treaty, just as it did seven years earlier when Nicaragua violated its sovereignty by sending troops across the border. In their conversations, Figueres's diplomats emphasized that without the assistance of the regional peacekeeping organization, a defenseless Costa Rica stood little chance against a country as well armed as Nicaragua.[118]

Figueres received support in his campaign against Somoza from an unlikely source. As mentioned, at that moment Batista was at odds with Trujillo. As a result, he refused a request for arms from Calderón Guardia. He told the *Diario de la Marina*, "we want peace in the Caribbean, we know that Figueres is a democrat and an anti-communist." Pleasantly surprised by what was an unexpected crack in La Internacional's united front, *La República* headlined the story.[119]

Tensions in the isthmus heightened when the Nicaraguans purchased twenty-five F-51 Mustang fighter planes from Sweden and the Venezuelan military sent a cache of arms to Managua. Throughout the fall, Nicaraguan planes repeatedly violated Costa Rican airspace, and its National Guard massed troops along the frontier.[120]

Woodward thought Figueres exhibited restraint out of justifiable concern for a domestic backlash. Any investigation would certainly dredge up his role in the April assassination attempt, providing grist for his opponents' political mill. "Such a censure would reawaken public disapproval within Costa Rica of suspected international meddling by the Figueres Government which seriously shook public confidence in the regime last summer." Figueres's reasoning for waiting to lodge a protest to the OAS, Woodward believed, was that it was better to wait "until such time as it is fairly certain that the potential attackers can be proved virtually flagrante delicto."[121]

Figueres did not have to wait long. On January 11, 1955, five hundred exiles, calling themselves the Authentic Anti-Communist Revolutionary Army, crossed into northwestern Costa Rica, occupied the village of La Cruz, and attacked nearby Villa Quesada. The rebels' plan was to move in undetected and declare this an "internal" rebellion, thereby muddying the OAS's jurisdiction in the matter. How credible such a claim would have been is debatable, given that Costa Rican authorities had for months warned of an invasion. But any hope of evading detection was blown when the Nicaraguan National Guard was caught red-handed airdropping arms and supplies to the rebels.

Tipping the Balance

On the day of the invasion a small rebel air force of three outdated World War II–era planes carried out bombing runs over several Costa Rican cities. The Calderonista rebels also set up a radio transmitter to broadcast messages that compared Figueres with Árbenz and urged Costa Ricans to join their cause.[122] The U.S. embassy reported that Costa Rican antiaircraft had shot down a plane said to have Venezuelan markings.[123] The Department (and the Costa Ricans) had good reason to suspect Venezuelan involvement. Warren cabled the Department that he had just met with Estrada, who refused to deny the presence of seven Venezuelan planes in Managua. Nor did he refute that those planes had carried arms, presumably for the rebels' use. The best the diplomat could extract from Estrada was a promise that "neither Nicaragua, [the] Dominican Republic [nor] Venezuela will send their soldiers into Costa Rica." But Estrada could not resist counting his chickens before they hatched. He told Warren that "Venezuela would recognize within two hours [the] new government following [the] overthrow [of] Figueres."[124]

AD, on the other hand, certainly felt that the Pérez Jiménez regime had been complicit. The CC issued a report confirming that Venezuelan airplanes had conducted bombing runs over Costa Rica's major cities. This was clear retaliation, the report claimed, for Figueres's decision not to send a delegation to Caracas.[125]

Somoza played innocent, publicly denying that he had anything to do with the exiles. But he admitted he was sorely tempted. Referring to the foiled assassination attempt in an interview with the *New York Times*, he declared that this was the first time in Latin American history that a president of one country "sent someone to assassinate another President." Trujillo's adversaries begged to differ. Somoza's first thought was to retaliate. "After all I am only human and the natural human reaction is to strike back when a man tries to kill you." Crying crocodile tears, he claimed to have resisted the impulse because "a great deal of innocent blood would have been shed."[126]

Pepe's boosters in the States again came to his aid. Berle cabled Dulles that he had made two trips to Costa Rica in the preceding months and had a good sense of the political climate there. There was no question in his mind that this was a "paramilitary operation from outside" and a clear violation of the Rio Pact. He urged Dulles to turn this matter over to the OAS peacekeeping machinery. "If the Rio Treaty does not work we shall inspire little confidence elsewhere in the world." In the aftermath of the intervention in Guatemala, it was especially crucial that the United States send the right signals: "all the hemisphere is watching the United States to see whether it will eventually line up with popular democracy or with a military dictatorship."[127]

In a public address to the nation, the Costa Rican ruler boasted that their cause was attracting widespread support all across the region. Hundreds of Colombian, Mexican, Cuban, and Puerto Rican soldiers returning from the Korean War "want to come and fight with us," and a campaign to recruit volunteers was underway in Havana. In Mexico City, "people are lining up outside our embassy asking how they can join our ranks." Ecuadorian soldiers, he added, also had inquired how they could enlist.[128] Meanwhile, the PRD leadership readied a contingent of Dominicans living in New York to join the battle, but federal authorities impeded their efforts. Instead, the Dominican exile organization organized a successful blood drive and staged several protests outside of Nicaragua's New York consulate.[129]

Faint echoes of Sandino's Latin American battalion resounded when a contingent of Cuban students traveled to Costa Rica in January to lend their support against the invaders, arriving just in time to fight on the northwestern front during the conflict's last days.[130] The head of the DRE, Echeverría, returned home inspired. Proclaiming itself democratic, strongly nationalistic, and anticommunist, the Directorio would play a pivotal role in the fight to oust Batista. In March 1956 Echeverría, whom Guerra describes as "the most dynamic central figure in civic mobilizations against Batista," gave a fiery speech, "Contra los dictadores de América" (Against America's Dictators), at an FEU meeting in the great hall of the University of Havana. He spoke eloquently of how this generation of student militants should pay homage to the ideas and deeds of Rodó, Ingenieros, and Sandino: "We, the men of America, the youth and students of Cuba, are not and should not be accomplices of tyrants. The solutions demanded by our America are not found in Inter-American conferences or false Pan-Americanism. . . . Here we are, the children of Ariel, the struggle of America is one and indissoluble! Whoever fights for freedom in Cuba is fighting against any dictatorship in America."[131]

With the outpouring of support for Costa Rica, Betancourt viewed this as a golden opportunity for reformers to press their advantage. He wrote the Costa Rican ambassador to the United States, Fernando Fournier Acuña, that this was the moment to "launch a major public opinion offensive in both Americas" on behalf of Costa Rica and the cause of democracy more generally. Exiled Adecos should lobby members of Latin American legislatures, intellectuals, and journalists, while Fournier must do the same in the United States. He underlined the urgency of his request by ending his missive with a reminder—"don't forget that the dictatorships have their own well-oiled lobbying machine."[132]

In a similar vein, on January 13, he wrote Romualdi, asking to schedule meetings with the presidents of the democratic labor movement in the United States (the AFL, the CIO, and the United Mine Workers). In his conversations, Romualdi should paint Costa Rica as a "victim of aggression," so as to elicit "public statements of support" from the leadership of these unions. The benefits of such affirmative statements, he predicted, would play well with Latin American labor unions and help to redress the strident criticism U.S. unions had taken for "following the flag" during the Guatemalan intervention. Romauldi carried out Betancourt's orders to a T; the very next day, the AFL issued a statement titled "Stop the War against Democratic Costa Rica!"[133]

As anticipated, Figueres requested urgent OAS assistance, accusing Nicaragua of a "systematic campaign of . . . aggression," support for the rebels, extensive anti-Costa Rican propaganda in its state-controlled media, troop movements along the border, and the closing of the San Juan River to its shipping. In response, the OAS quickly convened a five-member investigating team, which flew to San José two days later. A Costa Rican request for military assistance initially met with a mixed response from the OAS Council of Consultation; not surprisingly, it was the dictatorships, led by Perón's Argentina, that asked for a more measured response.[134]

But when it was learned that a Nicaraguan P-47 Thunderbolt was conducting bombing raids in Costa Rican territory, Figueres again asked the OAS team for additional aircraft to defend the country.[135] On the investigating team's recommendation, the Eisenhower administration agreed to sell Costa Rica four F-51 Mustangs for $1 apiece and hastily dispatched the planes from a Texas airbase. In a noticeable show of support for Figueres, the fighters were flown by U.S. Air Force pilots, who "gave Costa Rican pilots a crash course in handling the aircraft." Astonishingly, by the next day the Costa Rican airmen were flying sorties against the rebels. The administration also shipped three thousand rounds of .50-caliber antiaircraft ammunition from the Southern Zone Command to Costa Rica.[136]

The fighter planes and the added firepower helped offset Nicaragua's military advantage. With the rebels' positions no longer defensible, both sides agreed to stand down. The OAS team set up a "security zone" on both sides of the border so that the intruders could return to Nicaragua, where they "surrendered" to authorities. Knowing full well how this would play in Washington, Figueres showed his gratitude for the administration's support by rounding up "communist party members and sympathizers."[137] Ironically, the administration's timely decision to provide aircraft to Costa Rica was one of the few times that U.S. military assistance was utilized to defend a nation against external aggression. Despite express restrictions to the contrary, the region's militaries invariably made use of the arms and equipment they received to combat internal threats.[138]

One factor that influenced Washington's decision to take sides was the proximity of the conflict to the Panama Canal. Adding to the uncertainty was that Panama, at that very moment, was in crisis. Just ten days before the Calderonista invasion, Remón was assassinated. Whatever conflicting signals the administration may have sent Costa Rica and Nicaragua during the summer and fall of 1954, there is little doubt that its timely decision to send arms and airplanes to Costa Rica once hostilities began helped bring an end to the crisis.[139]

Moderates across the region rallied around Figueres. An editorial in *Bohemia* praised the "resolute" Costa Rican president for standing up to La Internacional. Settling this dispute was a significant test for the OAS, which "not that long ago watched helplessly as Guatemala was overrun." There were no excuses this time, because unlike Guatemala, where "Árbenz's tolerance of communists was the pretext," Figueres's anticommunist credentials were unimpeachable.[140]

Galíndez was thrilled. In his syndicated column the usually measured, analytical commentator crowed that this an undisputed triumph for democracy. He noted that he had waited to write until the outcome was decided because he did not want his longtime friendship with Figueres to "cloud my judgment." But this turn of events was worth celebrating; it was "the first great victory for the democratic cause . . . in a long time." He was heartened by the numbers of volunteers coming forward in Latin American capitals, and he congratulated the OAS and the United States for their roles in ending the conflict. "If this precedent becomes a tradition," he added with tongue firmly in cheek, "perhaps democrats should express their gratitude to Nicaragua's dictator."[141]

One unresolved question was whether Somoza, as a reward for his assistance with the Guatemalan coup, had received the go-ahead from the CIA to launch the invasion of Costa Rica. Figueres, Berle, and Woodward definitely thought so. Berle was dubious about the administration's motives. He wrote in his diary that Somoza had felt "he had an open season to do what he liked." Although he had no proof, it was not out of the realm of possibility that the "CIA in talking to Somoza might have intimated that as a quid pro quo for help [with Guatemala], the United States would be philosophical about a venture into Costa Rica."[142]

Figueres later accused CIA pilots of aiding the Calderonistas: "the same mercenary aviators who took part in the attack on Guatemala" ran

sorties and strafed "eleven defenseless towns in our territory." The airmen, who flew some of the same planes that were used in Operation PB-
SUCCESS, Pepe surmised, felt indebted to Somoza for his assistance in
ousting Árbenz. It is possible that familial ties may have had something
to do with it. One of the CIA's pilots who had participated in the Guatemalan campaign had married into the Calderón Guardia family.[143]

At a time when the State Department came to the aid of the Costa
Ricans, CIA agents were apparently working at cross-purposes, materially
contributing to the rebel cause. It is hard to imagine that the administration's willingness to assist both sides in the conflict was unintentional.
Somoza had been a loyal ally; Figueres was no innocent. If not for the criticism the United States received for the Guatemalan intervention, it was not
a given that the administration would have helped Costa Rica. As Matthews
related, the State Department may have wanted an end to hostilities between the neighboring countries, but it "had no intention of antagonizing
dictators in Venezuela, Nicaragua, the Dominican Republic and Cuba."[144]

Pepe took some solace in the support he received from the OAS. As
the historian Kirk Bowman has argued, the abolition of the military seven
years earlier redounded to Figueres's benefit. If Costa Rica had retained
its military—as weak as it was—the OAS would have been less likely to
get involved. It also denied the CIA an opportunity to sow the seeds of
dissatisfaction within a military, as it was wont to do elsewhere. On the
other hand, the absence of armed forces probably encouraged domestic
opposition to Figueres to ally itself with the Somoza-backed rebels.[145]

Privately, in a letter that was circulated to his friends a few weeks
after the ceasefire, Figueres waxed philosophical about the "mutual misunderstanding" resulting from the "victory of the democratic forces."
Whereas Latin Americans were by and large hopeful that the U.S. was
"leaning toward the democratic side," he lamented that many in the U.S.
"were not even aware of this fight." Offended by suggestions that he
meet with Somoza, Figueres admitted to "mixed feelings" about how the
conflict had ended. While grateful for U.S. assistance, he did not think
that the administration understood "the magnitude of the victory it has
achieved." He correctly predicted that the State Department and the
OAS would attempt to "hush the whole affair."[146]

The investigative team's report concluded that Costa Rica was the victim of aggression, but it refused to assess responsibility. The team understood that neither party was blameless. But there was more to its decision
not to cast aspersions. In early February 1955, the Ecuadorian member of

the OAS team, José Chiriboga, privately explained to Holland why their report had tread so carefully. Yes, "there was no doubt that Somoza was guilty of aggression," and he was convinced that the dictator, of whom he was personally "very fond," would continue his efforts to overthrow the Figueres government "in some new form until it was overthrown." But "branding him as an aggressor might not only be resented in Nicaragua," he explained. Here, Chiriboga was alluding to La Internacional. There was insufficient evidence, however, to implicate the other dictatorships in its report. More importantly, this was a "time of trial" for the fledgling peace-keeping organization, and it was incumbent upon the investigating team to "find the magic formula" that would protect "the OAS' prestige . . . without irrevocably alienating some of its members."[147]

Chiriboga's observation about La Internacional's sensitivity on this matter was accurate. Three days after his conversation with Holland, the Venezuelan foreign minister, Aureliano Otáñez, told Bernbaum that his nation would strongly repudiate the report if it concluded that "foreign intervention had been involved." If Venezuela—or other countries for that matter—were implicated, his country "would be supported in its attitude by a sufficiently large number of other countries to create a serious split, jeopardizing the future of the OAS."[148]

Holland agreed with the team's decision to shield the details of the rivals' headlong actions. In return, the assistant secretary of state pressed the two heads of state for a face-to-face meeting, where they could publicly make a display of burying the hatchet. Holland hoped that Nixon, who was about to undertake a goodwill tour through the Caribbean and Central America, could play peacemaker and broker such an encounter. Berle was called upon to be an interlocutor between the two heads of state, a move that he later regretted, because he put his friend Figueres in a no-win situation. Don Pepe, however, had little interest in meeting with Somoza, especially since pockets of resistance remained in the countryside until well into February. Nixon instead met with each leader separately. Platitudes were agreed to, but little was resolved.[149]

Figueres was upset that the U.S. had used its influence to persuade the OAS not to issue sanctions or to condemn Nicaragua, Venezuela, and the Dominican Republic for their precipitous actions. The administration missed a golden opportunity to take a principled stand against dictatorship, the Costa Rican president claimed.[150]

The OAS's reluctance to condemn either party satisfied no one. Even Ulate's newspaper expressed outrage with the OAS report. *El Dia-*

Costa Rican President José Figueres (right), Vice President Richard Nixon, and Assistant Secretary of State for Inter-American Affairs Henry Holland, c. 1955. Courtesy of Bill Holland.

rio de Costa Rica argued that by absolving the Nicaraguan head of state of any responsibility when he had permitted the Calderonistas to train on his soil, the commission was encouraging him to plot again. In fact, "the whole report appears to have been carefully worded in order not to annoy or displease the ruler of Nicaragua." The same held true for Figueres. As a result, "both countries will continue to suffer."[151]

Over the course of the next few weeks, critics were quick to point out the glaring inconsistencies in U.S. foreign policy. Pedro Gringoire's column in *Excélsior* made the case that Washington was reaping what it had sowed. First it had armed the militaries, and then it had sent arms to Costa Rica to defend itself. Washington must have realized that tyrants who made use of those weapons to repress their own people were an inherent threat to the stability of the region's democracies.[152] Another column lamented the ripple effects of the Guatemalan coup, which had destabilized the isthmus. The result was "the sorry sight of the United States trying to silence its own weapons in Central America."[153]

The Costa Rican leader may have been upset that the CIA and the State Department were not on the same page, but Somoza had every right to feel betrayed by his patrons. On January 20, 1955, his ambassador Sevilla Sacasa hand-delivered a forceful note from the dictator to the Department requesting that the administration sell Nicaragua four F-51s, on the same terms as it had to Costa Rica. Given his "great distrust" of Figueres, it was imperative that his country be prepared to defend itself. At a meeting with officers from the Bureau of Inter-American Affairs and the Offices of Regional American Affairs and Middle American Affairs, Sevilla Sacasa "pled at great length and with great emotion along the lines that the United States' friendship with Nicaragua was at a test." Department officials reminded him that even with the recent shipment of aircraft to Costa Rica, Nicaragua had a significantly larger air force than its neighbor.[154]

In the aftermath of the failed invasion, the Venezuelans engaged in a startling degree of finger-pointing, considering their complicity. The chargé d'affaires in its embassy in Managua told his counterpart in the U.S. embassy that the rebel leadership was incompetent and that his government was "dissatisfied with the part played in the attempt by President Somoza." After relating how his nation's military had transported a number of Costa Rican rebels from Venezuela to take part in the "revolution," he assured the North American diplomat that "the matter is by no means over and cannot be as long as Figueres is President and he and Rómulo Betancourt continue to be a threat" to his government. A North American diplomat in the Caracas embassy later confirmed the Venezuelan government's displeasure with Somoza, and not just "for bungling the invasion." It was convinced that the Nicaraguan dictator had pocketed a "goodly share of their recent contribution to that effort."[155]

The Venezuelans and their Calderonista allies were unwilling to let matters rest. The following spring a Honduran national, Abraham Perry Becker Borjas, who had met with Calderonista leaders on two occasions in California and Nicaragua in 1955, was hired to carry out an audacious, if poorly designed, attack on Figueres, his vice president, a member of his cabinet, and Ulate. Becker Borjas was to disguise himself as a priest, gain entrance to the archbishop's residence in San José, and then, at knifepoint, demand that Monsignor Rubén Odío call the president's office to set up an immediate meeting with Figueres and the others. Nothing went according to plan and Costa Rican authorities easily foiled the plot. According to Dominican diplomats, the money for the scheme, came from Pérez Jiménez.[156]

The threats would keep coming, reformers insisted, until the United States pressured the dictatorships to stop plotting. Indeed, Washington employed a double standard when it came to democrats and dictators. While Estrada was given the red-carpet treatment in the United States, policymakers in Washington considered the exile leadership disruptive and requiring of constant surveillance. After the U.S. pressured Betancourt to leave Costa Rica, he moved to San Juan, but even as a guest of Muñoz Marín he was subject to monitoring by U.S. authorities and harassment from La Internacional.

In February 1956, U.S. officials informed the Venezuelan that they had credible intelligence of a plot to murder him. To protect Betancourt and his family, Muñoz moved them to a small cottage on a peninsula a short distance from the capital. The property, surrounded by a high fence, "was buttressed by guard posts manned by police."[157] Betancourt and his allies brushed off the threat, but the State Department, as it had done before in Costa Rica, began to work on an exit strategy for the Venezuelan.

Perhaps not so coincidentally, the Department received complaints from Pérez Jiménez and Trujillo that Betancourt was plotting an insurrection from Puerto Rico. If true, that was a violation of U.S. neutrality laws. With plans in the works for Figueres, Grant, Romauldi, and Muñoz Marín to meet with Betancourt in San Juan, Holland decided that even the appearance of such a summit among five prominent leaders of the democratic movement would elicit a bellicose response from La Internacional. The reformers strenuously objected to a State Department plan to force Betancourt to leave the island. They insisted that the meeting was not to foment rebellion, but to organize a second Interamerican Conference on Democracy and Freedom. It was crucial that Betancourt, the leading light of the democratic movement, be present for the planning meetings, they argued.[154] In a letter to George Meany, Monge intimated that Pérez Jiménez and Trujillo had concocted the story in the first place as a pretext meant to "flush Rómulo Betancourt out [of Puerto Rico] to get him to a country where political assassination can be practiced more easily." Pepe registered concern about Betancourt's suggested landing spot, Mexico City. He wrote Alexander, "Once he is there, Pedro Estrada's thugs will not have any difficulty assassinating him."[159]

In protest, Grant and Romualdi promptly cancelled their trips.[160] Figueres sent an angry note to Holland that although he was sure that the State Department's decision was well intended, it was outrageous that "the Venezuelan gestapo has the power to harass democratic leaders even when they are in a U.S. territory." Why was it that the State Department was so willing to appease dictators "at the expense of democratic friends?"[161]

This did not sit well with the assistant secretary of state, who refused to answer the note or meet with Fournier. Figueres must have appeared ungrateful to Holland, since the Department had just sided with Costa Rica during the recent flare-up with Nicaragua. Pepe, though, was just as miffed. While grateful for the U.S. support against his neighbor, he privately wrote Alexander that he found it hard to believe that Somoza "would have prepared the invasion if he didn't have a green light from some people . . . in the Government of the United States."[162]

Pepe's visit went on as scheduled, but Muñoz Marín took the hint and left the island for the duration of Figueres's visit. It was an uncomfortable situation for all concerned, especially for the governor, who had invited the Costa Rican president in the first place. Pepe bemoaned his good friend's plight in a letter to Alexander. The governor, who was a frequent target of La Internacional because Puerto Rico's door remained open to the refugees, was caught between a rock and a hard place. On the one hand, he needed to remain on good terms with his patrons in Washington to get what he needed for the island, but his commitment to the cause of democracy in the region and his unfailing "friendship and loyalty" to reformers, put him at odds with policymakers. When Washington so publicly undercut his authority, as it did in this case, Pepe lamented, "they undermine our struggle, and once again they weaken this great man."[163]

Trujillo trod carefully when it came to Muñoz. He knew how well thought of he was in Washington. Instead, the Dominican general instructed his loyalists in the Congress and in the press to attack the Puerto Rican leader obliquely. An editorial in the Trujillo-funded newspaper *El Diario de Nueva York* titled "Política peligrosa" (Dangerous Policy) allowed that while Muñoz served his people well and was an inspiration to other Latin American leaders, he also was guilty of "directly intervening in the internal affairs of other American nations." In a similar vein, B. Carroll Reese, former chair of the Republican National Committee and a congressman from Tennessee, carped that Muñoz's position as the "highest-ranking representative" of a territory made such meddling especially problematic for the U.S. government.[164]

Betancourt was an easier target. The offensive included a speech in defense of Trujillo on the floor of the Senate by Russell Long (Democrat-Louisiana), while other supporters of the generalissimo in the House and the Senate lashed out against the Puerto Rican leader for harboring "adventurers" and "communists" like the "sinister" Betancourt.[165]

In the face of such criticism, Figueres felt it important to show his support for his two friends. "The State Department does not comprehend that there is a brotherhood of democrats in the hemisphere." Yes, Latin America is powerless to "do anything, without the United States," he added, "but the United States has to have a creative and positive attitude toward Latin America."[166]

Despite the administration's best efforts, Betancourt returned to San Juan in April 1956 and within a month, still another plot to assassinate him was reported. Pérez got wind of the scheme, which included an unusual degree of cooperation between Ciudad Trujillo, Caracas, and Havana. In May 1956, Estrada and twenty members of the SN flew to the Dominican Republic. This trip finalized plans to eliminate the AD chief first and then to go after Figueres. As part of the discussions, Pérez Jiménez agreed to broker a truce between Batista and Trujillo. Trujillo put up half a million dollars to hire Cuban hitmen, who, along with Estrada's agents, would abduct Betancourt in San Juan and bring him not to Venezuela but to Ciudad Trujillo. This would follow the same script employed by the Dominicans two months earlier when Galíndez vanished.[167] Pérez felt there was a direct correlation between the United States' dithering in its investigation of the Galíndez case and how emboldened Trujillo and other members of La Internacional had become of late.[168]

Pérez also conveyed what he knew about the threat to Allan Stewart at the U.S. embassy in San José. In a memo to his superiors titled "Alleged Plot to Assassinate Rómulo Betancourt," the diplomat relayed that Pérez was alarmed "because Trujillo is thorough when he enters upon any adventure." Apparently, he added, the Venezuelan head of state was also playing peacemaker to resolve a dispute between the Dominican

Los Tres Amigos: José Figueres, Luis Muñoz Marín, and Rómulo Betancourt.
Courtesy Fundación Luis Muñoz Marín, San Juan, Puerto Rico.

ruler and Somoza. Trujillo was said to be irate over how his Nicaraguan
counterpart had bungled the January 1955 invasion of Costa Rica and
kept funds meant for the Calderonistas. Now, owing to Pérez Jiménez's
intercession, Stewart could report that "the differences among the four
dictators . . . have been resolved."[169]

Pérez pleaded with Betancourt to take this plot seriously, since the
scheme had all the resources—financial and material—needed to complete the job. "This news is absolutely reliable, take precautions." In addition, he discouraged his mentor from agreeing to interviews, especially
with Cubans who might have ties to Dominican or Venezuelan officials,
and he promised to alert Puerto Rican authorities. Betancourt again
downplayed the plot, and in a letter to Grant pointed to the irony of
Pérez Jiménez's whining that civilian governments should not allow a

safe harbor for exiles like him when he had just given political asylum to the recently deposed Perón.[170]

Betancourt left Puerto Rico for the second time in a matter of months in the fall of 1956, not because of the threat to his life but because he learned that the House Un-American Activities Committee, which included Republican members supportive of the Venezuelan strongman, was on its way to the island to interrogate him, as well as Puerto Rican politicians.[171] Betancourt thought it would be "humiliating" for a former president of Venezuela and the head of one of its most prominent political parties to testify. Certainly, his past membership in the Costa Rican Communist Party would come up in the hearings. The circus-like proceedings, he fretted, also could have consequences for his own party. Given the divisions within AD, some members might use the hearings to undercut him. As it was, youthful elements were desirous of fraternizing with communists, and many were only too willing to criticize Washington, something Betancourt was anxious to head off, so as not to jeopardize his efforts to win the backing of the Eisenhower administration. Finally, at a time when by all rights the struggle to overthrow Pérez Jiménez must occupy all their energies, his testifying before HUAC would be an unnecessary sideshow. "It would be absurd," he wrote Grant and Romualdi, to have to "dedicate time and energy to a marginal battle. . . . I cannot and ought not subject myself to such a shameful humiliation." He packed up his books and papers and departed for Mexico.[172]

Betancourt may have tried to put the best face on his perilous situation, but he also took precautions. After receiving death threats from Trujillo's minions during a short stay in New York in the fall of 1957, he asked Muñoz Marín to contact Immigration Services to ask for a license to carry a handgun. After the governor put in a good word for him, Immigration Services requested a permit for Betancourt from the New York City Police Department. Later, Betancourt thanked Muñoz, joking that although he thought the danger overblown, his friends were "always worried about a 'Galindazo.' " Nevertheless, he took no chances, changing where he spent the night frequently during his stay in New York.[173]

Meanwhile, Figueres's allies were dwindling. Betancourt, Prío, and Arévalo had all been removed from power. Costa Rica could objectively count on support from only three small countries with progressive governments—Bolivia, Uruguay, and Ecuador.[174] Figueres's brash personality and principled stands made him a lightning rod at home and abroad. His critics claimed that by assisting Nicaraguan exiles he had precipitated the crisis and now he was taking full advantage to silence the domestic opposition. When *La Nación* reported that Echandi had had a hand in the invasion, rabidly nationalistic Ticos burned down the politician's office, and "he was beaten and nearly lynched." Such extremism helped turn public opinion against Figueres. A congressional investigation into whether Echandi's and another congressional deputy's actions were treasonous dragged on for months, polarizing the body politic and leading some to the conclusion that Figueres's administration was guilty of a witch hunt.[175]

A chastened Figueres made public gestures suggesting that he was willing to refrain from future adventurism. Under the aegis of the OAS, he opened negotiations with Somoza. The result was an agreement to monitor activities of the rebels and to resolve disputes amicably. Surprisingly, Costa Rica even resumed diplomatic relations with the Dominican Republic and Nicaragua, and in March 1955, Pepe sent a representative to a UN-sponsored conference on social security in Caracas, almost a year to the day after his refusal to attend the inter-American meetings.[176]

But he refused to normalize relations with the Pérez Jiménez regime, not until the dictator made some gesture to address the "insult" of the June leaflet-dropping incident, Foreign Minister Mario Esquivel informed Woodward. More to the point, a Costa Rican official told embassy staffer Alex Cohen that his government believed that if Costa Rica resumed relations, the Venezuelan embassy would, along with Nicaragua's embassy, "become another center for plotting." The feeling was apparently mutual in Venezuela. The State Department concluded in May 1955 that "prospects for a resumption of normal relations appear slim, at least for the near future." As late as that fall, Cohen thought that Costa Rican rebels training in Nicaragua still enjoyed "moral, material and financial support from Pedro Estrada."[177]

It was easy to chalk up the border war between Costa Rica and Nicaragua as just another chapter in the ongoing personal feud between two heads of state. Nixon surely did, dismissing it as "a personal feud between two men, neither of whom was quite big enough to run his own country and both of whom were ambitious to run all the other countries in the Caribbean area." Of the two leaders, the vice president had a somewhat higher opinion of the dictator because he "really desires to do what the United States wants him to do. Figueres, on the other hand, merely wants to do what he thinks is most advantageous."[178] After Nixon's visit to Managua and San José, he continued on to Ciudad Trujillo, where, addressing a joint session of the Dominican Congress, he graciously thanked a contemptible regime "for combatting the pernicious forces of communism."[179]

Conclusions

It was during Nixon's trip through the Caribbean in 1955 that he coined a phrase that became a future talking point for the administration. In response to criticism that Washington preferred to ally itself with dictatorships, Nixon recommended an "*abrazo* for democrats and a formal handshake for dictators." To his way of thinking, making such a distinction signaled the administration's clear preference for democratic rule. Critics would remark that such gestures, while better than the alternative, rang hollow as long as military and economic assistance gave despots the resources they needed to prolong their rule. Yes, symbols were important, reformers allowed, but actions spoke far louder. And what good was a correct handshake, his critics insisted, when in the next breath the vice president deigned to compare the "remarkable" Batista to Abraham Lincoln, as he did at a state dinner in Havana. While it was true that both leaders came from humble beginnings, that's where the comparison ended. Such gratuitous remarks cost the Eisenhower administration dearly in the court of Latin American public opinion.[180]

Betancourt's outspokenness continued to draw unwanted attention. In May 1955, he received word of the tragic death of his longtime compatriot Eloy Blanco, who was killed in a car accident in Mexico City. A memorial was planned, and Betancourt, who was then living in San Juan, was asked to deliver the eulogy. Just as he was about to leave the island, he received unsettling news from Mexico City's chief of police, who had received intelligence that SN agents were on their way from Venezuela to Mexico with orders to murder him. Sadly, he remained in Puerto Rico, unable to attend his good friend's funeral.[181]

Still, by the end of 1955, Betancourt and his peers had reason to be optimistic. "The dictatorial tide is regressing," he confided to his compatriot "Juan." Perón had been deposed, a military coup in Brazil had failed, Batista was "in crisis," in Peru students and workers had taken to the streets in protest the policies of the dictator Odría, and "even in Somozaland, there are rumors of rebellion."[182] Authoritarian regimes found themselves increasingly on the defensive by the middle of the decade.[183]

CHAPTER THIRTEEN

Latin America's Representative in the U.S. Congress

Dictators are like cyclists; when they stop pedaling, they fall.

—ATTRIBUTED TO SPANISH PRIME MINISTER ANTONIO MAURA
MONTANER

IN THE SPRING OF 1957, Representative Charles Porter received an unusual offer in the mail from an admirer in Latin America, one too good to pass up. An inspector for the last twenty-five years for the Cuban Electric Company in Havana, Héctor Consuegra Lima, was so appreciative of the congressman's willingness to speak out against the Eisenhower administration's coddling of dictators that he offered him a specially made gun holster gratis. He had read an article in Havana's *El Mundo* that the lawmaker was now carrying a firearm for protection to his office on the Hill. The District of Columbia police warned Porter not to make light of the "threatening letters and anonymous phone calls" he was receiving. "Even a congressman should not consider himself immune from the long arm of Trujillo's vengeance."[1]

Proud to inform Porter that he had invented a "complete carrier and two-loader," the inspector said he would be delighted to send one as a "GIFT, entirely free of charge to you . . . without any commercial publicity motives" (caps in original). Up to now, building this device had been a hobby, but Consuegra Lima would be honored if the young politician accepted one. He'd be only too happy to mail or hand-deliver it. Perhaps there was someone Porter knew who lived in Havana? Or if not, he'd drop it off at "the American embassy." His loader was guaranteed to increase the firing volume of Porter's two-inch barrel Colt handgun by five hundred percent, he boasted. It "loads in two or three seconds. . . . It's so easy a child or a blind man can use it." Porter accepted the inspector's kind offer, even providing specifics about his snub-nosed .38 revolver in his reply.[2]

Given Trujillo's notorious track record of plots to assassinate Latin American heads of state, it is an open question whether he would have tried to eliminate a U.S. politician. An ominous unsigned letter Porter received from a supporter of the tyrant certainly seemed to suggest so: "Mr. Parker [sic], better stop your pushing against Trujillo, you maybe have an accident. . . . Even in your condition of a congressman, a fight against the chief is too dangerous. Trujillo has enough money to buy your body in the same way he bought the bodies of Galíndez [and] Requena."[3]

It was the FBI that first encouraged Porter to carry a firearm. The Capitol Police and their law enforcement colleagues in the District of Columbia arrived at the same conclusion. Porter consented to carry the gun, but at first tried to keep it from his family, so as not to alarm them. But an aide leaked the story, defying the representative's instructions.[4]

Extraordinary precautions were taken for a session of the House in late February 1957 when Porter first revealed the threat against his life: gallery passes to Dominicans were denied; tours of the House side of the Capitol building were cancelled for the day; and plainclothes police were positioned in the galleries.[5]

Months later Porter admitted that he had stopped packing the gun, but not because the danger had passed. "I decided that if anyone was determined enough to kill me, I could not completely protect myself whatever I did."[6] He continued to speak out, despite the risk. In fact, he had just returned from a trip to Puerto Rico, where he attracted enthusiastic crowds and favorable press. He delivered a fiery speech at the University of Puerto Rico that had Dominican exiles cheering him on. "If I were a Dominican, I'd be a revolutionary," he told a rapt audience. "This would be true if I were a Pole, a Hungarian, a Russian, [or] a Czechoslovakian."[7]

His return to Washington was not as affirming. A colleague from across the aisle admonished Porter for exercising poor judgment in agreeing to meet with "dissident, disjointed and frustrated Dominican expatriates." But what really "sickened and appalled" Rep. Reese was the incendiary content of the upstart lawmaker's remarks. To which Porter had a retort at the ready: "I suppose our American revolutionaries could have been so described. ... Do I foment revolution against dictators? Yes, gladly and will until I die. Trujillo has been emboldened by the respectability accorded him by many Americans ... our coddling of dictators south of the border has already cost us dearly in prestige and capacity for leadership in Latin America."[8]

Liberals like Porter lifted up their voices at an opportune moment for Latin American reformers. Between 1952 and 1961, ten dictators either stepped down voluntarily or were driven from office. Except for a shared aversion to communism, the liberal critique of the Eisenhower administration's policy differed from the peace progressives of the 1920s and 1930s. The Borahs, Shipsteads, and Wheelers of that earlier era spoke out against U.S. intervention and played their part in bringing an end to the era of gunboat diplomacy, but they said little about the Harding, Coolidge, and Hoover administrations' propping up of regional strongmen. During the late 1950s, liberals in Congress, the labor movement, the press, and academia not only signaled their displeasure with the administration's nonintervention policy, which, they contended, only strengthened the hand of autocrats, but they advocated for civilian rule. With dictators falling by the wayside, progressive politicians on both sides of the border had reason to believe that democracy was finally on the march.

Porter's meteoric rise from relative obscurity could not have happened without the assistance of the region's reformers. Their alliance was not just a mutual admiration society; by mid-1958, Porter and his Latin American allies succeeded in putting the Eisenhower administration on the defensive. This chapter explores Porter's ascendancy, his embrace of the reformist agenda, and the limits of the liberal critique of U.S. foreign policy. His emergence occurred at a pivotal moment, just as Venezuela and Colombia were transitioning from authoritarianism to democratic rule. A closer examination of such "pacted" or consociational democracies illustrates why civilian rule was so tenuous in mid-twentieth-century Latin America. Policymakers in Washington were mindful of the implications of the democratic wave, but of two minds about how to respond. The democratic transitions in Colombia and Venezuela, in particular, influenced the administration's initial wait-and-see response to the Cuban Revolution.

One-Man FBI

It must have struck the congressman as odd that within a year of being sworn in as the junior member of his state's delegation he was now touted as "Latin America's Representative in the U.S. Congress." Nothing in his past had prepared him for such a role. The first Democrat to carry the Fourth District in seventy-five years, the bespectacled, thirty-seven-year-old attorney spoke no Spanish, and other than a brief stint reporting for the *Yank* (a weekly published by the U.S. Army) while briefly stationed in the Canal Zone during World War II, he had little in the way of firsthand experience. (Although, as he fondly recalled, he did acquire a taste for Cuban cigars while stationed in Panama). Nor was he given an opportunity to serve on the House Subcommittee on Inter-American Affairs, a post that would have given him valuable exposure to the region.[9]

In a 1986 oral history, Porter explained how a foreclosure on the family home during the Great Depression contributed to his pronounced sense of moral outrage. His father, who worked a number of jobs for the Southern Pacific Railroad, had his hours cut and could no longer afford to pay the mortgage. That his "hardworking, deserving" dad should have his home taken from him through no fault of his own—a house he had built himself—seemed patently unfair to the youngster, and kindled an early interest in a career in public service.[10]

Images seared into his mind while walking through Buchenwald, Dachau, and Auschwitz during the last days of World War II had an impact as well. Serving as a war crimes special investigator for the European Theater of Operations, his visits to the camps left an indelible mark. He recoiled in horror at seeing the cages where prison guards kept well-fed monkeys while prisoners were left to starve. "He rarely talked about the camps and never talked about what he saw in them, though he did say he could never get their images out of his mind," his son Samuel related in his eulogy at his father's funeral in 2006.[11]

As a result of what he witnessed in Europe, Porter became an early proponent of arms control and nuclear disarmament. During his first, unsuccessful run for the House in 1954, he called for Communist China's admittance into the United Nations. He was convinced that the achievement of a lasting peace could only be realized if all the great powers were present at the negotiating table. Although polling indicated that his constituents disagreed, he continued to advocate for China's inclusion into the international organization.[12]

Were it not for pressing constituent business, it is highly unlikely that he would have taken on the role of denigrator-in-chief of the administration's Latin American policy. In fact, when the case that turned his career upside down came about, just two months after he was sworn in as a representative, he initially paid it little heed. It was not until nine months after the disappearance of Galíndez, when the parents of a twenty-three-old pilot from Eugene approached him for assistance in locating their son, who had gone missing in the Dominican Republic, that he first became aware of the scandal. The Murphys' son, Gerald, employed by Dominican National Airlines, had vanished, his recently purchased, brand-new convertible found abandoned "on a cliff overlooking shark-infested waters" near a slaughterhouse in Ciudad Trujillo. As was the case with Galíndez, Murphy's body was never found.[13]

It was soon apparent that the disappearances were linked; the FBI revealed that the young pilot had rented a Beechcraft plane for eight hundred dollars in cash and then flown the aircraft carrying the Columbia University professor from Amityville, New York to the Dominican Republic. Nor were Galíndez and Murphy the only ones murdered, pronounced dead, or who disappeared in the cover-up. Also dead under mysterious circumstances—all within a four-month span in late 1956— were the fellow pilot who flew the last leg of the flight from Monte Cristi to Ciudad Trujillo, the nurse attending to the drugged dissident, a night watchman on duty at the airport where the plane took off, a mechanic at the West Palm Beach airport where the Beechcraft refueled, and the young pilot's best friend on the island, the man Murphy regarded as his "protector," intelligence chief Colonel Salvador Cobían Parra.[14] It was, however, the disappearance of his constitutent—the affable young flyboy who, by some reports, "knew too much"—that prompted Porter to investigate the case.

Murphy may have been naïve, but he was no innocent. Dominican authorities paid him the very handsome sum of ten thousand dollars to transport the professor to the island. Less known was that just two months before he vanished the pilot also was a willing participant in Trujillo's attempt to destabilize the Batista regime, first by conducting a reconnaissance mission near Santiago de Cuba to determine if Dominican C-46 planes could successfully land somewhere near the city; then by hand-delivering thirty thousand dollars and explosives to a contact at the University of Havana. The pilot's fiancée, Sally Caire, later told U.S. authorities that Murphy had mentioned that the funds and explosives were destined for the 26th of July movement (a charge that Castro heatedly denied). Other accounts, however, have it that the delivery went to members of the DRE. In either case, Trujillo's "contribution" paid dividends that October when the head of Cuban military intelligence, Antonio Blanco Rico, and two other military officers were gunned down as they were leaving Meyer Lansky's Montmartre nightclub and casino in Havana.[15] Murphy's surreptitious activities in Cuba were subsequently corroborated by J. Edgar Hoover in an update on the investigation that he filed with Brownell.[16]

In Porter's telling, the young pilot was not complicit in Galíndez's abduction; instead, he was kept in the dark about his mission by his handlers. Murphy was "gentle, conscientious, honest . . . a splendid young man."[17] Once he had learned the particulars of the crime, Porter was consumed by the case—not only seeking justice for the family but assuming the role of moral conscience of the House of Representatives, at least as it related to U.S policy in the region. The congressman was stumped by the administration's reluctance to confront the dictator about his many transgressions. "In a few short weeks, my files bulge" with examples of Trujillo's "dogged pursuit of his opponents. . . . What must the FBI files be like?" he wondered out loud.[18]

One journalist captured Porter's take-no-prisoners style well: a "lean, livewire type with a lot of nervous energy, a gift for the fluent phrase and a share of natural cockiness, he was born to heckle, speak his mind . . . and give hell to the other side."[19] Unfortunately, his brash demeanor and a conspicuous lack of deference did little to endear him to his colleagues in the House—on either side of the aisle. His flouting of convention prompted Speaker of the House Sam Rayburn (Democrat-Texas) to deadpan near the end of Porter's first term: "My, you've been evident." Undeterred, the upstart later admonished future speaker John McCormack (Democrat-Massachusetts) for accepting a "medal at a champagne supper at the Dominican embassy." There were consequences for such impertinence. His request to serve on the House Foreign Affairs Committee at the start of his second term was ignored. Instead, he was buried on the Post Office and Civil Service Committee, a staffer recalled.[20]

"Never at a loss for words, or causes," Porter did not have to look far for a role model.[21] His political mentor, Senator Wayne Morse, best known for his early opposition to the Vietnam War, was an unconventional maverick. Elected to the Senate as a Republican in 1944, Morse left the party in 1952 over his opposition to McCarthyite witch hunts.

Convinced that the party had been hijacked by dangerous extremists, Morse was one of seven Republicans to sign Margaret Chase Smith's "Declaration of Conscience." Like an earlier generation's "conscience of the Senate," Borah, the "egoistical, fiercely ambitious" Morse prided himself on his contrarian nature. For instance, he set a record in 1953 by filibustering on the floor of the Senate for 22 hours and 26 minutes (without a bathroom break). According to his biographer, Morse was "too argumentative, too self-centered, [and] too ready to assail colleagues" to scale Borah's political heights. Although Morse became a polarizing figure in the national arena, in the short run he was a boon for Oregon's moribund Democratic Party. After decades in the political wilderness, the party, Porter included, swept to victory at the polls on their senator's coattails in 1956. Nicknamed the Tiger of the Senate, Morse ultimately served ten years in that chamber as a Republican, two as an independent, and twelve as a Democrat.[22]

Porter idolized the irascible Morse. Meanwhile, the senator helped raise funds for Porter's campaigns and contributed one thousand dollars of his own money to the representative's coffers. He also took the political newcomer under his wing. Until they parted ways over policy toward Cuba, Porter was very solicitous of his mentor. "It is my hope that, with guidance from experienced friends like yourself," Porter wrote Morse," I'll ... have a better opportunity to reflect on ... the great issues coming before Congress, I certainly don't want to be a disappointment to you."[23]

The two were on the same page when it came to the administration's policy toward dictators. As chair of the Subcommittee on Latin America of the Senate Foreign Relations Committee, Morse held hearings in which he repeatedly jousted with State Department officials. To his way of thinking, "the major cause of the trouble we are having with the other republics of the western hemisphere is due to the support we gave for many years to right-wing dictators in these countries."[24] He pointedly questioned Rubottom during his confirmation hearings in early 1957 about policymakers' pandering to the Trujillos of the hemisphere. The senator also objected to the administration's exclusive emphasis on trade and private capital to promote Latin American development, questioning why the region received so little foreign aid in comparison to other global hot spots.[25] In this, he was not alone; a growing number of Democratic colleagues, including Fulbright, Albert Gore, Sr., Humphrey, George Aitken, George Smathers, and Frank Church, argued that funds earmarked for bilateral military assistance would be put to much better use addressing

President Kennedy meets with Charles O. Porter of Oregon in
the Oval Office, August 16, 1961. Abbie Rowe. White House
Photographs. John F. Kennedy Presidential Library and
Museum, Boston, MA.

the region's social and economic needs. Another young Democrat, John
Kennedy, his eyes on a presidential run, disagreed; although the arms
were of little strategic use against the Soviets, they were useful as a carrot
that could ensure the loyalty of Latin America's militaries.[26]

Porter may have lacked Morse's seniority, but he was no less cantankerous. A local political commentator remarked that in a short span the
student had surpassed his teacher in sheer obstinacy. "In a mere four
years in Congress ... Porter managed to do what it took his mentor,
Wayne Morse, twenty-four years to accomplish. He rendered himself
unelectable by the exercise of his big mouth. That he was unassailably
and prematurely correct on every major issue of our times must be small
comfort as he contemplates the wreckage of his career."[27]

Ultimately, what undid Porter politically was that he was too liberal
for his district. His positions on disarmament and China and his initially
favorable attitude toward Fidel Castro led to grumbling that he was
far more interested in foreign policy than in attending to his constituents'
needs. The Cuban Revolution's radicalization gave Porter's political

opponents ammunition aplenty, contributing to his defeat at the polls in 1960 after only two terms served. Although he stood for his House seat five more times, his district never again returned him to Congress.

For the most part, his constituents appreciated the lengths he took to assist the Murphy family but were by turns bewildered and dismayed by his growing preoccupation with Latin American affairs. When he was quizzed about whether his time spent on this work kept him from addressing matters closer to home, he stuck to his guns. "I told my constituents before they elected me that I intended to devote one-third of my time to working on peace." Ironically, the more national attention Porter received, the more it hurt him back home. Charges that he was "getting too big for his britches" or that he was not paying sufficient attention to the district's bread and butter, the lumber industry, were used against him by his political opponents.[28]

During his four years in Congress, Porter saved the sharpest rhetorical arrows in his quiver for the strongman Trujillo. Never at a loss for colorful descriptions, the Dominican exile Silfa labeled Porter a "one-man FBI."[29] Whether in the press, on radio, television, the floor of the House, on the stump, or during his visits to Latin American countries, he repeatedly accused the dictator of running a private mafia of assassins and then hushing up his crimes by buying off U.S. congressmen and the press. Typical was this riposte in *Coronet:* "The shocking fact is that a high paid organization of killers is at large in our country, operating chiefly in New York City and Miami, whose job it is to assassinate or intimidate the enemies of Trujillo in the United States. They don't draw the line at expatriate Dominicans. They will murder Americans too."[30]

Porter was a godsend to Silfa and his compatriots in the PRD. The congressman's crusade, he chortled, metastasized into a "malign tumor," impairing Trujillo's political wellbeing.[31] In Porter's mind, there was a direct correlation between service to his constituents and the making of foreign policy: "By [my] making these opinions, which are not lightly held, known and incorporated into our foreign policy, it may well be that many other American boys may be saved from the fate of my constituent, Gerry Murphy. Another result may be that the United States will attain a position of moral leadership commensurate with its economic power and its political responsibilities in the world."[32]

It was Figueres who coined the nickname Porter later embraced: "Although you were elected by the State of Oregon, you have become Latin America's representative to the U.S. Congress, press, and public opinion.

The life of your constituent, pilot Murphy, was a high price to pay, but it was paid for a necessary, belated awakening of conscience in the United States, to the worst problem that confronts the democratic cause in the American Republics: indigenous dictatorship."[33] *Time* magazine ran with Figueres's nickname in a story with the catchy title of "Dictator Hater." The piece zeroed in on the representative's testimony before a federal grand jury in a case linked to Galíndez's abduction, where he "earnestly" told the grand jurors that they should "consider indicting Trujillo himself."[34]

Fortuitously for Porter and the region's reformers, his campaign coincided with a sharp decline in the number of countries ruled by autocrats. Military or personalistic dictatorships were toppled or fell of their own volition in Argentina, Peru, Colombia, Honduras, Venezuela, Cuba, Guatemala, El Salvador, Panama, Haiti, and the Dominican Republic. Nine of the eleven countries transitioned to civilian rule, although in several instances democratic governance proved short-lived (see table 2).

The Democratic Wave

Not since the end of World War II had there been an analogous shift toward civilian rule. Just as in the 1920s and 1930s, secondary and university students spilled out onto the streets to demand an end to authoritarian rule. Several despots hastened their demise by running afoul of an institution that historically was a pillar of their regimes—the Catholic Church. In the Venezuelan and Colombian cases, uprisings resulted from their dictators' ungainly attempts to prolong their stay in power.[35]

Militaries played a key role in the removal of several dictators. Citing incompetence, corruption, and repression, high commands abandoned their chiefs at critical junctures. In some cases, officers lingered until the last possible moment before joining a civilian-initiated rebellion, waiting until it was apparent that the strongman's position was no longer tenable. In other cases, they were proactive, leading by example. A number of officers were even named to important cabinet posts in transitional or interim governments.[36]

However, the removal of a despot never foreclosed the possibility of a political comeback. Many strongmen amassed millions in ill-gotten gains that could be repurposed to retake power. Ciudad Trujillo became the preferred landing spot for ex-dictators. Perón, Rojas Pinilla, Pérez Jiménez, Batista, and the Haitian General Paul Magloire all relocated there after their ousters.[37]

Table 2. Democratic wave, 1952–1961

Dictator	Country	Date Removed	Result*
Hugo Ballivián	Bolivia	April 1952	revolutionary government
José Remón	Panama	January 1955	civilian government
Juan Perón	Argentina	September 1955	junta/civilian government
Manuel Odría	Peru	July 1956	civilian government
Gustavo Rojas Pinilla	Colombia	May 1957	junta/civilian government
Carlos Castillo Armas	Guatemala	July 1957	junta/civilian government
Military Junta	Honduras	December 1957	civilian government
Marcos Pérez Jiménez	Venezuela	January 1958	junta/civilian government
Fulgencio Batista	Cuba	December 1958	civilian/revolutionary governments
Rafael Trujillo	Dominican Republic	May 1961	civilian government

* Although Perón achieved the presidency via the ballot box, he is included here because of marked authoritarian tendencies. Vargas is not, because his second term in office (1950–1954) was more populist than autocratic.

A case in point was the ever-disruptive Perón, who, throughout his stay in Caracas as a guest of the Venezuelan dictator and then after Pérez Jiménez's ouster, from the safety of Ciudad Trujillo, brazenly schemed to reclaim the presidency of Argentina.[38]

There was more than a hint of irony in the democratic manner in which Trujillo treated his guests. Just as he was said to have charged Machado for relocating to the Dominican Republic in 1934, so too was it rumored that he exacted a substantial fee for lodging his more recent arrivals. Ex-dictators were all housed in the National Palace, in quarters set aside for visiting "friends of rank."[39] And when space was at a premium in the Dominican capital, Madrid and Caracas (until Pérez Jiménez's ouster in January 1958 shut that door) provided refuge and a base of operations from which former dictators could operate.[40]

Latin American reformers were quick to applaud the democratic surge. At a dinner held at the Carnegie International Center in New York City in January 1957 celebrating the publication of his opus, *Venezuela: política y petróleo*, Betancourt declared that Latin America was at "a moment full of promise."[41] A half a year later, in a letter to his friend Muñoz, he was optimistic about the prospects of finally realizing his long-held dream of ridding the hemisphere of dictatorships. After graciously thanking the governor for providing him with a safe haven that had made it possible to complete his manuscript, he confided that although the outlook was encouraging for the region in general and for his homeland, where popular resentment to Pérez Jiménez had reached fever pitch, it was premature to declare victory. He had witnessed these waves before and knew they did not always take. "One cannot count on victory," as Cuban fanatics of *la pelota* (the Cuban term for *beisbol*) always say, "until the final out" has been recorded.[42]

He did feel that there was something markedly different about this wave. Not only were protests against autocratic regimes on the rise, but with McCarthyism receding in the United States, Betancourt thought that the political climate in Washington was finally undergoing a much-needed corrective.[43] Fearless voices like Porter's lifted his spirits, giving the nomadic exile hope. In a letter to *Iberica*'s Kent, he praised the representative, a case in point of how "the heresy of a few are now converted into official orthodoxy."[44]

In February 1958, a manifesto signed by 57 writers, educators, journalists, and politicians, including five former presidents, hailed the "growing reconquest of civil democracy." The Colombian Arciniegas, a colleague of Galíndez's at Columbia, announced the initiative. The cosigners pledged to support democratic governance, individual liberties, self-determination, and economic justice. The declaration cautioned against backsliding and, echoing the principles first enunciated in the Larreta Doctrine, called for "mutual defense against dictatorships."[45]

A Welcome Breath of Fresh Air

That Porter and his allies struck a nerve was evident by the Dominican ruler's forceful response. Or as the lawmaker explained in his less-than-understated manner: "Trujillo's henchmen first tried to scare me. Then they tried to bribe me."[46] The harassment extended all the way to his home state. In the *Coos Bay Times*, the Pan America Anti-Communist Association, a Dominican front organization, took out an ad denouncing the congressman as "a left-wing McCarthy who is conducting a one-man war against the friendly governments of Generalissimo Franco of Spain, Batista of Cuba, Generalissimo Trujillo of the Dominican Republic and Somoza of Nicaragua."[47] Porter later identified two other organizations—the Dominican Cultural Society and the Ateneo—which, like the Pan America Anti-Communist Association, "functioned under the aegis of his [Trujillo's] consular corps." Their responsibilities included provocations against, and surveillance of, political enemies, intelligence gathering, picketing, and letter-writing campaigns.[48]

Intimidation and character assassination of the lawmaker came in various guises. Sometimes Porter received "eerie after-midnight calls," threatening harm if he did not back off, while at other times he had to contend with "Dominican intervention" in his electoral campaigns. A *Washington Post* editorial noted that the congressman was not the only representative who warranted special treatment. "With a nice show of bipartisanship, [Trujillo] has singled out one Democrat [Porter] and two Republicans as enemies of Trujilloland who have been marked for defeat." Charles Brownson (Republican-Indiana), Alvin Bentley (Republican-Michigan), and Porter revealed to their colleagues in the House that the Dominican secretary of state for commerce and industry, Arturo Despradel, had threatened officials in their respective states with severe economic consequences if their troublesome representatives won reelection.[49] Oregon's governor, Robert Holmes, decried the harassment and the "thinly veiled threats of economic embargo" against his state. Although the Dominican Republic had purchased only $196,000 in goods from Oregon only the year before, the governor was upset enough to take the matter up with the secretary of state, asking him to lodge a "vigorous protest" with the Dominican government.[50]

Porter seemed to invite retaliation, lashing out against the regime's tarring of Galíndez's reputation, for instance. When Trujillo branded the Basque a communist to fend off criticism that he was responsible for his abduction, Porter was one of the few congressmen to defend the professor. Having read his columns, Porter knew that such a smear was demonstrably false. Galíndez's "writings stand as an eloquent testimonial to his anti-communism and his profound love of freedom and human rights."[51] Knowing how highly Porter thought of Galíndez, Grant asked the representative to be the keynote speaker at the memorial service for Galíndez in Manhattan on the second anniversary of his abduction. Although his duties kept him from attending, he cabled remarks to be read that night. "Martyrs like Jesús de Galíndez inspire us all to greater efforts. He lives in the hearts of his many friends, old and new. His enemies have their backs to the wall and I predict that their final punishment in this world will come before another year passes."[52]

The representative refused to be cowed by the threats, continuing to speak out in the press and on the floor of the House. He appeared on a riveting hourlong radio broadcast in May 1957, produced and narrated by Edward R. Murrow, called "The Galíndez-Murphy Case: A Chronicle of Terror." CBS News wisely took precautions when it taped the broadcast, going to unusual lengths to protect the identity of its informants—using pseudonyms, distorting their voices, and filming the interviews in secret locations. Murrow later recalled that the broadcast was the most disquieting of his career, owing to the informants' palpable fear.[53]

In an article in *Ibérica*, Porter demanded action from the administration, warning that "by our silence and inaction we do grievous damage to the moral basis of our government." Then, in a turn of phrase that could have been scripted by Latin American reformers, he added that the struggle was not "between the free world and communism" but "the free world and any tyranny, communistic or otherwise. . . . Our failure to call a . . . tyrant a tyrant in the Dominican Republic hinders us . . . if the ultimate victory is to be won, tyranny, whether it be communism, fascism or Trujilloism, must be resisted with resolution and fortitude."[54]

In a draft of an essay he submitted to the *New Republic* (which went unpublished), he fleshed out ideas that later became talking points at his speaking engagements. He endorsed Betancourt's idea of a *cordon sanitaire* against dictatorships and objected to the State Department's "present perversion of the doctrine of non-intervention." Its "see no evil, hear no evil, and condemn no evil" policy toward its neighbors was not only counterproductive but hypocritical. Why was it acceptable, he asked, to oust "pink" governments like Guatemala, while the Department considered speaking ill of Pérez Jiménez's Venezuela or Batista's Cuba to be a "calculated and distinctly unwelcome intervention in their internal affairs?" Furthermore, how could the administration square its hands-off stance with its bilateral mutual defense assistance programs with Latin American militaries? Such agreements, Porter allowed, were clearly interventionist—and rightfully so, as far as he was concerned—since they incorporated restrictive language prohibiting U.S. weapons from being used by militaries against their own populations. Porter peppered the State Department on this point, and, in the process, shined a light on the Batista regime's misuse of U.S. arms against Cuban civilians. Believing that the U.S. should never employ force or economic might to overthrow a government, the congressman insisted that the administration's strict adherence to nonintervention was two-faced and counterproductive.[55]

The badgering by Porter and other congressmen was not in vain. Batista's violation of the mutual arms agreement was subsequently taken up by the Senate Foreign Relations Committee. Hearings were held right after U.S. authorities had announced the indictment of Prío on gun-running charges. The Democratic whip, Mike Mansfield, pressed Rubottom about the apparent inconsistency of continuing to send arms to a "military dictatorship" which was using U.S.-made weapons against civilians, while the duly elected Prío, who had been ousted by Batista, "is put in jail for trying to overthrow that government." Soon after the hearings concluded, the administration announced the suspension of arms shipments to the regime.[56]

Porter's observations about the misappropriation of U.S. military assistance resonated throughout the region. In an interview with St. George for *Look Magazine* in February 1958, a defiant Castro conveyed a similar message: "By furnishing arms to these usurpers of power—the men of the infamous 'International of Sabers,' tyrants like Pérez Jiménez of Venezuela, the exiled Rojas Pinilla of Colombia, Trujillo of the Dominican Republic—you kill the democratic spirit of Latin America. Do you think your tanks, your planes, the guns you Americans ship Batista in good faith are used in hemispheric defense? He uses them to cow his own defenseless people! How can he contribute to 'hemispheric defense'? He hasn't even been able to subdue us."[57]

The young congressman's campaign also hit a nerve with Trujillo's stateside supporters. Years later, he vividly recalled the time right after he had burst into national prominence, when a retired four-star marine general paid a visit to his office on the Hill. The former commander reminded the lawmaker what a loyal friend and ally Trujillo was to the United States. Not only did the Dominican Republic let the U.S. military use its waters and territory for maneuvers and permit us to establish a missile base, but it reliably voted with the U.S. in the UN. The way the general heard it, Murphy was just an adventurer. The congressman should focus on the big picture. Interviewed in 1986, Porter had lost none of his feistiness in his retelling of the story. "He's telling me, what the hell do I care whether your guy [Murphy] died down there." To Porter, the commander's cynicism encapsulated the administration's cold, calculating approach. The general's attitude was "we don't care what you do to your people. We don't care if you're shooting them, torturing them; that's your business."[58]

To be sure, Porter's policy prescriptions were hardly radical. While he agreed with Vice President Nixon's earlier call for *abrazos* for democrats and a "formal handshake" with dictators, he insisted that the administration take meaningful steps to enforce such symbolic gestures.

Tolerating, conciliating, and condoning dictators had to stop, and the administration should also refrain from praising and decorating despots or their aides.[59]

That Porter was swimming upstream on these matters, however, was confirmed by a memo that Rubottom sent to Foster Dulles. Openly criticizing Trujillo could backfire, he explained. The Dominican government "might retaliate against . . . our investors in the Dominican Republic, whose holdings total nearly 100 million dollars . . . [and] our guided missile testing facility there which the Department of Defense considers vital." Better to handle this discreetly, Richard Stephens, the chargé d'affaires in Ciudad Trujillo, wrote, with a stern warning of future consequences if such actions reoccurred. Instead, the administration withheld material assistance, turning down a Dominican request to have its squadron of F-47 fighter planes modernized and postponing the sale of thirteen F-80 jets.[60]

The State Department responded to Porter's complaints the way Trujillo had responded to Galíndez, by playing the red card. Rubottom lectured "Charley" that the Department's "scrupulous observance of the principle of non-intervention" was in keeping with the demands of Latin American governments and that Porter's criticisms, coming as they did from a member of Congress, "inevitably lend themselves to those communist and other elements unfriendly to the United States." The very same criticisms were heard on "Moscow Radio." "Our enemies are only too eager to portray such statements as official confirmation of their own propaganda line."[61]

Porter bristled at such patronizing counsel. In a speech titled "Defects of United States Policy in Latin America," he shot back:[62]

Why did our Department of State deal politely and lightly with a vicious Western Hemisphere tyrant caught red-handed in a bloody crime against an American citizen? . . . A policy that leads to condoning the most flagrant abuses of human rights and decency can never be successful in halting communism. At the outset I was warned by high State Department officials, as well as by some of my most respected colleagues in Congress, that in the interest of 'hemispheric solidarity' I should soft-pedal this case. I was told that hemispheric defense against international communism demanded close cooperation among all the American governments, regardless of the internal nature of those governments.

I was reminded how resentful our Latin American neighbors are of any kind of intervention by the United States.

He also had little patience for the secretary of state, who he felt had little interest in the region and thought of "the twentieth-century Latin American struggle for liberty as a nineteenth-century battle for power between the 'ins' and the 'outs.' "[63] He called on Foster Dulles to voice his disapproval of Trujillo publicly. He kept up the pressure even after the secretary had to step down because of ill health. In a July 1959 letter to Dulles's successor, Christian Herter, he suggested several ways to accomplish this objective: by withdrawing our ambassador, downgrading the embassy, cutting off military or technical funding, and printing warnings on passports that travel to the island was not without risk. At the very least, the president should express "our disdain for this police state."[64] The administration should even consider hitting Trujillo, the island's largest sugar producer, where it would hurt the most, by terminating the Dominican sugar quota.[65]

It was not enough to criticize dictators, he remarked; our government must also stand up and be counted with those fighting for democracy. It should praise "the heroic achievements of men and women throughout the hemisphere who are sacrificing their lives for the principles set forth in our own Bill of Rights."[66]

The State Department considered the representative a nuisance. In a confidential memo titled "Correspondence with Charles O. Porter," Rubottom and an aide who worked on the Cuba desk carped about "the tremendous man-hours in the preparation of replies" to the congressman's numerous demands for information, not to mention the repetitive nature of his inquiries. A frustrated assistant secretary wanted to discourage "future useless correspondence with Porter on matters involving our policy on Latin America, with which Mr. Porter appears to be in inexorable disagreement." In a follow-up memo he concluded that the best way to handle matters from here on out was to meet with Porter for periodic lunches, while keeping the correspondence to a minimum. Given "the congressman's propensity for making most of it [our correspondence] public, I think we should answer perfunctorily all those queries which we do not want publicized, [only] going into considerable detail in answering those which we want made public."[67]

Rubottom and his aides may have grumbled about Porter, but their misgivings about Trujillo's aggressions echoed those of the representative. A January 1958 memo from the director of the Office of Middle American Affairs, William Wieland, reported that relations between Washington and Ciudad Trujillo were "increasingly strained," as a result of the regime's obstruction in the Galíndez-Murphy investigation, improper activities by its diplomats and agents in the U.S., and its persistent meddling across the region.[68]

Porter must have felt that at times he was tilting at windmills, because he encountered stiff opposition from his colleagues. After his provocative speech on the floor of the House in February 1957, eight of Trujillo's congressional supporters attacked him for displaying "a hostile attitude toward a friendly power." At that time, not one congressman came to his defense. Later that summer, Porter's bill to suspend technical and military assistance to "dictatorship countries" was easily defeated.[69]

If his views failed to gain traction in Congress, his crusade was hailed as a welcome breath of fresh air by Latin Americans across the political spectrum. AD exiles residing in New York complimented Porter for seeing the "larger picture. It's not just a Santo Domingo problem, it is something that afflicts many Latin American countries," they noted in a lengthy letter. To better educate the congressman on their struggle to depose Pérez Jiménez, they cited chapter and verse of human rights violations in their homeland.[70]

In Puerto Rico, he had a memorable private audience with the cellist Pablo Casals, who congratulated the lawmaker for speaking out. Casals, who vowed never to perform in countries that had recognized Franco, was especially pleased with Porter's forceful condemnation of the Spanish strongman. The renowned cellist recounted advice he once gave the great humanitarian Albert Schweitzer. The doctor had an obligation to lend his "great international prestige on behalf of good causes." Casals counseled Schweitzer, "you have a duty to act." The cellist's pointed message was not lost on the congressman.[71]

The journalist Daniel James, who wrote a scorching polemic of Árbenz's Guatemala—*Red Design for the Americas*—urged Porter to keep the pressure on and to "not ... falter in your fight." Stationed in Mexico City, James explained that the local press was keenly following Porter's speeches. "Trujillo is a symbol of everything evil down here, and most Latinos are convinced that only the State Department keeps him going. I'd say there is a growing appreciation here of your courageous fight."[72]

Porter was startled by and somewhat uncomfortable with the accolades he received from Latin Americans. In his speech on the floor of the

House in July 1957 he described why he was of two minds: "Mail from eighteen of the twenty American Republics unanimously cheered my position. I received many invitations to visit Latin American countries. The *only* opposition in my mail came from two self-styled anti-communist leagues here in the United States, which are Trujillo-paid propaganda mills. This widespread Latin American approval of my stand at once heartened and perturbed me. Naturally I was encouraged. . . . On the other hand, the burning popularity in Latin America of my position attested to the sad fact that our policy is out of touch with Latin American realities" (emphasis in original).[73]

With Porter earning rave reviews in the region, reformist politicians hitched their political fortunes to his. Over the course of 1957 and 1958, Figueres, Betancourt, Muñoz Marín, Santos, Ricardo Arias (Panama), and Villeda all extended invitations to Porter to visit. His brief trips (with returns to Washington in between to attend to House business) came with all the trappings of state visits. Owing to his growing popularity, domestic opponents of those extending the invitations were wary of criticizing him. Even so, Porter found himself buffeted by political headwinds wherever he went. Occurring at a moment when political sparks were about to fly between Costa Rica, Nicaragua, and the Dominican Republic, the representative did his best to remain above the fray—with only limited success. What triggered this fresh round of sniping was the assassination of Somoza García on September 21, 1956.

We Are the Ones Considered Troublemakers

A day after the Nicaraguan dictator was nominated for his third term as president, a young poet, Rigoberto López Pérez, shot Somoza four times at close range at a campaign event. The assailant was immediately killed by the dictator's bodyguards. Whelan sent a helicopter to pick up Somoza and return him to the capital. Then, at the ambassador's request, Eisenhower dispatched a medical team to Managua including two surgeons, a bone specialist, and an anesthetist from Gorgas Military Hospital in the Canal Zone and a doctor from Walter Reed Army Hospital in Bethesda. With his condition worsening, the dictator was subsequently rushed to the Canal Zone. Despite the team's best efforts, Somoza never recovered.[74]

Eisenhower offered "personal regrets" for the strongman who, he said, "constantly emphasized both publicly and privately, his friendship for the United States." The secretary of state also conveyed his condolences, noting that Somoza's "constantly demonstrated friendship to the U.S. will never be forgotten."[75] Such generous words and deeds were not lost on opponents at home and abroad. As a Venezuelan exile residing in Buenos Aires phrased it: "If assassination is not occasion for rejoicing, neither is it grounds for publicly praising a notorious tyrant."[76] To add insult to injury, in early November, during a three-week trip to the States to inspect military installations, Somoza's son Tachito, who assumed command of the National Guard right after his father's death, met with the president, "albeit on the golf course." He was then awarded the Legion of Merit.[77]

In fact, the decoration was handed out to Latin American military officers with such regularity that the absence of conferral came to be considered a slight. Bestowal of the award on such a despised figure was precisely the kind of symbolic excess that Porter and reformers abhorred.[78] In this case, the timing of the honor was especially problematic. Among the dissidents rounded up immediately after Somoza's death was the head of the political opposition, Pedro Joaquín Chamorro. Falsely accused of participating in the plot to kill the elder Somoza, the longtime head of the Conservative Party and the editor of the Managua daily *La Prensa* was jailed for several months. During his confinement he was repeatedly tortured, at times by the man who just had been awarded the Legion of Merit.[79]

Owing to the longstanding animosity between the elder Somoza and Figueres, speculation was rife in Managua that the latter had had a hand in the assassination. (Figueres's audience in the Vatican with the Pope on the day of the shooting did nothing to dispel such rumors in the local press.) In fact, according to the French ambassador, Raymond Pons, Tachito believed that the assassination was just a warning shot across the bow from their neighbors.

What was now being planned across the region, Somoza Debayle was convinced, was something much bigger, comparable in scale to the Caribbean Legion's earlier efforts to rid the region entirely of dictatorships in the late 1940s. The Somozas were aware that members of Castro's 26th of July movement were training and stockpiling weapons in Mexico and Costa Rica in preparation for an amphibious landing in eastern Cuba in late November 1956. (Just five months earlier Fidel had made a fundraising trip to San José, meeting with the leadership of the PLN and Cuban exiles residing in the Costa Rican capital). Once Batista was overthrown the rebels would set their sights on Nicaragua. In fact, Castro did precisely that after he took power in January 1959, arming, funding, and training dozens of Nicaraguan exiles (the forerunners of the Sandinistas) committed to overthrowing the family dynasty.[80]

Pons also learned from a source close to the presidential palace that Whelan was (not for the first time) working at odds with his superiors in Washington. Even before the elder Somoza's death, the ambassador was "whispering in the ears" of his sons, feeding them troubling intelligence that Figueres's properties were now training sites for "future revolutionaries," and urging the brothers to take "preventative" steps against their neighbor. Pons also informed his foreign minister that in the weeks immediately after the assassination the pro-Somoza press in the capital was busy preparing Nicaraguans for another round of hostilities. Without offering any proof, press reports cast aspersions on Figueres for Somoza's assassination and whipped up anti-Tico sentiment by reminding readers that with Árbenz removed from power and Guatemala no longer a safe haven for political refugees, Costa Rica was now home to "the lion's share of exiles from authoritarian regimes (Cuba, Dominican Republic, Colombia, Venezuela, Nicaragua, Guatemala, etc.)."[81]

The Costa Rican government agreed with Pons, especially about Whelan. In an unattributed memorandum that Figueres shared with Muñoz Marin, the U.S. ambassador was branded as meddlesome, exercising undue influence over the Somoza family, much in the manner of his predecessors, Crowder, Welles, Caffery, and Peurifoy. Figueres and his lieutenants were certain that Whelan was behind the eleven bombing runs conducted by CIA pilots over Costa Rican territory the year before. The memo also reprised the Costa Rican government's claim that the Eisenhower administration erred in not assigning responsibility for those attacks. Since the Somozas and their accomplices were never held accountable, was it any wonder that Tachito felt emboldened to try again? "Now, we find ourselves facing a new threat . . . egged on by the same Ambassador Whelan. And we are the ones that are considered troublemakers by the State Department."[82]

Rubottom was aware of the criticism, yet Whelan remained a fixture in Managua. In fact, the assistant secretary praised Whelan's deft stewardship. "You have been left in Nicaragua as Ambassador for seven years and this has been interpreted widely as U.S. support of the Somoza family, including President Luis [Somoza], because of your well-publicized and quite understandable affection for them. . . . I know that we can count on you to handle your side of it in your usual Whelan-style diplomacy, which is as good as any I know."[83] To be sure, Whelan was not the only ambassador accused of "undue cordiality." Arthur Gardner and Earl Smith (ambassadors to Cuba) and Joseph Farland (Dominican Republic) were similarly accused of toadying up to Batista and Trujillo. But the ambassador's decade of service in Managua gave ample ammunition to Figueres and his allies, who painted him as a disruptive influence and a throwback to an age of invasive proconsulship.[84]

Given the political vacuum created by the death of their father, it is understandable why the Somoza brothers were on alert, in case this "veritable army of political refugees" reached out to elements of the domestic opposition.[85] While Luis, whom the Nicaraguan Congress designated to fulfill his father's term in office the day after his death, extended an olive branch to Figueres, his brother planned another invasion in early December 1956. Two thousand recruits were added to the Guard, effectively doubling its size. The U.S. embassy and its military mission reported that "intensive training" in guerrilla tactics was taking place on the Somozas' "immense personal properties." Pons surmised that Anastasio Jr. viewed this as a golden opportunity to attend to unfinished business, exacting "retribution for the failed invasion" of January 1955. Throughout the last months of 1956, the press campaign against Figueres and the training of the Guard intensified in "lock step."[86]

A North American foreign service officer stationed in Costa Rica felt that the exiles also deserved blame for increasing tensions between the two countries. The refugees deliberately "publish things," Alex Cohen reported, to foster "an atmosphere of intranquility [sic]," thereby creating diplomatic headaches for the host country that had extended them a "generous exile." As guests, they should "refrain from making statements that can be construed as political activities."[87]

A U.S. military attaché stationed in the San José embassy thought the stories circulating in the Managua press that Nicaraguan exiles in Costa Rica were about to stage another invasion were frankly overblown. It would be reckless of the Figueres administration either to encourage or not to do all within its power to thwart another border crossing, because the Nicaraguan National Guard had more than twice the number of soldiers than the Costa Rican militia, and its air force had fifty aircraft (including thirty fighters and two light bombers) compared to their neighbors' three P-51s. U.S. military intelligence estimated that Nicaraguan forces were "probably a match . . . for any two other Central American countries."[88]

Nicaragua had Washington to thank for its military superiority. It received more military grant aid than any other country in Central America during the 1950s. But the attaché saw no evidence of preparations. This did not, of course, preclude small groups of Nicaraguan exiles from moving across the border from Costa Rica to carry out terrorist attacks, he supposed, but it was far more likely that the unsubstantiated claims were the byproduct of an unsettled situation in Nicaragua. By turning up the criticism of Figueres in the official press, the Somozas sought to "focus attention outward," as a pretext to "crack down on the [domestic] opposition."[89] The military attaché's assessment was accurate, because no attack was forthcoming. The Somozas simply changed tactics.

For one, they opened up an arms bazaar. Taking advantage of better financing and lower prices, Nicaragua purchased aircraft and armaments from Western European countries, Japan, and Israel, keeping some hardware for its own military and selling the remainder to colleagues in La Internacional, among others. Almost half of the fighter aircraft purchased from Sweden just before the 1955 war with Costa Rica, for instance, were resold to the Dominican Republic and Indonesia. Similarly, Nicaraguan purchases of Israeli armored cars were resold less than a year later to Batista. The trend was worrisome to Nicaragua's neighbors and the United States. When Somoza acquired a large number of Armalite automatic rifles from Holland and Sweden in 1957, El Salvador and Honduras asked the United States to sell their militaries a comparable number of rifles. The State Department fretted that Nicaragua's actions "will result in the deterioration of Central American relations and a possible arms race."[90]

Castro expressed his frustration as well; not just with La Internacional, but with their enablers. When U.S. officials announced that they were withholding arms shipments to Batista in March 1958, the rebel lamented on a "Radio Rebelde" broadcast that the ban would not hinder Batista from readily obtaining arms elsewhere. "The result is in no way altered. The United States sells them [the arms] to Somoza and Trujillo. Somoza and Trujillo sell them to Batista." He was absolutely correct. Arms shipments from the other members of La Internacional and several Western European countries more than made up the difference.[91]

In addition to the arms buildup, Somoza and Trujillo tried to eliminate the Costa Rican president in May 1957. More convoluted and transnational than earlier attempts, this latest scheme was the handiwork of Bernardino and Abbes García, with assistance from Somoza Debayle. *El gángster* hired three Cuban gunmen to carry out the hit, with Bernardino promising to provide "a plane, arms and the use of a landing field in Costa Rica," owned by a Calderón Guardia supporter.[92] One of the conspirators, Juan Manuel Delgado y Chaves (a.k.a. El Francés) was a former pilot in the Cuban air force with ties to Prío. Another, Herminio Díaz García, was a member of the 26th of July movement. Jesús González Cartas (a.k.a. El Extraño, the Odd One), was a notorious figure in the Cuban underworld who had been hired to "do dirty jobs for Trujillo before." All three were rabid anti-Batistianos.

The conspirators flew to San José by different routes, with two originating on the island and Díaz García from Mexico, where he had been training with Castro's rebels. Additional proof that this was a La Internacional–sponsored plot was that Díaz García traveled under a false name, bearing a Venezuelan passport. Costa Rican authorities apprehended the three men a few days after their arrival, just as they were staking out the presidential palace. They had drawn attention to themselves by foolishly squandering large sums of money in the Costa Rican capital. So confident of success were the assailants that they told authorities they planned on contacting other anti-Batista exiles in San José after the attack. Trujillo's lieutenants apparently had promised that after the job was completed they were to be provided with money, planes, and arms to aid their efforts to overthrow the Cuban dictator.[93]

El Francés and Díaz García came clean to Costa Rican authorities, revealing that they were promised two hundred thousand dollars for the job (with five thousand paid up front). They admitted that they originally had discussed abducting the Costa Rican president "in the Galíndez style." When that was judged too risky, the conspirators decided to assassinate Figueres. Among the items seized by authorities and entered into evidence at the trial was a .45-caliber pistol with a silver-and-gold-plated handle engraved "Generalissimo Trujillo, to his friend General Jesús González Cartas."[94] They also confessed that at first Bernardino had encountered resistance from Luis Somoza, but his younger brother had few qualms, agreeing to provide "the plane for the mission and to facilitate the secret flights." Meanwhile, Bernardino promised he would run interference to ensure that the men would not face extradition to Cuba after the fact.[95]

The court gave the three plotters what amounted to a slap on the wrist—handing down six-month sentences. Not surprisingly, both the Dominican and Nicaraguan governments vehemently denied their involvement.[96]

Betancourt was convinced that the plot's timing was the result of the heat Trujillo was feeling from the Galíndez and Murphy cases. He warned Figueres, "as with any cornered shooter, he now is more dangerous than ever."[97] What was curious was that immediately after the arrests, the Costa Rican president asked his ambassador to the United States, Gonzalo Facio Segreda, to inform the State Department that he had asked Porter to come to Costa Rica to talk with one of the would-be assailants. El Francés had confidential information that he was willing to share with the congressman about Murphy's activities in Cuba prior to his disappearance. He had overlapped with Murphy for a month while both were employed as copilots by the Dominican National Airlines.[98]

Thinking out loud in a group cable to his embassies in the isthmus, Rubottom was puzzled as to why Figueres had approached Porter instead of following protocol and relaying his concerns about Nicaragua's and the Dominican Republic's participation in the assassination plot to the Department. Didn't the Costa Rican president understand that this was clearly beyond the purview of a lawmaker's duties? With the Dominican Republic now backpedaling from the fallout from the disappearances, Rubottom felt that drawing attention to this attempt on Figueres's life "would merely add" to the "alleged Dominican excesses now receiving wide publicity in United States." By involving Porter in this case in such a public manner, it was obvious that the Costa Rican president's intent was to tie this plot to the others. But it also suggested how little influence Figueres had with the State Department. Figueres, Rubottom speculated, "apparently wishes [to] appeal emotionally to the United States, [the] hemisphere and Costa Rican public opinion by emphasizing [the] similarity [of the] current plot to [the] Murphy-Galíndez case." With the congressman sure to raise a ruckus, "the publicity would not stop with the Dominicans and . . . other Central American countries would be drawn into the argument over real and fancied past grievances, which would be counterproductive." It was crucial, he concluded, that the Department reveal nothing in either "formal declarations or oral comments" to the congressman.[99]

What Porter billed as a fact-finding mission to Costa Rica became a celebration of the lawmaker's campaign against dictatorships. On June 13, 1957, five thousand Ticos, U.S. Ambassador Woodward, and a slew of dignitaries turned out to welcome Porter at El Coco Airport just outside of San José. Porter's brief remarks at the airport were met with approving chants from the crowd of "*Viva a la democracia; abajo con Trujillo*" (Long Live Democracy; Down with Trujillo). He was then whisked downtown to give a speech later that afternoon before a special session of the legislature. In his address, where he repeated his attacks on the region's dictators, he remarked that with investigations into the Murphy and Galíndez cases at a standstill in the States, he was hopeful that his questioning of the prisoner the following day would get the investigation off the schneid. After receiving an ovation from the deputies, Porter was escorted to the U.S. embassy, where Woodward held a reception in his honor. The final event that first night was a state dinner hosted by Figueres at the presidential palace.[100]

Admiring columns appeared in the local papers. Notable was an open letter to Porter published in *La República* by Chamorro congratulating Porter for singlehandedly rehabilitating Washington's image in the eyes of many Latin Americans. The congressman had put his "finger on the open wound of the Americas—tyrannies." He was hopeful that, thanks to Porter's campaign, the U.S. Congress would not be as complacent as it had been in the past.[101] Another piece, by the Puerto Rican politician José Ángel Ciliberto, appeared in the same newspaper. Ciliberto had witnessed the effusive reception Porter had received earlier that month in Puerto Rico and had come away singularly impressed. "Since the days of FDR," he wrote, "no North American politician has struck such a responsive chord in Latin America as Charles Porter."[102]

Showering praise on their guest of honor, however, did not stop opposition newspapers, such as Ulate's *Diario de Costa Rica* and *La Nación*, from attacking Figueres's adventurous foreign policy. The opposition press seized upon a Drew Pearson column that speculated that this latest assassination attempt was a fabrication. One critic went as far as to compare Figueres to Trujillo, which provoked a withering rebuke from the editorial writers at *La República*. Another column in *El Diario de Costa Rica* characterized Figueres as an agitator always seeking to disrupt the peace. How ironic was it that the man responsible for abolishing the nation's military had transformed the country into an armed camp? "We are governed by an administration in which ploughshares are converted into swords."[103] Fueling the broadsides against the president was that the country was in the midst of a hotly contested electoral campaign. The popular Figueres could not succeed himself as president, and his party had been unable to coalesce behind one candidate. One of two PLN candidates would run as an independent that fall, giving the opposition party, led by Echandi, an excellent opportunity to defeat the PLN in the election.[104]

On Porter's second day in the capital he met first with union leaders at the main hall of the Confederación de Trabajadores Rerum Novarum, the nation's largest anticommunist labor union. Afterward he was taken to San José's Central Penitentiary, where Delgado y Chaves and his accomplices were being held until their arraignment. He later confided to Facio Segreda that he intended to share what he learned from the Cuban pilot with the FBI.[105] During his stay in the Costa Rican capital, Porter also found time to sit for interviews with the local press and to lay a floral wreath on a plaque commemorating the death of Hungarians who had recently rebelled against the Soviet-backed regime.[106]

After lunch at La Lucha, he spoke with the leadership of exile organizations. That Porter met with dissidents in Costa Rica so soon after the tongue-lashing he received in the House of Representatives for meeting with Dominican exiles in San Juan was a testament to either his tenacity or his inexperience. He certainly understood that encounters with such groups were problematic. In a letter to Muñoz Marín before his visit to the island, the congressman admitted that "associating myself with any one of the several organized groups working for Trujillo's downfall" could be awkward, especially since he knew so little about each exile organization. He asked the governor for whatever "informal, off-the-record advice" he could offer.[107]

If the prospect of criticism troubled him, it never stopped him from doing what he thought was right. Porter was particularly impressed with how dedicated the Venezuelan refugees he met with in San José were to their cause. In fact, he took time to meet with exiles in each of the countries he visited: "In Costa Rica, Colombia, Panama and Puerto Rico, I met many young Venezuelans from all walks of life—lawyers, engineers, farmers, architects—who are forced into a life of exile for the simple crime of urging free elections, the basic tenet we proclaim so proudly in Europe, Asia and the Far East. These Venezuelans are the minutemen of Venezuela . . . or if you prefer, the freedom fighters."[108]

After returning home from Costa Rica, Porter once again defended himself against charges of grandstanding. In a speech on the floor of the House upon his return from the isthmus, he responded by drawing a clear distinction between Costa Rica and the Dominican Republic. In the former, the legislature that honored him "is not a congress screened by the president as it is in the farce that calls itself a congress in the country misleadingly known as the Dominican Republic." Costa Rica, indeed, had "a healthy, vociferous opposition," and he relished the opportunity to meet with Echandi.[109] Furthermore, in a move that probably angered Rubottom, he not only shared what he learned from El Francés with investigators, but he turned over copies of the translated affidavits of the gunmen's testimony that Costa Rican authorities had provided him with to Pearson, who, like Porter, was a critic of the administration's policy.[110]

Two weeks after his Costa Rican visit, Porter arrived in Colombia, at an auspicious moment. Just a month before, Colombians had mobilized to overthrow Rojas Pinilla. While in Bogotá, the representative was the guest of Santos, whose newspapers *El Tiempo* and *El Espectador* were just reopening after months of a government-imposed shutdown.[111] An editorial in the former celebrated the congressman's visit. Titled "The Authentic Good Neighbor," it cast Porter as the protagonist in a *Mr. Smith Goes to Washington*–style drama taking place in the U.S. Congress, one where the little-known politician was pitted against an entrenched political establishment.[112]

As was the case in San José, Porter received an enthusiastic welcome in Bogotá. The lawmaker learned of how a popular uprising a month before had brought down the dictator in a week's time. The arrest of a rival presidential candidate had sparked student demonstrations in the streets of the capital. Sympathy strikes were called throughout the country. In an effort to suppress the unrest, police and soldiers killed dozens of demonstrators in the capital, igniting public outrage. A general strike then ensued, and when demonstrators again took to the streets, Rojas Pinilla ordered his forces to restore order. Clashes between the protestors and the police cost fifty additional lives. After some demonstrators took refuge in a church in a fashionable section of the city, the police set off tear gas inside the sanctuary, offending religious sensibilities. When Cardinal Crisanto Luque issued a pastoral letter criticizing the dictatorship, the military's high command persuaded Rojas Pinilla that it was time to step down.[113]

A year later Porter traveled to Venezuela, arriving just six months after another strongman, Pérez Jiménez, was forced to flee the country. His brief visits to Colombia and Venezuela only reinforced his opposition to the administration's policy. A comparison of the two countries' paths toward civilian governance underscores the lengths reformers went to keep *golpes* at bay and preserve democratic rule. What came next in these two politically fractured nations must have been scarcely believable to many Venezuelans and Colombians, as bitter political rivals patched up their differences and established coalition governments. The compromises negotiated by Venezuelan and Colombian political parties ensured democracy's survival in their respective countries. Those concessions, however, hampered democrats' efforts to roll out badly needed reforms.

Pacted Democracies

On his return from Bogotá, Porter was pleased to report that the Colombians, "in an unprecedented demonstration of the will for democracy," had initiated a successful nonviolent campaign to depose "a dictator armed with U.S. hardware."[114] Popular unrest against the dictator was fueled by his censorship of the press, the increasing politicization of the military, his refusal to lift a state of siege decree, and an ill-considered decision to place "Caesar-like" busts of himself in the main squares of towns and villages. But what really stoked resentment and cost the regime allies within the military was his ham-fisted attempt to reelect himself. According to historian Robert Karl, toward the end of his four-year-rule Rojas Pinilla was so bereft of support that he had to "browbeat his top subordinates [in the military] into publicly affirming the extension of his presidency."[115]

The archconservative Gómez, whom Rojas Pinilla had replaced in 1953, and other Conservative Party politicians joined forces with their bitter rivals, the Liberals, to oppose this dictator's reelection.[116] The leaders of both parties decided that the best way to restore democratic rule was to craft a plan in advance, explaining how the two parties intended to jointly govern the country in the future. Over the course of several meetings between Gómez and Liberal Party head Lleras Camargo, the parties agreed to alternate the presidency over the next sixteen years. This intra-elite pact mandated that posts in all three branches of government were to be divided equally between the two parties (while expressly excluding other political parties from a role in government). In a rare display of unanimity for such a polarized society, 95 percent of the voters endorsed the pact in a plebiscite.[117]

There were notable similarities in how Colombia and Venezuela transitioned to civilian rule. The combination of grassroots uprisings and disaffected military officers—what Rangel referred to as "two movements joined at the hip like Siamese brothers"—unseated unpopular dictators who overstayed their welcome.[118] Scheming against Pérez Jiménez began a full year before his removal from power.[119] Opposition to the discredited regimes was broad and deep, encompassing the Catholic Church, businessmen, the military, students, and the urban poor. In addition, an economic downturn coincided with the succession crisis in both countries. Plummeting commodity prices—oil in the case of Venezuela and coffee in Colombia—did the dictators no favor.[120]

In addition, profligate spending habits by the dictators triggered fiscal crises, discouraging even their most loyal supporters. In Colombia, the general lost credibility among his fellow officers, many of whom "believed in the original pacifying and non-partisan mission that brought him to power" and who now recoiled at how Rojas Pinilla and his clique had used their positions for personal gain. Promotions were predicated on loyalty to the chief, not merit.[121] The same was true in Venezuela. As the military historian Winfield Burggraaff noted, it was an open question whether junior officers in the armed forces were more upset with the venality for moral reasons or if they were just envious, or some combination of the two. No matter the motivation, the "flaunting of ill-gotten wealth" eroded whatever legitimacy Pérez Jiménez and Rojas Pinilla still had.[122]

Interim governments, midwifed by military officers, oversaw the transition to civilian rule in Colombia and Venezuela. To guard against a counterrevolution, the juntas purged military and civilian loyalists from the defeated regime, repealed repressive measures, restored freedoms, permitted exiles to return, enacted modest reforms, and organized elections. The democratic administrations that followed the provisional governments had to walk a fine line, however. While the high commands were the lynchpins of the dictatorships, they also were instrumental in showing the tyrants to the door. If democracy was to take root, those very same officers needed to be gently ushered off the political stage without unduly tarnishing their reputations. As a result, the new civilian governments chose not to prosecute past abuses, and the high commands were given assurances that moving forward under civilian rule they would have the institutional autonomy they desired to manage their own affairs.

Interservice rivalries, personality clashes, and factionalism within the armed forces opened the door to strategic alliances between the political parties and the military.[123] Although militaries, in theory, held themselves to be above tawdry politics, officers not infrequently were just as partisan as civilians. In fact, in Venezuela, there were close ties between officers in the armed forces and the political parties. Fuenmayor, for instance, claimed that seven hundred officers were "involved in [AD] party activities."[124]

Separating the military from the political sphere was more challenging in Venezuela, where the head of the junta, Rear Admiral Wolfgang Larrazábal, ran for the presidency in December 1958. His popularity ran up against memories of what had transpired in 1948, when, promises to the contrary, a military junta had refused to relinquish power. Coupled with a longstanding tradition of military involvement in politics, this explains why, for some Venezuelans, it was almost axiomatic to appeal to the high command's patriotism. As Rafael Caldera, the head of the conservative Comité de Organización Electoral Independiente (COPEI), put in in June 1959: "Venezuelans are so accustomed to see the army as a factor in their daily lives, so accustomed to make the army the arbiter of their political contests, that at each moment the most varied groups for the most dissimilar ends attempt to involve the army in new adventures to change our political reality."[125] It turned out not to be the case this time, however. Even though he was runner-up to Betancourt, Larrazábal accepted the results and ensured an orderly transition of power.[126]

In both countries, accommodations also were reached with the Catholic Church. In Colombia, a provision of the December 1957 plebiscite reaffirmed Roman Catholicism as the state religion, a status Liberals had nixed in 1936. In return, the church, which up to then had been a vocal supporter of the Conservative Party, ceased to be partisan. In Venezuela, AD buried the hatchet with the church, as Betancourt (1959–1963) and his successor, Leoni (1963–67), not only increased its government subsidies, but their administrations took pains to assure the hierarchy of its institutional prerogatives.[127]

To no one's surprise though, coup plotting reared its head in both countries. In the months after Porter's visit to Bogotá, Rojas Pinilla schemed to return himself to power. Unlike other deposed despots, he was not content with conniving from afar. Upon his return to Colombia, his loyalists plotted the assassinations of Lleras Camargo and members of the military junta. After the second plot, Rojas Pinilla was arrested by authorities. The Colombian Senate created a National Investigative Commission to examine presidential malfeasance during the dictator's tenure. This took some political courage. Promising to "vindicate his honor," Rojas Pinilla sent a chilling message that once he regained the presidency "rivers of blood will flow and there will not be enough lampposts in Bogotá for all those designated for hanging."[128]

Notwithstanding the threats, the commission found that during Rojas Pinilla's four years in office the personal holdings of the dictator, family members, and business associates had grown astronomically. The Senate tried and convicted the dictator of abuse of power and enrichment in office, stripping him of his military rank, titles, pension, and citizenship. This earned Rojas Pinilla the dubious distinction of becoming the first ruler of a Latin American government ever to be convicted of crimes committed while in office.[129]

In Venezuela, coups were headed off by the junta's ability to retain the loyalty of much of the military. But that took negotiations between prominent civilian leaders, Larrazábal, and the ringleaders of the plots, coupled with massive street demonstrations in support of democratic rule. The overwhelming preoccupation with a military coup explains why Venezuelans of all social classes were willing to take to the streets to insist that the armed forces remain in the barracks.

A case in point was a July 1958 plot to overthrow the junta masterminded by the minister of defense, Colonel Jesús María Castro León, who claimed that Larrazábal had become a captive of leftists. Two days before the coup was to occur, fifteen armed men broke into Betancourt's home with the intention of apprehending and detaining him until the *golpe* was over. When they discovered he was not at home, the men searched the premises looking for incriminating materials that could be used to discredit the AD chief. Castro León's goal was not just to oust the provisional junta but to reinstate a pérezjimenista-type regime. In his memoirs he complained that political polarization had infected the armed forces. Within the military, he added, there were supporters of each of the major political parties. Such "political cannibalism" had to be eradicated to preserve the institution's integrity.[130]

The rebellion faltered as a result of a nationwide one-day general strike and an enormous demonstration repudiating *golpismo* in the Plaza del Silencio in Caracas. As the leadership of the major parties stood in unison and one after another denounced the plot, the protestors called on the military to arm them.[131] In the face of the united front, Castro León and seven of his colleagues capitulated. Subsequently expelled from Venezuela, they followed their former chief, Pérez Jiménez, to Ciudad Trujillo.[132] A second *golpe* just forty-five days later included some of the same principals, and it, too, failed. It was far costlier than the previous one, though, as eighteen were killed and one hundred injured in the fighting. An investigation determined that the plotters this time intended to assassinate Larrazábal, Betancourt, and Machado.[133]

Coup plotting continued to bedevil Venezuelan politics. This was partly a byproduct of a tradition dating back to the independence era of leniency toward instigators of rebellions. When Castro León's plot was uncovered, for instance, Larrazábal accepted his former defense minister's resignation and his public apology, but then allowed him to leave the country. Castro León continued to draw his full salary while in exile. The public was furious at this slap on the wrist. After the second rebellion was squelched, public opinion again demanded accountability, especially considering that one of the leaders of that uprising had been exiled along with Castro León less than two months before. All Larrazábal would concede to, however, was that in the future, plotters could face prison terms, the loss of rank, and criminal prosecution.[134]

Betancourt's ascension to the presidency was never a certainty. The junta and the armed forces lobbied against his return from exile. His homecoming in February 1958 also did not sit well with some members of his own party, who still blamed him for the 1948 coup and felt that he was too conciliatory to the oligarchy and the military. Included in his second wife's memoirs is a telling 1957 psychological profile of her husband that explains why Betancourt rarely evoked neutral reactions from contemporaries. "He is 100 percent politician, fundamentally a man of action, a passionate and vehement man. . . . He is tough, sure of himself and of his convictions."[135]

In a fiercely contested presidential campaign, Betancourt took his message to the farthest reaches of the country. Over the course of 45 days, he delivered 132 speeches and gave almost two dozen press conferences. In his addresses, he praised the armed forces for their role in overturning the dictatorship, invoked those who died in the struggle, but promised that acts of vengeance would not be tolerated if he were elected. With that said, he pledged to prosecute Pérez Jiménez and his confederates, whom he mocked as "Ali Baba and the Forty Thieves," to the full extent of the law.[136] Despite polling a dismal fourth in the capital, Betancourt received 49 percent of the vote, besting Larrazábal and Caldera. Acción Democrática earned majorities in both houses of Congress.[137]

Betancourt learned from the mistakes he and his party had made during AD's three years in power. Sectarianism gave way to compromise, and the military was co-opted rather than spurned. Venezuela, Betancourt contended, should not follow the Mexican path, where one party, the PRI, had dominated politics for decades. If democracy was to flourish in Venezuela, the other signatories of the power-sharing agreement that became known as the Pact of Punto Fijo—COPEI and the Unión Revolucionario Democrática (URD)—must prosper politically. As he noted soon after his victory at the polls: "Inter-party discord was kept to a minimum, and in this way the leaders revealed that they had learned the hard lesson that despotism gave to all Venezuelans."[138]

The same went for AD itself, as Betancourt expressly repudiated Gallegos's promise to rule in the interests of the party. National unity and the institutionalization of democratic norms, he argued, must take precedence over the implementation of a given party's platform. The architect of the Punto Fijo agreement believed that ensuring the preservation and strengthening of democratic rule was more important than his own party's agenda. This aggravated militants, who, after a decade out of power, were champing at the bit to bring about transformative change. The very notion of power sharing with a longtime rival like the more conservative COPEI was loathsome to leftist-leaning *muchachos*. Despite the criticism, Betancourt stubbornly defended his position, even threatening to resign on two occasions if AD's leadership went against his wishes.[139]

Hard-won lessons explain why party leaders in both countries felt that it was in their interest to engineer complex power-sharing arrangements with their rivals. While Colombia had a tradition of coalition governments to draw on, Venezuela, with the exception of the *trienio*, had been governed by personal or military dictators since independence.[140] Unlike Colombia, where the Liberal and Conservative Parties had alternated in power for almost the entirety of the country's history, Venezuela's political parties were late to emerge, and only one, AD, actually had experience governing.[141] In fact, military rule was the exception in Colombia. Prior to the coup that brought Rojas Pinilla to power, the military had intervened in politics only once in the preceding fifty years.

Venezuela's transition to civilian rule was especially meaningful to those who had risked their lives during the preceding ten years. In a revealing letter to Muñoz Marín, written just a month after Pérez Jiménez fled, Betancourt reflected on how much had changed in Venezuela since he had left in 1948. This moment was "among the most thrilling and complex" of his public life. Unlike the *trienio*, however, relations among the major political parties were "cordial," and when obstacles surfaced, he, Caldera, and URD's leader Villalba were able to resolve them.[142]

On the eve of his return to Venezuela after a decade in exile, Betancourt gave a speech to a New York audience titled "America and the Dictatorships," in which he cautioned that the democratic wave now sweeping the region demanded vigilance and unity, otherwise the militaries would soon retake power. Opportunities like this were rare, and it was incumbent upon democrats throughout the hemisphere to seize the moment and not let this opportunity go to waste. "If the [political] parties once again engage in a knife fight, a propitious climate for a relapse will result." If the price of unity was compromise, he added, that was a small price to pay for democracy's survival.[143]

Over time, policy differences between the governing party and the loyal opposition narrowed in each country, and orderly transitions of power proceeded with little incident. After the URD left the governing coalition in 1961, only AD and COPEI remained. Those parties alternated in power over the next three decades. After 140 years of nearly uninterrupted dictatorship, Venezuela unexpectedly became one of a handful of stable democracies in the region.

The communists, of course, were not invited to participate in the pacts. In Venezuela, this presented a thorny challenge because the PCV had grown much stronger during Pérez Jiménez's tenure. Before 1948, the party had been "marginalized and small . . . in the political sphere as well as the unions," Betancourt noted. "Now, after ten years of an implacable dictatorship, which brandished anti-communism as its shield, the communists appear to have infiltrated into many places."[144] The dictatorship, Betancourt concluded, had been a "much better breeding ground" for the PCV than the *trienio*.[145]

His assessment was corroborated by an NIE report; Pérez Jiménez's regime feared AD far more than the communists and "was willing to use communist hostility toward AD for its own ends."[146] Years later, Pérez corroborated that analysis. The SN may have harassed the PCV's leadership, but it left the party apparatus intact. As a result, the communists made significant inroads with professionals and the urban poor, especially in the dictatorship's last year. By one estimate, party membership exploded from one thousand in 1957 to nine thousand a year later. Aware that they had an enemy in Betancourt, the communists threw their support to Larrazábal in the election.[147]

Betancourt assured the State Department that AD had no intention of collaborating with the Venezuelan Communist Party now or in the future. Along with the State Department, Betancourt was unhappy with the PCV's presence in the Junta Patriótica (JP), a clandestine organization that opposed the dictatorship, composed of representatives from the major parties and influential sectors of society.[148] But the PCV's leading role in the JP and its visibility during the uprising were perfectly understandable. Unlike the other parties, the communists had given the appearance of collaborating with the dictatorship, or at least had not openly opposed it. As a result, they were not persecuted to the extent that the other parties were. The subtext of Betancourt's remarks must have been obvious to Rubottom and his aides. Washington's support for Pérez Jiménez had backfired; unless measures were taken, the communists would become a force to reckon with in Venezuelan politics.[149]

There were three notable differences between the two countries: the details written into the pacts, the role played by the popular sectors in bringing about regime change, and the pervasive violence afflicting rural Colombia. Negotiating the transition to democratic rule in Colombia was a top-down affair, carried out by elites from both parties in consultation with the military junta, with little input from other sectors of society. The opposite was the case in Venezuela, where popular classes repeatedly took to the streets to make their demands heard during the revolt against the dictator and then again during the transitional phase.

Opposition to Pérez Jiménez was further inflamed by resentment of his labor policies. During the 1950s, seven hundred thousand Spanish, Portuguese, and Italian immigrants had arrived in Venezuela, attracted by well-paying jobs on massive public works projects. The regime's preference for hiring foreigners angered un- and underemployed Venezuelans, who took out their frustrations by looting and burning businesses owned by Italians and Spaniards right after the dictator's ouster. The 23rd of January popular uprising came at a high cost—three hundred dead and one thousand wounded.[150]

Nothing commensurate occurred in Colombia, where the popular classes remained sidelined after Rojas Pinilla stepped down. On the other hand, violence was endemic in the country's rural areas. *La Violencia* (1948–1974) cost the lives of an estimated three hundred thousand Colombians while displacing hundreds of thousands more.[151] Feuding political parties could no longer rein in their own, as "hereditary hatreds" took on a life of their own. According to historian Marco Palacios, the bloodletting was "less acts of war" than "atrocities and vengeances." Peasant bands of fighters had little interest in territorial advantage, let alone winning a war. During the quarter-century of strife, a department's capital never changed hands. Instead, retaliating, remedying grievances, and defending one's kin's honor or community were of greater import.[152]

After seizing power, Rojas Pinilla had implemented an amnesty for "political crimes"—defined as attacks against the government or the armed forces or crimes precipitated by partisan politics. The truce occasioned a brief lull in the fighting. That 6,500 peasants turned in arms attests to the parameters of the conflict.[153] But the carnage soon recurred in the countryside, as armed bands of paramilitaries (called *pájaros*, or birds), with the connivance of local political bosses and the police, terrorized rural communities. *Pájaros* took advantage of the unrest to hatch elaborate extortion rackets. In return for protection, the paramilitaries demanded a portion of the crops, or in some cases, coerced landowners to sell their properties at "ridiculously" low prices. Some armed bands turned Marxist. As the historian Luis Herrán-Ávila noted, Rojas Pinilla's amnesty successfully disarmed the principal rebel groups but failed to pacify the countryside or stanch persistent demands for social and economic justice.[154]

Lleras Camargo, who was elected president in August 1958, placed the blame for his nation's "flames of madness" on his own political party and its rival: the Liberal and Conservative parties had "unleashed, ordered, stimulated [the violence] without any risk, by remote control."[155] One of the first steps taken by the junta that succeeded Rojas Pinilla was to establish a fact-finding committee to investigate the causes of the conflict. Over the course of the next several years, the seven-person national commission canvassed the country by automobile, horseback, helicopter, and foot, interviewing twenty thousand victims and rebels.[156]

The Colombian pact also stipulated that a Conservative politician serve first as president. But infighting among various factions of that party was so great that its leadership could not settle on a candidate. In a move that must have been as shocking to everyday Colombians as it was to elites of both parties, the Conservative Gómez prevailed upon a reluctant Liberal, Lleras Camargo, to accept the initial presidency of the new National Front government.

The potential for disruption was so great in Colombia that political elites felt it wiser to share power with those they despised than to risk the potential of a revolutionary situation that might open the door to more extremist solutions, either from the right or the left. While voting remained competitive, especially at the local and regional levels, with alternation in power operational, the violence normally associated with electoral campaigns would diminish, the pact's supporters contended.[157]

Thankfully, Lleras Camargo was a voice of reason at a profoundly destabilizing moment in the country's history. He was everything the pompous, vain Rojas Pinilla was not—conciliatory, transparent, self-deprecating, and honest to a fault. The military dictatorship was anomalous: reminding his countrymen of their history, he declared, "Colombia is unfertile land for dictatorship." A power-sharing arrangement, he contended, offered Colombians their best chance for a lasting political peace: "Colombians evidently cannot permit themselves the luxury, after such long years of institutional disorder, of reestablishing the political game as though nothing had happened. Politically there is no other way out ... [than] a government of the two parties, not for the purpose of opening another campaign for both of them to seek total power, but to acquiesce in a national regime in which neither predominates."[158] A glum Cabot thought Lleras faced almost insurmountable obstacles: "a virtual[ly] bankrupt government, a frightful violence in the countryside, [and] a country exhausted by ten years of bitter partisan strife." Tackling these matters would require Solomonic collaboration with bitter adversaries. "He realizes, of course, that he must have our support in many matters, but he also realizes that, given the alternatives, we have practically no choice other than to give him that support ... the probable alternative to Lleras is chaos, and in the coming years it may be quite hard to prevent precisely that."[159]

Designed to curtail political conflict, the Colombian and Venezuelan pacts guaranteed the signatories cabinet posts in the new governments and access to positions in the bureaucracy. The Colombian power-sharing arrangement went so far as to mandate political parity from the federal government to the municipalities. But progressive voices in both countries soon became disillusioned with the "pactocracies" because the compromises required to forge unity throttled any chance for meaningful change.[160]

Such consociational regimes are, by definition, conservative in character. As political scientist Terry Karl noted, by institutionalizing the status quo, the pact "demobilizes social forces while limiting the extent to which all actors can wield power in the future."[161] In the Venezuelan case, AD had to make significant concessions to overcome the concerns of its chief competitors, including a no-reelection clause, because the two opposition parties knew that at least in the short run, they were likely to lose any election to their well-established rival. But in return for those carrots, the presidency did not alternate as it did in Colombia; voters selected their presidents. Another difference between the neighbors: the signatories of Punto Fijo agreed on an aspirational "minimum program" even before assuming power, committing the parties to a progressive agenda, including full employment; a massive public housing program; a new labor code; significant expenditures on health, education, and social security; and subsidies on staples and housing. In both cases, democratic rule became possible only when elites became satisfied that the rules of the political game would do them minimal harm.[162]

The U.S. role also differed in Venezuela. It did not lift a finger to prevent the Venezuelan strongman (and Estrada) from moving to the States after his brief three-week stay in the Dominican Republic. This infuriated the JP, which felt that both must come back to face charges. Such was the revulsion that many Venezuelans felt that in the days immediately after their hurried exit from the country, demonstrators looted the homes of Pérez Jiménez and Vallenilla Lanz, set the SN's headquarters on fire, and beat, and in a few grisly cases, publicly executed SN agents and informers.[163]

Conclusions

To its credit, the Eisenhower administration took a wait-and-see approach during the Venezuelan transition to democracy. Some scholars claim that Betancourt's allies in the State Department were successful in altering the longstanding perception that the AD chief could not be trusted.[164] But this seems doubtful. For the previous decade, the administration did everything in its power to demonstrate its support for the Pérez Jiménez regime while treating Betancourt and AD as untrustworthy agitators. Berle felt that the AD chief had every reason to harbor a grudge but was tactful enough to keep those feelings to himself. "The State Department ... had tried to drive Betancourt out of the hemisphere for years. There was a time when the only house he could get a courteous dinner was mine in New York, What he had felt about the State Department, to his honor, he never told me, and he never muttered a syllable of bitterness against it. But on all personal grounds, he had every cause to be bitter. He's a bigger man than that."[165]

Only at the eleventh hour, in the last months of 1958, did the State Department engage with Betancourt seriously, at a point when few good options remained. It was Larrazábal's acceptance of the PCV's support for his run for the presidency that forced Washington's hand. From that point on, Betancourt became the clear preference. By then, it was apparent that he and AD would play a dominant role in any post–Pérez Jiménez government.

Two factors dictated Washington's restrained response: the *desideratum* that the oil industry be protected at all costs and a nonnegotiable requirement that the communists be excluded from political participation. It was not just Larrazábal's and Betancourt's assurances on these matters that convinced Washington, it was their actions. The oil fields were secured, and the communists were barred from participating in both the interim junta and the civilian governments.

The Eisenhower administration was well aware that a more heavy-handed response might backfire and bring with it popular mobilizations that domestic elites and Washington both feared. Oil raised the stakes. Just as it had done in Bolivia, the administration calculated the risks of intervention and chose a more deliberate approach. How much the rapidly unfolding Cuba situation played into the administration's thinking in Venezuela is more difficult to gauge, but it is instructive that at least until mid-1959, the administration took a similar wait-and-see approach to the 26th of July movement.

The jury was out in Washington as to whether fledgling civilian governments were strong enough to ward off communist infiltration. With policymakers fixated on how to prevent leftists from taking advantage of the newfound freedoms that civilian rule offered, Eisenhower and Foster Dulles decided to entrust Nixon with the task of shoring up relations with the newly minted democracies.

Initially, reformers were optimistic that the political tide had turned. Seizing the moment, they embraced liberals like Porter and Morse, who urged that assistance earmarked for the region's armed forces be redirected toward economic development and called for a reappraisal of the administration's policy. Meanwhile, Trujillo's thuggish actions abroad helped Porter and his colleagues make their case.

Not all Democrats, however, were amenable. Lobbied hard by the region's dictators, hawkish southern congressmen attacked their liberal colleagues for being soft on communism. State and Defense Department officials and Republican challengers back home joined the chorus. Even though McCarthyism was on the wane, liberal politicians still remained vulnerable.

What forced the administration to reconsider its policy toward the region, however, was not the liberal critique. It was the dramatic shift toward civilian rule in the hemisphere. The democratic surge meant that fences needed to be mended with neighbors. To this end, Eisenhower dispatched his vice president to the region in the spring of 1958 to shore up support among moderate politicians. Nixon's goodwill mission, however, demonstrated in no uncertain terms how far the United States had fallen in the estimation of many Latin Americans.

CHAPTER FOURTEEN

The Hour of the Sword No Longer Tolls

The one issue that is charged with perhaps the most intense emotion in Latin America is the attitude of the United States toward dictatorships. It has given dictators money . . . supplied them with planes and tanks, for which they had no use unless it was to employ them against their own people. It has praised dictators publicly. . . . Tens of thousands of people in Latin America have had relatives killed or have suffered imprisonment and torture at the hands of dictators. And they come from the classes that produce political leadership: students, professional men and businessmen, trade union officials.

—LUIS MUÑOZ MARÍN

You remember those people who threw rocks at Nixon. I'd like to believe it was just Nixon's personality, but they were sending us a message. We can't embrace every tinhorn dictator who tells us he's anti-communist while he's sitting on the necks of his own people.

—JOHN F. KENNEDY

In the spring of 1958, Eisenhower and his ailing secretary of state asked Nixon to attend the inauguration of Argentina's Arturo Frondizi on their behalf. Sending a high-ranking member of the administration, they believed, signaled support for democratic rule while it appeased domestic and foreign critics. Champing at the bit to take on greater responsibilities, Nixon, who had represented the administration at the Brazilian Juscelino Kubitschek's inaugural two years earlier without incident, initiated conversations with the State Department in the months leading up to Frondizi's swearing in about the possibility of combining the trip to Buenos Aires with a "goodwill" tour of South American countries.[1] Some foreign service officers questioned the vice president's motives. Cabot dismissed the trip as little more than a publicity stunt to "wow the yokels back home in the election year."[2]

Whether or not the two-and-a-half-week trip (April 27–May 15) actually bolstered Republican prospects in the upcoming midterm elections, Nixon's goals were commendable. He expressed a desire to interact, not just with politicians but with a broad cross-section of Latin American society, including businessmen, the press, organized labor, educators, and students. He was especially "anxious to meet the man on the street." Nor did the vice president intend to shy away from controversial topics, such as commodity prices, tariffs, quotas, and foreign aid.[3]

By any measure the trip was an unqualified disaster. Met by hostile crowds, especially in Lima and Caracas, Nixon and his colleagues blamed the unruly reception on communist agitators. But there was more to it than that. The democratic wave of the late 1950s gave voice to many who had been silenced by years of repression. Washington's coddling of dictators, in particular, had energized a new generation of student activists.

While the Nixon debacle prompted hand-wringing in Washington, it was not the final word on the subject. Latin Americans realized that North American politicians were not cut from the same cloth. Coming so soon afterward, Congressman Charles Porter's trip could not have been more different. Taken together, the two visits, a scant seven weeks apart, prompted a long-overdue reappraisal of U.S. policy.

A Prizefighter's Gesture

What was problematic for a paternalistic Cold Warrior like Nixon was the trend toward democratic rule. That might not be in a country's best interest, he later related, "particularly in those Latin American countries which are completely lacking in political maturity."[4] On the other hand, Nixon thought highly of the militaries, considering them the region's "great stabilizing force." The generals he encountered were among "the ablest and most dedicated leaders in the hemisphere." While he admitted that some officers were a threat to democratic rule, he was confident that "more of them are using their power and prestige to support free governments."[5]

The final schedule had Nixon and his wife, Pat, visiting eight countries, five of which had transitioned recently to civilian rule. That there was apprehension about his reception was borne out by the secrecy surrounding the itinerary. The schedule was kept under wraps until the last minute, as were the visits to universities. As Nixon explained in his memoir *Six Crises*, this was done to ensure that "hard core communist agitators would have no advance warning of my coming."[6]

In fact, the vice president was welcomed warmly in several countries, but in Uruguay, Argentina, and Bolivia, the reception was decidedly mixed. At the National University in Montevideo, for instance, a student castigated Nixon about U.S. support for repressive dictatorships. At the University of Buenos Aires, students criticized Washington for its role in the Guatemalan intervention. While not responding directly to that question, Nixon did allow that the U.S. had made mistakes in the past and would do so in the future, but that "dictators are repugnant to our people." His one stop in a country governed by an autocrat, Paraguay, should have given the vice president pause. There Nixon witnessed the arrest of student protestors by plainclothes police on the streets of Asunción. When the dictator, Stroessner, was questioned later about the arrests, he explained to the press that the demonstrators were communists. When pressed on how he knew that, he muttered, "because I say so."[7]

Nixon's trip triggered unrest, even in countries he did not visit. Violence broke out, for instance, in Panama on May 2, when students entered the Canal Zone and planted seventy Panamanian flags on the grounds. Protests recurred after authorities removed the flags. Nine demonstrators were killed by National Guard troops sent in to quell the protests.[8]

The stopovers in Peru and Venezuela illustrated just how incensed Latin Americans were with U.S. policy. What those two countries had in common was that the U.S. had backed repressive dictatorships and that those nations had recently undergone, or, in the case of Venezuela, was undergoing a transition to democratic rule.

The State Department was taken by surprise by the hostile Peruvian reaction. Even though the two countries did not see eye to eye on several issues, Rubottom predicted that the vice president would receive "a more gracious and friendly welcome" there than elsewhere. Peruvian authorities, however, were certainly aware of the potential for trouble. This was evident in how they played down his visit and kept the motorcade's route a secret.[9]

Trouble began soon after the entourage's arrival on May 7. That night, protestors made their sentiments known outside the Nixons' hotel. The next morning, the vice president placed a floral wreath with a U.S. flag affixed to it at a monument to one of the heroes of Peruvian independence, José de San Martín. As he returned to the hotel, demonstrators tore up the wreath, desecrating the flag in the process.[10]

Whether Nixon would even meet with students was an open question. Student leaders at San Marcos objected to their rector's invitation for Nixon to speak on campus. By neglecting to consult with the student directorate about the invitation, the rector had broken with longstanding tradition. Student leaders made their feelings known three days before the vice president arrived, issuing a public statement in which they declared the vice president persona non grata on campus. In their manifesto, they explained why he and the policies he represented did not deserve a public forum at *their* university. Students criticized the Eisenhower administration's imposition of tariff restrictions on mineral imports and its dumping of stockpiles of domestic cotton, which had led to a precipitous decline in world market prices for one of Peru's chief exports. But almost half of the statement's clauses criticized U.S. support for dictatorships. The decoration of Odría was an especially sore point, since the dictator had "persecuted, imprisoned and assassinated leaders who fought for the liberty of our people." The manifesto was signed by students of all political persuasions—communists, socialists, Apristas, and moderates.[11]

Even though Rubottom and U.S. ambassador to Peru Theodore Achilles were aware of the manifesto and had heard that the students intended to prevent the vice president's party from entering the campus, they advised Nixon not to cancel the visit, so as not to give "communist agitators" a propaganda windfall. The usually combative Nixon, who rarely shied away from a fight, expressed concern about the potential for violence at San Marcos. In fact, discussions with Rubottom and Achilles continued long into the night about whether he should go to the university. He asked his aides to speak with the rector about withdrawing the invitation, but when the two sides did not agree on how best to walk back the offer without either losing face, Nixon decided to meet with students. Years later, he defended the decision. "My intuition backed by considerable experience," he later remarked, "was that I should go."[12]

His intuition failed him. As Nixon and his entourage approached the university's locked gates, he was met by two thousand students and "a barrage of invective and stones, bottles, eggs and oranges." After an unsuccessful attempt to wade into the crowd and speak with the students, Nixon and his aides retreated back to their vehicles. Standing up in the back seat of his car, with his hands in "a prize-fighter's gesture," he chastised the students for not debating with him, calling them cowards.[13] His entourage wisely decided to back away and head to the nearby Catholic university, the Pontificia Universidad Católica del Perú. There he walked into two classes unannounced, demanding "to take on all comers." After the first class refused to meet with him, the second class agreed, but a small number of students showed their dissatisfaction by jeering and booing the vice president. Later in the day, he was accosted by rock- and tomato-throwing demonstrators as he and his aides walked through the Plaza San Martín.[14]

Nixon and the State Department blamed the confrontations on communists, and embarrassed authorities took swift action, rounding up fourteen party members. Postmortems by the State Department insisted that since the tactics employed and the slogans on the banners in different countries were similar, the protests were all "communist-inspired and staged." With the exception of Venezuela, there was little in the way of evidence to corroborate that charge, however.[15] After reflecting on the debacle for a week, Achilles came to a different conclusion. The government, he hypothesized, was well aware that hostilities were not just possible, but probable—"the pot was already boiling." Authorities were "hoping to utilize [the] visit to seek more U.S. loans and may not have been averse [to the] prospect of mild communist, anti-U.S. demonstrations."[16]

If Achilles blamed the Peruvian government, a local writer, Ezequiel Ramírez Novoa, placed the onus on Nixon. If anyone should be singled out for acting as an *agent provocateur*, it was not communists but the vice president himself. He and his aides knew the students' position. "If an in-

Nixon argues with student, Universidad de San Marcos, Lima,
Peru, May 8, 1958. National Archives and Records
Administration (NARA) and DVIDS Public Domain Archive.

dividual is aware that he has been declared persona non grata by an institution, he is obliged not to set foot on the premises." In the opinion of
Ramírez Novoa, Nixon reaped what he sowed.[17]

Why was Peru such a hotbed of anti-American sentiment? For the
first time in decades, Peruvians were enjoying a democratic spring, making it possible for political parties, unions, the media, and citizens to express opinions without fear of reprisal.[18] Nixon may have placed the
blame where he did, but thanks to detailed briefing books he received on
each of the countries he visited, he was aware that many Peruvians felt
aggrieved about the United States. Although communists did participate
in the demonstrations, it was the Apristas who led the protests. In fact,
the president of San Marcos's student directorate was an APRA member.

Over the years, Haya de la Torre had warmed to both the United
States and the desirability of foreign investment. Comparing the corporate
dollars that came to a country like Peru to the irrigation of crops, he argued that those funds were essential to cultivating healthy crops but had to
be "channeled and controlled" so that they would not spill over the river-
banks and flood the fields.[19] His opposition to communism never wavered,
but his stance on the military blew hot and cold. At times he thought it an

implacable obstacle to the pursuit of democratic rule; at other times, the armed forces were considered fertile ground for recruitment and a potential ally in the party's ongoing efforts to obtain legalization.[20]

By the late 1950s, APRA was beset by factionalism. As one journalist noted, the movement's more radical elements were disillusioned with the party's "middle-aged respectability and willingness to compromise." Some were unhappy with Haya's decision to collaborate with the civilian government of Manuel Prado Ugarteche in return for the party's legalization and some modest reforms for urban workers, always APRA's core constituency. Exasperated by the leadership's increasingly mainstream positions, a splinter group, calling itself APRA-Rebelde, would break away in 1959. Their anti-imperialist, antifeudal platform remained faithful to Haya's original message that he first articulated in the mid-1920s. These youthful militants later formed the Movimiento de Izquierda Revolucionaria and struck an uneasy alliance with Peruvian communists.[21]

What all Apristas agreed on, however, was that the U.S. should alter its stance toward dictatorships. During Nixon's visit, an APRA newspaper, *La Tribuna*, wrote an open letter to the vice president, in which it voiced its objection to the Eisenhower administration's bestowal of decorations on Batista, Trujillo, Stroessner, Pérez Jiménez, and Odría.[22]

After the fiasco in Lima, the crowds were more hospitable in Quito and Bogotá, although the atmosphere was tense in the latter. The U.S. embassy in Bogotá reported rumors of a possible attempt on the vice president's life. There was concern that Colombian students would try to emulate their Peruvian peers. But "the greatest danger" was said to come from the followers of the recently deposed Rojas Pinilla, who were intent on embarrassing the interim junta.[23] Nixon's arrival in the Colombian capital came at an anxious moment—just six days after Lleras Camargo and four members of the junta had been briefly abducted by the former dictator's supporters, and one day before elections were to be held.[24]

The State Department may have been surprised by the reaction in Peru, but it was well aware that anti-American sentiment was cresting in Venezuela. Dulles, however, was anxious to include Caracas on Nixon's itinerary, owing to the "special and strategic interests we have there" and the country's recent transition to democratic rule.[25] Still, Rubottom tried to dissuade Nixon. "We felt that things had not settled down enough in Venezuela and there was still this aftermath of ill feeling about alleged U.S. 'support' for Pérez Jiménez." At the very least, he recommended, Venezuela should be the first stop, not the last, so that organizers of the demonstrations would have less time to prepare. But the vice president knew that the large colony of North Americans in Venezuela would welcome his visit, and for that reason he envisioned Caracas as an upbeat finale to the trip.[26]

The decision to add Venezuela to the itinerary confirmed just how tone-deaf the administration was. A decade of support for a heinous regime and the presence of Pérez Jiménez and his henchman in Miami at that moment had poisoned the well. With the Venezuelan media unshackled since his overthrow, one exposé after another testified to the dictatorship's countless cruelties. The Caracas press also played up Pérez Jiménez's ostentatious lifestyle in exile, citing his four-hundred-thousand-dollar mansion on Pine Tree Drive in Miami Beach, a full complement of servants, around-the-clock surveillance of his compound by off-duty Miami policemen, and a fleet of cars at his family's disposal.[27]

Therefore the timing of Nixon's visit could not have been worse. Seven weeks earlier, an impolitic letter from former ambassador Warren to Estrada surfaced, instantly becoming front-page news in Venezuela. Written during the dictatorship's final days, on State Department letterhead, and sent from the diplomat's current posting in Ankara, Turkey, it was discovered in the recently ransacked SN archives. In his brief note, Warren conveyed his "warmest New Year's wishes" to the reviled Estrada and congratulated him on putting down a military rebellion ten days earlier. Like Whelan, Warren was a longtime advocate of dictators, serving as ambassador to Somoza before his stint in Venezuela between 1951 and 1956. Venezuelans remembered that it was Warren who had presented the Legion of Merit to Pérez Jiménez in 1954.[28]

The U.S. government said nothing about the letter, but the publication of a photostatic copy in the PCV's *Tribuna Popular* in mid-March was political dynamite. As the journalist Tad Szulc recalled, it "was something of a bombshell. It handed the Communist Party, which was busy … spreading its influence in universities, factories, unions and intellectual groups, just the issue it needed to set in motion an effective anti-United States campaign." Throwing gasoline on the fire was a poorly timed announcement by the State Department just a week afterward, confirming that the United States had, in fact, granted visas to Pérez Jiménez and Estrada.[29]

On the defensive, the State Department took pains to explain that its treatment of Pérez Jiménez was not in any way exceptional. After all, as an internal memo noted, the U.S. was not alone in providing visas for ex–heads of state. Latin American nations "generally display high regard for the traditional doctrine of asylum for political refugees." Over the last two decades, thirteen former heads of state, dictators and democrats alike, had been admitted to the United States "on visas permitting them to establish permanent or extended residence." Included on that list were four Venezuelans—two militarists (Medina Angarita and López Contreras) and two civilian politicians (Gallegos and Betancourt). With respect to Pérez Jiménez, it was Venezuela's provisional junta that had issued the ex-dictator a diplomatic passport just four days after he left the country and had not revoked or canceled it until six months later. Nor, as yet, had the junta invoked "the perfectly valid extradition treaty" between the two countries.[30] Practicing the kind of deception it had accused Porter of, the Department felt it better not to divulge the data on the visas, but recommended feeding the tip to a "friendly newspaperman . . . who could use it without attribution, or as a last resort get a friendly congressman to write the Department asking for information." Such misdirection would give the Department plausible deniability while ensuring "that none of the other governments named might resent our putting the finger on them publicly."[31]

Nixon was well aware of what a liability Pérez Jiménez was to the administration, referring to him at one point as "the most despised dictator in all of Latin America." But he defended the decision to grant him sanctuary because, in his words, the United States did "not believe that deposed rulers, no matter how despicable, should be put before firing squads without trial."[32]

All of this should have given the vice president and the State Department pause, but there were still other reasons to cancel the trip's last leg. As had their compatriots at the University of San Marcos, just before Nixon's arrival students at Caracas's Central University issued a statement that Nixon was "an undesirable visitor to Simón Bolívar's homeland." They declared themselves in solidarity with fellow student organizations in the region that had expressed dissatisfaction with Nixon's visit. The vice president, the statement read, was the representative of a government that aided dictatorships. The Eisenhower administration not only had decorated the Venezuelan despot but then had inflamed passions by giving "the assassins Pérez Jiménez and Estrada" asylum. Echoing the students at San Marcos, they objected to Nixon visiting their campus. When Larrazábal was asked what he thought of the demands, his answer appeared to give the students a wide berth: "If I were a student, I'd be protesting too."[33]

In addition to the student opposition to Nixon's visit, the CIA learned that local members of the Communist Party had hired a gunman to assassinate him.[34] The Department also was aware of the likelihood of large demonstrations in Caracas. But as Rubottom recalled, "by that time it was too late to call the thing off without seeming to run away."[35] When North American officials received assurance from authorities that there would be sufficient protection, they decided to soldier on. The only concessions made were to order closed limousines and to cancel his scheduled visit to Central University. The decision not to use open vehicles probably saved lives.[36]

Justifiably proud of overthrowing the dictatorship, hundreds of nationalistic Venezuelans chose this moment to express themselves in a most unfortunate manner. From the moment Nixon's Air Force DC-6 touched down at Maiquetía Airport on the 13th, roughly five hundred demonstrators made their intentions clear. With no Estrada to quietly escort the vice president from the airport as he had Foster Dulles four years earlier during the Inter-American meetings, the Nixons were left to face angry crowds. Demonstrators on the airport's observation deck jeered "*Nixon fuera*" (Nixon go home) and hurled garbage and spat tobacco juice on the pair as they walked toward the terminal.

Authorities also failed to provide a large enough police detail for the motorcade's twelve-mile trip from the airport to Caracas. Near a scheduled stop on the way to the Panteón Nacional, where the vice president was to lay a wreath on Bolívar's tomb, vehicles were placed along the route to obstruct the motorcade, making it impossible to proceed. As the limousines slowed to a halt, several hundred protestors besieged the convoy. Demonstrators threw rocks and trash, while some protestors wielding baseball bats and lead pipes smashed the windows of Nixon's Cadillac, injuring the Venezuelan foreign minister, a secret service agent, and Vernon Walters, who served as a translator and advisor for Nixon during the trip.[37] As the vehicles inched forward, several more waves of protestors assaulted the motorcade. The final wave of attacks lasted twelve harrowing minutes as protestors rocked Nixon's vehicle, nearly overturning it. Only the timely arrival of a small detachment of soldiers firing shots in the air allowed the motorcade to escape. A spontaneous decision to forego the ceremony at the Panteón and drive directly to the embassy under the circumstances was prudent. Venezuelan troops, who searched the six thousand demonstrators waiting for the motorcade at the Panteón, collected two hundred Molotov cocktails.[38]

Protestors attack the Nixons' limousine, Caracas, Venezuela, May 13, 1958.
Richard Nixon Foundation Collection of Audiovisual Materials, Richard
Nixon Presidential Library and Museum, Yorba Linda, CA.

For the rest of the Nixons' visit, the junta stationed armored cars and
tanks in front of the embassy. At a luncheon later that same day before
more than two dozen "important opinion leaders," a defiant vice president gave a "rousing anti-communist speech." Most of his subsequent
meetings took place inside the embassy.[39] Nixon decided to cut short his
stay, though. There were discussions about taking a helicopter from
nearby Carlota Airport to Maiquetía, but Nixon was told that Pérez Jiménez had left by helicopter from that military airport. Since he "did not
want any such odious comparison made after my departure," Nixon decided instead to retrace his path to Maiquetía with the benefit of beefed-
up security.[40]

Unsure if the vice president needed assistance or "if the Venezuelan
government might not want some aid from us," Eisenhower rushed
troops from North Carolina to Guantánamo in Cuba and Ramey Air
Force Base in Aguadilla, Puerto Rico and directed the Navy to send a

task force to the area.[41] Both Rubottom and Nixon objected to the deployment, concerned that it would embarrass their hosts.[42]

As it turned out, Eisenhower did not need to worry. Authorities provided much better security for the return trip to the airport. Unlike the day before, "the city seemed deserted except for tanks or armored vehicles stationed at every intersection," Nixon remembered. The liberal use of tear gas drove protestors away. "I observed only four or five civilians during the entire ride."[43]

The fallout from Eisenhower's big stick response was immediate. A *New York Times* editorial predicted that the communists would benefit from the display of military might because it "ignores the psychological and historical context. . . . News of United States troops moving southward conjures up in every Latin mind instant recollections of the bad old days of 'intervention' and of 'dollar diplomacy.' "[44]

The entire affair was deeply troubling to many in Venezuela. The governor of Caracas's federal district was fired, and two civilian members of the junta resigned, citing the abysmal performance of the security detail.[45] Additional heads rolled when Larrazábal shuffled his cabinet. In a somber radio address two days after Nixon returned home, Betancourt called it an "ignoble hour" in the country's history and blamed the incident on "irresponsible agitators." Those acting in such an uncivilized manner, he added, "play into the hands of the friends of dictatorship," who ply the falsehood that the nation was not ready for democracy. Now was the time for all Venezuelans to close ranks and show their support for the junta.[46] After having had some time to reflect on the wellsprings of his countrymen's discontent, Betancourt later placed the blame for the calamity where it belonged—on the Eisenhower administration's inexcusable support for the dictator. Protestors "found a ready atmosphere because when they said: 'Nixon, no!' there was nobody in Venezuela who was prepared to say: 'Nixon, yes!' "[47]

A defensive-sounding Venezuelan ambassador to the United States, Héctor Santaella, met with Rubottom a week after the trip. He shifted the blame to the Department for granting visas to Pérez Jiménez and Estrada. They deserved to stand trial for their crimes, Santaella insisted. "Not even [Lavrentiy] Beria or the Gestapo had committed greater atrocities than those perpetrated by Pérez Jiménez and Estrada." His countrymen "find it hard to understand why the United States, with its democratic traditions, permits Pérez Jiménez to live in luxury in Miami and openly flaunt his wealth." As a result, rumors were swirling in his country that the former dictator was plotting a return, "with the acquiescence and assistance of the United States." When Rubottom suggested that it might be advantageous if the Venezuelan government issued a statement explaining U.S visa policy, the ambassador scoffed—it would be "political suicide" for any official to do that; the two were "political dynamite."⁴⁸

Porter seconded Venezuelan demands, writing Attorney General William Rogers to inquire about what steps the administration was taking to "get him [Pérez Jiménez] out of the United States." After that story broke, Estrada, suspecting that his days in the United States were numbered, fled the country.⁴⁹

This was a fragile moment for Venezuela; rumors of a coup were in the air and the democratic transition was far from assured. It is instructive that when a coup was launched two months later, the very first item on the plotters' lengthy list of grievances referred to the junta's "shameful" handling of Nixon's visit.⁵⁰

Elections were still seven months away. A sliver of light was provided by none other than Nixon, who remarked that the administration now would look favorably on a Venezuelan request for Pérez Jiménez's extradition.⁵¹ Mitigating against a prompt request from the junta, however, was that the matter was sure to be an explosive issue in the upcoming political campaign.⁵²

The mood in the United States, however, was completely different. Outrage at the indignities the Nixons had suffered was leavened with "praise for the way he had comported himself under the most trying circumstances." Indeed, the vice president was hailed as a conquering hero. Ike arranged a "gala welcome" fit for a distinguished head of state. Civil servants were even given a busman's holiday so that they could line the route from Washington National Airport to the White House. Crowd estimates ranged from fifteen thousand at the airport to eighty thousand along the streets.⁵³

At a cabinet meeting the following day, Nixon gave the first of several briefings. In his opinion, Latin Americans were more upset with the U.S. for harboring "refugee dictators than various economic complaints," and that more needed to be done to win over students, who were all too susceptible to Soviet propaganda.⁵⁴ Six days later at an NSC meeting, he reiterated that "dictatorship now constitutes the most emotional issue in Latin America," but he expressed dissatisfaction with the democratic leaders he encountered. "They are very naïve about the nature and the

Dwight Eisenhower welcomes Vice President and Mrs. Richard Nixon
upon their return from a goodwill tour of South America. Greeting
them are John Foster Dulles and Julie and Tricia Nixon. May 15, 1958.
National Park Service Photo. Courtesy of the USNA, Eisenhower
Presidential Library, Abilene, Kansas.

threat of Communism, so much so that their attitude is frightening. They
regard the communists as nothing more than a duly constituted political
party." But it was not just the political classes. Members of the middle
class, intellectuals, labor leaders, and the media "were so weary of dictatorships that they felt that the danger of the old-fashioned dictatorship
was much more to be feared than any danger from communism." It
would be wise, he added, if future messaging drove home the point that
communism was nothing more than a "foreign-controlled dictatorship."[55]

Nixon's reflections were telling. They suggested that he and Porter
did not disagree on what was at the heart of Latin American objections to
U.S, policy. Where they differed was that Porter believed that the U.S.
must change its ways by jettisoning its support for dictatorships and by
publicly embracing democratic rule. The vice president's Cold Warrior

mindset precluded him from reaching the same conclusion. Even Foster Dulles thought the vice president's analysis simplistic. Commenting at the NSC meeting several weeks later about the surge in democratic governance around the world and specifically in Latin America, the secretary again betrayed a fundamental distrust of democratic rule. The new democracies were but babes in the woods, he remarked, "who have practically no capacity for self-government and indeed are like children facing this problem [the threat of Communism]."[56] Privately to Herter, he expressed skepticism about Nixon's instant policy prescriptions. "It was a bit presumptuous for Nixon to think he could go down there for a couple of days in many countries and think he has all the answers."[57] His brother, however, begged to differ. "There would be trouble in Latin America, if there were no communists," Allen Dulles told him. The agency had "no evidence that Moscow inspired or directed the attacks on Nixon."[58]

The House and Senate Foreign Affairs Committees met to consider the sorry state of U.S.-Latin American relations. Porter and Rep. Robert Byrd invited Figueres to speak before the House committee. Afforded the limelight, the former president did not hold back. This, he declared, was a watershed moment in U.S.-Latin American relations, but "it did not come out of nowhere." While he deplored what happened to the vice president, "when a people have used all of the means at their disposal to express themselves, the last resort they are left with is to spit." Yes, "Venezuelan zealots" behaved reprehensibly, but it was because "people cannot spit on a foreign policy, which is what they meant to do."[59]

Figueres then brought the reformers' longstanding complaint about the administration's double standards up to date: "If you talk of human dignity to Russia, why do you hesitate so much to talk [of] human dignity to the Dominican Republic? Your generals and your admirals and your high civilian officials are royally entertained there. ... But our women are raped, our men are castrated, and our professors are kidnapped from the classrooms of Columbia University. This is what some of your lawmakers call 'cooperation to fight communism.' "

He reminded committee members that Estrada, of all people, had been wined and dined by the State Department. "Spitting is a despicable practice. ... But what about moral spitting? When your government invited Pedro Estrada, the Himmler of the Western Hemisphere, to be honored in Washington, did you not spit in the faces of all Latin American democrats?" By contrast, his government, over the objections of policymakers in Washington, had refused on principle to send a delegation to Caracas.

Figueres's explosive testimony had the desired effect, energizing his allies in Washington and in the press. Porter dismissed communist influence as a red herring and called for a reappraisal of the administration's policy in the region. "To listen to Mr. Dulles, the Caracas riots would never have occurred if only the Venezuelan Government had supplied an adequate and efficient police force. . . . If we learned anything from the Caracas incident . . . the cooperation of a dictator will avail us nothing if he sits upon the powder keg of his own people's fury."[60]

The liberal press also scolded the administration. According to Matthews, it was not the "nefarious work of communists," nor was Nixon or the State Department at fault, "or Latin American ingratitude," for that matter. The four countries where the reception was the most antagonistic—Argentina, Peru, Colombia, and Venezuela—all had recently ousted strongmen. "They remember vividly the United States did not help them, but showed favor to their dictators." While commending Nixon for his "courage and patience" in defending himself against the protestors, he chided the vice president and the State Department for misjudging their audience: "If Mr. Nixon is to be criticized, it is for his basic misconception that he could go around Latin America debating with university students as if he were taking on debating teams at Harvard, Columbia or Stanford Universities. Students in all Latin American countries are passionately involved in politics, and there is among them a strong element of radicalism and even communism."[61]

Lippmann, who had aptly labeled the goodwill mission a "diplomatic Pearl Harbor," expressed similar sentiments. The vice president may have been stoned in only two countries, "but there was bad will, and plenty of it, everywhere. We are merely deluding ourselves if we pretend that only a few hoodlums led by communists are unfriendly." Besides, what was the State Department thinking by arranging a goodwill visit to an area "where anti-Americanism was rampant," he asked rhetorically.[62] Dripping with sarcasm, the old Latin American hand Berle doubled down on the criticism: "So, at long last the administration . . . discovers that it cannot lavish decorations and cordiality on avaricious dictators like Pérez Jiménez and chiefs of police like Estrada, who are local symbols of oppression and cruelty, and still expect the friendship of the peoples of the countries involved."[63]

Career foreign service officers with experience in the region came to different conclusions about Nixon's trip. Briggs was at a loss as to what the vice president's thinking was: "Instead of . . . confining his interviews to responsible government officials plus those recommended by our respective diplomatic missions, the Vice President . . . stopped his cavalcade to harangue crowds . . . and . . . argued on street corners with students . . . like an American candidate touring the boondocks."[64] In a letter to his superiors in the Department, Whelan disagreed. He thought all the hand-wringing in Washington and calls for a reexamination of policy were, on the one hand, a "fine example of Christian humility," but "Latinos seem to be mistaking this for [an] admission of basic guilt, and are responding to it as children would. Some sort of spanking seems called for to sober them up and bring them to [the] realization [that] they bear a larger share of responsibility for cracks in hemispheric solidarity."[65]

As Whelan's impolitic reaction indicates, policymakers continued to exhibit a pronounced insouciance about the state of U.S.–Latin American relations. Nowhere was this more apparent than the comments of Sam Waugh, the president of the Export-Import Bank, who accompanied the Nixons on the trip. He was stunned by the hostile reception. By all rights, they should have been well received in Venezuela, Waugh wrote. "American capital had spent millions of dollars in developing the oil and mineral resources of Venezuela and the country has been one of our best customers for years. . . . I couldn't have been more wrong."[66]

North Americans had reason to be appalled by the treatment the vice president received in Caracas and Lima. It was not the last time the Nixons' limousine would be attacked. In January 1969, antiwar protestors rained smoke bombs, beer bottles, and rocks on the president's and cabinet members' vehicles during the inaugural parade down Pennsylvania Avenue. In a scene reminiscent of Caracas, Secret Service agents fended off "projectiles with their bare hands."[67] Despite lining the parade route with troops from the District of Columbia's National Guard and the Army's 82nd Airborne Division, authorities could not prevent demonstrators from marring the inaugural.[68]

Nor had Nixon learned his lesson about the perils of wading into crowds filled with hostile demonstrators. Just as at San Marcos twelve years before, the President made himself an unwanted guest at the Lincoln Memorial in the early hours of May 9, 1970, where hundreds of student activists were camping out prior to a massive antiwar demonstration. Unlike in Lima, this time Nixon at least enjoyed the element of surprise, resulting in a much tamer reception. Before a crowd of sleepy, stunned onlookers, he delivered a rambling, incoherent monologue, veering from the benefits of travel abroad, Cambodia, recollections of World War II, and his intention to open relations with China to surfing and college football. One student dismissed the impromptu encounter. The president was someone decidedly out of touch with the matter at hand. "He wasn't really concerned with why we were here."[69] Not surprisingly, Nixon recalled the encounter differently. His goal, he suggested, had been to lift the students "out of the miserable intellectual wasteland in which they now wander aimlessly around."[70] Just as he had during his travels through Latin America, he misread his audience. Both encounters revealed an insensitive, defensive statesman, lacking the requisite awareness needed to change perceptions about his administration's policies.

A Household Word

Seven weeks after Nixon's tumultuous visit to Caracas, Porter was accorded celebrity status during his own three-day visit. His timing was perfect. On the heels of the Nixon debacle, his presence gave Venezuelans an opportunity to redeem themselves. While this may have contributed to the enthusiastic welcome, other factors better explain the very different responses to the two North American politicians.

Interestingly, Porter and Nixon had a history. In September 1952, the budding politician helped organize a sizable protest of the then–vice presidential candidate's campaign appearance at the Eugene railway station during a whistle-stop tour. At the time, Nixon was under fire for allegedly accepting improper campaign contributions from wealthy donors, funds that enabled his family to live beyond their means. The vice presidential candidate denied the allegations, insisting that he was of humble origins. His wife, he added for good measure, had to settle for a "respectable" cloth coat, not mink.

A reported two thousand demonstrators came out to heckle Nixon. In his remarks at the station, Nixon played to his base, denouncing the demonstrators as communists. Porter and his colleagues came up with some clever signage that day. Holding aloft a double-sided sign that read "No Mink Coats for Nixon—Just Cold Cash" and "Sh-h-h! Anyone Who Mentions the $16,000 [in campaign contributions] is a Communist," Porter and other protestors were attacked by Nixon supporters. In the scuffle his placard was ripped to bits. He displayed his uncanny knack for generating publicity, though, by promptly marching down to the police station and filing a complaint against the unruly protestor.[71]

On the defensive nationally, Nixon faced calls to resign. Five days after the story broke, he took to the airwaves to rebut the charges. Speaking to an audience of sixty million Americans—the largest television audience up to that point—he delivered his famous "Checkers" speech, so named because he insisted that the only political gift he had ever accepted was a cocker spaniel puppy named Checkers, which he intended to keep, to the delight of his daughters. The speech scored well with the public, and his spot on the ticket was assured. Years later, Porter was still upset with himself over the confrontation: "If we had known that we were going to ensure that Dick Nixon would become president of the United States. . . . Just because I had decided that we ought to go down and picket the [expletive]."[72]

Now, less than two months after the vice president's trip, Porter traveled to Caracas. Unlike Nixon, who was saddled with the burden of the administration's past association with the dictator, Porter's principled stance against authoritarianism gave citizens an opportunity to send an emphatic message to Washington that changes in its relationship with Venezuela and other countries in the region were overdue. An editorial titled "Ambassador from Oregon" in the *Times* hit the nail on the head: Venezuelans had nothing against Nixon per se; instead, "they were reacting to ten years of excessive American friendliness to the hated and brutal dictatorship of General Pérez Jiménez. Porter is an enemy of dictators and for that he is being honored." It did not hurt that the congressman was, in the words of a local journalist, already a "household word" to Caraqueños.[73]

Several months earlier, Porter scored points by insisting that the administration should congratulate Venezuelans for restoring democracy and that it should encourage the junta to honor its pledge to hold elections. In a speech on the floor of the House titled "A Shift for the Better in Our Latin American Policy," he predicted that although such a statement would raise hackles with regional dictators, it was critical that policymakers articulate their support in a timely way for the junta, which had restored freedom of speech, done away with the SN, and freed political prisoners. He called on the administration to categorically and publicly express its "disapproval of police states."[74]

Eisenhower met him halfway: in an unusual statement for an administration that rarely made a practice of commenting on transitions of power, he congratulated Venezuela on its return to democratic rule. But he had nothing to add about Pérez Jiménez or dictatorships more generally. The State Department chimed in, seeking to thread a needle of its own making. "While we're not in a position to intervene in the internal developments of the countries of Latin America," the Department was nonetheless pleased when any country chose the democratic path.[75] Still, the timing of the President's and the State Department's messages, nearly three months before Nixon's trip, was significant. Even if it was only a change in rhetoric, it was the first sign that the campaign by Porter and other liberal allies to alter the administration's policy was bearing fruit.

The day before he left for Caracas, Porter stopped in at the State Department for a briefing, as he did before all his trips abroad. Rubottom reviewed recent Venezuelan history and handed him a confidential summary of communist activities. The assistant secretary was concerned that the PCV's "increased influence" might trigger a military coup. Also worrisome was the "strong anti-American tenor" of the local press, which the Department believed was "infiltrated by communists." Rubottom was apprehensive about Larrazábal's apparent reluctance "to face up to the dangers of communism." Proof of this was the junta's decision to legalize the PCV over the Department's strenuous objections.[76] Larrazábal's justification of the students' actions no doubt irked officials as well.[77]

Porter asked the assistant secretary whether Venezuelan communists "were part of the international conspiracy" or might be "merely persons who sought social and political reforms for domestic reasons." Rubottom assured him that it was the former. His concerns with Larrazábal were validated when the PCV backed the admiral in the upcoming electoral campaign. Larrazábal's political coalition came in a strong second to Betancourt, winning several state legislatures and the Caracas and Maracay city councils.[78]

Knowing he would be questioned in Venezuela about Pérez Jiménez's status, Porter queried the assistant secretary as to whether there were any updates and whether it was possible for the ex-dictator to come to the Hill to face questioning. Rubottom thought that a bad idea. Although he did not explain his reasoning, one could see why the administration did not want to draw attention to its past ties to the unpopular ruler. When Porter asked why the administration was not investigating whether there were grounds for the ex-dictator's "exclusion from the United States," Rubottom deflected the question—the matter was in the hands of the Venezuelan government, and so far it had not provided evidence "which would have a bearing on his activities here."[79]

While Porter promised Rubottom that he would be careful not to "associate with any political party or group and to avoid any statements," in Caracas, just before he left, he made some tough-minded comments about the ex-dictator that were given wide play in the Venezuelan press. Pérez Jiménez, the congressman remarked, was alleged to have made off with 250 million dollars from public coffers "as he fled for his life." He predicted that "the best lawyers and public relations counsel money can buy cannot ever clear his name."[80]

The only note of caution about Porter's visit was a troubling report in a Caracas paper the day before he left. There were rumors of a possible attempt on the congressman's life, or, failing that, of a "mercenary demonstration encouraged by the Dominican government." Speculation was undoubtedly sparked by the recent visit to Caracas by the Dominican head of security, Espaillat. Authorities promised that extra precautions would be taken to protect the lawmaker.[81]

They did not have to worry. Carrying banners proclaiming "Viva la libertad," "Abajo los tiranos" (Down with Tyrants), and "Happy to Have you with us, Mr. Porter," two hundred Venezuelans, including a contingent of Dominican and Cuban exiles, were on hand to welcome him when his plane touched down at Maiquetía, at six in the morning, no less. That first day, with the help of an interpreter, he gave an expansive two-hour press conference at the Hotel Tamanaco, hosted by the Venezuelan Newspapermen's Association. A write-up afterward captured someone comfortable in his own skin. Wearing a "light gray suit, horn-rimmed glasses, while smoking an aromatic, fine cigar of enormous size which in his small mouth looks even bigger," the North American politician spoke with "great assurance," answering some questions forthrightly while giving more politic answers to others. He won friends by stating that he was happy to arrive in time for Venezuela's July 5th Independence Day festivities: "What better way to celebrate" than right after the Venezuelan people had recaptured their liberty. "If I had been alive during the time of Bolívar, I would have been a soldier fighting for independence."[82]

Questioned about the former dictator's status, he replied that he doubted Pérez Jiménez would remain in the States much longer. "His presence is a nuisance. I personally am campaigning to get him out immediately." In response to a question about the U.S. role in the Guatemalan intervention, he was much more forthright than the vice president. Porter thought the CIA-led coup was a "a mistake, a hasty action" because, in his opinion, the communist threat there was overblown. "I hope to God there won't be any repetition" of that kind of "old-style" intervention.

His reply to a question about whether he was concerned about the rise of communism in Venezuela would have made Rubottom cringe. Although many in the United States thought that communist influence was indeed a problem, Porter was of the opinion that it was "greatly exaggerated." In the next breath, however, he condemned dictatorships on the right and the left and applauded the country's three major political parties for voicing their opposition to the PCV.[83]

Porter's itinerary was chock-full of meetings with the leadership of the three major political parties, Larrazábal, the Chamber of Commerce, labor unions, students, artists, and Juan Bosch. Proof that the representative was treated as if he were a head of state, Porter went to the Panteón to lay a wreath on Bolívar's tomb, something that Nixon was unable to accomplish. He even found time to attend a reception in his honor at the Centro Vasco de El Tigre, which appreciated his investigation into the disappearance of its countryman, Galíndez. Venezuelans, of course, were well aware of Porter's interest in the Galíndez case, but a reporter for the *Times* thought the enthusiasm for the congressman had less to do with that abduction than with his prodding of the U.S. Immigration Service to investigate Pérez Jiménez's status.[84]

Porter also participated in a three-hour roundtable with Central University students. In stark contrast to Nixon's confrontational approach, a relaxed Porter enjoyed the give-and-take. He commented on the camaraderie among the students, who ran the gamut from conservative-minded to PCV supporters, and warned his audience that "communism could very well mean a return to the tactics and tyranny" of Pérez Jiménez. A reporter from the English-language *Caracas Journal* drew an implicit comparison to Nixon's interactions with students. It was obvious that Venezuelan students respected and admired the lawmaker; "they at least listen when he talks."[85]

In an open-ended interview with *El Nacional*'s reporter, Luis Esteban Rey, Porter expanded on his views about the North American fixation with the communist threat in Latin America. In the United States, "communists are put in the same bag as democratic leftists and nationalists." This reminded him of the McCarthy witch hunts, where liberals were lumped together with communists. Senator McCarthy and his supporters, Porter contended, "practiced a false anti-communism; they were averse to free speech and open thinking and were against any inconformity."

He was, however, noncommittal in his response to a question about the relative merits of different types of dictatorships. How could

Venezuelans be persuaded, Rey wondered, that "the most pressing danger to liberty is international communism, when it is no secret to anyone that ... [right-wing] dictatorships have formed an 'Internacional' dedicated to undermining democratic regimes in neighboring countries." Even though Porter dodged that question, Rey came away impressed. The representative was genuinely interested in learning about Venezuela, "without preconceptions, without prejudices.[86] Small wonder his countrymen had taken to referring to the congressman as their nation's "unofficial ambassador in Washington."[87]

El Universal's reporter, José González González, had a similar reaction after his one-on-one interview. In comparison to Nixon and Dulles, Porter "comes without bias and is received without prejudices." Venezuelans, he noted, were already aware what the "realist" Porter stood for. This trip was an opportunity for him to learn about Venezuela.

By far, the highlight of the visit was an appearance at a July 4th AD rally held at the Nuevo Circo, a Caracas bullring that often had been the site of significant political rallies. Porter and Betancourt shared the stage, each speaking before a crowd of twenty thousand of the party's faithful. It was the first mass meeting of Adeco supporters since the November 1948 coup. In an address titled "The Democratic Hour," Betancourt praised those in attendance for their steadfast opposition to the dictatorship. Venezuela, he added, was proud to be a part of the democratic wave sweeping the hemisphere. He listed the string of recent democratic victories— Frondizi, Siles Zuazo, Prado, Lleras Camargo, and Villeda Morales. In a clear reference to La Internacional, he chortled, "The hour of the sword no longer tolls." Only three dictatorships still cast their shadow on the region—the calcified regime in Santo Domingo; Cuba, which at that moment was in the midst of an insurrection; and Stroessner in Paraguay.[88]

With coup plotting still a concern, the AD chief denounced "the profiteers of disorder" who yearn not to bring back "the fugitive" (Pérez Jiménez) but to "reestablish a system similar to his." He railed about those who tossed anonymous pamphlets and handbills from "speeding automobiles." Their objective was to stoke fear that the country was awash in "social chaos, collective anarchy, [and] absolute insecurity for investors." Such scurrilous propaganda erroneously claimed that the political parties, especially AD, were "infiltrated to the marrow by communist ideology." He noted that communists were not proscribed from participating in the political arena because "we believe that witch hunts ... are contrary to the very essence of a democratic government." But he reminded the crowd that AD, "not yesterday, not today, nor tomorrow, has or will have" anything to do with the PCV.[89]

Porter's remarks that night demonstrated that he was a quick study. After apologizing for speaking in English, he applauded Larrazábal for his pledge to hold elections and heaped praise on Betancourt, Caldera, and Villalba and their respective parties for their commitment to democratic governance. Just as he had at the university and at the press conference, he called out the communists. "I was shocked to learn that a number of educated Venezuelans, including many journalists, are sympathetic to communism. Or they proclaim their neutrality and profess to be disgusted with both the United States and the Soviet Union." Alluding to the administration's past support for Pérez Jiménez, he allowed that his own government had "made mistakes," though they were of "the head, not of the heart." Few Venezuelans would have agreed with that assessment.[90]

Porter went on to congratulate his audience for ousting "the tyrant," framing the action as part of an unmistakable trend. Ending his speech on an upbeat note, he reiterated his support for Venezuela as it transitioned to civilian rule.[91] Porter was moved by the "sea of white handkerchiefs" in the bullring that night, an honor bestowed on *toreadores* for gallantry. After his return to Washington, he ruminated on the significance of that gesture with a journalist. "In Venezuela, the most honored form of greeting is the waving of white handkerchiefs. It signifies friendship, respect, warmth."[92]

The lawmaker concluded his trip by taking to the airwaves on Radio Caracas TV, where he reprised the message he had delivered at the bullring.[93] By any measure, his visit was an unqualified success. Even Rubottom, no admirer, admitted as much in a meeting he had with Muñoz Marín in Washington. When the governor mentioned that Porter's visit was very well received and "his words were helpful in presenting American views in a favorable light," the assistant secretary agreed, but immediately took credit for prepping Porter so well before his visit.[94]

Conclusions

Nixon later wrote that "Caracas was a much-needed shock treatment which jolted us out of dangerous complacency."[95] Proof of that was evident in August, when Eisenhower welcomed a new Venezuelan ambassador and, in his comments, expressed sentiments that Latin American reformers had been yearning to hear for quite some time. "Authoritarianism and autocracy of whatever form are incompatible with the ideals of our great leaders of the past." To reinforce the point, the president followed up with open letters of support to democratic presidents in the region. Furthermore, he directed the State Department and the Immigration Service to initiate deportation proceedings against Pérez Jiménez.[96]

It is unclear how much the stark contrast in reception of Nixon's and Porter's visits played into the administration's reassessment of U.S.–Latin American relations. But Porter certainly had reason to feel validated. The president had just addressed several of the congressman's top demands—a public denunciation of autocracy, praise for democrats, and a commitment to expel the former dictator.

Later that summer, the Senate Foreign Relations Committee held hearings on the administration's Latin American policy. At Fulbright's behest, the committee wrote an open letter to the president asking for a reconsideration of its military assistance programs. That aid, the letter read, "endangered the very values of individual freedom which we seek to safeguard."[97] While Batista's misuse of U.S. arms in his fight against the 26th of July movement prompted the committee's reassessment, lawmakers understood that it had implications for other countries in the region.

It soon became apparent that the president was unwilling to go that far. In November, Eisenhower appointed a commission to study the question, but he stacked the deck. Chaired by a retired general, the commission included three former generals, a retired admiral, and a former assistant secretary of defense. To no one's surprise, the Draper Commission concluded that military and economic assistance were two sides of the same coin. "Without internal security and the general feeling of confidence engendered by adequate military forces, there is little hope for economic progress." The commission's findings became grist for those in the administration who wanted to increase, not decrease, military assistance. Aid to the region actually increased in fiscal year 1959–1960. Rubottom disingenuously claimed that with military dictatorships on the wane, the charge that U.S. assistance was keeping despots in power was without merit.[98]

While Morse and Church wanted to terminate all military assistance to the region, the Senate Foreign Relations committee as a whole refused to go that far. Instead, a watered-down amendment was appended to the Mutual Security Act, which, on the one hand, stipulated that U.S. materiel could not be used for internal security, but gave the president the prerogative to make exceptions as needed.[99]

If the administration continued to prop up Latin American militaries as a first line of defense against the communist threat, it also began to address longstanding economic grievances. Over the last eighteen months of Eisenhower's second term, his administration agreed to support international price agreements for commodities, increase the lending limits of both the World Bank and the Export-Import Bank, and announced the creation of a new Inter-American Development Bank.

The changes coincided with a timely proposal, just a month after Nixon's trip, from two reformers, Kubitschek and Lleras Camargo, who called for an ambitious, hemispherewide initiative to tackle the problem of economic underdevelopment. Failing to address that intractable problem had significant consequences for the long-term viability of democratic governance in the region and for hemispheric security. The Brazilian president presented Operation Pan America to a meeting of the region's foreign ministers in Washington that September. It called for six hundred million dollars in assistance annually so that living standards could be raised from three hundred dollars to five hundred dollars per person over the next two decades. Initially, officials in the administration thought the proposal was a nonstarter; it appeared to offer little more than a reworking of earlier calls for a Marshall Plan for the region.[100]

Coming as it did on the heels of a general reconsideration of policy toward Latin America, however, it is clear that Operation Pan America influenced the administration's decision to liberalize its lending practices. Proof of that came at a September 1960 OAS meeting, where member states signed the Act of Bogotá, affirming the Brazilian ruler's call for a massive commitment of loans with flexible payment terms. During the meetings, U.S. officials announced that the administration was allocating an additional five hundred million dollars to a newly created Social Progress Trust Fund that would be administered by the Inter-American Development Bank. Although monies were not made available until the first months of Kennedy's presidency, the fund was a tacit, if belated, admission that the Eisenhower administration's faith in "trade, not aid" as the sole answer to Latin American fiscal and economic needs was misguided.[101]

The U.S. also agreed to float Venezuela a badly needed $250-million-dollar loan to help stabilize its finances.[102] But that credit only partially offset the pernicious impact of a mandatory quota on oil imports, which Eisenhower announced in March 1959. Designed to protect domestic oil producers, the executive order proved to be an unwelcome housewarming gift, coming as it did just as Betancourt was inaugurated.

The oil quota triggered a recessionary tailspin and wreaked havoc with the head of state's ambitious agenda. Over the next eight years, the country's share of the U.S. market declined by 25 percent.[103]

Another indication that change was in the air were the stunning results of the U.S. midterm elections. A tectonic shift occurred, with the Democrats increasing their margin in the House from 33 to 130 seats and in the Senate from 2 to 30, the largest swing in that body's history. Porter easily won a second term, and beginning that January, Fulbright assumed the chairmanship of the Senate Foreign Relations Committee. Coupled with Eisenhower's lame duck status, the Democratic rout ensured that foreign policy initiatives would merit greater scrutiny.[104] But congressional liberals were hamstrung by the expansive nature of their party. On matters of national security, prominent anticommunist southern politicians like Senators John Eastland (Democrat-Mississippi) and Allen Ellender (Democrat-Louisiana) were philosophically closer to Republicans. According to Hoover, both were in Trujillo's hip pocket.[105]

For the first time, reformers had reason to believe that an entirely democratic Latin America was within reach. By late 1958, Batista's hold on power was tenuous; Trujillo was approaching his thirtieth year in power, and his increasingly erratic behavior was costing him the backing of traditional bulwarks of his regime. With Venezuela and Colombia added to the democratic column, Porter turned his attention to the administration's Cuba policy. At first glance, conditions in Cuba looked comparable to what had occurred in Venezuela and Colombia. Grievances against a U.S.-backed dictatorship had prompted a popular uprising. Castro's triumph on January 1, 1959, was hailed throughout the hemisphere.

By the end of the decade, Nixon's nostrum of "*abrazos* for democratic leaders and a formal handshake for dictators" meant something altogether different than it had just five years earlier. A slogan many reformers initially had interpreted as a hopeful sign that the administration finally was coming to its senses about the dangers inherent in coddling dictators now carried a very different connotation to proud Latin Americans, many of whom had put their lives on the line to overthrow a dictator.

The United States had much to live down. If policymakers failed to take heed that this was a far more nationalistic moment, they did so at their political peril. Recognizing how out of sync such a formulation was, Betancourt summarily dismissed Nixon's remedy as an artifact of an "old inoperative diplomacy."[106] As the dean of development economics, Albert Hirschman, so perceptively noted, perhaps a stiff handshake might be preferable to reformers after all: "It is a measure of our naivete that Nixon's proposal ... was hailed as a tremendous advance in our thinking about U.S.-Latin American relations. It did not occur to anyone, it seems, that the democratic leaders might not particularly care for our *abrazo;* that, in the particular atmosphere of nationalistic exaltation in which these leaders frequently come to power, they might even fear it as a kiss of death, since their political appeal may in part rest on their not being embraced by us."[107]

It should not come as a surprise that U.S. military commanders in the field looked askance at the reformers. As the head of the U.S. Caribbean Command Center in the Canal Zone (soon to be renamed the Southern Command) noted in October 1959: "On the whole, Latin American professional politicians must be regarded with suspicion, both as to their patriotic motives and their professed friendship for the United States. The increasing popularity of ultra-nationalistic (and invariably anti-American) platforms as the only safe vehicle for election, lends added value to the influence of the indigenous military as a moderating factor."[108]

This nationalistic moment recalled the earlier tempest between Braden and Perón. To old hands at the State Department's Latin American desk, "ultranationalism" was as much of a concern as communism. The latter fueled the former. When stoked, such fervor had the potential to spread like wildfire. Mann, the former chief of the Division of River Plate Affairs when Perón effectively parried Braden's criticism of his ties to Nazis by playing the nationalist card, mused that if the United States confronted a one-two punch of hypernationalism and communist infiltration, it might have to eschew nonintervention and resort to more muscular methods. With economic nationalism on the lips of so many regional politicians during the 1950s, it was incumbent upon policymakers to explain why it was in the enlightened self-interest of Latin Americans to cooperate with the United States. "Our purpose should be to arrest the development of irresponsibility and extreme nationalism and their belief in their immunity from the exercise of United States power."[109]

Nationalistic Latin American youth were not alone in their struggle. The retrenchment of colonial rule after World War II in Africa, Asia, and the Caribbean Basin carried with it an implicit indictment of capitalism's inequalities. By comparison, socialism offered the prospect of a more just and less exploitative future. To many adolescents, the United States was the chief culprit of an international economic order that systematically disadvantaged the Global South.[110]

No one proved more adept at stoking anti-Americanism for political gain than Fidel Castro. His strident message resonated across the region, forcing moderate politicians to make choices they would have preferred to avoid. It did not take long for the Cuban Revolution to stymie their best-laid plans.

CHAPTER FIFTEEN

Cuban Conundrum

I used to think of Betancourt as a leftist, and now he is beginning
to look like a rightist.

—DWIGHT EISENHOWER, 1960

BEFORE A RAUCOUS CROWD of one hundred thousand at the Plaza del Silencio in Caracas, Fidel Castro thanked Venezuelans for their generous support during the insurrection against Batista. Not only did they send arms
and funds to his 26th of July movement, but local radio stations, such as
Radio Rumbos and Radio Continente, aired recordings of Radio Rebelde's
broadcasts while the capital's newspapers kept the public abreast.[1]

Fidel came to Venezuela in late January 1959 at the behest of the
Federación de Estudiantes Venezolanos, who invited the commander-
in-chief of Cuba's Revolutionary Armed Forces to participate in the first
anniversary celebrations of the restoration of democratic rule. At every
opportunity during his three-day visit to Caracas, he expressed his gratitude to Venezuelans for their contributions to the fight against Batista.
The popular mobilization against Pérez Jiménez had been a source of inspiration to his movement, instilling confidence at a time when it was
sorely needed. The strategy of a general strike was borrowed from Venezuela as well, although, as he sheepishly admitted, Cuba's shutdown
of businesses and services was not nearly as effective as Venezuela's.
He pledged that "if Venezuela once again finds itself under the boot of a

471

tyrant, it can count on the Cubans." At a moment when many in the crowd were uneasily glancing over their shoulder at the grim prospect of another *golpe*, that pledge struck a responsive chord.[2]

In fact, support for the rebel cause extended well beyond what Fidel mentioned. By April 1958, twenty-three solidarity committees were operating across seventeen states. A fund with the catchy slogan "Bolívar's March to the Sierra Maestra" caught on, monies poured in, and demonstrations in the streets of the capital on behalf of the rebel cause were commonplace. Placards with the message "Batista, now it's your turn!" appeared around the capital. The JP contributed fifty thousand bolívares (Venezuela's currency), and AD-in-exile and Figueres's PLN pulled out all the stops to lend a hand. Arms stockpiled in Costa Rica intended to liberate Venezuela and no longer needed after Pérez Jiménez was chased from power were redirected to the Sierra Maestra.[3]

Solidarity did not just bubble up from the grassroots. The junta winked and nodded as exiles brazenly flew arms and funds from Maiquetía to the Sierra Maestra.[4] One memorable mission in early December 1958, the sixth of seven from Venezuela that year, carried seven tons of arms and future president of Cuba Manuel Urrutia Lleó and his family. Also on board for the seven-hour flight was the Dominican Enrique Jiménez Moya, who, like Fidel, had participated in the Cayo Confites expedition. Representing the Unión Patriótica Dominicana de Venezuela, Jiménez Moya carried a letter for Castro requesting training for a small number of "carefully selected" members who would take the fight to Trujillo "once the situation in Cuba is resolved favorably." Castro readily agreed to train the Dominicans.[5]

There was even an unconfirmed report that the provisional government sold six airplanes to the rebels for one dollar each. The Cuban government claimed to have shot down one of the planes transporting arms over its airspace. So fed up was Batista with the junta's poorly disguised favoritism that he recalled his ambassador. The United Press reported that after Cuban diplomats had vacated the embassy, 150 supporters of the 26th of the July Movement "symbolically" occupied the premises, punctuating their mock takeover with cheers for Castro and stirring renditions of the national anthems of both countries.[6]

The Cuban *comandante* expressed his thanks for the arms shipments in an emotional letter to Larrazábal. After two years of hard fighting, of payloads confiscated and "compatriots lost," to now receive these weapons was "like a dream." So grateful was Fidel for all the aid rendered that he named a brigade after Venezuela's native son, Bolívar.[7]

Fidel appeared to be under the weather that night at El Silencio, his voice so hoarse that he held forth for only two hours. He first recounted the similar paths the two countries had taken. Both had lived through illegitimate coups d'état followed by years of ruthless repression. In both cases, popular rebellions drove the despots from power. U.S. policy toward the dictatorships was similar and all too familiar. He criticized North American lawmakers for approving the sale of arms to both regimes and then for looking the other way, while Estrada, Masferrer, and their ilk tortured and murdered at will. Fidel also drew a bright line that night between the warm reception he was enjoying in the capital and the tomatoes and rotten eggs hurled at a certain foreign dignitary, whom he did not need to identify. The difference in treatment, he suggested, was proof of the increasing political awareness and sophistication of Latin Americans.

In addition, he deplored the chronic *golpismo* that plagued the body politic of much of the hemisphere. Coups were profoundly undemocratic, rendering the *pueblo* impotent and robbing them of any say in a new government. They amounted to a phony bait-and-switch, he explained, peddled as a short-term fix that invariably mutated into prolonged bouts of authoritarian rule. Cognizant that some Venezuelan officers had deserted the dictator to join the opposition and that the military-led junta had just staged free and fair elections and had overseen an orderly transition of power, he qualified his biting remarks about the region's militaries by drawing a distinction between "patriotic" soldiers willing to take the field alongside his guerrilla fighters, and cabals intriguing behind closed doors.

His principal message to the crowd that evening, however, was the *desideratum* of continental unity, an ideal, he reminded them, first advanced by Bolívar. "The peoples of America know that if they do not want to once again be victims of tyranny, if they do not want again to be victims of aggression, they must unite." Not since Sandino had a Latin American leader uttered such a defiant hemispheric call to arms. The parallel went beyond rhetoric. Just as a multinational legion had come to life in the Segovias in the late 1920s, so too would young, idealistic Latin Americans journey to Cuba in the first months of 1959, where they were given a primer in guerrilla warfare by Bayo and Che before returning to their homelands to foment revolution.

Castro then feigned surprise that ever since he set foot in Venezuela, so many people on the street had approached him, chanting, "Trujillo, Trujillo next." Were there that many Dominicans residing in Caracas, he joked? No, answering his own question, they were not all Dominicans, many were the same Venezuelans who had responded so nobly to Cuba and who were now ready to lend support to their Dominican brethren. And just as batistianos were at that very moment being held accountable for their offenses in Cuba, once Trujillo, Somoza, and Stroessner were defeated, they and their henchmen must answer for their crimes.[8]

In fact, Castro's condemnation of La Internacional was a matter of public record well before the victory over Batista. As early as April 1958, he had framed his movement in transnational terms on a Radio Rebelde broadcast. "If the dictators help each other, why shouldn't the people give each other a hand. Don't we sincere democrats throughout America have the obligation to help each other? Haven't we paid heavily enough for the sin of our indifference toward ... tyrants. ... Isn't it understood that in Cuba we are fighting a battle for the democratic ideal of our continent?"[9] Statements like these were music to the ears of greying reformers like Betancourt, Figueres, and Muñoz Marín.

This was Castro's first visit abroad in an official capacity. Scarcely two weeks earlier, his band of *barbudos* (bearded ones) had marched victorious into Havana. Now he was the toast of the Venezuelan capital, overshadowing all the other festivities. Fifty thousand well-wishers turned out to welcome him and his fifty-strong security detachment at the airport, and cheering throngs in the capital besieged the scruffy young Cubans wherever they went. The newly appointed Cuban ambassador to Venezuela, Francisco Pividal Padrón, was struck by the number and diversity of exiles who welcomed Castro's entourage at the airport: all carrying banners and proudly waving their nations' flags were Puerto Rican *independentistas*, Dominican expatriates, anti-Somocistas, and Haitian refugees forced to flee Duvalier's reign of terror. The massive crowds certainly put the recent receptions for Porter and Nixon in perspective. The charismatic thirty-two-year-old *comandante* stayed in character throughout his stay; wherever he went he wore olive-green combat fatigues, cap, and boots, and when he rode the cablecar to the Pico de Ávila overlooking the city, he took his rifle and sidearm along, claiming lightheartedly to reporters that he would feel naked without them in the mountains.[10]

Speaking at a special session of the Venezuelan Congress the day before, Castro echoed Betancourt's call for a *cordon sanitaire* against dictatorships, and he restated his plea for a continental alliance of the new democracies. He also lashed out at La Internacional's undeclared war without borders, correctly identifying the Dominican strongman as its chief instigator. Fidel assured lawmakers that if Latin Americans were united in their resolve, "no dictatorship would stand a chance." Did this mean that he was willing to lead such a coalition, the *New York Times*'s correspondent asked later? In his reply, Castro clarified his remarks. He was ready to back "a military movement against the remaining dictatorships," but not to lead such an undertaking, a statement he walked back in the coming months.[11]

Fidel also received a rousing welcome at the Central University, where he shared the stage of the Aula Magna (lecture hall) with the poet laureate Neruda. For the occasion, the Chilean read his "Un canto para Simón Bolívar." Penned in 1941, the poem commemorates the sacrifice and heroism of fallen Republican combatants during the Spanish Civil War. In its final stanza, the Liberator reappears once every century just as *el pueblo* reawakens from its slumber, a coda tailor-made for such an auspicious time. Alluding to the man of the hour, Neruda added that "the great thing about freedom is that it always produces the man who becomes its best symbol."[12]

As if on cue, the university's rector announced the creation of a new solidarity committee in support of Dominican exile organizations. Members of the university's choir, the Orfeón Universitario sang the school hymn and then presented Fidel with a blue beret, a symbol of youthful resistance dating back to the Generation of 1928's struggle against Gómez. Patterned on the Basque blue beret, the cap initially honored one of that region's most renowned native sons, the writer Miguel de Unamuno.[13] To show his appreciation, Castro immediately donned *la boina veintiochera*, as it was popularly referred to in Venezuela. After conveying the importance of assisting Dominicans in their fight to liberate their homeland, he introduced Jiménez Moya. Fidel boasted that the Dominican-born *barbudo* would soon be commanding an expeditionary force of guerrilla fighters that would finish with Trujillo once and for all.

Ever the showman, Castro did some good-natured fundraising. He turned the beret upside down on the lectern and then tossed in five bolívares. Also donating to El Comité para la Liberación Dominicana were the rector and Larrazábal. This matter was personal for Venezuela's provisional president. His uncle, Carlos Larrazábal Blanco, was an outspoken antitrujillista who was forced to flee the island in 1946. Soon Fidel's cap was filled to the brim with contributions from the audience.[14] He commended the students, calling them "the defenders of all just causes who had been in the vanguard of freedom on our continent," and urged those in attendance to pour their energies into defeating the region's remaining dictatorships.

Donning *la boina veintiochera*, Fidel Castro addresses Central University
students, Caracas, January 1959. Andrew St. George papers, Cuban Revolution
Collection (MS 650), Manuscripts and Archives, Yale University Library.

He hoped that the next time he and the students met it would be at the entrance to the venerable Universidad de Santo Domingo. There, at the
gates of the first institution of higher learning in the New World (founded
in 1538), they would celebrate the Dominican people's liberation.[15]

Despite a jam-packed schedule, Castro squeezed in a visit with Dominican exile leaders at the residence of the Cuban ambassador, where
he reportedly told them that volunteers should come to Cuba as soon as
possible to begin their training and that, unlike Cayo Confites, this time
Dominicans would assume a leadership role in any invasion.[16]

To maintain the momentum, the rector announced the launch of "El
Millón Universitario" fundraising campaign. A splashy kickoff was held
at the university's Olympic Stadium, where each of the university's ten
thousand students was charged with raising one hundred bolívares for
the cause. A Dominican diplomat dutifully reported to Trujillo that professors and students were manning a table near the university clock
tower. Small Dominican flags were placed on the tower's twenty rungs,
one flag added for each five thousand bolívares contributed.[17]

The outpouring of support for Fidel was so astonishing that President-elect Betancourt kidded that if the young Cuban had been on the ballot in the recent elections, no candidate would have stood a chance. But privately he was furious with Castro's speech at El Silencio. He was especially unhappy with the young Cuban's comments about the region's armed forces. Given Venezuela's history, Betancourt knew that provocations of this sort would not be well received in the barracks. The two met privately for an hour and a half at Betancourt's home Las Mercedes. According to a Cuban historian present at the meeting, Betancourt broached the Dominican problem with his Cuban counterpart, and the two leaders discussed how best to bring about an end to the "Era of Trujillo."[18]

Castro also revealed his government's precarious balance sheet, owing to Batista's plundering of the treasury. Could the Betancourt administration lend Cuba three hundred million dollars or, failing that, make oil available at discounted prices? It was revealing that Fidel asked for assistance from Venezuela while resolutely refusing offers from the Eisenhower administration during his April visit to the States.

The Venezuelan commiserated with the *comandante*. Pérez Jiménez had left his country in a similar predicament. In fact, the outgoing junta was negotiating presently with New York banks for an emergency two-hundred-million-dollar loan to cover the shortfall it had inherited. Betancourt declined gifting the oil, explaining that foreign oil companies deducted royalty payments for country-to-country deliveries. He needed those revenues, he explained, because he, like Castro, had an ambitious domestic agenda in mind. Venezuela would be happy to sell Cuba oil, though. By all accounts, Castro did not take the rejection well.[19]

The hopes and aspirations surrounding the Cuban Revolution felt decidedly different from those of other democratic transitions. Fidel's repeated calls for continental unity against authoritarianism and the regime's early forays against the last few members of La Internacional appeared to validate moderate politicians' initial support for the revolution. Watchful waiting, however, gave way to progressive disillusionment, especially after Cuba's embrace of the USSR. As this chapter argues, the Cuban Revolution boxed in reformers in dispiriting ways. Coupled with the unanticipated emergence of the United States and Cuba as parties to the region's ongoing border wars and a slew of military *golpes* between 1962 and 1964, the few democracies still standing at mid-decade were forced to tack to the right and reassess their support for the revolution. Moderates were quickly disabused of any aspirations they had of

Betancourt and Castro agree to disagree, January 1959. Andrew St. George
papers, Cuban Revolution Collection (MS 650), Manuscripts and Archives,
Yale University Library.

remaining on the sidelines during the Cold War. Under withering pressure at home from conservatives and their militaries to sever relations
with Havana and to roll back leftist mobilizations, the handful of democracies that survived the rash of coups had little choice but to place themselves squarely within the U.S. orbit.

Civilian politicians were quick to expound upon their reservations
about Cuba privately, but Castro's popularity among their constituents
raised the political cost of making such grievances public. This was especially so after the Bay of Pigs, which, for many Latin Americans, conjured up painful memories of gunboat diplomacy. Playa Girón also made
it much more difficult for moderates to align themselves with Washington's diplomatic efforts to isolate Cuba. Reformers were appalled by "the
perfect failure," but not because they did not wish Fidel gone. As had
been the case with Árbenz, it was the means, not the end, that mattered.
The exception to the rule was Figueres. No longer sitting in the presidential chair, the opinionated Tico could sound off publicly about the
revolution's leftist turn.

Havana's and Washington's participation in the Caribbean Basin's undeclared border wars also complicated the political calculus for reformers. The revolution proved as polarizing as it was electrifying. As long as Fidel kept his sights squarely on their mutual enemies, the region's democracies were willing to lend a hand. They were familiar with the methods an increasingly aggressive Cuba utilized abroad; after all, fomenting instability, relentless propagandizing, the assiduous cultivation of domestic proxies, and the encouragement of military *golpes* had long been Trujillo's stock-in-trade. It was only when Cuba aided and abetted popular mobilizations against their own governments that reformers mustered sufficient political courage to voice their misgivings out loud.

Two unrelated events—the assassination of Trujillo in mid-1961 and the missile crisis—gave civilian politicians the political opening they needed to distance themselves publicly from Cuba. In both cases, moderates and the United States were on the same page. The Kennedy administration's liberal-democratic rhetoric and the goodwill engendered by the announcement of the Alliance for Progress also emboldened reformers to collaborate more openly with policymakers in Washington.

The most distressing trend for reformers, of course, was the abrupt end to the democratic wave. After years in exile, at a moment when there was a great deal of optimism that a democratic corner had been finally turned, this indeed was a bitter pill to swallow. The abrupt end to civilian rule did not mean a return to power of discredited caudillos, though. Instead, it afforded a new generation of professional, politically motivated generals the chance to seize power and govern. Over the course of the 1960s, high commands fully committed themselves to the Cold War binary and, owing to ample arms and counterinsurgency training from the United States, waged a ruthless war against domestic enemies. Only those democratic leaders agile (and accommodating) enough to co-opt their military establishments completed their terms in office.

When You Have a Revolution, You Kill Your Enemies

At the outset, reformers were bullish on the Cuban Revolution, and for good reason. During Fidel's visits to Venezuela in January and to the United States three months later, he presented himself as one of them. His agenda—economic nationalism, social justice, agrarian reform, literacy and public health campaigns, the repudiation of authoritarianism, and an alliance of hemispheric democracies—was comparable to their own. The Eisenhower administration may have objected to Cuba's material and moral support for Dominican, Nicaraguan, Panamanian, and Haitian exiles, but not so moderates, who initially applauded and then quietly backed Cuban efforts to depose some of the region's most despised tyrants.[20]

Social democrats also were reluctant to condemn the trials and executions of former members of Batista's army, even as they winced at the public spectacle and disagreed with their rushed and arbitrary manner. They empathized with the Cuban public's demands for justice and agreed wholeheartedly with Fidel that the expressions of outrage about "show trials" and "kangaroo courts" from congressmen and the media in the United States were the height of hypocrisy. Defenders of the revolution wondered, where was the righteous indignation when Batista's military and police perpetrated atrocities? As Matthews noted, the Cuban people were cognizant of the administration's complicity in the repression. "Our [military] officers in Cuba went on hobnobbing with some of the most hated associates of Batista, and our officers in Washington dined and decorated these men. The bitterness that this caused in Cuba was incalculable. To the Cubans we were teaching Batista's henchmen how to kill other Cubans—and honoring them in the bargain."[21]

To counter mounting criticism of the trials in the States, Muñoz Marín pleaded for "the greatest possible forbearance" for the changes underway in Cuba. While the governor did not condone the executions, he asked U.S. citizens to "put themselves in the shoes" of those who had lost loved ones or friends. Critics in the press and on the Hill, he pointed out, never mentioned that "Batista used to murder without jury trials."[22]

Porter felt the same way. Ever since he first objected to arm sales to the Batista regime in March 1957, ordinary Cubans had reached out, sharing horrific stories of what they experienced or witnessed. Right after Batista's exit, he and Adam Clayton Powell, Jr. traveled to Cuba, the only two lawmakers to accept Castro's standing invitation to members of Congress and the media to witness the trials. The Cuban government even sent a plane to Miami to transport the two congressmen to Havana. Porter, who, unlike Powell, did not have the luxury of a safe seat, knew that he was taking a political risk by traveling to Cuba. His decision to go put him at odds with his mentor, who had blasted Castro for practicing "the same police state methods" as the dictator he had just defeated. Porter countered that Morse was guilty of ethnocentrism when faulting Castro for not adhering to North American conceptions of jurisprudence.[23]

While the lawmakers were in Havana, images of "mutilated, brutalized bodies and mass graves" filled the pages of *Bohemia*, fueling national outrage and demands for retribution and revolutionary justice. Castro's intelligence chief shared with the congressmen dossiers containing graphic evidence of the dictatorship's brutal counterinsurgency campaign. Front and center were atrocities by Masferrer's *Tigres*. Porter was moved by what he saw. "They are beyond description," he told an audience at the Cleveland City Club upon his return. The evidence brought back painful memories of his work as a war crimes special investigator during World War II. Like the Nazis, "Masferrer and his sadistic underlings" had the temerity to shamelessly document their reprehensible actions.[24]

Even so, the lawmakers decided not to attend any of the trials. In his memoir, Powell, who was an early booster of the 26th of July movement, explained that he thought better of it because he did not want to be a part of the "spectacle."[25] Porter was so disheartened by what he learned about the trials while he was in Havana that he shared his procedural objections with Castro just before the latter headed off to Venezuela.[26] As he had prior to his trip to Caracas, before he left for Havana Porter huddled with State Department officials to inquire if it was appropriate to attend a mass rally where there was likely to be U.S. bashing. The Department initially wavered on its answer, and it was not until just before the rally that the embassy sent a note conveying its "strong desire" that he not attend. Porter admitted to some "soul searching" about the embassy's recommendation, but both he and Powell decided to attend the rally, which attracted a reported five hundred thousand Cubans. During Castro's speech, those in attendance signaled their overwhelming support for the continuation of the trials when he asked for a show of hands as to whether they approved of the "shooting of the assassins."[27]

In testimony given in executive session before the Senate Committee on Foreign Relations in late January, Allen Dulles was more sanguine about the Cuban public's demand for retribution. "When you have a revolution, you kill your enemies. There were many instances of cruelty and oppression by the Cuban army, and they certainly have the goods on some of these people. Now, there probably will be a lot of injustice. It will probably go much too far, but they have to go through this."[28]

The brouhaha over the trials and executions in the press and Congress did little to sway North American public perception of Fidel, however. His eleven-day, six-city tour of Washington, New York, Princeton,

Boston, Montreal, and Houston in April was a revelation. Fifteen hundred welcomed him at National Airport in DC, while twenty thousand carried him on their shoulders from New York's Pennsylvania Station to his nearby hotel. Despite a jam-packed schedule, he found time to sightsee (the New York Stock Exchange, the Empire State Building, and the Bronx Zoo), meet with baseball icon Jackie Robinson, receive the keys to the city, and introduce himself to a national viewing audience by appearing on *Meet the Press*.[29]

New York's Hispanic community came out thirty-five-thousand-strong for his Central Park rally. Speaking in Spanish to the considerable number of Dominican émigrés in the crowd, he empathized with their plight and let them know that they were welcome in Cuba. "We, too, were exiles," he allowed. At Columbia University's School of Journalism, Castro denounced Trujillo for harboring Batista, and in the next breath noted that impunity was not just a Latin American failing. Without mentioning Galíndez by name, he reminded the students and faculty present, "you know this too well, seeing as one of the professors of this university was assassinated by Trujillo and nothing happened." At the very least, he insisted, the U.S. government had a moral obligation to censure tyrants. Fidel's harping on this matter was not solely based on principle. He was aware that ex-batistianos had followed their chief to the Dominican Republic, where, with Trujillo's connivance, they were now plotting to retake power.[30]

In meetings with members of the House and Senate Foreign Relations Committees, Nixon, and State Department officials, and during an extraordinary three-hour chat with a CIA agent in his hotel room in New York, the message to the Cuban leader was the same: beware of communists. Even Porter buttonholed Castro at the Cuban embassy, inquiring whether there was any truth to the rumors that instructors at Camp Columbia were utilizing Marxist instructional materials. Castro was livid afterward, venting to his aides, "Do you believe that? This is my army. I started it from nothing and I control it. ... Don't you think I would be the first to be worried if I thought another power was taking it away from me?" He came away convinced that officials were obsessed with communists. Nixon was so disturbed by Castro's naivete that he became one of the earliest proponents in the administration of outfitting and training a contingent of Cuban exiles to overthrow the regime.[31]

Before the year was out an increasingly hostile Castro was painted in the North American press as "a pistol-packing, trouble-making" adolescent in need of discipline. Cubans were quick to point out that such a stereotype was remarkably similar to those attributed to *mambises* opposed to North American assistance in 1898. As one student of diplomatic history has noted, "American leaders reacted to the rise of Fidel Castro and others like him with a mix of impatience, contempt and hostility. Leaders and people of the third world assumed familiar guises; children for the knowing American to tutor, miscreants for U.S policemen to curb and if necessary to call for account."[32]

In a matter of months, the revolution's leftward trajectory—its strident anti-U.S. rhetoric, the indefinite postponement of elections, the silencing of organized labor and the press, the suppression of student protest, the removal of moderates from leadership positions in the government, the sponsorship of insurgency abroad, and its embassies' meddling in the internal affairs of its neighbors—all raised significant concerns with moderates. As with Árbenz, the presence of communists in Fidel's inner circle troubled Betancourt and his peers. As he related to Schlesinger, unlike in Venezuela, "the absence of well-organized democratic political parties" in Cuba best explains why Castro had little choice but to rely on the PSP. It was "the only disciplined political organization available to carry out his policies and defend his regime."[33]

Privately, reformers shared their concerns with policymakers in Washington. In a confidential memo, the Aprista leader and journalist Andrés Townsend Ezcurra warned that the revolution represented an existential threat to the United States and the region. If unchanged, Washington's traditional politics of containment—centered on an alliance with the region's dictatorships and oligarchies—would result in the eventual "Fidelization" of the continent. It behooved the U.S. to ally with reformist political parties. Before it was too late, the U.S. must choose between reactionaries or broad-based popular parties. Although APRA, AD, and the MNR had been anti-imperialist in the past, they were reliably anticommunist. While these parties on occasion pursued reforms inimical to U.S. interests, he admitted, aligning with moderates would prove more durable and efficacious because "only they can ideologically mobilize . . . the masses against communism." But Washington must encourage civilian governance by renouncing coups d'état wherever and whenever they occurred.[34]

Publicly, though, moderates held their tongues. They remembered how their muted objections to the dour Árbenz in 1954 had elicited strident criticism from both the left and the right. Now in a position to govern, they surmised that it would be ruinous to take on the popular *comandante*. This explains why they were so reluctant to support Washington's initial efforts to isolate Cuba at the OAS. The sole exception was Figueres, who became the first reformer to publicly break his silence.

Dean of Revolutions

Few anticipated that relations between the Cuban revolutionaries and Figueres would sour so quickly. Immediately after their victory, Fidel and Che publicly thanked him for his support during the insurrection. The Costa Rican responded in kind, defending Castro's stance on the trials and the executions. In a column that was given wide play in Cuba, he noted that for far too long, impunity had gone unpunished. "No one who knew the extremes of barbarism to which the recent tortures in Cuba, Venezuela and other 'republics' have gone, will be able to deny in conscience that the corrective methods must be extreme. . . . There is not the slightest doubt in each city and each town, who were the principal assassins."[35] The proceedings, he contended, acted as a necessary deterrent to those considering the use of such methods in the future. He also agreed with Castro that the trials and executions would "allay the passions" of the Cuban people, who "might otherwise resort to lynch law," as had occurred in Cuba in 1933 after Machado fled and in Venezuela in the days right after Pérez Jiménez resigned.[36]

To show their gratitude for his support at a time when the revolution faced fierce criticism in the foreign press, Franqui, on behalf of the 26th of July movement, extended invitations to visit the island to Figueres and several other PLN leaders. As it did for Porter and Powell, the Cuban government dispatched a military plane to San José on March 19, 1959, to collect the Costa Ricans.[37]

The visit began on a positive note, as Figueres and his colleagues were accorded full military honors and a parade was held in their honor. The 26th of July newspaper, *Revolución*, praised Figueres, calling him "a prominent figure of the democratic ideal in Latin America." He gave a televised interview, in which he walked back his earlier support for the show trials, but also criticized the United States for appearing to be the "accomplice of dictators."[38]

But matters quickly took a turn for the worse. Before a massive gathering of workers in Havana, Figueres shared the podium with Castro; David Salvador, the secretary-general of the Confederation of Cuban Workers; and President Urrutia. In his remarks, Figueres placed the Cuban Revolution within the democratic wave sweeping the region.

Though he knew that Castro had repeatedly pushed back the date for holding elections, he emphasized the importance of the ballot, calling it "the only source of permanent sovereignty for a people." He then upbraided the *comandante* for his "exaggerated" attacks on the United States. "Fidel should calm down," he lectured. Figueres warned Cubans to beware of the twin perils of demagoguery and dictatorship and urged the regime to set aside its differences with Washington. For historical and cultural reasons, Cuba's, and indeed, Latin America's rightful place during the Cold War was with the West. As he had done with *el pulpo*, he encouraged the Cubans to negotiate their differences with foreign companies.[39]

Figueres could afford to be more forthcoming than his peers, since at that moment he did not hold public office. His candid remarks also appeared to anticipate Cuba's departure from the United States' sphere of influence, occurring as they did a month before Raúl Castro asked the USSR for assistance with the regime's intelligence apparatus and a full year before any formal agreements were signed between the two countries.

In retrospect, Don Pepe's advice did not come as a shock. Just before he traveled to the island, he expressed reservations about what was occurring in Cuba, even questioning whether Fidel was mature enough to govern. Disquieting news about the revolution's trajectory reached him in the form of a report from Monge, who had just returned from a fact-finding trip to the island, where he met with leaders of the Cuban labor movement. Monge confided to Figueres that he was "completely disenchanted with what he had observed."[40]

Not surprisingly, Figueres's advice that day came off as patronizing and offensive to nationalistic Cubans, whose battle cry during the insurrection had been "Cuba for Cubans." So incensed was Salvador that he ripped the microphone from Figueres's grasp before he could finish speaking. Taking exception to Figueres's comment about where Cuba should position itself during the Cold War, he fired back: "We cannot be with the Americans who today are oppressing us."[41] A "visibly disturbed" Figueres was then allowed to conclude his remarks.[42]

Fidel retorted with a blistering two-hour rebuttal, defending Cuba's right to set its own sovereign course in international affairs and justifying its decision to remain neutral in the conflict between the superpowers. He dismissed Figueres's accusations out of hand. "Everyone knows I'm not a demagogue," he told the crowd. It was obvious that Figueres was duped by the North Americans. Does Don Pepe have so short a memory; had not Washington armed Somoza, who then used those weapons to attack his homeland? Even someone supposedly "free of fears and prejudice" like the Costa Rican leader had been taken in by an unprecedented hemispherewide campaign designed to first impugn and then destroy the revolution. Furthermore, Fidel predicted that an invasion was imminent—either from Santo Domingo or Florida—organized by "Trujillos or Masferrers." Broadcast live on radio and television, the public spat attracted a national audience.[43]

In the weeks ahead, neither side let the matter rest, each taking to the airwaves in their respective capitals. In a televised interview, Fidel spent thirty minutes of his four-hour appearance lambasting Figueres. He called attention to a coffee *finca* the former president had acquired while in office. A real revolutionary, he added, would never have left large landholdings untouched.[44] What could a reactionary *hacendado* and a profiteer teach Cubans about revolution? (That claim, incidentally, was later corroborated by the U.S. embassy in San José.) Instead of standing in solidarity with a small nation like Cuba in relation to the United States, this self-styled "dean of revolutions" only offered reproaches, Castro fumed. He then belittled the amount of aid Figueres's administration had provided during the insurrection. In fact, Don Pepe's administration had provided logistical support to Huber Matos and nine other M-26 militants when they flew ten tons of rifles, machine guns, mortars, ammunition, grenades, dynamite, and medical supplies from Costa Rican territory to the Sierra in May 1957. According to Barquín, who later broke with the fidelistas, that shipment was instrumental in staving off the army's offensive later that summer. Even after Figueres's term of office expired in May 1958, he continued to mobilize support, raising seventy thousand dollars at an exposition titled "Cubans in Costa Rica."[45]

Next, Castro contrasted his respectful demeanor in Venezuela with Figueres's condescending remarks. Unlike Figueres, he had refrained from commenting on domestic matters. Cubans were much too polite to their guest. If the Costa Rican had lectured Venezuelans the way he talked to Cubans, he would have been met with rocks, hisses, and boos. Finally, he labeled the former president "an agent of imperialism." In fact, Fidel's accusation was spot-on: the Costa Rican was working hand-in-glove with the CIA. The U.S. ambassador to Cuba, Philip Bonsal, summed up the *comandante*'s tirade in a few words: "violent, passionate, rude and personally insulting."[46]

Stung by Castro's attacks, "an angry and emotional" Figueres responded in kind at his *finca*, La Lucha, on the eleventh anniversary of the 1948 uprising. He told hundreds of his supporters that Cuba's revolution paled in comparison to what Costa Rica had accomplished under PLN rule. To shouts of "Abajo, Fidel Castro," he railed against the "anti-yankee" or "communistic" rhetoric emanating from Havana. "We did not make use of charlatanry as many young revolutionaries are doing today . . . [it is just] empty talk, demagoguery and insane projects." Finally, he distinguished between the godless communists' infiltration of certain revolutionary movements and Costa Rica's Western, Christian, and democratic revolution.[47] Privately, he alerted the U.S. ambassador to Costa Rica, Whiting Willauer, that a "dedicated nucleus" of Cuban communists was intent on precipitating a U.S invasion of the island—"a Hungary in reverse"—an allusion to the Soviets' repressive response to a reformist movement in that Eastern bloc country.[48]

Figueres's claims rang hollow. Demeaning Cuba's revolutionary project at such an early stage was premature at best. Besides, with the exception of Figueres's elimination of the military, few would have characterized what occurred during his tenure in office as especially revolutionary.[49] Soon after the rally, the PLN issued a statement denouncing dictatorship whether it be on the right or the left. A U.S. diplomat stationed in San José thought that typical of the arrogance of the party's leadership. Figueres and his aides believed themselves to be the "self-proclaimed guardians of Latin American democracy."[50] Suffice it to say, the Cubans felt exactly the same way.

Figueres's friends came to his aid. Porter lectured Castro that democrats like Figueres, Betancourt, and Muñoz Marín "should be your most trusted advisors."[51] His suggestion, however, fell on deaf ears. The dispute was indicative of a generational gulf between the young Cubans and the reformers. Schlesinger, now an advisor to Kennedy, found ample evidence of that "disturbing tendency" during a three-week fact-finding trip throughout Latin America in February and early March 1961. Even though conservatives considered AD and APRA "parties of red revolution," young intellectuals regarded them as "tired, played out [and] irrelevant."[52]

Coming as it did so soon after the revolution's triumph, the disagreement was a harbinger of what more was to come. Cuba's radicalization during Castro's first year left reformist politicians especially vulnerable to attacks from domestic adversaries on the right, who made hay over their reluctance to criticize Cuba, and from the left, who labeled them everything from *vendepatrias* to stalking horses for North American imperialism. Typical was an editorial in the Costa Rican Communist Party's newspaper, *El Adelante*. Whereas Figueres believed that "submission to the imperialistic policies of the United States is unavoidable," Castro "conceives and advances the possibility of independent policies based upon respect for the sovereignty of our countries."[53]

Berle characterized the unseemly back-and-forth as an "overt turning point," noting that a number of Cubans who had fought alongside Castro in the Sierra Maestra read the writing on the wall and chose that moment to leave the island. He felt that it was past time for the administration, which had treated Latin America's democratic leaders with "notorious shabbiness, had decorated and flattered their enemies, and had been anything but enthusiastic" when they assumed office, to reverse course, cut their ties to the region's remaining dictatorships, and support these reformers.[54]

Figueres later walked back his criticisms of Cuba's revolution, but only so far: "If he [Fidel] is for democratic principles, we will stick by him," he remarked.[55] Toeing a noncommittal line on Cuba grew increasingly problematic for moderates when it became clear, by March 1960, that Cuba had cast its lot with the Soviet bloc, and that the military and economic assistance reformers needed from Washington came with certain expectations in regard to Havana. Within a few years, the region's reformers all echoed Figueres's complaints.

Open Season on Despots

The Cuban Revolution complicated the Caribbean Basin's war without borders, a deeply embedded feature of the geopolitical landscape since the 1920s. Havana and Washington scrambled the conflict's parameters, doing so in ways that no Latin American statesman could have forecast in 1959.

Castro's overarching goal was to spread the gospel of the revolution by providing material and moral support for guerrilla insurgency. The literature emphasizes Che's role in training Latin American insurgents, but as Bayo noted when he first met Fidel in Mexico in July 1955, from the outset the young man was smitten with the idea. Through the years, the doyen of guerilla warfare noted that he had "thousands of conversations with utopian idealists" who dreamed of overthrowing either a Franco, a Somoza, or a Trujillo. Those conversations, Bayo added, invariably "dissipated just as soon as they were uttered, like a cigarette's smoke rings dis-appear as it escapes the mouth's prison that has given it life." But Fidel was different: he was a student of the subject, having combed through two of Bayo's memoirs, underlining passages devoted to strategy and tac-tics. That was why Bayo was "intoxicated by his [Fidel's] enthusiasm" and agreed to train his followers in Mexico. The triumph of his charges against Batista's army seemed to lend credence to the notion that under the right circumstances, guerrilla warfare permitted a weaker opponent to level the playing field against a more heavily armed opponent.[56]

Bayo returned to his native Cuba after the revolution's triumph and was promptly appointed director of the School of Revolutionary Train-ing. Reporting to Che, he put together a training manual titled *140 Questions on Guerrilla Warfare*, which became required reading for Latin American exiles at Che's training academies. Castro's backing of four poorly designed, hastily thrown together insurgencies between April and June 1959—all but one targeting dictatorships—was an early indication that replicating the Cuban model would not be easy.[57]

Ideology and objectives aside, the revolution's export of revolution bore an uncanny resemblance to Trujillo's bellicose foreign policy. Making the most of firepower and funds obtained from their respective patrons in Washington and Moscow, both the Dominican and Cuban regimes aimed to replace hostile governments with allies, and when that proved unrealistic, the operative goal was the destabilization of those governments from within. Rather than try to defeat their enemies militarily, the objective was to wreak havoc. They accomplished this with the assistance of domestic proxies, who were either ideologically compatible or receptive to emoluments.

Interestingly, both Cuba and the Dominican Republic pinned their hopes on forcing the hand of national militaries. The trujillista model pressured the neighbors' security forces to stop harboring dissidents. If governments refused to do so, the next step was to foment regime change. With Cuba, the goal was less transparent. By encouraging insurgency, the Cubans sought to undermine and destabilize bourgeois democratic gov-ernments, thereby obliging their nations' armed forces to step in and seize power. Having a more repressive regime in place, the argument went, was far more likely to hasten an authentic revolutionary mobilization.

Neither regime was entirely successful in achieving its goals—the Cu-bans less so than the Dominicans, owing to an aggressive response by the United States that frustrated their ambitions at every turn. But even as the two strongmen met with setbacks, Dominican and Cuban aggressions roiled the region and forced their political enemies to redirect precious resources from social and economic reforms to the armed forces, thereby undercutting the popularity and viability of the new democracies. The two regimes also proved extraordinarily resilient. If the goal of a dictatorship is survival, Trujillo and Castro could offer eloquent testimonials.

Even as relations between Cuba and the United States turned colder, it was business as usual for the region's remaining dictatorships and their detractors. Heartened by the democratic wave, moderates set out to dislodge the last remaining despots. Indeed, reformers initially were convinced they had a reliable ally in Fidel Castro. On the basis of his rhetoric and actions, the Cuban appeared to be just as committed as they were to making the Caribbean Sea a dictator-free zone.

The reformers' resolve was soon sorely tested. La Internacional may have been in disarray, with Perón, Batista, Pérez Jiménez, Odría, and Rojas Pinilla now in exile, but the dictators and their supporters believed that this was a temporary state, one that would be rectified in short order. Moreover, both Trujillo, always the chief disruptor, and the Somoza brothers remained firmly entrenched, as potent a threat to regional stability as ever.

Trujillo focused on the immediate threat—Fidel Castro. The Dominican ruler showed his true colors in early 1958 when he came to Batista's defense after the U.S. temporarily banned arms sales. An airbridge was established between March and December of that year as dozens of Cuban planes—both military and commercial carriers—flew to the Dominican Republic to pick up rifles, carbines, hand grenades, mortars, bazookas, bombs, and napalm. By the end of October, Cuban aircraft were running five flights a day to Ciudad Trujillo. Batista's aide José Suárez Núñez claimed that the Cuban government purchased five million dollars' worth of Dominican arms during the dictatorship's final months. Trujillo, who permitted the Cuban government to defer payment, was said to be deeply involved in the operational planning of the airbridge. (He was fit to be tied when he learned that rifles that bore his San Cristóbal foundry imprint wound up in the hands of Castro's *barbudos*, presumably sold to them by profiteers.) In return, Batista's secret police provided Dominican diplomats with intelligence on exiles in Cuba. With the Cuban regime in its death throes that December, Trujillo stepped up again, offering Batista four thousand troops, with half to be sent to the Sierra Maestra and the rest to Santa Clara, where the Cuban army was trying desperately to hold off Che Guevara's column. Batista declined, curiously informing the Dominican envoy, "I do not treat with dictators."[58] At first glance, Batista's characterization is puzzling, but he never considered himself an autocrat. He viewed himself as a populist reformer who was unafraid to employ the *mano dura* when it was required.[59] Even though Batista rejected the offer, Trujillo was once again there when needed, when on New Year's morning 1959, Batista and his entourage needed a landing spot.

In the midst of the airlift, the Dominican foreign minister alerted the State Department that the insurrectionists were "thoroughly infiltrated with militant Communists," a gross exaggeration to be sure, but one that U.S. authorities understandably discounted, since Trujillo had so often cried wolf about communists.[60]

The Dominican head of state had no interest, though, in practicing watchful waiting when it came to Castro. Once he obtained intelligence that the Cubans were training Dominican exiles, he quickly assembled an anticommunist Caribbean Legion, composed of mercenaries from the hemisphere's dictatorships, batistianos, former members of Franco's Blue Division who had fought alongside the German army during Operation Barbarossa, anticommunist Croat partisans, and North American and European pilots and technicians. During the spring and summer of 1959, Cuban former general José Eleuterio Pedraza put the legionnaires through their paces at Dominican bases while Cuban air force pilots tutored their Dominican colleagues. The State Department cabled its diplomats in the region that Trujillo "has attempted to obtain arms from various sources abroad, including this country, and has been reported to have infiltrated agents into Cuba for [the] purpose of organizing internal support for [the] counterrevolution."[61]

Castro was certain that an invasion was imminent. The day after Batista fled the island he addressed the Dominican threat in a speech in Santiago de Cuba. "If Santo Domingo becomes an arsenal of counterrevolution, if Santo Domingo becomes a base for conspiracies against the Cuban Revolution," it would reap what it sowed. Dominicans "have learned from the Cuban example that it is possible to fight against tyranny and defeat it." "Our example," he added for good measure, is "what dictators fear the most."[62]

One of Castro's first requests of his new finance minister was to locate funds in order to purchase arms. His minister tracked down monies that the members of Batista's high command had hidden offshore in European banks. Given the revolutionary regime's dire fiscal condition and the need to rebuild the country after the insurrection, it is revealing that one of its first moves was to use those funds to purchase more than five million dollars' worth of arms from Belgium to defend itself from Dominican aggression.[63] Castro had legitimate cause for concern. The Dominican armed forces were the most formidable in the Caribbean, boasting a twenty-thousand-man army and an air force that included thirty-eight British Vampire jets, as well as U.S. P-47s and AT-6 trainers.[64]

An outlandish plot to oust Castro was hatched in a Miami hotel room in April 1959.[65] Attending were the Dominican consul general in Miami, Augusto María Ferrando; Batista's former national police chief, Manuel Benítez; Dominic Bartone, an arms smuggler and fixer for Jimmy Hoffa's Teamsters; and a thirty-one-year-old North American soldier of fortune from Toledo, Ohio, William Morgan.[66] The latter was something of a folk hero in Cuba, having fought with the Second Front of the Escambray during the insurrection. Prior to throwing in his lot with the Second Front, Morgan had bounced in and out of prison in the States and reputedly had ties to a local crime syndicate in Toledo. The Second Front, an offshoot of the DRE, had an uneasy relationship with the rival 26th of July movement, and when Castro assumed power, its head, Eloy Gutiérrez Menoyo, and Morgan were effectively marginalized. Trujillo believed that Morgan and Gutiérrez Menoyo could be turned; the overlooked, unrewarded leaders might warm to the idea of collaborating with an invading force against a regime that was barreling leftward.[67]

Morgan agreed to the sales pitch, receiving "tens of thousands of dollars" stuffed into paper bags from Ferrando. Much of the preparations for this operation involved the acquisition and transport of arms to the remnants of the Second Front. In fact, Morgan personally commandeered a yacht from Miami to Havana filled with arms provided by Bartone. One account claimed that Trujillo put up more than a million dollars, with the monies going toward the purchase of .30- and .50-caliber machine guns, automatic rifles, and ammunition.[68]

The FBI found out about the preparations and brought Morgan in for questioning during one of his trips to Miami. He informed agents that he had turned down a foreign government's offer of a million dollars to overthrow the Castro regime and assured them that on principle, the Second Front would never collaborate with ex-batistianos. Castro was not a communist and deserved a fair chance, he added. Besides, Fidel was so popular that any plot to oust him was guaranteed to fail.

Despite his assurances to the FBI, preparations for the invasion continued. Over the course of the next six weeks, an intricate plot was set in motion. Leaving from a Dominican airbase, a thousand-man strike force would fly to the city of Trinidad at the foot of the Escambray Mountains, with Morgan and his compatriots waiting at a dirt airstrip for their arrival. The *Americano* then was to lead the force up into the mountains, where they would meet up with a re-formed Second Front.

Pedraza and the Dominican spy chief, Abbes, coached Morgan on the particulars, communicating via shortwave radio from the Dominican Republic. The Dominican SIM provided the American *comandante* with three radio transmitters and 20-meter directional antennas so he could keep in contact with his handlers in Ciudad Trujillo.[69] In anticipation of the strike force's arrival on Cuban soil, Dominican planes dropped dozens of crates of weapons to the Second Front. In early August, Morgan pleaded with Pedraza and Abbes to send even more weapons, boasting that the Second Front now was in control of a vast swath of territory and was preparing to seize Trinidad.

Trust was in short supply. Trujillo's spies in Cuba gleaned intelligence that the Cuban government was rounding up suspects, including two former senators whom the dictator had identified as prospective rulers of a post-Castro regime. That intelligence was accurate. In anticipation of the invasion, the regime detained a thousand former members of Batista's army.[70] Interestingly, Castro received advance warning of the planned assault from an unlikely source. Bonsal had relayed details of what the FBI had learned to the Cuban foreign minister, Roa. Concerned that reprisals might be taken against Americans living in Cuba if the U.S. were somehow linked to the plot, Bonsal wanted Roa to know that his government had nothing to do with it.

Smelling a trap, Trujillo put off Morgan for the moment, informing him that his force would be delayed until conditions improved. Instead, he dispatched a personal emissary to Cuba to ascertain the reliability of Morgan's claims. Even after he received a favorable report, a wary Trujillo decided to test the waters again by sending two small teams a few days apart, each flight carrying arms for the Second Front.[71] After the first flight went well, the second plane carrying weapons and ammunition left from the Dominican Republic on August 13. This time a small party of ten Dominican soldiers and Cuban exiles was met on the airstrip not just by Morgan and Gutiérrez Menoyo but Castro and his army. A brief firefight ensued, in which four were killed, ten were wounded, and the rest were taken prisoner by Cuban forces.[72]

To the delight of many who despised Trujillo, Castro paraded his captives before a national television audience and played taped conversations between Morgan and Abbes.[73] During a five-hour debriefing carried live on television and radio, Castro called Morgan "the hero of the hour." The *Americano* turned over to authorities the seventy-eight thousand dollars he had received from Ferrando.

An embarrassed Trujillo put a one-hundred-thousand-dollar bounty on Morgan's head. In response, Cuban authorities ringed Morgan's home with armed guards.[74] Meanwhile, the dictator's supporters in the North American media and the Congress closed ranks, branding the *Americano* a communist and a common criminal who had violated the 1939 Neutrality Act by running guns from U.S. territory. Despite all of his attempts at damage control, the strongman never quite recovered from the humiliation. As a close confidant put it, the Trinidad debacle was the generalissimo's "Bay of Pigs."[75]

Morgan was well acquainted with Trujillo's methods. In a televised interview with an NBC reporter, he acknowledged that he "wouldn't live twenty-four hours in Miami." When asked why, he replied, "Well, he kidnapped Galíndez and Murphy ... at least here, I am allowed to carry a gun. ... I have my own people."[76] Alluding to a recent report that the Dominican government had paid the Mutual Broadcasting System $750,000 to air 425 minutes per month for 18 months of "news favorable to the government," he lashed out at the dictator in an interview with a reporter from *Revolución*. "We have seen how his money poisons the United States, buying the press ... to defend his rotten regime. Those same dollars penetrate the Congress and many of his men, like [Senators] Eastland, Smathers, and [Representative] Francis Walters [Democrat-Pennsylvania], have influence in the Department of State."[77]

Coincidence or not, a week after the failed raid, Batista left the Dominican Republic for good, moving to Portugal. Trujillo effectively had sidelined him during the operation. The Cuban alluded to it briefly in a memoir, denying that he had anything to do with the plot.[78] His son later claimed that his father was convinced that the scheme was ill-advised, for two reasons: Castro's popularity, and because nationalistic Cubans would surely rise up against any invasion led by the despised Dominican ruler. That the two strongmen did not see eye to eye was not surprising. The Trujillo-Batista relationship always blew hot and cold, never more so than during his eight-month-stay in the Dominican capital. According to press reports, soon after he landed in Ciudad Trujillo, Batista was moved out of the National Palace to the Hotel Jaragua, where he remained under (admittedly comfortable) house arrest in a suite until Trujillo extracted full repayment for the weapons he had sent Batista the year before. The U.S. had it on good authority that Batista had been "subjected to considerable pressure, extortion and threats" from his Dominican counterpart and feared for his life if he stayed any longer on the island. Unlike Trujillo's other infamous house guests, the Cuban strongman skulked off the island that August, with nary a Dominican official present at the airport to see him off.[79]

The Trinidad operation bore a striking resemblance to the Trujillo-Prío joint scheme in 1956. In both cases, the Dominican leader attempted to buy off deposed members of a discredited government anxious to regain power. His motivation was similar in each case: to subvert the regime while foiling the ambitions of Dominican exiles residing in Cuba. The only difference this time was that the recipient of his largesse was an American with an unusual backstory.[80]

Collaborating with former dictators, of course, was standard operating procedure for Trujillo; recall his support for Machado in 1934, López Contreras in 1945, and Castillo Armas in 1954, to list the most conspicuous examples. Morgan's place in the revolutionary firmament did not linger. Fourteen months later, he was arrested, tried, and found guilty of counterrevolutionary activities. In March 1961, he was shot and killed by a firing squad.[81]

Rekindling a Deadly Vendetta

After the setback, Trujillo set his sights on his longtime rival, Betancourt. As he had during the *trienio*, Betancourt's February 1959 inaugural address kept faith with fellow exiles and with democratic governments that had provided a safe haven to Adecos.[82] He reaffirmed his commitment to the doctrine that bore his name: "Regimes which do not respect human rights, which violate the liberties of their citizens and tyrannize them with political police ought to be subjected to a rigorous *cordon sanitaire* and eradicated by the collective peaceful action of the Inter-American juridical community." It was in Venezuela's national interest to promote the defense and extension of representative democracy throughout the hemisphere. Those high-minded sentiments were enshrined in the 1961 Constitution.[83]

The day after the inauguration Betancourt met with Rubottom, U.S. Ambassador to Venezuela Edward Sparks, and former New York governor Thomas Dewey, who were all in Caracas for his swearing-in. Betancourt explained that he intended to raise "the question of expelling the dictator-ship countries" from the OAS at the regional organization's next meeting. In an indication of how strongly he felt, he threatened to pull Venezuela out of the OAS if the resolution was defeated.[84]

The Venezuelan government's diplomatic offensive included raising awareness of the harm posed by the venality of dictatorial regimes. At the United Nations and the OAS, its diplomats insisted that ex-dictators relin-quish their ill-gotten gains and return them to the countries in question. While officials were alluding to Pérez Jiménez, the Venezuelan government was making a broader case that corruption was inherently destabilizing for regional peace. Too often the funds were used to bankroll attempts to re-take power and overthrow governments. A legal precedent for the extradi-tion of stolen wealth already existed, the Venezuelan diplomats asserted. The Nuremberg justices had held the political and military leadership of the Third Reich accountable for its actions, and assets seized by the Nazis were, to the extent possible, returned to their legitimate owners.[85]

Betancourt was well aware that Trujillo would stop at nothing to subvert his presidency, partly because his victory at the polls presaged a freer hand for exile organizations based in Caracas. His presumption about Dominican interference was borne out over the course of the next eighteen months, culminating in still another assassination attempt that barely missed its mark.

The harassment began right after the inauguration and never sub-sided. Betancourt presented Sparks with a fulsome bill of particulars. Like clockwork, every morning at 6:30 a.m. the Dominican government radio station, La Voz Dominicana, spewed a "vitriolic diatribe" against him and his administration that was heard all around Venezuela. Owing to his mil-itary's monitoring, he had the daily transcripts to prove it.[86] Like the pub-lications produced during the *trienio*, tracts with provocative titles, such as *Rómulo Betancourt, amenaza roja* (red threat), began to appear on the shelves of Caracas booksellers. Written by exiles residing in Ciudad Tru-jillo, they recycled canards that Betancourt was a communist and a ho-mosexual. Furthermore, authorities detained a Norwegian freighter in Maracaibo after it made "an extended port of call" in the Dominican Re-public. A search of the vessel found seditious propaganda "of Dominican origin."[87] Finally, Betancourt argued that the Dominican regime was in clear violation of asylum laws. Trujillo had refused to grant exit permits to allow the safe conduct of thirteen Dominican dissidents granted asylum by Venezuela. The asylees had been stuck in limbo in the Venezuelan embassy in Ciudad Trujillo since January. Diplomats inside the embassy complained that local authorities were not only obstructing deliveries of food and medicine but had prevented Dominican employees who staffed the embassy from entering the premises.[88]

What the Venezuelan president neglected to mention, however, was that local radio stations, such as Radio Barquisimeto, Radio Rumbo, and Radio Continente, were returning the salvos, their signals strong enough to reach the island. One program, titled "The Hour of Dominican Liberty," appealed to different segments of Dominican society, with separate messages for peasants, the clergy, and the military, all urging them to rise up and overthrow the dictatorship.[89]

According to the first secretary of the U.S. embassy in Caracas, the Venezuelan president "left no doubt of Venezuela's sympathies" for Dominican exiles.[90] This time it was not just the former AD chief who spoke up on their behalf. COPEI, the URD, and the PCV all issued statements criticizing Trujillo. Then Castro gave his blessing to a plot to overthrow the despot. Cuban organizers flew to New York and Caracas to recruit Dominican exiles. The enlistees traveled to Pinar del Río in western Cuba to train for the invasion.[91]

Betancourt had a premonition of disaster and sought to dissuade the Cubans. Soon after his meeting with Castro in Caracas he dispatched Pérez to Havana to inform him that if he went ahead with the invasion, whatever assistance Betancourt's administration provided would be sub rosa, because if he appropriated arms from the Venezuelan military, it was certain to raise suspicions with the high command that the weapons might be used against the armed forces. Pérez did assure Fidel that if Trujillo invaded Cuba, Venezuela was prepared to come to its defense.[92]

The Cubans and the Dominican exiles stubbornly persisted, but with grievous results. Under the command of Jiménez Moya, the Army of Dominican Liberation, composed of more than two hundred exiles and eighteen Cuban *barbudos*, launched a combined aerial and amphibious assault on the island in mid-June 1959. Betancourt quietly contributed two hundred thousand dollars, a military pilot, and a C-46 twin-engine aircraft to the expedition. As he had predicted, the Dominican military easily and viciously repulsed the invasion. Those who were not killed were captured and tortured and then paraded before the official media, where they recanted the error of their ways.[93]

In response to a plea from a Dominican exile for assistance in obtaining the release of the prisoners, Betancourt was at pains to explain why he could not lend his government's support: "I have great affection for all of them. Theirs is a journey spiritually linked to my struggles, to my best years. . . . But I cannot do anything when I see that my effort is going to be useless."[94] In truth, his hands were tied. Only months after the inauguration, he had not yet won the loyalty of some in the high command. If such a gamble backfired it would provide grist for his political enemies.[95]

Citing Cuban and Venezuelan aggression, Trujillo lodged a protest with the OAS. Bringing the matter up at such a venue, Rubottom felt, would be a distraction from the real problem at hand—Cuba's export of revolution. In a memo to Foster Dulles in late June 1959, he pondered what might result if the United States were placed in the uncomfortable position of having to defend the principle of nonintervention *and* the Trujillo regime by voting to sanction Cuba and Venezuela for their actions. "The strong tide of pro-democratic and anti-dictator sentiment . . . conflicts with the principle of non-intervention and there is no doubt that any effort to take action [at the OAS meeting] which will in effect defend the Trujillo dictatorship will be widely condemned in public opinion in Latin America as in the United States." Fortunately for the administration, he succeeded in persuading Trujillo to withdraw his protest.[96] That August, at a meeting of foreign ministers of the OAS, the Venezuelan foreign minister made the case for expelling the Dominican Republic from the organization. Cuba's foreign minister, Roa, endorsed his old friend's effort to isolate the dictator, but the measure failed.[97]

Trujillo did not stand down. According to a confidential memorandum from Farland, the despot continued to aid and abet Venezuelan exiles "with money and arms." In fact, the Dominican government had purchased three jets from Canada for the former Venezuelan minister of defense, Castro León, who was in Ciudad Trujillo gearing up for yet another coup attempt.[98]

The Castro León plot may well have been La Internacional de la Espada's last gasp. In planning the operation, Trujillo had the backing of Perón, Pérez Jiménez (then in exile in the United States), and Francisco Franco. The historian Bernardo Vega has unearthed an extraordinary letter from the Dominican head of state to Pérez Jiménez in September 1959, in which Trujillo affirmed the need to coordinate decisive action against communist incursions in the region. He included details of an elaborate plan to galvanize what remained of the autocratic coalition. An emissary of Pérez Jiménez was charged with recruitment of former members of the SN and the Venezuelan military-in-exile, while the Spanish ambassador to the Dominican Republic was said to be enlisting two thousand legionnaires stationed in Spanish Morocco. Trujillo promised to contact Central American allies (i.e., the Somozas), while Perón, then comfortably ensconced in the Dominican capital, would enlist colleagues in the Southern Cone.[99]

Seven months later, Castro León led several hundred soldiers across the Colombian border and seized a minor military installation in Táchira State, three hundred miles from the capital. He went on local radio stations, declaring that he and his followers were in revolt against the "communist" Betancourt. Trujillo prematurely recognized the "new" government and announced the restoration of diplomatic relations. Within days, though, the rebellion crumbled, thanks to the timely response of the National Guard and a local militia composed of five hundred campesinos loyal to Betancourt's government, which set up roadblocks to deter the rebels' advance. After Castro León fled into the mountains, it was two peasants loyal to the government who captured him and turned him over to authorities. Pérez was convinced that if Castro León had been able to establish a foothold in Táchira, Trujillo would have sent planes and armaments to bolster the insurrectionists.[100]

As in the response following Castro León's first attempted coup nine months earlier, a massive crowd turned out for a rally in defense of democratic rule at El Silencio. Amid chants of al paredón (to the wall) from the angry crowd, speakers from each of the major political parties, including the PCV, deplored the attempted coup and called for swift and robust punishment of the perpetrators. Read aloud at the rally was a message from the president of Cuba, Osvaldo Dorticós Torrado, reminding Venezuelans of Fidel Castro's pledge at the same venue the year before that their nation was ready to assist the Venezuelan government if needed.[101]

Speaking to a national audience after the attempt was foiled, Betancourt reminded his countrymen that Venezuelan law proscribed capital punishment. Tweaking Fidel, he summarily rejected calls to execute Castro León and his followers, promising that the conspirators would be prosecuted to the full extent of the law. This time Castro León was found guilty and given a long prison sentence, but many of his followers received much lighter punishments. Years later, Fuenmayor took Betancourt to task for his short-sightedness, insisting that the Cuban approach, though brutal, was ultimately far more effective. Most of the conspirators apprehended in Venezuela "escaped unscathed and today walk our streets as if they were honest, upstanding citizens," he complained. "And tomorrow, when some other dictatorship represses us, the same gentlemen will once again serve as henchmen, torturers and murderers in the employ of new tyrants."[102]

The uprising's timing turned heads. Two days after Castro León's force crossed into Venezuela, Betancourt and the IADF hosted a major conference of two hundred democratic leaders from April 22 to 26 in Maracay, 120 kilometers west of Caracas. A long-anticipated sequel to the 1950 Havana Conference, twenty-one nations sent delegates, among them the president of British Guiana, Cheddi Jagan; Figueres; Allende; Frei; Bosch; Berle; and Porter. Although the primary topic of conversation was Cuba, the Táchira rebellion's import was not lost on the participants. In opening the conference, Betancourt dismissed the coup as a shabby attempt meant to take away Venezuelans' "well-earned right to live in liberty." With Pérez Jiménez in mind, he called for a revision of existing asylum laws. It was frankly preposterous, he declared, that former dictators were rewarded in this way. "They are men who do not speak to any audience or write a line in any newspaper; they conspire . . . to regain power, aided . . . by the huge accumulated fortunes looted from the treasuries of the country they tyrannized." Such fugitives from justice were unworthy of asylum. Bogged down in bickering about Cuba, conference delegates, however, could only muster a generic resolution condemning the region's four remaining dictatorships, while issuing a call for the collective defense of democratic governance.[103]

Whether or not Trujillo timed the uprising to disrupt the conference, he certainly was angered by Betancourt's stunning declaration a few weeks earlier, in which he intentionally linked the resolution of the region's two outstanding challenges—the Dominican Republic and Cuba. The Venezuelan head of state pledged "to take the lead on Cuba" with other Latin American leaders, but only after "the Trujillo problem was resolved with United States cooperation."[104]

The Eisenhower administration was of two minds about what it called the "Betancourt theory." On the one hand, it did not appreciate the Venezuelan's holding it hostage by linking the two, but up to that point policymakers had had precious little success enlisting hemispheric support for its anti-Castro offensive. Betancourt's statement not only increased the pressure on Trujillo, but it opened a door that Washington would, over the course of the next six months, walk through to good effect. By linking Castro and Trujillo, the United States could, at the very least, hope to inoculate itself against the charge that it was concerned only with leftist dictatorships.[105]

Two months after Castro León's unsuccessful uprising, Trujillo put in motion a two-part plan even more audacious than the Galíndez abduction: first, employ Venezuelan nationals to assassinate Betancourt, and then stage a coup and install a friendly government. According to regime insider Joaquín Balaguer, the plot "was prepared with as much care as the Galíndez kidnapping."[106] Trujillo and Abbes provided the exiles with weapons and two green suitcases containing a detonating device and sixty pounds of ammonium nitrate.[107] The plotters flew from the island to Venezuela in a commercial cargo plane, first unloading the arms that would be used in the *golpe* at a remote cattle ranch before proceeding to Caracas.[108]

On Armed Forces Day, June 24, 1960, a time when the plotters felt certain of Betancourt's itinerary, explosives were placed in the trunk of a 1954 Oldsmobile sedan parked along the intended route of the presidential motorcade. The perpetrator of the bombing, Luis Cabrera Sifontes, waited three hundred meters away with a radio transmitter. When Betancourt's black Cadillac passed by, he detonated the bomb, killing two, including the president's aide-de-camp and an innocent bystander. The force of the explosion was so great that it hurled the president's vehicle into the air and across the median, landing on the other side of the road without flipping over. That saved the lives of all but one of the passengers, who were able to escape before flames engulfed the vehicle. As Betancourt later recounted to Schlesinger, when the bomb exploded, "a sheet of fire descended on the presidential car," and he instinctively "threw his hands over his face to protect himself."[109]

Miraculously, Betancourt and several others in the motorcade's entourage survived the blast.[110] The president suffered second-degree burns on his face and hands, a lesion in his right eye, and a ruptured eardrum. He required surgery, but managed to address the nation the following evening. With halting speech impaired from burns on his lower lip, he spoke of an unholy alliance between those traitors banished from power by the January 23 uprising and the Dominican Republic. "This absurd regime," not content to persecute and humiliate its own people, acted with impunity abroad. This latest attempt, he assured the nation in typical "Betancourtese," was but "the last flick of a tail of a prehistoric dinosaur." He called on the OAS to "asphyxiate" the Trujillo regime once and for all. If the organization did not sanction the Dominican Republic for its actions, Venezuela promised to do so unilaterally. With rumors swirling that he was too incapacitated to govern, the Venezuelan head of state went before the cameras again on July 16. With hands heavily bandaged, he delivered a feisty address to the nation. At a tense moment, the president managed to inject some much-needed levity, comparing his bandaged hands to those of the popular Venezuelan light welterweight champion Carlos "Morocho" (dark-haired) Hernández, who at that moment was set to defend his title in Rome. Even inveterate political enemies, who never missed an opportunity to berate Betancourt, marveled at the "great courage" he displayed in the face of adversity. More significantly, his coolness under fire shored up support for him within the armed forces.[111] If the assassination had succeeded, it was unclear to many Venezuelans whether democratic rule would have persevered.

The best that Trujillo's mouthpiece, *El Caribe*, could offer was, "he who sows the wind, harvests storms."[112] Shockingly, the Venezuelan government had received ample warning of the plot from multiple sources, including the Argentine and U.S. governments and its own ambassador to Spain, but as with Nixon's visit, it failed to provide sufficient protection.[113] The response from the United States was predictable. Sounding much like his predecessors in the Department during the heyday of the Caribbean Legion, a frustrated Rubottom scolded Latin American diplomats: "we cannot allow individual groups of 'liberators' to pass judgment on the governments of particular countries" and launch paramilitary attacks on regimes they reject.[114]

At first glance, the bombing seemed little more than the latest episode in a long-running feud. But the Cuban Revolution and the United States response to it relegated the vendetta to the zero-sum politics of the Cold War. That July, the NSC was the scene of animated discussions about whether the United States should sever relations with Cuba and the Dominican Republic at the same time. Nixon spoke out forcefully against the idea, arguing that lumping the two together would alienate the dictator's supporters in Congress. Nixon argued that it would be prudent to sever relations with Cuba first. Betancourt was an opportunist who would desert the United States after he got what he wanted on the Dominican Republic.[115]

Concerned that OAS sanctions might trigger a political vacuum, unrest, and a Cuban-style overthrow of the Trujillo regime, Herter did his best to persuade Latin American governments to force the strongman out by holding supervised elections. After eight years of subscribing to the principle of nonintervention, the administration appeared ready to pivot, arguing that an exception in this case was warranted. This was not because it had any illusions about bringing democratic rule to the island. But it did suggest that the administration and Betancourt were finally on the same page about the need to remove Trujillo first before addressing Cuba.[116]

But the OAS Council of Foreign Ministers was unwilling to renounce nonintervention, a keystone of hemispheric relations since 1933. It rejected Herter's proposal to bring about regime change in the Dominican Republic at a meeting in San José in August. Meddling in the internal affairs of a country, even one as reprehensible as the Trujillo regime, was not the regional organization's mission, they contended. The foreign ministers did, however, believe that attempting to assassinate the sitting president of a member state warranted stiff punishment. Facing a united front, Herter dropped his proposal, but not before obtaining a concession that a discussion of Cuban aggression would take place immediately after the Dominican deliberations were completed. With the Dominican Republic and Venezuela abstaining, for the first time in its history the council unanimously recommended severing diplomatic relations with one of its member states, imposing partial economic sanctions, and suspending the sale of arms to the Trujillo regime. The sanctions would remain in effect as long as the Dominican Republic "constituted a danger to peace and security" in the region (that is, while Trujillo remained in charge).[117]

The wily dictator's response was to shop for arms in Europe and, to soften the impact of the sanctions, he lobbied his supporters in the U.S. Congress to redirect Cuba's allotment of the sugar quota to the Dominican Republic. Just as the OAS imposed sanctions, the U.S. Congress increased the Dominican Republic's share of the allotment from 27,000 to 350,000 tons. Eisenhower was so upset with Trujillo's backers on the Hill that he pushed through a punitive excise tax on Dominican sugar.[118]

Despite his diplomatic victory in San José, Betancourt's idea of a *cordon sanitaire* never caught on with his peers. With some exceptions, most governments continued to profess nonintervention. The usual questions were raised about who would determine which governments were or were not democratic. There also was the perception that given the United States' overweening influence in hemispheric affairs, if the OAS adopted the Betancourt Doctrine, it would afford Washington even greater latitude to interfere than it already had. For domestic reasons, statesmen were reluctant to approve measures that could be interpreted as caving in to the hegemon. Better to err on the side of nonintervention, the reasoning went, than to meddle in the internal affairs of a member state.[119]

The policy, then, of isolating dictatorships remained, with some exceptions, largely a Venezuelan initiative. During his five-year term, Betancourt suspended diplomatic relations with Argentina, Ecuador, El Salvador, Honduras, Peru, and the Dominican Republic, because, in each case, military coups had overturned democratically elected governments. He also broke off relations with three dictatorships—Cuba, Nicaragua, and Paraguay. There were significant domestic ramifications to severing relations with the Castro regime. Just as Figueres's persistent interference in his neighbors' affairs had triggered a backlash in Costa Rica, so, too, did the Betancourt Doctrine become a contentious issue at home among leftists and conservatives alike. That decision was decidedly unpopular with elements of his governing coalition, including members of his own party, who broke away from AD and set up their own party. As a result, AD forfeited its congressional majority.[120]

The Victim's Playbook

More so than the Nixon trip, the Cuban Revolution prompted a sober reappraisal of U.S. policy. With the exception of the Guatemalan intervention, up until 1959, the Eisenhower administration sought to curtail and restrain belligerents through diplomatic means. That approach changed dramatically over the next five years.

Allen Dulles had foreseen the likelihood of reversing course as early as April 1959, when he alerted Herter to the training of exiles in Cuba and to Castro's determination to overthrow the remaining dictatorships in the Basin. This was a fluid situation that bore watching, the CIA director mused, one that could go either of two ways. The region might go communist, or it could evolve into an "anti-American third force. . . . In either case, the United States Government would find itself associated firmly in the public mind of Latin America with the extreme right, especially as the friend and supporter of Dominican dictator Trujillo." No matter which situation presented itself, it could injure U.S. interests.[121] Even though Castro publicly espoused the creation of a nonaligned bloc, Dulles noted, he was in fact behind the "communist-dominated revolutionary groups conspiring against the Dominican Republic and Nicaragua." In addition, his backing of Haitian exiles against the Duvalier regime might result in the establishment of a base there that could then be used to launch attacks against the Dominican Republic. This, of course, had always been Trujillo's nightmare scenario, one that he had feared ever since he came to power. To counter that threat, the CIA reported that Trujillo had approached Duvalier and, with the Haitian leader's consent, had stationed Dominican troops along its border and positioned his navy's patrols in Haitian waters.[122]

Dulles also was concerned about the composition of such a "third force." It had all the makings of another Caribbean Legion. His commentary bears quoting in full because it illustrates how the onset of the Cold War dovetailed with the region's ongoing border wars.[123]

> Moderate forces led by Rómulo Betancourt of Venezuela and former President Figueres of Costa Rica are opposed to Fidel Castro's domination of this movement, and are, themselves, organizing groups of non-communist Nicaraguan and Dominican revolutionaries. Revolutionary activity of this kind would undoubtedly bring from the country attacked, a request for intervention by the OAS to avert a regional war. ... The United States, as the strongest member of the OAS, could very easily acquire an ideological stigma difficult to avoid. Reiteration of the view that the United States is the supporter of dictators in Latin America has brought about an estrangement of even the moderate leftists, a situation which abets the cause of those who want to bring the Caribbean political scene under communist domination.

Dulles's memo was prescient in all respects but one. He was aware that Figueres and Betancourt were at that moment lending support to anticommunist exiles, dissidents who had nothing to do with the Cuban-trained guerrillas. Although the two leaders shared Castro's goal of removing Trujillo and the Somozas from power, they were uneasy with the revolution's drift. Dulles, however, failed to account for the possibility that Venezuela might, in the months to come, play a double game by providing logistical support for the Cuban-backed invasion of the Dominican Republic in June 1959. Betancourt justified his actions because he felt that until Trujillo was removed from power, the region would never know peace. If that meant helping the Dominican exiles Castro was whipping into shape as a fighting force, so be it.

Given his distaste for the Cuban regime, Figueres and his PLN colleagues decided to strike first against the Somozas, thereby preempting
another group of rebels about to depart from Cuba. Figueres plotted
with an old ally, Chamorro. In late May 1959, 110 Nicaraguans, mostly
members of the latter's Conservative Party, were transported by two airplanes from a training base in Costa Rica to a remote mountain hamlet
east of the Nicaraguan capital, Managua. The National Guard, however,
learned of the plot and quickly contained it. Three weeks later, a separate
Cuban-trained group of sixty Nicaraguan and Cuban leftists landed in
southern Honduras on Nicaragua's northern border. Although guard
units were dispatched to meet that threat, their presence along the frontier proved unnecessary because the Honduran military surrounded the
rebels on its side of the border. In the firefight that ensued, six guerrillas
were killed, fifteen wounded, and the remainder surrendered to authorities. Among the wounded was the future leader and ideologue of the
Frente Sandinista de Liberación Nacional (FSLN), Carlos Fonseca.
Even if the two groups had coordinated with each other, it is doubtful
that the Somozas' hold on power was ever in serious jeopardy.[124]

Even though Cuban-backed rebels failed to overthrow four different
governments in the spring of 1959, the administration exercised restraint
with the new regime, just as it did with Venezuela and Colombia after
the removal of their dictators. That did not last long, however. As Rubottom later confided, by the summer of 1959, once the administration concluded that it could not work with the regime, it began making plans to
oust Castro. "It didn't make much difference whether Castro was communist or not. He was . . . bitterly hostile to the United States."[125]

Throwing caution to the wind, the Eisenhower administration insinuated itself into the region's border wars. Its objectives were twofold:
first to remove Castro from power, and failing that, to punish the island
economically and stoke domestic unrest, thereby diminishing the attractiveness of its example; and second, to discourage other governments
from emulating Cuba's revolutionary path. Removing Castro from power
became an obsession for both the Kennedy and Johnson administrations.
As Secretary of Defense Robert McNamara recalled, "we were hysterical
about Castro at the time of the Bay of Pigs and thereafter."[126]

"No more Cubas," became the unofficial mantra of both Democratic
and Republican administrations for the next three decades. A critical
component of the United States' strategy entailed enlisting and, if need
be, coercing client states to help accomplish its aims. Diplomatic persua-

sion included implied threats to cut off aid to reticent governments. The upshot, then, of the leftward tilt of the revolution and the United States' confrontational rejoinder was that neutrality was no longer an option for Latin American governments.

Washington's bellicose response—the covert and overt tactics employed, including the arming and training of a surrogate expeditionary force, sabotage, material support for the domestic opposition, economic and diplomatic warfare, and a concerted propaganda campaign—was very reminiscent of past border wars, although the resources the United States committed were, of course, far greater.

If Trujillo had lived that long, one could imagine the Dominican ruler applauding the odious creativity of the Kennedy administration's Operation Mongoose. The bombing of railway bridges, factories, and storage tanks, the burning of cane fields, the seeding of clouds, hit-and-run attacks carried out up and down the Cuban coastline by CIA-funded paramilitary organizations, and the funding and arming of the domestic resistance all wreaked havoc on Cuban society. And that did not include what one expert on U.S.-Cuban relations has aptly labeled "spoiling operations," in which farming and industrial equipment imported from European manufacturers was deliberately tampered with and rendered defective before shipment to the island. The operation's size—a budget of fifty million dollars, employing four hundred CIA workers and thousands of Cuban exiles—testifies to its significance.[127] Nor did the grand bargain that Kennedy and Khrushchev reached during the missile crisis put an end to the harassment campaign. The Soviet premier protested that the hostilities were a violation of Kennedy's no-invasion pledge, but the United States did not relent until 1965, when President Lyndon Johnson finally shut down Operation Mongoose.[128]

Increasingly autonomous and lethal, anti-Castro paramilitaries, subsidized by the Agency, amounted to an updated Caribbean Legion. Commando groups, such as the Movimiento de Recuperación Revolucionaria, Junta Revolucionaria Cubana, and Alpha 66, reconfigured the region's endless border wars. Washington's client states, including the civilian governments of Peru, Costa Rica, and Venezuela, gave these expatriate cells ample room to maneuver. In Venezuela, for example, five armed members of the AAA entered the Cuban embassy in the capital "in broad daylight" and vandalized the premises. The Venezuelan press reminded its readers that the group's leader, Sánchez Arango, and other officials in Prío's government had given succor to Adecos in exile during the 1950s. For the Betancourt administration to turn its back on the Triple A now in its hour of need, the journalist editorialized, was unthinkable.[129]

On occasion, the "armed raids and infiltrations of [Cuban] saboteurs" posed problems for the Kennedy and Johnson administrations. The paramilitaries' interdiction of neutral shipping, for example, angered Western European allies. By the mid-1960s, the exile organizations, once a creature of U.S. policy, had to be reined in by their patrons. Efforts by the adversaries to contain each other resulted in a stalemate, but "also boxed in and pushed democrats to the right, ensuring their downfall."[130]

Viewed through this prism, the Bay of Pigs was but the war's latest manifestation. Just as Guatemala's neighbors (and the Dominican Republic and Venezuela) had assisted the CIA and Castillo Armas during Operation PBSUCCESS, so, too, did Guatemala, Honduras, and Nicaragua provide logistical support for the 2506 Brigade. The housing and training of Cuban exiles in Guatemala was particularly unpopular. When word leaked out about the existence of a training base for the Brigade, it immediately brought to the surface memories of past humiliation. Members of the high command were upset that President Ydígoras Fuentes made the decision without even consulting them. So pronounced was the disgust with the operation that nearly a third of the army rebelled against their president. Ultimately, the uprising was snuffed out by loyal troops; the timely assistance of CIA pilots, who flew B-26 bombers intended for the Cuban campaign; and members of the 2506 Brigade. Those conspirators fortunate to escape soon reconstituted themselves as guerrillas and proved to be a thorn in the side of the Guatemalan military for years to come. If Ydígoras Fuentes's decision to permit Cuban exiles to train on Guatemalan soil was not controversial enough, his willingness to deploy the CIA and its surrogates to fight against members of the army ensured that his days in power would be numbered.[131]

Figueres, Betancourt, and Muñoz Marín tried to dissuade the U.S. government from carrying out the attack. Not because they thought it would end as poorly as it did, but because they knew that Latin American popular opinion was so firmly opposed to U.S. intervention and that it was incumbent upon Washington first to demonstrate good intentions by repudiating its decades-long support for repressive regimes. A unilateral intervention, Betancourt fretted, would undermine an already fragile inter-American system. Just a day before the invasion, AD leadership, cognizant of how unpopular the prospect of an invasion was with its rank and file, issued a statement condemning intervention in the strongest possible terms.[132]

Figueres also expressed displeasure with reports that an invasion was imminent, predicting a setback for inter-American relations. Like Betancourt, he believed that it made more sense to get rid of Trujillo first before confronting Castro; otherwise, Latin Americans would wonder why it was that the U.S. tolerated right-wing dictatorships but not leftists. It would be "Guatemala all over again," he warned.[133] Moderates, in particular, were "left out to sea," he wrote Betancourt, because the United States and reformers had very different goals. "Between our friends and us there is a difference . . . [their] vision is paramilitary. . . . We are committed to strengthening democracy and hemispheric solidarity. I foresee difficulty for the democratic cause."[134]

After the press reported in late December 1960 that an invasion of Cuba was imminent, a downcast Muñoz Marín wrote Betancourt, prophesying disaster for democrats and for inter-American relations more generally. He deplored the involvement of "Trujillistas and Somocistas" in the preparations. Echoing Figueres, he decried the United States' objective of "simply security. . . . [We] . . . are fighting for a political system and for permanent principles. They don't have a political vision, nor even a philosophical one." He also forecast dark days ahead for the cause.[135]

The three democrats proved able prognosticators. Two weeks after the Bay of Pigs, they tried to put their best face on the disaster, issuing a joint declaration that, although unsurprising in its principles, revealed how out of touch they were with mainstream public opinion. As many Latin Americans publicly rejoiced after the Cuban victory, "The Declaration of San José" stubbornly justified the intervention even as it criticized the United States. Yes, the statement began, Kennedy may have inherited the operation, but it was not solely his fault. Rather, the defeat was the result of a "legacy of indifference" and a failure to communicate between the United States and its partners in the hemisphere. Cuba was a front, albeit an important one, in the Cold War, but Latin Americans should not delude themselves into thinking that a "third" position was tenable in this conflict.[136]

As for the intervention, the issue for moderates was the means, not the end. Launching an invasion of a totalitarian state was defensible, but what was unacceptable—and here we can discern Figueres's input—was that the brigade received assistance from the Somozas. Washington must stop "lavishing aid on our most hated enemies." The very existence of a Trujillo, a Stroessner, and a Somoza "violates the principles and treaties of the inter-American system." Concluding the declaration with a rhetorical flourish, they called on the OAS to sanction the region's dictatorships: "We do not accept the thesis that one brand of tyranny is worse than the other. For our tortured brothers the pain is no greater in the left arm than the right. Our fallen patriots in Havana are not any more dead than our murdered students in Managua. It is not any worse to kill in the name of a world revolution than in the name of a feudal dynasty."[137]

As students in the 1920s, Haya and Betancourt were outspoken anti-imperialists who repudiated gunboat diplomacy. Now they could only find fault with Washington's methods. While it was true that their views had moderated in the interim, "The Declaration" also speaks to how little room reformers had to maneuver after 1959. In fact, what really angered Figueres was that reformers, as was the case in 1954, were kept out of the loop. What kind of an alliance was it "if our friends will not believe that we can be trusted with secrets. I may disagree with something, but I can still be trusted to keep quiet about it."[138]

Betancourt was hopeful that the Cuban people would rise up against Castro's regime, just as Venezuelans did. In a frank exchange with Kennedy during the latter's visit to Venezuela in December 1961, he pledged his administration's continuing support for "the resistance movement . . . within its resources" on the island. What must not happen, he warned the young president, was another unilateral action like the Bay of Pigs. The Venezuelan president, of course, was not alone in predicting that the revolution would not last. Both he and Kennedy sorely underestimated the depth of domestic support for Castro.[139]

Testifying to the lengths that Betancourt and Figueres went to eliminate Castro was their participation in an unsuccessful assassination plot just two months after Playa Girón. Operation Condor was audacious in its conception: murder both Castro brothers and Guevara. Also involved in the plot were Ydígoras Fuentes and the CIA. Not to be confused with a later operation of the same name—a 1970s CIA-backed campaign of political repression against leftist subversives by Southern Cone military governments—this earlier Condor hired two former members of Batista's police force and a third man from Puerto Rico (then residing in Havana) to carry out the assassinations. In the event that it succeeded, Condor was to be followed by "an external attack on Cuba by trained forces . . . which at this time was being staged on Costa Rican soil." The CIA had recommended one of the hitmen and facilitated communications between Guatemala City and the assailants. Fortunately for the Cuban premier, Soviet intelligence obtained a copy of a memorandum describing the plan worked up by Ydígoras Fuentes's intelligence chief and shared it with their Cuban allies. The operation had been approved by the Guatemalan and Venezuelan presidents and the former Costa Rican chief executive at a meeting in Costa Rica. Although this was one of many unsuccessful attempts on Castro's life, it illustrates the degree to which the United States and reformers were now complicit in the region's border wars. As the chief of Kennedy's Latin American desk, Edwin Martin, acknowledged in his memoirs, Figueres "played a major role in shaping our thinking."[140]

Washington's intrusion in the Basin's border wars was not solely fixated on Cuba, although that remained its overriding preoccupation. To bolster the profile of reformers, the CIA provided funds for a political journal, *Combate*, which began publication in the summer of 1958. Figueres, Betancourt, and Haya de la Torre were members of the journal's maiden editorial board. *Combate*'s editor, Monge, had dreams of an updated *Reportorio Americano*, but as the journal's content increasingly became a vehicle for anticommunist propagandizing, he resigned in frustration. The Agency also provided funds for an affiliated Institute of Political Education, which opened its doors in 1960. The institute's purpose was to school and train party cadres in democratic principles to counter what organizers argued was the communist indoctrination students imbibed at Latin American universities. Invitations were extended to virtually every liberal democratic party in the hemisphere to send its most promising activists. Each party selected one or two of its militants to receive scholarships to attend. During the first year, twenty-seven students from fifteen political parties in ten countries attended. The leading lights of the region's democracies were brought in to lead workshops and to teach ten-week courses. Both *Combate* and the institute were housed in Costa Rica.[141]

Collaboration between the administration and the reformers went well beyond political education. After years of tolerating the Dominican head of state, the administration abruptly reversed course in early 1960. Once again, Cuba dictated its actions. As Eisenhower astutely observed, "until Trujillo is eliminated, we cannot get our Latin American friends to reach a proper level of indignation in dealing with Castro." By April

1960—a month before Trujillo attempted to murder Betancourt—the president had authorized a contingency plan to realize the overthrow of the longtime U.S. ally.[142]

The plan entailed quietly identifying and cultivating civil-military leadership groups on the island which could fill the vacuum left by his departure, uniting competing exile groups, and, if Trujillo refused to step down, laying the groundwork for an armed invasion. To address the last two features of the plan, Operation Santo Domingo was formulated. Figueres, Betancourt, and Muñoz Marín were enlisted to iron out the details with logistical assistance from a member of the administration's Task Force on Latin American Affairs, Richard Goodwin, and CIA agent Cord Meyer. An oversight committee was established with representatives from many of the region's reformist parties in order to put a Latin American veneer on what was a North American–led operation.[143]

Among the talking points at the first meeting, held in October 1960 in Puerto Rico, were the creation of a coalition government in waiting and how best to ensure that Trujillo family members were excluded from any future government. An anti-Trujillo propaganda blitz would be launched from an office in Santurce, Puerto Rico. The press campaign would then be beamed to the Dominican Republic from a radio station in Ponce on Puerto Rico's southern coast. Muñoz Marín's lieutenant, Morales Carrión, was charged with initiating discussions among the contentious exile groups. The different organizations—each with a different agenda for a post-Trujillo future—were cobbled together into the Vanguardia Revolucionaria Dominicana. Venezuelan authorities quietly permitted the opening of a training base at a *finca* owned by a longtime Dominican exile. Even so, disagreements emerged about the wisdom and practicalities of an armed invasion. When some leftist exiles tried to take matters into their own hands, Betancourt's minister of the interior, Pérez, threatened to deport them.[144]

Figueres was frustrated with the snail's pace of Operation Santo Domingo. He wrote Betancourt on Christmas Day 1960 that he had fulfilled his part of the bargain, traveling to Venezuela twice and the United States three times to jump-start planning, but "the truth is, they [U.S. officials] haven't made up their mind and they spend their time talking."[145]

With the operation stalled, the administration made several attempts to persuade Trujillo to relinquish power and enjoy a comfortable retirement elsewhere. In each case, the administration dispatched special envoys who had personal relationships with the dictator. Among them were

Smathers and Pawley, who, along with the dictator, held shares in Dominican petroleum and nickel companies. Trujillo rebuffed any and all appeals to surrender power, including an offer of asylum in the United States "with his fortune [to be] deposited in a foundation headed by U.S. and Latin American leaders." Eight months later, he rejected similar offers to retire to Morocco or Portugal. Better to die in power than emulate Batista and Pérez Jiménez, he told a French journalist.[146]

The unsuccessful attempts to persuade the dictator to step down laid bare the administration's indecision about how best to bring about the desired regime change. Pawley and Smathers made the case to the administration that Trujillo should be given the opportunity to hold elections and make a graceful exit. In a May 1960 meeting with State Department officials, the two expressed concerns that pushing the Dominican ruler to resign was tantamount to opening the door for communists to take over. Then, they contended, the U.S. would have no option but to send troops to the island. The hardline Pawley, who had played such a crucial role in Operation PBSUCCESS, added that he much preferred working with Trujillo than with Betancourt. State Department officials, however, were dubious that the dictator would actually follow through with free and fair elections.[147]

Even Washington's subsequent decision to cut off arms sales and pull its military missions off the island failed to have the desired effect. Trujillo simply turned to European arms suppliers, and in a move that defied logic to anyone unfamiliar with his methods, over the course of several months in late 1960 and early 1961 he extended an olive branch to the Castro regime. Each side agreed to suspend public attacks on the other. (Abbes was even dispatched to Moscow to confer with Soviet officials, although the Soviets and other Eastern Bloc countries refused to grant him visas.) Dominicans must have been bewildered when they heard La Voz Dominicana and a new radio station run by the SIM, Radio Caribe, now praising the Cuban Revolution and attacking the ungrateful Eisenhower administration. It was equally startling for many Cubans to hear Guevara, whose manual on guerrilla warfare was penned with despots like Trujillo in mind, declare over the airwaves in January 1961 that Trujillo was "now our friend." The dictator's rationale for this unusual, short-lived détente between two regimes in Washington's crosshairs was to send the administration a message not to take his loyalty for granted. In truth, the Cubans (and the Soviets) never felt comfortable with a public embrace of Trujillo, but for several months the feuding between the two island nations subsided.[148]

When the dictator hinted, as he had several times in the past, that he might be willing to turn over the reins of government to a subordinate, the consul general and de facto CIA chief of station, Henry Dearborn, recommended that the administration reject the offer.[149] As long as Trujillo remained in the Dominican Republic, "as Governor of Santiago province or dog-catcher," he wrote Mann in October 1960, he remained an existential threat. Dearborn thought that even if the administration could somehow prevail upon Trujillo to leave the island that he would never go gently into retirement. "If he has his millions and he is a free agent he will devote his life from exile to preventing stable government in the Dominican Republic, to overturning democratic governments and establishing dictatorships in the Caribbean, and to assassinating his enemies." Echoing Porter's sentiments, the colorful chief of station left little doubt about what he thought the only solution was to such an intractable problem: "If I were a Dominican . . . I would favor destroying Trujillo as being the first necessary step in the salvation of my country and would regard this, in fact, as my Christian duty. If you recall Dracula, you will remember it was necessary to drive a stake through his heart to prevent a continuation of his crimes. I believe sudden death would be more humane than the solution of the [Papal] Nuncio who once told me he thought he should pray that Trujillo would have a long and lingering illness."[150]

As Dearborn acknowledged, coaxing Trujillo to relinquish power was a fool's errand. A narcissist surrounded by sycophants who told him only what they thought he wanted to hear, Trujillo believed to his core that he was the best man to govern his country. As the political theorist Guillermo O'Donnell noted about "caudillo-führers," by definition such rulers are distrustful and untrustworthy and never relinquish power willingly. As a result, they either die in office (Gómez), are ousted by force (Perón, Machado, Pérez Jiménez, Batista, Somoza Debayle), or are assassinated (Somoza García, Trujillo).[151]

Dearborn was cleared in June 1960 to cultivate two groups of domestic dissidents: an action group to carry out the assassination and a political group to assume the reins of power after Trujillo was eliminated.[152] The attempt on Betancourt's life lent the request added urgency. Further evidence that the administration was committed to the despot's removal was a decision that permitted Dominican exiles to broadcast anti-Trujillo programming from Radio Swan, a CIA-run station off the coast of Honduras.[153]

The decision to aid the conspirators was part of a pattern by the Eisenhower and Kennedy administrations of employing covert assets to eliminate heads of state. Planning for the murders of three other heads of state—Castro, Vietnam's Ngo Dinh Diem, and the Congo's Patrice Lumumba—began at roughly the same time. While Castro and Lumumba were leftists, what they had in common with Diem and Trujillo was that policymakers concluded that their continued presence in power was a threat to the national interest.[154]

In July 1960 Rubottom was demoted and named ambassador to Argentina and Wieland was fired, both scapegoated for the loss of Cuba to the Soviets. Berle wrote in his diary that he suspected that Pawley, who had the president's ear, had pressured Eisenhower to make these changes at Trujillo's behest. That September, Pawley testified before Congress that Wieland deserved to be sacked for allowing Castro to come to power and for agreeing to OAS sanctions against the Dominican Republic. Nor was he happy with Rubottom's replacement, Mann, who he believed was far too chummy with Betancourt.[155]

While Pawley defended Trujillo, the administration moved ahead with its plans to bring about an orderly transfer of power. In December 1960, Richard Bissell, the CIA's deputy director and architect of the Bay of Pigs operation, convened the 5412 Committee, a special group charged with oversight of CIA covert activities. The committee recommended that the Agency furnish the conspirators with weapons. Dearborn received the green light on January 19, 1961, the last day of the Eisenhower administration. Three carbines and three .38-caliber revolvers were smuggled in diplomatic pouches "to neutralize Trujillo." Subsequent requests from the conspirators for submachine guns and other "more exotic" weapons were turned down, however.[156] In a March 1961 cable, Dearborn justified his and his government's actions. "Political assassination is ugly and repulsive, but everything must be judged in its own context. The United States used the atom bomb on Hiroshima and that was ugly and repulsive—unless one stops to consider that it was used to save thousands of lives in the long run."[157]

As with the Bay of Pigs, the Kennedy administration inherited the ongoing operation and needed to decide whether to follow through or shut it down. Testifying before the Church Committee in its investigation of political assassinations in 1975, Secretary of State Dean Rusk admitted that Cuba had influenced the administration's deliberations about Trujillo. "The excesses of Batista led to concern that the Dominican Republic might also eventually fall victim to a Castro-style Communist regime."[158]

The Kennedy administration was so worried that Trujillo's removal would result in political instability that it reached out to Betancourt and

Lleras Camargo to seek their militaries' participation in a joint intervention should leftists threaten to seize power in the Dominican Republic. Betancourt was willing to commit his air force and navy in the event of another Cuban invasion of the Dominican Republic, but objected to the U.S. request for a joint declaration. He preferred that each nation issue its own rationale for participation. Cognizant of how collaboration with the United States would be interpreted at home, he hedged, indicating that Venezuela would participate only if the OAS authorized a peace-keeping force.[159]

Aware that an assassination attempt was in the works, U.S. officials wrestled with conflicting objectives—maintaining plausible deniability of their involvement while making sure that the Dominican Republic did not become another Cuba. After the Bay of Pigs, the Kennedy administration, uneasy about who might fill the vacuum if Trujillo were eliminated, did an about-face and instructed Dearborn to actively discourage the action group.

The CIA station chief was dumbfounded: for more than a year, he and other U.S. officials "had been nurturing the effort to overthrow Trujillo." It was, he complained, "too late to consider whether United States will initiate overthrow of Trujillo." Goodwin counseled the station chief to walk a fine line: "remain in the good graces of the dissidents" but avoid "any action which might further involve the United States in the anticipated assassination."[160] While the administration had no qualms about eliminating Castro, not so with Trujillo. No doubt the prospect of another failure so soon after the Bay of Pigs influenced the decision to reverse course.

Dearborn's efforts to persuade the conspirators to stand down, however, failed. Understandably, frustration had set in with Washington's fickleness. The conspirators curtly informed him that their plans were well advanced and that this was "their affair and it could not be turned off to suit the convenience of the United States government." In a last-minute maneuver designed to distance his administration, Kennedy cabled Dearborn on May 29, 1961, stating that under no circumstances should the United States government be complicit in political assassination. That note eventually saw the light of day, but to be safe, the State Department ordered Dearborn and his staff to destroy earlier correspondence with the plotters.[161] Two days later, fourteen conspirators intercepted the dictator's 1959 Chevrolet late in the evening and riddled his body with bullets.[162]

The Kennedy administration, however, did not bathe itself in glory when it did not lift a finger to stop Ramfis and Abbes's brutal vengeance against the conspirators.[163] It must have had an inkling of what was to come because a week after the assassination, Dearborn was ordered to leave the island immediately. "Since the Trujillo family continued to be powerful and since I was known to be in touch with the dissidents," he recalled in a 1975 interview, "there was no knowing what conclusion the Trujillo intelligence apparatus might come to." The plain-spoken CIA station chief certainly had no regrets about his actions. With the dictator, "on the skids … it was our purpose to cultivate the pro-U.S. dissidents so that the future government of the Dominican Republic would be pro-U.S. rather than anti."[164] It is ironic that the actions taken by the U.S. government to rid itself of a recalcitrant head of state, including the knitting together of a unified domestic opposition, the enlistment of proxies, the delivery of weapons to plotters, sanctions, attempts to ease out the dictator, and encouragement of and involvement in the act of magnicide itself, were straight out of the victim's playbook.

With the tyrant dead, stakeholders struggled to make sure that Castro-supported leftists *and* members of Trujillo's extended family and cronies did not fill the political vacuum. When he first learned of the assassination, Muñoz Marín immediately wrote Morales Carrión, now deputy assistant secretary of state for inter-American affairs, urging the administration to refrain from awarding asylum to key trujillistas. To be avoided at all costs was a repetition of the anti-American backlash that had occurred in Venezuela after Pérez Jiménez and Estrada were allowed to settle in south Florida. But leaving Balaguer or Ramfis in charge also was unacceptable to the governor. Over the course of that fall, the governor and his lieutenants emerged as interlocutors, meeting with exiles and tendering advice to policymakers in Washington about how best to force the remaining trujillistas out and manage the transition. With its chief target removed from the equation, though, Operation Santo Domingo closed up shop.[165]

In truth, reformers were selective when it came to U.S. interference in the internal affairs of other countries. Few batted an eye, for instance, when the Kennedy administration dispatched a naval task force off the coast of the Dominican capital in November 1961 in order to discourage a coup that would have placed Trujillo's relations in charge. On board the eight warships were twelve thousand marines at the ready, and fighter jets from the task force flew ominously over the shoreline. The

Caribbean had not witnessed such saber rattling since Roosevelt sent warships to Cuba in 1933. Trujillo's relations took the hint and left the island, but not before shamelessly lining their pockets.[166] Reformers, who had worked tirelessly to remove the Dominican ruler and his family, did not have much time to savor their victory. A rapid succession of coups d'état upended their goal of a dictator-free zone.

A Plague of *Golpes*

Eight democracies fell between 1962 and 1964, an abrupt end to a wave that began so auspiciously with the Bolivian Revolution. Two additional states—the pacted democracies of Venezuela and Colombia—withstood coups, but not without making significant concessions to their armed forces. Predictably, coup plotters contended that civilian governments were too weak to confront the communist threat. This, of course, was pro forma—La Internacional regularly invoked the red scare—but Cuba's stunning shift to the Soviet camp lent credibility to what up to then had been largely a debating point. Unlike civilian politicians, who had to appeal to voters, high commands could fearmonger at will. For decades, militaries had remained silent when dictators incorporated communists into their governments, but in the wake of the Cuban Revolution, anything less than a *mano dura* toward leftists by civilian politicians was judged a sign of weakness by hawkish high commands. There were, of course, pragmatic reasons to cry wolf as well. Given Washington's preoccupation with preventing another Cuba, military establishments were well aware that a dedicated strategy to repress domestic leftists kept the arms pipeline open.[167]

But that claim obscures more than it reveals. Of the eight countries where military coups succeeded, only Guatemala contended with a guerrilla insurgency of even limited duration, and leftist rebels there never mounted a serious threat. A case in point of claims of creeping leftist influence was the Dominican Republic, where the military was quick to cry red as a pretext for ousting Juan Bosch in 1963. But it was Bosch's unsuccessful efforts to alter a deeply ingrained authoritarian culture, his frustrations with the slow pace of reform, incompetence, a reluctance to compromise, his prickly relationship with North American investors, and a U.S. ambassador whose modus operandi recalled proconsuls of the past that better explain why the Dominican Republic's first democratically elected president in forty years was removed from office after only seven months in power. Too often, Bosch spoke his mind when circumstances dictated restraint or compromise. Some PRD loyalists, who had waited so patiently for this opportunity, could be heard griping, "*Juan no sirve nada*" (Juan is good for nothing). When rumors of a *golpe* swirled, the Kennedy administration's muted response was telling. While Bosch certainly did not endear himself when he allowed leftist exiles to return to the island and participate in politics, he never surrounded himself with leftists as Árbenz had. Bosch might have pointed out that allowing communists to participate in the political arena was not an issue for Betancourt, who had insisted that not doing so ran the risk of driving them underground.[168]

Ironically, the country most at risk of a successful leftist rebellion was Venezuela, and in that case Betancourt and Leoni not only prevailed against *la guerrilla* but survived multiple coup and assassination attempts—not all of them from the right. While guerrilla insurgencies in the countryside and urban terrorism resulted in major defections within their own party, it also unified what remained of AD's political coalition while retaining the all-important loyalty of the armed forces.[169] As one analyst noted, for many Venezuelans the guerrilla threat transformed AD's image at home overnight; once thought of as "the Antichrist and extreme radical of the 1940s," the party was now regarded as "a bulwark of modernization and stability." Owing to Betancourt's solicitous demeanor and a "gift for command," the military establishment came to trust the man who not long before they could not countenance.[170] Stewart, now elevated to ambassador to Venezuela, explained the great lengths that the president went to win over the armed forces.[171]

> Every Thursday Betancourt devoted his afternoons to meetings with any military officer or noncom who wanted to come to see him at Miraflores Palace with whatever problem in the world he had, whether personal or whether he was concerned about policies. And he very patiently went through the policy things, told them why he was doing this, what the reasons were. Or if the guy had a personal problem, he saw that the personal problem was attended to. ... Even if they were against his policies, he would hear them out and then patiently explain why he was doing it the way he was. He had only one rule, that there should be no disrespect to the commander-in-chief; so, if any officer or non-com showed disrespect, then he would be arrested and prosecuted, no bones about that.

Betancourt also made himself available to the rank and file on his frequent travels across the country. By giving so generously of his time, "he built up a great loyalty in the armed forces, not to mention the fact that he knew the good officers and people that supported him and had them in charge of the key military establishments and key posts. So that his relationship with the military was unique and something that other presidents should consider because it really saved his neck."[172]

Even though the region's armed forces pressured democratic governments to take the domestic left seriously, the red scare in and of itself does not explain why the region's political center of gravity shifted toward the right. What, then, explains this resurgence of authoritarianism? A number of factors carry greater explanatory power: the fragility and ineffectiveness of the new democracies, political polarization, a high command's anxiety over which political party might emerge victorious in an upcoming election, calls for military intervention by civil society, and the armed forces' monopoly of power. If militaries needed additional reasons to crush incipient unrest, the fate of former batistianos in the months after the triumph of the revolution provided it.

The perpetrators of this wave of coups were not the personalistic caudillos of the past. Trujillo's death and the exile of several members in good standing of La Internacional dovetailed with the increasing professionalization and the politicization of the region's militaries, a trend Rangel first documented in the early 1950s. Those trends gained traction in the early 1960s, thanks in large part to the Kennedy administration's conviction that the region's militaries needed to be retooled and retrained to confront the twin threats of rural insurgency and urban terror.

Perhaps most surprising was the role played by civilians in pressuring militaries to intervene in domestic politics. By one count, there were 35 attempted coups against Arturo Frondizi's presidency in Argentina (1958–1962), many instigated by domestic opponents of the administration.[173] In some cases, it was the oligarchy and its media advocating military intervention, but at other times it was the left that deliberately provoked unrest. Disgruntled civilian interest groups that conspired with the armed forces to foment a coup invariably petitioned the military to cede power back to civilians as soon as possible. But civil society's ability to force the issue was circumscribed because of the military's monopoly of power. Unlike the earlier decades of the century, when militaries served as personal armies to strongmen, autonomous high commands now took such lobbying under advisement. The combination of modernization and professionalization and the military's extreme aversion to political instability meant that institutional considerations were given pride of place.[174]

Civilian politicians also had difficulty navigating the highly charged political environment. Endeavoring to please both sides of the spectrum, Frondizi satisfied no one. On the one hand, he implemented a fiscally prudent economic stabilization plan, which included significant cuts in public spending, the elimination of subsidies on public services, and the devaluation of the currency. Those measures endeared him to businessmen, foreign investors, multilateral lenders, and the Kennedy administration. Foreign investment increased, and inflation fell from 114 percent in 1959 to 13.5 percent two years later. Those policies, however, were not uniformly popular, and coupled with the granting of concessions to foreign oil, cost him the support of organized labor and progressives. In addition, his reluctance to sever relations with Cuba angered the high command. What sealed his fate, however, was his high-stakes decision to allow the Peronists to participate in the 1962 congressional and provincial elections. When the party did far better than anticipated, the military, which deemed the Peronists a far greater threat than the communists, demanded that he annul the elections. Although he made last-minute concessions to save his presidency, he failed to mollify the armed forces and was ousted in March 1962. Better politicians than Frondizi might not have been able to thread Argentina's fractious political needle, but he did himself no favors by alienating the one institution he needed to survive. Even after he was forced out, the military's scheming to influence the political arena did not abate.[175]

Elsewhere, civilian pressure did not always achieve the desired result. Just as AD had cozied up to disaffected pérezjimenistas in the armed forces during the 1950s, the Movimiento Izquierdista Revolucionario (MIR), a breakaway offshoot, cultivated junior officers during the early 1960s. For AD, which had spent a decade conspiring with officers to regain power, the shoe was now firmly on the other foot. In the spring of 1962, two *golpes* led by progressive officers linked to the MIR were defeated by forces loyal to the government. That, however, did not put an end to the plotting, as a number of the rebellious officers joined the armed struggle.

The sectarian, generational divide that plagued AD was present among leftists as well. Early on, oldline Venezuelan communists warned the "impatient," inexperienced Miristas not to engage in putsches. The MIR responded by chiding their elders; perhaps they should spend less time policing deviationists and devote more of their energies to making the revolution. Yet when the PCV did an about-face and announced that it was joining the insurgency, the decision proved disastrous. Many members of the party's Central Committee were rounded up and jailed, and over the course of an ill-conceived armed struggle, the PCV squandered the good will it had engendered in ousting Pérez Jiménez. In truth, the Venezuelan left was its own worst enemy.[176]

With a few notable exceptions when the armed forces pursued reformist agendas, the coups benefited national oligarchies. In such cases, the juntas impeded or scrapped the implementation of social and economic programs begun by civilian predecessors. Even where democracies survived, resistance to what the high commands perceived as leftist giveaways slowed the pace of reform. The pivot back to authoritarian rule also helps explain why the Kennedy administration's ballyhooed Alliance for Progress initiative stumbled out of the gate and why it encountered indifference from generals and oligarchs alike.

Often the stated reasons for a coup were the ineffectiveness, weakness, or corruption of a civilian government. But here again, motivations and rhetoric did not line up neatly. In Peru, Honduras, Ecuador, and Guatemala, where *golpes* took place a year or less before elections were scheduled to be held, militaries acted preemptively, either to call off upcoming elections or to invalidate a vote that had just taken place. In each case, the triumph of a particular political party or a candidate was considered inimical to institutional interests. In Brazil, the armed forces acted to prevent President João Goulart from extending his term of office, whereas the Ecuadorian military intervened to prevent the return of a former president it had deposed two years earlier. Similar concerns surfaced in Guatemala when rumors of ex-president Arévalo's return from exile preoccupied the high command. In Peru, the armed forces nullified the results of an election in 1962 because they were convinced that the Apristas, who had garnered a plurality of the votes in a disputed election, would exact revenge for past repression. Nor was this a new trend. In fact, a longitudinal study of military *golpes* during the twentieth century found that just under 40 percent were carried out either six months before or after an election.[177]

Even in countries that escaped coups and remained ostensibly democratic, the military often wielded outsized influence. Civilian governments were kept on a short leash. Any effort to pare down a bloated military budget was guaranteed to raise hackles. Pitting factions of the military against itself, more often than not, ended infelicitously for civilian governments. Or as Schlesinger inelegantly put it, "civilian governments exist on the army's sufferance."[178]

Military establishments were, by definition, complex bureaucratic organisms. More so than strongmen, they answered to different constituencies. In addition to traditional interservice rivalries, differences of opinion existed among officers about the wisdom of the institution's involvement in politics. In some cases, ideological differences undermined military cohesion and unity. In Argentina, factions within the armed forces feuded for years about whether or not to legalize the Peronist Party. Civilian politicians played upon such rifts. Those reformist administrations that remained in power sought to divide and conquer by frequently shifting and rotating officers or, as in the case of Bolivia's MNR and Venezuela's AD, by showering resources on newly formed national police forces.

The creation of alternative fighting forces, as military historian Edwin Lieuwen noted, was a strategy that civilian administrations adopted at their peril, because military establishments considered paramilitaries and, in some cases, the police a threat to their prerogatives. The only reformist politician savvy enough to profitably employ such a strategy was Betancourt, and in that country the existence of a concerted insurgency assuaged concerns among the high command that the newly empowered National Guard was a threat to its interests.[179]

There was a stiff price to pay for catering to the military, the Catholic Church, and business interests. Progressives in his own party skewered Betancourt for failing to deliver on his campaign promises. During the last months of Betancourt's presidency, a party loyalist, Gumersindo Rodríguez, wrote him and offered a frank assessment of AD's tenuous situation, one that readily applied to any of the region's reformist parties. Speaking for many of his peers, Rodríguez admitted that although the Cuban issue was divisive, that was only one of many factors contributing to an exodus of militants to the MIR and the PCV: "It's been a tumultuous few years. It pains me that I don't have the same admiration for you that I once had. Those of us who were with AD when we were *muchachos* had a very passionate confidence in our leaders and principally in you. ... It was precisely the party's Jacobinism that attracted many of us." During the struggle against the dictatorship, Rodríguez allowed, it was easy to maintain "the most absolute loyalty to the party." But ever since AD achieved power in 1959 the administration's pragmatism and its rightward retreat had muddled the party's message, raising legitimate concerns among militants about the old guard's commitment to a peaceful, democratic revolution. The absence of clarity in this regard raised questions about "what type of society we want." Rodríguez was appalled by Betancourt's frequent resort to the suspension of constitutional liberties; the limits placed on press freedoms of the Communist newspaper *La Tribuna Popular*, the MIR's *Izquieridista*, and the URD's *Clarín;* the bans on outdoor political meetings; the broad discretionary power in the detention of suspects; and the police raids of homes without the need for a warrant. Communists, he added, had been quick to pounce on this assault on political liberties "to lure the young away from the party."[180]

Other exceptions to the spate of coups—Mexico, Costa Rica, Uruguay, Chile, and Cuba—were thought to be free from the taint of military interference in the political sphere. But even where a well-established tradition of civilian governance existed, such as in Uruguay and Chile, militaries in the early 1970s ousted democratically elected governments and established brutal dictatorships of significant duration. Moreover, just because a military did not play a pivotal role in its nation's body politic was not enough to assure democratic governance. Mexico and Cuba, for instance, experienced revolutionary mobilizations that effectively gutted standing armies in the 1910s and in 1959, respectively. Each replaced its existing army with a revolutionary force that was loyal and that remained subservient to the one-party state. The result was an enduring political, rather than military, dictatorship in each country. A surprising but revealing commentary is that only tiny Costa Rica managed to avoid autocratic rule during the second half of the Cold War.

Although La Internacional's loose alliance of strongmen never reconstituted itself, that did not mean that militaries did not pool resources, especially when it came to tracking the whereabouts of leftist insurgents. Well before the creation of Operation Condor in the mid-1970s, Southern Cone militaries were sharing intelligence. The impetus for such cooperation came from Brazilian general Artur da Costa e Silva, who first warned of the transnational character of a leftist diaspora. A case in point of successful collaboration was the assistance given to Bolivia's military during Che Guevara's doomed guerrilla insurgency in 1967. Border sweeps conducted by Bolivia's neighbors made it logistically impossible for Cuba to resupply Che's rebel force.

As the *golpes* proliferated, Betancourt reached out to democratic politicians across the region. In letters to the president of Mexico, Adolfo

López Mateos, and Bolivia's Paz Estenssoro in July 1962, he warned that moderates must make their case before the OAS or face the consequences. "If collective measures are not taken to stop this contagious epidemic of militarist coups, the time may come when even the most . . . established democracies will suffer."[181] He took up the matter with Kennedy as well, cautioning that if Washington did not take a tougher stance against the wave of coups, more Cubas were in the offing. Since 1948, dictatorships had resulted in repression, corruption, and incompetent governance; the growing radicalization of the region's youth; and a "visible deterioration in relations" between the United States and its neighbors. He contended that the Kennedy administration's inconsistent practice of withholding recognition of certain military juntas while recognizing others only made matters worse. Such behavior undercut faith in democratic governance.[182]

After the Peruvian coup, Venezuela and its democratic allies in Colombia, Honduras, Costa Rica, and the Dominican Republic all severed relations with the Peruvian junta and collectively asked the United States to back an OAS resolution condemning *golpes* and reaffirming "the democratic solidarity of the Americas." But the Kennedy administration nixed the idea because it felt that any blanket condemnation of coups would tie its hands. In his reply, Kennedy noted that while he shared the Venezuelan president's concerns, recognition was a knotty problem. Even Latin American governments could not agree on how best to address the matter. After all, he added, coups essentially were domestic matters and external pressure only went so far.[183] Years later, U.S. Ambassador to Peru James Loeb expressed regret about the refusal to support Betancourt's resolution. It was not only a missed opportunity to demonstrate the administration's commitment to democratic rule, but he was confident that if the U.S. had used its diplomatic muscle to persuade other governments to follow suit, the outcome would have been different.[184]

Washington's litmus test for recognition was whether it considered a junta or a military ruler sufficiently anticommunist. For instance, recognition was not withheld after the Argentine military removed Frondizi because, as Rusk explained to Betancourt, "my fear is that the failure to do this will only play into the hands of the extremists."[185] When asked why the administration denounced and delayed recognition of certain coups (Peru, Honduras, and the Dominican Republic) while recognizing others (Argentina, Guatemala, and Ecuador), the best Kennedy could offer was "[we] haven't got a consistent policy because the circumstances are sometimes inconsistent."[186] By the last year of his presidency, he had given up on the notion that withholding recognition would deter coups or bend the region's military establishments to the United States' will. Assistant Secretary of State Martin did his best to formalize the equivocal response. While the U.S. was opposed to *golpismo*, it recognized that it was powerless to "create effective democracy" or to keep "a man in office by use of economic pressure or even military force, when his own people are not willing to fight to defend him."[187]

Betancourt was enough of a realist to understand that he could push Kennedy only so far. While Venezuela could afford to be idealistic, the United States did not have that luxury. As he related to Stewart, "we know that there are certain considerations as a world power that you have to take into consideration that we don't have to. We can be Don Quixotes if we want to but you can't and I understand that." On the other hand, that did not stop him from calling Stewart on the carpet and "giving me a chewing out, the likes of which you have never heard, when we would recognize a regime. Once he'd gotten it out of his system, then that was forgotten."[188]

While Kennedy's visits to four of the region's democracies met with a far more favorable response than Nixon's trip, his administration's military assistance program was viewed with increasing skepticism. As the emphasis on hemispheric defense, a cornerstone of U.S. policy since World War II, gave way to counterinsurgency training, internal security measures, and civic action programs, critics charged that Latin American militaries had become little more than glorified policemen, and repressive ones at that.[189]

Illustrative of that trend was rural Colombia, where "banditry has become a way of life." As criminal gangs roamed the countryside, residents, fearing for their lives, refused to cooperate with the military. Pacifying the countryside thus became a high priority for Lleras Camargo's administration, which reached the conclusion that until rural zones were demilitarized, implementing an agrarian reform was impossible. Of special concern to the United States was that "communist and pro-Castro elements have penetrated many of the [rural] gangs." In November 1959, the U.S. military dispatched a team of antiguerrilla warfare experts to survey the problem. Its report recommended specialized training for the military. Their findings pulled no punches; after years of violence, the public had little confidence in state institutions. The survey team's report recommended specialized training for the military in psychological war-

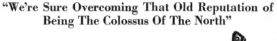

"We're sure overcoming that old reputation of being the
Colossus of the North," published October 5, 1963. A
1963 Herblock Cartoon, © The Herb Block Foundation,
and Prints & Photographs Division, Library of Congress,
LC-DIG-ppmsca-17189.

fare and a tactical unit to address crime and insurgency. Meanwhile, a
Colombian military offensive called Operation Marquetalia targeted the
so-called autonomous republics—swaths of mountainous terrain under
the control of Liberal guerrillas. The campaign proved militarily successful, but it sowed the seeds of one of the longest and most devastating
guerrilla insurgencies in Latin American history. In addition, the military
implemented a civic action program to improve its reputation among the
rural poor. The army was now charged with everything from building

John Kennedy and Rómulo Betancourt attend land grant ceremony
at Resettlement Project in La Morita, Venezuela. Cecil Stoughton.
White House Photographs. John F. Kennedy Presidential Library and
Museum, Boston, MA.

roads to running sanitation and public health campaigns to promoting
rural education.[190] Detractors insisted that the far more expansive and
costly military assistance programs amounted to new wine in old bottles,
because just as in the past, the "arms and training bolstered militarism,
and dictatorship was understood to be an unpleasant but acceptable consequence."[191]

For all the Kennedy administration's high-minded rhetoric about
agrarian reform, expanding education, improving health services, and reforming tax codes, the Alliance for Progress rollout was marred by a mo-
rass of bureaucracy. Betancourt was especially frustrated with "the
endless paperwork." In February 1962, he vented privately to Muñoz
Marín, comparing the arrogance of Alliance technicians sent to his country with "the Texans," who came during the early days of his country's oil
boom. "And this, Luis, for a country that is one of the focal centers of
Castro's activity in the Caribbean area, and where there is a general anti–
North American attitude."[192]

Nine months after he was inaugurated, Kennedy asked his advisors
"to increase the intimacy" between the Pentagon and Latin American
militaries. During the decade, an average of thirty-five thousand Latin
American officers, enlisted men, and police officers a year came to the
Canal Zone or the States for training.[193] In places where security was

thought to be at risk, such as northeastern Brazil or Honduras, the administration soft-pedaled the Alliance for Progress mandate for agrarian reform. In the latter, civilian president Villeda Morales's efforts to implement a new decree that permitted the national government to confiscate fallow lands, a law that he believed was in keeping with the Alliance's directives, was derailed by the Kennedy administration and the United and Standard Fruit Companies. Taken together, an inconsistent recognition policy, counterinsurgency training, and the strategic leveraging of military and economic assets meant that in practice, the Kennedy and Johnson administrations tolerated working with "regimes and groups that were undemocratic, conservative and frequently repressive."[194]

The July 1962 Peruvian coup was notable in this regard. After decades of shunning APRA, the U.S. openly supported Haya's candidacy because he disavowed communism during the campaign while his opponent, Fernando Belaúnde Terry, did not. But the Peruvian military's hatred of APRA rivaled the Argentine military's abhorrence of the Peronists, and officers conveyed their objections to an Aprista government in no uncertain terms to Loeb. He actively discouraged the military from seizing power, but his efforts went for naught. Soon after Haya eked out a victory at the polls, thirty tanks rumbled into Lima's Plaza de Armas. The military demanded that President Prado step down, even though he had only one month remaining in his term, and then it annulled the elections. After the *golpe* the Kennedy administration, claiming that the junta had dealt the democratic cause in Latin America "a ruinous setback," withheld recognition and suspended military and economic aid.[195]

But the Peruvian junta took U.S. posturing in stride, as well it should have. It noted that the Kennedy administration initially had made similar noises about withholding recognition and cutting off military aid after Frondizi's ouster and then quietly had reconsidered months later. Policymakers did the same with Peru, but not before extracting a pledge from the junta that it hold elections in the near future. Unlike many of its peers, however, this junta was unusually reform-minded and far from repressive. It committed to holding elections and relinquishing power, and it lived up to its promise a year later.[196]

When moderate Belaúnde Terry assumed power in 1963, the Johnson administration did little to assist him, especially after negotiations broke down between the government and the U.S.-based International Petroleum Company. To pressure Belaúnde to accept more favorable terms, Mann intentionally slow-tracked Agency for International Development

(AID) loans to Peru between 1964 and 1966. A settlement was reached in August 1968, but the nationalistic backlash that resulted from that agreement contributed to still another military coup in 1968.[197]

Loyal allies, like Bolivia's MNR, once considered an exemplar of liberal democratic reform and a major recipient of U.S. aid, were now left to twist in the wind as coup plotters circled. As happened with AD in Venezuela, progressive elements deserted the party, citing the country's unseemly dependence on Washington. Evidence was not lacking. In the late 1950s and early 1960s, U.S. advisors had overseen virtually all phases of the Siles Zuazo (1956–1960) and Paz Estenssoro (1960–1964) administrations. Petroleum and mining codes were rewritten to Washington's specifications, and a highly unpopular monetary stabilization program, which slashed employment in key sectors of the economy, was implemented. U.S. technical assistance teams were twice as large as those sent to much larger countries like Chile, Colombia, and Brazil.

After Paz amended the constitution so that he could run again in 1964, the armed forces pounced. U.S. military advisors, who had helped rebuild the armed forces, were said to have been whispering in the ears of Bolivian generals. Ironically, it was U.S.-funded civic action programs that enabled coup leader General René Barrientos Ortuño to build a base of support in the countryside. After the *golpe*, the Johnson administration funneled funds to Barrientos, which helped secure his victory at the polls in the 1966 presidential elections.[198]

The U.S. was even more hands-on in Chile, where investment by U.S.-based multinational companies reached seven hundred million dollars in 1960. The Kennedy administration's response to Allende's near-upset in the 1958 presidential election was to shower economic assistance on the victor, Jorge Alessandri (1958–1964). Johnson then earmarked millions of dollars and a team of campaign strategists to help the moderate Christian Democratic candidate Frei win the 1964 elections. That party traced its roots back to the 1930s, when Catholic students broke away from the Conservative Party to form the Falange Nacional. The Christian Democrats' commitment to social justice was rooted in the papal encyclicals *Rerum Novarum* (1891) and *Quadragesimo Anno* (1931) and the ideas of the French philosopher Jacques Maritain, which decried both capitalist inequality and atheistic communism. Chilean priests educated in Europe brought those teachings back to their homeland. Like reformist parties elsewhere, Christian Democrats' big tent contained both progressive and moderate wings, which disagreed about the best path forward.[199]

Frei, the leader of the party's moderate wing, nevertheless promised Chileans a "Revolution in Liberty." The centerpieces of his agenda were an ambitious agrarian reform and the "Chileanization" of the copper industry, the country's principal source of foreign exchange. Buoyed by higher copper prices during the first two years of his administration, Frei moved assertively to expand services for the poor and to address social and economic inequality.

By promising to create one hundred thousand new yeoman farmers, however, candidate Frei raised unrealistic expectations for his agrarian reform. But although he fell far short of his goal—only one in five of the rural poor obtained land—agricultural productivity, unionization, and employment spiked, and real income for rural households tripled. For the first time, peasants felt empowered. As the best scholarly study of the reform notes, it was "the most significant redistribution of private wealth in Chilean history."[200]

Policymakers in Washington were not as troubled by the reform, since North American ownership of land was minimal in Chile. As a result, they kept the aid pipeline open and trumpeted the reform as an Alliance for Progress success story. The reform, however, angered the landed elite, who felt betrayed after they had thrown their support to Frei while drawing fire from the left for not going far enough to break up large landed estates. The polarizing reform, coupled with sliding copper prices during the last years of Frei's administration and fissures within the party itself, diminished its prospects for the 1970 elections.

Matters took a turn for the worse for the United States when Allende secured a narrow victory at the polls in 1970. Since he received only a plurality of the vote, his victory had to be confirmed by the congress. Just before that vote, the constitutionalist general René Schneider was murdered during a botched kidnapping. With rumors swirling that the CIA was complicit in the plot, nationalistic Chileans pressured their legislators to cast their votes for Allende. The backlash also ensured that constitutionalists within the military prevailed, at least over the short term. For the next three years, Schneider's successor, General Carlos Prats González, managed to keep putschist plotters within the military at bay.[201] But Allende's election, a Marxist assuming power through the ballot box, was a nightmare scenario for the Nixon administration. The administration moved aggressively to destabilize Allende's Popular Unity government and then it played a supportive role in the 1973 coup that brought General Augusto Pinochet to power.

Conclusions

By the end of the 1960s, military regimes governed fifteen countries. Betancourt, of course, had been through this before. In his July 1963 letter to Kennedy, he drew parallels between the current moment and 1948, when a number of nascent democracies were jettisoned from power. There were indications, however, that this latest shift to authoritarian rule was qualitatively different from the earlier one. Four factors best explain why this trend toward autocracy represented an existential threat to the long-term prospects for democracy in the hemisphere: the militaries' determination to protect and defend their institutional interests; the exemplary character of the Cuban Revolution and its commitment to exporting its model; Washington's involvement in the region's border wars; and reformers' willingness to assist the Kennedy and Johnson administrations' efforts to contain Castro.

As Castro had predicted, *golpistas* promised to rule for a short time and then promptly reneged. While the Cuban Revolution did not trigger the takeovers, it did act as a useful cudgel that militaries repeatedly wielded against civilian politicians. Castro's export of revolution— between 1959 and 1961, insurgencies patterned on the *foco* model were active in more than a dozen countries—lent urgency to U.S.-funded counterinsurgency training and legitimized the belief in some quarters that a military government was better equipped to defeat leftist uprisings. Three of the five civilian presidents confronting sustained guerrilla activity failed to complete their terms, but not because insurgents were particularly successful. In Bolivia, Guatemala, and Peru, guerrillas failed to win over campesinos, who either turned against them or actively aided the government. Guerrilla operations in the countryside and urban terror resulted in significant collateral damage, undermining support for the rebel cause. Furthermore, insurgents committed the cardinal sin of leftists everywhere—they squabbled and fractured. Local communist parties, in particular, resented Cuban meddling. Matters came to a head at a secret meeting of Latin American communist parties in Havana in November 1964, where the hosts were sharply criticized for their patronizing and overbearing methods.[202]

Although Trujillo's assassination eliminated a major source of instability, the United States' involvement in the Caribbean Basin's border wars more than filled that vacuum. With Trujillo removed from the equation, the path was cleared for Washington and its allies—reformers

and dictators alike—to give their undivided attention to Cuba. Even the
Soviet Union's removal of the missiles of October (in exchange for Kennedy's pledge not to invade the island) did not deter the United States.

By removing almost all the last vestiges of La Internacional from political office, the democratic wave inadvertently opened the political door
for military regimes. The new regimes were very different from their
predecessors, however. Of all the strongmen who were ousted in the late
1950s, only Perón regained power, and he spent nearly two decades in
exile before the military government permitted him to return. His election in July 1973 proved short-lived, lasting only nine months before he
passed away. Political comebacks by Rojas Pinilla, Pérez Jiménez, and
Odría all failed miserably. Castillo Armas, Somoza, and Trujillo were assassinated in office, while Batista lived out his last years in obscurity.

The challenges facing civilian governments during this turbulent period were formidable. As constraints on the media were lifted, politicians
had to fend off vitriolic attacks from both the left and the right. Politicians warned that scurrilous reporting paved the way for coups, but that
did little to dissuade the fourth estate. Efforts to censor the press resulted in charges of hypocrisy being leveled against civilian governments.

Since militaries were often complicit in an outgoing caudillo's repressive apparatus, civilian politicians had to move gingerly when implementing guardrails to rein in the armed forces' worst instincts. They dared not
investigate, let alone prosecute, officers involved in meting out repression. In countries where popular rebellions drove out dictators, such as
Colombia and Venezuela, armed forces were, for a time, chastened. But
arrogant, thin-skinned officers, defensive about their role in propping up
unpopular autocrats, rarely reacted well to criticism from civilian politicians. Setting up a legislative committee to monitor the armed forces, for
instance, was regarded with deep suspicion by high commands, which
zealously sought to defend institutional autonomy. Moreover, the ever-
present prospect of coup plotting convinced presidents that it was in their
self-interest to appoint members of the high command to the post of defense minister, further politicizing the institution.

Another problem facing the new civilian rulers was that their political parties were, with some exceptions, weak, "with few or no roots in the
past."[203] Established parties, such as the Christian Democrats in Chile
and Colombia's Liberal and Conservative Parties, were able to respond
to or deflect complaints from affiliated unions, peasant confederations,
and student federations. But, militants, upset with their party's stance on

Cuba and a perceived tone-deafness in their party's leadership, voted with their feet, joining leftist organizations. Intense pressure from the military, conservatives, and Washington led to crackdowns on dissidents as politicians tried with mixed results to employ both the carrot and the stick to diminish the attractiveness of clandestine operations.

Democracies also walked a fine line when it came to implementing their agendas. If they moved too precipitously on reforms, whether it be land expropriations or raising taxes, they risked alienating businessmen and landowners. If, however, they moved too slowly, their impatient base turned on them. Not surprisingly, most politicians erred on the side of caution. There were exceptions where reforms helped preserve democratic rule. Betancourt's administration, for instance, distributed one hundred thousand parcels to peasants and invested heavily in health, sanitation, and education in the countryside. Such reforms diminished the popularity of leftist movements and laid the groundwork for decades of democratic rule.

The Kennedy and Johnson administrations did not fundamentally differ from their predecessors. They had little patience for politicians who proved themselves unequal to the task of rooting out leftist subversion. As one scholar of the period put it, Kennedy and Johnson "supported the *golpistas*, enthusiastically in some cases, and with varying degrees of embarrassment in others."[204] Governments thought to be leftist-leaning, such as that of Goulart and the Dominican government, were actively undermined or forcibly overthrown. The U.S. funded Goulart's political rivals, bolstered anticommunist labor unions, and dispatched Vernon Walters to prod the military to stage a coup. Not only did the U.S. promise the armed forces immediate recognition and additional aid, but Johnson ordered the deployment of a carrier task force off the Brazilian coast to further discourage the president's backers. After the coup, it reopened the aid spigot. Between 1964 and 1966, the U.S. dispersed $950 million to Brazil's repressive military government.[205]

By mid-decade, reformist governments had, with a few exceptions, given way to authoritarian rule. The new military regimes were unlike anything the region had ever witnessed. Reformers may have anticipated that another democratic surge would soon return them to office, but Cold War convulsions precluded that possibility.

Conclusion

B Y THE EARLY 1960s, reformers appeared to have reached the promised land. Populists, throwback caudillos, and modernizing military regimes beat a hasty retreat. For social democrats who now held the governing reins, this moment surely called for celebration. After years of imprisonment, torture, and extended exile, reformers now had the chance to establish and consolidate democratic rule, address their country's most pressing needs, and advance their agendas. There was another reason to feel optimistic—a Democratic president in the White House who seemed far more amenable than his predecessors.

Yet in the span of a few years, most were rudely shown the door, never to appear on the political stage again. The dream of a continent free from dictatorship was never realized. A frustrated Frances Grant, who worked tirelessly for the democratic cause, surveyed the wreckage in 1965 and pondered whether it was worth it. "All of us who are in this field seem to be on a kind of treadmill, which turns, but hardly ever moves ahead. Do we really make progress?"[1]

Why was democracy so fragile? And what changed to make this promising surge so fleeting? The short answer is the Cuban Revolution. Castro's decision to relinquish his nation's secure, if dependent, place in the United States' sphere of influence for an uncertain future in the Soviet bloc, its export of revolution, and Washington's single-minded determination to isolate and punish Cuba placed all of these young democracies in a vise. Until January 1, 1959, Washington's warnings about the communist threat had fallen on deaf ears, and for good reason.

The region's small communist parties were weak and discredited. But that threat was now a reality.

Just as a belated Cold War made its presence felt, reformers contended with powerful centrifugal and centripetal forces that made it next to impossible to meet their citizens' rising expectations. While democrats always knew they had to overcome a well-heeled oligarchy opposed to reform, they also had their hands full coping with wounded but still dangerous militaries blamed for their complicity with dictatorships, and "the innate suspicion of the U.S. government."[2]

Since civilian politicians promised more than they delivered, they left the door ajar to criticism from progressives in their own political parties, who asked themselves whether the long struggle to defeat strongman rule was worth such modest, incremental change. Such political cannibalism took its toll as embittered factions peeled off from reformist parties and joined leftist insurgencies. To survive such a tumultuous environment, reformers came down hard on both urban terrorism and rural insurgency. The formula the few civilian governments that survived the plague of coups employed was to appease their armed forces by repressing the left and by slow-pedaling the pace of reform.

Moderates can be excused for initially dragging their feet on Cuba. Fidel did not just say what they wanted to hear, he walked the walk. As mentioned, in his first year in power, he supported expeditions against three of the most despised despots—Trujillo, Somoza, and Duvalier. Given Fidel's popularity among their constituents, it would have been political suicide early on for reformist politicians to appear to cave to U.S. pressure by isolating Cuba diplomatically. As the Nixon visit clearly illustrated, Washington's standing in the region was at a low ebb, and not just with the left. The Bay of Pigs debacle compounded the problem. Its manifest unpopularity briefly stiffened the resolve of Latin American governments as they staked out a more autonomous position.

Washington surely realized how politically precarious it was for reformers to follow its lead. But as far as it was concerned, if the Cuban Revolution was permitted to prosper, its demonstration effect might win new converts. As a result, the Kennedy and Johnson administrations used every economic, military, and diplomatic tool at their disposal to forge a united front similar to Roosevelt's Fortress America during World War II.

As Castro switched allegiance, as U.S. pressure intensified, and as militaries ramped up pressure on their governments to cut ties with Havana, one by one the new democracies relented and fell into line. The

missile crisis and Castro's continuing support for insurgency gave politicians the cover they needed to break off relations, but they did not save
the eight democratic governments.

As noted, the broad parameters of U.S. policy toward the region
were fashioned decades earlier, and all of its requisite elements—the protection of nationals and their business interests, the maintenance of a
sphere of influence initially centering in the Caribbean littoral but later
expanding into South America, the mitigation of communist influence,
the promotion of stability by strengthening the region's militaries, and
the bending of Latin American governments to its political and economic will—did not substantively change. In this sense, even a belated
Cold War was not an aberration. There were only two brief interludes
when Washington reconsidered its age-old policy: the twenty-month period between 1945 and 1947 when Braden publicly criticized and reduced assistance to dictatorships, and Jimmy Carter's human rights
policy. On both occasions, domestic hawks undermined those well-
meaning efforts, arguing that morality had no place in the making of foreign policy. And in each case, dictators simply waited out what they were
convinced would be an inevitable return to the status quo ante.

To be sure, a country's foreign policy reflects more than the perspectives and policies of a given administration. Critics in Congress, the
media, academia, the labor movement, and the public at large voiced
objections to interventionism and their government's coddling of
dictators. Faultfinders on the Hill, like Borah, Wheeler, Morse, and Porter, railed at their nation's foreign policy. On occasion, they achieved
modest successes in reining in excesses, but they never objected to the
policy itself.

Latin America's Democratic Crusade has examined in some detail the region's ongoing border wars, which pitted La Internacional de la Espada
against a coalition composed of the region's democracies and political exiles. The dictators destabilized democratic governments and pursued, harassed, and eliminated dissidents abroad. In this battle, democracies were
far from shrinking violets. Offering a safe haven for political refugees,
they not only looked away as exiles propagandized, plotted, and launched
implausible expeditions, they provided arms and monies. From the 1920s
until the end of the Cold War, this undeclared war raged on. Try as it did,
Washington was often powerless to restore stability to the region, offering
ample proof that Latin American governments—dictatorships and democracies alike—acted on their strategic interests as they saw fit.

The Cold War's tardy arrival only inflamed longstanding animosities. What did change after 1959 was that Washington and Havana were now actively engaged in these disputes, raising the stakes for all concerned. Their participation complicated in no small way what up to that point had been a transnational struggle between democrats and dictators.

So intent were democratic leaders on eliminating the scourge of autocracy that they defied Washington's wishes and sent funds and arms to ill-defined insurrections whose future direction was in doubt. In the case of Costa Rica in 1948, they accomplished their objective. Figueres shared their values and became a voluble spokesman for the democratic cause. With Cuba in 1959, the goal was achieved when Batista was removed from power, but the regime that emerged was not what they had anticipated. Once burned, moderates nevertheless repeated the error twenty years later when democracies threw their support behind the Sandinistas. Again, the immediate objective was achieved, but the repercussions for regional stability were devastating.

Postscript

Urban terrorism and guerrilla insurgency not only put the remaining civilian governments on the defensive, but it also spawned ideologically driven military governments. More so than in the past, the enemy within monopolized the attentions of the hemisphere's armed forces. Leftist extremism—kidnappings, bombings, targeted assassinations, robberies, the ransoming of corporate executives—unleashed a multipronged, counterrevolutionary response well out of proportion to the threat posed. In Central America, the toll was biblical—a staggering three hundred thousand dead, a million refugees, national economies laid to waste.[3]

Once again, the Brazilian military dictatorship (1964–1985) was the trendsetter. Its National Security Doctrine, a blueprint for many of the region's military governments, emphasized that the armed forces were "guardians of the national interest." Blending French counterinsurgency theory with rabid anticommunism, the new military governments directed their attention to internal enemies of the state. Unlike fascist and populist leaders, who used political parties to mobilize their supporters, the new bureaucratic-authoritarian regimes, which first gained a foothold in the Southern Cone and then spread throughout the hemisphere, discouraged politicking, suspended or abolished elections, dismantled unions, purged universities, and silenced the opposition. The dirty wars of the late 1960s and 1970s targeted dissidents and eradicated leftist ideas wherever they were nurtured.

Military regimes did not just focus on the left. Reformist political parties and their affiliated unions and peasant federations were considered part of the problem. According to the Brazilian theorist Fernando Henrique Cardoso, in such a stultifying climate " 'representative democracy' sounds only marginally less frightening than opening the front door to the devil, an appropriate metaphor given that the military see themselves as the defenders of Christian and occidental values against the worldwide menace of communism."[4]

Reformist military regimes in Peru, Panama, Ecuador, and Bolivia bucked the reactionary trend. All were staunchly anticommunist, which provided breathing space with Washington. They also benefited from a brief period of détente between the two superpowers and the Nixon administration's preoccupation with the war in Vietnam. Reformist or not, these regimes paid scant attention to democratic norms. For instance, Peru's Revolutionary Government of the Armed Forces nationalized U.S. oil companies, implemented an ambitious agrarian reform, assumed ownership of key domestic industries, restored relations with Cuba, and normalized diplomatic relations with the Soviet Union. This unusual top-down experiment lasted seven years before conservative officers, displeased with the junta's progressive direction and ineffectiveness, overthrew their superiors. Reformist military governments elsewhere met similar fates.[5]

Another outlier was Chile's armed forces, which, within a span of three years, pivoted from constitutionalist generals defending Allende's democratic road to socialism to a right-wing junta that brutally suppressed the left. Even Frei's Christian Democrats, who welcomed the coup, were taken back by the ferocity of the repression.[6] Interestingly, while the Nixon administration did its utmost to punish Allende economically, it never cut off assistance to the armed forces, even during the time when constitutionalist generals held sway. At an NSC meeting on Chile in 1970, Nixon pulled no punches: "I will never agree with the policy of downgrading the military in Latin America. They are power centers subject to our influence. . . . We want to give them some help. . . . Build them up with consultation. I want [the] Defense [Department] to move on this. We'll go for more budget if necessary." His administration then helped the coup plotters end one of the region's most enduring democracies.[7]

A Cold Warrior like Nixon and the chief architect of his foreign policy, Henry Kissinger, were dubious about whether democratic governments could withstand leftist subversion. The two eschewed direct confrontation in the region, preferring to work with proxies who quashed unrest. If concerted action was required, the Nixon administration resorted to covert methods and economic warfare. This disposition for indirection, however, did not conceal what was in plain sight to long-time observers of U.S.–Latin American relations. During the Cold War, Washington was *the* principal source of regional instability. The U.S. aided in the overthrow of twenty-four governments: four times by its own military, three via covert action, and in seventeen instances it abetted or encouraged militaries or the political opposition to mount coups d'état. All but three occurred after 1959, proof of how the Cuban Revolution fundamentally altered the dynamic. In the first decade after Castro took power, the U.S. was complicit in nine *golpes* staged by Latin American militaries. Not included in this count were unsuccessful operations, such as the Bay of Pigs or other occasions when the Kennedy and Johnson administrations stepped in to prevent friendly governments from being ousted. As the historian John Coatsworth observes, "These actions enhanced the capacity of U.S. leaders to shape events throughout the region by making intervention a credible threat, even in countries where it had not yet occurred. As a consequence, for over forty years, Latin Americans were ruled by governments more conservative (and thus reliably anti-Communist) than Latin American voters were inclined to elect." Suffice it to say, such interference had the effect of inflaming the left and lending its cause greater legitimacy, especially among the young.[8]

Although the U.S. and Latin American militaries shared similar goals and worked together, it is a mistake to conclude that the former dictated the latter's mission or their actions. One of the best studies of this period notes that it was precisely its "homegrown nature that gave the National Security Doctrine its ideological power and endowed it with such devastating force." Indicative of the limits of U.S. influence was Jimmy Carter's human rights initiative. Carter declared that his administration would no longer ally with authoritarians and that the region's democracies would be reliable partners in the fight against subversion. This, of course, was precisely what reformers had been preaching for decades. Carter's fleeting, Bradenesque approach—lecturing dictatorships for their atrocious human rights violations, employing carrots and sticks to pressure Somoza Debayle either to curb repression or stand down, initiating dialogue with

Cuba—failed to persuade. Rather than succumb to the administration's diplomatic jawboning, seven defiant military regimes renounced U.S. aid and purchased their armaments elsewhere, while openly mocking the moralistic young president they derisively labeled "Jimmy Castro."[9]

Unfortunately, by the time Carter took office, democrats were an endangered species. The only holdovers left from the late 1950s surge were Costa Rica and the two pacted democracies, Venezuela and Colombia. Although elections were held in Mexico and the Dominican Republic, those nation-states were democracies in name only. Mexico's one-party regime conducted its own dirty war against its left and stubbornly resisted efforts to open up its political system, while the Dominican Republic was ruled with an iron fist by the Trujillo acolyte Balaguer. Dominicans experienced déjà vu as the combination of military patrols and an updated La 42, a paramilitary group called La Banda, ruthlessly crushed dissent. More than three thousand Dominicans were murdered between 1966 and 1974. Balaguer may have blamed the repression on "uncontrollable forces," but funding for La Banda came out of the military's intelligence budget.[10]

Unlike the United States, the Soviets acknowledged their limitations. After withdrawing its nuclear missiles from Cuba, the Soviet Union practiced restraint up until the last decade of the Cold War, and even then it plied its influence selectively. Always uneasy about Cuba's support and training of guerrillas, the USSR shunned costly investments in a region it had always viewed as peripheral to its strategic and economic interests. Moscow steered clear of leftist insurgencies, advised Havana to follow suit, and provided only a modicum of assistance to Allende's socialist experiment. Soviet policy did not materially change until the 1980s, when Moscow began funneling arms (via North Korea, Vietnam, Eastern Europe, and Cuba) to the Sandinistas, but even then, it did so only after Somoza was ousted. Even then it steered clear of other insurgencies, such as Peru's Maoist-inspired *Sendero Luminoso* (Shining Path) and Guatemala's leftist rebels.[11]

Much to Washington's chagrin, many Latin American countries, democracies and anticommunist military regimes alike, resumed diplomatic and economic relations with the USSR during the late 1960s and 1970s. Only pariah states like Pinochet's Chile, Stroessner's Paraguay, Duvalier's Haiti, and Guatemala's military dictators did not.[12]

Sectarianism and fissures continued to bedevil the left. By the end of the 1960s, orthodox communist parties, following Moscow's line, had largely distanced themselves from the armed struggle, hurting their credibility with a new generation of student militants. The Venezuelan PCV, for instance, backed off from insurgency and grew increasingly critical of Castro's self-appointed role as arbiter of "what is and what is not revolutionary in Latin America." Traditional communist parties also had to contend with an emerging "New Left" that melded ideas from Marx, Gramsci, Mao, and liberation theologians and heaped scorn on the domestic bourgeoisie, foreign investors, the U.S. government, *and* on Moscow and the region's communist parties.[13]

If Che's martyrdom in Bolivia in 1967 inspired the faithful, it also was a cautionary tale, prompting a tactical reassessment. Except for the Central American isthmus and Colombia, where rural *focos* continued to proliferate, cities now became the principal sites of contestation. The lone holdouts—guerrilla insurgencies in El Salvador, Guatemala, Peru, and in Nicaragua, where the Sandinistas established a revolutionary government—all met their demise. Perhaps the most surprising outcome was the FSLN's willingness to respect the will of the people and relinquish power after their humbling defeat at the polls in 1990.

Only three reformist governments—Costa Rica, Venezuela, and Colombia—persevered and managed to outlast the era's convulsions. In Costa Rica, Figueres's PLN won five of seven presidential elections between 1962 and 1990. The absence of a military afforded successive administrations the opportunity to invest in its citizens, while the creation of a Central American Common Market in 1960 proved an economic boon to the isthmus as a whole and to Costa Rica especially. Owing to gains in gross domestic product and foreign investment, unemployment and consumer price indexes remained low, and infant mortality, literacy, life expectancy, and educational indicators all improved. Even on the occasions when the PLN's opponents governed, they never substantively altered that development model.[14]

A far more unlikely success story was Venezuela. The two remaining signatories of the Pact of Punto Fijo, AD and COPEI, alternated in power for forty years. Even so, democratic governance was a shell of what AD had promised its citizens. Instead of making the most of soaring oil prices during the 1970s, Betancourt's longtime lieutenant, Pérez, squandered the windfall and presided over an administration that rivaled the corruption of the Gómez and Pérez Jiménez years. AD's leadership governed with a heavy hand, its cadres designating candidates for regional and local offices, judgeships, and heads of unions, universities, and professional organizations. Since the executive committees of the national parties presented voters with slates of candidates rather than individual names, elected candidates often felt a greater sense of obligation to the party than to their constituents. Those deviating from the party's line were dealt with severely. Disillusioned Venezuelans had every right to question the purported benefits of democratic rule.[15]

In Colombia, the region's other pacted democracy, the problems were different, but the results were similarly unsatisfying. Although alternation of the two political parties continued as scripted, the cumbersome checks and balances first crafted by Lleras Camargo and Gómez led to dispiriting political gridlock. The ruthless pacification of the interior between 1962 and 1965 left much of central and southern Colombia "traumatized and militarized."[16]

Periodic flare-ups in the Caribbean Basin showed no indication of letting up. During the late 1970s, an unlikely assortment of governments—Venezuela, Mexico, Costa Rica, Panama, and Honduras—decided that Somoza Debayle had to go. Cuba was the last to sign on, refusing to contribute military assistance until three Sandinista factions agreed to set aside their differences and create a unified front against the dictatorship. Just as activists had found their way to Froylán Turcios's bookshop in Tegucigalpa during the late 1920s, now leftist militants, "frustrated by the lack of progress in their own revolutions," appeared at Sandinista headquarters in San José to offer their services. Argentine Montoneros, for instance, fled their country's Dirty War, jumping at the chance to join the fight against La Internacional's lone holdout. They even donated a million dollars to the FSLN cause.[17]

Proof of how the struggle against dictatorship was passed down as a birthright, both Figueres's son and the son of the populist commander of Panama's National Guard, Omar Torrijos, were among the many enlistees.[18] Past violations of national sovereignty by the Somozas were all the motivation that Costa Rica needed to permit Sandinista rebels to use their territory as both a safe haven and a staging ground for incursions across their border.

So despised was the last Somoza that even repressive Honduran military governments winked and nodded as the FSLN opened a two-front war against the dictator. Torrijos did his share by facilitating the movement of Cuban arms to the rebels, and the combination of the OPEC oil embargo, rising prices, and new discoveries of oil made it possible for Venezuela and Mexico to provide arms and funding for the Sandinista cause. In late 1977, Pérez agreed to provide the FSLN with a monthly stipend of one hundred thousand U.S. dollars.[19]

The assassination of longtime Nicaraguan dissident Pedro Joaquín Chamorro in January 1978, however, altered Pérez's calculus. He withdrew his ambassador to Nicaragua and immediately wrote Carter urging that both the United States and Venezuela intercede in the conflict before matters got out of hand. Two months later they discussed the unsettled situation again during Carter's visit to Venezuela. If nothing was done, Pérez warned, "Somoza could end up playing Batista to a Sandinista Castro." While Carter did not disagree with the comparison, he preferred less invasive measures (for example, freezing U.S. aid; encouraging Somoza to permit an OAS human rights investigating team). As one study notes, the Carter administration's initial reticence to pressure Somoza created a political vacuum that democratic states rushed to fill.[20]

Pérez did not hide his hand. In July 1978, he met with Somoza on a small island off the Venezuelan coast. When the despot proudly showed off an encouraging note he had just received from Carter, Pérez did not equivocate: "I don't care what Carter says. Our position is firm. You have to go."[21] It was only natural for him to work closely on this matter with two PLN presidents, Daniel Oduber Quirós (1974–1978) and Rodrigo Carazo (1978–1982), whom he had befriended during his Costa Rican exile in the 1950s.

For Pérez, the opportunity to depose the last member of La Internacional was too tempting to resist. As late as 1984, when he was well aware of the leftist drift of the Sandinista revolution, he defended his decision to send arms and monies to the FSLN. "I would never regret having supported the struggle against Somoza, even if the Sandinista movement changes into a communist movement and tried to establish a communist government in Nicaragua." U.S officials, Pérez added, never understood why he and his peers were willing to take that risk. "The U.S. is not very knowledgeable. [It] does not know how much blood, how many sacrifices, how much struggle, how much frustration generations of Latin Americans have gone through."[22] When Somoza responded to a September 1978 Sandinista offensive by bombing suspected FSLN targets in northern Costa Rica, Pérez rushed bombers and interceptors to Carazo's government. Perhaps unaware of the Venezuelan president's past history with dictators, a State Department report advanced its own theory for why Pérez was so invested in removing the dictator from power. "[He] wants to have influence with the Sandinistas and a serious commitment to them is the only way of achieving and holding this influence. Whether Pérez has thought through the consequences of such [involvement] is unclear." As for Mexico's willingness to back the FSLN, this was not the first time that an ambitious president had sought to exert influence in the isthmus. Recall Calles's support for Central American liberals during the 1920s.²³

Unlike the Coolidge administration, which pressured Calles to stand down and then had Stimson impose a solution in Nicaragua, Carter was unable to dissuade those governments supporting the Sandinistas to pull back, nor was his administration successful in engineering regime change. Regional governments sympathetic to the FSLN insisted that Nicaraguans decide their own political fate. As a member of Carter's NSC staff, Robert Pastor, put it: "We tried a multilateral approach toward finding a moderate solution, but Panama, Venezuela, Costa Rica and Mexico were determined to help play a different role toward Somoza. Nothing we did deterred them."²⁴ Given the unsatisfactory results the last time that reformist governments had backed an insurrection in Cuba, one might have anticipated that at the very least, the Costa Rican and Venezuelan governments would have exercised greater restraint. But La Internacional's last remaining strongman was too inviting a target for them to remain on the sidelines.

After the failure of a fall 1978 offensive, the FSLN's three factions came hat in hand to Havana. The Cubans held up their end of the bargain.²⁵ A report by a special commission of the Costa Rican legislature concluded in 1981 that more than sixty flights carrying "approximately one million pounds of arms and munitions" had entered Costa Rica from Venezuela and Cuba (via Panama) in the last seven months of the insurrection alone. Sixty percent of the weapons smuggled through Costa Rica originated in Cuba. Carazo, the report concluded, had approved "the entire operation." Interestingly, the commission criticized the president for neglecting to inform the public of the arms smuggling, not for aiding the Sandinistas. In fact, many Ticos applauded their government's efforts to depose Somoza. Indeed, the Costa Rican head of state aggressively defended his actions, declaring, "Don't let anyone think that I am ashamed of what I did to free Costa Rica from the threats of Somoza and to free the world from the shame of that dictator."²⁶ In July 1979, Somoza gave up the fight; his parting gifts: a crushing foreign debt and a barren national treasury.

The Sandinista victory in July 1979 greatly exacerbated conflict in the isthmus. Three thousand National Guardsmen found refuge in

Honduras, Guatemala, and El Salvador and immediately began plotting their return. The new revolutionary government in Managua inflamed tensions further by assisting leftist rebels in neighboring El Salvador, while the U.S. now jumped into the fray, arming and funding a proxy army, the Contras, whose leadership included prominent National Guard members. Reversing course were Honduras's military government and Costa Rica, both of which concluded that their neighbor's revolutionary regime was a destabilizing force. Costa Rican president Luis Monge (1982–1986) may have claimed that his official policy was "unarmed neutrality," but in fact, Eden Pastora's Revolutionary Democratic Alliance (*Alianza Revolucionaria Democrática*, ARDE) was given ample room to maneuver along the country's northern border. According to the journalist Martha Honey, ARDE was "protected by a network of CIA operatives and collaborators within the Monge government."[27]

The Contras received assistance from an unlikely source: Argentina's military junta. This did not come entirely out of the blue. During the late 1970s, the Argentine military offered instruction to officers from Southern Cone countries in methods it had perfected during its successful Dirty War against the left. By 1977, its advisors were training Somoza's secret police in interrogation techniques while monitoring exiled dissidents in the isthmus. In that cohort was the Nicaraguan Ricardo Lau, who was allegedly hired by the Salvadoran death squad leader Roberto D'Aubuisson to carry out the assassination of Archbishop Oscar Romero in March 1980.[28]

Then, a year after the FSLN's victory, the Argentines opened training centers in Guatemala City and Tegucigalpa, where their advisors tutored the Honduran national police, members of Salvadoran and Guatemalan death squads, and Nicaraguan exiles. As *Washington Post* reporter Christopher Dickey explained, the Argentine junta "acted as if they had discovered a great truth, the final solution for communism, and they wanted to apply it beyond their borders. It was no longer just a question of chasing old enemies. . . . They saw themselves rolling back the advances of the Soviets in the new world war that was already begun, a war without frontiers." The trainers were far from idle bystanders. They took to the field alongside the Contras, blowing up bridges in Nicaragua and joining the fray in El Salvador and Guatemala, where they helped military governments track and disappear leftist dissidents.[29]

As the political scientist Ariel Armony noted, initially the Argentines acted independently, but when Washington concluded that it could no longer tolerate the Sandinista regime, the CIA contributed funding, arms, maps, and satellite imagery. Similar to the preparations for the Bay of Pigs, Argentine instructors trained former Nicaraguan guardsmen in base camps in Florida. The mutually beneficial arrangement ended abruptly, however, when the Reagan administration chose not to remain neutral in the 1982 Falklands/Malvinas conflict. That so angered the junta that it shut down the training center. From that point on, the Agency assumed oversight of the Contra army.[30]

In a conspicuous example of how the Cold War grafted itself onto the earlier transnational struggle between democracies and dictatorships, Somoza Debayle was assassinated in Asunción, Paraguay, thirteen months after he fled Nicaragua. Tachito went the way of Trujillo, ambushed and then riddled with bullets while traveling through the streets of the Paraguayan capital. Unlike the Dominican ruler's assassination, though, the assailants were not avenging Nicaraguans but a breakaway offshoot of Argentina's Ejército Revolucionario del Pueblo (ERP). The leftist militants had fought alongside the Sandinistas during the final offensive, and after the victory was secured, they joined an elite FSLN commando unit with the foreboding name of the Nucleus of Steel. Led by a former ERP combatant, the strike force subsequently tracked the exiled dictator to Paraguay.[31]

The Cold War's last decade witnessed yet one more democratic wave, as thirteen dictatorships relinquished power to civilian governments between 1979 and 1990. But this surge felt qualitatively different than its predecessors. Rarely is it the case that military governments that win wars so decisively are so uniformly discredited. As abhorrent their crimes, as disgraced as these regimes were, they stepped down for reasons having little to do with atrocious human rights violations. Latin America's "lost decade," a perfect storm of economic mismanagement, currency devaluations, debt crises, and IMF bailouts, better explains this latest democratic wave. Blame was rightfully laid at the doorstep of the region's ineffectual military governments.

North American encouragement of the democratic trend did have an impact on certain military regimes. This was especially true in Pinochet's Chile, where U.S. diplomats pressured the dictator to hold a plebiscite. Pinochet consented only because he was convinced he would win handily. Elsewhere, the administration's efforts bore fruit because many of the region's governments were drowning in debt. Reagan made relief contingent on a government's willingness to reduce tariff barriers and open up the country to foreign investment. Unfortunately, Washington's neoliberal agenda only heightened income disparities, an alarming trend that came back to haunt the new democracies.

Unlike previous transitions from dictatorship to civilian rule, when optimism abounded and meaningful reform was anticipated, this democratic turn came at a time of collective exhaustion and circumscribed expectations. In some countries, a major accomplishment for a new democracy was simply to prevent a *golpe* and have its president complete his or her term in office. Even where a military no longer governed, it remained a potent political actor and cast a long and often disapproving shadow over the new government. This helps explain why so few political leaders held past military governments accountable for their egregious actions.

Again, the exception sheds light on the rule. To the surprise of many observers, Argentine president Raúl Alfonsín's administration successfully prosecuted the leadership of the Dirty War juntas (1976–1982). The public nature of the trials and the convictions of the generals, however, prompted a backlash from an embittered military, which felt that it deserved gratitude, not humiliation. It did not take long after the verdicts were rendered for the conspiring to start, and when the *Carapintada* (painted faces) revolt broke out in 1987, Alfonsín backpedaled, ordering an end to any prosecutions of junior officers alleged to have taken part in the atrocities. The lessons learned by other armed forces from the Argentine experience were to demand airtight protections from prosecution before stepping down and to resort to intimidation if civilian politicians dared to hold the generals accountable.[32] Not surprisingly, this transition to democratic rule was gradual and incomplete. A decimated left was in no position to make demands, further diminishing the prospects for reform.

It is incorrect, however, to assign blame for Latin America's Cold War to democracy's failure to take root. Extremists on the right and the left, repressive authoritarians, and timid reformers all shared collective responsibility for the failure of a decades-long struggle to achieve sustainable democratic governance.

Second Acts

Second acts in politics are rarely successful. The best proof of this adage was Juan Perón's brief, if tumultuous, return to Argentina after eighteen years in exile. Perhaps no leader could have unified a country as badly polarized as Argentina was in 1973, but in eight short months he managed to aggravate longstanding divisions on the right and the left and set the stage for the depredations that followed.[33]

To a lesser degree, the same could be said of José Figueres, whose second term as president, between 1970 and 1974, was mired in controversy and accusations of scandal. As happened in Venezuela, dissension within the PLN ranks, largely along generational lines, undercut Figueres's legitimacy. Younger party members complained that he and other leading lights of the party's founding generation had used their positions to feather their own nests and had forsaken their commitment to peasants and workers.[34] Never one to take criticism well, Figueres became even more officious, paying little heed to the legislature and the courts and repeatedly lashing out at the press. Often blurring the lines between the personal and the political, he spent much of this presidency defending or deflecting alleged conflicts of interest and lapses in judgment. In a bald-faced move that one might have anticipated from the despots he so despised, Figueres tried unsuccessfully to amend the constitution so that he could run for yet another term in 1978. Perhaps his peccadillos would have been more excusable if he could have pointed to solid accomplishments, but unlike his first term, his administration advanced few new initiatives.

Figueres, however, was intent on recapturing his leadership role in inter-American affairs. But his reputation took a tumble when an exposé in *Ramparts Magazine* documented that the Institute for Political Education was a CIA front organization. Rarely one for obfuscation, Figueres freely admitted that he knew that the Agency provided funding. The institute's founders, he argued, went into this partnership with the CIA with their eyes wide open and did so because the end more than justified the means. If democratic governance was to prevail in Latin America, its practitioners needed resources to educate and mobilize the next generation of democrats. After all, he added, this was precisely how international communism had captured the imagination of many young Latin Americans. Moreover, if dictators collaborated with each other, so too must democrats. As he later recalled, "we had to organize and we needed and welcomed U.S. funds. There was [*sic*] never any restrictions on our activities and though the United States never fully took us into its confidence, we were allies in a struggle against the communists and the dictators."[35]

That Figueres was considered toxic for accepting funds from the CIA was not the sole factor explaining his inability to revive his former role as an interlocutor in hemispheric affairs. With civilian governments so few in number, he was bereft of allies who shared his vision. His friends Betancourt and Muñoz Marín were long since retired from political office. Furthermore, Figueres's counsel was no longer welcomed at the State Department during the Nixon years. Indeed, his relations with Washington came full circle; once regarded as untrustworthy and a loose cannon by Foster Dulles, then praised by Kennedy as a paladin for the democratic cause, now he was shunted aside and treated as if he were irrelevant. Given his temperament, Don Pepe surely would have preferred wrong to inconsequential. Incapable of being ignored, during the early 1970s he interjected himself and his country into tempest-in-a-teapot controversies, mostly of his own making, and made cringeworthy statements that shocked his longtime supporters.

Figueres's decision to establish diplomatic relations and sign trade pacts with the Soviet Union and other Eastern bloc countries created a firestorm at home. He defended the decision, contending that Costa Rica needed new markets for its coffee. Although stopping short of restoring relations with Cuba (or China), for the first time he acknowledged that Castro's revolution was here to stay. Perhaps even more surprising, he praised some of the new military regimes, insisting that they were preferable to the personalistic regimes of the past. For the moment, he even buried the hatchet with Somoza Debayle, insisting that the son should not be held responsible for the sins of his father. Such head-spinning reversals on matters that had been articles of faith just a short time before elicited condemnation from many Costa Ricans.

Three years after his second term ended, the wily Figueres reverted to form. With an insurrection underway next door, the former president could not resist the urge to meddle. Angry that Somoza Debayle had violated Costa Rican sovereignty by sending the National Guard across the Costa Rican border to hunt down members of the FSLN, he once again opened up Lucha sin fin to the rebels. According to Pastora, then the Sandinista commander of the FSLN's southern front, the former president "gave us 300 M-1 rifles, rockets, bazookas, 50 machine guns, [and] 300,000 bullets."[36]

Unlike Figueres, Betancourt never ran for president again. Initially, he tried to remain aloof by taking a self-imposed exile in Europe between 1964 and 1971, but the role of elder statesman did not suit him. He had invested too much in AD to walk away, especially when factionalism threatened to tear the party apart. Professing to be a peacemaker, he too often played kingmaker, bestowing his blessing on presidential candidates. His meddling did little to restore party unity and contributed to AD electoral defeats in 1968 and 1978. He also had little success persuading party leaders that they should keep the Punto Fijo coalition alive. Scarred by his experience during the *trienio*, he felt that it was incumbent upon AD to ensure the existence of a viable political opposition by continuing the practice of reaching across the aisle and incorporating members of COPEI in their administrations. In a letter to Alexander in June 1969, he expressed concern that democratic norms were not sufficiently ingrained: "the formula of the AD-COPEI coalition is the only one capable of stabilizing democratic institutions." His plea went unheeded, as future AD administrations went it alone.[37]

However, on other occasions, his politicking paid dividends. By refusing to dispel rumors that he intended to run for president in 1972 until just days before AD's nominating convention, he discouraged some candidates in his own party from running so that his preference, Carlos Andrés Pérez, would be the party's standard bearer in the upcoming elections. But when his choice presided over a corruption-marred five years, he promptly turned against him. Whether a source of unity or discord, Betancourt remained active in party politics until his death from a massive stroke in 1981.[38]

Narrowly defeated in 1960, Charles Porter nevertheless was bullish about his future prospects. With a Democratic administration about to assume power in 1961, he had reason to feel optimistic. Just three weeks after the elections, he wrote Betancourt that "I would like very much to have something to do with the formulation of the new Latin American policy."[39] If not Rubottom's job as assistant secretary for inter-American affairs, perhaps an ambassadorship might be the ticket. If the lame duck congressman had his druthers, Venezuela was his preferred destination. He actively campaigned for the position with colleagues in Washington, reaching out to Morse and Adlai Stevenson, among others. He even lobbied Venezuelan acquaintances, mentioning his interest to Betancourt's foreign minister, Falcón Briceño, and informing the editor of the English-language *Caracas Journal* that his selection would send an unmistakable message that the Kennedy administration "intended to be against dictators."[40]

By backing Hubert Humphrey for president in the 1960 campaign, however, he did not endear himself to the new administration. What really hurt his chances was that he had, in his own words, "insulted" powerful southern Democratic senators for their support for dictators.

Kennedy had no appetite for a nasty confirmation hearing. Berle recommended him for a job with AID in Peru, but Porter demurred because the position required a four-year commitment and he did not want to tie his hands if he tried to reclaim the House seat he had narrowly lost in 1962. An article in *Time* titled "No Time for Charlie" noted that the lame duck congressman applied for twenty-three patronage jobs with the Democratic National Committee, but as Porter lamented, "they haven't given me the time of day." Instead, he took a brief consultancy with the Food for Peace program, and he and Alexander co-authored a book, *The Struggle for Democracy in Latin America.*[41]

He was never again elected to public office, although not for lack of trying. He failed to secure the party's nomination for his Fourth District seat on three occasions (1962, 1964, 1976), and the two times he succeeded in securing the nomination (1966, 1972), he was beaten in the general election. His one Senate bid in 1980 was similarly unsuccessful.

He kept his hand in Latin American affairs, speaking out against human rights violations in Cuba and Chile. For example, he represented families of Cuban political prisoners in their efforts to secure the release of their loved ones. During a 1963 trip to the island, he presented Castro with a petition for a general amnesty of political prisoners on humanitarian grounds. Castro had benefited from just such a pardon in 1955 after the unsuccessful attack on the Moncada barracks. Fidel promised to look into the matter, but results were not forthcoming.[42] When Porter asked the State Department two years later to validate his passport so he could return to the island to follow up on the stalled petition, his request was turned down because, according to Mann, it would be misunderstood as a "softening of U.S. policy." As the assistant secretary explained, even though Porter would be traveling as a private citizen, it would convey "the impression that would gain currency that the [U.S.] Government was interested in making a deal with the Cuban regime where it would release political prisoners in exchange for our relaxation of pressures upon it." Porter was furious, because the administration had permitted another attorney to negotiate the release of 9,700 Bay of Pigs prisoners. The former congressman continued to work on the families' behalf, but he never returned to the island.[43]

Porter also continued to pursue justice for Jesús Galíndez and Gerry Murphy, even after the former was declared officially dead by the U.S. government in August 1963. While Porter was attending Bosch's presidential inauguration in February 1963, a former prison guard told him that he had witnessed Murphy's garroting by two SIM agents in a jail storeroom and that he knew who the culprits were and the location of the cemetery where Murphy was buried. Upon his return home, Porter wrote Bosch, explaining how "very favorably impressed" he was with the eyewitness, but that the man needed the government's protection "because he fears reprisals." He urged the president to have his minister of justice reopen the investigation. Evidence is lacking on whether Bosch or his successors followed up on Porter's request. Neither disappearance was ever resolved.[44]

Until his death in 2006, the gadfly never stopped fighting for causes he believed in. On national matters, he voiced strong opposition to the Vietnam War, dueled with the CIA and the FBI to obtain his files, and even authored a resolution calling for the impeachment of five Supreme Court justices because, he argued, their decision in *Bush v. Gore* invalidated regular recount procedures in the 2001 election.

Locally, he fought against nuclear power plants and noxious paper mills, and for the decriminalization of marijuana. He was best known, however, for leading a thirty-year fight to remove a fifty-one-foot cement cross from a municipal park in Eugene. Porter argued that placing the cross on public property sent "a compelling, biased message that it endorses Christian religious tradition and is not religiously neutral." In 1997 the Ninth Circuit Court agreed, a testament to his lifelong pursuit of justice.[45]

Dramatis Personae

Reformers

Arciniegas Angueyra, Germán, Colombia, Minister of Education, Liberal Party

Arévalo Bermejo, Juan José, Guatemala, President, 1945–50, Revolutionary Action Party

Betancourt Bello, Rómulo, Venezuela, junta president, 1945–47; President, 1959–63, AD

Bosch Gaviño, Juan, Dominican Republic, President, 1963, PRD

Cárdenas del Río, Lázaro, Mexico, President, 1934–40, National Revolutionary Party, Party of the Mexican Revolution

Figueres Ferrer, José "Pepe," Costa Rica, President, 1953–58, 1970–74, PLN

Frei Montalva, Eduardo, Chile, President, 1964–70, Christian Democratic Party

Frondizi Ércoli, Arturo, Argentina, President, 1958–62, Radical Party

Gaitán, Jorge Eliécer, Colombia; assassinated April 1948, Liberal Party

Goulart, João Belchior Marques, Brazil, President, 1961–64, Labor Party

Grau San Martín, Ramón, junta president, 1933–34; President, 1944–48, Auténtico Party

Haya de la Torre, Víctor Raúl, Peru, APRA

Kubitschek de Oliveira, Juscelino, Brazil, President, 1956–61, Social Democratic Party

Lleras Camargo, Alberto, Colombia, interim president, 1945–46; President, 1958–62, Liberal Party

Lleras Restrepo, Carlos, Colombia, President, 1966–70, Liberal Party

Muñoz Marín, Luis, Puerto Rico, Governor, 1948–64, Popular Democratic Party

Paz Estenssoro, Víctor, Bolivia, President, 1952–56, 1960–64, 1985–89, MNR

Prío Socarrás, Carlos, Cuba, President, 1948–52, Auténtico Party

Santos Montejo, Eduardo, Colombia, President, 1938–42, Liberal Party

Siles Zuazo, Hernán, Bolivia, President, 1956–60, 1982–85, MNR

Villeda Morales, Ramón, Honduras, President, 1957–63, Liberal Party

Dictators

Batista y Zaldívar, Fulgencio, Cuba, 1940–44, 1952–58
Carías Andino, Tiburcio, Honduras, 1924, 1933–49
Castillo Armas, Carlos, Guatemala, 1954–57
Duvalier, François, Haiti, 1957–71
Estrada Cabrera, Manuel, Guatemala, 1896–1920
Gómez Castro, Laureano, Colombia, 1950–53
Gómez Chacón, Juan Vicente, Venezuela, 1908–35
Hernández Martínez, Maximiliano, El Salvador, 1931–44
Ibáñez del Campo, Carlos, Chile, 1927–31, 1952–58
Leguía y Salcedo, Augusto, Peru, 1919–30
Machado y Morales, Gerardo, Cuba, 1925–33
Odría Amoretti, Manuel, Peru, 1948–56
Pérez Jiménez, Marcos, Venezuela, 1953–58
Pinochet Ugarte, Augusto, Chile, 1973–90
Rojas Pinilla, Gustavo, Colombia, 1953–57
Trujillo Molina, Rafael, Dominican Republic, 1930–61
Somoza García, Anastasio "Tacho," Nicaragua, 1936–56
Somoza Debayle, Luis, Nicaragua, 1956–63
Somoza Debayle, Anastasio "Tachito," Nicaragua, 1967–72, 1974–79
Stroessner Matiauda, Alfredo, Paraguay, 1954–89
Ubico Castañeda, Jorge, Guatemala, 1931–44

Populists

Perón, Juan Domingo, Argentina, President, 1946–55, 1973–74; titular head of
    La Internacional de la Espada
Torrijos Herrera, Omar, Panama, Commander, National Guard; de facto ruler of
    Panama, 1969–81
Vargas, Getúlio, Brazil, President, 1934–45, 1951–54

Progressive Voices

Alexander, Robert, Rutgers University economist
Beals, Carleton, journalist and author
Frank, Waldo, writer, critic of North American materialism
Galíndez Suárez, Jesús de, Basque exile; outspoken critic of Trujillo; abducted
    and murdered by the regime, March 1956
Grant, Frances, Secretary, Inter-American Association of Democracy and Free-
    dom
Ingenieros, José, Argentine public intellectual
Kent, Victoria, editor, *Ibérica* magazine
Krehm, William, Canadian journalist

Lippmann, Walter, syndicated columnist

Matthews, Herbert, *New York Times* Latin American correspondent

Mistral, Gabriela, Nobel Prize–winning Chilean poet

Palacios, Alfredo, Argentine socialist

Romauldi, Sergio, AFL-CIO labor ambassador to Latin America

Tannenbaum, Frank, historian, professor of Latin American history, Columbia University

Turcios, Froylán, Honduran bookdealer; editor; journalist; ally of Sandino

Ugarte, Manuel Baldomero, Argentine socialist *pensador*

Prominent Leftists

Allende Gossens, Salvador, Chile, President, 1970–73

Árbenz Guzmán, Jacobo, Guatemala, President, 1950–54

Fonseca Amador, Carlos, Nicaragua, rebel; ideologue; founder of the FSLN

Mariátegui, José Carlos, Peru, Marxist intellectual; founder of the Peruvian Communist Party

Neruda, Pablo, Chile, Nobel Prize–winning poet; member of the Communist Party

Costa Ricans

Calderón Guardia, Rafael, President, 1940–44

Carazo Odio, Rodrigo, President, 1978–82

Echandi Jiménez, Mario, President, 1958–62

Facio Segreda, Gonzalo, Ambassador to the United States, 1956–58

Fournier Acuña, Fernando, Ambassador to the United States, 1955–56

Monge Álvarez, Luis, PLN stalwart; head, ORIT; President, 1982–86

Oduber Quirós, Daniel, PLN politician; President, 1974–78

Ulate Blanco, Otilio, President, 1950–53

Cubans

Bayo y Giroud, Alberto, Spanish Civil War veteran; member of Caribbean Legion; instructed Fidel, Che, and others in guerrilla warfare in Mexico

Carpentier y Valmont, Alejo, writer; critic of the Machado regime

Chibás Ribas, Eduardo "Eddy," student activist; senator; radio journalist; founder of the Ortodoxo Party

De la Torriente Brau, Pablo, Communist public intellectual; critic of Machado

Franqui, Carlos, Communist militant; opposed Machado; joined the 26th of July movement; edited the underground paper *Revolución* during the insurrection and continued in that role after 1959

Guiteras Holmes, Antonio, key cabinet member and progressive voice in Grau's provisional government, 1933–34; head of TNT and Joven Cuba

Gutiérrez Menoyo, Eloy, led the Second National Front of Escambray, a guerrilla army that opposed first Batista and later Castro

Mañach y Robato, Jorge, prominent moderate intellectual and politician; critic of Machado and Batista

Martí Pérez, José, poet and revolutionary whose writings and martyrdom inspired student militants

Martínez Villena, Rubén, poet; cofounder of the PCC; critic of Machado

Matos Benítez, Huber, *comandante*, ran guns from Costa Rica to Cuba during the insurrection; later broke with Castro, arrested, served twenty years in prison

Masferrer Rojas, Rolando, head of an action group, MSR; chief of a brutal paramilitary organization, Los Tigres

Mella McPartland, Julio Antonio, student leader; Communist militant; founder, La Universidad Popular José Martí; exiled to Mexico, where he was assassinated by assailants sent by Machado

Morgan, William (U.S. citizen), member of the Second National Front of Escambray

Pedraza y Cabrera, José Eleuterio, Cuban military officer who participated in an unsuccessful trujillista plot to oust Castro

Quevedo y de la Lastra, Miguel Ángel, owner and director of *Bohemia*

Roa García, Raúl, leader of Ala Estudiantil; journalist; foreign minister, 1959–76

Sánchez Arango, Aurelio, member of the DEU directorate; Prío's minister of education; founder, Acción Armada Auténtica

Varona, Enrique José, public intellectual; politician; professor and mentor to Cuban student radicals; critic of Machado

Dominicans

Abbes García, Johnny, Director, Trujillo's Servicio de Inteligencia Militar (SIM)

Almoina Mateos, José (Spaniard), Trujillo's personal secretary; later a critic of regime; murdered 1960

Balaguer Ricardo, Joaquín, Trujillo's chief lieutenant and troubleshooter; writer; President, 1960–62, 1966–78, 1986–96

Bernardino y Evangelista, Félix (aka *El gángster*), member of LA 42; notorious hitman

Espaillat, Arturo "Navajito," Director, SIM

Estrella Ureña, Rafael, Trujillo's vice president; later staged an unsuccessful expedition against the regime

Jiménez Moya, Enrique, participant, Cayo Confites expedition; enlisted in the 26th of July movement against Batista; fought and was killed during the unsuccessful June 1959 invasion of the Dominican Republic

Landestoy Félix, Carmen "Carmita," author, critic of regime

Miolán, Ángel, PRD leader

Morales Córdova, Ángel, politician, diplomat, exile leader

Ramírez Alcántara, Miguel Ángel, member, Caribbean Legion; fought in Figueres's army in Costa Rica
Requena, Andrés, diplomat; journalist; critic of Trujillo; novelist; murdered 1952
Rubirosa Ariza, Porfirio, diplomat
Sánchez Rubirosa, Ernesto, diplomat
Silfa Canario, Nicolás, PRD leader
Vásquez, Horacio, President, 1924–30

Guatemalans

Arana Castro, Francisco, colonel, rival of Árbenz, assassinated 1949
Asturias Rosales, Miguel Ángel, novelist, *pensador*
Ydígoras Fuentes, Manuel, President, 1958–63

Haitians

Lescot, Élie, President, 1941–46
Magloire, Paul, general; President, 1950–56
Roumain, Jacques, writer; critic of Trujillo
Vincent, Sténio, President, 1930–41

Mexicans

Calles, Plutarco Elías, President, 1924–28
Fabela Alfaro, Isidro, jurist; diplomat; critic of U.S. intervention and of dictatorships
Morones Negrete, Luis, Minister of Industry; union leader, secretary-general of the Confederación Regional Obrera Mexicana (CROM)
Obregón Salido, Álvaro, President, 1920–24
Padilla Nervo, Luis, Foreign Minister, diplomat
Sáenz Garza, Aarón, Foreign Minister, 1924–28
Vasconcelos Calderón, José, Secretary of Education, 1921–24

Nicaraguans

Chamorro Cardenal, Pedro Joaquín, journalist; head of the Conservative Party; critic of Somozas, assassinated 1978
López Pérez, Rigoberto, poet; assassin of Somoza García
Sevilla Sacasa, Guillermo, diplomat

Peruvians

Belaúnde Terry, Fernando, President, 1963–68, 1980–85
Pavletich Trujillo, Esteban, Aprista turned communist

Prado Ugarteche, Manuel, President, 1939–45, 1956–62
Sánchez Sánchez, Luis Alberto, prominent Aprista
Seoane Corrales, Manuel, prominent Aprista

Puerto Ricans

Morales Carrión, Arturo, Undersecretary of State, 1953–61; U.S. Deputy Assistant Secretary of State, 1961–64
Moscoso Mora, Teodoro, politician and diplomat; Ambassador to Venezuela, 1961

Venezuelans

Aponte Hernández, Carlos, fought with Sandino and Guiteras, PCV
Caldera Rodríguez, Rafael, President, 1964–69, 1994–99, COPEI
Capriles Ayala, Miguel Ángel, newspaper publisher
Carnevali Rangel, Luis Alberto, secretary-general, AD underground
Castro León Contreras, General Jesús, coup plotter; Minister of Defense, 1958
Delgado Chalbaud Gómez, Carlos, head of the 1948 military junta, assassinated 1950
Estrada Albornoz, Pedro, director, SN, 1951–58
Falcón Briceño, Marcos, Foreign Minister, 1960–64, AD
Fuenmayor Rivera, Juan Bautista, PCV leader and historian
Gallegos Freire, Rómulo, novelist, President, 1947–48, AD
González Martínez, César, Ambassador to the United States, 1952–58
Larrazábal Ugueto, Wolfgang, president, provisional junta, 1958
Leoni Otero, Raúl, President, 1964–70, AD
López Contreras, José Eleazar, President, 1936–41
Machado Morales, Gustavo, PCV leader
Medina Angarita, Isaías, President, 1942–45
Otero Silva, Miguel, student activist, novelist, journalist
Pérez, Carlos Andrés, secretary to Betancourt; Minister of the Interior, 1959–63; President, 1974–79, 1989–93
Rangel Bourgoin, Domingo Alberto, AD militant and public intellectual; later broke with the party and helped establish the MIR
Ruíz Pineda, Leonardo, secretary-general, AD underground
Vallenilla Lanz Planchart, Laureano, Minister of the Interior, 1952–58
Villalba Gutiérrez, Jóvito, Generation of 1928 student leader; later head of URD

U.S. Government

Acheson, Dean, Secretary of State, 1949–53
Achilles, Theodore, Ambassador to Peru, 1956–60
Atwood, Rollin, Director, Office of South American Affairs, 1952–55

Berle, Jr., Adolf, Assistant Secretary of State, 1938–44; Ambassador to Brazil, 1945–46; member, Latin American Task Force during Kennedy administration; friend to reformers

Bernbaum, Maurice, Foreign Service officer, Latin American desk; Ambassador to Ecuador, 1960–65; Ambassador to Venezuela, 1965–69

Bonsal, Philip, career diplomat, postings included Cuba, 1959–61

Borah, William, Senator, Republican-Idaho, 1907–40

Braden, Spruille, Ambassador to Colombia, 1939–42; Ambassador to Cuba, 1942–45; Ambassador to Argentina, 1945; Assistant Secretary of State for Western Hemisphere Affairs, 1945–47

Briggs, Ellis, career diplomat, various postings

Brownell, Jr., Herbert, Attorney General, 1953–57

Byrnes, James, Secretary of State, 1945–47

Cabot, John, Assistant Secretary of State for Inter-American Affairs, 1952–54

Caffery, Jefferson, Ambassador to El Salvador, 1926–28; Ambassador to Colombia, 1928–33; Assistant Secretary of State, 1933; Ambassador to Cuba, 1934–37; Ambassador to Brazil, 1937–44

Crowder, Enoch, Special Envoy and Ambassador to Cuba, 1919–27

Dearborn, Henry, CIA station chief and Consul General, Dominican Republic, 1960–61

Donnelly, Walter, Ambassador to Venezuela, 1947–50

Duggan, Laurence, Chief of the Division of Latin American Republics during the Roosevelt administration

Dulles, Allen, Director, CIA, 1952–61

Dulles, John Foster, Secretary of State, 1952–59

Eastland, James, Senator, Democrat-Mississippi, 1941, 1943–78

Eisenhower, Milton, brother of the president and unofficial advisor on Latin American matters

Ellender, Allen, Senator, Democrat-Louisiana, 1937–72

Farland, Joseph, Ambassador to the Dominican Republic, 1957–59

Fulbright, J. William, Senator, Democrat-Arkansas, 1945–74

Gardner, Arthur, Ambassador to Cuba, 1953–57

Goodwin, Richard, member, Kennedy's Task Force on Latin American Affairs; Deputy Assistant Secretary of State for Inter-American Affairs, 1961–63

Herter, Christian, Secretary of State, 1959–61

Hill, Robert, Ambassador to Costa Rica, 1953–54

Holland, Henry, Assistant Secretary of State for Inter-American Affairs, 1954–57

Hoover, J. Edgar, Director, FBI, 1924–72

Hughes, Charles Evans, Secretary of State, 1921–25; member, U.S. delegation to Inter-American Conference in Havana, 1928

Hull, Cordell, Secretary of State, 1933–44

Humphrey, George, Secretary of the Treasury, 1953–57

Humphrey, Hubert, Senator, Democrat-Minnesota, 1949–64, 1971–78

Kellogg, Frank, Secretary of State, 1925–29

Loeb, James, Ambassador to Peru, 1961–62

Long, Russell, Senator, Democrat-Louisiana, 1948–87

Mann, Thomas, veteran State Department hand; Assistant Secretary of State for Western Hemisphere Affairs, 1964–65

Marshall, George, Secretary of State, 1947–49

Martin, Edwin McCammon, Assistant Secretary of State for Western Hemisphere Affairs, 1962–64

Martin, John Barthlow, Ambassador to the Dominican Republic, 1962–63

Meyer, Cord, CIA agent, Operation Santo Domingo

Miller, Edward, Assistant Secretary of State for Inter-American Affairs, 1949–52

Morrow, Dwight, Ambassador to Mexico, 1927–30

Morse, Wayne, Senator, Republican-, Independent-, Democrat-Oregon, 1945–69

Munro, Dana, foreign service officer with postings in Nicaragua and Haiti

Patterson, Robert, Secretary of War, 1945–47

Pawley, William, confidant and advisor to Eisenhower; friend and business partner of Trujillo

Peurifoy, John, Ambassador Extraordinary and Plenipotentiary to Guatemala, 1953–54

Porter, Charles, Representative, Democrat-Oregon, 1956–60

Reese, B. Carroll, Representative, Republican-Tennessee, 1921–31, 1933–47, 1951–61; chair, Republican National Committee, 1946–48

Rubottom, Jr., Roy, Assistant Secretary of State for Inter-American Affairs, 1957–60

Rusk, Dean, Secretary of State, 1961–69

Schlesinger, Jr., Arthur, historian; member, Kennedy's Latin American Task Force

Shipstead, Henrik, Senator, Farmer-Laborer Party, 1923–41; Republican, 1941–47, Minnesota

Smathers, George, Senator, Democrat-Florida, 1951–69

Smith, Earl, Ambassador to Cuba, 1957–59

Smith, Walter Bedell, Director, CIA, 1950–53; Undersecretary of State, 1953–54

Sparks, Edward, career diplomat, various postings

Stimson, Henry, Special Envoy to Nicaragua, 1927; Secretary of State, 1927–31

Walters, Vernon, military officer; special aide and translator for Nixon during his 1958 trip to the region; Special Envoy to the Brazilian military

Warren, Fletcher, Ambassador to Nicaragua, 1945–47; to Venezuela, 1951–56

Welles, Sumner, Special Envoy to Cuba, 1933; Undersecretary of State, 1936–43

Wheeler, Burton, Senator, Democrat-Montana, 1923–47

Whelan, Thomas, Ambassador to Nicaragua, 1951–61

Woodward, Robert, Ambassador to Costa Rica, 1954–58

Notes

Abbreviations

AABD	Adolf A. Berle Diary
AAPS	*Annals of the American Academy of Political and Social Science*
AHR	*American Historical Review*
AM	*Atlantic Monthly*
CA	*Cuadernos Americanos*
CCPL	Calvin Coolidge Presidential Library, Northampton Public Library, Northampton, MA
CH	*Current History*
CHCW	*Cambridge History of the Cold War*
CHLA	*Cambridge History of Latin America*
COP	Charles O. Porter Papers, University of Oregon Library, Eugene, Oregon
CR	*Congressional Record*
DCR	*Diario de Costa Rica*
DH	*Diplomatic History*
EPL	Dwight D. Eisenhower Presidential Library, Abilene, Kansas
FA	*Foreign Affairs*
FLMM	Fundación Luis Muñoz Marín, Trujillo Alto, Puerto Rico
FPR	*Foreign Policy Reports*
FRB	Fundación Rómulo Betancourt, Caracas, Venezuela
FRG	Frances R. Grant Collection, Rutgers University Library
FRUS	*Foreign Relations of the United States*
FTC	Frank Tannenbaum Collection, Columbia University Library
HAHR	*Hispanic American Historical Review*
IAEA	*Inter-American Economic Affairs*
JCP	Jefferson Caffery Papers, Edith Garland Dupré Library, University of Southwestern Louisiana, Lafayette, Louisiana

JFDOHP   John Foster Dulles Oral History Project, Seely G. Mudd
         Manuscripts Library, Princeton University
JFKPL   John F. Kennedy Presidential Library, Boston, MA
JISWA   *Journal of Interamerican Studies and World Affairs*
JLAS   *Journal of Latin American Studies*
LAP   *Latin American Perspectives*
LARR   *Latin American Research Review*
LR   *La República* (Costa Rica)
MRV   Biblioteca del Ministerio de Relaciones, Dirección de Política
         Internacional, Palacio de Miraflores, Caracas, Venezuela
NL   *New Leader*
NR   *New Republic*
NYT   *New York Times*
OHS   Oregon Historical Society
RA   *Repertorio Americano*
RG, NA   Record Group, National Archives and Records Administration,
         Suitville, MD
TA   *The Americas*
TPL   Truman Presidential Library and Museum, Independence, Missouri
WP   *Washington Post*

Introduction

1. Memorandum, Telephone Conversation, Bettinger, Miller, and Snow, May 13, 1958, *FRUS, 1958–1960*, 19 vols. (Washington, DC: Government Printing Office, 1991), V: 233–235; and Eldon Kenworthy, "Eisenhower Will Lead a Gala Welcome Today," *NYT*, May 15, 1958.
2. José González González, "Porter," *El Universal* (Caracas), July 8, 1958; and Allan Stewart, oral history, October 23, 1967, 26, JFKPL. https://www.jfklibrary.org/asset-viewer/archives/JFKOH/Stewart%2C%20C%28harles%29%20Allan/JFKOH-CAS-01/JFKOH-CAS-01. Accessed October 21, 2021.
3. Porter presumably was referring to Luis Somoza, who assumed power in 1957 after his father's assassination. Porter's speech, July 4, 1958, Box 35, File, Trip, Venezuela #2, July 1958, COP.
4. Quoted in Alfredo Coronil Hartmann, *Rómulo Betancourt: La vida como pedagogía* (Caracas: Editorial Gráficas Alfa, 1987), 18.
5. *Tempestad en el Caribe* (Mexico City: n.p., 1950).
6. Quoted in William Walker, "Mixing the Sweet with the Sour: Kennedy, Johnson and Latin America," in *The Diplomacy of the Crucial Decade: American Foreign Relations during the 1960s*, ed. Diane Kunz (New York: Columbia University Press, 1994), 42.
7. Allen Wells, *Tropical Zion: General Trujillo, FDR, and the Jews of Sosúa* (Durham: Duke University Press, 2009), chapter 15.

8. Greg Grandin, "Off the Beach: The United States, Latin America and the Cold War," in *A Companion to Post-1945 America*, ed. Jean-Christophe Agnew and Roy Rosenzweig (Malden, MA: Blackwell, 2006), 426–445, 426. Cf. Vanni Pettinà's *Historia mínima de la Guerra Fría en América Latina* (Mexico City: El Colegio de México, 2018), which, like this study, contends that the conflict was a late arrival and that the Cuban Revolution was a watershed.

9. Gilbert Joseph and Daniela Spenser, eds., *In from the Cold: Latin America's New Encounter with the Cold War* (Durham: Duke University Press, 2008); Grandin and Joseph, eds., *A Century of Revolution: Insurgent and Counterinsurgent Violence During Latin America's Cold War* (Durham: Duke University Press, 2010); Virginia Garrard-Burnett, Mark Atwood Lawrence, and Julio Moreno, eds., *Beyond the Eagle's Shadow: New Histories of Latin America's Cold War* (Albuquerque: University of New Mexico Press, 2013); and Thomas Field, Jr., Stella Krepp, and Pettinà, eds., *Latin America and the Global Cold War* (Chapel Hill: University of North Carolina Press, 2020).

10. For example, Stephen Rabe, *Eisenhower and Latin America: The Politics of Anticommunism* (Chapel Hill: University of North Carolina Press, 1988); idem, *The Most Dangerous Area in the World: John F. Kennedy Confronts Communist Revolution in Latin America* (Chapel Hill: University of North Carolina Press, 1999); idem, *The Killing Zone: The United States Wages War in Latin America*, 2nd ed. (New York: Oxford University Press, 2015); Alan McPherson, *Intimate Ties, Bitter Struggles: The United States and Latin America since 1945* (Washington, DC: Potomac Books, 2006); and Michael Grow, *U.S. Presidents and Latin American Interventions: Pursuing Regime Change in the Cold War* (Lawrence: University Press of Kansas, 2008). Works that discuss U.S.–Latin American relations over a longer period include Lars Schoultz, *Beneath the United States: A History of U.S. Policy toward Latin America* (Cambridge: Harvard University Press, 1998); David Schmitz, *Thank God They're on Our Side: The United States and Right-Wing Dictatorships, 1921–1965* (Chapel Hill: University of North Carolina Press, 1999); and his sequel, *The United States and Right-Wing Dictatorships, 1965–1989* (New York: Cambridge University Press, 2006). Odd Arne Westad's impressive *The Global Cold War: Third World Interventions and the Making of Our Times* (New York: Cambridge University Press, 2005) emphasizes the last decades of the Cold War when superpower conflict in Asia, Africa, and Latin America was at its apex.

11. Two exceptions are Hal Brands, *Latin America's Cold War* (Cambridge: Harvard University Press, 2012) and Patrick Iber, *Neither Peace nor Freedom: The Cultural Cold War in Latin America* (Cambridge: Harvard University Press, 2015).

12. For example, Robert Alexander, *Rómulo Betancourt and the Transformation of Venezuela* (New Brunswick: Transaction Books, 1982); idem, *Prophets of the Revolution: Profiles of Latin American Leaders* (New York: Macmillan, 1962);

Charles Ameringer, *Don Pepe: A Political Biography of José Figueres of Costa Rica* (Albuquerque: University of New Mexico Press, 1978); Frederick Pike, *The Politics of the Miraculous in Peru: Haya de la Torre and the Spiritualist Tradition* (Lincoln: University of Nebraska Press, 1986); and Luis Alberto Sánchez, *Haya de la Torre y El APRA: Crónica de un hombre y un partido* (Santiago: Editorial del Pacífico, 1955). Exceptions to this trend include Steve Stein, *Populism in Peru: The Emergence of the Masses and the Politics of Social Control* (Madison: University of Wisconsin Press, 1980); Manuel Caballero, *Rómulo Betancourt, político de nación* (Caracas: Alfadil Ediciones, Fondo de Cultura Económica, 2004); and Lillian Guerra, *Heroes, Martyrs, and Political Messiahs in Revolutionary Cuba, 1946–1958* (New Haven: Yale University Press, 2018).

13. Some of the best research on the region's border wars is by Latin American and European scholars. For example, Eliades Acosta Matos, *La telaraña cubana de Trujillo*, 2 vols. (Santo Domingo: Archivo General de la Nación, 2012); Gustavo Salcedo Ávila, "Conflictos en el Caribe: Eisenhower y Pérez Jiménez, historia de cooperación y enfrentamiento," *Revista Politeia* 48, 35 (2012): 33–62; Loris Zanatta, *La internacional justicialista: auge y ocaso de los sueños imperiales de Perón*, trans. Carlos Catroppi (Buenos Aires: Sudamericana, 2013); Jorge Ibarra Guitart, *Las relaciones cubano-dominicanos, su escenario hemisférico (1944–1948)* (Santo Domingo: Archivo General de la Nación, 2011); Mu-Kien Sang et al., eds., *La política exterior dominicana, 1844–1961*, 3 vols. (Santo Domingo: Secretaría de Estado de Relaciones Exteriores, 2000); and Maria Teresa Romero, *Venezuela en defensa de la democracia, 1958–1998: El caso de la Doctrina Betancourt* (Caracas: Fundacion de la Cultura Urbana, 2005). The sole book in English that treats the reformers as participants in a transnational movement is Ameringer, *The Democratic Left in Exile: The Antidictatorial Struggle in the Caribbean, 1945–1959* (Coral Gables: University of Miami Press, 1974).

14. Alan Angell, "The Left in Latin America since c. 1920," in *Latin America: Politics and Society since 1930*, ed. Leslie Bethell (New York: Cambridge University Press, 1998), 75–144, especially 83.

15. There is a voluminous scholarship on Latin American populism. Some useful primers are Federico Finchelstein, *From Fascism to Populism in History* (Berkeley: University of California Press, 2017); Raanan Rein, "From Juan Perón to Hugo Chávez and Back: Populism Reconsidered," in *Shifting Frontiers of Citizenship: The Latin American Experience*, ed. Mario Sznajder, Luis Roniger, and Carlos Ferment (Leiden: Brill, 2012), 289–309; Carlos de la Torre, *Populist Seduction in Latin America*, 2nd ed. (Athens: Ohio University Research in International Studies, 2010 [2000]); Carlos Vilas, ed., *La democratización fundamental: El populismo en América Latina* (Mexico City: Consejo Nacional para la Cultura y las Artes, 1995); Michael Conniff, ed., *Latin American Populism in Comparative Perspective* (Albuquerque: University of New Mexico Press, 1982); and Alan Knight, "Populism and Neo-Populism in Latin America. Especially Mexico," *JLAS* 30:2 (May 1998): 223–48. For a

helpful critique, see Ian Roxborough, "Unity and Diversity in Latin American History," *JLAS* 16:1 (May 1985), 1–26.

16. Two works that tease out the dyadic relationship between populist politicians and their followers are Daniel James, *Resistance and Integration: Peronism and the Argentine Working Class, 1946–1976* (New York: Cambridge University Press, 1988); and Javier Auyero, *Poor People's Politics: Peronist Survival Networks and the Legacy of Evita* (Durham: Duke University Press, 2001).

17. Notable exceptions were Cárdenas's nationalization of the oil industry and Perón's takeover of British-owned railways.

18. E.g., Stein, *Populism in Peru;* and Marco Palacios, *El populismo en Colombia* (Bogotá: Editorial Siusinza, 1971).

19. Richard Turits, *Foundations of Despotism: Peasants, the Trujillo Regime, and Modernity in Dominican History* (Stanford: Stanford University Press, 2003); Lauren Derby, *The Dictator's Seduction: Politics and the Popular Imagination in the Era of Trujillo* (Durham: Duke University Press, 2009); and Jeffrey Gould, *To Lead as Equals: Rural Protest and Political Consciousness in Chinandega, 1912–1979* (Chapel Hill: University of North Carolina Press, 1990).

Chapter One. The Poet and the Rebel

Epigraph 1: Quoted in Paco Taibo II, *Tony Guiteras* (Mexico City: Editorial Planeta, 2008), 379.

Epigraph 2: Gregorio Urbano Gilbert, *Junto a Sandino* (Santo Domingo: Alfa y Omega, 1979), 21.

1. Although Turcios offered no proof of the review's readership and while the broad discrepancy in the circulation numbers raises questions about their veracity, there is ample anecdotal evidence to corroborate the editor's claim that his journal elicited considerable interest abroad. For Turcios's claims, see Medardo Mejía, *Froylán Turcios en los campos de la estética y el civismo* (Tegucigalpa: Editorial Universitaria, 1980), 165–166, 192.

2. Darío Euraque, *Reinterpreting the Banana Republic: Region and State in Honduras, 1870–1972* (Chapel Hill: University of North Carolina Press, 1996), 4; Thomas Dodd, *Tiburcio Carías: Portrait of a Honduran Political Leader* (Baton Rouge: Louisiana State University Press, 2005), 30; and Arthur Ruhl, *The Central Americans: Adventures and Impressions between Mexico and Panama* (New York: Charles Scribner's Sons, 1928), 136.

3. Among *Ariel's* notable contributors were the Mexican intellectual José Vasconcelos, the Cuban firebrand Julio Antonio Mella, Haya, the Puerto Rican educator Eugenio María de Hostos, and the Argentine socialist Manuel Ugarte. Turcios, *Album secreto de Froylán Turcios*, ed. Roberto Sosa (Tegucigalpa: Litografía López, 2009).

4. *Repertorio Americano*, a Costa Rican journal comparable to *Ariel*, was an irregular news outlet for Sandino's missives. See Eugenio García Carrillo, *El*

hombre del Repertorio Americano (San José: Universidad Autónoma de Centro América, 1981); and Jussi Pakkasvirta, *Un continente, una nación: Intelectuales latinoamericanos, comunidad política y las revistas culturales en Costa Rica y en el Perú (1919–1930)* (Helsinki: Academia Scientiaru Fennicam 1997), 142–157.

5. Sandino to Turcios, September 20, 1927, and idem, December 29, 1927, in Sergio Ramírez, ed., *Sandino: The Testimony of a Nicaraguan Patriot, 1921–1934*, trans. Robert Conrad (Princeton: Princeton University Press, 1990 [1984]), 105–107, 144–155, quotes, 106, 144.

6. Oscar-René Vargas, *Floreció al filo de la espada: El movimiento de Sandino, 1926–1939: Once ensayos de interpretación* (Managua: El Amanecer, 1995), 216.

7. For example, Sandino to Turcios, May 20, 1928, in Arturo Taracena Arriola, "Aporte documental al *pensamiento vivo de Sandino*. Tres nuevos textos," *Revista de Historia* 20 (1989): 263–273, especially 270–272.

8. Neill Macaulay, *The Sandino Affair* (Chicago: Quadrangle Books, 1967), 95.

9. Marco Aurelio Navarro-Génie, *Augusto "César" Sandino: Messiah of Light and Truth* (Syracuse: Syracuse University Press, 2002), 53–54; and McPherson, *The Invaded: How Latin Americans and Their Allies Fought and Ended U.S. Occupations* (New York: Oxford University Press, 2014), quote, 79.

10. *RA* 16:14 (April 14, 1928) and 16:22 (June 9, 1928); and Richard Salisbury, *Anti-Imperialism and International Competition in Central America, 1920–1929* (Wilmington: Scholarly Resources, 1989), 139.

11. Michelle Dospital, *Siempre más allá . . . : El movimiento Sandinista en Nicaragua, 1927–1934*, trans. Verónica Krugel (Managua and Paris: Instituto de Historia de Nicaragua and Centro Francés de Estudios Mexicanos y Centroamericanos, 1996), 28.

12. Quoted in Jaime Quezada, ed., *Gabriela Mistral: Escritos políticos* (Mexico City: Fondo de Cultural Económica, 1994), 21.

13. *RA* 16:14 (April 14, 1928) and 23:2 (July 13, 1931).

14. Martín Bergel, "El anti-antinorteamericanismo en América Latina (1898–1930): Apuntes para una historia intelectual," *Nueva Sociedad* 236 (November–December 2011): 152–167, especially 160.

15. Donald Hodges, *Intellectual Foundations of the Nicaraguan Revolution* (Austin: University of Texas Press, 1986), 135. To speak of a Latin American Legion, as Sandino later admitted, was technically incorrect, because the foreign recruits were dispersed among his army's battalions. Dospital, *Siempre más allá . . .*, 53. See also Armando Amador, *Nicaragua y Sandino: Las banderas de Gustavo Machado* (Caracas: Ediciones Centauro, 1984), 79; and Gregorio Selser, *Sandino: General of the Free*, trans. Cedric Belfrage (New York: Monthly Review Press, 1981 [1978]), 94.

16. Dospital, *Siempre más allá . . .*, 55.

17. Quoted in McPherson, *The Invaded*, 216–217.

18. Selser, *El pequeño ejército loco: Sandino y la operación México-Nicaragua* (Mexico City: Bruguera Mexicana de Ediciones, 1980 [1978]); and Michel Gobat,

Confronting the American Dream: Nicaragua under U.S. Imperial Rule (Durham: Duke University Press, 2005), 236.

19. Quoted in McPherson, *The Invaded*, 109.

20. Cruse, "Situación actual de Sandino," February 13, 1928, and idem, "Situación de Sandino," November 17, 1928, in R. R. Isaguirre and A. Martínez, eds. *Sandino y los U.S. Marines: Reportes de los agregados militares y comandantes marines en acción* (Tegucigalpa: Guaymuras, 2000), 169–171, 288.

21. Gilbert, *Junto a Sandino*, 21, 144; and Navarro-Génie, *Augusto "César" Sandino*, quote, 53.

22. Quoted in Rodolfo Cerdas Cruz, *La hoz y el machete: La Internacional Comunista, América Latina y la revolución en Centroamérica* (San José, Costa Rica: Editorial Universidad Estatal a Distancia, 1986), 236n52.

23. Charles Howlett, "Neighborly Concern: John Nevin Sayre and the Mission of Peace and Goodwill to Nicaragua, 1927–1928," *TA* 45:1 (July 1988): 19–46, quote, 25; and John Nelson, *The Peace Prophets: American Pacifist Thought, 1919–1941* (Chapel Hill: University of North Carolina Press, 1967), 34.

24. Quoted in McPherson, *The Invaded*, 218.

25. Volker Wünderich, *Sandino, una biografía política* (Managua: Nueva Nicaragua, 1995), 180–181.

26. Beals, "This is War, Gentlemen!" *Nation* 126:3275 (April 11, 1928): 403–406.

27. Beals, "With Sandino in Nicaragua," *Nation* 126:3268 (February 22, 1928): 205.

28. Beals, *Glass Houses: Ten Years of Free-Lancing* (Philadelphia: J. B. Lippincott, 1938), 294. His six-part series in *The Nation* during February–March 1928 was translated into Spanish and published as *Con Sandino en Nicaragua* (San José: Edición del Comité Pro-Sandino, 1928) and later revised and republished as *Banana Gold* (Philadelphia: J.B. Lippincott, 1932). Quotes are taken from the latter, 189–190, and 193. More than forty U.S. newspapers and the Latin American, European, and Australian press carried Beals's columns. McPherson, *The Invaded*, 196–197.

29. Selser, *Sandino: General of the Free*, quote, 141–142.

30. Ana Cairo, ed., *Mella: 100 años*, 2 vols. (Santiago de Cuba: Ediciones Oriente, Ediciones La Memoria, 2003): I: 74–75.

31. *El Dictamen* (Veracruz, Mexico), October 1929, in Ramírez, ed., *Sandino: The Testimony*, 276–278, quote, 277.

32. Munro to Kellogg, December 26, 1927, *FRUS, 1927*, 3 vols. (Washington, DC: Government Printing Office), III: 451.

33. Kellogg to Summerlin, December 31, 1927. *FRUS, 1927*, III: 453.

34. Kellogg to Summerlin, January 4, 1928, *FRUS, 1927*, III: 559–560.

35. Euraque, *Reinterpreting the Banana Republic*, 57.

36. Summerlin to Kellogg, July 2, 1928, *FRUS, 1928* (Washington, DC: Government Printing Office), III: 581–582; The U.S. Minister to El Salvador, Jefferson Caffery sent a similar cable to Kellogg ten days later. Caffery to Kellogg, July 12, 1928, *FRUS 1928*, III: 580–581.

37. Ricardo Melgar Bao and Mariana Ortega Breña, "The Anti-Imperialist League of the Americas between the East and Latin America," *LAP* 35:2 (March 2008): 9–24.

38. Robert Ferrell, *The Presidency of Calvin Coolidge* (Lawrence: University Press of Kansas, 1998), 138–139.

39. Salisbury, *Anti-Imperialism*, 137–139; and Mejía, *Froylán Turcios*, 183, 333.

40. Cruse, "Situación de Sandino," August 27, 1928, in Isaguirre and Martínez R., *Sandino y los U.S. Marines*, 204; and José Antonio Funes, "Froylán Turcios y la campaña de Sandino en la revista *Ariel* (1925–1928)," *CA* 133 (2010/2013): 181–208, especially 194.

41. Alberto Ghiraldo, *Yanquilandia bárbara: La lucha contra el imperialismo* (Madrid: Historia Nueva, 1929), 176ff. quote, 178.

42. Telegram, Eberhardt to Stimson, May 8, 1929, *FRUS, 1929* (Washington, DC: Government Printing Office, 1944), III: 564.

43. Buell, "Reconstruction in Nicaragua," *FPR* 6 (November 12, 1930): 315–343, 339–345.

44. Ibid., quote, 340. Mejía Colindres vacillated on curbing incursions by Sandino's forces. See Euraque, *Reinterpreting the Banana Republic*, 56, 58.

45. Buell, "The United States and Central American Revolutions," *FPR* (July 22, 1931), 187–204, especially 194–195.

46. Ibid., 194–195; and Funes, "Froylán Turcios," 181–186, quote, 186.

47. Wünderich, "El nacionalismo y el espiritualismo de Augusto C. Sandino en su tiempo," in *Encuentros con la historia*, ed. Margarita Vanini (Managua: Instituto de Historia de Nicaragua-UCA, 1995), 313–331, especially 285–286.

48. Quoted in ibid., 288.

49. Funes, "Froylán Turcios," 189.

50. Ibid.

51. Rama, *Rubén Darío y el modernismo* (Caracas: Biblioteca de la Universidad Central de Venezuela, 1970), 76.

52. Quoted in Ruhl, *The Central Americans*, 163.

53. Vasconcelos, Mistral, and Haya dabbled in theosophy. Eduardo Devés Valdés and Melgar Bao, "Redes teosóficas y pensadores (políticos) latinoamericanos, 1910–1930," *CA* 6:78 (November–December 1999): 137–152, especially 145; Marta Elena Casaús Arzú, "La creación de nuevos espacios públicos a principios del Siglo XX: La influencia de redes intelectuales teosóficas en la opinión pública centroamericana (1920–1930)," in *Las redes intelectuales centroamericanas*, ed. Marta Elena Casaús Arzú and Teresa García Giráldez (Guatemala City: F and G Editores, 2005): 71–121, especially 79–82.

54. Wünderich, *Sandino, una biografía política*, quote, 81.

55. LeGrand, "Living in Macondo: Economy and Culture in a United Fruit Company Banana Enclave in Colombia," in *Close Encounters of Empire: Writing the Cultural History of U.S.-Latin American Relations*, ed. Gilbert Joseph, Catherine LeGrand, and Ricardo Donato Salvatore (Durham: Duke University Press, 1998), 333–368, especially 350.

56. Amartya Sen, "Tagore and His India," *New York Review of Books* 44:11 (June 26, 1997). http://www.nybooks.com.ezproxy.bowdoin.edu/articles/archives/1997/jun/26/tagore-and-his-india/?insrc=toc. Accessed August 1, 2014; and Ketaki Kushari Dyson, *In Your Blossoming Flower-Garden: Rabindranath Tagore and Victoria Ocampo*, 2nd ed. (New Delhi: Sahitya Akademi, 1996 [1988]), 68ff.

57. Wünderich, *Sandino, una biografía política*, 143–144, 149; and idem, "El nacionalismo y el espiritualismo," 281–282.

58. Jorge Arías Gómez, *Farabundo Martí: Esbozo biográfico* (San Salvador: Editorial Universitaria Centroamérica, 1972), 55.

59. Ghiraldo, *Yanquilandia bárbara*, 157–158, 170–171, quote, 157.

60. Mejía, *Froylán Turcios*, 160, 169, 171.

61. Dodd, "The United States and Nicaragua," *AAPS* 132 (July 1927): 134–141, quotes, 135; and Kenneth Grieb, *Guatemalan Caudillo: The Regime of Jorge Ubico, 1931–1944* (Athens: Ohio University Press, 1979), 82–83.

62. Buell, *The Central Americans* (New York: Foreign Policy Association, 1930), quote, 24.

63. Knut Walter, *The Regime of Anastasio Somoza, 1936–1956* (Chapel Hill: University of North Carolina Press, 1993), 18; and Conrad, "Translator's Introduction," in Ramírez, ed., *Sandino: The Testimony*, 13–14.

64. "Manifesto to the Nicaraguan People," August 26, 1927, in Ramírez, ed., *Sandino: The Testimony*, 92.

65. Sandino to Turcios, March 14, 1928, in Ramírez, ed., *Sandino: The Testimony*, 187–189, quote, 188.

66. Conrad, "Translator's Introduction," "Guidelines for the Organization of the Army in Defense of the National Sovereignty of Nicaragua," September 2, 1927, and "Letter to Colonel Pompilio Reyes, November 27, 1927, in Ramírez, ed., *Sandino: The Testimony*, 13n27, 95–97, and 130–131, quote, 131.

67. Ingenieros, *Antimperialismo y nación*, ed. Oscar Terán (Mexico City: Siglo XXI, 1979), 439.

68. Mejía, *Froylán Turcios*, 105–106.

69. Quotes taken from Turcios to Sandino, October 11 and October 27, 1927, in Mejía, *Froylán Turcios*, 171, and Wünderich, *Sandino, una biografía política*, 124.

70. Porfirio Sánchez to Turcios, March 14, 1928, in Instituto de Estudio del Sandinismo, *El sandinismo: documentos básicos* (Managua: Nueva Nicaragua, 1983), 169; Salvador Mendieta, *El problema unionista de Centro-América y los gobiernos locales* (Quetzaltenango, Guatemala: Talleres Tipográficos, 1930); and Salisbury, "The Anti-Imperialist Career of Alejandro Alvarado Quirós," *HAHR* 57:4 (November 1977): 587–612, especially 591ff.

71. Carlos Deambrosis Martins, "La expulsión de Haya de la Torre de Guatemala," in Haya de la Torre, *A donde va a Indoamérica?* 2nd ed. (Santiago, Chile: Editorial Ercilla 1935 [1935]), 275–280, quote, 278.

72. Wünderich, *Sandino, una biografía política*, 180.

73. Ibid., 50, 180.

74. Sandino to Turcios, November 21, 1928, in Ramírez, ed., *Sandino, The Testimony*, 211–212.

75. Turcios to Sandino, December 28, 1928, and Sandino to Turcios, January 7, 1929, in Ramírez, ed., *Sandino; The Testimony*, 228–230 and 228.

76. Quoted in Funes, "Froylán Turcios," 202.

77. Macaulay, *The Sandino Affair*, 96; and Alejandro Bolaños Geyer, *Sandino* (Masaya, Nicaragua: self-published, 2002).

78. Nicola Miller, *In the Shadow of the State: Intellectuals and the Quest for National Identity in Twentieth-Century Spanish America* (London: Verso, 1999), 176–177.

79. Rodó, *Ariel*, trans. Margaret Sayers Peden (Austin: University of Texas Press, 1988 [1900]).

80. Norberto Galasso, *Manuel Ugarte y la lucha por la unidad latinoamericana*, 2nd ed. (Buenos Aires: Ediciones Corregidor, 2001 [1974]), 45.

81. Lippmann, "Vested Rights and Nationalism in Latin America," *FA* 5:3 (April 1927): 353–363, quote, 356. *Repertorio Americano* beat the drum for the internationalization of the Canal between 1927 and 1931, inviting intellectuals to contribute columns for its feature, "Canales interoceánicos: Panama, Nicaragua."

82. Bergel, "El anti-antinorteamericanismo en América Latina."

83. Miller, *In the Shadow of the State*, 178–179; and Blanco Fombona, *Ensayos históricos*, ed. Rafael Castellanos (Caracas: Biblioteca Ayacucho, 1981), 435–448.

84. Edward Perry, "Anti-American Propaganda in Hispanic America," *HAHR* 3:1 (February 1920): 17–40, quote, 27.

85. Mejía, *Froylán Turcios*, 181.

86. Sandino, "An Open Letter to President Herbert Hoover," March 6, 1929, in Ramírez, ed., *Sandino, The Testimony*, 239–242, quotes, 240 and 241.

87. Quoted in Bergel, "El anti-antinorteamericanismo en América Latina," 164.

88. Max Friedman, *Rethinking Anti-Americanism: The History of an Exceptional Concept in American Foreign Relations* (New York: Cambridge University Press, 2012), 6; and McPherson, ed., *Anti-Americanism in Latin America and the Caribbean* (New York: Berghahn, 2006), introduction.

89. Abel, "Martí, Latin America and Spain," in *José Martí: Revolutionary Democrat*, ed. Christopher Abel and Nissa Torrents (Durham: Duke University Press, 1986), 139–140.

90. Miller, *In the Shadow of the State*, 180–181; and Rama, *The Lettered City*, 90.

91. Haya de la Torre, *Por la emancipación de América Latina: Artículos, mensajes, discursos (1923–1927)* (Buenos Aires: M. Glezier, 1927), 107–115.

92. María de las Nieves Pinillos, ed., *Manuel Ugarte: Biografía, selección de textos y bibliografía* (Madrid: Ediciones de Cultura Hispánica, 1989), 109–113; Ugarte, *La nación latinoamericana*, ed. Norberto Galasso (Caracas: Biblioteca Ayacucho, 1987 [1978]); and Eliff Lara Astorga, "Cartas entre Manuel

Ugarte e Isidro Fabela: El dolor de las ideas," *Literatura Mexicana* 19:1 (2008): 139–160, especially 140–143.

93. De las Nieves Pinillos, *Manuel Ugarte*, 115–116; Lara Astorga, "Cartas entre," 143; and Galasso, *Manuel Ugarte y la lucha*, 378–380. For a synopsis of Ugarte's travels, see J. Fred Rippy's introduction to Ugarte, *The Destiny of a Continent*, trans. Catherine A. Phillips (New York: AMS Press, 1970 [1923]). On the Parisian student organization, see Taracena Arriola, "La Asociación de Estudiantes Latinoamericanos de Paris (1925–1933)," *Anuario de Estudios Centroamericanos* 15: 2 (1989): 61–80.

94. Miller, *In the Shadow of the State*, 184–187; and Terán, "El primer antimperialismo latinoamericano," *Punto de Vista* 4:12 (1981): 3–10, especially 8.

95. Ugarte, *The Destiny of a Continent*, 142; and idem, "Dangers Latent in our Latin American Policy," *CH* 26:6 (September 1, 1927): 897–901.

96. Quoted in Beals, "Latin American Nations' Failure to Attain Unity," *CH* 26:6 (September 1, 1927): 862–870.

97. Quoted in Galasso, *Manuel Ugarte y la lucha*, 192.

98. Pablo Yankelevich, "Una mirada argentina de la Revolución Mexicana: La gesta de Manuel Ugarte (1910–1917)," *Historia Mexicana* 44:4 (April–June 1995); 645–676, quote, 666.

99. One of Vasconcelos's innovations as Secretary of Education was to offer professors from other countries pedagogical training in Mexico. John Haddox, "La influencia de José Vasconcelos sobre Victor Raúl Haya de la Torre," in *El APRA: De la ideología a la praxis*, ed. Heraclio Bonilla and Paul Drake (Lima: Centro Latinoamericano de Historia Económica y Social, Center for Iberian and Latin American Studies, UCSD, and Editorial Gráfica Nuevo Mundo, 1989), 47–70, especially 51; and Bergel and Ricardo Martínez Mazzola, "América Latina como práctica: Modos de sociabilidad intelectual de los reformistas universitarios (1918–1930)," in *Historia de los intelectuales de América Latina*, ed. Carlos Altamirano, 2 vols. (Buenos Aires: Katz Editores, 2010) II: 119–145, especially 130.

100. Yankelevich, *Miradas australes* (Mexico City: Instituto Nacional de Estudios Históricos de la Revolución Mexicana, 1997), 257ff., quote, 257.

101. "Letter from General José Vasconcelos regarding the Tyrant of Venezuela," in José Rafael Pocaterra, *Gómez: The Shame of America: Fragments from the Memoirs of a Citizen of the Republic of Venezuela in the Days of Her Decadence* (Paris: Imp. Nicolas Renault, 1929 [1927]), 246.

102. "Letter from General José Vasconcelos"; Naudy Suárez Figueroa, "El joven Betancourt: La social democracia venezolana de 1928 a 1930," *Nueva política* 14 (1974): 3–129, especially 20n26; Melgar Bao, "Redes del exilio aprista en México (1923–1924), una aproximación," in *México, país refugio: La experiencia de los exilios en el Siglo XX*, ed. Yankelevich (Mexico City: INAH-Plaza y Valdés, 2002): 245–263; Brian McBeth, *Dictatorship and Politics: Intrigue, Betrayal and Survival in Venezuela, 1908–1935* (Notre Dame: University of Notre Dame Press, 2008), 165, 206, 213; and Amalia Lluch

Pérez, *Luis Muñoz Marín: poesía, periodismo y revolución (1915–1930)* (San Juan: La Universidad del Sagrado Corazón, La Fundación Luis Muñoz Marín, 1999), 184–186.

103. Melgar Bao, "Redes del exilio aprista," 248.

104. Quoted in Yankelevich, *Miradas australes*, 290.

105. Colombi, *Viaje intelectual: Migraciones y desplazamientos en América Latina (1880– 1915)* (Rosario, Argentina: Beatriz Viterbo Editora, 2004), 15–16, quote, 171; and Bergel and Martínez Mazzola, "América Latina como práctica," 137.

106. Frederick Pike, "Latin America and the Inversion of United States Stereotypes in the 1920s and 1930s: The Case of Culture and Nature," *TA* 42:2 (October 1985): 131–162, especially 151–152; and Jefferson Cowie, "The Emergence of Alternative Views of Latin America: The Thought of Three U.S. Intellectuals," Duke-UNC Program in Latin American Studies, Working Paper #3 (September 1992), especially 34. For evidence of Latin Americans' glowing reactions to Frank's lecture tour, see Hispanic Institute in the United States, *Waldo Frank in América Hispana*, ed. M. J. Benardete (New York: Instituto de Las Españas, 1930).

107. Frank, "What Is Hispano-America to Us?" *Scribner's Magazine* 87:6 (June 1930): 579–586, especially 583–586.

108. Ibid., 585.

109. Pike, "Latin America and the Inversion," 150.

110. Manuel Solís Avendaño and Alfonso González Ortega, *La identidad mutilada: García Monge y el Repertorio Americano, 1920–1930* (San José: Editorial de la Universidad de Costa Rica, 1998), 66–67; and Pike, "Latin America and the Inversion," 151–152.

111. Frank, *Memoirs of Waldo Frank*, ed. Alan Trachtenberg (Amherst: University of Massachusetts Press, 1973), 156, 166.

112. García Calderón, "Dictatorship and Democracy in Latin America," *FA* 3:3 (April 1925): 459–477, especially 473–474.

113. García Calderón, *Latin America: Its Rise and Progress*, trans. Bernard Miall (London: T. Fisher Unwin, 1924 [1913]), 365, 368.

114. On Ingenieros, see Terán's splendid introduction in Ingenieros, *Antimperialismo y nación*, 1–118; Alexandra Pita González, *La Unión Latino Americano y El Boletín Renovación: Redes intelectuales y revistas culturales en la década de 1920* (Mexico City: El Colegio de México, Universidad de Colima, 2009), 43ff; Francisco Zapata, *Ideología y política en América Latina* (Mexico City: El Colegio de México, 2001), 41–54; and Devés Valdés, *El pensamiento latinoamericano en el siglo XX: Entre la modernización y la identidad*, 2 vols. (Buenos Aires: Editorial Biblos, Centro de Investigaciones Diego Barros Arana, 2000), I: 59.

115. Richard Walter, *Student Politics in Argentina: The University Reform and its Effects, 1918–1964* (New York: Basic Books, 1968), 72–73; and Haya de la Torre, "The Student Movement of Latin America," *Bulletin of the Pan American Union* 60 (November 1926): 1105–1108, especially 1107.

116. Raúl Roa, *Bufa subversiva* (Havana: Ediciones la Memoria del Centro Cultural Pablo de la Torriente Brau, 2006 (1935]), 38–39.

117. Quoted in Ibid., 37–38. See also Juan Carlos Portantiero, *Estudiantes y política en América Latina: El proceso de la reforma universitaria (1918–1938)* (Mexico City: Siglo Veintiuno, 1978), 74.

118. Pita González, "La circulación de bienes culturales en una publicación (y una red) Latinomericanista: *El Boletín Renovación,*" in *Revistas en América Latina: Proyectos literarios, políticos y culturales,* ed. Regina Crespo (Mexico City: UNAM, Centro de Investigaciones sobre América Latina y el Caribe, 2010): 118–147, especially 123.

119. Quoted in Pita González, *La Unión Argentina,* 42.

120. Asturias, "El imperialismo económico de los Estados Unidos y nosotros," *RA* 18:7 (February 16, 1929); and Taracena Arriola, "La Asociación," 75, 79n53.

121. Bergel, "Nomadismo proselitista y revolución: Notas para una caracterización del primer exilio aprista (1923–1931)," *Estudios Interdisciplinarios de América Latina* 20:1 (2009): 41–66, especially 45.

122. *RA*, October 13, 1928.

123. Dospital, *Siempre más allá . . .,* 45.

124. Reprinted in *RA* 17:2 (July 14, 1928). See also Devés, *El pensamiento latino-americano,* I: 175–176.

125. Wünderich, *Sandino, una biografía política,* 180–181.

126. Taracena Arriola, "La Asociación General," 68.

127. Ibid., 68–70; and, Goebel, *Anti-Imperial Metropolis: Interwar Paris and the Seeds of Third World Nationalism* (New York: Cambridge University Press, 2015), 132.

128. Goebel, *Anti-Imperial Metropolis,* 130.

129. Quoted in Ramón de Belausteguigoitia, *Con Sandino en Nicaragua: La hora de la paz* (Managua: Editorial Nueva Nicaragua, 1981 [1934]), 158.

130. Navarro-Génie, *Augusto "César" Sandino.*

131. Gould, "*Indigenista* Dictators and the Problematic Origins of Democracy in Central America," in *The Great Depression in Latin America,* ed. Paolo Drinot and Knight (Durham: Duke University Press, 2014), 188–212, especially 199.

132. McPherson, *The Invaded,* 57.

133. Cerdas Cruz, *La hoz y el machete,* 217.

134. Cerdas Cruz, *Sandino, el APRA y la Internacional Comunista: Antecedentes históricos de la Nicaragua de hoy* (Lima: Comisión Nacional de Ideología y Doctrina del Partido Aprista Peruano, Edmissa, 1983), 27.

135. Diplomatic historian Walter LaFeber illustrates this point in his discussion of the Wilson administration's opposition to an oil concession between the Costa Rican government and British investors in 1919. *Inevitable Revolutions: The United States and Central America* (New York: Norton, 1993 [1983]), 56–60.

136. Dospital, *Siempre más allá . . .*, 46–47; Wünderich, *Sandino, una biografía política*, 188; and Instituto de Estudio, *El sandinismo*, 65.

137. Dodd, *Tiburcio Carías*, 33, 38; and James Morris, *Honduras: Caudillo Politics and Military Rulers* (Boulder: Westview Press, 1984), 9.

138. Buell, *The Central Americans*, 17–18.

139. James Dunkerley, *Power in the Isthmus: A Political History of Modern Central America* (London: Verso, 1988), 67; and Edward Boatman-Guillan, " 'In Honduras a Mule is Worth More than a Congressman," in *Honduras: Portrait of a Captive Nation*, ed. Nancy Peckenham and Annie Street (New York: Praeger, 1985), 38–43.

140. Euraque, *Reinterpreting the Banana Republic*, 50; and James Mahoney, *The Legacies of Liberalism: Path Dependence and Political Regimes in Central America* (Baltimore: The Johns Hopkins University Press, 2001), 226ff.

141. Funes, "Froylán Turcios," 193.

142. Sandino to Turcios, June 10, 1928, quoted in Selser, *Sandino: General of the Free*, 107–108.

143. Wünderich, *Sandino, una biografía política*, 175; and Navarro-Génie, *Augusto "César" Sandino*, 18.

144. Bolívar's call for an inter-American alliance came at the Congress of Panama in 1826. The idea resurfaced periodically, especially when European and North American interventions rattled the region. Ricaurte Soler, "Manual Ugarte: Bolivarismo contra imperialismo," *Casa de Las Americas* 26:152 (September–October 1985): 120–128. On Sandino's "Plan for the Realization of Bolívar's Ultimate Dream," see Karl Bermann, ed., *Sandino Without Frontiers: Selected Writings of Augusto César Sandino on Internationalism, Pan-Americanism, and Social Questions* (Hampton, VA: Compita, 1988), 10; and Wünderich, *Sandino, una biografía política*, 181.

145. Dospital, *Siempre más allá . . .*, 48.

146. Quoted in Hodges, *Intellectual Foundations*, 86–87.

147. Dospital, *Siempre más allá . . .*, 110–111.

148. After his death in 1943, his remains were returned to his homeland and he was interred in Tegucigalpa. Dodd, *Tiburcio Carías*, quote, 205.

Chapter Two. The Obligation to Think

Epigraph: Roa, *Retorno a la alborada*, 2 vols. (Havana: Universidad de Las Villas, 1964), I: 233.

1. Walter, "The Intellectual Background of the 1918 University Reform in Argentina," *HAHR* 49:2 (May 1969): 233–253, especially 247.

2. "La juventud Argentina de Córdoba a los hombres libres de Sudamérica," in Portantiero, *Estudiantes y política*, 131–136, especially 132; and Raymond Craib, *The Cry of the Renegade: Politics and Poetry in Interwar Chile* (New York: Oxford University Press, 2016), 57.

3. Quoted in Haya de la Torre, "The Student Movement," 1105–1108, 1106.

4. Quoted in Orlando Albornoz, "Models of the Latin American University," in *The Latin American University*, ed. Joseph Maier and Richard Weatherhead (Albuquerque: University of New Mexico Press, 1979), 123–134, 125–126.

5. González, *La reforma universitaria*, 5 vols. (Buenos Aires: Ediciones de La Revista Sagitario, 1927), I: 71–72 and II: chapter 4; and David Spencer, "Student Politics and University Reform," in *Student Politics in Latin America*, ed. idem (Philadelphia: United States National Student Association, 1965), 9–13.

6. Portantiero, *Estudiantes y política*, 30–31. For Palacios's comments, see Antonio Herrero, *Alfredo L. Palacios: Carácteres, valores y problemas de su personalidad y su acción social: Reforma universitaria Ibero-Americanismo* (Buenos Aires: M. Gleizer, 1925), 78. For precursors to the university reform, Bergel and Martínez Mazzola, "América Latina como práctica,"126–127.

7. Joseph Tulchin, "Origins of Student Reform in Latin America: Córdoba, 1918," *Yale Review* 56:4 (June 1972): 575–590; Chris Hamilton, "Origins of the University Reform Movement: Student Politics in Argentina between 1918 and 1922," in *Student Politics in Latin America*, 14–20; and Pablo Buchbinder, "El movimiento reformista de 1918: Una aproximación desde la historia interna de las instituciones universitarias," *Ibero-Amerikanisches Archiv* 26:1/2 (2000): 27–58.

8. Alistair Hennessy, "Students in the Latin American University," in *The Latin American University*, 147–184, especially 149; Walter, *Student Politics in Argentina*, quote, 27; and del Mazo, ed., *La Reforma Universitaria*, 3rd ed., 3 vols. (Lima: Universidad Nacional Mayor de San Marcos, 1976 [1941]).

9. Rama, *The Lettered City*, ed. and trans. John Chasteen (Durham: Duke University Press, 1996 [1984]), 58.

10. Jean Franco, *The Modern Culture of Latin America: Society and the Artist* (Hammondsworth, Middlesex, England: Penguin, 1970 [1967]), 82, 118–119; Goebel, "Decentering the German Spirit: The Weimar Republic's Cultural Relations with Latin America," *Journal of Contemporary History* 44:2 (April 2009): 221–245; and Alberto Flores Galindo, *La agonía de Mariátegui: La polémica con la Komintern* (Lima: Editorial Revolución, 1991 [1980]), 43.

11. Haya de la Torre, "La reforma universitaria," in *Construyendo el Aprismo: Artículos y cartas desde el exilio*, ed. idem (Buenos Aires: Colección Claridad, 1933), 155–166, especially 156.

12. Walter, "The Intellectual Background."

13. Craib, *The Cry of the Renegade*, 60.

14. Hamilton, "Origins of the University Reform Movement," 19.

15. Sánchez, *Haya de la Torre y El APRA*, 79.

16. Walter, *Student Politics*, 70; Haya de la Torre, "The Students Movement," 1107; and Albornoz, "Models of the Latin American University," 127.

17. Portantiero, *Estudiantes y política*, 73.

18. Walter, "The Intellectual Background," 240.

19. Galasso, *Manuel Ugarte y la lucha*, 322; and Walter, "The Intellectual Background," 236n7 and 237n9.

20. Quoted in Walter, "The Intellectual Background," 243 and 244.

21. González, *La reforma universitaria*, I: 71–72; Tulchin, "Origins of Student Reform," 583; and Robert Whitney, *State and Revolution in Cuba: Mass Mobilization and Political Change, 1920–1940* (Chapel Hill: University of North Carolina Press, 2001), 88.

22. Sánchez, "El estudiante, el ciudadano, el intelectual y la Reforma Universitaria Americana," in del Mazo, ed., *La reforma universitaria*, III: 127–131, quote, 128.

23. Jeffrey Klaiber, "The Popular Universities and the Origins of Aprismo, 1921–1924," *HAHR* 55:4 (November 1975): 696–697; Enrique Cornejo Koster, "Crónica del movimiento estudiantil peruano," in del Mazo, ed., *La reforma universitaria*, II: 11–36; and Miller, *In the Shadow of the State*, 68–69.

24. Quoted in Galasso, *Manuel Ugarte y la lucha*, 346. On Palacios's trip to Peru, see Pita González, *La Unión Latino Americana*, 121; and Bergel and Martínez Mazzola, "América Latina como práctica," quote, 137.

25. Eugenio Chang-Rodríguez, *La literatura política de González Prada, Mariátegui y Haya de la Torre* (Mexico City: Ediciones de Andrea, 1957); David Sobrevilla, *Manuel González Prada. Free Pages and Hard Times: Anarchist Musings*, trans. Frederick Fornoff and ed. Sobrevilla (New York: Oxford University Press, 2003), xliv; and Steven Hirsch, "Peruvian Anarcho-Syndicalism: Adapting Transnational Influences and Forging Counterhegemonic Practices, 1905–1930," in *Anarchism and Syndicalism in the Colonial and Postcolonial World, 1870–1940: The Praxis of National Liberation, Internationalism, and Social Revolution*, ed. idem and Lucien van der Walt (Leiden: Brill, 2010): 227–272.

26. Stein, "De la clase a la política: Victor Rául Haya de la Torre y la institucionalización de la protesta social en los años veinte," in *El APRA: de la ideología*, 23–45, especially 29–31.

27. Ibid., 29–31; Murillo Garaycochea, *Historia del APRA, 1919–1945* (Lima: Editora Atlántida, 1976), 21–22; and David Parker, "Peruvian Politics and the Eight-Hour Day: Rethinking the 1919 General Strike," *Canadian Journal of History/Annales canadiennes d'histoire* 30 (December 1995): 417–438.

28. Betancourt, "Panorama de los movimientos estudiantiles de Latino-América y sus proyecciones," *RA* 20:11–12 (March 15 and March 22, 1930): 75–92.

29. Quoted in Klaiber, "The Popular Universities," 700–703; Haya de la Torre, *Por la emancipación*, 10; and Raúl Chanamé O., "Haya de la Torre y las universidades populares," in *Vida y obra de Victor Raúl Haya de la Torre*, ed. Raúl Chanamé O., Hugo Vallenas M., María Teresa Quiroz (Lima: Instituto Cambio y Desarrollo, 1990): 1–92, especially 29–30.

30. For precursors, see Klaiber, "The Popular Universities," 694–695; Chang-Rodríguez, *La literatura política*, 222; and John Inness, "The Universidad Popular Mexicana," *TA* 30:1 (July 1973): 110–122.

31. Stein, "De la clase," 42.
32. Portantiero, *Estudiantes y política*, 79; Murillo Garaycochea, *Historia del APRA*, quote, 40; and Hirsch, "Peruvian Anarcho-Syndicalism," 242.
33. Quoted in José Chavarría, *José Carlos Mariátegui and the Rise of Modern Peru* (Albuquerque: University of New Mexico Press, 1979), 78.
34. Quoted in Chanamé O., "Haya de la Torre y las universidades populares," 40.
35. Ibid., 33; and Iñigo García-Bryce, *Haya de la Torre and the Pursuit of Power in Twentieth-Century Peru and Latin America* (Chapel Hill: University of North Carolina Press, 2018), 141.
36. Klaiber, "The Popular Universities," 705; and Cornejo Koster, "Crónica del movimiento estudiantil peruano."
37. Stein, "Populism in Peru: APRA, the Formative Years," in *Latin American Populism in Comparative Perspective*, 113–134, quote, 118.
38. Stein, "De la clase," 37.
39. *Claridad* magazines also appeared in Argentina, Chile and Brazil. Miller, *Soviet Relations with Latin America, 1959–1987* (New York: Cambridge University Press, 1989), 26.
40. Ricardo Portocarrero, "Introducción a *Claridad*," in idem, *Claridad. Edición en facsimile* (Lima: Editora Amauta, 1994), 7–18; and Franco, *The Modern Culture of Latin America*, 149–150.
41. Mariátegui, *Los siete ensayos de interpretación de la realidad peruana* (Lima: Biblioteca Amauta, 1928), 89ff.
42. Stein, *Populism in Peru*, 130, 136–137 and 140.
43. García-Bryce, *Haya de la Torre and the Pursuit of Power*, 20.
44. Flores Galindo, *La agonía de Mariátegui*, 8; Melisa Moore, *José Carlos Mariátegui's Unfinished Revolution: Politics, Poetics and Change in 1920s Peru* (Lewisburg, PA: Bucknell University Press, 2014), 32–34; and Charles Walker, "Lima de Mariátegui: Los intelectuales y la capital durante el oncenio," *Socialismo y participación* 35 (September 1986): 71–88.
45. Haya de la Torre, "The Student Movement," 1105.
46. Haya de la Torre, "Las universidades populares de la reforma," in del Mazo, ed., *La reforma universitaria*, II: 42.
47. Basadre, *La vida y la historia: Ensayos sobre personas, lugares, problemas*, 2nd ed. (Lima: Industrial, 1981 [1975]), quote, 273.
48. Alfonso Quiroz, *Corrupt Circles: A History of Unbound Graft in Peru* (Washington, DC, and Baltimore: Woodrow Wilson Center Press and the Johns Hopkins University Press, 2008), 230–231.
49. Stein, "De la clase," 38; Peter Klarén, *Modernization, Dislocation, and Aprismo: Origins of the Peruvian Aprista Party, 1870–1932* (Austin: University of Texas Press, 1973), 102; and Eudocio Ravines, *The Yenan Way* (New York: Charles Scribner's Sons, 1951), 15.
50. Portocarrero, "Introducción de *Claridad*," 14; Chang-Rodríguez, *La literatura política*, 275; Murillo Garaycochea, *Historia del APRA*, 44; and Stein, "Populism in Peru: APRA," 120.

51. Mariátegui, *Seven Interpretive Essays on Peruvian Reality*, trans. Marjory Urquidi (Austin: University of Texas Press, 1971 [1928]), 107.

52. Quoted in Pike, *The Politics of the Miraculous in Peru*, 49.

53. Cornejo Koster, "Crónica del movimiento estudiantil peruano," quote, 31.

54. Quiroz, *Corrupt Circles*, 232–233.

55. Haya de la Torre, "El pensamiento de la nueva generación antiimperialista latinoamericana contra el enemigo de fuera y contra el enemigo de dentro," in idem, *Por la emancipación*, 107–115, quote, 112; and "Cada gobierno latinoamericano es un Virreynato del Imperio Yanqui," in idem, 161–166.

56. Daniel Masterson, *Militarism and Politics in Latin America: Peru from Sánchez Cerro to Sendero Luminoso* (Westport, CT: Greenwood Press, 1991), 31.

57. Bergel, "Nomadismo, proselitista," 43.

58. García-Bryce, *Haya de la Torre and the Pursuit of Power*, 142.

59. Klaiber, "The Popular Universities," 707; Walker, "Lima de Mariátegui," 80; Cornejo Koster, "Crónica del movimiento estudiantil peruano," 32; Alexander, *Prophets of the Revolution*, 75; and Murillo Garaycochea, *Historia del APRA*, 50–51.

60. Quoted in Kushari Dyson, *In Your Blossoming Flower-Garden*, 91. See also Krishna Dutta and Andrew Robinson, *Rabindranath Tagore: The Myriad-Minded Man* (New York: St. Martin's, 1996), 256; and Pita González, *La Unión Latino Americana*, 220.

61. Mariátegui, *Seven Interpretive Essays*, quotes, 107, 109.

62. Melgar Bao, "Cominternismo intelectual: Representaciones, redes y prácticas político-culturales en América Central, 1921–1933," *Revista Complutense de Historia de América* 35 (2009): 135–159, especially 143,

63. Klaiber, "The Popular Universities," 705; and Mariátegui, "La reforma universitaria," (1928), in del Mazo, ed., *La reforma universitaria*, III: 112–118, quote, 112.

64. Franco, *The Modern Culture*, 97 and 99.

65. *El tema de nuestro tiempo* (Madrid: Espasa-Calpe, 1956). The theory has been much debated. See Alan Spitzer, "The Historical Problem of Generations," *American Historical Review* 78:5 (December 1973): 1353–1385; Jean-François Sirinelli, "The Concept of an Intellectual Generation," in *Intellectuals in Twentieth-Century France: Mandarins and Samurais*, ed. Jeremy Jennings (London: Macmillan, 1993), 82–93; and Portantiero, *Estudiantes y política*, 82–83.

66. Quoted in Caballero, *Rómulo Betancourt, político de nación*, 47.

67. José Luis Romero, "University Reform," in *The Latin American University*, 135–146, quote, 141; and González, *La reforma universitaria*, I: 34ff.

68. Portantiero, *Estudiantes y política*, 81–84.

69. De las Nieves Pinillos, ed., *Manuel Ugarte*, prologue; and Miller, *In the Shadow of the State*, 91–92.

70. Craib, *The Cry of the Renegade*, 9–11, quote, 10.

71. Inman, *Problems in Pan Americanism* (New York: George H. Doran, 1925 [1921]), 31.

72. Hobsbawm, "Nationalism and Nationality in Latin America," in *Pour une histoire économique et sociale internationale: mélanges offerts à Paul Bairoch*, ed. Bouda Etemad, Jean Batou, and Thomas David (Geneva: Editions Passé Présent, 1995): 313–323, quote, 313.

73. Miller, *In the Shadow of the State*, 91.

74. Craib, *The Cry of the Renegade*, 35.

75. Unless otherwise indicated, the following discussion of Haya's travels through Mexico and Central America draws on Salisbury, *Anti-Imperialism and International Competition*, 145–151.

76. Although Haya and his followers dated APRA's origin to a conference he gave to the Federation of Mexican Students in 1924 in the Mexican capital, most scholars now agree that the first cell was created in Paris in 1926 or early 1927. Melgar Bao, "Redes del exilio aprista," 255; Bergel, "Nomadismo, proselitista y revolución," 63n1; and Goebel, *Anti-Imperial Metropolis*, 207. For his most cogent statement of principles, see Haya de la Torre, "What is the APRA," *Labour Monthly* 8:12 (December 1926): 756–759.

77. Flores Galindo, *In Search of an Inca: Identity and Utopia in the Andes*, trans. and ed. Carlos Aguirre, Charles Walker, and Willie Hart (New York: Cambridge University Press, 2010 [1986]), 192–193, quote, 192.

78. Nelson Manrique, *¡Usted fue aprista! Bases para una historia crítica del APRA* (Lima: Fondo Editorial Pontificia Universidad Católica, 2009), 74.

79. García-Bryce, *Haya de la Torre and the Pursuit of Power*, 26ff.

80. Stein, "Populism in Peru: APRA," 126–129, quote, 129 and 178; and Pike, *The Politics of the Miraculous*, 7–8.

81. Bergel, "Nomadismo proselitista y revolución," quote, 42; and idem, "La desmesura revolucionaria. Prácticas intelectuales y cultura vitalista en los orígenes del APRA peruano (1921–1930)," in *Historia de los intelectuales*, II: 301–324, quote, 320.

82. Stein, "Populism in Peru: APRA," 125–126, quote, 125.

83. Quoted in Seoane, *Nuestros fines (version taquigráfica de una conferencia prohibida)*. (Lima: F. y E. Rosay, 1931), 22.

84. Geneviève Dorais, "Coming of Age in Exile; Víctor Raúl Haya de la Torre and the Genesis of the American Popular Revolutionary Alliance, 1923–1931," *HAHR* 97:4 (November 2017): 651–679, especially 663–665; and Stein, "Populism in Peru: APRA," 125.

85. Manrique, *¡Usted fue aprista!*, quote, 86.

86. Seoane, *Nuestros fines*, quote, 22.

87. Pike, "The Old and the New APRA in Peru: Myth and Reality," *IAEA* 2 (Autumn 1964): 3–44, quote, 24–25.

88. Bergel, "La desmesura revolucionaria," II: 301–324, quote, 320.

89. Adam Anderle, "Algunos problemas de la evolución del pensamiento antimperialista en Cuba entre las dos guerras mundiales: Comunistas y Apristas," *Acta Universitatis Szegediensis de Attila József Nominatae: Acta Histórica* 2 (1975): 3–80, especially 14.

90. Bergel, "La desmesura revolucionaria," 307; Klaiber, "The Popular Universities," 705; Salisbury, "The Middle American Exile of Víctor Raúl Haya de la Torre," *TA* 40:1 (July 1983): 1–15, especially 4; Pakkasvirta, "Víctor Raúl Haya de la Torre en Centroamérica: ¿la primera y última fase del aprismo internacional?" *Revista de Historia* 44 (July–December 2001): 1–9, especially 2; and Murillo Garaycochea, *Historia del APRA*, 53.

91. Klarén, *Modernization, Dislocation*, 116.

92. Bergel, "Manuel Seoane y Luis Heysen: Avatares del estilo reformista peruano en la Argentina de los viente," *Allpanchis* 68 (2006): 141–174, especially 156–157.

93. Sánchez, *Haya de la Torre y El APRA*, 203–223.

94. Publication of the manuscript was delayed for seven years. Many of its ideas were expressed in his lectures and columns during this earlier period, however. Haya de la Torre, *El antiimperialismo y el APRA*, 4th ed. (Lima: Fondo Editorial del Congreso del Peru, 2010 [1935]).

95. Basadre, "Introduction," to Mariátegui, *Seven Interpretive* Essays, quotes, xxii.

96. Adys Cupull, *Julio Antonio Mella en los mexicanos* (Mexico City: Ediciones El Caballito, 1983), 15, 37.

97. Christine Hatzky, *Julio Antonio Mella (1903–1929): Una biografía*, trans. Jorge Luis Acanda (Santiago de Cuba: Editorial Oriente, 2008 [2004]), 313–316.

98. Ibid., 211; and Mella, "¿Qué es el ARPA?," in *J. A. Mella: Documentos y artículos*, ed. Instituto de Historia del Movimiento Comunista y la Revolución Socialista de Cuba (Havana: Editorial de Ciencias Sociales, Instituto Cubano del Libro, 1975), 10–11 and 370–403.

99. Quoted in Alexander, *Prophets of the Revolution*, 81.

100. Hatzky, *Julio Antonio Mella (1903–1929)*, 169–170; Goebel, *Anti-Imperial Metropolis*, 207ff; and Kersffeld, "Latinoamericanos en el Congreso Antiimperialista de 1927: Afinidades, disensos y rupturas," *Journal of Iberian and Latin American Research* 16:2 (December 2010): 151–163, especially 156–159.

101. Quoted in Pakkasvirta, *Un continente*, 94.

102. Flores Galindo, "Aprismo y comunismo, 1930–1931," *Cuadernos socialistas* 2 (May 1979): 32–38; and Moore, *José Carlos Mariátegui's Unfinished Revolution*, 11.

103. For Vasconcelos's recollections of the conference, see his *El desastre: tercera parte de Ulises criollo*, 4th ed. (Mexico City: Ediciones Botas, 1938), 743ff. On Haya's eclecticism, see Pike, "The Old and the New APRA," 18–20.

104. Matthew Worley, "Courting Disaster? The Communist International in the Third Period," in *In Search of Revolution: International Communist Parties in the Third Period*, ed. idem (London: Taurus, 2004), 1–18; and Alexander, *Trotskyism in Latin America* (Stanford: Hoover Institution Press, 1973), 6.

105. Hatzky, *Julio Antonio Mella (1903–1929)*, 36; and Westad, *The Global Cold War*, 53; and Angell, "The Left in Latin America," 79, 82.

106. Flores Galindo, *In Search of an Inca*, 185, 193, quote, 185.

107. Mariátegui also ran afoul of the defenders of the new orthodoxy. Miller, *In the Shadow of the State*, 120–121; Flores Galindo, *La agonía de Mariátegui*, 45–48; and Pike, *The Politics of the Miraculous*, quote, 67.

108. Quoted in Klarén, *Modernization, Dislocation*, 112.

109. Ibid., 113n26.

110. Anderle, "Algunos problemas, 12.

111. Tomás Straka, "*Cuadernos Americanos* y la democracia venezolana: Una relación de setenta años." *CA* 36:2, no. 140 (April–June 2012): 11–36, especially 19.

112. Haya de la Torre, "La protesta de Haya de la Torre," and "Una rectificación y una denuncia," *RA 17:13* (October 6, 1928); Deambrosis Martins, "La expulsion"; and Pakkasvirta, "Víctor Raúl Haya de la Torre," 17.

113. Taracena Arriola, "El APRA, Haya de la Torre y la crisis del liberalismo guatemalteco en 1926–1929," *Revista de Historia* 25 (1992): 9–25; and Sánchez, *Haya de la Torre y El APRA*, 220.

114. Gould and Aldo Lauria-Santiago, *To Rise in Darkness: Revolution, Repression, and Memory in El Salvador, 1920–1932* (Durham: Duke University Press, 2008), quote, 50.

115. Haya de la Torre, "Una rectificación y una denuncia"; and Sánchez, *Haya de la Torre y El APRA*, 223.

116. Ana María Botey and Rodolfo Cisneros, *La crisis de 1929 y la fundación del Partido Comunista de Costa Rica* (San José: Editorial Costa Rica, 1984), 65.

117. Both quoted in García Carrillo, *El hombre del Repertorio Americano*, 97, 98.

118. Gómez, *Rómulo Betancourt y el Partido Comunista*, 26–28; García Carrillo, *El hombre del Repertorio Americano*, 98; and Pakkasvirta, "Víctor Raúl Haya de la Torre," 18.

119. "La protesta de Haya de la Torre," *RA* 17:11 (September 7, 1928). See also Taracena Arriola, "El primer Partido Comunista de Guatemala (1922–1932)," *Araucaría de Chile* 27 (1984): 71–91, especially 80.

120. Haya de la Torre, *El antiimperialismo y el APRA*, 101.

121. Haya de la Torre, "La protesta de Haya de la Torre," *RA* 17:11 (September 7, 1928).

122. Quoted in Alexander, *Prophets of Revolution*, 277.

123. *RA* 14:15 (April 23, 1927).

124. During his Parisian exile, Asturias was a tireless advocate for the popular university. For example, "El más alto deber de los guatemaltecos," "Un llamamiento a los obreros de Guatemala," "A los alumnus de la Universidad Popular de Guatemala," and "Las primeras realizaciones," in idem, *Paris, 1924–1933. Periodismo y creación literaria*, ed. Amos Segala (Paris: Colección Archivos, 1988), 18–19, 19–20, 20–22, and 75–76.

125. *RA* 18:7 (February 6, 1929); Franco, *The Modern Culture of Latin America*, 125; and Weiss, *The Lights of Home*, 34–36.

126. Stephen Henighan, "Two Paths to the Boom: Carpentier, Asturias, and the Performative Spirit," *Modern Language Review* 94:4 (October 1999): 1009–

1024, quote, 1016–1017. See also Taracena Arriola, "Miguel Ángel Asturias y la búsqueda del 'alma nacional' Guatemalteca. Itinerario político, 1920–1933," in Asturias, *Paris, 1924–1933,* 679–708; and Georges Pillement, "El París que Asturias ha visto y vivido," in Asturias, *Paris, 1924–1933,* 743–757, especially 744.

127. Henighan, *Assuming the Light: The Parisian Literary Apprenticeship of Miguel Ángel Asturias* (London: Legenda, European Humanities Research Centre, University of Oxford, 1999), 152–153; and John Beverley and Marc Zimmerman, *Literature and Politics in the Central American Revolutions* (Austin: University of Texas Press, 1990), 20.

128. See Flores Galindo, "Aprismo y comunismo," 35ff; and Portocarrero, "Introducción a *Claridad,*" 11.

129. Barry Carr, "Radicals, Revolutionaries and Exiles: Mexico City in the 1920s," *Berkeley Review of Latin American Studies* (Fall 2010): 26–30, especially 27.

130. Haya de la Torre, *El antiimperialismo y el APRA,* 146.

131. Letter, Haya de la Torre to Turcios, February 5, 1928, and "Concerning Nicaragua, There's Only One Possibility: To Assist Them with Fighters and Money," in Haya de la Torre, *¿A donde va a Indoamérica?* 265–269, quote, 268. See also Cerdas Cruz, *Sandino, el APRA,* 59.

132. Dospital, *Siempre más allá . . .,* 51; and Taracena Arriola, "Aporte documental," 264ff.

133. Quoted in Dospital, *Siempre más allá . . .,* 58.

134. Salisbury, *Anti-Imperialism and International Competition,* 149–150.

135. Haya de la Torre, "Carta al Presidente de Panama," and "Opiniones de un hombre de 30 años," in *¿A donde va a Indoamérica?* 65–69, and 81–83; and Alexander, *Prophets of the Revolution,* 81–82.

136. Deambrosis Martins, "La expulsión de Haya de la Torre de Guatemala," in *¿A donde va a Indoamérica?* 275–280.

137. Salisbury, "The Middle American Exile," 15.

138. Stein, "De la clase," 40; and Masterson, *Militarism and Politics,* 41ff.

139. García-Bryce, *Haya de la Torre and the Pursuit of Power,* 45–47.

Chapter Three. The Generation of 1928

Epigraph: Roa, "Rómulo Betancourt: El Combatiente," in *Rómulo Betancourt: pensamiento y acción,* ed. Betancourt (Mexico City: Beatriz de Silva, 1951), 51–72, quote, 60.

1. Betancourt, *Venezuela, Oil and Politics,* trans. Everett Bauman (Boston: Houghton Mifflin, 1979 [1956]), 42–44, and quote, 46.

2. Quoted in John Martz, *Acción Democrática: Evolution of a Modern Political Party in Venezuela* (Princeton: Princeton University Press, 1966), 23.

3. Ameringer, *The Democratic Left in Exile,* 23; and William Krehm, *Democracies and Tyrannies of the Caribbean* (Westport, CT: Lawrence Hill, 1984 [1948]). 216.

4. Óscar Sambrano Urdaneta, "Introducción," in Miguel Otero Silva, *La fiebre*, 6th ed. (Caracas: Biblioteca Popular Venezolana, 1961 [1939]).

5. *The Magical State: Nature, Money, and Modernity in Venezuela* (Chicago: University of Chicago Press, 1998), 91; and Caballero, *Rómulo Betancourt, político de nación*, 67–68.

6. Quoted in Rama, *The Lettered City*, 92.

7. Suárez Figueroa, "El joven Betancourt," 11, 19, 23.

8. Eduardo Schaposnik, *La democratización de las Fuerzas Armadas Venezolanas* (Caracas: Fundación Gonzalo Barrios, 1985), 23; Betancourt, *Venezuela: Política y petroleo*, 3rd ed. (Barcelona: Editorial Seix Barral [1956] 1979), 89; and Caballero, *Rómulo Betancourt, político de nación*, 74.

9. Villalba, "La Federación de Estudiantes y la reforma universitaria (1936)," in *Estudiantes y política en América Latina*, 278–282, especially 280–281; Miguel Tinker Salas, *Venezuela: What Everyone Needs to Know* (New York: Oxford University Press, 2015), 70–71; and Suárez Figueroa, El joven Betancourt," 13.

10. Tinker Salas, *Venezuela: What Everyone Needs to Know*, 71.

11. María de Lourdes Acedo and Carmen Nones Mendoza, *La generación del 1928 (estudio de una élite política)* (Barcelona: Talleres de Ediciones Ariel, 1967), 90–91.

12. Capriles, *Memorias de la inconformidad*, 2nd ed. (La Victoria, Venezuela: Grabados Nacionales, 1973 [1973]), 152–153.

13. Otero Silva, *La fiebre*, 86; and Judith Ewell, *Venezuela: A Century of Change* (Stanford: Stanford University Press, 1984), 86.

14. Germán Carrera Damas, *Rómulo histórico: La personalidad histórica de Rómulo Betancourt vista en la instauración de la república popular representativa y en la genesis de la democracia moderna de Venezuela* (Caracas: Editorial Alfa, 2013), 71, 78; "La semana del estudiante y sus proyecciones," in *Rómulo Betancourt: Semblanza de un político popular*, ed. Escritores de Venezuela (Caracas: Ediciones Caribe, 1948), 19–23.

15. Rosalba Méndez, "¿Un período histórico?" in *Juan Vicente Gómez y su época*, ed. Elías Pino Iturrieta (Caracas: Monte Avila, 1988), 25–49, especially 28; and Acedo de Sucre and Nones Mendoza, *La generación de 1928*, 92ff.

16. Quoted in Carrera Damas, *Rómulo histórico*, 90.

17. Quoted in Ewell, *The Indictment of a Dictator: The Extradition and Trial of Marcos Pérez Jiménez* (College Station: Texas A&M University Press, 1981), 13.

18. Betancourt, *Hombres y villanos* (Caracas: Grijalbo, 1987), 131.

19. Aragorn Miller, *Precarious Paths to Freedom: The United States, Venezuela and the Latin American Cold War* (Albuquerque: University of New Mexico Press, 2016), 17.

20. Alexander, *Prophets of the Revolution*, 109; and Pedro Pereira, *En la prisión: Los estudiantes de 1928* (Caracas: Ávila Gráfica, 1952).

21. Betancourt, "El sentido y la orientación del movimiento universitario en Venezuela de 1928: Conforme a uno de sus protagonistas," in *Programas políticos*

venezolanos en la primera mitad del Siglo XIX, ed. Suárez Figueroa, 2 vols. (Caracas: Universidad Católica Andrés Bello, 1977), I: 59–71, especially 60.

22. A hectare equals 2.47 acres.

23. Betancourt and Otero Silva, *En las huellas de la pezuña* (Santo Domingo, 1929); and Sosa y Eloi Lengrand, *Del garibaldismo estudiantil a la izquierda criolla: Los orígenes marxistas del proyecto de A. D. (1928–1935)* (Caracas: Ediciones Centauro, 1981), 43, 57, 105. On Gómez's monopolistic practices, Doug Yarrington, "Political Transition in an Age of Extremes: Venezuela in the 1930s," in *The Great Depression in Latin America,* 160–187, quote, 162–163; and Luis Troconis Guerrero, *La cuestión agraria en la historia nacional* (San Cristóbal, Venezuela, 1966), 139–140.

24. Betancourt, "El sentido y la orientación," in *Programas políticos,* quote, 69.

25. Nicolás Silfa, *Guerra, traición y exilio,* 3 vols. (Barcelona: Manuel Girona, 1981), II: 111.

26. For example, "Lista de algunos de las víctimas del despotismo venezolano: Asesinados en las mazmorras de La Rotunda, Caracas"; and "Noticia sobre algunos de los movimientos revolucionarios habidos en Venezuela contra el régimen de Juan Vicente Gómez," *RA* August 15, 1931.

27. *RA* September 15, September 22, and October 6, 1928.

28. Thomas Rourke, *Gómez: Tyrant of the Andes* (New York: William Morrow, 1936), 158–159.

29. Muñoz Marín, "Tyranny and Torture in Venezuela," *Nation* 120:3119 (April 15, 1925): 412–414, quote, 412.

30. Suárez Betancourt, "El joven Betancourt," 30.

31. Santiago Castro Ventura, *Trujillo vs. Betancourt: ¡Rivalidad perpetua!* (Santo Domingo: Editora Manatí, 2008), 21–31; Alexander, *Rómulo Betancourt and the Transformation of Venezuela,* 52–53; and Julio Portillo, *Venezuela-República Dominicana: relaciones diplomáticas, 1844–1984* (Caracas: Editorial Ex Libris, 1991), quote, 179.

32. Romero, *Venezuela en defensa de la democracia,* quote, 65–66.

33. "Manifesto: Protesta por la desaparición en Cuba de Francisco Laguado Jaime," in *El comienzo del debate socialista: El pensamiento político venezolano del Siglo XX: Documentos para su estudio,* ed. Ramón Velásquez, 12 vols. (Caracas: Congreso de la República, 1983), XII: 285–287; Horacio Ferrer, *Con el rifle al hombro* (Havana: El Siglo XX, 1950), 261–262; and Rolando Rodríguez García, "El pensamiento y la acción de Julio Antonio Mella," *Revista Bimestre Cubana* 9 (1998): 147–155, especially 147.

34. The timing of *Venezuela: Política y petróleo*'s publication in 1956 probably explains Betancourt's reluctance to acknowledge his leftist roots. At that moment, again in exile, he was seeking to obtain U.S. support for AD's campaign to depose Pérez Jiménez.

35. Quoted in Suárez Figueroa, "El joven Betancourt," 103–104.

36. Ibid., quote, 80n157.

37. Ibid., 44ff. On dissimulation, see Caballero, *Rómulo Betancourt, político de nación*, 132.

38. Caballero, *Rómulo Betancourt, político de nación*, 100.

39. Ibid., 101–104.

40. Philip Taylor, Jr., *The Venezuelan golpe de estado of 1958: The Fall of Marcos Pérez Jiménez* (Washington, DC: Institute for the Comparative Study of Political Systems, 1968), 27; Daniel Hellinger, *Venezuela: Tarnished Democracy* (Boulder: Westview Press, 1991), 50–51; and Steve Ellner, "Venezuela," in *Latin America between the Second World War and the Cold War, 1944–1948*, ed. Bethell and Roxborough (New York: Cambridge University Press, 1992), 147–169, especially 154.

41. Sosa and Lengrand, *Del garibaldismo estudiantil*, 16ff.

42. Caballero, "El hombre Gómez: Un retrato enemigo," in *Juan Vicente Gómez y su época*, 11–23, quote, 23.

43. Sosa and Lengrand, *Del garibaldismo estudiantil*, 120–125; and Suárez Figueroa, "El joven Betancourt," 53–54.

44. Arturo Sosa, "Prólogo," *El comienzo del debate socialista*, XII: xxv–xl.

45. Steven Schwartzberg, "Rómulo Betancourt: From a Communist Anti-Imperialist to a Social Democrat with U.S, Support," *JLAS* 29:3 (October 1997): 613–665, especially 618–625.

46. Arturo Gómez, *Rómulo Betancourt y el Partido Comunista de Costa Rica, 1931–1935* (Caracas: Fondo Editorial de Humanidades y Educación, Universidad Central de Venezuela, 1985), 32, 40; idem, *Rómulo Betancourt contra la dictadura de Juan Vicente Gómez: Repertorio Americano, Costa Rica* (Caracas: Ediciones Centauro, 1982), 12–13 and 63; and Caballero, *Rómulo Betancourt, político de nación*, 128.

47. Carrera Damas, *Rómulo histórico*, 82–86. In a series of interviews and in correspondence with Alexander, Betancourt denied that he ever supported Stalin and the Soviet Union while a member of the Costa Rican Communist Party. Alexander, *Venezuela's Voice for Democracy: Conversations and Correspondence with Rómulo Betancourt* (New York: Praeger, 1990), 128ff.

48. "Jornada de apreciación de la vida y obra de Rómulo Betancourt," Portuguesa State, Venezuela, February 20–21, 1988, Section VII, Series 1, Archivo Individuo Especial, Cartapacio #76, FLMM; and Coronil Hartmann, *Rómulo Betancourt: La vida como pedagogía*.

49. Gómez, *Rómulo Betancourt y el Partido Comunista de Costa Rica*, 142, 173.

50. Luis Chesney Lawrence, "La cultura en los programas políticos venezolanos: Mariano Picón Salas y Rómulo Betancourt," *Anales de la Universidad Metropolitana* 5:1 (2005), 143–158, quote, 151.

51. Otilio Ulate, *Hacia donde lleva a Costa Rica El Señor Presidente Figueres? Replica documentada de D. Otilio Ulate a las imputaciones del Señor Figueres y clarificación de responsabilidades ante el juicio de los costarricenses* (San José: n.p., 1955), 12–13.

52. Gómez, *Rómulo Betancourt y el Partido Comunista de Costa Rica*, 11; and Iván Molina, "Los primeros años de *Trabajo*, el periódico del Partido Comunista de Costa Rica," *Amnis: Revue de civilisation contemporaine Europe/Amériques* 4 (2004): 137–50. https://journals.openedition.org/amnis/736. Accessed February 20, 2019.

53. The letter is reprinted in Ulate, *Hacia donde lleva*, 14.

54. Mirela Quero de Trinca, "Rómulo Betancourt: Una vida de exilio," *Tiempo y espacio* 49 (January–June 2008), 75–88; Gómez, *Rómulo Betancourt y el Partido Comunista de Costa Rica*, quote, 105; and Sosa and Lengrand, *Del garibaldismo estudiantil*, 149.

55. Roa, "Rómulo Betancourt, el combatiente," quote, 59.

56. Quoted in Ameringer, *The Democratic Left in Exile*, 26.

57. José Antonio Catalá and Domingo Alberto Rangel, *Gustavo Machado: Un caudillo prestado al comunismo* (Caracas: El Centauro, 2001), 74; and Caballero, *Latin America and the Comintern, 1919–1943* (Cambridge: Cambridge University Press, 1986), 159.

58. Catalá and Rangel, *Gustavo Machado*, 76, 81.

59. Lino Morán Beltrán, Lorena Velásquez, and Vileana Meleán, "Gustavo Machado y los orígenes del marxismo en Venezuela" (March 3, 2006), 6, 8. http://www.google.com/search?client=safari&rls=en&q=C:%5CSciELO%5Cserial%5Crf%5Cn49%5Cbody%5Cart_02.htm&ie=UTF-8&oe=UTF-8. Accessed 3/28/2013.

60. Quoted in Carr, "Radicals, Revolutionaries and Exiles," 27.

61. McBeth, *Dictatorship and Politics*, 213, quote, 162; and Hatzky, *Julio Antonio Mella (1903–1929)*, 301.

62. Hellinger, *Venezuela: Tarnished Democracy*, 49; Suárez Figueroa, "El joven Betancourt," 40; and Melgar Bao, "El exilio venezolano en México," *Memoria* 110 (April 1998): 37–45.

63. Machado, "Los estudiantes venezolanos y la revolución," in *El comienzo del debate socialista*, XII: 209–216.

64. Sandino to the U.S. Section of the All-America Anti-Imperialist League, May 20, 1928, in Ramírez, ed., *Sandino: The Testimony*, 200–201.

65. Quoted in Morán Beltrán et al., "Gustavo Machado," 9.

66. Amador, *Nicaragua y Sandino*, 53.

67. Quoted in Cerdas Cruz, *Sandino, el APRA*, 40n51. Taracena Arriola claims that Machado hid his communist affiliation from Sandino. See "Aporte documental," 264.

68. Amador, *Nicaragua y Sandino*, 49.

69. Cerdas Cruz, *Sandino, el APRA*, 95.

70. Tinker Salas, *Venezuela: What Everyone Needs*, 74; and René Hartmann de Betancourt, *Rómulo y yo: Instantes de la democracia venezolana* (Barcelona: Ediciones Grijalbo, 1984), 102–103.

71. Caballero, *Rómulo Betancourt, político de nación*, 142.

72. Ramón Hernández and Roberto Giusti, eds., *Carlos Andrés Pérez: memorias proscritas* (Caracas: Los Libros de El Nacional, 2006), 15.

73. Rabe, *The Road to OPEC: United States Relations with Venezuela, 1919–1976* (Austin: University of Texas Press, 1982), 46–47; Caballero, *Rómulo Betancourt, político de nación*, 155; and Silvia Mijares, *Organizaciones políticas de 1936: su importancia en la socialización política del venezolano* (Caracas: Academia Nacional de la Historia, 1980), 63.

74. Elisabeth J. Freidman, *Unfinished Transitions: Women and the Gendered Development of Democracy in Venezuela, 1936–1996* (University Park: Pennsylvania State University Press, 2000), chapter 2.

75. Ewell, *Venezuela: A Century*, quote, 76, and 90.

76. Ibid., quote, 84–85.

77. Caballero, *Rómulo Betancourt, político de nación*, 165–167; and Hartmann, *Rómulo y yo*, 107.

78. *El libro rojo: La verdad de las actividades comunistas en Venezuela* (Caracas: Centauro, 1936).

79. Hellinger, *Venezuela: Tarnished Democracy*, 51; Coronil, *The Magical State*, 94ff; Escritores de Venezuela, *Rómulo Betancourt: Semblanza de un político*, 119–129; Hartmann, *Rómulo y yo*, 110; and Mijares, *Organizaciones políticas*, 78.

80. Quero de Trinca, "Rómulo Betancourt," 7.

81. Ellner, "Factionalism in the Venezuelan Communist Movement, 1937–1948," *Science and Society* 45:1 (Spring 1981): 52–70, especially 53–54; and Hernández and Giusti, *Carlos Andrés Pérez: memorias proscritas*, 17.

82. Quero de Trinca, "Rómulo Betancourt"; and Caballero, *Rómulo Betancourt, político de nación*, 181.

83. Alexander, *Venezuela's Voice for Democracy*, 130.

84. Section V, Series 2, Governor of Puerto Rico, 1949–1964, Correspondencia Particular, Folder 54, FLMM.

85. Terry Karl, "Petroleum and Political Pacts: The Transition to Democracy in Venezuela," Working Papers, #107, 1982, Wilson Center, Latin American Program, Washington, DC, 5–6.

86. Caballero, *Rómulo Betancourt, político de nación*, 204.

87. Ibid.

88. Juan Carlos Rey, *Personalismo o liderazgo democrático: El caso de Rómulo Betancourt* (Caracas: Fundación Rómulo Betancourt 2008), 25–26; and Levine, "Venezuela since 1958: The Consolidation of Democratic Politics," in *The Breakdown of Democratic Regimes: Latin America*, ed. Juan Linz and Alfred Stepan (Baltimore: The Johns Hopkins University Press, 1978): 82–108, especially 88.

89. Stanley Serxner, *Acción Democrática of Venezuela: Its Origin and Development* (Gainesville: University of Florida Press, 1959), quote, 4n13.

90. Quoted in Martz, "The Generation of '28,' " 32.

91. Méndez, "¿Un período histórico?" in *Juan Vicente Gómez*, 43.

92. Portantiero, *Estudiantes y política*, 14.

Chapter Four. Polestar

Epigraph: Quoted in Roa, *Bufa subversiva*, xxxix.

1. Louis Pérez, Jr., *Cuba Under the Platt Amendment* (Pittsburgh: University of Pittsburgh Press, 1986), 195; Leland Jenks, *Our Cuban Colony: A Study in Sugar* (New York: Vanguard Press, 1928); Alan Dye and Richard Sicotte, "U.S.-Cuban Trade Cooperation and its Unraveling," *Business and Economic History* 28:2 (Winter 1999): 20–31; Dye, *Cuban Sugar in the Age of Mass Production* (Stanford: Stanford University Press, 1998), 2, 7; Steven Palmer, José Antonio Piqueras, and Amparo Sánchez Cobos, "Introduction: Revisiting Cuba's First Republic," in *State of Ambiguity: Civic Life and Culture in Cuba's First Republic*, ed. idem (Durham: Duke University Press, 2014): 1–21, especially 4; and " 'O,' Cuba and the United States," *FA* (January 1, 1927): 231–244, especially 232–234.

2. Pérez, Jr., *On Becoming Cuban: Identity, Nationality, and Culture* (Chapel Hill: University of North Carolina Press, 1999); idem, *Cuba in the American Imagination: Metaphor and the Imperial Ethos* (Chapel Hill: University of North Carolina Press, 2008), quote, 212; and Julio Le Riverend, *La República: dependencia y revolución* (Havana: Instituto del Libro, 1969), 229.

3. Whitney, *State and Revolution in Cuba*, quote, 22.

4. Quoted in Pérez, Jr., *The Structure of Cuban History: Meanings and Purposes of the Past* (Chapel Hill: University of North Carolina Press, 2013), 122.

5. Frank Argote-Freyre, *Fulgencio Batista: From Revolutionary to Strongman* (New Brunswick: Rutgers University Press, 2006), 26.

6. Julio García Oliveras, *José Antonio Echeverría: la lucha contra Batista*, 2nd ed. (Havana: Editoral Política, 2001 [1979]), 11.

7. Dopico, "The 3:10 to Yuma," in *Anti-Americanism*, ed. Andrew Ross and Kristin Ross (New York: New York University Press, 2004): 47–68, quote, 49.

8. Russell Porter, " 'Cuba Libre': The New Challenge," *NYT*, September 17, 1933.

9. Gail Hanson, "Ordered Liberty: Sumner Welles and the Crowder-Welles Connection in the Caribbean," *DH* 18:3 (1994): 311–332, especially 320.

10. Philip Wright, *The Cuban Situation and Our Treaty Relations* (Washington, DC: Brookings Institution, 1931), 42.

11. Ferrell, *The Presidency of Calvin Coolidge*, 123; Pérez, Jr., *Cuba Under the Platt Amendment*, 190–192, 207, and 209; and León Primelles, *Crónica cubana, 1919–1922: Menocal y la Liga Nacional, Zayas y Crowder, fin de la Danza de los Millones y reajuste* (Havana: Editorial Lex, 1958), 120. The political cartoon is depicted in Hanson, "Ordered Liberty," 324.

12. Quoted in Pérez, Jr., *Cuba and the United States: Ties of Singular Intimacy*, 3rd ed. (Athens: University of Georgia Press, 2003 [1990]), 168. For a blistering critique of Crowder's tenure, see Emilio Roig de Leuchsenring, *Historia de la enmienda Platt: Una interpretación de la realidad cubana*, 2 vols. (Havana: Cultural, 1935): I: 274–280.

13. Beals, *The Crime of Cuba* (Philadelphia: J. P. Lippincott, 1934), 230–231.

14. Quoted in Jenks, *Our Cuban Colony*, 238.

15. Merle Curti and Kendall Birr, *Prelude to Point Four: American Technical Missions Overseas, 1838–1938* (Madison: University of Wisconsin Press, 1954), 109.

16. Quoted in Robert Freeman Smith, *The United States and Cuba: Business and Diplomacy, 1917–1960* (New York: Bookman Associates, 1960), 103.

17. "Manifesto de los estudiantes de derecho contra el nombramiento de Crowder, Doctor Honoris Causa de la Universidad," in *Las luchas estudiantiles universitarias, 1923–1934*, ed. Olga Cabrera and Carmen Almodóvar (Havana: Editorial de Ciencias Sociales, 1975), 65–68; Jaime Suchlicki, *University Students and Revolution in Cuba, 1920–1968* (Coral Gables: University of Miami Press, 1969), 20; and David Lockmiller, *Enoch H. Crowder: Soldier, Lawyer, and Statesman* (Columbia: University of Missouri Press, 1975), 223.

18. José Tabares del Real, *La revolución del 30: Sus dos últimos años* (Havana: Editorial de Arte y Literatura, 1971), 99; and Roa, *Bufa subversiva*, lviii.

19. Primelles, *Crónica Cubana, 1919–1922*, 568–569.

20. Luis Aguilar, *Cuba 1933: Prologue to Revolution* (Ithaca: Cornell University Press, 1972), 72–73; and Roa, *Retorno a la alborada* (Havana: Imprimex, 1963), I: 235.

21. Alejandro De la Fuente, *A Nation for All: Race, Inequality and Politics in Twentieth-Century Cuba* (Chapel Hill: University of North Carolina Press, 2001), 147.

22. K. Lynn Stoner, *From the House to the Streets: The Cuban Women's Movement for Legal Reform, 1898–1940* (Durham: Duke University Press, 1991), 133.

23. Jules Benjamin, "The *Machadato* and Cuban Nationalism, 1928–1932," *HAHR* 55:1 (February 1975): 66–91, especially 76; Cairo, *El Grupo Minorista y su tiempo* (Havana: Editorial de Ciencias Sociales, 1978); Sheldon Liss, *Roots of Revolution: Radical Thought in Cuba* (Lincoln: University of Nebraska Press, 1987), 65, quote, 82; Harry Swan, "The 1920s: A Decade of Intellectual Change in Cuba," *Review/Revista Interamericana* 82:2 (Summer 1978): 275–288.

24. Quoted in Carlos Ripoll, *La generación del 23 en Cuba: Y otros apuntes sobre el vanguardismo* (New York: Las Americas Publishing, 1968), 34.

25. Pablo de la Torriente Brau, *Pluma en ristre*, ed. Roa (Havana: Ministerio de Educación, Dirección de Cultura, 1949), xlii.

26. Ripoll, *La generación del 23*, 111.

27. Roa, "Adios al maestro," in idem, *La revolución del 30 se fue a bolina* (Havana: Instituto del Libro, 1969), 89–97, quote, 91.

28. Hugh Thomas, *Cuba: The Pursuit of Freedom* (New York: Harper & Row, 1971), 592; and Lionel Soto, *La revolución del 33*, 3 vols. (Havana: Editorial Pueblo y Educación, 1985): I: 344, 364.

29. The scholarship on Mella is prodigious. The most dispassionate and well-researched biography is Hatzky, *Julio Antonio Mella (1903–1929)*, 10, 62.

30. Pérez, Jr., *Cuba Under the Platt Amendment*, 235.

31. Instituto, *J. A. Mella*, 5; and Soto, *La revolución del 33*, I: 120.

32. Thomas, *Cuba: The Pursuit of Freedom*, 565; Suchlicki, *University Students*, 21; and David Raby, "The Cuban Pre-Revolution of 1933: An Analysis," Occasional Papers, Institute of Latin American Studies, University of Glasgow 18 (1975), quote, 11.

33. Hatzky, *Julio Antonio Mella (1903–1929)*, 115–116; and Cairo, ed., *Mella: 100 años*, I: 55–56.

34. Soto, *La revolución del 33*, I: 106ff; Liss, *Roots of Revolution*, 84; Le Riverend, *La República*, 212–213; and George Howland Cox, "Machado, Welles and the Cuban Crisis," in *The Caribbean Area*, ed. A. Curtis Wilgus (Washington, DC: George Washington University Press, 1934): 195–209, especially 202.

35. Aguilar, *Cuba 1933*, 74.

36. Portantiero, *Estudiantes y política*, 91.

37. Guerra, "The Struggle to Redefine Martí and 'Cuba Libre' in the 1920s," in *The Cuban Republic and José Martí*, ed. Mauricio Font and Quiroz (Lanham, MD: Lexington, 2006): 34–50, especially 41.

38. "Víctor Raúl Haya de la Torre," in Instituto, *J. A. Mella*, 76–77; Whitney, *State and Revolution*, 45–47; and Boris Goldenberg, "The Rise and Fall of a Party: The Cuban CP (1925–1959)," *Problems in Communism* 61 (July–August 1970): 61–80, especially 64.

39. Hatzky, *Julio Antonio Mella (1903–1929)*, 123.

40. Miller, *In the Shadow of the State*, 115.

41. Sánchez, *Haya de la Torre y El APRA*, quote, 41.

42. "Aspectos del problema social en el Perú," in Haya de la Torre, *Por la emancipación*, 39–47, especially 46–47.

43. "Mensaje a la Universidad Popular José Martí," in Ibid., 49–54; Alexander, *Prophets of the Revolution*, 79; Melgar Bao, "Militancia Aprista en el Caribe: La sección Cuba," *CA* 7:37 (January–March): 208–226, especially 215; and García-Bryce, *Haya de la Torre*, 21–22.

44. Mella, "Víctor Raúl Haya de la Torre," *Juventud* 2–3 (November–December 1923), 11. For the Peruvian diplomat's reaction, see Anderle, "Algunos problemas," 7.

45. Bergel and Martínez Mazzola, "América Latina como práctica," 131.

46. Roa, "José Ingenieros," in *15 años después*, ed. idem (Havana: Editorial Librería Selecta, 1959), 408–420, especially 408.

47. Hatzky, *Julio Antonio Mella (1903–1928)*, 34, 131–133.

48. Whitney, *State and Revolution*, 39, 50; Melgar Bao, "La recepción del orientalismo antiimperialista en América Latina," *CA* 109 (2005): 11–41; idem, "El exilio venezolano," 41; and Hatzky, *Julio Antonio Mella (1903–1929)*, 171–172.

49. Hilda Tisco Lindley, "De los orígenes del APRA en Cuba: El testimonio de Enrique de la Osa," *CA* 7:37 (January–February 1993): 198–207, especially 204–205; de la Osa, *Visión y pasión de Raúl Roa* (Havana: Editorial de Ciencias Sociales, 1988), 15; and Melgar Bao, "Militancia Aprista," 218–219.

50. Roa, *Retorno a la alborada*, quote, I: 115; and Taibo II, *Tony Guiteras*, 378–379.
51. Goldenberg, "The Rise and Fall of a Party," 65.
52. Hatzky, *Julio Antonio Mella (1903–1929)*, 136.
53. Mella, "Machado: Mussolini tropical," in Instituto, *J. A. Mella*, 169–170; and Roa, *Retorno a la alborada*, I: 234, II: 68.
54. Quoted in Pérez, Jr., *The Structure of Cuban History*, 165.
55. Hatzky, *Julio Antonio Mella* (1903–1929), 144.
56. Alejandra Bronfman, *Measures of Equality: Social Science, Citizenship, and Race in Cuba, 1902–1940* (Chapel Hill: University of North Carolina Press, 2004), 201n78.
57. Stoner, *From the House to the Street*, 115, 119–120.
58. Schoultz, *That Infernal Little Cuban Republic: The United States and the Cuban Revolution* (Chapel Hill: University of North Carolina Press, 2009), quotes, 30, 31.
59. Beals, *Glass Houses*, 309–310; Juan Pérez de la Riva et al., *La república colonial*, 2 vols. (Havana: Editorial de Ciencias Sociales, 1975–1979), II: 352; and Pérez, Jr., "In Defense of Hegemony: Sumner Welles and the Cuban Revolution of 1933," in *Ambassadors in Foreign Policy: The Influence of Individuals on U.S.-Latin American Policy*, ed. C. Neale Ronning and Albert Vannucci (New York: Praeger, 1987), 28–48, especially 31.
60. De la Fuente, *A Nation for All*, 79–80, quote, 80; and Bronfman, *Measures of Equality*, 149.
61. Stoner, *From the House to the Streets*, 71.
62. Benjamin, "The *Machadato*," 72–73; Hatzky, Julio Antonio Mella (1903–1929), 84; Aguilar, *Cuba 1933*, 82ff; and Le Riverend, *La República*, 201–204.
63. Fernando Ortiz, *Las responsablidades de los Estados Unidos en los males de Cuba* (Washington, DC: Cuban Information Bureau, 1932).
64. Roig de Leuchsenring, "Significación internacional de Cuba en el continente americano," *Cuba contemporanea* 41 (July 1926): 213–237, especially 233.
65. Hatzky, *Julio Antonio Mella (1903–1929)*, 143.
66. Pérez, Jr., *Rice in the Time of Sugar: The Political Economy of Food in Cuba* (Chapel Hill: University of North Carolina Press, 2019), chapter 3.
67. Tabares del Real, *Guiteras*, 2nd ed. (Havana: Editorial de Ciencias Sociales, 1990 [1973]), 69.
68. Guerra, "The Struggle to Redefine Martí," 43; Argote-Freyre, *Fulgencio Batista*, 36; and Alberto Baeza Flores, *Las cadenas viene de lejos: Cuba, América Latina y la libertad* (Mexico City: Editorial Letras, 1960).
69. Quoted in Tabares del Real, *Guiteras*, 69.
70. Roa, "La generación inmolada," in idem, *15 años después*, 188–202, quote, 189.
71. Hatzky, *Julio Antonio Mella (1903–1929)*, 182; and Patrick Radden Keefe, *Say Nothing: A True Story of Murder and Memory in Northern Ireland* (New York: Doubleday, 2019), 149.

72. Stoner, "Ofelia Domínguez Navarro: The Making of a Cuban Socialist Feminist," in *The Human Tradition in Latin America: The Twentieth Century*, ed. William Beezley and Ewell (Wilmington: Scholarly Resources, 1987), 119–140, especially 126.

73. Hatzky, *Julio Antonio Mella (1903–1929)*, 183; and Ada Ferrer, *Cuba: An American History* (New York: Scribner, 2021), 227.

74. Franqui, *Diary of the Cuban Revolution*, trans. Georgette Felix et al. (New York: Viking Press, 1980 [1976]), 37; and García Oliveras, *José Antonio Echeverría*, 80.

75. Kersffeld, "La Liga Antiimperialista de las Américas: Una construcción política entre el Marxismo y el Latinoamericanismo," in *El comunismo: Otras miradas desde América Latina*, ed. Elvira Concheiro Bórquez, Massimo Mondones and Horacio Crespo (Mexico City: UNAM, Centro de Investigaciones Interdisciplinarias en Ciencias y Humanidades, 2007), 151–166, especially 158–159.

76. On hunger strikes, see Keefe, *Say Nothing*, 149–150. On Mella's release, see Roa, *Retorno a la alborada*, I: 118–121; and Tabares del Real, *La revolución del 30*, 215.

77. Hatzky, *Julio Antonio Mella (1903–1929)*, 174ff; Daniela Spenser, *The Impossible Triangle: Mexico, Soviet Russia and the United States in the 1920s* (Durham: Duke University Press, 1999), 172; and Ladislao González Carbajal, *Mella y el movimiento estudiantil* (Havana: Editorial de Ciencias Sociales, 1977), 59ff.

78. Hatzky, *Julio Antonio Mella (1903–1929)*, 191, 194; and Carr, *Marxism and Communism in Twentieth-Century Mexico* (Lincoln: University of Nebraska Press, 1992), 334n1.

79. Cox, "Machado, Welles," 202.

80. Soto, *La revolución del 33*, I: 366; and Gerardo Machado y Morales, *Ocho años de lucha: Memorias* (Miami: Editorial Cubana Luis J. Botifoll, 2006 [1982]), 19.

81. Quoted in Gonzalo de Quesada y Miranda, *¡En Cuba libre! Historia documentada y anecdótica del machadato*, 2 vols. (Havana: Seoane, Fernández y Cía, 1938), I: 113–114.

82. Cairo, ed., *Mella: 100 años*, I: quote, 141–142.

83. Roa, *Bufa subversiva*, 246ff; and Miller, *In the Shadow of the State*, 72.

84. Buell, "Cuba and the Platt Amendment," *FPR* 5:3 (April 17, 1929), 39; *Problems of the New Cuba. Report of the Commission on Cuban Affairs* (New York: Foreign Policy Association, 1935), 9ff; Pérez de la Riva et al., *La república colonial*, II: 249ff; and Russell Fitzgibbon, *Cuba and the United States, 1900–1935* (Menasha, WI: Collegiate Press and George Banta, 1935), 187.

85. Aguilar, *Cuba 1933*, 65–66, 88; Benjamin, "The *Machadato*," 67, 78; Pérez, Jr., *Cuba Under the Platt Amendment*, 275; and Jorge I. Domínguez, "Seeking Permission to Build a Nation: Cuban Nationalism and U.S. Response under the First Machado Presidency," *Cuban Studies* 16 (1986): 33–49, especially 37.

86. Fitzgibbon, " '*Continuismo* in Central America and the Caribbean," *Inter-American Quarterly* 2 (July 1940): 56–74.

87. Roa, "La generación inmolada," 191.

88. Suchlicki, *University Students*, 24–25.

89. Hatzky, *Julio Antonio Mella (1903–1929)*, 242.

90. Quoted in Aguilar, *Cuba 1933*, 90.

91. Whitney, *State and Revolution*, 63.

92. "El Directorio Estudiantil Universitario contra la prórroga." In Cabrera and Almodóbar, *Las luchas estudiantiles*, 199–204; and Whitney, *State and Revolution*, quote, 57–58.

93. Beals, *The Crime of Cuba*, 256.

94. Phillips, *Cuba: Island of Paradox* (New York: McDowell, Obolensky, 1959), 51; and McPherson, *The Invaded*, 209.

95. *NYT*, January 11, 1928, 12.

96. De Quesada y Miranda, *¡En Cuba libre!* 121; Sánchez, *Haya de la Torre y El APRA*, 206; and Vasconcelos, "Disparos reveladores," *RA* 16:6 (February 11, 1928).

97. Roig de Leuchsenring, *Historia de la enmienda Platt*, I: quote, 283, and 286–287.

98. Welles, *A Time for Decision* (New York: Harper & Brothers, 1944), 187.

99. Lewis Gannett, "The Love Feast at Havana," *Nation* 126:3265 (February 1, 1928): 117–118.

100. Cuba folder, CCPL; and Stewart Beach, "Diplomacy in Action at Havana," *The Independent* 120: 4053 (February 4, 1928): 118–119.

101. "Machado's Speech," *NYT*, January 17, 1928.

102. *Report of the Delegates of the United States of America to the Sixth International Conference of American States* (Washington, DC: Government Printing Office, 1928), 63.

103. Quoted in Robert Johnson, *The Peace Progressives and American Foreign Relations* (Cambridge: Harvard University Press, 1995), 223–224.

104. Quoted in Aguilar, *Cuba 1933*, 88.

105. Cuba Folder, CCPL.

106. Marial Iglesias Utset, "A Sunken Ship, a Bronze Eagle, and the Politics of Memory: The 'Social Life' of the USS Maine in Cuba (1898–1961)," in *State of Ambiguity*, 22–53, especially 44–45; and de Quesada y Miranda, *¡En Cuba Libre!* 124–125.

107. "Lindbergh Stamp in Cuba," "Machado Will Greet Flier," "Parley Delegates to Visit Cuban Shrine," "Cuba to Give Flier its Highest Award, "Havana Awaits Lindbergh," "Machado Lauds Our Policy," "Lindbergh Air Host to Cuban Notables," and "Lindbergh Notes that Flight Today Marks Year Since He Quit Air Mail," *NYT*, January 13, 1928, January 28, 1928, February 1, 1928, February 3, 1928, February 8, 1928, February 8, 1928, February 12, 1928, and February 13, 1928, respectively. For an overview of the entire junket, see A. Scott Berg, *Lindbergh* (New York: Putnam, 2008), 172ff.

108. Raquel Tibol, ed., *Julio Antonio Mella en El Machete: Antología parcial de un luchador y su momento histórico* (Mexico City: Fondo de Cultura Popular, 1968), 9–11, 40, 47.

109. Moshe Temkin, *The Sacco and Vanzetti Affair: America on Trial* (New Haven: Yale University Press, 2009), 47ff. On demonstrations in Mexico, see Lisa McGirr, "The Passion of Sacco and Vanzetti: A Global History," *Journal of American History* 93:4 (March 2007): 1085–1115, especially 1095. For comparable protests elsewhere in Latin America, see Laurence Duggan, *The Americas: The Search for Hemisphere Security* (New York: Henry Holt, 1949), 54.

110. Carr, *Marxism and Communism*, 37–38.

111. Carr, "Radicals, Revolutionaries and Exiles," 29.

112. Thomas, *Cuba: In Pursuit of Freedom*, 588; Roa, *Bufa subversiva*, 332; and Goldenberg, "The Rise and Fall of a Party," 64n10.

113. Goebel, *Anti-Imperial Metropolis*, 133–134; and Jason Weiss, *The Lights of Home: A Century of Latin American Writers in Paris* (New York: Routledge, 2003), 37.

114. Miller, *In the Shadow of the State*, 115; and Mella, "Los falsos maestros y discípulos," in Instituto, *J. A. Mella*, 118–120.

115. Rodríguez García, "El pensamiento y la acción," 151.

116. Ibid., 150; Carr, "Radicals, Revolutionaries and Exiles," 28; Hatzky, *Julio Antonio Mella (1903–1929)*, 172–173; and McBeth, *Dictatorship and Politics*, 206, 213.

117. Hatzky, *Julio Antonio Mella (1903–1929)*, 291–292, 306.

118. Iber, *Neither Peace*, 26–27.

119. There is some debate as to whether Mella resigned or was expelled from the PCM. Cf. Hatzky, *Julio Antonio Mella (1903–1929)*, 274; and Spenser, *The Impossible Triangle*, 173–174.

120. Hatzky, *Julio Antonio Mella (1903–1929)*, 336ff; and Thomas, Cuba: *The Pursuit*, 588n13.

121. Beals, *The Great Circle: Further Adventures in Free-Lancing* (Philadelphia: J. B. Lippincott, 1940), 215.

122. *Julio Antonio Mella (1903–1929)*, 320.

123. Ibid.

124. "Ante la farsa electoral: Nuestra oposición al intento de legalizar el golpe de estado fascista," in Instituto, *J. A. Mella*, 487–491.

125. Froilán González and Adys Cupull, *Julio Antonio Mella en medio del fuego: un asesinato en México* (Havana: Casa Editora Abril, 2006); Spenser, *The Impossible Triangle*, 173; and Beals, *The Great Circle*, 217.

126. Bertram Wolfe, *The Fabulous Life of Diego Rivera* (New York: Cooper Square Press, 2000 [1963]), 230–233, quote, 232.

127. "105 días presos," in de la Torriente Brau, *Pluma en ristre*, 25–26.

128. Ibid., quotes, 23, 25.

129. De Quesada y Miranda, *¡En Cuba libre!* 171.

130. Niurka Pérez Rojas, *El movimiento estudiantil universitario de 1934–1940* (Havana: Editorial de Ciencias Sociales, 1975), 17; and Russell Porter, "'Cuba libre.'"

131. Roa, "Rafael Trejo y el 30 de septiembre," and "Rafael Trejo," in idem, *La revolución del 30 se fue a bolina*, 17–23 and 131–150; Stoner, *From the House to the Street*, 116–117; Justo Carrillo, *Cuba 1933: Students, Yankees, and Soldiers*, trans. Mario Llerena (Miami: North-South Center, University of Miami, 1994), 4–6; and Aguilar, *Cuba 1933*, quote, 103.

132. Quoted in Aguilar, *Cuba 1933*, 104–105; and Cox, "Machado, Welles," 202.

133. *RA* 22:1 (January 3, 1931); and Frank, "What Is Hispano-America to Us?" 585.

134. Roa, *Bufa subversiva*, 104; and de la Osa, *Visión y pasión de Raúl Roa*, 5.

135. Ofelia Domínguez (Navarro), *50 años de una vida* (Havana: Instituto Cubano del Libro, 1971).

136. Goldenberg, "The Rise and Fall of a Party," 63; Philip Dur and Christopher Gilcrease, "U.S. Diplomacy and the Downfall of a Cuban Dictator: Machado in 1933," *JLAS* 34:2 (May 2002): 255–283, 257; and Pérez, Jr., "In Defense of Hegemony," 29.

137. Gillian McGillivray, "Cuba: Depression, Imperialism, and Revolution, 1920–1940," in *The Great Depression in Latin America*, 246–275, especially 247; and Pérez, Jr., "In Defense of Hegemony," especially 28–29.

138. Pérez, Jr., "The Military and Political Aspects of the 1933 Cuban Revolution: The Fall of Machado," *TA* 31:2 (October 1974): 172–184, especially 174–175; and Ortiz, *Las responsabilidades*, 4.

139. Ortiz, *Las responsabilidades*, 4.

140. Beals, *The Crime of Cuba*, 282.

141. Phillips, *Cuba: Island of Paradox*, 5.

142. Ortiz, *Las responsabilidades*, quote, 4.

143. Whitney, *State and Revolution*, 73–74 and 77–78; and Ferrer, *Con el rifle al hombro*, 294–295.

144. Lima, *La odisea de Rio Verde* (Havana: Cultural, 1934); Le Riverend, *La República*, 272; and De Quesada y Miranda, *¡En Cuba libre!* II: 22.

145. Antonio Guiteras y Holmes, *Antonio Guiteras: Su pensamiento revolucionario*, ed. Cabrera (Havana: Editorial de Ciencias Sociales, 1975), 15–16; and Whitney, *State and Revolution*, quote, 72.

146. Pettinà, *Cuba y Estados Unidos, 1933–1955: del compromiso nacionalista al conflicto* (Madrid: Catarata, 2011), 32; and Le Riverend, *La República*, 275.

147. Although critical of Machado, Hart Phillips scolded student activists as if they were spoiled children. *Cuban Sideshow* (Havana: Cuban Press, 1935), 9, 83, and 116ff.

148. Francisco López Segrera, "Orígenes, desarrollo y frustración de La Revolución de 1933," in *Los partidos políticos burgueses en Cuba neocolonial, 1899–1952*, ed. Ramón de Armas, idem, and Germán Sánchez Otero (Havana: Editorial de Ciencias Sociales): 89–139, especially 96–100.

149. Pérez de la Riva, *La república neocolonial*, II: 371–372.

150. For his reporting, James Phillips earned the sobriquet *El Testigo* (The Witness). Jorge Oiler Oller, "El testigo del asesinato de los hermanos Valdés Daussá," http://www.cubaperiodistas.cu/fotorreportaje/108.htmm. Accessed July 25, 2015; de Quesada y Miranda, *¡En Cuba libre!* II: 142–143; and Phillips, *Cuban Sideshow*, 15ff.

151. De Quesada y Miranda, *¡En Cuba libre!* II: 142–143; Phillips, *Cuban Sideshow*, 15ff; and Beals, *The Crime of Cuba*, 292–293.

152. Whitney, *State and Revolution*, 83.

153. Quoted in Pérez, Jr., "The Military and Political Aspects," 176.

154. Hull to Welles, May 1, 1933, *FRUS, 1933* (Washington, DC: Government Printing Office, 1952), V: 279.

155. Ibid., and Welles to Hull, May 13, 1933, *FRUS, 1933*, V: 285, 287–290; Jorge Ibarra Guitart, *La mediación del 33: Ocaso del machadato* (Havana: Editora Política, 1999), chapter 1; and Carlos Rafael Rodríguez, "La Misión Welles," in *La lucha anti-imperialista de Cuba* (Havana: Editorial Popular de Cuba y del Caribe, 1960): 15–102.

156. Welles to Hull, May 13, 1933, *FRUS, 1933*, V: 287–290, quotes, 289, 290, 291.

157. Welles to Hull, June 21, 1933, *FRUS, 1933*, V: 311–313, quote, 312.

158. Carrillo, *Cuba 1933: Students, Yankees, Soldiers*, 37, 42–47.

159. Welles to Phillips, June 26, 1933, *FRUS, 1933*, V: quote, 315–316.

160. Charles Thomson, "The Cuban Revolution: Fall of Machado," *FPR* 11:21 (December 18, 1935): 250–260, especially 252; de Quesada y Miranda, *¡En Cuba libre!* II: 186–188; and Ameringer, *The Cuban Democratic Experience: The Auténtico Years, 1944–1952* (Gainesville: University Press of Florida, 2000), 4–5.

161. Welles to Acting Secretary of State William Phillips, June 2, 1933, *FRUS, 1933*, V: 299–301; Pérez, Jr., "In Defense of Hegemony," 34–35; Dur and Gilcrease, "U.S. Diplomacy and the Downfall," 265, 268; and Schoultz, *In Their Own Best Interest: A History of the U.S. Effort to Improve Latin Americans* (Cambridge: Harvard University Press, 2018), quote, 124.

162. Aguilar, *Cuba 1933*, 146.

163. In his memoirs, Welles rationalized his heavy-handedness in forcing Machado out and blamed the Hoover administration for turning a blind eye to the repression. *A Time for Decision*, 194.

164. McGillivray, "Cuba: Depression," 257.

165. Welles, *A Time for Decision*, 194.

166. Hanson, "Ordered Liberty."

167. Raúl Rodríguez Aguiar, *El bonchismo y el gangsterismo en Cuba* (Havana: Editorial de Ciencias Sociales, 2000), 88; and Ferrer, *Cuba: A National History*, 235–236.

168. Guerra, *Heroes, Martyrs, and Political Messiahs*.

169. Machado's arms never reached their destination. U.S. occupation authorities in Haiti intercepted the weapons, indirectly contributing to Vásquez's

demise and Trujillo's rise to power. Krehm, *Democracies and Tyrannies*, 175; and Fitzgibbon, "*Continuismo* in Central America," 58.

170. De la Torriente Brau published a pamphlet documenting Trujillo's complicity in the conspiracy. *Los títeres de Ferrara* (Havana, 1935), 23–25. See also Roa, *15 años después*, 218.

Chapter Five. Mexican Impasse

Epigraph: Quoted in Richard Millett, *Guardians of the Dynasty* (New York: Maryknoll, 1977), 52.

1. Much of the following draws on the excellent scholarship of Jürgen Buchenau. See *In the Shadow of the Giant: The Making of Mexico's Central America Policy, 1876–1930* (Tuscaloosa: University of Alabama Press, 1996); and *Plutarco Elías Calles and the Mexican Revolution* (Lanham, MD: Rowman and Littlefield, 2007).

2. Friedrich Katz, *The Life and Times of Pancho Villa* (Stanford: Stanford University Press, 1998), chapter 15.

3. Douglas Richmond, *Venustiano Carranza's Nationalist Struggle, 1893–1920* (Lincoln: University of Nebraska Press, 1983), 212–215.

4. Meyer, *The Mexican Revolution and the Anglo-American Powers: The End of Confrontation and the Beginning of Negotiation*, trans. Sandra del Castillo (La Jolla: Center for U.S.-Mexican Studies, University of California, San Diego, 1985), 2; and Hermila Galindo, *La doctrina Carranza y el acercamiento indolatino* (Mexico City, 1919).

5. "Sandino to the Rulers of Latin America," August 4, 1928, in Ramírez, ed., *Sandino: The Testimony*, 204–206, quote, 206.

6. The one exception to this rule was Obregón's willingness to provide arms and funding to Venezuelan rebels.

7. Buchenau, "Calles y el movimiento liberal en Nicaragua," *Boletín* (Fideicomiso Archivos Históricos Plutarco Elías Calles y Fernando Torreblanca) 9 (March 1992): 1–32, especially 6–7.

8. Linton Wells, "Mexico's Bid for Supremacy in Central America," *NR* (May 18, 1927), 348–350, quote, 349.

9. Quoted in Emily Rosenberg, *Financial Missionaries to the World: The Politics and Culture of Dollar Diplomacy, 1900–1930* (Cambridge: Harvard University Press, 1999), 140.

10. Buchenau, "Calles y el movimiento," 16–17.

11. Colonel James H. Reeves, "Situación histórica de Nicaragua," January 3, 1927, and A. Bloor, "Intervención Mexicana en los asuntos de Nicaragua," March 19, 1927, in Isaguirre and Martínez, eds., *Sandino y los U.S. Marines*: 44–50 and 75–80, respectively; McBeth, *Dictatorship and Politics*, 163; and Salisbury, "Mexico, the United States and the 1926–1927 Nicaraguan Crisis," *HAHR* 66:2 (May 1986): 319–339, especially 321–323.

12. Wells, "Mexico's Bid," 349–350.

13. Salisbury, *Anti-imperialism and International Competition*, 77ff., quotes, 81.

14. Idem, "Mexico, the United States," 328.

15. Ferrell, *The Presidency of Calvin Coolidge*, 135.

16. Quoted in Gobat, *Confronting the American Dream*, 142.

17. Wallace Thompson, "The Doctrine of the 'Special Interest' of the United States in the Region of the Caribbean Sea," *AAPS* 132 (July 1927): 153–159, quote, 157–158.

18. Gobat, *Confronting the American Dream*, 141–142.

19. Joseph Baylen, "American Intervention in Nicaragua, 1909–1933: An Appraisal of Objectives and Results," *Southwestern Social Science Quarterly* 35 (January 1954): 128–154, especially 153n129.

20. The clause was named after nineteenth-century Argentine jurist Carlos Calvo. Ferrell, *The Presidency of Calvin Coolidge*, 125; and Johnson, *The Peace Progressives*, 127–137, quotes, 133.

21. Frank Tannenbaum, *Mexico: The Struggle for Peace and Bread* (New York: Knopf, 1950), 270–272.

22. Frank Fox, *J. Reuben Clark: The Public Years* (Provo, UT: Brigham Young Press, 1980), 477–478 and 490–491; Beals, "Whose Property is Kellogg Protecting?" *NR* (February 23, 1927): 8–11, especially 8–9, 132ff; Stanley Ross, "Dwight Morrow and the Mexican Revolution," *HAHR* 38:4 (November 1958): 506–528, especially 511; and Meyer, *México y los Estados Unidos, en el conflicto petrolero (1917–1942)* (Mexico City: El Colegio de México, 1972), 240–242.

23. Quoted in Robert Freeman Smith, *The United States and Revolutionary Nationalism, 1916–1932* (Chicago: University of Chicago Press, 1972), 234–235.

24. Knight, *U.S.-Mexican Relations, 1910–1940: An Interpretation* (La Jolla: Center for U.S.-Mexican Studies, University of California, San Diego, 1987), 80–84, quote, 84.

25. John W. F. Dulles, *Yesterday in Mexico: A Chronicle in Revolution, 1919–1936* (Austin: University of Texas Press, 1961), 319–320.

26. Meyer, *México y los Estados Unidos*, 221, 247; *Mexico Before the World: Public Documents and Addresses of Plutarco Elías Calles*, trans. and ed. Robert Murray (New York: Academy Press, 1927); and William Walling, *The Mexican Question: Mexican and American-Mexican Relations under Calles and Obregón* (New York: Robins Press, 1927).

27. Ethan Ellis, *Frank B. Kellogg and American Foreign Relations, 1925–1929* (New Brunswick: Rutgers University Press, 1961), 55; and Rosenberg, *Financial Missionaries*, 140–141.

28. Dulles, *Yesterday in Mexico*, 316–317; and James Callahan, *American Foreign Policy in Mexican Relations* (New York: Macmillan, 1932), 596.

29. Quoted in Schoultz, *In Their Own Best Interest*, 86.

30. Ibid., quotes, 96–97.

31. James Horn, "El embajador Sheffield contra el presidente Calles," *Historia Mexicana* 20:2 (October–December 1970): 265–284, quote, 274; Meyer, *The*

Mexican Revolution and the Anglo-American Powers, 30; Ellis, *Frank B. Kellogg*, 24; and Richard Melzer, "The Ambassador Simpático: Dwight Morrow in Mexico, 1927–1930," in *Ambassadors in Foreign Policy*, 1–28, quote, 6.

32. Horn, "U.S. Diplomacy and 'The Specter of Bolshevism in Mexico' (1924–1927)," *TA* 32:1 (July 1975): 31–45, especially 32–24 and 39–40.

33. John Britton, *Revolution and Ideology: Images of the Mexican Revolution in the United States* (Lexington: University Press of Kentucky, 1995), 83–84; Helen Delpar, *The Enormous Vogue of Things Mexican: Cultural Relations between the United States and Mexico, 1920–1935* (Tuscaloosa: University of Alabama Press, 1992), 51–52; idem, "Frank Tannenbaum: The Making of a Mexicanist, 1914–1933," *TA* 45:2 (October 1988): 153–171, especially 162.; and Charles Hale, "Frank Tannenbaum and the Mexican Revolution," *HAHR* 75:2 (May 1995): 215–246, especially 238–239.

34. Horn, "U.S. Diplomacy," 41–42; and, Salisbury, "Mexico, the United States," quote, 320.

35. Haring, *South America Looks at the United States* (New York: Macmillan, 1928), 146–147.

36. Ellis, *Frank B. Kellogg*, 36.

37. Lamar Beman, ed., *Selected Articles on Intervention in Latin America* (New York: H. W. Wilson, 1928), quote, 102; and Harold Denny, *Dollars for Bullets: The Story of American Rule in Nicaragua* (New York: Dial Press, 1929), quote, 252.

38. Quoted in Salisbury, *Anti-Imperialism and International Competition*, 90–91.

39. Quoted in Millett, *Guardians of the Dynasty*, 52.

40. Ellis, *Frank B. Kellogg*, 39–40.

41. Quoted in Spenser, *The Impossible Triangle*, 89.

42. Ibid., 171–172.

43. Meyer, *México y los Estados Unidos*, 233, 257.

44. Callahan, *American Foreign Policy*, 607.

45. Buchenau, *Plutarco Elías Calles and the Mexican Revolution*, 134; Spenser, *The Impossible Triangle*, 90–91; Knight, *U.S.-Mexican Relations*, 134; and Ferry, *The Presidency of Calvin Coolidge*, quote, 128.

46. George Philip, *Oil and Politics in Latin America: Nationalist Movements and State Companies* (Cambridge: Cambridge University Press, 1982), quote, 38; and Meyer, *México y los Estados Unidos*, 230.

47. LeRoy Ashby, *The Spearless Leader: Senator Borah and the Progressive Movement in the 1920s* (Urbana: University of Illinois Press,1972), 95–99; and MacPherson, *The Invaded*, 205.

48. Rosenberg, *Financial Missionaries to the World*, 150.

49. Quoted in Lynne Olson, *Those Angry Days: Roosevelt, Lindbergh, and America's Fight over World War II, 1939–1941* (New York: Random House, 2013), 60; and Johnson, *The Peace Progressives*, quote, 123.

50. María del Carmen Collado, *Dwight W. Morrow: Reencuentro y revolución en las relaciones entre México y los Estados Unidos, 1927–1930* (Mexico City: Instituto

Mora and the Dirección General del Acervo Histórico Diplomático de la Secretaría de las Relaciones Exteriores, 2005), quote, 33.

51. Borah, "What the Monroe Doctrine Really Means," *Colliers* 75 (January 31, 1925), 25.

52. Never a model of consistency, Borah flip-flopped on the desirability of intervention in Nicaragua. Ashby, *The Spearless Leader,* quotes, 109 and 210.

53. Quoted in Selser, *El pequeño ejército loco,* 61–62.

54. Johnson, *The Peace Progressives,* 125, 128.

55. Lippmann, "Concerning Senator Borah," *FA* 4:211 (1925–1926): 211–222, quote, 213.

56. Philip, *Oil and Politics in Latin America,* 38; and William Appleman Williams, *The Tragedy of American Diplomacy* (New York: Dell, 1962 [1959]).

57. Ellis, *Frank B. Kellogg,* 41.

58. Johnson, *The Peace Progressives,* 124.

59. Ashby, *The Spearless Leader,* 212, quote, 17; and Johnson, *The Peace Progressives,* 132.

60. Quoted in Margot Louria, *Triumph and Downfall: America's Pursuit of Peace and Prosperity* (Westport, CT: Greenwood Press, 2001), 92.

61. Johnson, *The Peace Progressives,* 233; and Delpar, "Frank Tannenbaum," quotes, 166–167.

62. Inman, *Intervention in Mexico* (New York: Association Press, 1919); Kenneth Woods, "Imperialistic America: A Landmark in the Development of U.S. Policy toward Latin America," *IAEA* 9 (January 1967): 55–72; and McPherson, *The Invaded,* 181.

63. Although Inman initially approved of the occupations of Haiti and the Dominican Republic, he later rejected all forms of interventionism. See his *Through Santo Domingo and Haiti: A Cruise with the Marines* (New York: Committee on Cooperation in Latin America, 1919); and idem, "Imperialistic America," *AM* 134 (July 1924): 107–116. See also Mary Renda, *Taking Haiti: Military Occupation and the Culture of U.S. Imperialism, 1915–1940* (Durham: Duke University Press, 2001), chapter 6; and Rosenberg, *Financial Missionaries to the World,* 132ff.

64. Virginia S. Williams, *Radical Journalists, Generalist Intellectuals and U.S.-Latin American Relations* (Lewiston, NY: Edwin Mellen Press, 2001), 61–62.

65. Woods, "Imperialistic *America*," 63.

66. Welles, "Is America Imperialistic?" *AM* 134 (September 1924); McPherson, *The Invaded,* 181; Rosenberg, *Financial Missionaries to the World,* 135–137; and Williams, *Radical Journalists, Generalist Intellectuals,* 60.

67. George Marabell, *Frederick Libby and the American Peace Movement, 1921–1941* (New York: Arno Press, 1975), 92–94, quote, 92.

68. Selser, *El pequeño ejéricito loco,* quote, 111; Rosenberg, *Financial Missionaries to the World,* 145–146 and 234; Scott Nearing and Joseph Freeman, *Dollar Diplomacy: A Study in American Imperialism* (New York: Arno Press, 1970

[1925]); and Alexander, "Labor and Inter-American Relations," *AAPS* 334 (March 1961): 41–53, especially 42.

69. Selser, *El pequeño ejércicto loco*, quotes, 63 and 64.
70. Quoted in Horn, "U.S. Diplomacy," 34.
71. Meyer, *México y los Estados Unidos*, 248.
72. Delpar, *The Enormous Vogue of Things Mexican*, 51–52.
73. Spenser, *The Impossible Triangle*, 138; and Beals, *Glass Houses*, 264–265.
74. Selser, *El pequeño ejércicto loco*, 61, 78 and 111.
75. Quoted in *RA* 18:3 (January 19, 1929).
76. Lippmann, "Vested Rights and Nationalism," 358, 362; and Johnson, *The Peace Progressives*, 212.
77. Selser, *Sandino, General of the Free*, 225n2.
78. Buchenau, *In the Shadow of the Giant*, 175–176.
79. Collado, *Dwight W. Morrow:* 28–30; Robert Freeman Smith, *The United States and Revolutionary Nationalism*, 241ff; and Lindbergh, "To Bogotá and Back by Air: The Narrative of a 9,500 Mile Flight from Washington over Thirteen Latin American Countries and Return, in the Single-Seater Airplane 'Spirit of St. Louis,' " *National Geographic* 53 (May 1928): 529–601, especially 529–531.
80. Robert Freeman Smith, "Thomas W. Lamont: International Baker as Diplomat," in *Behind the Throne: Servants of Power to Imperial Presidents, 1898–1968*, ed. Thomas J. McCormick and LaFeber (Madison: University of Wisconsin Press, 1993), 101–125, especially 117; and Ron Chernow, *The House of Morgan: An American Banking Dynasty and the Rise of Modern Finance* (New York: Atlantic Monthly Press, 1990), 241–243.
81. Warren Cohen, *Empire without Tears: America's Foreign Relations, 1921–1933* (New York: Knopf, 1987), 68.
82. Fox, *J. Reuben Clark*, quote, 479.
83. Ibid., 490ff; and Ross, "Morrow and the Mexican Revolution," 514–515.
84. Collado, *Dwight W. Morrow*, 67–68.
85. Mella, "Lo que significa el vuelo de Lindbergh," in Tibol, *Julio Antonio Mella en El Machete*, 178–180.
86. Meyer, *The Mexican Revolution and the Anglo-American Powers*, 31; and Ferrell, *The Presidency of Calvin Coolidge*, 130.
87. Quoted in Robert Freeman Smith, *The United States and Revolutionary Nationalism*, 243.
88. Knight, *U.S.-Mexican Relations*, quotes, 93, 144.
89. LaFeber, *The American Age: United States Foreign Policy at Home and Abroad since 1750* (New York: Norton, 1989), 342.

Chapter Six. Something New in American History

Epigraph: Dodd, "The United States and Nicaragua," 136.
1. Quoted in Schoultz, *In Their Own Best Interest*, 101.

2. Walter, *The Regime of Anastasio Somoza, 1936–1956,* 18; Conrad, "Translator's Introduction," in Ramírez, ed., *Sandino: The Testimony,* 13–14; and Ferrell, *Frank B. Kellogg* in *The American Secretaries of State and Their Diplomacy,* ed. idem and Samuel Flagg Bemis, 20 vols. (New York: Cooper Square Publishers, 1963), XI: 55.

3. Baylen, "American Intervention in Nicaragua," 138, 138n50; and "Somoza of Nicaragua Rules Country Like a Feudal Fief," *NYT,* January 13, 1955.

4. Andrés Pérez, "Henry L. Stimson in Nicaragua: The Historical Context and Political Significance of his Mission," in *Henry L. Stimson's American Policy in Nicaragua: The Lasting Legacy* (New York: Markus Wiener, 1991), 67–104, especially 78; and Elting Morison, *Turmoil and Tradition: A Study of the Life and Times of Henry L. Stimson* (Boston: Houghton Mifflin, 1960), 274.

5. Telegram, Eberhardt to Kellogg, January 24, 1927, *FRUS,* III: 303–304.

6. Andrew Bacevich, Jr., "The American Electoral Mission in Nicaragua, 1927–1928," *DH* 4 (July 1980): 241–261, especially 245–254, quotes, 250, 254.

7. John Findling, *Close Neighbors, Distant Friends: United States-Central American Relations* (New York: Greenwood Press, 1987), 89.

8. Jeremy Kuzmarov, "Modernizing Repression, Police Training, Political Violence, and Nation-Building in the 'American Century,'" *DH* 33:2 (April 2009): 191–221, especially 194.

9. Morison, *Turmoil and Tradition,* quote, 276–277.

10. Quoted in Rafael de Nogales, *The Looting of Nicaragua* (New York: Robert McBride, 1928), 241.

11. Sandino, "An Open Letter to President Herbert Hoover," in Ramírez, ed., *Sandino, The Testimony,* quote, 242.

12. Buchenau, "Calles y el movimiento liberal," 23.

13. Paul Boeker, "American Policy in Nicaragua," in *Henry L. Stimson's American Policy,* 25.

14. Buell, "Reconstruction in Nicaragua," quote, 332; and Findling, *Close Neighbors, Distant Friends,* 79.

15. Buell, "Reconstruction in Nicaragua," 332.

16. Gobat, *Confronting the American Dream,* 47.

17. Millett, *Guardians of the Dynasty,* 41–47, 70, quote, 41.

18. Buell, *The Central Americans,* quote, 9.

19. Buell, "Reconstruction in Nicaragua," 332; and Mahoney, *The Legacies of Liberalism,* 232–233.

20. Quoted in Richard Clinton, Jr., "The United States and the Caribbean Legion: Democracy, Dictatorship and the Origins of the Cold War in Latin America, 1945–1950" (Ph.D. dissertation, Ohio University, 2001), 45.

21. Bacevich, Jr., "The American Electoral Mission," quotes, 251, 252.

22. Ibid., 261; and Thomson, "The Caribbean Situation: Nicaragua and El Salvador," *FPR* 19:13 (August 30, 1933): 142–148, especially 144.

23. Quoted in McPherson, *The Invaded,* 200.

24. Ibid., 200.

25. Beman, ed., *Selected Articles.*

26. January 3, 1928, in Beman, *Selected Articles*, 247.

27. Broun, "It Seems to Heywood Broun," *Nation* 126 (January 18, 1928): 62.

28. Ted Vincent, "The Harlem to Bluefields Connection: Sandino's Aid from the Black American Press," *Black Scholar* 16:3 (May–June 1985): 36–42, especially 40.

29. Van Gosse, *Where the Boys Are: Cuba, Cold War America and the Making of a New Left* (London: Verso, 1993), 17.

30. Dulles obtained his data from Milton Offutt, *The Protection of Citizens Abroad by the United States* (Baltimore: The Johns Hopkins University Press, 1928).

31. Dulles, "Conceptions and Misconceptions Regarding Intervention," *AAPS* 144 (July 1929), 103–104.

32. Quoted in Ronald Pruessen, *John Foster Dulles: The Road to Power* (New York: Free Press, 1982), 22–23. See also Nancy Lisagor and Frank Lipsius, *A Law unto Itself: The Untold Story of the Law Firm Sullivan & Cromwell* (New York: William Morrow, 1988), 65, 95.

33. Dunkerley, *Power in the Isthmus*, 64.

34. Johnson, *The Peace Progressives*, quotes, 134, 137; and Millett, *Guardians of the Dynasty*, 117.

35. Richard Grossman, "Solidarity with Sandino: The Anti-Intervention and Solidarity Movements in the United States, 1927–1933," *LAP* 36:6 (November 2009): 67–79.

36. Johnson, *The Peace Progressives*, 137; McPherson, *The Invaded*, 200–207; and Grossman, "Solidarity with Sandino," 75.

37. Johnson, *The Peace Progressives*, 127–137, quote, 127.

38. Grossman, "Solidarity with Sandino," especially 68–70.

39. Ibid., 71–73, quote, 73.

40. *RA* 14:107 (October 13, 1928); and Schoultz, *Beneath the United States*, 266.

41. Quoted in McPherson, *The Invaded*, 204.

42. Selser, *El pequeño ejército loco*, 147.

43. Eberhardt to Kellogg, May 7, 1928, *FRUS*, III: 573–574.

44. Norman Davis, "Wanted: A Consistent Latin American Policy," *FA* 9:4 (July 1931): 547–568.

45. Leandro Morgenfeld, *Vecinos en conflicto: Argentina y Estados Unidos en las Conferencias Panamericanas, 1880–1955* (Buenos Aires: Ediciones Continente, 2011), 78ff; and Inman, "Pan American Conferences and Their Results," *Southwestern Political and Social Science Quarterly* 4 (1923–1924): 238–266.

46. Schoultz, *In Their Own Best Interest*, 113–114.

47. Morgenfeld, *Vecinos en conflicto*, 185–186.

48. Welles, *A Time for Decision*, 187; McPherson, *The Invaded*, 208; and Rosenberg, *Financial Missionaries of the World*, 130.

49. Inman, "Imperialistic America," 115; Andrew Cleven, "Pan-American Problems at the Havana Conference," *CH* 27:6 (March 1, 1928): 858–867,

especially 865; and Gene Sessions, "The Clark Memorandum Myth," *TA* 34:1 (July 1977): 40–58, especially 42.

50. Quoted in Schoultz, *Beneath the United States*, 286–288.

51. "Message to the Pan-American Congress," January 17, 1928, in Ramírez, *Sandino: The Testimony*, quote, 158.

52. Macaulay, *The Sandino Affair*, 102.

53. David Bryn-Jones, *Frank Kellogg: A Biography* (New York: G. P. Putnam's Sons, 1937), 197.

54. Salisbury, *Anti-Imperialism and International Competition*, 120–122.

55. De Quesada y Miranda, *¡En Cuba libre*, I: 122.

56. Quoted in Morgenfeld, *Vecinos en conflicto*, 197.

57. Bryn-Jones, *Frank Kellogg*, quote, 197.

58. *Report of the Delegates* 13–15; Salisbury, *Anti-Imperialism and International Competition*, 120–122; and Merlo Pusey, *Charles Evans Hughes*, 2 vols. (New York: Macmillan, 1951), II: 554–560.

59. *Report of the Delegates*, 11–13; Inman, *Building an Inter-American Neighborhood* (New York: National Peace Conference, 1937), 9; and Salisbury, *Anti-Imperialism and International Competition*, 120–122.

60. Quoted in *Report of the Delegates*, 13–15. Hughes elaborated on his views afterward in *Our Relations to the Nations of the Western Hemisphere* (Princeton: Princeton University Press, 1928), 75–84.

61. *Report of the Delegates*, 13–15.

62. Grandin, "Your Americanism and Mine: Americanism and Anti-Americanism in the Americas," *AHR* 111:1 (October 2006): 1042–1066, especially 1051.

63. Guerrero justified his decision to withdraw the resolution in *RA* 17:7 (August 18, 1928); and 17:8 (August 25, 1928).

64. Quoted in Clinton, Jr., "The United States and the Caribbean Legion," 15–16.

65. Lippmann, "Second Thoughts on Havana," *FA* 6:4 (July 1928): 541–554.

66. Inman, *Inter-American Conferences, 1826–1954*, 126.

67. Soto-Hall, *Nicaragua y el imperialismo norteamericano: Contraste entre la insolencia norteamericana y la vergonzosa tolerancia de los gobiernos de América Latina* (Buenos Aires: Artes y Letras, 1928), 116.

68. Roosevelt, "Our Foreign Policy: A Democratic View," *FA* 6:4 (July 1928): 573–587, quotes, 584, 585; and McPherson, *The Invaded*, 210–211.

69. Mills, "Our Foreign Policy: A Republican View," *FA* 6:4 (July 1928): 555–572.

70. Salisbury, *Anti-Imperialism and International Competition*, 120–123.

71. Wünderich, *Sandino, una biografía política*, 27–29.

72. Dospital, *Siempre más allá*, 114; and Navarro-Génie, *Augusto "César" Sandino*, 46.

73. Wünderich, *Sandino, una biografía política*, 168, 187, 221–222.

74. Quoted in Dospital, *Siempre más allá . . .*, 110–111.

75. Quoted in Wünderich, *Sandino, una biografía política*, 175.

76. Navarro-Génie, *Augusto "César" Sandino*, 64.

77. Carlos Fonseca, "Viva Sandino," in Bermann, ed., *Sandino without Frontiers*, 107–121, especially 111.

78. Vargas, *Floreció al filo de la espada*, 228.

79. Navarro-Génie, *Augusto "César" Sandino*, 79.

80. Quoted in Bermann, ed., *Sandino without Frontiers*, 8. See also Wünderich, *Sandino, una biografía política*, 224; and Melgar Bao, "Una cultura política en formación: Los Cominternistas Centroamericanos," in *El comunismo*, 385–421, especially 402–404.

81. Interview with *El Dictamen* (Veracruz, Mexico), October 1929, in Ramírez, ed., *Sandino: The Testimony*, 276–278.

82. On the Good Neighbor Policy, see Bryce Wood, *The Making of the Good Neighbor Policy* (New York: Columbia University Press, 1961); Irwin Gellman, *Good Neighbor Diplomacy: United States Policies in Latin America, 1933–1945* (Baltimore: The Johns Hopkins University Press, 1979); and David Green, *The Containment of Latin America: A History of the Myths and Realities of the Good Neighbor Policy* (Chicago: Quadrangle Books, 1971).

83. Clark, *Memorandum on the Monroe Doctrine* (Washington, DC: Government Printing Office, 1930), ix–xxv, quote, xix; Schoultz, *Beneath the United States*, 258, 290–291; McPherson, *The Invaded*, 209–210; and Sessions, "The Clark Memorandum Myth," 47.

84. Clark, *Memorandum*, quote, xx.

85. Ellis, *Frank B. Kellogg*, 101–103.

86. Joan Hoff Wilson, *Herbert Hoover: Forgotten Progressive* (Boston: Little Brown, 1975), 200–201.

87. Alexander DeConde, *Herbert Hoover's Latin-American Policy* (Stanford: Stanford University Press, 1951), quotes, 13, 14; and Harry Hill, *President-elect Herbert Hoover's Good Will Cruise to Central and South America, this Being a Log of the Trip Aboard the U.S.S. Maryland* (San Francisco: The Book Press, 1929).

88. Quoted in Williams, *The Tragedy of American Diplomacy*, 154.

89. McPherson, *The Invaded*, 210–211.

90. *RA* 18:5 (February 2, 1929).

91. Clinton, Jr., "The United States and the Caribbean Legion," 26.

92. Schoultz, *In Their Own Best Interest*, quote, 120.

93. Quoted in LaFeber, *Inevitable Revolutions*, 69. See also DeConde, *Herbert Hoover's Latin-American Policy*, 53–54, 63–65; and Vargas, *Al floreció*, 178.

94. Welles, "Inter-American Relations," address, Center of Inter-American Studies, George Washington University, Washington, DC, December 19, 1934, 3.

95. Quoted in Davis, "Wanted: A Consistent Latin American Policy," 550–551. Cf. Dennis, "Revolution, Recognition and Intervention," *FA* 9:2 (January 1931): 204–221.

96. Telegram, Eberhardt to Kellogg, April 20, 1927, *FRUS*, III: 323–324.

97. Charles Stansifer, "Application of the Tobar Doctrine to Central America," *TA* 23:3 (Jan 1967): 251–272.

98. Duggan, *The Americas*, 56.

99. Salisbury, "Domestic Politics and Foreign Policy: Costa Rica's Stand on Recognition, 1923–1934," *HAHR* 54:3 (August 1974): 453–478, especially 467 and 473.

100. Dennis, "Revolution, Recognition and Intervention"; Buchenau, *Mexican Foreign Policy*, 154–155; and Isaac Joslin Cox, *Nicaragua and the United States, 1909–1927* (Boston: World Peace Foundation, 1927), 750–751.

101. Buell, *The Central Americans*, quote, 28.

102. Salisbury, "Domestic Politics and Foreign Policy," 467–468.

103. Cohen, *Empire without Tears*, 30–31.

104. Herbert Feis, *The Diplomacy of the Dollar: First Era, 1919–1932* (Baltimore: The Johns Hopkins University Press, 1950), 9–12; and Buell, *The Central Americans*, 13–14.

105. Buell, The United States and Central American Revolutions," 202–203, quote, 203.

106. The general went by his mother's surname, due to the absence of his father's legal title. Krehm, *Democracies and Tyrannies*, 7.

107. Grieb, "The United States and the Rise of General Maximiliano Hernández Martínez," *JLAS* 3:2 (November 1971): 151–172, especially 154, 158; and Schmitz, *Thank God*, 63ff.

108. Schmitz, *Thank God*, quote, 64–65.

109. Bernardo Vega, "Asalto de Trujillo al poder," in Academia Dominicana de la Historia, *Historia general del pueblo dominicano*, ed. Roberto Cassá, 6 vols. (Santo Domingo: Academia Dominicana de la Historia, 2014): V: 57–120, quote, 89.

110. Gellman, *Secret Affairs: Franklin Roosevelt, Cordell Hull, and Sumner Welles* (Baltimore: The Johns Hopkins University Press, 1995), chapter 8; and Benjamin Welles, *Sumner Welles: FDR's Global Strategist* (New York: St. Martin's Press, 1997), quote, 131.

111. Quoted in Clinton, Jr., "The United States and the Caribbean Legion," 24.

112. Quoted in Schoultz, *In Their Own Best Interest*, 109.

113. Eric Roorda, *The Dictator Next Door: The Good Neighbor Policy and the Trujillo Regime in the Dominican Republic* (Durham: Duke University Press, 1998), quotes, 43, 45; and Vega, ed., *Correspondencia entre Ángel Morales y Sumner Welles* (Santo Domingo: Archivo General de la Nación and Academia Dominicana de la Nación, 2013), 36.

114. Roorda, *The Dictator Next Door*, quote, 60.

115. Schoultz, *In Their Own Best Interest*, quote, 85.

116. Since the treaty's adoption the U.S. had withheld recognition on three occasions—in Honduras (1924), Nicaragua (1925), and Guatemala (1930). L. Woolsey, "The Recognition of the Government of El Salvador," *American Journal of International Law* 28:2 (April 1934): 325–329, especially 328.

117. Philip J. Williams and Walter, *Militarization and Demilitarization in El Salvador's Transition to Democracy* (Pittsburgh: University of Pittsburgh Press, 1997), 19.

118. Telegram, Stimson to Curtis (for Caffery), December 18, 1931, *FRUS, 1931,* 3 vols. (Washington: Government Printing Office, 1946), quote, II: 202–203.

119. Dur, "US Diplomacy and the Salvadoran Revolution of 1931," *JLAS* 30:1 (February 1998), 95–119, quote, 105; and idem, *Jefferson Caffery of Louisiana: Ambassador of Revolutions, an Outline of His Career* (Lafayette, LA: Southwestern Louisiana Press, 1998).

120. Schmitz, *Thank God,* 66.

121. Williams and Walter, *Militarization and Demilitarization,* 19.

122. Telegram, Caffery (through Curtis) to Stimson, December 30, 1931, *FRUS, 1931,* II: 210–212, especially 211.

123. Grieb, "The United States and the Rise of General Maximiliano Hernández Martínez," 159; Salisbury, "Domestic Politics and Foreign Policy," 469–474; Schmitz, *Thank God,* quote, 65–66; and Findling, *Close Neighbors, Distant Friends,* 80.

124. Dur, "US Diplomacy and the Salvadoran Revolution," quote, 109; and Erik Ching, *Authoritarian El Salvador: Politics and the Origins of the Military Regimes, 1880–1940* (Notre Dame: University of Notre Dame Press, 2014), 252–253.

125. LaFeber, *Inevitable Revolutions,* 74.

126. Thomas Anderson, *Matanza: El Salvador's Communist Revolt of 1932* (Lincoln: University of Nebraska Press, 1971); Gould and Santiago, *To Rise in Darkness: Revolution, Repression and Memory in El Salvador, 1920–1932* (Durham: Duke University Press, 2008); and Ching, *Authoritarian El Salvador.*

127. *Power in the Isthmus,* 93, 108n23.

128. Schmitz, *Thank God,* 61; Ching, *Authoritarian El Salvador,* quote, 276; and Dunkerley, "El Salvador, 1930–1989," in *Political Suicide in Latin America and Other Essays,* ed. idem (London: Verso, 1992), 49–82, especially 54–55.

129. Leon Zamosc, "The Landing that Never Was: Canadian Marines and the Salvadoran Insurrection of 1932," *Canadian Journal of Latin American and Caribbean Studies* 21 (1986): 131–147, quote, 133.

130. Lindo-Fuentes et al., *Remembering the Massacre,* 64–67.

131. Grieb, "The United States and the Rise of General Maximiliano Hernández Martínez," 165, 167.

132. Schmitz, *Thank God,* 69, 72.

133. Quoted in Ching, *Authoritarian El Salvador,* 257.

134. Grieb, "The Myth," 339.

135. Jonathan Hartlyn, "The Trujillo Regime in the Dominican Republic," in *Sultanistic Regimes,* ed. H. E. Chehabi and Juan Linz (Baltimore: The Johns Hopkins University Press, 1998), 50–112, especially 90.

136. Clinton, Jr., "The United States and the Caribbean Legion," quotes, 37–38 and 78.

137. Max Friedman, *Rethinking Anti-Americanism*, quote, 129.
138. Matthews, "Diplomatic Relations," in *The United States and Latin America*, ed. idem, 2nd ed. (Englewood Cliffs: Prentice-Hall, 1963 [1959]), 121–175, quote, 135.
139. Matthews, *Half of Spain Died: A Reappraisal of the Spanish Civil War* (New York: Charles Scribner's Sons, 1973), 176ff.

Chapter Seven. Tony Guiteras

Epigraph 1: Osa, *Visión y pasión*, quote, 40.
Epigraph 2: Rodríguez, "La Misión Welles," 95.
1. Tabares del Real, *Guiteras*, 40–52.
2. Ibid., 100. Guiteras's sister Calixta Guiteras Holmes hints that Fidel got his idea for the attack on the Moncada Barracks from her brother. *Biografía de Antonio Guiteras* (Havana: Municipio de La Habana, 1960), 8.
3. Tabares del Real, *La revolución del 30*, 255; and idem, *Guiteras*, 127.
4. Taibo II, *Tony Guiteras*, 17–18.
5. Tabares del Real, *Guiteras*, 92–93; and Liss, *Roots of Revolution*, 116.
6. Pérez, Jr., "The Military and Political Aspects," 182, quote, 183; Schoultz, *Beneath the United States*, quote, 297; Hanson, "Ordered Liberty," 320; and de Quesada y Miranda, *¡En Cuba libre!* I: 10.
7. Braden, *Diplomats and Demagogues: The Memoirs of Spruille Braden* (New Rochelle: Arlington House, 1971), 297–298.
8. Welles to Hull, August 14, 1933, *FRUS, 1933*, V: 363; López Segrera, "Orígenes, desarrollo y frustración," 117; and Suchlicki, *University Students*, 34.
9. Aguilar, *Cuba 1933*, 153, 157–159; Matías Franco Varona, *La revolución del 4 de Septiembre: datos para la historia tomados del carnet de un reporter militar que actuó en los hechos, desde la caída de Machado hasta el advenimiento de Mendieta* (Havana: Imprenta Marvel, 1934); and Ferrer, *Cuba: A National History*, 236–237.
10. McGillivray, "Cuba: Depression," 256.
11. Pérez, Jr., "In Defense of Hegemony," 40.
12. Beals, "The New Crime of Cuba," *NR* (July 3, 1935): 216–219, quotes, 217, 218.
13. Welles to Hull, August 15, 1933, *FRUS, 1933*, V: 365–366, quote, 366.
14. Whitney, *State and Revolution*, 84; and Ferrer, *Cuba: A National History*, quote, 236.
15. Pérez Jr., *Army Politics in Cuba, 1898–1958* (Pittsburgh: University of Pittsburgh Press, 1976), 76–81; Enrique Fernández, *La razón del 4 de septiembre*, 2nd ed. (Havana: n.p. 1950 [1935]); and Ferrer, *Cuba: A National History*, 237.
16. Pérez, Jr., *Army Politics*, 83, 85; and Thomson, "The Cuban Revolution: Reform and Reaction," *FPR* 11:22 (January 1, 1936): 262–276, especially 262.
17. Quoted in Thomas, *Cuba: The Pursuit*, 640.

18. Soto, *La revolución del 33*, III: 365n1.

19. Ibid., III: 85.

20. Welles to Hull, September 17, 1933, *FRUS, 1933*, V: 443–445, quote, 444.

21. Welles to Hull, September 18, 1933, *FRUS, 1933*, V: 446–448, quote, 447.

22. Daniels to Hull, September 6 and 9, 1933, *FRUS, 1933*, V: 394, 414–415; and E. David Cronon, "Interpreting the New Good Neighbor Policy: The Cuban Crisis of 1933," *HAHR* 39:4 (November 1959): 538–567, quotes, 551–552.

23. Welles to Hull, September 25, 1933, *FRUS, 1933*, V: 458–459, quote, 459.

24. Quoted in Schoultz, *Beneath the United States*, 300.

25. Memo, Acting Assistant Secretary of State Caffery, September 13, 1933, *FRUS, 1933*, V: 428–31, quote, 430.

26. Quoted in Schoultz, *Beneath the United States*, 302; and Hull, *Memoirs of Cordell Hull*, 2 vols. (New York: Macmillan, 1948), I: 315.

27. Argote-Freyre, *Fulgencio Batista*, 77.

28. Antoni Kapcia, "The Siege of the Hotel Nacional, Cuba, 1933: A Reassessment," *JLAS* 34:2 (May 2002): 283–309, especially 300; McGillivray, "Cuba: Depression," 259; and Schoultz, *That Infernal Little Cuban Republic*, 32.

29. Duggan, *The Americas*, 63.

30. Cronon, "Interpreting the New Good Neighbor Policy," 547–550; and Thomson, "The Cuban Revolution: Reform and Reaction," 263.

31. Beals, "American Diplomacy in Cuba," *Nation* 138 (January 17, 1934): 68–70, quote, 69; and Thomas, *Cuba: The Pursuit*, 648–649, 670. On U.S. pressuring of other Latin American governments to withhold recognition, see Carrillo, *Cuba 1933: Students, Yankees, and Soldiers*, 283–284.

32. Quoted in Argote-Freyre, *Fulgencio Batista*, 86.

33. Tabares del Real, *Guiteras*, 161.

34. Beals, "Cuba's John Brown: 'Guiteras' Soul Goes Marching On,' " *Common Sense* (July 28, 1935), 6–8, quote, 6.

35. Quoted in Taibo II, *Tony Guiteras*, 17.

36. Tabares del Real, *Guiteras*, 213; and Phillips, *Cuban Sideshow*, 275.

37. De La Fuente, *A Nation for All*, 195.

38. Whitney, *State and Revolution*, 107, 113–115; McGillivray, "Cuba: Depression," 259–260; Tabares del Real, *Guiteras*, 165–166, 177; and Ferrer, *Cuba: A National History*, 243–244.

39. Whitney, *State and Revolution*, 112.

40. Argote-Freyre, *Fulgencio Batista*, 90.

41. Quoted in Aguilar, *Cuba 1933*, 178.

42. Welles to Hull, September 19, 1933, *FRUS, 1933*, V: 449.

43. Pérez, Jr., *Army Politics*, 86; and idem, *The Structure of Cuban History*, 167.

44. Quoted in Williams, *The Tragedy of American Diplomacy*, 174.

45. Quoted in Jesús Arboleya, *The Cuban Counter-Revolution*, trans. Rafael Betancourt (Athens: Ohio University Center for International Studies, 2000 [1997]), 17.

46. Roa, "Mongonato, Efebocracia, Mangoneo," November 10, 1933, in idem, *La revolución del 30 se fue*, quote, 85.
47. Whitney, *State and Revolution*.
48. Cairo, ed., *Mella: 100 años*, I: quote, 155.
49. Phillips, *Cuba: Island of Paradox*, 81–82; Thomas, *Cuba: The Pursuit*, 656; Taibo II, *Tony Guiteras*, 265–268; and Argote-Freyre, *Fulgencio Batista*, 72.
50. Ferrer, *Con el rifle al hombro*, 385; and Cupull, *Julio Antonio Mella en los mexicanos*, 90–94.
51. Kapcia, "The Siege of the Hotel Nacional," 307–308.
52. Quoted in Aguilar, *Cuba 1933*, 185.
53. Welles to Hull, September 16, 1933, *FRUS, 1933*, V: 440–442, quote, 441.
54. Pérez, Jr., "In Defense of Hegemony," 40.
55. Thomson, "The Cuban Revolution," 264–265.
56. Welles to Hull, September 10, 1933, *FRUS, 1933*, Vol. 5: 416–418, quote, 417.
57. Russell Porter, "Grau Says Cuba Deserves to be Recognized by the United States," *NYT*, October 29, 1933.
58. Thomson, "The Cuban Revolution," 267; and Beals, "American Diplomacy," 68.
59. Quoted in Pérez, Jr., *Cuba Under the Platt Amendment*, 331; and Whitney, *State and Revolution*, 118.
60. Schmitz, *Thank God*, quote, 79–80.
61. Welles to Hull, November 2, 1933, *FRUS, 1933*, V: 508–509, quote, 508.
62. Aguilar, *Cuba 1933*, 192n22.
63. Ibid., quote, 177; and Carrillo, *Cuba 1933: Students, Yankees, and Soldiers*, 244ff.
64. Carrillo, *Cuba 1933: Students, Yankees, and Soldiers*, 258.
65. Quoted in Gellman, *Roosevelt and Batista: Good Neighbor Diplomacy in Cuba, 1933–1945* (Albuquerque: University of New Mexico Press, 1973), 76.
66. Gordon Connell-Smith, *The United States and Latin America: An Historical Analysis of Inter-American Relations* (London: Heinemann Educational Books, 1974), 164.
67. Dur, "Conditions for Recognition," *Foreign Service Journal* (September 1985): 44–46, quote, 44; and Pettinà, *Cuba y Estados Unidos*, 1933–1945, 52.
68. Aguilar, *Cuba 1933*, 224.
69. Caffery, "Adventures in Diplomacy," Box 69–2, JCP.
70. Robert Corrigan, "An Appreciation of a Diplomat," *Foreign Service Journal* (November 1967), 22–27 and 50–51; and Ellis Briggs, *Proud Servant: The Memoirs of a Career Ambassador* (Kent: Kent State University Press, 1998), 82–97.
71. De La Torriente Brau, "Posthumous Elegy of Colonial Batista," *Three Americas* 1 (January–February 1936): 17–23, quote, 20.
72. E. Wilder Spaulding, *Ambassadors Ordinary and Extraordinary* (Washington, DC: Public Affairs Press, 1961), quote, 261.

73. In his memoirs, Caffery related that Miguelito had been gifted to him by a former president of Colombia. "Adventures in Diplomacy," Box 69–2, JCP.

74. Aguilar, *Cuba 1933*, quote, 224.

75. Grau San Martín, "The Cuban Terror," *Nation* 140:3639 (April 3, 1935): 381–382, quote, 381.

76. Acosta Matos, *La telaraña cubana*, quote, I: 153.

77. Caffery's daily reports on the transition are found in *FRUS, 1934* (Washington, DC: Government Printing Office, 1952), V: 95–107. See also Gellman, *Roosevelt and Batista*, 79–85.

78. Dur speculates that Welles encouraged Phillips to turn down the request because he was miffed that Caffery had accomplished what he failed to achieve—Grau's departure. "Conditions for Recognition."

79. Gruening, *Many Battles: The Autobiography of Ernest Gruening* (New York: Liveright, 1973), 168–169.

80. Partial newspaper clippings, Box 38–1, JCP.

81. Schoultz, *In Their Own Best Interest*, 138–139.

82. Gellman, *Roosevelt and Batista*, quote, 133.

83. Whitney, "The Architect of the Cuban State: Fulgencio Batista and Populism in Cuba, 1937–1940," *JLAS* 32:2 (May 2000): 439–459, quote, 458.

84. Guiteras, "Septembrismo," *Bohemia* (April 1, 1934), 30–38; Aguilar, *Cuba 1933*, quote, 177–178; and Whitney, *State and Revolution*, 145.

85. Rolando Bonachea and Nelson Valdés, "Introduction," in *Revolutionary Struggle, 1947–1958: Selected Words of Fidel Castro*, ed. idem (Cambridge: MIT Press, 1972), 14.

86. Quoted in Beals, "Cuba's John Brown," 6.

87. Taibo II, *Tony Guiteras*, 368.

88. Quoted in Goldenberg, "The Rise and Fall of a Party," 70.

89. Taibo II, *Tony Guiteras*, 344, 376; and Cerdas Cruz, *La hoz y el machete*, 233.

90. Gellman, *Roosevelt and Batista*, 88, quote, 96.

91. Ibid., 111.

92. Whitney, *State and Revolution*, 145; and Thomson, "The Cuban Revolution," 274.

93. Caffery, "Adventures in Diplomacy," Box 69–2, and partial newspaper clippings, Box 38–2, JCP; and "No puede cometerse delito más grave que atentar contra un delegado extranjero," *Diario de la Marina*, May 28, 1935.

94. Roberto Herrera Soto and Rafael Romero Castañeda, *La zona bananera del Magdalena: Historia y léxico* (Bogotá: Imprenta Patriótica del Instituto Caro y Cuervo, 1979), 11; and Palacios, *Between Legitimacy and Violence: A History of Colombia, 1875–2002*, trans. Richard Stoller, 2nd ed. (Durham: Duke University Press, 2007 [2006]), 83.

95. J. Fred Rippy, *The Capitalists and Colombia* (New York: Vanguard Press, 1931), 18off; Herrera Soto and Romero Castañeda, *La zona bananera*, 43; Judith White, *Historia de una ignominia: La United Fruit en Colombia* (Bogotá: Editorial Presencia, 1978), 81, 93–94; and Miguel Urrutia, *The Development*

of the Colombian Labor Movement (New Haven: Yale University Press, 1969), 100–107.

96. Stephen Randall, *The Diplomacy of Modernization: Colombian-American Relations, 1920–1940* (Toronto: University of Toronto Press, 1977), 132ff.

97. LeGrand, "El conflicto de las bananeras," in *Nueva historia de Colombia*, ed. Álvaro Tirado Mejía, 6 vols. (Bogotá: Editorial Planeta, 1989): III: 183–217; Eduardo Posada-Carbó, "Fiction as History: The *bananeras* and Gabriel García Márquez's *One Hundred Years of Solitude*," *JLAS* 30:2 (May 1998): 395–414, especially 403. Cortés Vargas defended his actions in *Los sucesos de las bananeras* (Bogotá: Imprenta de la Luz, 1929). For a leftist organizer's account, see Alberto Castrillón, *Ciente veinte días bajo el terror militar: A la huelga de las bananeros* (Bogotá: Revista Universidad, 1929).

98. Herbert Braun, *The Assassination of Gaitán: Public Life and Urban Violence in Colombia* (Madison: University of Wisconsin Press, 1985), 57–58; W. John Green, *Gaitanismo, Left Liberalism, and Popular Mobilization in Colombia* (Gainesville: University Press of Florida, 2003), 61; and Richard Sharpless, *Gaitán of Colombia: A Political Biography* (Pittsburgh: University of Pittsburgh Press, 1978), 57ff.

99. De La Torriente Brau, "Posthumous Elegy," 20–21.

100. Dur, "US Diplomacy and the Salvadoran Revolution," 106.

101. Briggs, *Proud Servant*, 87.

102. Jorge I. Domínguez, *Cuba: Order and Revolution* (Cambridge: Belknap, 1978); and Briggs, *Proud Servant*, 98, 104.

103. Pérez, Jr., *Army Politics in Cuba*, quote, 110–111; and Domínguez, *Cuba: Order and Revolution*, 79ff.

104. Pérez Rojas, *El movimiento estudiantil universitario*, especially 40, 64–65.

105. J. D. Phillips, "Batista Talks of the Future of Cuba," *NYT*, April 14, 1935; and Gellman, *Roosevelt and Batista*, 94.

106. Gellman, *Roosevelt and Batista*, 124.

107. *Problems of the New Cuba*, p. 16; and Harold Sims, "Cuba," in *Latin America between the Second World War*, 217–242, especially 219.

108. Thomson, "The Cuban Revolution," 273–274.

109. Sánchez Arango, "The Recent General Strike in Cuba," *Three Americas* 1:4 (June 1935): 10–15, quote, 13; and Pérez Rojas, *El movimiento estudiantil universitario*, 71.

110. Sánchez Arango, "The Recent General Strike," 13; Tabares del Real, *La revolución del 30*, 595–598; and Samuel Farber, *Revolution and Reaction in Cuba, 1933–1960: A Political Sociology from Machado to Castro* (Middletown, CT: Wesleyan University Press, 1976), 47–48.

111. Whitney, *State and Revolution*, 132–133; Thomas, Cuba: *The Pursuit*, 699; and Sims, "Cuba," 219–220.

112. Pérez, Jr., *Army Politics*, 107.

113. J. D. Phillips, "Batista Talks of the Future."

114. Sims, "Cuba," 219.

115. Guiteras, *Antonio Guiteras*, 52–53; Tabares del Real, *La revolución del 30*, 620; Thomas, *Cuba: The Pursuit*, 700; Taibo II, *Tony Guiteras*, 419; and Germán Sánchez Otero, "La crisis del sistema neocolonial en Cuba, 1934–1952," in *Los partidos políticos burgueses*, 141–268, especially 203.

116. Beals, "Cuba's John Brown," quotes, 6; and Gellman, *Roosevelt and Batista*, 128.

117. Huber Matos, *Como llegó la noche* (Barcelona: Fabula Tusquets, 2002), 201.

118. José Suárez Núñez, *El gran culpable: ¿Cómo 12 guerrilleros aniquilaron a 45,000 soldados?* (Caracas: Libreria Cervantes, 1963), quote, 89.

119. De La Torriente Brau, *Los títeres*, 29.

120. Phillips, "Batista Links His Destiny with Cuba's," *NYT*, October 14, 1934.

121. Guerra, *Heroes, Martyrs*, 22; Edwin Lieuwen, *Arms and Politics in Latin America* (New York: Council on Foreign Relations, Praeger, 1960), 98; and Ferrer, *Cuba: A National History*, 250.

122. Pérez, Jr., *Army Politics*, quotes, 105, 106.

123. Pérez, Jr., "The Military and Political Aspects," 184.

124. Guerra, *Heroes, Martyrs*; and Whitney, "The Architect of the Cuban State," 450ff.

125. Angell, "The Left in Latin America," 99–100.

126. De la Torriente Brau, *Pluma en ristre*, xx.

127. Pérez Rojas, *El movimiento estudiantil, passim*.

128. *Problems of a New Cuba*, 150–154.

129. Aguiar Rodríguez, *El bonchismo y el gangsterismo*, 1, 118–126; and Bonachea and Valdés, "Introduction."

130. Pérez Rojas, *El movimiento estudiantil*, 201ff; and Iber, *Neither Peace nor Freedom*, 121.

131. Suchlicki, *University Students*, 59.

132. Aguiar Rodríguez, *El bonchismo y el gangsterismo*, 1–8.

133. Ameringer, *The Cuban Democratic Experience*, 12; and Whitney, "The Architect of the Cuban State," 452.

134. Arthur Whitaker, "Pan America in Politics and Diplomacy," in *Inter-American Affairs, 1944: An Annual Survey*, ed. idem (New York: Columbia University Press, 1945), 42–44.

135. Guerra, *Heroes, Martyrs*, 21.

136. *Relations between the United States and Cuba*, Publication #577 (Washington, DC: Government Printing Office, 1934).

Chapter Eight. Your Words Inspired

Epigraph: Patterson to Dean Acheson, *FRUS, 1947*, 8 vols. (Washington, DC: Government Printing Office, 1948), VIII: 108.

1. David Rock, "Introduction," in *Latin America in the 1940s: War and Postwar Transitions*, ed. idem (Berkeley: University of California Press, 1994), 1–14, especially 5; and Whitaker, "Pan America in Politics," 44ff.

2. Bethell and Roxborough, "The Impact of the Cold War on Latin America," in *Origins of the Cold War: An International History*, ed. Melvyn Leffler and David Painter, 2nd ed. (New York: Routledge, 2005 [1994]), 299–316, especially 300–301.

3. Victor Villanueva, *La sublevación aprista del 48: tragedia de un pueblo y de un partido*, 4th ed. (Lima: Editorial Milla Batres, 1973 [1956]).

4. Finchelstein, *From Fascism to Populism*, 111; and Rock, "War and Postwar Intersections: Latin America and the United States," in *Latin America in the 1940s*, 15–40, especially 21.

5. Quoted in Finchelstein, *From Fascism to Populism*, 151.

6. Glenn Dorn, "Perón's Gambit: The United States and the Argentine Challenge to the Inter-American Order, 1946–1948," *DH* 26:1 (Winter 2002): 1–20, quote, 6–7.

7. See Bethell and Roxborough, "The Postwar Conjuncture in Latin America: Democracy, Labor and the Left," in *Latin America between the Second World War*, 1–32, especially 10; and Angell, "The Latin American Left," 102–103.

8. Grandin, "Off the Beach," 434.

9. Wood, *The Dismantling of the Good Neighbor Policy* (Austin: University of Texas Press, 1985), 95–96.

10. Quoted in Schoultz, *That Infernal Little Cuban Republic*, 36.

11. Lieuwen, *Arms and Politics*, 229; and Tannenbaum, "An American Commonwealth of Nations," *FA* (July 1944): 577–654, especially 584.

12. Duggan, *The Americas*, 180–181.

13. Gaddis, *The Last Years of the Monroe Doctrine, 1945–1993* (New York: Hill and Wang, 1994), quote, 226–227; and Wells, *Tropical Zion*, 270–271.

14. Robert Freeman Smith, "United States Policy-Making during the Truman Administration," *Continuity: A Journal of History* 16 (Fall 1992): 87–111, quote, 92.

15. Unless otherwise indicated, quotations in this section are taken from Clinton, Jr.'s excellent dissertation, "The United States and the Caribbean Legion."

16. Wood, *The Dismantling*, quote, 95.

17. Rabe, "Inter-American Military Cooperation, 1944–1951," *World Affairs* 137:2 (Fall 1974): 132–149, especially 136; George Butler to Byrnes, November 18, 1946, *FRUS, 1946*, XI: 810; and Ameringer, *The Caribbean Legion: Patriots, Politicians, Soldiers of Fortune, 1946–1950* (University Park: Pennsylvania State University Press, 2004 [1996]), 13.

18. Robert Freeman Smith, "United States Policy-Making," 90.

19. Michael Krenn, *The Chains of Interdependence: U.S. Policy Toward Central America, 1945–1954* (Armonk, NY: M. E. Sharpe, 1996), 149–150, quote, 149; and Paul Coe Clark, Jr., *The United States and Somoza, 1933–1956: A Revisionist Look* (Westport, CT: Praeger, 1992), 143–145.

20. Clark, Jr., *The United States and Somoza*, 94.

21. Pérez Jr., "International Dimensions of Inter-American Relations, 1944–1960," *IAEA* 27:1 (1973): 47–68, quote, 51; Gould, "Nicaragua," in *Latin*

America between the Second World War," 243–279, especially 244; and Clark, Jr., *The United States and Somoza,* chapter 4.

22. Walter, *The Regime of Anastasio Somoza,* 239; and Millett, *Guardians of the Dynasty,* 203.

23. Margarita López Maya, *EE.UU. en Venezuela: 1945–1948* (Caracas: Universidad Central de Venezuela, Consejo de Desarrollo Científico y Humanístico, 1996), 70.

24. Quoted in Ameringer, *The Caribbean Legion,* 14.

25. Trujillo funded the publication of a polemic titled *I Accuse Braden.* Ameringer, *The Democratic Left in Exile,* 56. Public relations firms on retainer with the dictator also tarred Braden in the *Miami Herald* and other newspapers. Gregorio Bustamante (pseudonym, José Almoina), *Una satrapía en el Caribe: Historia punctual de la mala vida del déspota Rafael Leónidas Trujillo* (Guatemala City: Ediciones del Caribe, 1949), 178.

26. Quoted in Lauro Capdevila, *La dictadura de Trujillo, República Dominicana, 1930–1961,* trans. Denise Armitano, 2nd ed. (Santo Domingo: Sociedad Dominicana de Bibliófilos, 2000 [1998]), 140.

27. Lieuwen, *The United States and the Challenge to Security in Latin America* (Columbus: Ohio State University Press, 1966), 13.

28. Briggs, *Proud Servant,* 194–195.

29. Luis Arías Núñez, *La política exterior en la era de Trujillo* (Santo Domingo: PUCCM, 1991), 142.

30. Capedvila, *La dictadura de Trujillo,* 141–142.

31. Roorda, *The Dictator Next Door,* 227–228; and Research Division of the Office of American Republics, "The Trujillo Regime in the Dominican Republic," December 31, 1946, in Vega, ed., *Los Estados Unidos y Trujillo, año 1946: Colección de documentos del Departamento del Estado y de las Fuerzas Armadas Norteamericanos,* 2 vols. (Santo Domingo: Fundación Cultural Dominicana, 1982), II: 73–163, especially 151. On illicit arms purchases from Cuba, see Acosta Matos, *La telaraña cubana de Trujillo,* II: 418.

32. Welles, "Intervention and Interventions," *FA* 26:4 (October 1947): 116–133, quote, 129.

33. Braden, *Diplomats and Demagogues,* 364–367. For a more nuanced perspective, see Wood, *The Dismantling,* chapter 6.

34. Michael McClintock, *Instruments of Statecraft: U.S. Guerrilla Warfare, Counter-insurgency, and Counter-terrorism, 1940–1990* (New York: Pantheon, 1992), quote, 17.

35. Michael Hunt, *The American Ascendancy: How the United States Gained and Wielded Global Dominance* (Chapel Hill: University of North Carolina Press, 2007), 124.

36. CIA funding of Italian opposition parties and a "media scare" campaign warning the electorate of the dangers of communist rule helped swing parliamentary elections to conservatives. Such tactics were later replicated in Latin America. Scott Anderson, *The Quiet Americans: Four CIA Spies at the*

Dawn of the Cold War—A Tragedy in Three Acts (New York: Doubleday, 2020), 147. See also Gaddis, *The Last Years of the Monroe Doctrine*, 10–11.

37. Chester Pach, Jr., "The Containment of U.S. Military Aid to Latin America, 1944–1949," *DH* 6:3 (Summer 1983): 225–243.
38. Bethell and Roxborough, "The Impact of the Cold War," 310.
39. Wood, *The Dismantling*, quote, 137.
40. Steven Topik and Allen Wells, "Introduction: Latin America's Response to International Markets during the Export Boom," in *The Second Conquest of Latin America: Coffee, Henequen, and Oil during the Export Boom, 1850–1930*, ed. idem (Austin: University of Texas Press, 1997), 1–36, especially 21.
41. Bethell and Roxborough, "The Postwar Conjuncture," 16–17.
42. Gould, "Nicaragua," quote, 276.
43. Gleijeses, "Juan José Arévalo and the Caribbean Legion," *JLAS* 21:1 (February 1989): 133–145, especially 134–135; and Juan José Arévalo, *Despacho presidencial: Obra póstuma del Doctor Juan José Arévalo Bermejo* (Guatemala City: Editorial Oscar de León Palacios, 1998), 47–48, quote, 126.
44. Bayo, *Tempestad*, quote, 19.
45. Quoted in Robert Levine, *Tropical Diaspora: The Jewish Experience in Cuba* (Gainesville: University Press of Florida, 1993), 134. See also Freda Kirchwey, "Caribbean Refuge," *Nation* 150 (1940): 466–468, especially 468.
46. Inaki Urquijo, *La tumba abierto: Los vascos y los Estados Unidos* (Bilbao, Spain: Servicio Central de Publicaciones del Gobierno Vasco, 1993), 89; and Turits, *Foundations of Despotism*, 197–198. On the 1942 strike, see Krehm, *Democracies and Tyrannies*, 177.
47. Bayo, *Tempestad*, 135–136; and Juan Ducoudray, "Cruz Alonso y su hotel de estrella y media," in *Réquiem por la utopia y otras saudades*, ed. idem (Santo Domingo: Editora Nomara, 2000), 60–64, quote, 61.
48. *Democracias y tiranías en el Caribe* became required reading for regional democrats. An updated English-language edition was published in 1984.
49. Carmen Kordick, *The Saints of Progress: A History of Coffee, Migration, and Costa Rican National Identity* (Tuscaloosa: University of Alabama Press, 2019), 219n2.
50. John Patrick Bell, *Crisis in Costa Rica: The 1948 Revolution* (Austin: University of Texas Press, 1971), 138ff.
51. Ameringer, *The Caribbean Legion*. Years later, Dominican exile leader Juan Bosch contended that a myth of the Legion's prowess was deliberately propagated and embellished by the region's dictators to rally support to their cause. Bosch, "La Legión del Caribe, un fantasma de la historia," in idem, *33 artículos de temas políticos* (Santo Domingo: Editora Alfa y Omega, 1988), 244–254.
52. Daniel Pécaut, "El populismo gaitanista," in *La democratización fundamental: El populismo en América Latina*, ed. Vilas (Mexico City: Consejo Nacional para la Cultura y las Artes, 1995), 501–522; Sharpless, *Gaitán of Colombia*; Braun, *The Assassination of Gaitán*; and Green, *Gaitanismo, Left Liberalism*.

53. Heraclio Bonilla and Paul Drake, "Introducción," in *El APRA: de la ideología a la praxis*, 11–19, especially 15.

54. Drake, "International Crises and Popular Movements in Latin America: Chile and Peru from the Great Depression to the Cold War," in *Latin America in the 1940s*, 109–140, especially 127.

55. Geoffrey Bertram, "Peru, 1930–c. 1960," *CHLA*, ed. Bethell, 11 vols. (New York: Cambridge University Press, 1991), VIII: 385–450, especially 414–430.

56. Masterson, *Militarism and Politics*, 46, 55.

57. García-Bryce, *Haya de la Torre*, 83–84, 158. On Haya's asylum case, see Norman Bailey, "Asylum and Haya de la Torre," *Journal of International Affairs* 9:1 (1955): 82–86.

58. Germán Arciniegas, *Entre la libertad y el miedo* (Mexico City: Cuadernos Americanos, 1953), 100.

59. "Jornada de apreciación."

60. Ewell, "Che Guevara and Venezuela: Tourist, Guerrilla Mentor, and Revolutionary Spirit," in *Che's Travels: The Making of a Revolutionary in 1950s Latin America*, ed. Drinot (Durham: Duke University Press, 2010): 148–180, quote, 162; and Darlene Rivas, *Missionary Capitalist: Nelson Rockefeller in Venezuela* (Chapel Hill: University of North Carolina Press, 2002).

61. Martz, *Acción Democrática*, 100.

62. Levine, "Venezuela since 1958," 89–90.

63. Alfredo Peña, *Conversaciones con Carlos Andrés Pérez*, 2 vols. (Caracas: Ediciones Ateneo, 1979), I: 84–85.

64. Ewell, *The Indictment of a Dictator*, 23; Serxner, *Acción Democrática of Venezuela*, 12; Edward Gibson, "Nine Cases of the Breakdown of Democracy," in *Democracy in the Americas: Stopping the Pendulum*, ed. Robert Pastor (New York: Holmes and Meier, 1989), 159–203, especially 161; and Rey, *Personalismo o liderazgo*, 35–37.

65. Martz, *Acción Democrática*, quote, 306.

66. Ewell, *Venezuela: A Century of Change*, 96, 99; Tinker Salas, *What Everyone Needs*, 82; and Avendaño, *El militarismo en Venezuela: La dictadura de Pérez Jiménez* (Caracas: Ávila Artes, 1982).

67. Even before the 1945 coup the UPM aspired to govern. Members signed a secret oath attesting to the military lodge's intentions. Taylor, Jr., *Thoughts on Comparative Effectiveness, Leadership and the Democratic Left in Colombia and Venezuela* (Buffalo: Council of International Studies, State University of New York at Buffalo, 1971), 15; and Gene Bigler, "The Armed Forces and Patterns of Civil-Military Relations," in *Venezuela: The Democratic Experience*, ed. Martz and David Myers (New York: Praeger, 1977), 113–133, quote, 117.

68. Gibson, "Nine Cases," 162–163; and Alexander, *The Bolivarian Presidents: Conversations and Correspondence with Presidents of Bolivia, Peru, Ecuador, Colombia, and Venezuela* (Westport, CT: Praeger, 1994) 229–230.

69. Caballero, *Rómulo Betancourt, político de nación*, 261–262. Initially, the U.S. embassy expressed concern about Pérez Jiménez, viewing him as a demagogue like Perón. Tinker Salas, *Venezuela: What Everyone Needs*, 86.

70. Simón Alberto Consalvi, *Rómulo Betancourt en la Conferencia de Bogotá, 1948* (Caracas: Fundación Rómulo Betancourt, 1948), 18.

71. Ibid.

72. Grandin, "Off the Beach," 435.

73. Quoted in Drake, "International Crises and Popular Movements," 133.

Chapter Nine. Give the Canary Birdseed and Listen to It Sing

Epigraph: Quoted in Sang et al., eds., *La política exterior dominicana, 1844–1961*, II: 309.

1. Vega, "Asalto de Trujillo al poder," in *Historia general*, V: 57–120.

2. More votes were cast in the tainted election than eligible voters, with Trujillo allegedly receiving 99 percent of the tally. Francis Pou de García, "Movimientos conspirativos de el papel de exilio en la lucha antitrujillista," *Clío* 78:177 (January–June 2009): 13–72, especially 15.

3. Research Division, "The Trujillo Regime," II: 85.

4. Gruening, "The Dictatorship in Santo Domingo: A 'Joint Concern,' " *Nation* (May 23, 1934), 583–585; and Beals, "Caesar of the Caribbean," *CH* 48:1 (January 1938): 31–34, especially 32.

5. Moya Pons, *The Dominican Republic: A National History*, 3rd ed. (Princeton: Markus Wiener, 2010 [1995]), 356.

6. Research Division, "The Trujillo Regime," II: 73–163; Bustamante, *Una satrapía en el Caribe*, 87; and Vega, *Trujillo y Haiti, Volume 4 (1946–1950): El complot contra Estimé* (Santo Domingo: Fundación Cultural Dominicana, 2009), 26.

7. Emilio Cordero Michel, "Movimientos de oposición a Trujillo en la década 1930–1939," *Clío* 78:178 (July–December 2009): 149–174, especially 153; Beals, "Caesar of the Caribbean," 32; and Thomson, "Dictatorship in the Dominican Republic," *FPR* 12:2 (April 1, 1936): 30–40, especially 32.

8. *Cementerio sin cruces* (New York: self-published, 1949), 20.

9. Landestoy, *¡Yo acuso también! Rafael Leonidas Trujillo, tirano de la República Dominicana* (Santo Domingo: Archivo General de la Nación, 2011 [1946]), 69.

10. Turits, *Foundations of Despotism*.

11. Howard Wiarda, *Dictatorship and Development: The Methods of Control in Trujillo's Dominican Republic* (Gainesville: University of Florida Press, 1968), 45–51.

12. Félix Aguirre Mejía, *Viacrucis de un pueblo: relato sinóptico de la tragedia dominicana bajo la férula de Trujillo*, 2nd ed. (Mexico City: Editorial Jus, 1960 [1951]), 48.

13. Albert Hicks, *Blood in the Streets: The Life and Times of Trujillo* (New York: Creative Age Press, 1946), 13–14; and Vega, "Asalto de Trujillo al poder," in *Historia general*, V: 115–116.

14. Aguirre Mejía, *Viacrucis de un pueblo*, 60, 64; and Moya Pons, *The Dominican Republic*, 355.

15. Vega, ed., *Correspondencia entre Ángel Morales y Sumner Welles*, 372; and Beals, "Caesar of the Caribbean," 33.

16. Vega, ed., *Correspondencia entre Ángel Morales y Sumner Welles*, quotes, 58 and 89–90.

17. Wells, *Tropical Zion*, introduction and chapter 1; and Gail Hanson, "Sumner Welles and the American System: The United States in the Caribbean, 1920–1940" (Ph.D. dissertation, State University of New York at Stony Brook, 1990), 181, 207.

18. Gellman, *Secret Affairs*, xi; and Roorda, *The Dictator Next Door*, 59–60, 105.

19. Gellman, *Secret Affairs*, 106.

20. Vega, "Las relaciones internacionales," in *Historia general*, V: 553–590, especially 559.

21. Quoted in Stuart McKeever, *Professor Galíndez: Disappearing from Earth: Governments, Complicity, and How a Kidnapping in the Midst of American Democracy Went Unsolved* (New York: CUNY, Dominican Studies Institute, 2018), 179.

22. Cassá, *En búsqueda del tiempo del exilio: Semblanza del Dr. Leovigildo Cuello* (Santo Domingo: Editora Taller, 1999), 14.

23. Vega, *Control y represión en la dictadura trujillista* (Santo Domingo: Fundación de Cultura Dominicana, 1986), 9–11.

24. Acosta Matos, *La telaraña cubana*, II: 446–447: and Pericles Franco Ornes, *La tragedia dominicana: análisis de la tiranía de Trujillo* (Santiago, Chile: Federación de Estudiantes de Chile, 1946).

25. Thomson, "Dictatorship in the Dominican Republic," 32; Research Division, "The Trujillo Regime," 138; and Francisco Girona, *Las fechorías del bandolero Trujillo: Estudio crítico de la vida y milagros del tirano de Santo Domingo* (Santo Domingo: Academia Dominicana de la Historia, 2013 [1937]), 128.

26. Paulino Ramos, "Luchas políticas durante la primera mitad de la dictadura (1930–1945)," in *Historia general*, V: 203–267, especially 204; Aguirre Mejía, *Viacrucis de un pueblo*, 62; and Vega, ed., *Correspondencia entre Ángel Morales y Sumner Welles*, 39–40. Bencosme's murder may not have been accidental. Trujillo had it in for his family. In 1930, Sergio's father, Cipriano, a wealthy landowner and a Vásquez supporter, led a rebellion against the regime. After the uprising was put down, Cipriano was killed. Three of Sergio's siblings also were subsequently murdered. Acosta Matos, *La telaraña cubana*, I: 256n55. For similar blood feuds against other dissident families, see Juan Balcácer, *Trujillo: El tiranicidio de 1961* (Santo Domingo: Taurus Historia, 2006), 77–78.

27. When New York detectives traveled to the island to track Chichi down, authorities said he did not exist. In fact, he was never seen again, although curiously his mother, in New York, continued to receive checks in the mail once a year from "her son" to allay suspicions. Jesús de Galíndez, *La era de*

Trujillo: Un estudio casuístico de dictadura hispanoamericana (Santiago, Chile: Editorial del Pacífico, 1956), 266; and Landestoy, *¡Yo acuso también!*, 58.

28. McKeever, *Professor Galíndez,* 10.

29. Vega contends that it was the Barletta affair, Trujillo's arrest of an Italian national, that led to the attempt on Morales's life. But the diplomatic fallout from that incident did not occur until almost a month after Bencosme's murder. Vega, *Almoina, Galíndez,* 35–36.

30. Naida García-Crespo, "Picturing 'the Tightest Little Tyranny in the Caribbean': The *March of Time* and a 1936 United States–Dominican Diplomatic Crisis," *Film History* 29:4 (Winter 2017): 89–111, especially 90ff.

31. John McManus, "An Affair of Honor," *NYT,* July 19, 1936.

32. Roorda, *The Dictator Next Door,* 106–108; and Raymond Fielding, *The March of Time, 1935–1951* (New York: Oxford University Press, 1978), 151–154.

33. Roorda, *The Dictator Next Door,* 107–108; Sang, ed., *La política exterior dominicana,* II: 42; and Acosta Matos, *La telaraña cubana,* I: 279.

34. Hicks, *Blood in the Streets,* xix–xx.

35. Vega, "Introducción," in Girona, *Las fechorías,* 11–28.

36. Wiarda, *Dictatorship and Development,* 128.

37. Franco Ornes, *La tragedia dominicana,* 17.

38. Vega, *Control y represión,* 63; and Aguirre Mejía, *Viacrucis de un pueblo,* 68.

39. For Linz's original conceptualization, see "Totalitarian and Authoritarian Regimes," in *Handbook of Political Science,* 8 vols., ed. Nelson Polsby and Fred Greenstein (Reading, MA: Addison-Wesley, 1975), III: 175–412, especially 217–218. For a reformulation, see Chehabi and Linz, "A Theory of Sultanism I," in *Sultanistic Regimes,* ed. idem (Baltimore: The Johns Hopkins University Press, 1998), 3–25, especially 7. On the strategic use of technology, see Hartlyn, "The Trujillo Regime in the Dominican Republic," in *Sultanistic Regimes,* 50–112, especially 96.

40. Vallenilla Lanz Planchart, *Escrito de memoria* (Mexico City: Editorial Mazatlán, 1967), 205.

41. Franco Ornes, *La tragedia dominicana,* 37; and Vega, *Control y represión, passim.*

42. Requena, *Cementerio sin cruces.*

43. McKeever, *The Galíndez Case* (Bloomington: AuthorHouse, 2013), 29.

44. Derby, *The Dictator's Seduction.*

45. No author, undated typescript, "Dominican Crisis," p. 4, Caja 16, Folder 135, FLMM; and Wiarda, *Dictatorship and Development,* 82ff.

46. Coronil, *The Magical State,* 84n16.

47. Derby, *The Dictator's Seduction* 2–3; Ángel Miolán, *Memorias: De la batalla contra la tiranía de Trujillo en la República Dominicana y Haití* (Santo Domingo: Impresora Valdez, 1995) 98; and Bustamante, *Una satrapía en el Caribe,* 98.

48. Nelson Moreno Ceballos, "Represión y crímenes," in *Historia general,* V: 591–630, especially 603ff; and Alan Rouquié, "The Military in Latin American Politics since 1939," in *Latin America: Politics and Society,* 145–218, especially 147.

49. Arturo Espaillat, *Trujillo: The Last Caesar* (Chicago: Henry Regnery Company, 1963), 39.

50. Johnny Abbes García, *Trujillo y yo*, ed. Orlando Inoa (Santo Domingo: Letragráfica, 2009), 80.

51. "Dominican Crisis," 4.

52. Acosta Matos, "El conglomerado burocrático y militar," in *Historia general*, V: 269–301, especially 294; Pou de Garcia, "Movimientos conspirativos," 18; and Alan Block, "Violence, Corruption, and Clientelism: The Assassination of Jesús Galíndez, 1956," *Social Justice* 16:2 (Summer 1989): 64–88, especially 76–78.

53. Frank Piñeyro, *Náufragos del odio: dos vidas en lucha contra las tiranías de Trujillo y Batista* (Santo Domingo: Editora Taller, 1995).

54. Ramón Vila Piola, *Esclarecimiento: La verdad sobre los sucesos políticos acaecidos en Santiago en el año 1934 y sus consecuencias* (Madrid: Graf. Uguina-Mélendez Valdéz, 1964), 15–26.

55. Miolán, *Memorias*, 134.

56. Vila Piola, *Esclarecimiento*, 15.

57. Miolán, *Memorias*, 147.

58. Miolán, *La revolución social frente a la tiranía* (Mexico City: n.p., 1938), 65–66; Cordero Michel, "Movimientos de oposición," 161–163; and Paulino Ramos, "Luchas políticas," 236.

59. Vega, ed., *Los Estados Unidos y Trujillo, 1946, Vol. 4*, quote, II: 98–99; Aguirre Mejía, *Viacrucis de un pueblo*, 281; and Cassá, "El proceso político de la segunda mitad de la dictadura (1945–1961)," in *Historia general*, V: 473–590, especially 481–482.

60. Luis Gómez Pérez, "La resistencia a la tiranía trujillista," in *Historia general*, V: 631–654, especially 640.

61. Peña Batlle, *Política de Trujillo* (Santo Domingo: Impresora Dominicana, 1954), 105–106.

62. Quoted in Vega, *Trujillo y Haiti, Vol. 4*, 76.

63. Ibid., 47.

64. *Vega, Trujillo y Haiti, Vol. I:* 113–116.

65. Vega, ed., *Trujillo y Haiti: 1930–1937* (Santo Domingo: Fundación Cultural Dominicana, 1995), 173; Edward Paulino, *Dividing Hispaniola: The Dominican Republic's Border Campaign Against Haiti, 1930–1961* (Pittsburgh: University of Pittsburgh Press, 2016), 52–53; and Rafael Darío Herrera, "La matanza de Haitianos de 1937," in *Historia general*, V: 303–333, especially 305–306.

66. Cassá, "Hacia una caracterización de la dictadura de Trujillo," in *Historia general*, V: 19–56, especially 31; and Paulino Ramos, "Luchas políticas," V: 220–222.

67. Letter, Buenaventura Sánchez et al. to Vincent, August 11, 1933, in Sánchez, *Trujillo: La agonía dominicana* (Santo Domingo: Editora Nacional, 2011 [1933]), 35–38; and Vega, *Trujillo y Haiti, Vol. 1*, 115–116, 151.

68. The following draws on Miolán, *Memorias*, 185–193.

69. Landestoy, *¡Yo acuso también!*, 70.

70. Vega, *Trujillo y Haití*, *Vol. 1*, 196.

71. Ibid., 155.

72. Miolán, *Memorias*, 193; and Jimenes Grullón, *Una gestapo en América: vida, tortura, agonía y muerte de presos políticos bajo la tiranía de Trujillo*, 3rd ed. (Havana: Editorial Lex, 1948 [1946]), 175.

73. Vega, *Trujillo y Haití*, *Vol. 1*, 196.

74. Ibid., 208.

75. Turits, *Foundations of Despotism*, 159.

76. Vega, *Trujillo y Haití*, *Vol. 1*, 154–155.

77. Ibid., *Vol. 4*, 114.

78. Ibid., *Vol. 4*, 32–64 and 93; Silfa, *Guerra, traición y exilio*, II: 95ff; and Turits, *Foundations of Despotism*, 160.

79. Vega, *Trujillo y Haití*, *Vol. 4*, quote, 156.

80. Published estimates of the death toll vary from four thousand to eighteen thousand. The literature on the massacre is prodigious. For a good synthesis, see Rafael Darío Herrera, "La matanza de Haitianos de 1937," in *Historia general*, V: 303–333. See also Vega, ed., *Trujillo y Haiti, 1930–1937*, 2 vols. (Santo Domingo: Fundación Cultural Dominicana, 1988, 1995). Interpretations that go against the grain are Derby and Turits, "Historias de terror y los terrores de la historia: la masacre haitiana de 1937 en la República Dominicana," *Estudios Sociales* (Santo Domingo) 26:92 (April–June 1993): 65–76; and Turits, "A World Destroyed, A Nation Imposed: The 1937 Haitian Massacre in the Dominican Republic," *HAHR* 82:3 (August 2002): 589–635.

81. Laurent Dubois, *Haiti: The Aftershocks of History* (New York: Metropolitan Books, 2012), 304–305.

82. Roorda, *The Dictator Next Door*, 213.

83. "The Dominican Crisis," 9.

84. Roorda, *The Dictator Next Door*, 105.

85. Vega, ed., *Correspondencia entre Ángel Morales y Sumner Welles*, 258.

86. Acosta Matos, "1934: La expedición de Mariel," *Boletín del Archivo General de la Nación* 62: 127 (May–August 2010): 57–67, especially 57–58.

87. Ibid., 60–61; and Vega, *Trujillo y Haiti*, *Vol. 1*, 150.

88. Silfa, *Guerra, traición y exilio*, I: 121–122; and Acosta Matos, "1934: La expedición de Mariel," 58. Machado's stay ended when he (allegedly) refused to make blackmail payments to Trujillo's brother Petán. Bustamante, *Una satrapía en el Caribe*, 97; and Jimenes Grullón, *Una gestapo*, 175.

89. One of the new hires, Miguel Francisco Sanabria, was implicated in Mella's murder. Acosta Matos, *La telaraña cubana*, I: 50n40.

90. Ibid., I: 59, 92–93.

91. Ibid., quote, I: 64.

92. Letter, Morales to Federico Velázquez, December 18, 1933, in Vega, *Control y represión*, 45–46.

93. Paulino Ramos, "Luchas políticas," 224–225.
94. Morales to Welles, December 24, 1934, in Vega, ed., *Correspondencia entre Ángel Morales y Sumner Welles*, 324.
95. Bosch, et al, "Cayo Confites y la lucha contra Trujillo," *Política, teoría y acción* 44 (November 1983): 1–28, especially 15.
96. Ibarra Guitart, *Las relaciones cubano-dominicanas*, 13–14; and Paulino Ramos, "Luchas políticas," 226.
97. Acosta Matos, *La telaraña cubana*, quote, I: 179.
98. Acosta Matos, "1934: La expedición de Mariel," 62ff.
99. Velázquez to Morales, December 22, 1933, in Vega, *Control y represión*, 48–49; Silfa, *Guerra, traición y exilio*, I: 122; and Paulino Ramos, "Luchas políticas," 225–226.
100. Vega, *Trujillo y Haití*, Vol. 1, quote, 151.
101. Ibarra Guitart, *Las relaciones cubano-dominicanas*, quote, 12; and Acosta Matos, "1934: La expedición de Mariel," 63.
102. Acosta Matos, "1934: La expedición de Mariel," quote, 66.
103. Iber, *Neither Peace nor Freedom*, 122.
104. Unless otherwise indicated, this section draws on Acosta Matos's fine-grained analysis of Cuban-Dominican relations, *La telaraña cubana*.
105. Bonachea and Valdés, "Introduction," 61.
106. Salvador Morales Pérez, *Almoina, un exilado gallego contra la dictadura trujillista* (Santo Domingo: Archivo General de la Nación, 2009), 301.
107. Ramón Barquín, *Las luchas guerrilleras en Cuba: de la colonia a la Sierra Maestra*, 2 vols. (Madrid: Editorial Playor, 1975), I: 76.
108. Vallenilla Lanz, *Escrito de memoria*, 148; and Goldenberg, "The Rise and Fall of a Party," 78.
109. Galíndez, "La opereta bufa de Trujillolandia," *Bohemia*, July 20, 1952. The quotation comes from a revised version of the article, "Un reportaje sobre Santo Domingo," *CA* 80:1 (March–April 1955): 37–56. See also Vega, *Almoina, Galíndez*, 62, 79.
110. Ramfis's paternity was the subject of speculation well before 1952. Journalist John Barthlow Martin mentioned it in an article published in 1938 and then repeated it in his memoir, *Overtaken by Events: The Dominican Crisis from the Fall of Trujillo to the Civil War* (Garden City: Doubleday, 1966), 49. Almoina and Requena mentioned it in their accounts and both, like Galíndez, paid the ultimate price. Bustamante, *Una satrapía en el Caribe*, 21; and Requena, *Cementerio sin cruces*.
111. As provocative as this theory is, there is evidence that suggests that Galíndez was on Trujillo's radar at least a year before "La opereta bufa" was published. In 1962, the FBI interviewed Trujillo insider Anselmo Paulino Álvarez, who mentioned that Trujillo "began to remark to his entourage that Galíndez was 'causing trouble' . . . and that something will have to be done about this . . . his remarks indicated to all who were familiar with his nature and modus operandi that sooner or later Galíndez would have to

pay with his life for having antagonized Trujillo." Untitled Memorandum, July 11, 1962, Section 15, Internal Security Division File, FBI, DOJ Case File 109–51–25, USNA, RG 60, Theories and rumors about the Galíndez case grew like wildfire in the exile community. For a sampling, see Fred Cooke, "Galíndez: The Riddle of the Mystery," *Nation* 185:3 (August 3, 1957): 43–46, quote, 44.

112. Aguirre Mejía, *Viacrucis de un pueblo*, 83.
113. Landestoy, *¡Yo acuso también!*, 229.
114. Sang, *La política exterior dominicana*, I: 182.
115. Morales Pérez, *Almoina, un exilado gallego*, 158.
116. Ibid., 314–318.
117. Arías Núñez, *La política exterior en la era de Trujillo*, 152–154.
118. On Cayo Confites, see Ameringer, *The Caribbean Legion;* Vega, ed., *Los Estados Unidos y Trujillo, año 1946:* Bosch et al., "Cayo Confites," 1–28; and José Diego Grullón, *La revolución traiconada* (Santo Domingo: Alfa y Omega, 1989). 47.
119. Mejía, *De Lilís a Trujillo: historia contemporánea de la República Dominicana* (Caracas: Editorial Elite, 1944); and Portillo, *Venezuela-República Dominicana*, 133.
120. Carlos Guerón, "La 'Doctrina Betancourt' y el papel de la teoría en política exterior," *Politeia* 1 (1972): 231–243, especially 235–237.
121. Peña Batlle, *Política de Trujillo*, 120.
122. Ironically, six hundred rifles came courtesy of Perón via Guatemala; Arévalo never told the Argentine president why he wanted the arms. Clinton, Jr., "The United States and the Caribbean Legion," 187, 191.
123. Jonathan Hansen, *Young Castro: The Making of a Young Revolutionary* (New York: Simon & Schuster, 2019), 99.
124. John Rys, "Tensions and Conflicts in Cuba, Haiti and the Dominican Republic between 1945 and 1959" (Ph.D. dissertation, American University, 1966), 79–80; and Bosch, "La Legión del Caribe," 247.
125. Galíndez, "La opereta bufa," quote, 30.
126. Capdevila, *La dictadura de Trujillo*, 184.
127. Bosch, "Cayo Confites," 13.
128. Bonachea and Valdés, "Introduction," 23.
129. Ewell, *Venezuela and the United States: From Monroe's Hemisphere to Petroleum Empire* (Athens: University of Georgia Press, 1996), 152; and Aaron Moulton, "Patronising the Counter-Revolution: Rafael Trujillo versus Venezuela's Trienio Adeco, 1945–1948," unpublished mss.
130. Capdevila, *La dictadura de Trujillo*, 189.
131. Clinton, Jr., "The United States and the Caribbean Legion," 203ff.
132. Quoted in Acosta Matos, *La telaraña cubana*, II: 505.
133. Espaillat, *Trujillo: The Last Caesar,* quote, 139.
134. Ibid.
135. Silfa, *Guerra, traición y exilio*, II: 278–280.

136. García Olivares, *José Antonio Echeverría*, quote, 279–280 and 300–302; and Hilda Berdayes García, ed., *Papeles del presidente: Documentos y discursos de José Antonio Echeverría Bianchi* (Havana: Casa Editora Abril, 2006), quote, 70–71 and 84–87.

137. Batista was concerned enough by the rumors that he sent Barquín to the Dominican Republic in March 1956 to spy on military installations and to determine if Trujillo was planning an invasion. Barquín, *Las luchas guerrilleras en Cuba*, I: 99, 170, 173, 174n4. See also Thomas, *Cuba: The Pursuit of Freedom*, 882–886; Pérez, Jr., *Army Politics in Cuba*, 147ff; Bonachea and Valdés, "Introduction," 67ff; and Robert Taber, *M-26: Biography of a Revolution* (New York: Lyle Stuart, 1961), 78ff.

138. Hernández and Giusti, eds., *Carlos Andrés Pérez: memorias proscritas*, 102.

139. Espaillat, *Trujillo: The Last Caesar*, 139–141.

140. *Hearings Before the Committee on Foreign Relations of the United States Senate 85th Congress, Second Session on Foreign Policy, February 8, 17, 18, 19, 26 and 27 and March 3, 5, 10, 58*. Part I. (Washington, DC: Government Printing Office, 1958), I: 354ff., quote, 357.

141. Quoted in Heberto Norman Acosta, *La palabra empeñada*, 2 vols. (Havana: Oficina de Publicaciones del Consejo de Estado, 2006), II: 263–264.

142. Jules Dubois, *Fidel Castro: Rebel—Liberator or Dictator?* (Indianapolis: Bobbs-Merrill, 1959), quotes, 129–130 and 132.

143. Bonachea and Valdés, "Introduction," 84–85n244 and 332–337. According to Ameringer, after accepting Dominican arms and money, Castro broke with Trujillo in December 1956. *The Democratic Left*, 169. See also Norman Acosta, *La palabra empeñada*, II: 57.

144. Sang, ed., *La política exterior dominicana*, II: 637.

145. Taber, *M-26*, 82.

146. Letter, Louise Crane to Porter, March 13, 1957, Box 24, File, General Correspondence, COP; and Norman Acosta, *La palabra empeñada*, II: 261, 301–302.

147. Telegram, Gardner to State Department, October 16, 1956, *FRUS, 1955–1957* (Washington, DC: Government Printing Office, 1987), VI: 835.

148. Dubois, *Fidel Castro: Rebel*, 148–149; and Vega, *Eisenhower y Trujillo* (Santo Domingo: Fundación Cultural Dominicana, 1991), 29 and 226–230.

149. Taber, *M-26*, 225–226.

150. Betancourt to Romauldi, Tomo XXIX:2 (April 2, 1956), #185, FRB.

151. The complete report can be found in Morales Pérez, *Almoina, un exilado gallego*, 299–352.

152. Alexander, "Stanley Ross and the Battle for N.Y. Puerto Ricans," *NL* 41:15 (April 14, 1958): 7–10, quote, 7. A copy of Ross's October 20, 1955, memo to Trujillo can be found in Section V: Serie 19 Material Informativo, Caja 16, Folder 131, FLMM.

153. Alexander, "Stanley Ross and the Battle," quotes, 7.

154. Crane, "A Memorandum on Jesús de Galíndez," Box 24, File, Murphy-Background Material Re. Galíndez, etc, COP.

155. "Mutual Case Spotlights Trujillo's U.S. Efforts," *WP*, September 1959, Box 15, File, Foreign Affairs, Dominican Republic, Record, Clips, Information, etc., COP.

156. Morales Pérez, *Almoina, un exilado gallego*, 225.

157. Bustamante, *Una satrapía en el Caribe*, 88.

158. Miolán, *El Perredé desde mi ángulo*, 2nd ed. (Caracas: Avila Arte, 1985 [1984]), 488.

159. Víctor Grimaldi, *Sangre en el barrio del jefe* (Santo Domingo: Editora Corripio, 2007), 25–26.

160. C. Harvey Gardiner, *La política de inmigración de Trujillo: Estudio sobre la creación de una imagen humanitaria* (Santo Domingo: Talleres de la Universidad Nacional Henríquez Ureña, 1979), 135–136.

161. Galíndez, "Datos sobre el asesinato de Manuel de Jesús ('Pipí') Hernández Santana, en La Habana, el 8 de agosto, 1955," undated, MC 671, 29:24, FRG.

162. Sang, ed., *La política exterior dominicana*, II: 635–636. For similarities between the Hernández murder and the abduction of Galíndez seven months later, see Grant to Peter Heinz, March 31, 1956, MC 671, 29:28, FRG.

163. Quoted in Morales Pérez, *Almoina, un exilado gallego*, 239.

164. *Yo fui secretario de Trujillo* (Buenos Aires: Editora y Distribuidora del Plata, 1950). On Almoina's predicament, see Morales Pérez, *Almoina, un exiliado gallego*, 239–271.

165. Constancio Cassá Bernaldo de Quirós, "Vida y obra de Jesús de Galíndez Suárez," in *Jesús de Galíndez. Escritos desde Santo Domingo y artículos contra el régimen de Trujillo en el exterior*, ed. idem (Santo Domingo: Comisión Permanente de Efemérides Patrias, Archivo General de la Nación, 2010), 17–32, especially 26–27.

166. Ibid., 99.

167. Peck, "Our Struggle Against Trujillo," *Liberation* (December 1957): 5–8, quotes, 5–6.

168. Elizabeth Manley, "The Galíndez Case in the Dominican Republic," *Oxford Research Encyclopedia of Latin American History*, 7. https://oxfordre.com/latinamericanhistory/view/10.1093/acrefore/9780199366439.001.0001/acrefore-9780199366439-e-354?rskey=1daNoD&result=1. Accessed 11/07/2016; and McKeever, *Professor Galíndez*, 4.

169. Galíndez began work for the FBI and the forerunner of the CIA, the OSS, in the Dominican Republic. Manuel de Dios Unanue, *El caso Galíndez: Los vascos en los servicios de inteligencia de EEUU* (Nafarroa, Spain: Editorial Txalaparta, 1999), 190.

170. Harrison Salisbury, "The Strange Correspondence of Morris Ernst and John Edgar Hoover, 1939–1964," *Nation* 239 (December 1, 1984).

171. Germán Ornes, *Trujillo: Little Caesar of the Caribbean* (New York: Thomas Nelson and Sons, 1958), quote, 310.

172. Inaki Bernardo Urquijo, *La tumba abierto: los vascos y los Estados Unidos* (Bilbao, Spain: Servicio Central de Publicaciones del Gobierno Vasco, 1993), 357; and Dios Unanue, *El caso Galíndez*, 52–65.

173. McKeever, *Professor Galíndez*, 64–66.

174. Ibid., 48.

175. Galíndez to Morales, January 15, 1955, MC 671, 29:25, FRG.

176. Matthew Crawford, Jr., FBI, Missing Person Report, February 23, 1957, Section 1, Internal Security Division File, DOJ Case File 109–51–25, RG 60, USNA.

177. Hoover to E. Tomlin Bailey, March 15, 1957, Section 2, Internal Security Division File, DOJ Case File 109–51–25, RG 60, USNA. On Navajita, see Vega, *Eisenhower y Trujillo*, 14.

178. FBI interviews with students, May 2, 1957, Section 3, Internal Security Division File, DOJ Case File 109–51–25, RG 60, USNA.

179. Galíndez to Morales, November 22, 1955, MC 671, 29:25, FRG.

180. Tannenbaum to Naranjo, April 3, 1956. Box 9, FTC.

181. Tannenbaum, "Galíndez," October 17, 1960, Box 9, FTC.

182. Matthews, "Galíndez Case: New Chapter in Dominican History," *NYT*, December 15, 1957.

183. Tannenbaum to Naranjo, April 3, 1956, Box 9, FTC.

184. Tannenbaum to Naranjo, May 31, 1956, Box 9, FTC.

185. Crane, "A Memorandum on Jesús de Galíndez."

186. IADF press release, undated, 29:25, MC671, FRG.

187. Moulton, "Patronising the Counter-Revolution"; Castro Ventura, *Trujillo vs. Betancourt;* Sang, *La política exterior dominicana*, Vol. II; and Federico Landaeta, *Cuando reinaron las sombras: Tres años de luchas contra el Romulato en Venezuela* (Madrid: Gráfico Clemares, 1955).

Chapter Ten. In Defense of Democracy

Epigraph 1: Memo, Director of the Office of South American Affairs, *FRUS, 1946*, IV: 396.

Epigraph 2: Oral History Interview, José Figueres Ferrer, by Donald McCoy and Richard McKinzie, July 8, 1970, Harry S. Truman Oral History Collection, 35, TPL. Accessed July 18, 2016. https://www.trumanlibrary.org/oralhist/ferrerjf.htm

1. Baldwin and Grant to Roosevelt, January 11, 1949, MC 671, Box 27–17, FRG.

2. Ewell, *Venezuela and the United States*, 155.

3. Planning Committees, 1949–1950, MC 671, Box 27–5, FRG.

4. Press release, April 17, 1950, MC 671, Box 27–5, FRG.

5. Havana, 1950, Planning 1 (of 2), MC 671, Box 27–15, FRG; and "Aid for Democracy Set Up in Havana," *NYT*, May 15, 1950.

6. García-Bryce, *Haya de la Torre*, 118–120 and 158.

7. "Speech Delivered by Mr. Rómulo Betancourt at the Close of the Interamerican Conference of Democracy and Freedom," May 1950, MC 671, 27:24, FRG.

8. Havana, 1050, Resolutions and Miscellany, MC 671, 27:23, FRG.

9. Cerdas Cruz, "Costa Rica," in *Latin America between the Second World War,* 280–299, especially 294ff; and Tord Hoivik and Aas Solveig, "Demilitarization in Costa Rica: A Farewell to Arms," *Journal of Peace Research* 18:4 (1981): 333–351.

10. Figueres expressed misgivings for reneging on his promise in *El espíritu del 48* (San José: Editorial Costa Rica, 1987), 319.

11. Rouquié, "The Military in Latin American Politics," 184.

12. Pérez, Jr., "International Dimensions," quote, 53; and Wood, *The Dismantling,* quote, 133.

13. Coronil, *The Magical State,* 162–163; and Tad Szulc, *Twilight of the Tyrants* (New York: Henry Holt, 1959), 207.

14. "The Day of the Race," *NYT,* October 12, 1955, 30; and Ewell, *Venezuela and the United States,* quote, 159.

15. Quoted in Wood, *The Dismantling,* 159–160.

16. Quoted in Rabe, "Dulles, Latin America, and Cold War Anticommunism," in *John Foster Dulles and the Diplomacy of the Cold War,* ed. Richard Immerman (Princeton: Princeton University Press, 1990), 159–188, especially 169.

17. Adolf A. Berle, Jr., "The Cuban Crisis: Failure of American Foreign Policy," *FA* 39:1 (October 1960): 40–55, quote, 49–50.

18. Rangel, Una interpretación de las dictaduras latinoamericanas," *CA* 13 (September–October 1954), 33–42.

19. Ibid.

20. Kolb, *Democracy and Dictatorship,* 94; Trinkunas, *Crafting Civilian Control,* 266n5; and Martz, *Acción Democrática,* quote, 101.

21. Memorandum by the Director of the Office of South American Affairs, *FRUS, 1952–1954* (Washington, DC: Government Printing Office, 1955), IV: 383.

22. Susanne Bodenheimer, " 'The Social Democratic Ideology in Latin America: The Case of Costa Rica's Partido Liberación Nacional," *Caribbean Studies* 10:3 (October 1970): 49–96, especially 79–80.

23. Rabe, "Eisenhower and Latin America: Arms and Dictators," *Peace and Change* 11:1 (April 1985): 49–61, especially 50–54; John Child, *Unequal Alliance: The Inter-American Military System, 1938–1978* (Boulder: Westview Press, 1980), 126; and Robert Holden, "The Real Diplomacy of Violence: United States Military Violence in Central America, 1950–1990," *The International History Review* 15:2 (May 1993): 283–322, especially 288.

24. Martha Huggins, *Political Policing: The United States and Latin America* (Durham: Duke University Press, 1998), 80, 84–85.

25. Charles Maechling, Jr., "Counterinsurgency: The First Ordeal by Fire," in *Low-Intensity Warfare: Counterinsurgency, Proinsurgency, and Antiterrorism in the Eighties,* ed. Michael Klare and Peter Kornbluh (New York: Pantheon, 1987), 21–48, especially 32.

26. Brands, *Latin America's Cold War,* 80.

27. Child, *Unequal Alliance,* 116, 124.

28. "U.S. Policy toward Latin America," August 20, 1956, NSC Series, Policy Papers Subseries, Box 1.8, White House Office, Office of the Special Assistant for National Security Affairs: Records, EPL.

29. Lieuwen, *Arms and Politics*, 230.

30. Santos, "The Defense of Freedom in Latin America," in *Responsible Freedom in the Americas*, ed. Ángel del Río (New York: Greenwood, 1968), 215–223, quote, 220–221.

31. Rabe, "Eisenhower and Latin America," 52–53, quote, 52.

32. Matthews, "Diplomatic Relations," 165.

33. Betancourt to Muñoz Marín, September 20, 1953, Section V, Series, Governor of Puerto Rico, 1949–1964, Correspondencia Particular, Cartapacio #36, FLMM.

34. "National Intelligence Estimate: The Caribbean Republics," August 24, 1954, *FRUS, 1952–1954*, IV: 397.

35. "A Report to the NSC by the Executive Secretary on U.S. Objectives and Courses of Actions with Respect to Latin America," March 6, 1953, NSC Series, Policy Paper Subseries, White House Office, Office of the Special Assistant for National Security Affairs: Records, Box 4, EPL.

36. Roy Richard Rubottom, Jr., oral history, p. 14, JFDOHP.

37. "Costa Rica: Policy Statement Prepared in the Department of State," March 3, 1951, *FRUS, 1951* (Washington, DC: Government Printing Office, 1952), II: 1314–1320, quote, 1318.

38. Quoted in Longley, "Resistance and Accommodation: The United States and the Nationalism of José Figueres, 1953–1957," *DH* 18:1 (January 1994): 1–28, especially 14.

39. Ernesto "Che" Guevara, *Latin American Diaries: The Sequel to the Motorcycle Diaries* (Melbourne, Australia: Ocean Press, 2011), quote, 56–57.

40. Silfa, *Guerra, traición y exilio*, I: 398.

41. Quoted in McKeever, *Professor Galíndez*, 30.

42. Galíndez, "Anti-comunismo negativo y positivo," *LR*, February 25, 1954.

43. Ibid.

44. Galíndez, "Vísperas de sangre en Cuba?" *LR*, March 31, 1954.

45. Lehman, "Revolutions and Attributions: Making Sense of Eisenhower Administration Policies in Bolivia and Guatemala," *DH* 21:2 (Spring 1997): 185–213, quote, 194–195; and Laurence Whitehead, "Bolivia since 1930," *CHLA* VIII: 509–586, especially 542–543.

46. Knight, "The Domestic Dynamics of the Mexican and Bolivian Revolutions," in *Proclaiming Revolution: Bolivia in Comparative Perspective*, ed. Merilee Grindle and Pilar Domingo (Cambridge, MA: David Rockefeller Center for Latin American Studies, 2003) 55–90, especially 70–71; and Whitehead, "Bolivia since 1930," 546.

47. Zanatta, "The Rise and Fall of the Third Position. Bolivia, Perón and the Cold War, 1943–1954," trans. Judith Evans, *Desarrollo Económico* 45:177 (April–June 2005), 1–27, especially 4; and Dorn, "Perón's Gambit," 17.

48. Dunkerley, *Rebellion in the Veins: Political Struggle in Bolivia, 1952–1982* (London: Verso, 1984), quote, 31; Whitehead, "Bolivia since 1930," 533; Cole Blasier, *The Hovering Giant: U.S. Responses to Revolutionary Change in Latin America, 1910–1985*, revised ed. (Pittsburgh: University of Pittsburgh Press, 1985), 128; and idem, "The United States and the Revolution," in *Beyond the Revolution: Bolivia since 1952*, ed. James Malloy and Richard Thorn (Pittsburgh: University of Pittsburgh Press, 1971), 53–110, especially 61.

49. Lehman, "Braked but not Broken: Mexico and Bolivia—Factoring the United States into the Revolutionary Equation," in *Proclaiming Revolution:* 91–113, especially 91 and 101; and Alexander, *The Bolivarian Presidents*, 16.

50. Blasier, *The Hovering Giant*, 130; and Zanatta, "The Rise and Fall," 15.

51. Finchelstein, *From Fascism to Populism*, 122–123.

52. "The Problem of Bolivia," *NYT*, June 17, 1953; and Blasier, *The Hovering Giant*, 134.

53. Burton Hersh, *The Old Boys: The American Elite and the Origins of the CIA* (New York: Scribner's, 1992), 339; Lehman, Revolutions and Attributions," 192; and idem, "Braked but not Broken," 103. For Atwood's statement, see "Bolivian Economic Problems," July 26, 1953, in House Committee on Foreign Affairs, *Selected Executive Hearings . . . 1951–1956*, 433.

54. James Siekmeier, *The Bolivian Revolution and the United States, 1952–Present* (University Park: Pennsylvania State University Press, 2010), 43ff.

55. Figueres, "The Problems of Democracy," 18.

56. Coatsworth, "The Cold War in Central America, 1975–1991," in *CHCW*, ed. Leffler and Westad, 3 vols. (New York: Cambridge University Press, 2010), III: 201–221, quote, 203.

57. Jim Handy, *Gift of the Devil: A History of Guatemala* (Toronto: Between the Lines, 1984), 135–136; and Mahoney, *The Legacies of Liberalism*, 215.

58. Dunkerley, "Guatemala, 1944–1954," in *Political Suicide*, 83–114, especially 105–106.

59. Norman LaCharité, Richard Kennedy, and Philip Thienel, *Case Study in Insurgency and Revolutionary Warfare: Guatemala, 1944–1954* (Washington, DC: Special Operations Research Office, American University, 1964), 85.

60. Kalman Silvert, *A Study in Government: Guatemala* (New Orleans: Tulane University Middle American Research Institute, 1954), 29–30; and LaCharité et al, *Case Study*, 96.

61. Dunkerley, "Guatemala," in *Latin America between the Second World War*, 300–326, especially 312.

62. Theories abound as to who murdered Arana and why. The most persuasive account is Gleijeses, "The Death of Francisco Arana: A Turning Point in the Guatemalan Revolution," *JLAS* 22:3 (October 1990): 527–552. Cf. Ameringer, *U.S. Foreign Intelligence: The Secret Side of American History* (Lexington, MA: Lexington Books, 1990), 252; and Silfa, *Guerra, traición y exilio*, II: 281, 283.

63. Dunkerley, *Power in the Isthmus*, 143; Ross Baker, *A Study of Status and Status Deprivation in Three Latin American Armies* (Washington, DC: Center for

Research in Social Systems, American University, 1967), 38–42; and Robert Kirkland, *Observing* Our Hermanos de Armas*: U.S. Military Attachés in Guatemala, Cuba and Bolivia, 1950–1964* (New York: Routledge, 2003), 66–67.

64. Gleijeses, "The Death of Francisco Arana," quote, 549.

65. Moulton, "The Dictators' Domino Theory: A Caribbean Basin Anti-Communist Network, 1947–1952," *Intelligence and National Security* 34:7 (2019): 945–961, especially 948–950; and idem, "Counterrevolutionary Friends: Caribbean Basin Dictators and Guatemalan Exiles against the Guatemalan Revolution," *TA* 76:1 (January 2019): 107–135.

66. Gleijeses, *Shattered Hope: The Guatemalan Revolution and the United States, 1944–1954* (Princeton: Princeton University Press, 1991), especially 67n67 and 81–83; and John Gillin and K. (Kalman) Silvert, "Ambiguities in Guatemala," *FA* 34:3 (April 1956): 469–481, especially 478.

67. Cardoza y Aragón, *La revolución guatemalteca* (Guatemala City: Editorial del Pensativo, 1994 [1955]), 48–49.

68. Handy, *Gift of the Devil*, 111–112; Baker, *A Study of Status*, 46–47; Pike, "Guatemala, the United States, and Communism in the Americas," *Review of Politics* 17 (April 1955): 232–261, especially 248; and Gordon Bowen, "U.S. Foreign Policy toward Radical Change: Covert Operations in Guatemala, 1950–1954," *LAP* 10:1 (Winter 1983): 88–102, especially 88.

69. Dunkerley, *Rebellion in the Veins*, quote, 4.

70. Shesko, *Conscript Nation: Coercion and Citizenship in the Bolivian Barracks* (Pittsburgh: University of Pittsburgh Press, 2020), chapter 7, quote, 163; Whitehead, "Bolivia since 1930," 548, 553; and Malloy, "Revolutionary Politics," in *Beyond the Revolution*, 111–156, especially 122. Huggins suggests that in the years after the revolution, U.S. preoccupation with the fourteen-thousand-strong mineworkers' union, which it considered vulnerable to communist penetration, contributed to a revival of the Bolivian military's fortunes. *Political Policing in Latin America*, 85.

71. NSC "Progress Report on United States Objectives and Courses of Action with Respect to Latin America," August 10, 1955, *FRUS, 1955–1957*, VI: 6–13, quote, 8.

72. Lehman, "Revolutions and Attributions," 199; and idem, "Braked but not Broken." On Milton Eisenhower's recommendation, see Blasier, *The Hovering Giant*, quote, 133.

Chapter Eleven. We Are Fighting in Difficult Circumstances

Epigraph: Forward to Betancourt, *Hacia América Latina democrática e integrada*, 2nd ed. (Caracas: Senderos, 1967 [1967]), 12.

1. Quoted in Ameringer, *The Democratic Left in Exile*, 155.

2. "Democracia y Caracas no se concilian," *LR*, February 20, 1954.

3. "Briefing on Central American Questions," May 22, 1953, United States Congress, House Committee on Foreign Affairs, *Selected Executive Session*

Hearings of the Committee, 1951–1956, Vol. 16, The Middle East, African and Inter-American Affairs (Washington, DC: Government Printing Office, 1980), 491.

4. Alexander, *Venezuela's Voice for Democracy*, 24.

5. Betancourt to Otilio Ulate, May 10, 1954, reprinted in Ulate, *Hacia donde lleva*, 14–15.

6. Ameringer, *The Democratic Left in Exile*, quote, 154.

7. Guillermo García Ponce and Francisco Camacho Barrios, *Diario de la resistencia y la dictadura, 1948–1959*, 2nd ed. (Caracas: Ediciones Centauro, 1982 [1980]), 47.

8. Ocarina Castillo D'Imperio, *Los años del buldozer: ideología y política, 1948–1958* (Caracas: Fondo Editorial Tropykos, Asociación de Profesores, U.C.V., and CENDES, 1990); and Ameringer, *The Democratic Left in Exile*, quote, 154.

9. Betancourt, *Venezuela: Política*, 577; and García Ponce and Camacho Barrios, *Diario de la resistencia*, p. 102.

10. Betancourt, "La opinión continental frente a la X Conferencia Interamericana," *CA* 71 (September–October 1953): 7–37; and José Vicente Abreu, *Guasina, donde el río perdió las siete estrellas: Relatos de un campo de concentración de PJ* (Caracas: José Agustín Catalá, 1969).

11. Comité Ejecutivo Nacional del Partido Acción Democrática, *Libro negro de una dictadura: Venezuela bajo el signo del terror, 1948–1952* (Mexico City: Editorial Centauro, 1952).

12. Betancourt, *Hombres y villanos*, quote, 146.

13. Catalá, *La denuncia: Crimenes y torturas en el régimen de Pérez Jiménez* (Caracas: José Agustín Catalá, 1969).

14. Schaposnik, *La democratización de las Fuerzas Armadas*, 26; Fuenmayor, *Historia de la Venezuela política contemporánea, 1899–1969*, 14 vols. (Caracas: Talleres Tipográficos de Miguel Ángel García e Hijo,1985), IX: 74–75; and Winfield Burggraaff, *The Venezuelan Armed Forces, 1935–1959* (Columbia: University of Missouri Press, 1972), 93.

15. On the January 1948 plot, see Moulton, "Building Their Own Cold War in Their Own Backyard: The Transnational, International Conflicts in the Greater Caribbean Basin, 1944–1954," *Cold War History* 15:2 (2015), 146; Castro Ventura, *Trujillo vs. Betancourt*, 81–82; and Portillo, *Venezuela-República Dominicana*, 140. Six months earlier the State Department had discouraged a similar plot, also initiated in the Dominican Republic. The most detailed, if one-sided, account of the two conspiracies is by a Venezuelan diplomat complicit in the plotting. Leonardo Altuve Carrillo, *Yo fui embajador de Pérez Jiménez* (Caracas: Talleres de Tipografía y Litografía Ortiz e Hijos, 1973), 180ff.

16. García Ponce and Camacho Barrios, *Diario de la Resistencia*, p. 94–95.

17. Agustín Blanco Muñoz, ed. *Pedro Estrada habló: La dictadura* (Caracas: Editorial José Martí, 1983), 108.

18. García Ponce and Camacho Barrios, *Diario de la Resistencia*, 93; and Burggraaff, *The Venezuelan Armed Forces*, 140.

19. Tinker Salas notes that the SN and the security departments of foreign oil companies shared intelligence. *Venezuela: What Everyone Needs*, 89–90.

20. Szulc, *Twilight of the Tyrants*, 293–294.

21. Silfa, *Guerra, traición y exilio*, II: 119.

22. García Ponce and Camacho Barrios, *Diario de la resistencia*, 90–91; López Maya, ed., *Antología política, 1948–1952* (Caracas: Fundación Rómulo Betancourt, Consejo Desarrollo Científico y Humanístico de la Universidad Central de Venezuela, 1990), V: 805–811; Avendaño Lugo, *El militarismo en Venezuela*, 218–219; Schaposnik, *La democratización de las Fuerzas Armadas Venezolanas*, 169; and Helena Plaza, *El 23 de enero de 1958 y el proceso de consolidación de la democracia representativa en Venezuela: Ensayo de interpretación sociopolítica* (Caracas: Garbizu & Todtmannn Editores, 1978), 21.

23. Burggraaff, *The Venezuelan Armed Forces*, 153.

24. Quoted in Schaposnik, *La democratización de las Fuerzas Armadas*, 159. See also Avendaño Lugo, *El militarismo en Venezuela*, 216; and Burggraaff, *The Venezuelan Armed Forces*, 152.

25. Quoted in Elisabeth J. Friedman, *Unfinished Transitions*, 110–111. On female participation in the resistance, see Fania Petzoldt and Jacinta Bevilacqua, *Nosotros también nos jugamos la vida: testimonios de la mujer venezolana en la lucha clandestina, 1948–1958* (Caracas: Editorial Ateneo de Caracas). On the repression of AD, see Fuenmayor, *Historia de la Venezuela política contemporanea*, IX: 151, quote, 75; and Glen Kolb, *Democracy and Dictatorship in Venezuela* (Hamden, CT: Archon Books, 1974), 97, 102. On license plates, see Szulc, *Twilight of the Tyrants*, 286.

26. Capriles, *Memorias de la inconformidad*, 356–357.

27. Ibid., 311, 324–326; and Szulc, *Twilight of the Tyrants*, 257.

28. For example, *Informaciones Venezolanas*, September 1, 1953, and *Acción Democrática habla al pueblo de Venezuela en su XII aniversario*, September 13, 1953, Section V, Series, 2, Governor of Puerto Rico, 1949–1964, Correspondencia Particular, Cartapacio #36, FLMM.

29. Matos, *Como llegó la noche*, quote, 71.

30. Peña, *Conversaciones con Carlos Andrés Pérez*, I: 111.

31. Quero de Trinca, "El tercer exilio de Rómulo Betancourt (1953–1958)," in *Antología del pensamiento político de Rómulo Betancourt*, 7 vols. (Caracas: Fundación Rómulo Betancourt, 2004), volume editor, idem, 12–44, especially VI: 19.

32. Letter, Betancourt to Luis Lander, January 14, 1950, López Maya, ed., *Antología política, 1948–1952*, V: 290–291.

33. Szulc, *Twilight of the Tyrants*, 293.

34. Abbes García, *Trujillo y yo*, quote, 148–149.

35. Schaposnik, *La democratización de las Fuerzas Armadas*, 141.

36. Hernández and Giusti, eds., *Carlos Andrés Pérez: memorias proscritas*, 91ff; "Ex-Venezuelan Reports Plot on Life," *NYT*, April 21, 1951; and Kolb, *Democracy and Dictatorship*, 95.

37. Betancourt, *Venezuela: Política*, 587–589; and López Maya, *Antología política, 1948–1952*, V: 570–584.

38. García Ponce and Camacho Barrios, *Diario de la resistencia*, p. 96; and Alfredo Angulo Reyes, "Relaciones Venezuela-Cuba: un caso de conflicto diplomático," *Boletín de la Academia Nacional de la Historia* 74: 296 (October–December 1991): 89–106, especially 99.

39. Letter, José Ángel Saviñón, Dominican Consul in San Juan, Puerto Rico, to the Dominican Foreign Ministry, Ciudad Trujillo, January 31, 1951, in Sang, ed., *La política exterior dominicana*, II: 295–295. On Cuban passports, see Hartmann, *Rómulo y yo*, 126. On Bosch's and Figueres's transfer of funds, see Bosch, "La Legión del Caribe," 253.

40. Quero de Trinca, "El tercer exilio," 19–20. A Venezuelan journalist tallied seventeen plots against Betancourt's life. Caballero, *Rómulo Betancourt, político de nación*, 320n8.

41. Vallenilla Lanz, *Memorias en escrito*, 203.

42. Norman Dupray (aka Fuenmayor), *Aves de rapiña sobre Venezuela: Análisis de la situación política contemporánea de Venezuela y de las causas por las cuales fué asesinado el coronel Carlos Delgado Chalbaud* (Buenos Aires: Talleres Gráficos de La Técnica Impresora S.A.C.I., 1958), 102.

43. Betancourt, *Hombres y villanos*, 265; Semán, *Ambassadors of the Working Class*, 270n95; and Castillo D'Imperio, *Los años del buldozer*, 83ff.

44. Coronil Hartmann, *Rómulo Betancourt: La vida como pedagogía*, 18; and Zanatta, *La internacional justicialista*, quote, 223.

45. Zanatta, *La internacional justicialista*, 323.

46. Alexander, "Labor and Inter-American Relations," 45–46; and Dorn, "Perón's Gambit," 4. Two played at this game. The Eisenhower administration subsidized trips to the U.S. taken by the leadership of anticommunist unions. Rabe, "Dulles, Latin America," especially 164.

47. Zanatta, "The Rise and Fall," quote, 7.

48. Franqui, *Diary of the Cuban Revolution*, 10; Zanatta, *La internacional justicialista*, 156; and Dorn, "Perón's Gambit."

49. Semán, *Ambassadors of the Working Class*, 4, 56, 154, and 217; Alexander, "Peronism and Argentina's Quest for Leadership in Latin America," *Journal of International Affairs* 9:1 (1955): 47–55, especially 55; and Andrés Cisneros and Carlos Escudé, "Historia general de las relaciones exteriores de la República Argentina," http://www.argentina—rr.ee.com/13/13–010.htm. Accessed February 8, 2013.

50. Quoted in Harold Peterson, *Argentina and the United States, 1810–1960* (New York: State University of New York Press, 1964), 431. See also Finchelstein, *The Ideological Origins of the Dirty War: Fascism, Populism, and Dictatorship in Twentieth Century Argentina* (New York: Oxford University Press, 2014), 68.

51. Rock, "Argentina, 1930–1946," in *CHLA*, VIII: 3–71, especially 52.
52. Schaposnik, *La democratización de las Fuerzas Armadas*, 32–33.
53. Capdevila, *La dictadura de Trujillo*, 179.
54. Roa, "Rómulo Betancourt, el combatiente"; Alexander, "Peronism and Argentina's Quest," 49; and Zanatta, *La internacional justicialista*, 187, 297. On plotting in Chile and Bolivia, see Zanatta, "The Rise and Fall," 10, 15; and Leonor Machinandiarena de Devoto and Carlos Escudé, "Las relaciones argentine-chilenas, 1946–1953, y las ilusiones expansionistas del peronismo," in *Argentina-Chile: desarrollos paralelos?* ed. Torcuato di Tella (Buenos Aires: Nuevohacer, 1997), 181–200.
55. Dorn, "Perón's Gambit," 10–18.
56. Zanatta, *La internacional justicialista*, 191–192, quote, 329.
57. Plaza, *El 23 de enero de 1958*, 16.
58. Rein, "Francoist Spain and Latin America, 1936–1953," in *Fascism Outside Europe: The European Impulse against Domestic Conditions in the Diffusion of Global Fascism*, 116–152, ed. Stein Ugelvik Larsen (New York: Columbia University Press, 2001), 121–123, quote, 121.
59. Lorenzo Delgado Gómez-Escalonilla, *Diplomacia franquista y política cultural hacia Iberoamérica, 1939–1953* (Madrid: Consejo Superior de Investigaciones Científicas, Centro de Estudios Históricos, Departamento de Historia Contemporánea, 1988), 10ff., quote, 25; and Ruth Ben-Ghiat, *Strongmen: Mussolini to the Present* (New York: Norton, 2020), 68.
60. Delgado Gómez-Escalonilla, *Diplomacia franquista*, quote, 131–132.
61. Marisol Saavedra, "Perón y Franco: afinidades, intereses y ideología: las relaciones hispano-argentinas entre 1946–1955," *Todo es historia* 35:409 (August 2001): 56–71, especially 60–64; and Matilde Eiroa San Francisco, "Acción exterior y propaganda: Las visitas de líderes latinoamericanos a Franco," *Revista Latinoamérica* 11:53 (June 2012): 111–134.
62. Schaposnik, *La democratización de las Fuerzas Armadas*, 60, 83.
63. Moulton, "Counterrevolutionary Friends," especially 117n51; and Andrew Schlewitz, "Imperial Incompetence and Guatemalan Militarism, 1931–1966," *International Journal of Politics, Culture and Society* 17:4 (Summer 2004): 580–614, especially 597.
64. Roa, "Vientos de fronda en Venezuela," in *15 años después*, ed. idem, 240–247, especially 246.
65. Dupray, *Aves de rapiña*, 95–96; and NIE report, "Conditions and Trends in Latin America," December 6, 1955, *FRUS, 1955–1957*, VI: 16–45, especially 43–44.
66. Vallenilla Lanz, *Escrito de memoria*, 203–204.
67. Ibid., 187.
68. Kolb, *Democracy and Dictatorship*, 113, quote, 42. Castro Ventura contends that Trujillo had a hand in the assassination of Delgado Chalbaud. His murder paved the way for Pérez Jiménez to take power, someone far more preferable to Trujillo than the relatively progressive Delgado Chalbaud. The

ringleader of the group that kidnapped and murdered Delgado Chalbaud, Rafael Simón Urbina, had close ties to Trujillo. *Trujillo vs. Betancourt*, 98, 126; and Szulc, *Twilight of the Tyrants*, 282.

69. Betancourt, "La opinión continental," quote, 6; and Caballero, *Rómulo Betancourt, político de nación*, 266.

70. Moulton, "Patronising the Counter-Revolution."

71. Kolb, *Democracy and Dictatorship*, 19–20; and *Venezuela: Política y petroleo*, 550.

72. Moulton, "Patronising the Counter-Revolution"; and Ewell, *Venezuela and the United States*, 151.

73. Betancourt, "La opinión continental," quote, 19.

74. Quoted in Betancourt, *Panamericanismo y dictadura: la opinión continental frente a la X Conferencia Interamericanna* (Mexico City: Cuadernos Americanos, 1953). See also Jorge Mañach, "Ante la Conferencia de Caracas," *LR*, February 26, 1954.

75. Betancourt, "El caso de Venezuela y el destino de la democracia en América," *CA* 4 (July–August 1949): 27–66, especially 54–55.

76. Betancourt to "Juan" (pseudonym), Tomo 19:1 (January 7, 1953), FRB.

77. Quoted in Fuenmayor, *Historia de la Venezuela política contemporanea*, X: 115, 152.

78. Quoted in Betancourt, "La opinión continental," 24–25. See also Mark Hove, "The Árbenz Factor: Salvador Allende, U.S.-Chilean Relations, and the 1954 U.S. Intervention in Guatemala," *DH* 31:4 (September 2007): 623–663, especially 631.

79. "Diputados condicionan asistencia de Costa Rica a la Conferencia de Caracas," *LR*, February 10, 1954.

80. Quoted in Betancourt, "La opinión continental," 26.

81. Quoted in Ameringer, *Don Pepe*, 117–118. See also Longley, *The Sparrow and the Hawk: Costa Rica and the United States during the Rise of José Figueres* (Tuscaloosa: University of Alabama Press, 1997), 137.

82. Gleijeses, *Shattered Hope*, 270.

83. "Ante la Reunión de la X Conferencia Interamericana de Caracas," *Informaciones Venezolanas*, September 1, 1953, Section V, Series 2, Governor of Puerto Rico, 1949–1964, Correspondencia Particular, Cartapacio #36, FLMM.

84. Betancourt to Alexander, 23:1 (January 17, 1954), #53, FRB.

85. Grant to Betancourt, 23:1 (January 12, 1954), #22; and Grant to Betancourt, 23:2 (February 11, 1954), #151, FRB.

86. Betancourt to Grant, February 17, 1954, 47:43, Rómulo Betancourt Correspondence, FRG.

87. Romauldi to Betancourt, October 28, 1952; and Betancourt to Romauldi, 28:1 (November 4, 1952), FRB.

88. Ellner, "Populism in Venezuela, 1935–48: Betancourt and the Acción Democrática," in *Latin American Populism*, 135–154, quote, 147.

89. Caballero, *Rómulo Betancourt, político de nación*, quote, 278.

90. Ellner, "Populism in Venezuela," 138.

91. Kolb, *Democracy and Dictatorship*, 23; and Alexander, *The Communist Party of Venezuela* (Stanford: Hoover Institution Press, 1969), 29ff.

92. Rangel, *La revolución de las fantasías*, 2nd ed. (Caracas: Ediciones Ofidi, 1988, [1966]), 126–127; and "Carta de Rómulo Betancourt al grupo de asilados en Cuba," in *La resistencia del partido del pueblo en el exilio, 1948–1958*, ed. Acción Democrática (Caracas: Gráficas Franco SRL, 2003), 19–21. On efforts to forge an alliance between the PCV and AD, see García Ponce and Camacho Barrios, *El diario desconocido*.

93. Quero de Trinca, "El tercer exilio," 18ff.

94. Ibid., 22.

95. Hartmann, *Rómulo y yo*, 31, 36.

96. Plaza, *El 23 de enero*, 152.

97. Caballero, *Rómulo Betancourt, político de nación*, 18; and Elisabeth J. Friedman, *Unfinished Transitions*, quote, 113.

98. Rangel, *La revolución de las fantasías*, 17–18, quote, 126; Ellner, "Leonardo Ruíz Pineda: Acción Democrática's *Guerrillero* for Liberty," *JISWA* 22:3 (August 1980): 389–392, quote, 389; Ameringer, "Leonardo Ruíz Pineda: Leader of the Venezuelan Resistance, 1949–1952," *JISWA* 21:2 (May 1979): 209–232.

99. Betancourt to Romauldi, 25:1 (October 13, 1954), #1, FRB; and Andrés Stambouli, *Crisis política: Venezuela, 1945–1958* (Caracas: Editorial Ateneo de Caracas, 1980), 149ff.

100. Memorandum of Conversation, Figueres and Robert Hill, February 6, 1954, *FRUS, 1952–1954*, IV: 839; and Kolb, *Democracy and Dictatorship*, 136.

101. Cerdas Cruz, "Costa Rica," 296 and quote, 298; and Kordick, *The Saints of Progress*, 120.

102. Kordick, *The Saints of Progress*, 121.

103. Gonzalo Facio, "Tenemos el mismo derecho que el editorialista para opinar," *LR*, February 12, 1954.

104. "Por la exclusiva voluntad del gobierno fue tomada decisión de no ir a Caracas, dice D. Otilio Ulate," *LR*, March 9, 1954.

105. Betancourt, letter to the editor, *DCR* 23:1 (February 3, 1954).

106. Longley, *The Sparrow and the Hawk*, 137; Kirk Bowman, "Democracy on the Brink: The First Figueres Presidency," in *The Costa Rica Reader: History, Culture, Politics*, ed. Steven Palmer and Iván Molina (Durham: Duke University Press, 2004), 175–182, especially 178; and Ameringer, *Don Pepe*, 118. Muñoz Marín also tried to get Figueres to change his mind, but to no avail. Diary entry, March 29, 1954, AABD (Hyde Park, NY: Franklin Delano Roosevelt Library, 1978), Roll 7.

107. Memorandum of Conversation, Figueres and Hill.

108. Ameringer, *Don Pepe*, 78, 111; and Alexander, *Prophets of the Revolution*, quote, 163.

109. Memorandum of Conversation with United Fruit Company executives, September 4, 1953, *FRUS, 1952–1954,* IV: 829.

110. Memorandum by Cabot to Robert Woodward, November 18, 1953, *FRUS, 1952–54,* IV: 832; and Longley, "Resistance and Accommodation," quote, 11.

111. Memorandum by Rollin Atwood and Jack Neal to Holland, July 22, 1954, *FRUS, 1952–1954,* IV: 393–394.

112. Ibid.

113. Longley, "Resistance and Accommodation," 14.

114. Berle diary entry, May 17, 1954, AABD; and "60 millones por año ganará Costa Rica," *LR,* June 5, 1954.

115. Jordan Schwarz, *Liberal: Adolf A. Berle and the Vision of an American Era* (New York: Free Press, 1987), quote, 317.

116. Woodward to Holland, October 27, 1955, *FRUS, 1955–1957,* VII: 10–18, quote, 10.

117. Oral history, R. Richard Rubottom, Jr., by Richard Challener, June 12, 1966, JFDOHP, 9; and Harold Bonilla, *Figueres and Costa Rica: An Unauthorized Political Biography* (San José: Editorial Texto Limitada 1975), 75.

118. Bowman, *Militarization, Democracy, and Development: The Perils of Praetorianism in Latin America* (University Park: Pennsylvania State University Press, 2002), 123–124.

119. Figueres, "The Problems of Democracy in Latin America," *Journal of International Affairs* 9:1 (1955): 11–23, quote, 15.

120. Bonilla, *Figueres and Costa Rica,* 106.

121. Schlesinger, "History of the Week," undated, Section VII, Series 1, Archivo Individual Especial, Cartapacio #170, FLMM.

122. Quoted in Ameringer, *Don Pepe,* 124.

123. Quoted in Diary entry, February 8, 1955, AABD.

124. Schoultz, *In Their Own Best Interest,* 190.

125. Diary entry, February 8, 1955, AABD.

126. K. A. Cuordileone, *Manhood and American Political Culture in the Cold War* (New York: Routledge, 2005), introduction.

127. Letter, Berle to Warren, April 7, 1953, AABD.

128. Schwarz, *Liberal: Adolf A. Berle,* viii.

129. Quoted in McKeever, *Professor Galíndez,* 53.

130. Immerman, *The CIA in Guatemala: The Foreign Policy of Intervention* (Austin: University of Texas Press, 1982), 145.

131. Kolb, *Democracy and Dictatorship,* quote, 136.

132. Elisabeth J. Friedman, *Unfinished Transitions,* 118.

133. Minutes of Meeting Between Representatives of the Department of State and the Department of Defense, August 12, 1953, *FRUS, 1952–54,* IV: 158.

134. Tulchin, "The United States and Latin America in the 1960s," *JISWA* 30:1 (Spring 1988): 1–36, especially 9.

135. Milton Eisenhower, *United States–Latin American Relations: Report to the President,* Department of State Publication #5290 (Washington, DC: U.S.

Government Printing Office, 1953); and Minutes of Cabinet Meeting, March 5, 1953, Cabinet Series, Box 3, Eisenhower Papers, EPL. On Humphrey, see Thomas Zoumaras, "Eisenhower's Foreign Policy: The Case of Latin America," in *Reevaluating Eisenhower: American Foreign Policy in the 1950s*, ed. Richard Melanson and David Mayers (Urbana: University of Illinois Press, 1987): 155–191, quote, 156.

136. Grow, *U.S. Presidents*, quote, 18.

137. Wood, *The Dismantling*, xi.

138. Cabot, *Toward Our Common American Destiny: Speeches and Interviews on Latin American Problems* (Medford, MA: Fletcher School of Law and Diplomacy, 1955), 118.

139. Memorandum by Kennan to John Foster Dulles, March 29, 1950, *FRUS, 1950*, 7 vols. (Washington, DC: Government Printing Office, 1976), II: 598–624, quote, 607; Roger Trask, "George F. Kennan's Report on Latin America 1950," *DH* 2:3 (July 1978): 307–311; and Derek Leebaert, *The Fifty-Year Wound: The True Price of America's Cold War Victory* (Boston: Little, Brown, 2002), 74.

140. Tim Weiner, *Legacy of Ashes: The History of the CIA* (New York: Doubleday, 2007), 95; and Nick Cullather, *Secret History: The CIA's Classified Account of Its Operations in Guatemala, 1952–1954*, 2nd ed. (Stanford: Stanford University Press, 2006 [1999]), 55.

141. Cabot, *First Line of Defense*, 90.

142. Quoted in Schoultz, *That Infernal Little Cuban Republic*, 57.

143. Quoted in Gleijeses, *Shattered Hope*, 271.

144. Coronil, *The Magical State*, quote, 184; and Rabe, *The Road to OPEC*, 121.

145. Betancourt, "La Conferencia de Caracas: Hora crítica de Panamericanismo," 34:1 (May 1954), #81, FRB.

146. Max Friedman, *Rethinking Anti-Americanism*, 136.

147. Tenth Inter-American Conference, Caracas, Venezuela, March 1–28, 1954. Report of the Delegation of the United States of America with Related Documents, Department of State Publication 5692 (Washington, DC: Government Printing Office, 1955), 52; and Immerman, *The CIA in Guatemala*, 147.

148. Blanche Wiesen Cook, *The Declassified Eisenhower: A Divided Legacy* (New York: Doubleday, 1981), quote, 269–270.

149. Quoted in Siekmeier, *Aid, Nationalism and Inter-American Relations: Guatemala, Bolivia, and the United States, 1944–1961* (Lewiston, NY: Edwin Mellen, 1999), 19.

150. Miller, *Soviet Relations*, 14.

151. Gleijeses, *Shattered Hope*, quote, 274; and Rabe, *Eisenhower and Latin America*, 51.

152. Rubottom, oral history, 9.

153. Max Friedman, "Fracas in Caracas: Latin American Diplomatic Resistance to United States Intervention in Guatemala in 1954," *Diplomacy and Statecraft* 21 (2010): 669–689, quote, 674.

154. Ibid., quote, 674; and North American Congress on Latin America, *Guatemala*, ed. Susanne Jonas and David Tobis (Berkeley: The Congress, 1974), 71.

155. Quoted in Rabe, *Eisenhower and Latin America*, 52.

156. Tenth Inter-American Conference, 9.

157. Quoted in Gleijeses, *Shattered Hope*, 275.

158. Max Friedman, "Fracas in Caracas," quote, 670.

159. Jerome Slater, *The OAS and United States Foreign Policy* (Columbus: Ohio State University Press, 1967), 118–121.

160. Cabot, *First Line of Defense*, 92.

161. *Excélsior*, March 2, 1954; and idem, "La conferencia de Caracas y la actitud anticomunista de México," *CA* 75:3 (May–June 1954): 7–44, especially 17–19, quotes, 36.

162. Report on the Caracas Conference, House Committee on Foreign Affairs, *Selected Executive Session Hearings . . .* 516.

163. Krenn, *The Chains of Interdependence*, quote, 183; and Rubottom, oral history, 9–10.

164. Rubottom, oral history, 10.

165. Annex 'A'—Detailed Developments, *FRUS, 1952–1954*, IV: 95; and Memorandum of Conversation by Holland with Venezuelan Ambassador to the United States César González, August 17, 1954, *FRUS, 1952–54*, IV: 1671.

166. Rubottom felt it unfair to single out the U.S. for decorating the Venezuelan dictator. Thirteen other Latin American governments, including the Árbenz administration, had done the same. Rubottom, oral history, 14–15. See also "Address of Rómulo Betancourt at a Meeting of European and Latin American Political Leaders on Behalf of International Democratic Solidarity," undated, Section VII, Series 1, Archivo Individuo Especial, Cartapacio #82, FLMM.

167. Rabe, "Dulles, Latin America," 171.

168. Kolb, *Democracy and Dictatorship*, quote, 143.

169. Alexander, "Communists Gain Strength in Guatemala," *NL* (May 24, 1953), 21–22, quote, 21.

Chapter Twelve. *La Lucha sin Fin* (The Never-Ending Struggle)

Epigraph: "Las pequeñas hermanas olvidadas," in Franco Ornes, *La tragedia dominicana*, v–vii, quote, vi.

1. Berle, diary entry, May 19, 1954, AABD.

2. Idem, "Memo: The Guatemalan Problem in Central America," March 31, 1953, AABD; and Iber, *Neither Peace nor Freedom*, 99–100.

3. Alexander, "Revolution in Guatemala," *NL* (January 5, 1953), 6–8. See also Gillin and Silvert, "Ambiguities in Guatemala," 471. After his ouster, Árbenz reminded his critics that unlike Cuba, Costa Rica, and Chile, communists never served in his cabinet. Roa, "Tiene la palabra Jacobo Árbenz," *Bohemia*

(November 26, 1954). http://librinsula.bnjm.cu/secciones/298/entrevistas/298_entrevistas_2.html. Accessed September 13, 2019.

4. Berle, Memorandum of Conversation with Figueres, Diary entry, March 31, 1953, AABD

5. Ibid.

6. Ibid.

7. Gleijeses, *Shattered Hope*, quote, 242.

8. Quoted in Schwarz, *Liberal: Adolf A. Berle*, 314.

9. Blanco Muñoz, *Pedro Estrada habló*, 295.

10. Betancourt, "Actividades de A.D. en el exterior," 34:1 (April 30, 1954), #38, FRB.

11. Ibid.

12. Ewell, "Che Guevara and Venezuela," 163.

13. Caballero, *Rómulo Betancourt, político de nación*, quote, 291.

14. Memorandum of the 199th Meeting of the National Security Council, May 27, 1954, NSC, Box 5, Eisenhower Papers, EPL.

15. Quoted in Max Friedman, *Rethinking Anti-Americanism*, 132.

16. Ameringer, *The Democratic Left*, 203.

17. Gleijeses, "Juan José Arévalo and the Caribbean Legion," *JLAS* 21:1 (February 1989): 133–145, quote, 144.

18. Longley, "Resistance and Accommodation," 17n81.

19. Quoted in Max Friedman, "Significados transnacionales del golpe de estado de 1954 en Guatemala: Un suceso de la guerra fría internacional," in *Guatemala y la guerra fría en América Latina, 1947–1977*, ed. Roberto García Ferreira (Antigua, Guatemala: Universidad de San Carlos, 2010), 19–28, quote, 27.

20. Galíndez, "La tragedia de Guatemala," *LR*, June 25, 1954; and Eduardo Crawley, *Nicaragua in Perspective*, 2nd ed. (New York: St. Martin's Press, 1984 [1979]), 111.

21. Galíndez, "La tragedia."

22. Ibid.

23. Ibid.; and Dunkerley, "Guatemala," 326.

24. Three weeks later, Galíndez wrote a follow-up, "En Guatemala ... ¿qué?" describing the overwhelmingly negative response throughout the hemisphere. *LR*, July 16, 1954. See also Hove, "The Arbenz Factor," 614n3. The exception among moderates was Muñoz Marín, who publicly spoke out against the coup. "El gobernador de Puerto Rico contra intervención a Guatemala," *LR*, June 9, 1954.

25. Cook, *The Declassified Eisenhower*, 226; and Grow, *U.S. Presidents*, 15. See also "Editorial note," *FRUS, 1952–1954, Guatemala* (Washington, DC: United States Government Printing Office, 2003), xxvi; Max Holland, "Private Sources of U.S. Foreign Policy: William Pawley and the 1954 Coup d'état in Guatemala," *Journal of Cold War Studies* 7:4 (Fall 2005): 36–73, especially 51–53. On the impact of Iran on CIA plans in Guatemala, see Cullather, *Secret History*, 38–43; and Anderson, *The Quiet Americans*, 327.

26. Quoted in Stephen Schlesinger and Stephen Kinzer, *Bitter Fruit: The Untold Story of the American Coup in Guatemala* (New York: Doubleday, 1982), 102.

27. García Ponce and Camacho Barrios, *Diario de la resistencia*, 177–178.

28. Vega, *Almoina, Galíndez*, 55–56; and Miguel Ydígoras Fuentes, as told to Mario Rosenthal, *My War with Communism* (Englewood Cliffs, NJ: Prentice-Hall,1953), 50. On Trujillo's request, see Rabe, *The Killing Zone*, 41.

29. Burton Hersh, *The Old Boys*, 339. On arms smuggling, see Stephen Streeter, *Managing the Counterrevolution: The United States and Guatemala, 1954–1961* (Athens: Ohio University Center for International Studies, 2000), 25–26; Cullather, *Secret History*, 32; Cook, *The Declassified Eisenhower*, 236–237; and Wood, *The Dismantling*, 141, 157.

30. Gerald Haynes, "CIA and Guatemala Assassination Proposals, 1952–1954," in "CIA and Assassinations: The Guatemala 1954 Documents," National Security Archive Electronic Briefing Book No. 4. https://nsarchive2.gwu.edu/NSAEBB/NSAEBB4/index.html. Accessed April 6, 2021; and Blasier, *The Hovering Giant*, 161.

31. Burton Hersh, *The Old Boys*, 346.

32. Memorandum from (name not declassified) of the Western Hemisphere Division, CIA to Frank Wismer, Document #12, July 9, 1952, and Memorandum from Jacob Seekford (pseudonym) to Colonel J. C. King, Doc. #18, September 18, 1952, *FRUS, 1952–1954, Guatemala*, 20–22 and 27, respectively; Moulton, "Building Their Own Cold War," especially 135; Gleijeses, *Shattered Hope*, 292; and Silfa, *Guerra, traición y exilio*, II: 142–143.

33. Tony Raful, *La rapsodia del crimen: Trujillo vs. Castillo Armas* (Mexico City: Grijalbo, 2017), 127.

34. Immerman, *The CIA in Guatemala*, 137.

35. Lawrence Wittner, *American Intervention in Greece, 1943–1949* (New York: Columbia University Press, 1982), 290–291; Theodore Couloumbis, *Greek Political Reaction to American and NATO Interests* (New Haven: Yale University Press, 1966), 53ff; and Flora Lewis, "Ambassador Extraordinary: John Peurifoy," *NYT*, July 18, 1954, quote.

36. Gleijeses, *Shattered Hope*, quote, 254; and Schlesinger and Kinzer, *Bitter Fruit*, 134–135.

37. Weiner, *Legacy of Ashes*, 102; and Holland, "Private Sources of U.S. Foreign Policy," 57–61.

38. Jean Edward Smith, *Eisenhower in War and Peace* (New York: Random House, 2013), 631; Evan Thomas, *The Very Best Men: Four Who Dared; The Early Years of the CIA* (New York: Touchstone, 1996), 129; and Holland, "Private Sources of U.S. Foreign Policy," 61–62. On the disinformation campaign, see David Atlee, *The Nightwatch* (New York: Ballantine, 1982).

39. Dunkerley, *Power in the Isthmus*, 150.

40. Gleijeses, *Shattered Hope*, 356 and 357n171.

41. Huggins, *Political Policing in Latin America*, 86.

42. Dunkerley, "Guatemala, 1944–1954." 109.

43. Max Friedman, *Rethinking Anti-Americanism*, 143–144.
44. Hove, "The Árbenz Factor," 651.
45. Memorandum by the Director of the Office of South American Affairs, *FRUS, 1952–1954*, IV: 398.
46. Schaposnik, *La democratización de las Fuerzas Armadas Venezolanas*, 173.
47. Memo, Foster Dulles to Eisenhower, July 8, 1954, John Foster Dulles Papers, Box 8, EPL.
48. "Guatemalan President Welcomed," *WP and Times Herald*, November 1, 1955; "Castillo Begins State Visit in U.S.," *NYT*, October 2, 1955; "Guatemalan Chief Pledges Charter," *NYT*, November 3, 1955; "Castillo in U.N. Address Urges All Nations to Coexist in Peace," *NYT*, November 4, 1955; "Diocese Honors Castillo at Mass," *NYT*, November 7, 1955; and "President, Walking, Greets Guests," *NYT*, November 10, 1955.
49. Quoted in Elisa Servín, "Frank Tannenbaum entre América Latina y Estados Unidos en la Guerra Fría," *Contracorriente* 13:3 (Spring 2016): 50–75, especially 60.
50. Letter, Figueres to Berle, July 11, 1954, AABD; and "Reconoció Costa Rica a la Junta de Gobierno de Guatemala," *LR*, July 6, 1954.
51. Berle diary entry, May 10, 1954, AABD.
52. Cerdas Cruz, "Costa Rica," quote, 290.
53. "Situation in Guatemala and Costa Rica," House Committee on Foreign Affairs, *Selected Executive Session Hearings ... 1951–1956*, 478; and Longley, "Resistance and Accommodation," 16n73.
54. Quoted in Longley, "Resistance and Accommodation," 7n22.
55. "Rubottom briefing for Acting Secretary of State," May 20, 1959, Rubottom Subject Files, 1957–59, Box 12, File, 1959, Costa Rica, RG59, USNA.
56. Jorge Salazar Mora, *Política y reforma en Costa Rica, 1914–1958* (San José: Editorial Porvenir, 1982), 205.
57. Memorandum by the Director of the Office of South American Affairs, *FRUS, 1952–1954*, IV: 396.
58. Pérez claimed that Washington discouraged Castillo Armas from inviting and honoring the Dominican ruler. Hernández and Giusti, eds., *Carlos Andrés Pérez: memorias proscritas*, 95.
59. Acosta Matos, *La telaraña cubana de Trujillo*, II: 670.
60. Vega, *Almoina, Galíndez*, 55–56; Moulton, "Militant Roots: The Anti-Fascist Left in the Caribbean Basin, 1945–1954," *Estudios Interdisciplinarios de América Latina y el Caribe* 28:2 (2017): 14–29, especially 23; and Acosta Matos, *La telaraña cubana de Trujillo*, II: 670.
61. "La verdad sobre el embajador Sánchez Rubirosa," and "Un embajador nongrato," in *LR*, July 29, 1958, and August 27, 1958. Most accounts identify Romeo Vásquez Sánchez as a lone assassin. But Silfa claims that the trujillista agent Carlos Gacel and the notorious Cuban *pistolero* Gildardo Montúfar Gutiérrez were at the scene when Castillo Armas was murdered. *Guerra, traición y exilio*, II: 148–149, 154. Montúfar was a person of interest to both

Mexican and Cuban authorities in the attempted murders of the Dominican dissident Tancredo Martínez García and Batista. Raful, *La rapsodia*, 77–80, quote, 88.

62. Memorandum, William Wieland to Rubottom, January 30, 1958, *FRUS*, *1958–1960*, (Washington, DC: Government Printing Office, 1991), V: Microfiche Supplement, #12.

63. "Guatemalan Plot Laid to Dominican," *NYT*, December 5, 1957, p. 23; Minutes, NSC meeting, August 1, 1957, Box 9, NSC Series, EPL. The most detailed account of the assassination is Crassweller, *Trujillo: The Life and Times*, 334–340. An insider account of the Trujillo regime bragged that "whole segments of the Guatemalan secret service were controlled more by Trujillo than by [Castillo] Armas." Espaillat, *Trujillo: The Last Caesar*, 127. Cf. Schlewitz, who suggests that members of Castillo Armas's political party in cahoots with disaffected military officers murdered the president. "Imperial Incompetence," 597.

64. Quoted in Schlesinger and Kinzer, *Bitter Fruit*, 236.

65. Streeter, *Managing the Counterrevolution*, quote, 60.

66. Monge, "El embajador de la República Dominicana es un pistolero que ultraja dignidad de Costa Rica," and idem, "Non grato," *LR*, June 19 and June 20, 1958; "En poder de la Asamblea, documentos sobre asesinato de Castillo Armas," *LR*, July 24, 1958; and "Political Activities of Former President José Figueres since May 8, 1958," Estep to State Department, Box 2983, File 718.00/5-258, RG 1955–1959, USNA.

67. Memo of Conversation, Sevilla-Sacasa, Mann, and John Ohmans, September 29, 1952, *FRUS*, *1952–1954*, IV: 1372–1375.

68. Hernández and Giusti, eds., *Carlos Andrés Pérez: memorias proscritas*, 96–98.

69. "Asunto: Adquisición de armas en México," and "Estudio preliminar: Las cartas cruzadas de Betancourt en el exilio (1948–1952)," in *Antología política, 1948–1952*, V: 509–510 and V: 3–26, especially 15, 19–20, respectively.

70. Letter, Alfredo (Ruíz Pineda) to Álvarez (Betancourt), March 19, 1952, in *Antología política, 1948–1952*, V: 592–595.

71. Hernández and Giusti, *Carlos Andrés Pérez: memorias proscritas*, 86–88; and Quero de Trinca, "El tercer exilio," 38n28.

72. Julia Sweig, *Inside the Cuban Revolution: Fidel Castro and the Urban Underground* (Cambridge: Harvard University Press, 2002).

73. Peña, *Conversaciones con Carlos Andrés Pérez*, I: 120–126.

74. Salcedo Ávila, "Conflictos en el Caribe," 45–46; and Peña, *Conversaciones con Carlos Andrés Pérez*, I: 118, 126.

75. Memo of Conversation, Sevilla-Sacasa, Mann, and Ohmans, September 29, 1952, *FRUS*, *1952–1954*, IV: 1374. For a discussion of the quid pro quo, see Salcedo Ávila, "Conflictos en el Caribe."

76. Ohmans to Hill, July 7, 1954, *FRUS*, *1952–54*, IV: 846.

77. Telegram, Maurice Bernbaum to the State Department, May 31, 1954, *FRUS*, *1952–54*: IV: 1666.

78. Ameringer, *The Caribbean Legion*, 71; and Stephen Earley, "Arms and Politics in Costa Rica and Nicaragua, 1948–1981," Research Paper Series, No. 9, Latin American Institute, University of New Mexico (May 1982), 6.

79. Martz, *Central America: The Crisis and the Challenge* (Chapel Hill: University of North Carolina Press, 1959), quote, 186; and "Siguen fabricando calumnias los periódicos de Somoza," *LR*, May 4, 1954.

80. Ameringer, *The Democratic Left*, 204.

81. Walter, *The Regime of Anastasio Somoza*, 230–233; Ameringer, *Don Pepe*, 117–126; idem, *The Democratic Left*, 206.

82. Ameringer, *The Democratic Left*, 210.

83. "Enérgicas declaraciones de Figueres sobre la nota Nicaragüense," *LR*, May 21, 1954; and "Aventuras internacionales y nacionales," *LR*, June 2, 1954.

84. Bowman, "Democracy on the Brink," 178–179, quote, 179.

85. Kolb, *Democracy and Dictatorship*, 139.

86. NSC Briefing, "Possible Costa Rican Coup," July 14, 1954, *FRUS, 1952–1954*, IV: 258; and Moulton, "Building Their Own Cold War," 135.

87. "'F,' 'H,' 'G' (pseudonyms) to Rómulo Betancourt," Tomo 23:1 (January 7, 1954), #17, FRB.

88. "Figueres Expresses Confidence," *NYT*, January 9, 1955.

89. "Indiscutible la intervención de Somoza y Pérez Jiménez en la anormal situación de Costa Rica," *LR*, January 12, 1955.

90. Miguel Acuña Valerio., *El 55: Te mataron hermano* (San José: Librería Lehmann, 1977), 182; and Silfa, *Guerra, traición y exilio*, II: 157.

91. Letter, Muñoz Marín to Figueres, July 29, 1954, Section V, Series 2, Governor of Puerto Rico, 1949–1964, Correspondencia Particular, Cartapacio #174, FLMM.

92. Telegram, Muñoz Marín to Eisenhower, November 27, 1954, and letter, idem to Paz Estenssoro, November 27, 1954, Section V, Series 2, Governor of Puerto Rico, 1949–1964, Correspondencia Particular, Cartapacio #174, FLMM.

93. "El Señor Somoza imputa a gobiernos y a personas lo mismo que el ha practicado," *LR*, April 8, 1954.

94. Telegram, Dulles to Embassy in Nicaragua, May 18, 1954, *FRUS, 1952–1954*, IV: 1383.

95. Interview, Woodward by Charles Stuart Kennedy, 1987. Costa Rica Country Reader. https://www.adst.org/Readers/Costa%20Rica.pdf. Accessed April 7, 2019.

96. Memo, Holland to Smith, *FRUS, 1952–1954*, IV: 1384–1385.

97. NSC Briefing, "Possible Costa Rica Coup," July 14, 1954.

98. Acuña Valerio, *El 55*, 30.

99. Cohen, "Background of Figueres-Somoza Feud."

100. Memo, Hill to State Department, August 6, 1954, *FRUS, 1952–1954*, IV: 857.

101. Memo, Atwood to Holland, July 22, 1954, *FRUS, 1952–1954*, IV: 374–376.

102. Ameringer, *The Democratic Left*, 211.
103. Telegram, Foster Dulles to embassy in Guatemala, July 9, 1954, *FRUS, 1952–1954*, IV: 850–851, quote, 851.
104. Telegram, Bernbaum to Department, July 9, 1954, *FRUS, 1952–1954*, IV: 372–373.
105. Dulles to Brownell, July 21, 1954, *FRUS, 1952–1954*, IV: 1668–1669.
106. Memorandum, Betancourt to CEN, February 22, 1955; and Betancourt, "Me voy de Costa Rica por propia decisión," *LR*, July 27, 1954. Bosch also left the country, continuing his exile in Santiago. Silfa, *Guerra, traición y exilio*, II: 158.
107. Memorandum, Betancourt to CEN, February 22, 1955.
108. NSC Briefing, "Possible Costa Rica Coup," July 14, 1954; Moulton, "Building Their Own Cold War," quote, 135; and Gambone, *Eisenhower, Somoza, and the Cold War*, 90.
109. Memo of telephone conversation, Holland to Whelan, July 28, 1954, *FRUS, 1952–1954*, IV: 1387.
110. Telegram, Dulles to the Embassy in Venezuela, July 10, 1954, *FRUS, 1952–1954*, IV: 373.
111. Memo of Conversation by Holland, August 17, 1954, *1952–1954*, IV: 1670–1671.
112. "Citation of Medal Presented to Pérez Jiménez," November 12, 1954, Box 16, COP.
113. Progress Report on NSC 5432/1, "United States Objectives and Courses of Action with Respect to Latin America," January 19, 1955, White House Office, Office of the Special Assistant for National Security Affairs: Records, Box 13, Policy Paper Subseries, EPL.
114. Ewell, *Venezuela and the United States*, 157.
115. Romauldi to Betancourt, Tomo 25:2 (December 3, 1954), FRB; and Salcedo Ávila, "Conflictos en el Caribe," quote, 42. This was not the first time that the Eisenhower administration had feted Estrada. In 1952, he was Foster Dulles's guest of honor at a reception in Washington, where he was presented with a "luxurious" album containing fifty-two photographs. García Ponce and Camacho Barrios, *Diario de la resistencia*, 187.
116. Bowman, *Militarization, Democracy, and Development*, 128.
117. Quoted in Clark, Jr., *The United States and Somoza*, 191.
118. Acuña Valerio, *El 55*, 22.
119. "Batista negó ayuda a Calderón para su 'revolución,'" *LR*, October 19, 1954.
120. "El *New York Times* editorializa sobre la actual situación en Costa Rica," *LR*, January 12, 1955; and Ameringer, *Don Pepe*, 120. On the sale of aircraft from Sweden, see Memo, Ohmans to Robert Newbegin, January 17, 1955, *FRUS, 1955–1957*, VII: 195–196.
121. Woodward to State Department, January 5, 1955, *FRUS, 1955–1957*, VI: 581–583, quotes, 582.

122. Ameringer, *Don Pepe*, 121–122; and Longley, "Resistance and Accommodation," 22.

123. "Report Being Drafted," *NYT*, January 14, 1955.

124. Telegram, Warren to State Department, January 9, 1955, *FRUS, 1955–1957*, VI: 585–586.

125. "Declaraciones del Comité Ejecutivo Nacional de AD," Tomo 28, complementos A–B (January 1955), #1, FRB.

126. "Nicaragua Offers Planes to Patrol," *NYT*, January 14, 1955.

127. Berle Diary, telegram, Berle to Dulles, January 12, 1955, AABD.

128. "Mensaje del Presidente Don José Figueres al país," *LR*, January 15, 1955.

129. Silfa, *Guerra, traición y exilio*, II: 161, 185–186.

130. García Oliveras, *José Antonio Echeverría*, 147; and Norman Acosta. *La palabra empeñada*, I: 77.

131. Quoted in García Oliveras, *José Antonio Echeverría*, 158–159; Guerra, *Heroes, Martyrs*, quote, 153; and Juan Nuiry Sánchez, *José Antonio: A través de su testamento político* (Havana: n.p., 1965).

132. Betancourt to Fournier, Tomo 26:1 (January 12, 1955), #20, FRB.

133. Betancourt to Romauldi, Tomo 26:1 (January 13, 1955), #21; and AFL statement, "Stop the War . . ." 26:1 (January 14, 1955), #21, FRB.

134. Slater, *The OAS and United States Foreign Policy*, 72–76.

135. The P-47 had been used by CIA pilots in the Guatemalan campaign. Ameringer, *U.S. Foreign Intelligence*, 255.

136. Quoted in Longley, "Resistance and Accommodation," 24; and telegram, Woodward to State Department, January 15, 1955, *FRUS, 1955–1957*, VI: 597–599.

137. Memo, Holland to Dulles, January 13, 1955, *FRUS, 1955–1957*, VI: 594–595.

138. Holden, "The Real Diplomacy of Violence," 312.

139. Acuña Valerio, *El 55*, 43.

140. "En defensa de Costa Rica," *Bohemia*, January 16, 1955.

141. Galíndez, "Un triunfo de la democracia," *LR*, January 27, 1955.

142. Berle Diary, February 8, 1955, AABD.

143. Ameringer, *Don Pepe*, quote, 124–125.

144. Ameringer, *The Democratic Left*, quote, 216.

145. Bowman, *Militarization, Democracy, and Development*, 131–132.

146. Figueres, "Mixed Feelings," Tomo 28: Complementos A–B (February 10, 1955), FRB.

147. Memo of Conversation, Holland and Chiriboga, February 1, 1955, 718.00/2–155, RG59, USNA.

148. "Venezuelan Position on Consideration by the COAS of the Report of the Investigating Committee to Costa Rica," Bernbaum to State Department, February 4, 1955, 718.00/2–155, RG59, USNA.

149. Telegram, Woodward to State Department, February 4, 1955, *FRUS, 1955–1957*, VI: 609–611; and Dulles to U.S. Embassy in Cuba, February 9, 1955, *FRUS, 1955–1957*, VI: 611–612.

150. Ameringer, *Don Pepe*, 124–125.

151. *DCR*, February 18, 1955, in Cohen to State Department, February 18, 1955, Box 2983, File 718.00 (W)/1–755, RG 59, 1955–1959, USNA.

152. "Excélsior de México analiza el conflicto con Nicaragua," *LR*, January 15, 1955.

153. David Wesley, "Nicaragua, Costa Rica y EEUU," *LR*, January 20, 1955.

154. Memorandum of Conversation, State Department, January 20, 1955, *FRUS, 1955–1957*, VII: 197–198.

155. C. J. Warner to State Department, March 21, 1955, and Charles Urruela to State Department, May 13, 1955, 718.00/2–155 and 718.00/5–655, RG59, USNA.

156. Sang, ed., *La política exterior dominicana*, II: 165–166.

157. Alexander, "Latin American Dictator Snipes at Exile," *WP*, January 20, 1957.

158. Grant to Betancourt, Tomo XXIX:2 (February 29, 1956), #125, FRB.

159. Monge to Meany, Tomo XXX:2 (August 19, 1956), #266, and Figueres to Alexander, Tomo XXIX:2 (March 1, 1956), #126, FRB.

160. Betancourt to Romauldi, Tomo XXVII (February 11, 1956), #79, FRB.

161. Figueres to Alexander, Tomo XXIX:2 (March 1, 1956), #126, FRB; and Ameringer, *Don Pepe*, quote, 133.

162. Figueres to Alexander, March 1, 1956; and Memo of Conversation, Fournier, Robert Newbegin and Park Wollam, File 718.00/1–1856, RG 59, 1956–1959, USNA.

163. Figueres to Alexander, March 1, 1956.

164. "Política peligrosa," *El Diario de Nueva York*, August 27, 1957.

165. Memorandum para el CC acerca de la situación de Rómulo Betancourt en Puerto Rico," Tomo XXXIV, Anexo C (September 15, 1957), #6, FRB. Grant thought attacking Betancourt and Muñoz was a clear ploy by Trujillo to divert attention away from the fallout from the Galíndez affair. Grant to Earl Hanson, November 15, 1957, MC671, 47:14, File, Puerto Rico, Earl Hanson, and Grant to Muñoz Marín, November 15, 1957, MC 671, 47:18, File, Munoz Marín, 1958–1965, FRG.

166. Figueres to Alexander, March 1, 1956.

167. Pérez to Betancourt, June 12, 1956, Tomo XXX:1 (June 12, 1956), #1.

168. "Discurso pronunciado por el compañero Carlos Andrés Pérez en el acto conmemorativo del décimo-quinto aniversario del Partido Acción Democrático ..." San José, Costa Rica, Tomo XXX:1 (September 13, 1956), #26, FRB.

169. "Alleged Plot to Assassinate Rómulo Betancourt," Stewart to State Department, June 15, 1956, File 718.00/1–1856, Box 2982, RG 59, 1956–1959, USNA.

170. Pérez to Betancourt, June 12, 1956, Tomo XXX:1 (June 12, 1956), #1, and Betancourt to Grant, Tomo XXX:2 (August 13, 1956), #252, FRB.

171. Krieg to Morales Carrión, November 6, 1957, Folder #55, Section V, Series 2, Governor of Puerto Rico, 1949–1964, Correspondencia Particular, FLMM.

172. Memorandum para el CC acerca de la situación de Rómulo Betancourt en Puerto Rico, September 15, 1957, Tomo XXXIIV: Anexo C, #6, FRB.

173. Muñoz Marín to José Monserrat, October 29, 1957, and Betancourt to Muñoz Marín, December 6, 1957, Section V, Series 2, Governor of Puerto Rico, 1949–1964, Correspondencia Particular, Folder 55, FLMM.

174. Berle to Nelson Rockefeller, January 12, 1955, AABD.

175. Ameringer, *Don Pepe*, 127–128; and Bowman, *Militarization, Democracy, and Development*, 131–134.

176. Acosta Matos, *La telaraña cubana de Trujillo*, II: 556.

177. Despatch, Allan Stewart, San José, Costa Rica Embassy to State Department, May 25 1955; Memo of Conversation, Álvaro Vindas and Cohen, "Costa Rica-Venezuela Relations," April 25, 1955; Office Memorandum, Ohmans to Richard Davis and Newbegin, "Costa Rica-Venezuela Relations," May 5, 1955; and Despatch, Cohen to State Department, "Possibilities for Improvement in Relations Between Costa Rica and Venezuela," October 3, 1955, File 618.00/12-655, RG 59, USNA.

178. Memo of Discussion at the 240th Meeting of the NSC, March 10, 1955, *FRUS, 1955–1957*, VI: 614–618, quote, 616.

179. Ameringer, *Don Pepe*, quote, 130.

180. Schoultz, *That Infernal Little Cuban Republic*, 56.

181. García Ponce and Camacho Barrios, *Diario de la resistencia*, 201.

182. Betancourt to "Juan," Tomo 28:1 (December 30, 1955), #236, FRB.

183. NIE Estimate, "Conditions and Trends in Latin America, *FRUS, 1955–1957*, VI: 16–45, especially 24.

Chapter Thirteen. Latin America's Representative in the U.S. Congress

Epigraph: Cited in Betancourt to Muñoz Marín, January 9, 1958, Folder 55, Section V, Series 2, Governor of Puerto Rico, 1949–1964, Correspondencia Particular, FLMM.

1. Consuegra Lima to Porter, undated, Box 24, File, Murphy Reactions from Cuba, *New York Post*, July 6, 1958, Box 15, File, Foreign Affairs, Dominican Republic, Record, Clips, Information, etc., COP; and "Representative Carries Pistol," *NYT*, March 7, 1957.

2. Consuegra Lima to Porter, undated, and Porter to Consuegra Lima, June 18, 1957, Box 24, File, Murphy Reactions from Cuba, COP.

3. Unsigned letter, March 14, 1957, Box 25, File, Murphy Reactions from New York-USA, COP.

4. Charles Porter, oral history, Digital Collections, Jim Strassmaier, interviewer, OHS. https://digitalcollections.ohs.org/informationobject/browse?creators=577433&topLod=0&query=Charles+O.+Porter&sqo=Charles+O.+Porter&sort=relevance&sortDir=desc, tapes 8:1 and 10:2. Accessed August 20–September 12, 2020.

5. "Trujillo Scored in House Debate," *NYT*, February 28, 1957.

6. *New York Post*, July 6, 1958.

7. *CR*, p. 8101 (June 13, 1957), Box 24, File, Foreign Affairs, Dominican Republic, Record, Clips, information, etc., COP; and "Porter en San Juan, Puerto Rico," *DCR*, June 9, 1957.

8. *CR*, p. 8101 (June 13, 1957), Box 24, File, Foreign Affairs, Dominican Republic, Record, Clips, information, etc., COP.

9. John Shott, "Biography of Charles O. Porter," Box 8, COP.

10. Porter, oral history, tape 1:1–2.

11. Samuel Porter, "Eulogy, Charles Porter"; "Charles Porter," obituary, *The Register-Guard*, January 20, 2006; Porter, oral history, tape 4:2.

12. Porter, oral history, tapes 4:2 and 7:2.

13. Porter, "Remarks on U.S. Policy and the Gerald Lester Murphy-Jesús de Galíndez Case," February 26, 1957, Box 24, File, Murphy, COP; and Porter, oral history, tape 10:2.

14. Miguel Vázquez, *Jesús de Galíndez: "El vasco" que inició la decadencia de Trujillo* (Santo Domingo: Taller, 1975), 93–95 and 104–105; Crassweller, *Trujillo: The Life and Times*, 317–318; Germán Ornes, *Little Caesar of the Caribbean*, 323; Joaquín Balaguer, *La palabra encadenada*, 2nd ed. (Santo Domingo: Editora Taller, 1985 [1975]), 414–415; Matthews, "Galíndez Case: New Chapter," *NYT*, December 15, 1957; Urquijo, *La tumba abierta*, 357; Szulc, "Witness Tells of Galíndez Pilot's Death," *NYT*, April 6, 1964; and McKeever, *Professor Galíndez*, 112–113.

15. State Department interview, Caire, December 19, 1956, Section 1, Internal Security Division File, DOJ Case File 109–51–25, RG 60, USNA. The Hungarian journalist Andrew St. George (later reputed to be a CIA agent) contended that Murphy was killed because he knew of Trujillo's plot to assassinate Batista, not his role in Galíndez's kidnapping. "Why Gerry Murphy was Really Murdered," *Real Magazine* (October 1957), 12–15 and 61–64. See also Bonachea and Valdés, "Introduction," 85–86; and Franqui, *Diary of the Cuban Revolution*, 113. It is unclear how much Porter knew about Murphy's activities in Cuba.

16. Hoover to Brownell, December 26, 1956, Section 3, Criminal Division File, DOJ Case File 109–51–25, RG 60, USNA. Norman Acosta posits that it was the DRE that carried out the hit on Blanco Rico. *La palabra empeñada*, II: 366.

17. St. George, "Why Gerry Murphy was Really Murdered," quote, 63; and Porter, oral history, tape 11:1.

18. Porter, "Remarks on U.S. Policy."

19. *New York Post*, July 6, 1958.

20. "Persistent as a Bulldog," editorial, *The Register-Guard*, January 4, 2006; Laura Olson, " 'A Beautiful Race Horse:' Remembering Charlie Porter," *The Eugene Weekly*, January 12, 2006; and Porter, oral history, tape 10:2. On McCormick's medal, Porter, "The Butcher of the Caribbean," 64.

21. "Persistent as a Bulldog," *The Register-Guard*, January 4, 2006.

22. Morse's objections to McCarthy were about means, not ends. He voted for the Smith, McCarran, and Communist Control Acts in 1948, 1950, and 1954, respectively. Wayne Drukman, *Wayne Morse: A Political Biography* (Portland: Oregon Historical Society Press, 1997), 202, quote, 7. See also Burton, *Democrats of Oregon: The Pattern of Minority Politics, 1900–1956* (Eugene: University of Oregon Press, 1970); A. Robert Smith, *The Tiger in the Senate: A Biography of Wayne Morse* (New York: Doubleday, 1962); Carlos Schwantes, *The Pacific Northwest: An Interpretive History*, 2nd ed. (Lincoln: University of Nebraska Press, 1996 [1989]); and Gordon Dodds, *Oregon: A Bicentennial History* (New York: Norton and American Association for State and Local History, 1977).

23. Drukman, *Wayne Morse*, 286.

24. Johnson, *Congress and the Cold War* (New York: Cambridge University Press, 2006), quote, 81.

25. Marvin Zahniser and W. Michael Weis, " 'A Diplomatic Pearl Harbor'? Richard Nixon's Goodwill Mission to Latin America in 1958," *DH* 13:2 (Spring 1989): 163–190, especially 167–168.

26. Willard Barber and Ronning, *Internal Security and Military Power: Counterinsurgency and Civic Action in Latin America* (Columbus: Ohio State University Press, 1966), 66; and Rabe, *The Most Dangerous Area*, 12.

27. Ron Abell, "Charles Porter, Smarter than Hell: A Political Disaster," *Willamette Week*, 2:19 (March 22, 1976), pp. 1, 3, 8, quote, 1. Porter's friendship with Morse chilled because of their disagreement about Castro and his refusal to back the senator in his unsuccessful bid for the presidency in 1960. Porter, oral history, tape 10:1.

28. Porter, oral history, tape 11:1; and *New York Post*, July 6, 1958.

29. Silfa, *Guerra, traición y exilio*, I: 499.

30. Porter, as told to Geoffrey Boca, "The Butcher of the Caribbean," *Coronet* 42 (July 1957): 50–66, quote, 52.

31. Silfa, *Guerra, traición y exilio*, I: 499.

32. *CR*, p. 8101 (June 13, 1957), Box 15, File, Foreign Affairs, Dominican Republic, Record, Clips, information, etc., COP.

33. Figueres to Porter, May 28, 1957, Box, 35, File, Trip to Costa Rica-1957, COP.

34. "Dictator Hater," *Time* (September 2, 1957).

35. Not included are several countries that experienced political transitions that did not ultimately result in democratic rule. In addition to Árbenz, the military ruler Magloire was removed from power in Haiti in December 1956, and François "Papa Doc" Duvalier was elected president in April 1957, but then established a brutal fourteen-year dictatorship. In El Salvador, after Colonel José María Lemus was removed from office, a military junta assumed power.

36. Luis Araquistáin, "Venezuela desde Europa," *El Universal* (Mexico City), December 20, 1958.

37. Szulc, *Twilight of the Tyrants*, 303–304.

38. Memorandum, "Venezuelan Foreign Policy: Interview of Representatives of National Editorial Association with Foreign Minister (Ignacio Luis Arcaya)," November 24, 1959, File 631.00/3–559, Box 2599, RG59, USNA; and Rubottom to Dulles, February 20, 1958, *FRUS, 1958–1960*, V: 464–465.

39. Suárez Novoa, *El gran culpable*, 135; and Acosta Matos, *La telaraña cubana*, II: 749.

40. Lieuwen, *Arms and Politics*, 149–150.

41. Betancourt address, Carnegie International Center, 34:2 (January 12, 1957), #166, FRB.

42. Betancourt to Muñoz Marín, 33:A (December 6, 1957), #81, FRB.

43. Ibid.

44. Betancourt to Kent, 32:2 (March 24, 1957) #146, FRB.

45. "New Order is Urged for Latin America," *NYT*, February 20, 1958.

46. *CR*, pp. 14229–14231 (August 11, 1959), Box 15, File, Foreign Affairs, Dominican Republic, Record, Clips, Information, etc., COP.

47. *CR*, A2773 (April 5, 1957), Box 24, File, Murphy, COP.

48. "Memorandum on the Dominican Dictatorship in Respect to the Case of Gerald Murphy," Box 24, Murphy-Background Material Re. Galíndez, etc., COP.

49. *WP*, October 3, 1958, Box 15, File, Foreign Affairs, Dominican Republic, Record, Clips, Information, etc., COP.

50. Press Release, Governor of Oregon, October 2, 1958, Box 15, File, Foreign Affairs, Dominican Republic, Record, Clips, information, etc., COP.

51. Porter, "Draft Remarks on U.S. Foreign Policy on the Occasion of the Anniversary of the Disappearance of Jesús de Galíndez," March 7, 1957, Box 24, File, Murphy, Gerald L., case file, COP.

52. Porter to Grant, January 28, 1958, and telegram, Porter to Grant, March 12, 1958, 29:32, MC 671, FRG.

53. Alberto Elósegui, *El verdadero Galíndez* (Bilbao: Ediciones A. Saldana Ortega, 1990), 137–138, 155.

54. *Ibérica*, March 15, 1957, quotes, 16, Box 25, File, Murphy Reactions from New York-USA, COP.

55. Porter, "Non-Intervention: The Dictator's Shibboleth," unpublished essay, Box 15, File, Foreign Affairs—Latin America #2, 1957, COP.

56. Blasier, "The Elimination of United States Influence," in *Revolutionary Change in Cuba*, ed. Carmelo Mesa-Lago (Pittsburgh: University of Pittsburgh Press, 1971), quote, 46. By one estimate Prío contributed a quarter of a million dollars to the 26th of July movement. Ferrer, *Cuba: A National History*, 295.

57. St. George, "Cuban Rebels," *Look Magazine*, February 4, 1958.

58. Porter, oral history, tape 11:1.

59. "Trujillo Scored in House Debate."

60. Ameringer, *The Democratic Left*, quote, 216; Rubottom to Dulles, February 20, 1957, *FRUS, 1955–1957*: VI: 908; and Dispatch, Stephens to State Department, January 16, 1957.

61. Rubottom to "Charley," August 20, 1958, Records of Assistant Secretary of State for Inter-American Affairs Roy R. Rubottom, Box 9, File, 1958, Porter, Congressman Charles O., RG 59, USNA.

62. Porter, "Defects of United States Policy in Latin America and Recommendations for a New Policy," July 15, 1957, Box 15, File, Foreign Affairs Latin America #1, COP.

63. *CR*, May 20, 1958, 9628–9630.

64. Porter to Herter, July 10, 1959, Box 24, File, Murphy, Gerald L. Case file, COP.

65. Elósegui, *El verdadero Galíndez*, 136; and Vázquez, *Jesús de Galíndez*, 84.

66. Porter, "Trujillo is Next," unpublished article, March 1959, Box 15, File, Foreign Affairs, Dominican Republic, Correspondence, COP.

67. Memo, Rubottom and Terrance Leonhardy, "Correspondence with Charles O. Porter," June 23, 1958, and memo, Rubottom and Stewart, "Correspondence with Congressman Porter," June 24, 1958, Box 9, File, 1958, Porter, Congressman Charles O., Records of Rubottom, RG 59, USNA.

68. Memo, Wieland to Rubottom, January 30, 1958, *FRUS, 1958–1960*, V: Microfiche Supplement, #12.

69. Porter, "Trujillo is Next," unpublished article, March 1959, Box 15, File, Foreign Affairs, Dominican Republic, Correspondence, COP; and Memo, Wieland to Rubottom, January 30, 1958.

70. AD-in-exile, New York to Porter, XXXII: 2 (April 5, 1957), #164, FRB.

71. In 1961 Casals made an exception and performed at the invitation of the Kennedys at the White House. Porter, oral history, tape 11:2.

72. James to Porter, Box 25, File, Murphy Reactions from Mexico, COP; and James, *Red Design for the Americas: Guatemalan Prelude* (New York: John Day, 1954).

73. Porter, "Defects of United States Policy."

74. Martz, *Central America: The Crisis*, 201.

75. Ameringer, *The Democratic Left*, 217; and Bernard Diederich, *Somoza and the Legacy of U.S. Involvement in Central America*, 2nd ed. (Princeton: Markus Wiener, 2007 [1981]), quote, 49.

76. Porter, "Defects of United States Policy."

77. Memo, Porter to Rosita Rieck Bennett, November 22, 1957, Box 15, File, Foreign Affairs-Latin America #2, 1957, COP; and Rubottom to Whelan, April 7, 1958, *FRUS, 1958–1960*, V: Microfiche Supplement #20.

78. Odría (1953), Pérez Jiménez (1954), Somoza Debayle (1956), and Cuban colonels Ramón Barquín (1955) and Francisco Tabernilla (1958) were just some of the officers awarded the Legion of Merit. Matthews, "Diplomatic Relations," 163.

79. Chamorro describes his treatment in Somocista prisons in *Estirpe sangrienta: Los Somoza* (Mexico City: Editorial Diogenes, 1980 [1957]). See also John Booth, "The Somoza Regime in Nicaragua," in *Sultanistic Regimes*, 132–152, especially 136.

80. Pons to Pineau, December 6, 1956, Section V:2, Governor of Puerto Rico, 1949–1964, Correspondencia Particular, Folder #55, FLMM. Among those training in Cuba were future founders of the FSLN Carlos Fonseca Amador, Tomás Borge Martínez, and Silvio Mayorga Delgado. On Castro's trip to Costa Rica, see Bonachea and Valdés, "Introduction," 80.
81. Pons to Pineau, December 6, 1956.
82. Unattributed Confidential Memo, August 8, 1957, Section V:2, Governor of Puerto Rico, 1949–1964, Correspondencia Particular, Folder #55, FLMM.
83. Rubottom to Whelan, April 7, 1958, *FRUS, 1958–1960*, V: Microfiche Supplement, #20; See also Clark, Jr., *The United States and Somoza*, 191.
84. Matthews, "Diplomatic Relations," 163.
85. Telegram, Rubottom to embassies in San José and Managua, September 14, 1956, Box 2594, File 617.18-1-556, RG 59, USNA.
86. Pons to Pineau, December 6, 1956.
87. Memo, Cohen to the State Department, "The 'Ups' and 'Downs' of Costa Rican-Nicaraguan Relations," July 6, 1955, Box 2594, File 617.009/3-1857, RG 59, USNA.
88. Memo, (no first name) Neal to Rubottom, December 11, 1956, Box 2504, File 617.18-556, RG 59, USNA.
89. Ibid.; and Holden, "The Real Diplomacy of Violence," 303.
90. Gambone, *Eisenhower, Somoza, and the Cold War*, 198–200, quote, 200.
91. Franqui, *Diary of the Cuban Revolution*, 299–300; and Barquín, *Las luchas guerrilleras en Cuba*, II: 534, 719.
92. "Memorandum sobre las actividades pro-trujillistas de los cubanos Policarpio Soler, Jesús Gonzalez Cartas (aka, 'El Extraño'), Herminio Díaz, Leonel Gómez y Juan Manuel Delgado (aka, 'El Francés'), September 21, 1958," in Julio César Martínez, *Quiénes y por qué eliminaron a Trujillo* (Santo Domingo: Ediciones Renovación, 1975), quote, 18; and James to Morris Ernst, January 22, 1958, Box 25, File, Murphy Reactions from Mexico, COP.
93. "Memorandum sobre las actividades," 54–55; and Crassweller, *Trujillo: The Life and Times*, 334.
94. James to Ernst, January 22, 1958; and "Memorandum sobre las actividades," 18.
95. Ameringer, *Don Pepe*, 139; and idem, *The Democratic Left*, 172–173.
96. Memo of conversation, Irving Davidson and Wollam, May 31, 1957, Box 2594, File 617.18-1-556, RG 59, USNA; and "Memorandum sobre las actividades," 54–55.
97. Betancourt to Figueres, 33:1 (May 21, 1957), #23, FRB.
98. "Antes que cualquier cosa soy revolucionario," *DCR*, June 15, 1957.
99. Telegram, State Department to embassies in San José, Guatemala City, Managua, San Salvador, and Tegucigalpa, May 22, 1957, Box 2983, File 718.00/3-457, RG 59, USNA.
100. "Cinco mil personas recibieron al Diputado Porter," "Charles Porter orgullo democracia," and "A la cárcel los asesinos," *LR*, June 15, 1957.

101. Chamorro, "Carta abierta," *LR*, June 14, 1957.
102. Ciliberto, "Porter y la democracia latinoamericana," *LR*, June 14, 1957.
103. "La oposición se enfrenta a que El Caribe siga siendo area de disturbios," *DCR*, June 16, 1957; and "Figueres quedó en ridículo ante el Representante Porter," *DCR*, June 18, 1957.
104. Bowman, "Democracy on the Brink," 182; and Martz, "Costa Rican Electoral Trends, 1953–1966," *Western Political Quarterly* 20:4 (December 1967): 888–909, especially 891n20.
105. Porter to Facio Segreda, June 26, 1957, Box 35, File, Trip to Costa Rica, 1957, COP; "Solo a 'El Francés' interrogo El Senador Charles O. Porter," *DCR*, June 19, 1957; and "Mi lucha es contra las dictaduras," *LR*, June 16, 1957.
106. "Antes que cualquier cosa"; and "Cinco mil personas."
107. Porter to Muñoz Marín, April 18, 1957, Box 24, File, General Correspondence, COP.
108. *CR*, May 20, 1958, 9628–9630.
109. Porter, "Defects of United States Policy."
110. Box 14, File, Foreign Affairs, Cuba 1957–April 1958, COP.
111. Palacios, *Between Legitimacy and Violence*, 152; Vernon Fluharty, *Dance of the Millions: Military Rule and Social Revolution in Colombia, 1930–1956* (Westport, CT: Greenwood Press, 1975 [1957]), 262ff; and Martz, *Colombia: A Contemporary Political Survey* (Chapel Hill: University of North Carolina Press, 1962), 204ff.
112. The piece was carried in the Costa Rican paper *La República*. "Un auténtico 'Buen Vecino,'" June 25, 1957.
113. Szulc, *The Winds of Revolution: Latin America Today—and Tomorrow* (New York: Praeger, 1963), 93–94; and Abel, "Colombia, 1930–1958," *CHLA*, VIII: 626.
114. "Porter, "Defects of United States Policy."
115. Karl, *Forgotten Peace: Reform, Violence, and the Making of Contemporary Colombia* (Berkeley: University of California Press, 2017), 30; Eric Hobsbawm, "The Revolutionary Situation in Colombia," *The World Today* 19:6 (June 1963): 248–258, especially 251; and Szulc, *The Winds of Revolution*, 93–94.
116. Richard Maullin, *Soldiers, Guerrillas, and Politics in Colombia* (Lexington, MA: D. C. Heath, 1973), 60.
117. Karl, *Forgotten Peace*, 33; and James Daniel, *Rural Violence in Colombia since 1946* (Washington, DC: Special Operations Research Office, 1965), 34.
118. Rangel, *La revolución de las fantasías*, 127.
119. Plaza, *El 23 de enero*, 91.
120. Tinker Salas, *The Enduring Legacy: Oil, Culture, and Society in Venezuela* (Durham: Duke University Press, 2009), 221. On the church-state controversy, see Stambouli, *Crisis política*.
121. Maullin, *Soldiers, Guerrillas*, 64; and Abel, "Colombia, 1930–1958," *CHLA*, VIII: 626.

122. Burggraaff, *The Venezuelan Armed Forces*, 150.

123. Ellner, "Venezuelans Reflect on the Meaning of the *23 de enero*," *LARR* 20:1 (1985): 244–256, especially 246–247.

124. Fuenmayor, *Historia de la Venezuela política contemporánea*, IX: 176.

125. John Johnson, *The Military and Society in Latin America* (Stanford: Stanford University Press, 1964), quote, 120.

126. No admirer of Betancourt, Rangel noted that the AD leader magnanimously proposed Larrazábal as a compromise choice to govern the country, but that the other parties insisted on open elections. *La revolución de las fantasias*, 296.

127. Robert Dix, "Consociational Democracy: The Case of Colombia," *Comparative Politics* 12:3 (April 1980): 302–323, especially 315–316.

128. Despatch, from Cabot to State Department, July 11, 1958, *FRUS, 1958–1960*, V: Microfiche Supplement, #9. Lleras Camargo told a Bogotá newspaper that Trujillo and Pérez Jiménez were backing Rojas Pinilla. "Está funcionando en el Caribe una 'internacional negra,' " *El Universal* (Bogotá), December 16, 1958, in Tomo 35: Complemento D, #24, FRB.

129. Szulc, *Twilight of the Tyrants*, 5, 208ff; J. León Helguera, "The Changing Role of the Military in Colombia," *Journal of Inter-American Studies* 3:3 (July 1961): 351–358, especially 357; and Martz, *Colombia*, 282–285.

130. "Atentado contra Rómulo Betancourt," July 26, 1958, Tomo 35: Complemento A:32, FRB; and Fuenmayor, *Historia de la Venezuela política contemporánea*, XII: 281.

131. Plaza, *El 23 de enero*, 112.

132. "Trescientos mil trabajadores fueron ayer al paro simbólico," *El Nacional* (Caracas), July 23, 1958; and "Más de ochenta mil Venezolanos se reunieron en El Silencio en grandiosa manifestación de unidad," *El Universal* (Caracas), July 24, 1958, in *Historia gráfica de Venezuela*, José Rivas Rivas, ed., 12 vols. (Caracas: Centro Editor, 1972), VII: 142–143 and 144. See also Taylor, Jr., *The Venezuelan golpe*, 56–61.

133. "Asesinar al Presidente Larrazábal y los líderes Betancourt y Machado decidieron los cabecillas de la conspiración," *El Nacional*, September 13, 1958, in *Historia gráfica*, VII: 194–195; and Plaza, *El 23 de enero*, 112.

134. Bigler, "The Armed Forces and Patterns," 121; and Edward Gude, "Political Violence in Venezuela, 1958–1964," in *When Men Revolt and Why: A Reader in Political Violence and Revolution*, ed. James Davies (New York: Free Press, 1970), 259–273, especially 267.

135. Quoted in Hartmann de Betancourt, *Rómulo y yo*, 442,

136. For example, Betancourt, "Reencuentro con el pueblo," in idem, *Posición y doctrina* (Caracas: Editorial Cordillera, 1959), 37–45.

137. Martz, *Acción Democrática*, 105.

138. Levine, *Conflict and Political Change in Venezuela* (Princeton: Princeton University Press, 1973), quote, 43; and Hartmann, *Rómulo y yo*, 159.

139. Rey, *Personalismo o liderazgo*, 40–43.

140. Wilde, "Conversations among Gentlemen," 60.

141. Alexander, *Venezuela's Voice for Democracy*, 131.

142. Betancourt to Muñoz Marín, February 21, 1958, Folder 55, Section V, Series 2, Governor of Puerto Rico, 1949–1964, Correspondencia Particular, FLMM.

143. Betancourt, "América y las dictaduras," in *Testimonio de la revolución en Venezuela, 1 de enero-23 de julio-1958*, ed. José Umaña Bernal (Caracas: Vargas, 1958), 174–177, quote, 175.

144. Betancourt to Muñoz Marín, February 21, 1958.

145. Ibid.

146. The quote comes from an undated NIE Estimate. Based on matters discussed in its text, it appears to have been written in the fall of 1958. *FRUS, 1958–1960*, V: Microfiche Supplement, #27.

147. Ewell, *Venezuela: A Century of Change*, 125. For Pérez's observations, see Alexander, *The Bolivarian Presidents*, 230. The PCV supported Larrazábal even though the admiral had requested support from the U.S. for a new "secret political investigative bureau" to monitor communist activity. Tinker Salas, *The Enduring Legacy*, 224.

148. Tinker Salas, *The Enduring Legacy*, 222.

149. Memorandum of Conversation, Rubottom, Betancourt, Bernbaum, Caldera, and Villalba, January 31, 1958, Rubottom Subject Files, 1957–1959, Box 10, File 1958, Venezuela, RG 59, USNA; and minutes of January 6, 1958, NSC meeting, NSC Series, Box 9, Ann Whitman File, EPL.

150. Burggraaff, *The Venezuelan Armed Forces*, 141; Ewell, *Venezuela: A Century of Change*, 112–113; Szulc, "Venezuela: Anti-U.S. Case History," *NYT*, May 17, 1958; and Plaza, *El 23 de enero*, 101.

151. For useful primers on *La Violencia*, see Germán Guzmán Campo, Orlando Fals Borda, and Eduardo Umaña Luna, *La violencia en Colombia: Estudio de un proceso social* (Bogotá: Ediciones Tercer Mundo, 1962); Charles Bergquist, Ricardo Peñaranda, and Gonzalo Sánchez, eds., *Violence in Colombia: The Contemporary Crisis in Historical Perspective* (Wilmington: Scholarly Resources, 1992); Sánchez and Donny Meertens, *Bandits, Peasants, and Politics: The Case of "La Violencia" in Colombia* (Austin: University of Texas Press, 2001); and Norman Bailey, "La Violencia in Colombia," *JISWA* 9:4 (October 1957): 561–575.

152. Palacios, *Between Legitimacy and Violence*, 137; and Abel, "Columbia, 1930–1958," *CHLA*, VIII: 616–620.

153. Hobsbawm, "The Revolutionary Situation," 248.

154. Palacios, *Between Legitimacy and Violence*, 164; Bailey, "*La Violencia* in Colombia," 568. 7; Maullin, *Soldiers, Guerrillas*, 62; and Herrán-Ávila, "Convergent Conflicts: The Cold War and the Origins of the Counterinsurgent State in Colombia (1946–1954)," in *Peripheries of the Cold War*, ed. Frank Jacobs (Würzburg, Germany: Königshausen & Neumann, 2015), 319–336, especially 327.

155. Wilde, "Conversations among Gentlemen," quote, 76n85; and John Peeler, *Latin American Democracies: Colombia, Costa Rica, Venezuela* (Chapel Hill: University of North Carolina Press, 1985), 57.

156. Herrán-Ávila, "Convergent Conflicts, 320; and Daniel, *Rural Violence in Colombia*, 106.

157. James Payne, *Patterns of Conflict in Colombia* (New Haven: Yale University Press, 1968), 178–179.

158. Fluharty, *Dance of the Millions*, quote, 303; and Harvey Kline, "The National Front: Historical Perspective and Overview," in *Politics of Compromise: Coalition Government in Colombia*, ed. R. Albert Berry, Ronald Hellman, and Mauricio Solaún (New Brunswick, NJ: Transaction, 1980), quote, 70.

159. Despatch, Cabot to State Department, July 11, 1958.

160. Brands, *Latin America's Cold War*, 20.

161. Karl, "Petroleum and Political Pacts."

162. Peeler, *Latin American Democracies*, 58, 92–93.

163. Tinker Salas, *Venezuela: What Everyone*, 91.

164. Rangel, *La revolución de las fantasías*, 156–158.

165. Berle, oral history, July 6, 1967, p.11, JFKPL. https://www.jfklibrary.org/asset-viewer/archives/JFKOH/Berle%2C%20Adolf%20A/JFKOH-AAB-01/JFKOH-AAB-01. Accessed October 21, 2021.

Chapter Fourteen. The Hour of the Sword No Longer Tolls

Epigraph 1: Muñoz Marín with Donald Robinson, "It's Later than We Think in Latin America," *Look*, July 18, 1958, 19–20.
Epigraph 2: Quoted in Richard Goodwin, *Remembering America: A Voice from the Sixties* (Boston: Little Brown, 1988), 147.

1. In his self-serving memoir Nixon presented himself as initially reluctant to attend the inauguration and had to be coaxed by Foster Dulles to visit other countries. *Six Crises* (New York: Doubleday, 1962), 184. Rubottom offers a more nuanced view of the pre-trip discussions. Rubottom, oral history, 38ff.

2. Unless otherwise indicated, what follows draws on Zahniser and Weis, " 'A Diplomatic Pearl Harbor.' " On Cabot, see Gellman, *The President and the Apprentice: Eisenhower and Nixon, 1952–1961* (New Haven: Yale University Press, 2015), quote, 495.

3. For an eyewitness account that portrays Nixon as heroic, see Vernon Walters, *Silent Missions* (New York: Doubleday, 1978).

4. Memorandum of Discussion at the 366th Meeting of the NSC, May 22, 1958, *FRUS, 1958–1960*, V: 239–246.

5. Nixon, *Six Crises*, 208.

6. Ibid., 186–187.

7. Szulc, *The Winds of Revolution*, 108.

8. Jonathan Brown, *Cuba's Revolutionary World* (Cambridge: Harvard University Press), 349.

9. Nixon, *Six Crises*, 193.

10. Szulc, *The Winds of Revolution*, 109–110.

11. Richard Patch, "Nixon in Peru: Comments on the Implications of Student Attacks on the Vice President," *American Universities Field Staff Reports*, West Coast South America Series, V:4 (May 20, 1958): 1–10, especially 4–7; E. (Ezequiel) Ramírez Novoa, *América Latina y Estados Unidos: Las aventuras de Mr. Nixon en Latinoamérica* (Lima: n.p., 1958), 25; and Bertram, "Peru, 1930–1960," 443.

12. Achilles to State Department, May 8, 1958, *FRUS, 1958–1960*, V: Microfiche Supplement, #24; and Nixon, *Six Crises*, 199.

13. Nixon, *Six Crises*, 202.

14. Walters characterized Nixon's visit to the Pontificia as celebratory, with students at one point hoisting him on their shoulders. *Silent Missions*, 324.

15. "Department of State: Vice President Nixon's Trip to South America," May 26, 1958, Annex C, Box 18, NSC Series, Policy Papers Subseries, EPL; and Nixon, *Six Crises*, 223.

16. Telegram, Achilles to State Department, May 16, 1958, *FRUS, 1958–1960*, V: Microfiche Supplement, #24.

17. Ramírez Novoa, *América Latina y Estados Unidos*, 26.

18. James Carey, *Peru and the United States, 1900–1962* (South Bend: University of Notre Dame Press, 1964), 186, 189.

19. Iber, *Neither Peace nor Freedom*, 96.

20. Pike, "The Old and the New APRA," 34–35.

21. Szulc, *The Winds of Revolution*, 91; and Julio Cotler, "Peru since 1960," *CHLA*, VIII: 451–508, especially 453–454.

22. Carey, *Peru and the United States*, 196, 199, 203.

23. "Department of State: Vice President Nixon's Trip."

24. Memo from Albert Gerberich to Terry Sanders, May 12, 1958, *FRUS, 1958–1960*, V: Microfiche Supplement, #9.

25. Dulles to Nixon, March 6, 1958, *FRUS, 1958–1960*, V: 223.

26. Rubottom, oral history, 38.

27. Ewell, "The Extradition of Marcos Pérez Jiménez, 1959–1963: Practical Precedent for Enforcement of Administrative Honesty?" *JLAS* 9:2 (November 1977): 291–313, especially 291.

28. Kolb, *Democracy and Dictatorship in Venezuela*, 181.

29. Szulc, "Venezuela: Anti-U.S. Case History"; and Kolb, *Democracy and Dictatorship in Venezuela*, 181ff.

30. Interoffice memo, John Devine to Rubottom, July 9, 1958, and interoffice memo, O. C. Anderson to Rubottom, "Refutation of Attacks and Criticism Based on our Treatment of Marcos Pérez Jiménez," July 11, 1958, File 1958, Venezuela, Folder 2, RG 59, USNA.

31. Interoffice memo, Anderson to Rubottom, "Refutation of Attacks and Criticism."
32. Nixon, *Six Crises*, 211.
33. "Acuerdo de los estudiantes universitarios sobre la llegada de Nixon," *El Nacional*, May 11, 1958, in *Historia gráfica de Venezuela*, VII: 111–112; Fuenmayor, *Historia de la Venezuela política contemporanea*, XI: 234, quote, 235; and Plaza, *El 23 de enero*, 108.
34. Gellman, *The President and the Apprentice*, 504.
35. Rubottom, oral history, 39.
36. Szulc, *The Winds of Revolution*, 111.
37. Memorandum of a Telephone Conversation between Burrows and Rubottom, May 13, 1958, *FRUS, 1958–1960*, V: 226–227; and Walters, *Silent Missions*, 330.
38. Memorandum of a Telephone Conversation, May 13, 1958, *FRUS, 1958–1960*, V: 226–227; McPherson, *Yankee No! Anti-Americanism in U.S.-Latin American Relations* (Cambridge: Harvard University Press, 2003), 29; Gellman, *The President and the Apprentice*, 505–506; and Schmitz, *Thank God*, 210.
39. Memorandum of a Telephone Conversation between Rubottom and Snow, May 13, 1958, *FRUS, 1958–1960*, V: 229–232; and Walters, *Silent Missions*, 336.
40. Nixon, *Six Crises*, 226.
41. Szulc, *The Winds of Revolution*, 113–114.
42. Memorandum of a Telephone Conversation among Bettinger, Miller, and Snow.
43. Eldon Kenworthy, "Eisenhower Will Lead a Gala Welcome Today," *NYT*, May 15, 1958; and Nixon, *Six Crises*, 227.
44. "Troop Movement," *NYT*, May 15, 1958.
45. Plaza, *El 23 de enero*, 109.
46. Betancourt, "La visita de Nixon," May 17, 1958, in *Combate* 1:1 (July–August 1958).
47. "Betancourt Viewpoint," *Christian Science Monitor*, April 12, 1962.
48. Memorandum of conversation between Rubottom, Santaella, and Bartch, May 20, 1958, Rubottom Subject Files, 1957–1959, Box 10, File 1958, Venezuela, RG 59, USNA.
49. Porter to Rogers, March 4, 1959, Box 24, File, Dictators-Extradition, COP.
50. Elvira Mendoza, "Una gran victoria de la junta y del pueblo," in *Testimonio de la revolución*, 259–274.
51. Operations Coordinating Board, "Report on Latin America," May 21, 1958, NSC 5613/1, Box 13, Policy Paper Subseries, White House Office, Office of the Special Assistant for National Security Affairs: Records, NSC Policy Series, EPL.
52. Ewell, "The Extradition of Marcos Pérez Jiménez," 292.
53. Kenworthy, "Eisenhower Will Lead."

54. Minutes of the Cabinet Meeting, White House, May 16, 1958, *FRUS, 1958–1960*, V: 238–239.

55. Memorandum of Discussion, *FRUS, 1958–1960*, V: 239–246 quotes, 240, 241 and 244.

56. Memorandum of Discussion of the 369th Meeting of the NSC, June 19, 1958, *FRUS, 1958–1960*, V: 27–32, quote, 28.

57. Quoted in Schmitz, *Thank God*, 213; and Gellman, *The President and the Apprentice*, 510–511.

58. Quoted in Rabe, *Eisenhower and Latin America*, 102.

59. "Statement of Señor José Figueres," House Committee on Foreign Affairs, June 9, 1958, Records of Rubottom, Subject Files 1957–1959, Box 4, 1958, RG59, USNA. See also Figueres, "No se puede escupir a una política exterior," *Combate* 1 (July–August 1958), 64–69; and "Figueres habla claro," *LR*, June 11, 1958.

60. *CR*, May 20, 1958, 9628–9630.

61. Matthews, "The Lessons of Latin America," *Foreign Policy Bulletin* 37:19 (June 15, 1958).

62. Lippmann, "Too Complacent," *Miami Herald*, May 22, 1958.

63. Cartapacio #24, Sección V: Serie 19, Caja 2, FLMM.

64. Briggs, *Proud Servant*, 362.

65. Whelan to State Department, May 28, 1958, *FRUS, 1958–1960*, V: Microfiche Supplement, #20.

66. Quoted in Rabe, *The Road to OPEC*, 135.

67. Lawrence Roberts, *Mayday 1971: A White House at War, a Revolt in the Streets, and the Untold History of America's Biggest Mass Arrest* (Boston: Houghton Mifflin, 2020), 34–35, 44–47.

68. Ben Franklin, "Young Demonstrators at Parade Throw Smoke Bombs and Stones at Nixon's Car," *NYT*, January 21, 1969; and Robert Dallek, *Nixon and Kissinger: Partners in Power* (New York: Harper Collins, 2007), 95.

69. Quoted in Dallek, *Nixon and Kissinger*, 203.

70. Quoted in Stephen E. Ambrose, *Nixon: The Triumph of a Politician, 1962–1972* (New York: Simon and Schuster, 1989), 357.

71. "Nixon Blames Smear for Revelation; Nixon Should Withdraw," and "Nixon Gives 'Basic Facts' on Fund, Defends Use of It," *WP*, September 20 and 21, 1952.

72. Porter, oral history, tape 7:1–2; and Dallek, *Nixon and Kissinger*, 22–23.

73. "Ambassador from Oregon," *NYT*, July 8, 1958; and *El Nacional*, July 5, 1958.

74. "A Shift for the Better in Our Latin American Policy," *CR*, February 18, 1958, A1443.

75. Rabe, *The Road to OPEC*, quote, 134.

76. Memo of Conversation, Rubottom, Porter, and John Hill, July 3, 1958, File, Venezuela, Folder 2, Box 10, Rubottom, Subject Files, 1957–59, 1958, Speeches, June–December, W Miscellaneous, RG 59, USNA; and Burrows to State Department, February 12, 1958, *FRUS, 1958–1960*, V: Microfiche Supplement, #27.

77. Richard Gott, *Guerrilla Movements in Latin America*, 2nd ed. (Oxford: Seagull, 2008 [1970]), 97.

78. Memo of Conversation, Rubottom, Porter, and Hill, July 3, 1958; and Gude, "Political Violence in Venezuela, 1958–1964," 267.

79. Memorandum of Conversation, Rubottom, Porter, and Hill, July 3, 1958.

80. Tomo 33: Complementos A, July 3, 1958, FRB.

81. "Visita a Venezuela del congresante norteamericano Charles O. Porter," *La Esfera*, July 3, 1958.

82. Transcript of Porter's press conference, Venezuelan Newspaper Association, July 4, 1958, Library of Congress Translation Service, Box 36, Trip-Venezuela 1958, COP; and *El Nacional*, July 5, 1958.

83. "Venezuela Hails Porter on Visit," *NYT*, July 7, 1958; "Transcript of Porter's press conference"; and *El Nacional*, July 5, 1958.

84. "Porter y la tiranía trujillista," *El Nacional*, July 5, 1958; and "Venezuela Hails Porter on Visit."

85. "Porter huésped de honor de la Universidad Central," *El Universal*, July 8, 1958; and "Porter Warns Students of Communist Danger," *Caracas Journal*, July 8, 1958.

86. Rey, "Mr. Porter y las esperanzas del pueblo venezolano," *El Nacional*, July 6, 1958.

87. Tinker Salas, *Venezuela: What Everyone Needs*, quote, 94.

88. Betancourt, "La hora de la democracia," in *Posición y doctrina*, 223–240, quote, 232–233.

89. Ibid.; *CR*, July 29, 1958, 1491–149; and Martz, *Acción Democrática*, 99.

90. Porter's speech, July 5, 1958, Box 35, File, Trip, Venezuela #2, July 1958, COP.

91. Ibid.

92. "Crowds Cheer Representative Porter in Venezuela," *Venezuela Up-to-Date* 7:10 (September–October 1958), Box 35, File, Trip, Venezuela #2, July 1958, COP.

93. Porter, "Democracy in Venezuela," *CR*, July 21, 1958, A14527.

94. Memorandum of Conversation with Rubottom, Muñoz Marín, Dr. Torres, and Mr. Reed, July 7, Rubottom, Subject Files, 1957–1959, Box 9, File 1958, Puerto Rico, RG 59, USNA.

95. Nixon, *Six Crises*, 228.

96. Rabe, *Eisenhower and Latin America*, quote, 105; and Ewell, "The Extradition of Marcos Pérez Jiménez," 296ff.

97. Quoted in Rabe, *Eisenhower and Latin America*, 106.

98. Ibid.

99. Ibid.

100. Szulc, *The Winds of Revolution*, 115–117.

101. Barber and Ronning, *Internal Security and Military Power*, 19; and LaFeber, "Thomas C. Mann," 179.

102. Rubottom to Cabot, January 31, 1959, Records of Rubottom, Subject Files 1957–1959, 1959, Box 12, RG 59, USNA.

103. Rabe, *The Road to OPEC*, 158.

104. Schoultz, *That Infernal Little Cuban Republic*, 82–83.

105. Porter, oral history, tape 14:2.

106. Ameringer, "The Foreign Policy of Venezuelan Democracy," in *Venezuela: The Democratic Experience*, 335–358, quote, 341.

107. Hirschman, "*Abrazo* vs. Coexistence: Comments on Ypsilon's Paper," in *Latin American Issues: Essays and Comments*, ed. idem (New York: Twentieth Century Fund, 1961): 59–63, quote, 61; and Weiner, *Enemies: A History of the FBI* (New York: Random House, 2012), 216–217.

108. Quoted in Holden, "The Real Diplomacy of Violence," 300.

109. Quoted in LaFeber, "Thomas C. Mann," 174.

110. Hunt, *American Ascendancy*, 200.

Chapter Fifteen.　Cuban Conundrum

Epigraph: Rabe, "The Caribbean Triangle: Betancourt, Castro, and Trujillo and U.S. Foreign Policy, 1958–1963," *DH* 20:1 (Winter 1996): 55–78, quote, 70.

1. Crowd estimates varied widely. Castro later claimed that three hundred thousand crammed into the Plaza. Gott, *Guerrilla Movements*, 99–100; and "Visita del Fidel Castro a Venezuela," January 1959, País Interior, Expediente #143, MRV. See also Francisco Pividal Padrón, *Los tres días de Fidel Castro en Venezuela, hace treinta años* (Caracas: Universidad Central de Venezuela, 1989), 28.

2. Unless otherwise indicated, what follows draws on Castro's speech at El Silencio. http://www.fidelcastro.cu/es/discursos/discurso-pronunciado-en-la-plaza-aerea-del-silencio-en-caracas-venezuela. Accessed October 14, 2020.

3. Manuel Urrutia Lleó, *Fidel Castro & Company, Inc: Community Tyranny in Cuba* (New York: Praeger, 1964), 25–26; "Una subscripción en favor de los revolucionarios de Cuba patrocina La Junta Patriótica," *El Universal*, March 26, 1958, in *Historia gráfica*, VII: 93. In 1959, one bolívar was worth 0.16 in U.S. currency. See also Hernández and Giusti, *Carlos Andrés Pérez*, 112; and Pividal Padrón, *El Movimiento 26 de Julio en Venezuela y quienes lo apoyaron* (Morelia, Mexico: Universidad Michoacana de San Nicolás de Hidalgo, 1996), 24.

4. "Cubanos, Fidelistas de toda la nación vinieron a entrevistarse con Urrutia," *La Esfera*, April 28, 1958; and Brown, *Cuba's Revolutionary World*, 225–226.

5. Quoted in Hamlet Hermann, *Fidel, Trujillo, USA: 1958–1961* (Santo Domingo: Editora Búho, 2014), 44. See also Delio Gómez Ochoa, *Constanza, Maimón y Estero Honda: La victoria de los caídos* (Santo Domingo: Alfa y Omega, 1998), 20, 25.

6. Untitled United Press report, April 10, 1958, Cuba, Situación Política, Expediente #59, MRV; G. H. Fisher, Second Secretary, Caracas embassy,

memorandum, "Venezuelan-Cuban Relations Strained," April 9, 1958, File 631.35/1–2958, Box 2599, RG 59, USNA; and Urrutia Lleó, *Fidel Castro & Company*, 17, 25.

7. Quoted in Hermann, *Fidel, Trujillo, USA*, 46.

8. Gott, *Guerrilla Movements*, xxviii; and Diederich, *Trujillo: The Death of the Goat* (Maplewood, NJ: Waterfront Press, 1990 [1978]), quote, 27.

9. Franqui, *Diary of the Cuban Revolution*, quote, 299–300.

10. Pividal Padrón claimed that one hundred thousand welcomed Castro at Maiquetía airport. *Los tres días de Fidel*, 16, 18.

11. "Castro Asks Move to Curb Dictators," and "Castro Urges U.S. to Revise Policy," *NYT*, January 25 and January 26, 1959.

12. *Diario Las Américas* (Miami), January 25, 1959, in Cuba, Situación política, Expediente #59, MRV; Luis Báez, "Crónica de un testigo sobre la visita del Fidel a Venezuela hace 50 años," *Cubadebate*, January 22, 2009, http://www.cubadebate.cu/opinion/2009/01/22/cronica-de-un-testigo-sobre-la-visita-de-fidel-a-venezuela-hace-50-anos. Accessed March 4, 2022; and Pividal Padrón, *Los tres días de Fidel*, quote, 40.

13. Hartmann, *Rómulo y yo*, 91.

14. Hermann, *Fidel, Trujillo, USA*, 31; and Diederich, *Trujillo: The Death of the Goat*, 27.

15. John Cates, First Secretary, Caracas Embassy, memorandum, "Venezuela Suspends Diplomatic Relations with the Dominican Republic," June 17, 1959, File 631.35/1–2958, Box 2599, RG 59, USNA; Castro Ventura, *Trujillo vs. Betancourt*, 178; and Hermann, *Fidel, Trujillo, USA*, quote, 95.

16. Miguel Guerrero, *La ira del tirano: Historia del atentado de Los Próceres* (Santo Domingo: Editora Corripio, 1994), 63; and Pou de García, "Movimientos conspirativos," 53–54.

17. Sang, *La política exterior dominicana*, II: 750, 754.

18. Castro Ventura, *Trujillo vs. Betancourt*, 179; and Juan Liscano, "Rómulo Betancourt ante sus obras y la historia," in *Multimagen de Rómulo: vida y acción de Rómulo Betancourt en gráficas*, ed. idem and Carlos Gottberg (Caracas: Orbeca, 1978).

19. Hartmann, *Rómulo y yo*, 150–151; Brown, *Cuba's Revolutionary World*, 226–227; and Guerrero, *La ira del tirano*, 125–126.

20. National Intelligence Estimate, June 25, 1959, *FRUS, 1958–1960*, V: 391–392.

21. Matthews, "Diplomatic Relations," 166.

22. Felix Belair, Jr., "Castro Defended by Muñoz Marín," *NYT*, January 20, 1959.

23. Ibid. For Morse's criticism, see "Morse Asks Cuba to End 'Blood Baths,' " *WP*, January 13, 1959.

24. In addition to the two congressmen, three hundred foreign journalists accepted the Cuban government's invitation to witness what it called Operation Truth. Hermann, *Fidel, Trujillo, USA*, 85; *CR*, March 2, 1959, 320–322;

Guerra, *Visions of Power in Cuba: Revolution, Redemption, and Resistance, 1959–1971* (Chapel Hill: University of North Carolina Press, 2012), 42; and Michelle Chase, "The Trials: Violence and Justice in the Aftermath of the Cuban Revolution," in *A Century of Revolution*, 163–198.

25. Powell, *Adam by Adam: The Autobiography of Adam Clayton Powell, Jr.* (New York: Dial Press, 1971), 190–191; and Porter, oral history, 11:2.
26. Porter, oral history, 11:2; and *CR*, March 2, 1959, 3200–3202.
27. *FRUS, 1958–1960*, VI: 378–381, quotes, 380, 381.
28. Quoted in Schoultz, *That Infernal Little Cuban Republic*, 87.
29. McPherson, "The Limits of Populist Diplomacy: Fidel Castro's April 1959 Trip to North America," *Diplomacy and Statecraft* 18 (2007): 237–268.
30. "Fidel Castro se refirió en Columbia a la muerte de Profesor de Galíndez," *El Universal*, April 22, 1959; and Philip Benjamin, "Castro Gets a Noisy Reception Here," *NYT*, April 22, 1959.
31. William Leogrande and Peter Kornbluh, *Back Channel to Cuba: The Hidden History of Negotiations between Washington and Havana* (Chapel Hill: University of North Carolina Press, 2014), 15–21; Rufo López-Fresquet, *My 14 Months with Castro* (Cleveland: World Publishing, 1966), 107; Kent Beck, "Necessary Lies, Hidden Truths: Cuba in the 1960 Campaign," *DH* 8:1 (Winter 1984): 37–59, especially 40–41. On Nixon's early support for what became Brigade 2506, see Matthews, *The Cuban Story* (New York: Braziller, 1961), 249. On Castro's response to Porter, Aleksandr Fursenko and Timothy Naftali, *"One Hell of a Gamble:" Khrushchev, Castro, and Kennedy, 1958–1964* (New York: Norton, 1997), quote, 9.
32. Hunt, *American Ascendancy*, quotes, 188, 190.
33. Typescript, Schlesinger, "Report to the President on Latin American Mission, February 12–March 3, 1961," Caja 8, File 67A, FLMM.
34. Confidential memorandum, Andrés Townsend Ezcurra, October 1960, Caja 8, File 67A, FLMM.
35. Matthews, *The Cuban Story*, quote, 294.
36. Ameringer, *Don Pepe*, 151.
37. Memorandum, Cohen to the State Department, "The Figueres–Fidel Castro Feud," File 618.00/12–655 Box 2594, RG59 USNA; and Ameringer, *Don Pepe*, 151.
38. Ameringer, *Don Pepe*, 153–154; Memo of Discussion, NSC meeting, March 26, 1959, *FRUS, 1958–1960*, VI; 6; and R. Hart Phillips, "Cuba Admonished about Executions," *NYT*, March 24, 1959.
39. Memorandum of Conversation, Francisco Aguirre and William Wieland, "Break between Prime Minister Fidel Castro and Former Costa Rican President Figueres," March 26, 1959, File 618.00/12–655, Box 2594, RG 59, USNA; Goldenberg, *The Cuban Revolution and Latin America*, 179; Brown, *Cuba's Revolutionary World*, 52; and Brands, *Latin America's Cold War*, 31.
40. Memorandum, Cohen to the State Department, "The Figueres-Fidel Castro Feud"; and Hunter Estep, "Former President Figueres Broadcasts Views on

Recent Latin American Developments," File 618.00/12–655, Box 2983, RG, 59, USNA.

41. Hermann, *Fidel, Trujillo, USA*, 26; and Ameringer, *Don Pepe*, 154–155.

42. Phillips, "Castro Bars Pledge to Join U.S. in War," *NYT*, March 23, 1959.

43. Castro, "No Hope for Counterrevolution," March 23, 1959, Latin American Network Information Center, http://lanic.utexas.edu/project/castro/db/1959/19590323.html. Accessed November 15, 2021; and Phillips, "Castro's Nationalism Disturbs Some Cubans," *NYT*, April 5, 1959.

44. Telegram, Bonsal to State Department, April 3, 1959, *FRUS, 1958–1960*, VI: 447–448.

45. Barquín, *Las luchas guerrilleras en Cuba*, II: 523; Martz, *Central America, The Crisis*, 250; and Ameringer, *Don Pepe*, 149, 156.

46. "Ante la Prensa," CMQ-TV, April 2, 1959, in Fidel Castro Ruz, "Figueres," *Humanismo* 8:55–56 (May–August 1959): 71–75; "Costa Rican Denies Charges by Castro," *NYT*, April 14, 1959; Memorandum, Cohen to the State Department, "The Figueres-Fidel Castro Feud"; and Bonsal to State Department, quote, 448. Years later Figueres admitted to working with the agency. "Costa Rican Link," *NYT*, March 10, 1975; and Ameringer, *Don Pepe*, 162.

47. Estep to State Department, Memorandum, "Former President Figueres."

48. Telegram, Willauer to State Department, March 30, 1959, *FRUS, 1958–1960*, VI: 442–444, quote, 443–44.

49. Estep to State Department.

50. Memorandum, "National Liberation Party Issues Statement on Dictatorships," March 16, 1959, File 618.00/12–655, Box 2594, RG59, USNA; and Estep to State Department, Memorandum, "Former President Figueres," April 13, 1959.

51. Quoted in Luis Marcano Salazar, *La política exterior del gobierno de Rómulo Betancourt (1959–1964)* (Caracas: Editorial de la Fundación Servicios y Proyecciones para la América Latina, 1998), 108.

52. Schlesinger, "Report to the President."

53. Cohen to State Department, April 21, 1959, File 618.00/12–655, Box 2594, RG 59, USNA.

54. Berle, "Latin America: The Hidden Revolution," *The Reporter* 20:1 (May 28, 1959), 17–20, quote, 19; and idem, "The Cuban Crisis," especially 45.

55. Ameringer, *Don Pepe*, quote, 158.

56. Bayo, *Mi aporte a la revolución cubana* (Havana: Imprenta Ejército Rebelde Havana, 1960), quotes, 15 and 20; and Matthews, *Revolution in Cuba: An Essay in Understanding* (New York: Charles Scribner's Sons, 1975), 70.

57. Brown, *Cuba's Revolutionary World*, 212.

58. Acosta Matos, *La telaraña cubana*, II: 645–649; Suárez Núñez, *El gran culpable*, 109; Thomas, *Cuba: The Pursuit of Freedom*, quote, 1021; Manuel Javier García, *Mis 20 años en el Palacio Nacional junta a Trujillo y otros gobernantes dominicanos*, 2 vols. (Santo Domingo: Ediciones de Taller, 1985, 1986), II: 273; and Barquín, *Las luchas guerrilleras en Cuba*, II: 534.

59. Pettinà, *Cuba y Estados Unidos*, 112–113.

60. *FRUS, 1958–1960*, VI: 293n2.

61. Espaillat, *Trujillo: The Last Caesar*, 144; Szulc, *Fidel: A Critical Portrait*, 499; Vega, ed., *Los Estados Unidos y Trujillo. Los días finales: 1960–1961. Colección de documentos del Departamento de Estado, la CIA y los archivos del Palacio Nacional Dominicano* (Santo Domingo: Fundación Cultural Dominicana, 2011), 250; idem, *Eisenhower y Trujillo*, 9; and State Department Telegram to All Missions in the American Republics, June 18, 1959, *FRUS, 1958–1960*, VI: quote, 535–536. Pedraza and the Dominican ruler had worked together before. He was alleged to have been part of Trujillo's plot to overthrow Grau in 1945. Barquín, *Las luchas guerrilleras en Cuba*, I: 75.

62. Quoted in Hermann, *Fidel, Trujillo, USA*, 71.

63. López Fresquet, *My 14 Months*, 81; Brown, *Cuba's Revolutionary World*, 52; and Szulc, *Fidel: A Critical Portrait* (New York: William Morrow, 1986), 497.

64. Diederich, *Trujillo: The Death of the Goat*, 28.

65. Unless indicated, this section draws on Aran Shetterly, *The Americano: Fighting with Castro for Cuba's Freedom* (Chapel Hill: Algonquin Books, 2007); David Grann, "The Yankee *Comandante*: A Story of Love, Revolution, and Betrayal," *The New Yorker*, May 21, 2012. https://www.newyorker.com/magazine/2012/05/28/the-yankee-comandante. Accessed November 5, 2020; and Michael Sallah and Mitch Weiss, *The Yankee Comandante: The Untold Story of Courage, Passion, and One American's Fight to Liberate Cuba* (Guilford, CT: Lyons Press, 2015), 144ff.

66. Pérez Jiménez is said to have contributed two hundred thousand dollars. Andrés Zaldívar Diéguez and Pedro Etcheverry Vásquez contend that Morgan's past ties to the mob best explain Bartone's presence at the meeting. Smarting from the loss of its casinos in Havana, the Mafia viewed the plot as an opportunity to recover its properties. *La conspiración trujillista: una fascinante historia* (Santo Domingo: Archivo General de la Nación, 2016), 218n287, 225ff.

67. Vega, *Los Estados Unidos . . . Los días finales*, 29.

68. Zaldívar Diéguez and Etcheverry Vásquez claim that the arms were procured by Bernardino and Porfirio Rubirosa, not Bartone. *La conspiración trujillista*, 237.

69. Fabián Escalante, *The Cuba Project: CIA Covert Operations, 1959–1962*, trans. Maxine Shaw, 2nd ed. (Melbourne, Australia: Ocean Press, 2004 [1995]), 25.

70. Brown, *Cuba's Revolutionary World*, 64.

71. Filiberto Olivera Moya, *La conjura trujillista* (Havana: Ediciones Verde Olivo, 1998), 24.

72. Ibid., 41.

73. Espaillat, *Trujillo: The Last Caesar*, 160.

74. "A Fighter with Castro: William Alexander Morgan," "Cubans Capture Invasion Plane; Accuse Trujillo," both in *NYT*, August 15, 1959; and "Castro is Lionized for Tricking Foes: American is Hailed," *NYT*, August 16, 1959.

75. Espaillat, *Trujillo: The Last Caesar,* 161.

76. Shetterly, *The Americano,* quote, 221–222.

77. Quoted in Ibid., 211–212. See also Douglass Cater and Walter Pincus, "The Foreign Legion of U.S. Public Relations," *The Reporter,* no. 30 (December 22, 1960): 15–22.

78. Batista, *Respuesta* . . . (Mexico City: Manuel León Sánchez, 1960), 373.

79. Acosta Matos, *La telaraña cubana,* II: 748–752; Abbes García, *Trujillo y yo,* 224n6; García, *Mis 20 años en el Palacio Nacional,* II: 94; Víctor Grimaldi, *Tumbaron al jefe,* 3rd ed. (Santo Domingo: n.p., 1999), 34–36; Memo of Discussion, NSC meeting, July 23, 1959, and C. Douglas Dillon to Eisenhower, July 27, 1959, *FRUS, 1958–1960,* VI: 567–568 and quote, 575; and "Batista Flies to Lisbon from Dominican Exile," *NYT,* August 20, 1959.

80. There is circumstantial evidence that Trujillo retaliated seven months later. Castro blamed the U.S. for the March 4, 1960, explosion of the French ship *La Coubre* in Havana harbor, which cost more than one hundred lives, but the insurance firm Lloyd's of London posited that Trujillo could have been responsible. Vega, *Los Estados Unidos . . . Los días finales,* 146.

81. Sallah and Weiss, *The Yankee Comandante,* 165; Brown, *Cuba's Revolutionary World,* 45; and Pedro Páramo (pseud.?), "Epílogo," in Gutiérrez Menoyo, *El radarista* (Madrid: Editorial Playor, 1985), 112–116. A former member of the Second Front told the CIA in 1961 that he believed that the decision to execute Morgan was the result of an unusual quid pro quo between Castro and Trujillo. After Morgan's death, Trujillo released from prison Cuban captain Delio Gómez Ochoa, who was captured during the unsuccessful June 14, 1959, invasion. Shetterly, *The Americano,* 281.

82. Guerrero, *La ira del tirano,* 59.

83. Guerón, "La 'Doctrina Betancourt' y el papel de la teoría," 237; and Ameringer, "The Foreign Policy of Venezuelan Democracy," quote, 336–337.

84. Memorandum of a Conversation among Betancourt, Rubottom, Dewey, Sparks, and Falcón Briceño, February 14, 1958, *FRUS, 1958–1960,* V: Microfiche Supplement, #27.

85. Ewell, *The Indictment of a Dictator,* 57.

86. Memorandum of Conversation between Arcaya and Burrows, "Dominican Asylees in Venezuelan Embassy at Ciudad Trujillo," May 18, 1959, File 631.35/1–2958, Box 2599, RG 59, USNA.

87. Memorandum of Conversation between Betancourt, Sparks, and Burrows, April 27, 1959, *FRUS, 1958–1960,* Microfiche Supplement, #27; Background Paper Prepared by Robert Redington, Office in Charge of U.S. OAS Delegation Matters, August 7, 1959, *FRUS, 1958–1960,* V: 322–333, especially 327; Aragorn Storm Miller, "Season of Storms: The United States and the Caribbean Context for a New Political Order, 1958–1961," in *Beyond the Eagle's Shadow,* 51–75, quote, 84; and Castro Ventura, *Trujillo vs. Betancourt,* 174.

88. Castro Ventura, *Trujillo vs. Betancourt,* 175–177.

89. Sang, *La política exterior dominicana*, II: 754.

90. John Cates to State Department, June 17, 1959, File 631.35/1–2958, RG 59, USNA.

91. Rys, "Tensions and Conflicts," 182.

92. Guerrero, *La ira del tirano*, 63.

93. Ibid., 60–61; Szulc, *The Winds of Revolution*, 123–124; Balcácer, *Trujillo; El tiranicidio*, 94; and idem, *Fidel: A Critical Portrait*, 499. Among the dead were Cubans, Guatemalans, and Venezuelans. Sang, *La política exterior dominicana*, II: 764. Castro was reportedly furious with Betancourt for not providing more assistance. Gómez Ochoa, *Constanza, Maimón*, 46.

94. Quoted in Castro Ventura, *Trujillo vs. Betancourt*, 190.

95. Hernández and Giusti, *Carlos Andrés Pérez*, 128.

96. Memo, Rubottom to Foster Dulles, June 25, 1959, *FRUS, 1958–1960*, V: 290–291.

97. Betancourt, "Mensaje al Señor Presidente de la Conferencia de Consulta de Cancilleres Americanos," August 12, 1959, and "Contacto con los hombres de las finanzas," in *Tres años de gobierno democrático, 1959–1962*, ed. idem, 3 vols. (Caracas: Imprenta Nacional, 1962), I: 98–99 and I: 79–85, especially 85; and Liss, *Diplomacy and Dependency: Venezuela, The United States, and the Americas* (Salisbury, NC: Documentary Publications, 1978), 212.

98. Farland to State Department, December 18, 1958, File 631.35/1–2958, RG 59, USNA.

99. Fuenmayor, *Historia de la Venezuela política contemporánea*, XII: 297–298; and Vega, *Los Estados Unidos . . . Los días finales*, 142–146. On Trujillo's arms purchases in late 1959, see Moya Pons, *El pasado dominicano* (Santo Domingo: Fundación J. A. Caro Álvarez, 1986), 326.

100. "Castro León nunca controlo totalmente a San Cristóbal," *El Nacional*, April 22, 1960," in *Historia gráfica*, VIII: 69–73; "Venezuela Reports a Rebellion Halted," *NYT*, April 21, 1960; Peña, *Conversaciones con Carlos Andrés Pérez*, I: 179; and Aragorn Storm Miller, "Season of Storms," 87–88.

101. "Manifestación de apoyo al gobierno," *El Nacional*, April 22, 1960, in *Historica gráfica*, VIII: 74–76.

102. Castro León died in prison in 1965. Gude, "Political Violence in Venezuela," 267; Betancourt, *Tres años*, 235; and Fuenmayor, *Historia de la Venezuela política contemporánea*, XIII: 299.

103. "Movimiento continental contra las tiranías," *El Nacional*, April 27, 1960, in *Historia gráfica*, VIII: 85–86; and Betancourt, "Por la democracia y la libertad de América," in *Tres años*, I: 229–232, quote, 231.

104. Rabe, "The Caribbean Triangle," 64.

105. Vega, *Los Estados Unidos . . . Los días finales*, 268.

106. Balaguer, *La palabra encadenada*, 303.

107. Castro Ventura, *Trujillo vs. Betancourt*, 211–213; Diederich, *Trujillo: The Death of the Goat*, 44; and Vega, *Los Estados Unidos . . . Los días finales*, 242.

108. Pérez, far from a neutral observer, contended that prior to the attempt, the "unscrupulous beast" Trujillo conducted a successful dry run of the detonation, replete with unsuspecting prisoners in the vehicle. "All died." Peña, *Conversaciones con Carlos Andrés Pérez*, I: 190.

109. "Capturados responables del atentado al presidente," *El Mundo* (Caracas), June 28, 1960, in *Historia gráfica*, VIII: 105; Catalá, ed., *Rómulo Betancourt: El atentado de Los Próceres* (Caracas: Ediciones Centauro, 1984); Sexta Reunión de Consulta de Ministros de Relaciones Exteriores, Acta Final, August 16–21, 1960, San José, Costa Rica (Washington, DC: Unión Panamericana, Secretaria General de la OEA, 1960); and Schlesinger, "Report to the President."

110. *La Voz Dominicana* jumped the gun, erroneously declaring Betancourt dead and reporting that insurgents had occupied Miraflores. Vega, *Los Estados Unidos . . . Los días finales*, 283.

111. Betancourt, *Tres años*, quotes, I: 354; Castro Ventura, *Trujillo vs. Betancourt*, 215–216; Guerrero, *La ira del tirano*, quote, 189; Gottberg, "Visto de cerca," in *Multimagen de Rómulo*; and Fuenmayor, *Historia de la Venezuela política contemporánea*, XII: 355. For the military's appreciation of Betancourt's courage, see (General) Alberto Müller Rojas, "Rómulo Betancourt y la política militar," in *Rómulo Betancourt: historia y contemporaneidad*, ed. Rafael Caldera (Caracas: Editorial Fundación Rómulo Betancourt, 1980), 407–426, especially 423.

112. Guerrero, *La ira del tirano*, quote, 143.

113. "Un cable de Washington anunciaba al gobierno el atentado," *El Nacional*, June 24, 1960, in *Historia gráfica*, VIII: 94; and Vega, *Los Estados Unidos . . . Los días finales*, 283.

114. Guerrero, *La ira del tirano*, 143; and Rabe, "The Caribbean Triangle," quote, 61.

115. Vega, *Los Estados Unidos . . . Los días finales*, 297–299; and Memo of Discussion, NSC meeting, July 7, 1960, *FRUS, 1958–1960*, VI: 980–991, especially 984.

116. Rabe, "The Caribbean Triangle," 67–68.

117. Ameringer, "The Foreign Policy of Venezuelan Democracy," quote, 338; and Wiarda, *Dictatorship and Development*, 155–156.

118. Norman Gall, "How Trujillo Died," *NR* (April 13, 1963), 19–20.

119. Liss, *Diplomacy and Dependency*, 188; Goldenberg, *The Cuban Revolution and Latin America*, 320; and Ameringer, "The Foreign Policy of Venezuelan Democracy," 338–339.

120. Ameringer, "The Foreign Policy of Venezuelan Democracy," 337–339.

121. Memorandum, Allen Dulles to Herter, April 15, 1959, *FRUS, 1958–1960*, V: 372–391.

122. Ibid; and Brown, *Cuba's Revolutionary World*, 52.

123. Memorandum, Dulles to Herter, April 15, 1959.

124. Brown, *Cuba's Revolutionary World*, 59ff; and Ameringer, *Don Pepe*, 151–153, 159–160.

125. MacPherson, "The Limits of Populist Diplomacy," 263n9; and Schoultz, *That Infernal Little Cuban Republic*, quote, 104.

126. Frank Costigliola, "US Foreign Policy from Kennedy to Johnson," in *CHCW*, II: 112–133, quote, 121.

127. Paterson, "Fixation with Cuba: The Bay of Pigs, the Missile Crisis and Covert War Against Castro," in *Kennedy's Quest for Victory: American Foreign Policy, 1961–1963*, ed. idem (New York: Oxford University Press, 1989), 123–155, especially 137–138; and Rabe, *The Killing Zone*, 73.

128. Rabe, *The Killing Zone*, 66, 78.

129. "Complot para boicotear la visita de Dorticós," *El Nacional*, May 30, 1960; and "Dos visitas funestas," *La Esfera*, May 31, 1960.

130. Brands, *Latin America's Cold War*, 68; and Brown, *Cuba's Revolutionary World*, 189–190.

131. Giovanni Ratz, "Military Factionalism and the Consolidation of Power in 1960s Guatemala," in *Beyond the Eagle's Shadow*, 51–75, especially 59–60.

132. Fuenmayor, *Historia de la Venezuela política contemporánea*, XIII: 200; and Brown, *Cuba's Revolutionary World*, 260.

133. Ameringer, *Don Pepe*, quote, 180.

134. Vega, *Los Estados Unidos . . . Los días finales*, 491–492.

135. Muñoz Marín to Betancourt, December 25, 1960, Folder #56, Rómulo Betancourt, Correspondencia Particular, FLMM.

136. "Carta para los firmantes de la 'Declaración de San José del 29 de abril, 1961,' " Tomo 38: Complemento D, FRB.

137. Ibid.

138. Ameringer, *Don Pepe*, quote, 179–180.

139. Memo of conversation, "Cuban problem, OAS Foreign Ministers Meeting," Caracas, December 16, 1961, *FRUS, 1961–1963* (Washington, DC: U.S. Government Printing Office, 1996), XII: 271–274, quote, 273.

140. Fursenko and Naftali, *"One Hell of a Gamble,"* 135; and Edwin McCammon Martin, *Kennedy and Latin America* (Lanham, MD: University Press of America, 1994), 24n3.

141. Ameringer, *Don Pepe*, 148, 163; and idem, *Democracy in Costa Rica* (New York: Praeger, 1982), 123–124.

142. Turits, *Foundations of Despotism*, 259. Diederich dates CIA contact with dissidents as early as December 1958. *Trujillo: The Death of the Goat*, xv. See also Memorandum of the Discussion of the 453rd Meeting of the NSC, July 25, 1960, *FRUS, 1958–1960*, Microfiche Supplement, Dominican Republic.

143. Ameringer, *Don Pepe*, 183.

144. "Memorándum sobre 'Operación Santo Domingo,' " October 11, 1961, Caja 16, Folder 139, FLMM; Walter Bonilla, *La revolución de abril y Puerto Rico* (Santo Domingo: Editora Cole, 2001), 21–22; Balcácer, *Trujillo: El tiranicidio*, 103; and Vega, *Los Estados Unidos . . . Los días finales*, 356–357, 418–419.

145. Vega, *Los Estados Unidos . . . Los días finales*, 491–492.

146. Balcácer, *Trujillo: El tiranicidio*, 143–144; Smith, *The Last Years of the Monroe Doctrine*, 124; and Rabe, *Eisenhower and Latin America*, 156.

147. Vega, *Eisenhower y Trujillo*, 85.

148. Max Frankel, "Castro and Trujillo Call Truce, Diplomats in Caribbean Believe," *NYT*, January 5, 1961; Rabe, "The Caribbean Triangle," 72; and Vega, *Eisenhower y Trujillo*, 182.

149. Senate Select Committee on Intelligence Activities (Church Committee), *Attempted Assassination Plots Involving Foreign Leaders: Interim Report of the Select Committee to Study Governmental Operations with Respect to Intelligence Activities* (Washington, DC: Government Printing Office, 1975), 194n1. https://www.intelligence.senate.gov/sites/default/files/94465.pdf. Accessed November 5, 2020.

150. Dearborn to Mann, October 27, 1960, *FRUS, 1958–1960*, Microfiche Supplement, Dominican Republic.

151. O'Donnell, "Transitions to Democracy: Some Navigation Instruments," in *Democracy in the Americas*, 62–75, especially 73.

152. As early as 1957, Farland, acting on instructions from the Dulles brothers and Undersecretary of State Herbert Hoover, Jr., quietly reached out to the domestic opposition. Vega, *Los Estados Unidos . . . Los días finales*, 22.

153. Bosch, "La muerte de Trujillo: secreto develado," in idem, *33 artículos*, 255–261, especially 258.

154. The Church Committee documented eight attempts against the life of the Cuban leader. Seymour Hersh, *The Dark Side of Camelot* (Boston: Little Brown, 1997), 185ff; Rabe, *The Killing Zone*, 69; and Thomas Powers, *The Man Who Kept the Secrets: Richard Helms and the CIA* (New York: Knopf, 1979), 147. The first assassination attempt against Castro was on September 2, 1960, but Soviet intelligence alerted the Cubans and the plot was foiled. That same month, the CIA initiated discussions with Mafia chiefs Sam Giancana and Santos Traficante to eliminate the Cuban leader. Fursenko and Naphtali, *"One Hell of a Gamble,"* 56, 62.

155. Vega, *Eisenhower y Trujillo*, 162–163.

156. Diederich's detailed account of the assassination differs in several respects from the Church Committee's findings. *Trujillo: The Death of the Goat*, 85. Cf. Senate Select Committee, *Attempted Assassination Plots*, 196–197, 204–205, 210.

157. Cable, Dearborn to State Department, March 22, 1961, *FRUS, 1961–1963*, XII: quote, 621.

158. Senate Select Committee, *Attempted Assassination Plots*, 192.

159. Vega, *Los Estados Unidos . . . Los días finales*, 645–646, 680, 707.

160. Senate Select Committee, *Attempted Assassination Plots*, quotes, 212.

161. Rabe, "The Caribbean Triangle," 73.

162. Senate Select Committee, *Attempted Assassination Plots*, quote, 206, 211; and Rabe, *Eisenhower and Latin America*, 161–162.

163. Only two conspirators survived Ramfis's and Abbes García's hideous settling of scores. Balcácer, *Trujillo: El tiranicidio*, 386–387.

164. Dearborn interview, Association for Diplomatic Studies and Training Foreign Affairs Oral History Project, Library of Congress, April 1975. https://tile.loc.gov/storage-services/service/mss/mfdip/2010/2010deao1/2010deao1.pdf. Accessed February 13, 2022.

165. Bonilla, *La revolución de abril*, 24–42.

166. Szulc, *The Winds of Revolution*, 222; and Rabe, *The Most Dangerous Area*, 40, 43.

167. Unless otherwise indicated, this section draws on Lieuwen, *Generals vs. Presidents: Neomilitarism in Latin America* (New York: Praeger, 1964); idem, *The United States and the Challenge to Security*; Barber and Ronning, *Internal Security and Military Power*; Johnson, *The Military and Society*; and Brands, *Latin America's Cold War*.

168. Michael Kryzanek, "Political Party Decline and the Failure of Liberal Democracy: The PRD in Dominican Politics," *JLAS* 9:1 (1977): 115–143, especially 119; Blasier, *The Hovering Giant*, 253; and Rabe, *The Most Dangerous Area*, 44–45.

169. Gude, "Political Violence in Venezuela," 273.

170. Gottberg, "Visto de cerca," in *Multimagen de Rómulo*; and Levine, "Venezuela since 1958," 98.

171. Stewart, oral history, JFKPL, quote, 26.

172. Ibid.

173. Peter Nehemkis, *Latin America: Myth and Reality* (New York: Knopf, 1964), 49–50.

174. Lieuwen, "Survey of the Alliance for Progress. The Latin American Military: A Study Prepared at the Request of the Subcommittee on American Republics Affairs of the Committee on Foreign Relations," United States Senate, October 9, 1967. (Washington, DC: Government Printing Office, 1967), 6.

175. Juan Carlos Torre and Liliana de Riz, "Argentina since 1946," in *CHLA*, VIII: 75–194, especially 112–113; and Rabe, *The Most Dangerous Area*, 57–58.

176. Fuenmayor, *Historia de la Venezuela política contemporánea*, XII: 70; Gott, *Guerrilla Movements in Latin America*, xxxv, 138; and Angell, "The Latin American Left," 109–110.

177. Egil Fossum, "Factors Influencing the Occurrence of Military Coups d'état in Latin America," *Journal of Peace Research* 4:3 (1967), 228–251, especially 234.

178. Walker, "Mixing the Sweet," quote, 48.

179. Martz, "The Party System: Toward Institutionalization," in *Venezuela: The Democratic Experience*, 93–112, especially 101–102.

180. Rodríguez to Betancourt, September 23, 1963, Tomo 40, FRB.

181. Betancourt to López Mateos and Paz Estenssoro, July 23, 1962, Tomo 39: Complemento B, FRB.

182. Betancourt to Kennedy, July 22, 1963, Tomo 40, Complemento B, FRB.

183. John Van Cleve, "The Latin American Policy of President Kennedy: A Reexamination: Case: Peru," *IAEA* 1 (Spring, 1977): 29–44, especially 43–44; and Martin, *Kennedy and Latin America*, 85.

184. Loeb, oral history, February 9, 1968, p. 19, JFKPL. https://www.jfklibrary.org/asset-viewer/archives/JFKOH/Loeb%2C%20James%20I/JFKOH-JIL-02/JFKOH-JIL-02. Accessed October 21, 2021.

185. Quoted in Rabe, *The Road to OPEC*, 147.

186. Van Cleve, "The Latin American Policy of President Kennedy"; and Willard Carpenter, "Latin America: The Return of the Military," *New University Thought* 1 (Summer 1964): 3–13, especially 5–6.

187. Rabe, "Controlling Revolutions," quote, 115.

188. Stewart, oral history, pp. 25–26.

189. Michael Shafer, *Deadly Paradigms: The Failure of U.S. Counterinsurgency Policy* (Princeton: Princeton University Press, 1988); and Kuzmarov, "Modernizing Repression."

190. Memorandum from Livingston Merchant to Eisenhower, December 31, 1960, *FRUS, 1958–1960*, V: Microfiche Supplement; Barber and Ronning, *Internal Security and Military Power*, quote, 6–7. Dennis Rempe, "Guerrillas, Bandits and Independent Republics: US Counter-insurgency Efforts in Colombia, 1959–1965," *Small Wars and Insurgencies* 6:3 (1995): 304–327; and Herrán-Ávila, "Convergent Conflicts," 329ff.

191. Holden, "The Real Diplomacy of Violence," 296–297; and Rabe, "Controlling Revolutions," 117.

192. Betancourt to Muñoz Marín, February 5, 1962, Tomo 39 (1962), Complemento B, FRB.

193. Rabe, *The Most Dangerous Area*, quote, 127, and 130.

194. Quoted in Rabe, "Controlling Revolutions," 122.

195. Van Cleve, "The Latin American Policy of President Kennedy," 36–39; and Rabe, *The Most Dangerous Area*, 116.

196. Brown, *Cuba's Revolutionary World*, 307–308.

197. Blasier, *The Hovering Giant*, 253–54.

198. Siekmeier, *The Bolivian Revolution*, 82, 98, 101; Blasier, *The Hovering Giant*, 139–143; and Malloy, "Revolutionary Politics," 143.

199. Fleet, *The Rise and Fall of Chilean Christian Democracy* (Princeton: Princeton University Press, 1985), 44–52 and 77–78.

200. Heidi Tinsman, *Partners in Conflict: The Politics of Gender, Sexuality, and Labor in the Chilean Agrarian Reform, 1950–1973* (Durham: Duke University Press, 2002), chapters 3–5, quote, 84.

201. Rouquié, "The Military in Latin American Politics," 169–170.

202. Westad, *The Global Cold War*, 176–177; and Brands, *Latin America's Cold War*, 27, 39.

203. O'Donnell, "Transitions to Democracy," 64; and Meyer, "Democracy from Three Latin American Perspectives," in *Democracy in the Americas*, 29–38, especially 34.

204. Brands, *Latin America's Cold War*, 57.
205. Rabe, *The Most Dangerous Area*, 66–71.

Conclusion

1. Quoted in Ameringer, *Don Pepe*, 228.
2. Wiarda, "The Crisis of the Latin American Democratic Left," *Dissent* 16 (November–December 1969), 528–536, quote, 536.
3. Coatsworth, "The Cold War in Central America, 1975–1991," in *CHCW*, III: 221.
4. Barber and Ronning, *Internal Security and Military Power*, 38; and Cardoso, "On the Characterization of Authoritarian Regimes in Latin America," in *The New Authoritarianism in Latin America*, ed. David Collier (Princeton: Princeton University Press, 1979), 33–57, quote, 45.
5. Carlos Aguirre and Drinot, eds., *The Peculiar Revolution: Rethinking the Peruvian Experiment Under Military Rule* (Austin: University of Texas Press, 2017); David Scott Palmer, *Peru: The Authoritarian Tradition* (New York: Praeger, 1980); and Abraham Lowenthal, *The Peruvian Experiment: Continuity and Change under Military Rule* (Princeton: Princeton University Press, 1979).
6. In fact, Frei's criticism of Pinochet may have contributed to his death in 1982. In January 2019 his doctors, chauffeur, and a former member of the secret police were found guilty of poisoning the former president. An appeals court subsequently set aside the convictions, citing insufficient evidence. Similar suspicions were raised about the death of Neruda twelve days after the coup. "Chile Court Overturns Convictions for 1982 Murder of Former President Frei," *The Guardian*, January 25, 2021. https://www.the-guardian.com/world/2021/jan/25/chile-court-murder-pinochet-era-president-frei. Accessed May 19, 2021.
7. Quoted in Tanya Harmer, *Allende's Chile and the Inter-American Cold War* (Chapel Hill: University of North Carolina Press, 2011), 69; and Rouquié, "The Military in Latin American Politics," 169–170.
8. Coatsworth, "The Cold War in Central America," quote, 220; and idem, "United States Interventions: What For?" *ReVista* 5:1 (Spring/Summer 2005), 1–6.
9. Brands, *Latin America's Cold War*, quote, 82, 174; Pastor, *Condemned to Repetition: The United States and Nicaragua* (Princeton: Princeton University Press, 1987); and Martha Cottam, "The Carter Administration's Policy toward Nicaragua: Images, Goals, and Tactics," *Political Science Quarterly* 107:1 (Spring 1992), 123–146, especially 136.
10. Moya Pons, *The Dominican Republic: A National History*, 391–392, 528; and Wiarda and Kryzanek, "Dominican Dictatorship Revisited: The Caudillo Tradition and the Regimes of Trujillo and Balaguer," *Revista/Review Interamericana* 7:3 (Fall 1977): 417–436. Citing a letter from CIA director Richard Helms to his covert operations chief, Desmond Fitzgerald, Weiner notes

that Balaguer served as a "trusted confidential source" to the FBI and that the CIA provided personnel and the funding he needed to defeat Bosch in the 1966 presidential election. *Enemies*, quote, 262–263.

11. Brands, *Latin America's Cold War*, 139, 198, 216, 261. The Sandinistas redirected Soviet military equipment received from the USSR and Cuba to the Salvadoran insurgency. Russell Crandall, *The Salvadoran Option: The United States in El Salvador, 1977–1992* (New York: Cambridge University Press, 2016).

12. Nicola Miller, *Soviet Relations with Latin America, 1959–1987* (New York: Cambridge University Press, 1989), 12–13. On Soviet aid to Chile see Jonathan Haslam, *The Nixon Administration and the Death of Allende's Chile: A Case of Assisted Suicide* (London: Verso, 2005).

13. Gould, "Solidarity under Siege: The Latin American Left," *AHR* 114:2 (April 2009): 348–375.

14. John Booth, *Costa Rica: Quest for Democracy* (Boulder: Westview Press, 1998), 157.

15. Guerón, "Introduction," in *Venezuela in the Wake of Radical Reform*, ed. Tulchin and Gary Bland (Washington, DC/Boulder: Woodrow Wilson Center/Lynne Reinner, 1993), 1–18.

16. Karl, *Forgotten Peace*, 219.

17. Gerardo Sánchez Nateras, "The Sandinista Revolution and the Limits of the Cold War in Latin America: The Dilemma of Non-Intervention during the Nicaraguan Crisis, 1977–1978," *Cold War History* 18:2 (2018): 111–129, especially 115.

18. Alan Riding, "A Reporter's Notebook: Managua Relaxes," *NYT*, July 23, 1979; and Ariel Armony, *Argentina, the United States, and the Anti-Communist Crusade in Central America, 1977–1984* (Athens: Ohio University Press, 1997), 80.

19. Sánchez Nateras, "The Sandinista Revolution," 115–116; Graeme Mount, "Costa Rica and the Cold War, 1948–1990," *Canadian Journal of History/Annales canadiennes de'historie* 50:2 (2015), 290–316, especially 300; and Brands, *Latin America's Cold War*, 182–183.

20. Anthony Lake, *Somoza Falling* (Boston: Houghton Mifflin, 1989), 25, 42–43, and 88; and Sánchez Nateras, "The Sandinista Revolution," 117, 121–122.

21. Quoted in Lake, *Somoza Falling*, 88.

22. Quoted in Pastor, *Condemned to Repetition*, 281.

23. Ibid., 60, 65; and quoted in Sánchez Nateras, "The Sandinista Revolution," 127.

24. Quoted in Brands, *Latin America's Cold War*, 185.

25. Sánchez Nateras, "The Sandinista Revolution," 126.

26. Quoted in Pastor, *Condemned to Repetition*, 125–126. See also Riding, "Arms Scandal is Charged in Costa Rica: Exposures Follow Crash," *NYT*, May 21, 1981, quote.

27. Honey notes that Monge agreed to support the Contras in return for badly needed economic assistance. An emergency $100 million IMF bailout was approved, and AID grants increased from $13 million in 1982 to $212 million a

year later. *Hostile Acts*, 59–62, 213, 237, quote, 11. See also Armony, *Argentina, the United States*, 74.

28. In addition to training, the junta approved the sale of arms to Central American military regimes, with the profits benefiting companies owned by high-ranking officers. Armony, *Argentina, the United States*, passim.

29. Christopher Dickey, *With the Contras: A Reporter in the Wilds of Nicaragua* (New York: Simon & Schuster, 1985), 89; Martin Andersen, *Dossier Secreto: Argentina's* Desaparecidos *and the Myth of the "Dirty War"* (Boulder: Westview, 1993), 303; and Armony, *Argentina, the United States*, 91, 96, 132.

30. Armony, *Argentina, the United States*, 103; and Mount, "Costa Rica and the Cold War," 312–313.

31. Claribel Alegría and Darwin Flakoll, *Death of Somoza: The First-Person Story of the Guerrillas who Assassinated the Nicaraguan Leader* (Willimantic, CT: Curbstone Press, 1996); and Diederich, *Somoza and the Legacy of U.S. Involvement*, epilogue.

32. Alison Brysk, *The Politics of Human Rights in Argentina: Protest, Change, and Democratization* (Stanford: Stanford University Press, 1994); Jaime Malamud Goti, *Game Without End: State Terror and the Politics of Justice* (Norman: University of Oklahoma Press, 1996); and Luis Roniger, *The Legacy of Human Rights Violations in the Southern Cone: Argentina, Chile, and Uruguay* (New York: Oxford University Press, 1999).

33. Andersen, *Dossier Secreto*.

34. What follows draws on Ameringer, *Don Pepe*, chapter 10.

35. Ameringer, *Don Pepe*, quote, 164–165.

36. Dickey, *With the Contras*, 38.

37. Alexander, *Venezuela's Voice*, 94, quote, 98–99.

38. Michael Coppedge, *Strong Parties and Lame Ducks: Presidential Partyarchy and Factionalism in Venezuela* (Stanford: Stanford University Press, 1994), 100–101.

39. Porter to Betancourt, November 28, 1960, Box 16, Foreign Affairs, Venezuela, COP.

40. Porter to Falcón Briceño, November 21, 1960, and idem to Jules Schwede, December 1, 1960, Box 16, Foreign Affairs, Venezuela, COP.

41. (New York: Macmillan, 1961). See also Porter, oral history, tape 12:1; and "No Time for Charlie," *Time*, January 13, 1961.

42. Porter, "An Interview with Fidel Castro," *Northwest Review* 6:4 (Fall 1963), 73–88, 105–10.

43. Porter to Morse, April 11, 1964, Porter to William Proxmire, September 3, 1964, and Porter to Mann, December 8, 1964, Box 47, Cuba trip, 1965, COP.

44. Porter to Bosch, August 13, 1963, and September 11, 1963, Box 48, Dominican visit, August 1–3, 1963, COP; and Porter to Szulc, March 18, 1964, DOJ Case File 109–51–25, Section 20, RG 60, USNA.

45. Abell, "Charles Porter, Smarter than Hell," 1, 3, 8; and Jim Feehan and Diana Elliott, "Former Lawmaker Charles Porter Dies," *Register-Guard*, January 3, 2006, A1, A9.

Acknowledgments

RESEARCHERS WHO HAVE WORKED in the field of international history are all too aware of their own limitations and the magnitude of their reliance on those who paved the way. While I am responsible for any factual errors and interpretive flaws, I owe a great deal to the specialists cited in the text and notes. The same can be said for the valuable comments and suggestions I received from the Press's reviewers. Translations from Spanish to English are mine as well, unless a published translation is noted.

To carry out a transnational study such as this, archivists and librarians are indispensable. Working at the Fundación Rómulo Betancourt in Caracas was a pleasure thanks to Mirela Quero de Trinca and Virginia Betancourt-Valverde. Also meriting thanks at other archives: Ana Patricia Segura Solís, Archivo Nacional de Costa Rica; Julio Quirós Alcalá, Fundación Luis Muñoz Marín; Amanda Moreno, Cuban Heritage Collection, University of Miami Library; Lauren Goss, University of Oregon Special Collections and Archives; Christopher Abraham, U.S. National Archives and Records Administration; Fernanda Perrone, Rutgers University Special Collections; Scott Jordan, Special Collections, University of Louisiana at Lafayette Library; Julie Bartlett Nelson, Forbes Library, Northampton, MA; Genevieve Coyle, Manuscripts and Archives, Sterling Library, Yale University; and Mary Burtzloff, Eisenhower Presidential Library. Pauline Klustad located images and obtained permissions from the Archivo General de la Nación, Santo Domingo, Dominican Republic. Bill Nelson Cartographic Services prepared the maps. Thanks as well to Bill Holland for sharing a picture of his dad and Pepe Figueres. I also benefited considerably from Philip Dur's research on Jefferson Caffery.

A jewel that deserves recognition is the staff at Bowdoin College's Hawthorne-Longfellow Library, who graciously tended to my numerous requests for materials. I'd especially like to commend Guy Saldanha and his staff at Interlibrary Loan, Carmen Greenlee, Barbara Levergood, Jaime Jones, and the late Judy Montgomery, who is sorely missed by our entire community. Matthew Stuart and the staff at Patten Free Library deserve special shout-outs for retrieving and processing books that arrived during the pandemic.

Since retiring in 2019, I've had time to reflect on how truly fortunate I was to work at Bowdoin for more than three decades. Inquisitive students in my courses followed me down rabbit holes and acted as sounding boards, while colleagues and staff were generous with their time and expertise. I especially want to thank Matt Klingle, Brian Purnell, Dave Hecht, David Gordon, Cara Martin-Tetreault, Jean Harrison, Rebecca Banks, Ann Ostwald, and Kathi Lucas. Kudos as well to Noah Bragg '15, who, at an early stage, provided helpful research assistance. The following former students, who have gone on to make their mark in their respective fields, took time out to answer queries and provide useful comments: Russell Crandall '94, Elizabeth Shesko '02, Kenneth Weisbrode '91, and Georgia Whitaker '14. Special thanks to Katharine Watson, Kathy and Chuck Remmel, and Charlotte and Joe Heil for their steadfast support and encouragement.

At crucial stages of the project, the College provided two Andrew W. Mellon sabbatical leave supplements and a Fletcher Family Research Award. I also benefited from an American Philosophical Society Franklin Research Award. In addition, I tested out ideas at the Universidad Católica Andrés Bello in Caracas; the University of California, Irvine; Pomona College; and Hartwick College, where students and colleagues posed questions that helped refine my thinking.

A number of scholars offered useful suggestions. I'm indebted to the late Charles Ameringer, Hal Brands, John Britton, Jonathan Brown, John Coatsworth, Robin Derby, Steve Ellner, Judith Ewell, Ben Fallaw, Eric Gettig, Michel Gobat, Piero Gleijeses, Lowell Gudmundson, Bill Holland, Patrick Iber, Aaron Moulton, Raanan Rein, Lars Schoultz, Michael Schroeder, and Tomás Straka.

Words cannot properly express my gratitude to David Carey, Russell Crandall, William Taylor, and Steven Topik, who read the entire manuscript and offered insightful commentary. David believed in this project before I did. Thanks, *compa!* Bill and Steve read so many drafts over the years that they have every right to cringe when they receive emails with attachments from me. To their credit and to my great benefit, they never once turned me down. I also received helpful comments from the following specialists who commented on chapter drafts: Jefferson Boyer, Lillian Guerra, Lou Pérez, Jr., Steve Stein, Miguel Tinker Salas, and Bill Vanderwolk. I can't thank Miguel enough for sharing his vast knowledge of Venezuelan history. His numerous contacts and recommendations opened doors during a memorable research trip to Caracas in 2012. Finally, I shudder to think where I'd be today if not for Steve Stein, who, as my advisor and mentor at the State University of New York at Stony Brook, took a green graduate student under his wing and gave him the confidence he so sorely needed to pursue this career.

My first stop on this twelve-year journey was a visit to the University of Oregon Library's Special Collections, where I first worked with the Charles O. Porter papers. During my stay in Eugene, I was introduced to the late congressman's son, Sam, who kindly responded to my inquiries about his father and provided materials that added immeasurably to my understanding of his dad's motivations and actions.

Saludos to Yale's acquisitions editor Jaya Chatterjee, who took a chance on such a lengthy book; to her editorial assistant Eva Skewes, who patiently mentored me in the intricacies of copyright permissions; and to production editor Joyce Ippolito, who guided this manuscript to the finish line. Once again, I'm greatly indebted to Eleanor Lahn, whose careful, painstaking copy edit improved a sprawling manuscript in countless ways. A *gran abrazo* to Michael Lettieri, who proofed the final manuscript. Thanks as well to our favorite artist, Andrew Abbott, for the illustration for the dust jacket.

I dedicate this book to David, Emily, and Anna, who made our trips to Latin America and beyond so rewarding, adventurous, and fun. Their curiosity, sense of humor, and enthusiasm continue to inspire. Last, thank you, Kathy, for sharing in my obsessions for more than four decades. I am so fortunate to spend my life with such a gentle, patient, empathetic person.

Index

Castro León, Jesús María, 433–34, 454, 498–99, 672n110

Catholic Church, 56, 160; democratic governance, support for, 327, 429, 430, 432, 523; strongman rule, allied with, 45 46, 59, 64, 65, 90, 116, 249, 337

Cayo Confites expedition, 275, 280–82, 286–87, 304, 472, 476

CBS News, 415

CC (Venezuela), 325, 332, 343, 344, 376–77, 386, 472

Cementerio sin cruces. See Requena, Andrés

CEN (Venezuela), 325, 332, 343, 344, 376

Center for Higher Military Studies (Peru), 309

Central American Common Market, 542

Central American Court of Justice, 38, 78

Central American union, 35–36, 52, 64, 78, 146, 147, 372

Central Intelligence Agency. *See* CIA

Central University (Venezuela), 2, 102, 350, 450, 451, 463, 475–76

Centro Ariel (Montevideo), 65, 151

Centro Vasco Americano (New York). *See* Galíndez, Jesús de

Centro Vasco de El Tigre (Caracas), 463. *See also* Galíndez, Jesús de

Chamorro, Emiliano, 49, 79, 185

Chamorro, Pedro Joaquín, 421, 427, 506, 544, 655n79

Chapultepec Conference (and Agreement), 237, 358

Chase National Bank, 121

Chibás, Eddie, 54, 124, 215, 226, 277, 283

Chicago Defender, 170

Chile, 3, 10, 84, 233, 290, 301, 340, 524, 533, 541, 547; Peronist influence, 315, 335, 337; student movement in, 47, 58, 62, 66, 67; U.S. relations, 530, 531, 539. *See* Tacna-Arica dispute; Inter-American Conference, Santiago

Chilean Communist Party, 233

Chilean military, 531, 539

Chilean Socialist Party, 104

China, 115, 351, 405, 409, 459, 550

Chiriboga, José, 391

Chorrillos Military Academy (Peru), 247, 329

Christian Democratic Party (Chile), 3, 530–31, 533–34, 539

Church, Frank, 408–9, 466, 515

CI, 66–67, 81, 93–95, 103, 122, 135; Latin America, parties in, 9, 73, 74, 81, 98, 117, 233, 252; sectarian position, adoption of, 73–75, 98, 118, 130; Sandino, relationship with, 36, 97, 181–83

CIA, 218, 243, 309, 328, 451, 486, 515, 547, 549, 553, 617n36; Costa Rica–Nicaragua conflict, 381, 390–91, 422; Cuban Revolution, response to, 504–7, 510–11, 670n81, 674n154; Dominican Republic, involvement in, 258, 677–78n10; Guatemalan intervention, role in, 16, 320, 352–53, 364–67, 508. *See also* Dulles, Allen; Galíndez, Jesús de: as informant for FBI and CIA

Ciliberto, José Ángel, 427

Civic Movement (Dominican Republic), 255

Claridad, 61, 579n39

Clarín (Venezuela), 524

Clark, J. Reuben, 161, 184

Cleveland Plain Dealer, 170

Club Femenino (Cuba), 121

Coatsworth, John, 317–18, 540

Cobían Parra, Salvador, 406

Cohen, Alex, 400, 423

Cold War, 17, 192, 218, 255, 313, 322, 502, 540; historiography, 7–8, 16, 84, 324, 365; late arrival in Latin America, 2–3, 6–7, 478, 485, 479,